Lecture Notes in Computer Science

Lecture Notes in Artificial Intelligence 16353

The series Lecture Notes in Artificial Intelligence (LNAI) was established in 1988 as a topical subseries of LNCS devoted to artificial intelligence.

The series publishes state-of-the-art research results at a high level. As with the LNCS mother series, the mission of the series is to serve the international R & D community by providing an invaluable service, mainly focused on the publication of conference and workshop proceedings and postproceedings.

Thanh Tho Quan · Chattrakul Sombattheera ·
Hoang-Anh Pham · Ngoc Thinh Tran
Editors

Multi-disciplinary Trends in Artificial Intelligence

18th International Conference, MIWAI 2025
Ho Chi Minh City, Vietnam, December 3–5, 2025
Proceedings, Part I

Springer

Editors
Thanh Tho Quan
Ho Chi Minh City University of Technology
(HCMUT), VNU-HCM
Ho Chi Minh City, Vietnam

Hoang-Anh Pham
Ho Chi Minh City University of Technology
(HCMUT), VNU-HCM
Ho Chi Minh City, Vietnam

Chattrakul Sombattheera
Mahasarakham University
Maha Sarakham, Thailand

Ngoc Thinh Tran
Ho Chi Minh City University of Technology
(HCMUT), VNU-HCM
Ho Chi Minh City, Vietnam

ISSN 0302-9743 ISSN 1611-3349 (electronic)
Lecture Notes in Artificial Intelligence
ISBN 978-981-95-4956-6 ISBN 978-981-95-4957-3 (eBook)
https://doi.org/10.1007/978-981-95-4957-3

LNCS Sublibrary: SL7 – Artificial Intelligence

This Springer imprint is published by the registered company Springer Nature Singapore Pte Ltd.
The registered company address is: 152 Beach Road, #21-01/04 Gateway East, Singapore 189721, Singapore

Preface

Artificial Intelligence (AI) has gone through its 69-year history so quickly. In recent years, AI has received tremendous global attention, largely due to its remarkable successes across a wide range of real-world applications. This momentum continues to accelerate research in AI, driven by the need to address new and emerging challenges. As a little part of AI history, the International Conference on Multi-disciplinary Trends in Artificial Intelligence (MIWAI) has gone through its 18-year history and has been incorporated into the *Lecture Notes in Artificial Intelligence (LNAI)* series for 14 years. Throughout its journey, MIWAI has remained dedicated to advancing high-quality research in AI while maintaining a broad perspective on its diverse applications. At its core, MIWAI upholds a strong belief that only rigorous, high-quality research can be effectively translated into real-world practice. This guiding principle continues to shape the conference's mission and commitment to fostering meaningful contributions to the global AI community.

This volume contains the papers presented at MIWAI 2025: The 18th International Conference on Multi-disciplinary Trends in Artificial Intelligence, held during December 3–5, 2025 in Ho Chi Minh City, Vietnam. MIWAI 2025 welcomed aboard a large program committee (PC) of 195 members from 26 countries of all 5 inhabited continents of the world: Africa, America, Asia, Europe, and Oceania/Australia. There were more than 780 authors, from 54 countries of all inhabited continents, participating in MIWAI 2025. Vietnam had the highest number of submissions (137), followed by India (40), Australia (12), Japan (10), and Malaysia (8). Vietnam had the most accepted papers (68), followed by India (11), Japan (6), and USA (3). The most popular keywords were deep learning, machine learning, large language models, computer vision, and natural language processing.

As always, the review process was carefully and deliberately conducted to ensure only high-quality papers were accepted to MIWAI 2025. Each paper was assigned to at least two two PC members, but they all received at least double-blind reviews. In addition, there were several rounds of suggestions, discussions and improvement attempts with regards to the quality of each paper between the authors and the MIWAI 2025 General and Program Co-Chairs in order to maintain the high quality standards of the conference before decisions were made. Outstanding papers (30) received 2 reviews, while most of the papers (145) received three reviews. The other papers received up to 5 reviews. The average number of reviews for a submission was 2.85. Every accepted paper also received additional comments from the General and Program Co-Chairs to improve it even further for the best possible technical quality.

The number of submitted papers was 306 and only 110 of them were accepted to be published in the proceedings. This makes the acceptance rate 35.95%.

We are profoundly grateful to all the authors for the time and effort devoted to preparing and submitting their high-quality research papers. We extend our heartfelt congratulations to the authors whose papers were accepted for presentation at MIWAI

2025. At the same time, we would also like to express our sincere appreciation to the authors whose papers were not accepted this year.

As a wise saying reminds us, *"Life is a remarkable journey filled with twists and turns; the only guarantee of success lies in one's determination and perseverance."* We encourage all authors to continue their pursuit of excellence, to carefully consider the reviewers' comments, and to refine and improve their work for future submissions. There will always be new opportunities to share and advance their research, and we wish them great success in their academic journey.

Finally, we would like to extend our deepest gratitude to all members of the Program Committee and reviewers for their valuable time, expertise, and insightful feedback shared with the authors. In particular, we express our special thanks to those who graciously reviewed additional papers beyond their assigned load, ensuring the quality and fairness of the review process.

October 2025

Thanh Tho Quan
Chattrakul Sombattheera
Hoang-Anh Pham
Ngoc Thinh Tran

Organization

Steering Committee

Arun Agarwal	Zen Technologies Ltd., India
Richard Booth	Cardiff University, UK
Patrick Doherty	Linköping University, Sweden
Rina Dechter	University of California, Irvine, USA
Leon Van Der Torre	University of Luxembourg, Luxembourg
Peter Haddawy	Mahidol University, Thailand
Jérôme Lang	Université Paris-Dauphine, France
Atul Negi	University of Hyderabad, India
Somnuk Phon-Amnuaisuk	Universiti Teknologi Brunei, Brunei
Paul Weng	Duke Kunshan University, China
Quan Thanh Tho	Ho Chi Minh City University of Technology (HCMUT), VNU-HCM, Vietnam

Conveners

Raghava Morusupalli	CVR College of Engineering, India
Chattrakul Sombattheera	Mahasarakham University, Thailand

General Co-chairs

Chattrakul Sombattheera	Mahasarakham University, Thailand
Jean-Daniel Zucker	Institute for Sustainable Development (IRD) and Sorbonne University, France
Quan Thanh Tho	Ho Chi Minh City University of Technology (HCMUT), VNU-HCM, Vietnam

Program Co-chairs

Henry Nguyen	Griffith University, Australia
Pham Hoang Anh	Ho Chi Minh City University of Technology (HCMUT), VNU-HCM, Vietnam
Ruibin Bai	University of Nottingham Ningbo China, China

Dayang Norhayati Abang Jawawi	Universiti Teknologi Malaysia, Malaysia

Publicity Co-chairs

Daphne Teck Ching Lai	Universiti Brunei Darussalam, Brunei
Panich Sudkhot	Zyntelligent Co., Ltd., Thailand

Local Organizing Co-chairs

Benjawan Intara	Mahasarakham University, Thailand
Tran Ngoc Thinh	Ho Chi Minh City University of Technology (HCMUT), VNU-HCM, Vietnam

Program Committee

Azizi Ab Aziz	Universiti Utara Malaysia, Malaysia
Chirag Agrawal	IEEE Member
Johanna Ahmad	Universiti Teknologi Malaysia, Malaysia
Isara Anantavrasilp	King Mongkut's Institute of Technology Ladkrabang, Thailand
Le Duc Anh	Center for Open Data in the Humanities, Japan
Ruibin Bai	University of Nottingham Ningbo China, China
Fabien Baldacci	University of Bordeaux, France
Akshata Bhat	Amazon, USA
Dharamsotu Bheekya	Geethanjali College of Engineering and Technology, India
Huynh Thi Thanh Binh	Hanoi University of Science and Technology, Vietnam
Tien-Dung Cao	School of Engineering, Tan Tao University, Vietnam
Thanh-Duc Chau	University of Science, HCMUS, Vietnam
Vo Thi Ngoc Chau	Ho Chi Minh City University of Technology (HCMUT), VNU-HCM, Vietnam
Yu-N Cheah	Universiti Sains Malaysia, Malaysia
Sook Ling Chua	Multimedia University, Malaysia
Broderick Crawford	Pontificia Universidad Católica de Valparaiso, Chile
Le Anh Cuong	Ton Duc Thang University, Vietnam
Hoa Khanh Dam	University of Wollongong, Australia

Thi Phuc Dang	Industrial University of Ho Chi Minh City, Vietnam
Thin Dang Van	University of Information Technology - HCM National University, Vietnam
Sy Hieu Dau	Ho Chi Minh City University of Technology (HCMUT), VNU-HCM, Vietnam
Iman Dehzangi	Rutgers University, USA
Nikhil Devnani	Apple, USA
Thanh-Dang Diep	Ho Chi Minh City University of Technology (HCMUT), VNU-HCM, Vietnam
Kejun Dong	China Internet Network Information Center, China
Duong Duc Tin	Ho Chi Minh City University of Technology (HCMUT), VNU-HCM, Vietnam
Nguyen Duy Ham	Khoa CNTT, trường Đại học Sài Gòn, Vietnam
Xuening Feng	Shanghai Jiao Tong University, China
Tasnim Ferdous	BRAC University, Bangladesh
Lee Kien Foo	Multimedia University, Malaysia
Luigi O. Freire	Universidad Técnica de Cotopaxi, Ecuador
Susmita Ghosh	Jadavpur University, India
Hock Guan Goh	Universiti Tunku Abdul Rahman, Malaysia
Hui-Ngo Goh	Multimedia University, Malaysia
Tilottama Goswami	Vasavi College of Engineering, India
The Anh Han	Teesside University, UK
Rohayanti Hassan	Universiti Teknologi Malaysia, Malaysia
Van Lam Ho	Quy Nhon University, Vietnam
Trong-Thuc Hoang	University of Electro-Communications, Japan
Tran Hong Tai	Ho Chi Minh City University of Technology (HCMUT), VNU-HCM, Vietnam
Jianshu Hu	Shanghai Jiao Tong University, China
Bui Thanh Hung	Industrial University of Ho Chi Minh city, Vietnam
Jae Young Hur	Jeju National University, South Korea
Nor Azura Husin	Universiti Putra Malaysia, Malaysia
Nguyen Huu Giao	SELabs, EPFL Innovation Park, Switzerland
Masayuki Ida	Aoyama Gakuin University, Japan
Suradej Intagorn	Mahidol University, Thailand
Nor Azliana Akmal Jamaludin	National Defence University of Malaysia (UPNM), Malaysia
Dayang Norhayati Abang Jawawi	Universiti Teknologi Malaysia, Malaysia
Yunpeng Jiang	Shanghai Jiao Tong University, China
Srinivas Jvs	DVR College of Engineering and Technology, India

Manasawee Kaenampornpan	Khon Kaen University, Thailand
Phan Tran Minh Khue	Ho Chi Minh City Open University, Vietnam
Nguyen Kieu Linh	Posts and Telecommunications Institute of Technology, Vietnam
Pham Kieu Nhat Anh	Ho Chi Minh City University of Technology (HCMUT), VNU-HCM, Vietnam
Binh Kieu-Do-Nguyen	EdgeCortix Company, Japan
Ven Jyn Kok	Universiti Kebangsaan Malaysia, Malaysia
Monchai Kooakachai	Chulalongkorn University, Thailand
Raja Kumar	Taylor's University, Malaysia
Hürevren Kiliç	Atilim University, Turkey
Weng Kin Lai	Tunku Abdul Rahman University of Management & Technology, Malaysia
Jérôme Lang	CNRS, LAMSADE, Université Paris-Dauphine, France
Long Tan Le	University of Sydney, Australia
Thai Le	Ho Chi Minh City University of Science, Vietnam
Thanh Van Le	Ho Chi Minh City University of Technology (HCMUT), VNU-HCM, Vietnam
Trong Nhan Le	Ho Chi Minh City University of Technology (HCMUT), VNU-HCM, Vietnam
Tung Le	University of Science, VNU-HCM, Vietnam
Boon Giin	Lee University of Nottingham Ningbo China, China
Jysoo Lee	King Abdullah University of Science and Technology, Saudi Arabia
Yunli Lee	Sunway University, Malaysia
Yu Li	University of Tsukuba, Japan
Nguyen Thi Thuy Loan	International University, VNU-Ho Chi Minh City, Vietnam
Nguyen Hong Buu Long	University of Science – VNU-HCMC, Vietnam
Xuân Bách Lê	Ho Chi Minh City University of Technology (HCMUT), VNU-HCM, Vietnam
Naga Sailaja Mahankali	ICS An Mai International University, Vietnam
An Mai	International University, VNU-HCM, Vietnam
Tai Tan Mai	Dublin City University, Ireland
Xuan Toan Mai	Ho Chi Minh City University of Technology (HCMUT), VNU-HCM, Vietnam
Sakorn Mekruksavanich	University of Phayao, Thailand
Jérôme Mengin	IRIT - Université de Toulouse, France
Raghava Morusupalli	CVR College of Engineering, India
Mahesh Munjala	CSL, USA
Le Nguyen Hoai Nam	VNUHCM - University of Science, Vietnam

Khanista Namee	King Mongkut's University of Technology North Bangkok, Thailand
Do Thanh Nghi	Can Tho University, Vietnam
Duc Minh Ngo	Qualcomm, Ireland
Vuong M. Ngo	Dublin City University, Ireland
Duc Dung Nguyen	Ho Chi Minh City University of Technology (HCMUT), VNU-HCM, Vietnam
Hien D. Nguyen	University of Information Technology, VHU-HCM, Vietnam
Hoang H. Nguyen	University of Tennessee at Chattanooga, USA
Hung Nguyen	Griffith University, Australia
Hung Son Nguyen	University of Warsaw, Poland
Huynh Tuong Nguyen	Industrial University of Ho Chi Minh City, Vietnam
Kiet Van Nguyen	University of Information Technology, Vietnamese National University - Ho Chi Minh City, Vietnam
Le Duy Lai Nguyen	Ho Chi Minh City University of Technology (HCMUT), VNU-HCM, Vietnam
Le Minh Nguyen	Japan Advanced Institute of Science and Technology, Japan
Quoc Duy Nam Nguyen	Osaka Metropolitan University, Japan
Truc Nguyen	National Renewable Energy Laboratory, USA
Viet Hung Nguyen	LIMOS CNRS, Clermont Auvergne University, France
Vinh-Tiep Nguyen	University of Information Technology, VNU-HCMC, Vietnam
Vinh Nguyen Dinh	FPT University, Can Tho, Vietnam
Thao Nguyen-Thi-Ai	Ho Chi Minh City University of Technology (HCMUT), VNU-HCM, Vietnam
George Obaido	University of California, Berkeley, USA
Oliver Obst	Western Sydney University, Australia
Jia Jan Ong	Tunku Abdul Rahman University of Management and Technology, Malaysia
Jun Pang	University of Luxembourg, Luxembourg
Stuart Perry	University of Technology Sydney, Australia
Hoang-Anh Pham	Ho Chi Minh City University of Technology (HCMUT), VNU-HCM, Vietnam
Nick Pham	Cardiff University, UK
Ninh Pham	University of Auckland, New Zealand
Phu Pham	HUTECH University, Ho Chi Minh City, Vietnam
Thien Pham	Ho Chi Minh City University of Technology (HCMUT), VNU-HCM, Vietnam

Trinh Tan	Dat Saigon University, Vietnam
Thanh Tuan Thai	Jeju National University, South Korea
Nguyen Thanh Cong	Ho Chi Minh City University of Technology (HCMUT), VNU-HCM, Vietnam
Vu The Huynh	Cinnamon Lab, Vietnam
Mai The Vu	Sejong University, South Korea
Nguyen Thi Ngoc Hoa	Ho Chi Minh City University of Transport, Vietnam
Van Thien Hoang	Ho Chi Minh City University of Technology (HCMUT), VNU-HCM, Vietnam
Pham Duc Thinh	ATMRI - NTU, Singapore
Tran Ngoc Thinh	Ho Chi Minh City University of Technology (HCMUT), VNU-HCM, Vietnam
Jaree Thongkam	Mahasarakham University, Thailand
Nguyen Tien Huy	University of Science Ho Chi Minh City, Vietnam
Long Phuoc	Ton Industrial University of Ho Chi Minh City, Vietnam
Manegaouindé Roland Tougma	Université Joseph Ki-Zerbo, Burkina Faso
Tuan Anh Tran	Ho Chi Minh City University of Technology (HCMUT), VNU-HCM, Vietnam
Nguyen Tran Minh Khang	University of Information Technology, VNU-HCM, Vietnam
Duy Tran Ngoc Bao	Ho Chi Minh City University of Technology (HCMUT), VNU-HCM, Vietnam
Tuan Phat Tran Truong	Ho Chi Minh City University of Technology (HCMUT), VNU-HCM, Vietnam
Hong Son Trang	Hoa Sen University, Vietnam
Le Hong Trang	Ho Chi Minh City University of Technology (HCMUT), VNU-HCM, Vietnam
Nguyen Hai Trieu Anh	NamiTech JSC, Vietnam
Van-Giang Trinh	Inria Saclay, EP Lifeware, France
Luu Anh Tuan	Nanyang Technological University, Singapore
Vo Tuan Binh	Ho Chi Minh City University of Technology (HCMUT), VNU-HCM, Vietnam
Nguyen Tuan	Dang Saigon University, Vietnam
Nguyen Tuan Khoi	Ho Chi Minh City University of Technology (HCMUT), VNU-HCM, Vietnam
Tran Thanh	Tung International University, VNUHCM, Vietnam
Suguru Ueda	Saga University, Japan
Mudita Uppal	Chitkara University, India
Huynh Van Thong	Chonnam National University, South Korea
Kieu Van Xuan	FPT Software, Vietnam

Truong Vinh Lan	Ho Chi Minh City University of Technology (HCMUT), VNU-HCM, Vietnam
Bay Vo	HUTECH University, Ho Chi Minh, Vietnam
Dang Khoa Vo	Industrial University of Ho Chi Minh City, Vietnam
Nhat Vo	Chonnam National University, South Korea
Phuong Vo	International University - VNUHCM, Vietnam
Tham Vo	Nguyen Tat Thanh University, Vietnam
Chalee Vorakulpipat	NECTEC, Thailand
Thuy Trang Vu	Monash University, Australia
Tu Vu	Chonnam National University, South Korea
Paul Weng	Duke Kunshan University, China
Mariusz Wzorek	Linköping University, Sweden
Yoke Leng Yong	HELP University, Malaysia
Noor Hidayah Zakaria	Universiti Teknologi Malaysia, Malaysia
Aniqua Nusrat Zereen	Mahidol University, Thailand
Chunlai Zhou	Renmin University of China, China

Additional Reviewers

Abdul Wahab, Norshahriah
Ahmad, Arniyati
Alsayed, Ahmed
An, Mai
Arbain, Rizal
Binh, Huynh Thi Thanh
Bredenfeld, Ansgar
Bui, Long
Bühl, Johannes
Chu, Nguyen-Hoang
Chu, Quang Huy
Dinh, Tran Van
Duong, Tran Dai
Hao, Do
Hoang, Thien
Huynh, Kha
Ivan, Mujuni
Jyothirmai, J.
Krause, Stefanie
Le, Duy Dong
Le, Truc Nhi
Li, Yu
Lorente Lemoine, Loic
Luu, Son
Mai, Xuan Toan
Marzukhi, Syahaniem
Mat Jusoh, Ruzanna
Nguyen, Minh-Phuong
Nguyen, Ngoc-Minh
Nguyen, Thuy An
Obaido, George
Quan, Thanh Tho
Samya, Dr.Banoth
Satyamurty, Ch. V. S.
Shamszaman, Zia Ush
Song, Shaoyang
The Vu, Mai
Xie, Yiqian
Xu, Yifan
Zeng, Linghan
Zhao, Wenhao
Zheng, Yingtao
Zhong, Junyan

Contents

Topological Activation Maps for Visual Representation Learning from Tabular Data

M. Achutha(✉) and Bhaskarjyoti Das(✉)

Department of Computer Science and Engineering (AIML), PES University, Bengaluru 560084, India
achutha2704@gmail.com, bhaskarjyoti01@gmail.com

Abstract. The transformation of non-image data into visual representations suitable for deep learning remains a challenging frontier in machine learning. Many existing methods map tabular data to images via global feature-space layouts, which can reduce instance-specific nuance. We propose Topological Activation Maps (TAMs), a new framework that couples global feature topology with per-instance activations for more faithful and interpretable data transformations. TAMs use a two-phase embedding: (i) kernel projection and Self-Organizing Map training establish a prototype grid capturing global feature relationships; (ii) each sample generates a unique activation map by interacting with this grid through Gaussian-weighted distances. This design preserves both dataset-level structure and sample-specific characteristics. On benchmark classification datasets, TAMs deliver competitive or superior accuracy compared with strong ensemble baselines while offering a complementary perspective on interpretability.

Keywords: Tabular Deep learning · Representation learning · Feature Extraction · Dimensionality Reduction

1 Introduction

The success of deep learning in computer vision has prompted sustained efforts to extend convolutional and attention-based architectures to tabular data. Unlike images, where spatial proximity carries semantic meaning—adjacent pixels belong to the same object, neighboring patches share texture—tabular features lack inherent geometry. Features are arbitrarily ordered, heterogeneous in scale and type, and their relationships are statistical rather than spatial. This fundamental mismatch poses a question: can we engineer meaningful spatial structure that leverages vision models' inductive biases without discarding the intrinsic characteristics of tabular data?

Existing approaches attempt this transformation through various strategies like Dimensionality reduction, Feature permutation and Embedding based methods. These methods optimize feature arrangements to align statistical similarity

T. T. Quan et al. (Eds.): MIWAI 2025, LNAI 16353, pp. 1–12, 2026.
https://doi.org/10.1007/978-981-95-4957-3_1

with pixel proximity, producing a single global layout. While these methods establish spatial structure, they encode all variation through pixel intensities at predetermined locations, potentially conflating global feature topology with sample-specific characteristics. [1–3]. We introduce Topological Activation Maps (TAMs), a framework that decouples these two aspects. TAM operates in two phases: first, it learns a global topological reference by projecting data into kernel space and training a Self-Organizing Map to arrange prototypes on a 2D grid; second, each sample generates its own activation map by measuring proximity to these prototypes via Gaussian-weighted distances. This design preserves dataset-level manifold structure in the prototype grid while encoding individual samples as unique spatial activation patterns—a "topological fingerprint" that captures both where a sample lies within the learned topology and how it deviates from learned prototypes. The transformation induces a hybrid kernel that combines feature-space geometry with spatial topology, enabling vision models to exploit their architectural biases.

We evaluate TAM across 11 UCI benchmark datasets spanning diverse characteristics—dimensionality, class balance, and problem type—comparing against tree-based ensembles, deep tabular models, and DeepInsight. TAM paired with modern vision architectures (BEiT, ConvNeXt, ResNet) achieves robust performance in 25 of 44 metric-dataset combinations, with particularly strong results on imbalanced datasets where the topology-preserving encoding effectively captures minority class structure. These results suggest that explicitly separating global topology from local variation provides a principled pathway for applying vision models to tabular data.

2 Related Work

The remarkable success of Convolutional Neural Networks (CNNs) in computer vision has motivated researchers to explore whether these architectures could be applied to tabular data. There have been several advancements in tabular deep learning [4–6], however the question persists: can meaningful spatial representations of tabular features be engineered for CNNs' hierarchical feature learning capabilities? Unlike images, where spatial proximity is meaningful, tabular features are arbitrarily ordered and heterogeneous, mixing continuous, categorical, and binary values across different scales and distributions. Converting tabular data into images addresses this by inducing pseudo-spatial relationships and standardizing features into uniform matrices suitable for deep learning architectures. [3,7].

Gómez-Martínez et al. [8] categorized existing methodologies into three categories based on their feature arrangement strategies. *Dimensionality Reduction-Based Methods* project features onto a 2D plane using manifold learning algorithms. DeepInsight [1] applies t-SNE or Kernel PCA to obtain feature coordinates, uses convex hull and rotation to frame the scatter plot, then maps features to pixels—often with collision averaging and resulting sparse images. REFINED [9] employs Multidimensional Scaling followed by hill-climbing optimization to preserve pairwise feature distances. *Embedding and Direct Encoding*

Methods employ diverse strategies beyond similarity optimization. SuperTML [10] renders feature values as text strings on images, natively handling mixed types and missing data while leveraging pretrained vision models. *Feature Permutation and Similarity-Based Methods* directly optimize feature placement by matching statistical relationships to spatial proximity. IGTD [2] frames arrangement as rank-matching: iteratively swapping features to minimize differences between feature similarity ranks and pixel distance ranks, producing compact, dense images. LM-IGTD [8] extends this by first augmenting low-dimensional datasets with stochastic noise features to create larger images, addressing the "low-dimensionality trap". Notably, VFP [11] contradicts this clustering principle, positioning highly correlated features far apart in a vortex pattern to prevent overfitting—revealing fundamental disagreement about optimal spatial structure. TabMap [12] creates a fixed, feature-centric grid and shows sample variations as changing intensities at preset locations.

In contrast, TAM learns a prototype topology in kernel space and projects each instance as a topological activation map over this manifold—encoding variation as spatial activation patterns rather than static intensities. In doing so, TAM links global structure and local geometry, distinguishing TAM as more than a feature-placement heuristic; it is a hybrid Dimensionality Reduction—cum—embedding based method with explicit globalâĂŞlocal coupling. Other notable approaches include NCTD's geometric transformations, Tab2Visual's bar-chart representations, and BIE's binary encoding with correlation-based reordering [13–15].

3 Methodology

As outlined in Algorithm 1, our proposed method transforms tabular data into 2D image representations through a structured, two-phase process. The first phase is concerned with learning a robust topological layout of the feature space. This involves projecting the data into a non-linear manifold using a kernel approximation and then training a Self-Organizing Map (SOM) [16] to arrange learned data prototypes onto a 2D grid which serves as a fixed reference map of the dataset's intrinsic structure. In the second phase, each individual data sample is transformed into a unique image by computing its proximity to every prototype on the reference grid, generating a smooth activation map.

3.1 Phase 1: Learning the Global Topological Grid

The goal of this phase is to construct a fixed grid of prototypes that faithfully represents the dataset's intrinsic topology. This involves a kernel space embedding followed by competitive learning.

Non-Linear Feature Space Embedding. To effectively model non-linear relationships, we first project the data $X \in \mathbb{R}^{n \times d}$ into a high-dimensional feature

Algorithm 1 Topological Activation Map (TAM)

Phase 1: Global Topology Learning

Input: $X_{\text{train}}, X_{\text{test}}, (g_x, g_y), (\gamma, m, \sigma)$
$X'_{\text{train}}, X'_{\text{test}} \leftarrow \text{Std}(X_{\text{train}}, X_{\text{test}})$
$\Phi \leftarrow \text{NystroemMapping}(X'_{\text{train}}, \gamma, m)$
  ▷ Learn RBF kernel projection
$X_{\text{train\_k}} \leftarrow \Phi(X'_{\text{train}})$
$X_{\text{test\_k}} \leftarrow \Phi(X'_{\text{test}})$
$\pi \leftarrow \text{FindFeatureOrder}(X_{\text{train\_k}})$
  ▷ Via hierarchical clustering
$X_{\text{train\_k}} \leftarrow X_{\text{train\_k}}[:, \pi]$
$X_{\text{test\_k}} \leftarrow X_{\text{test\_k}}[:, \pi]$
$W_{\text{init}} \leftarrow \text{PCA-Init}(X_{\text{train\_k}}, g_x, g_y)$
$W \leftarrow \text{TrainSOM}(X_{\text{train\_k}}, W_{\text{init}})$
  ▷ $W \in \mathbb{R}^{g_x \times g_y \times m}$

Phase 2: Activation Map Generation

function GENERATE(X_{k}, W, σ)
  $I \leftarrow \{\}$
  for each sample $x_i \in X_{\text{k}}$ **do**
    $A_i \leftarrow \left[\exp(-\frac{\|x_i - W_{p,q}\|^2}{2\sigma^2})\right]_{(p,q)}$
      ▷ Create $g_x \times g_y$ map
    $A'_i \leftarrow \text{Normalize}(A_i)$
      ▷ Scale to [0, 1]
    $I_i \leftarrow \text{Colormap}(A'_i)$
      ▷ Convert to 3-channel
    $I \leftarrow I \cup \{I_i\}$
  end for
  return I
end function

$I_{\text{train}} \leftarrow \text{Generate}(X_{\text{train\_k}}, W, \sigma)$
$I_{\text{test}} \leftarrow \text{Generate}(X_{\text{test\_k}}, W, \sigma)$

Return $I_{\text{train}}, I_{\text{test}}$

space induced by an RBF kernel. We use the Nyström method to efficiently approximate this projection, yielding a new representation:

$$X_{\text{k}} = K_{nm} V(\Lambda + \epsilon I)^{-1/2} \in \mathbb{R}^{n \times m} \quad (1)$$

where $K_{nm}[i, j] = \exp(-\gamma\|x_i - z_j\|^2)$ is the kernel matrix between the n data points and m landmark points $\{z_j\}$, while V and Λ are the eigenvectors and eigenvalues of the landmark-only kernel matrix K_m and ϵ is a small tolerance factor for numerical stability. This formulation provides a computationally tractable embedding where Euclidean distances better reflect the data's manifold structure.

Feature Reordering for Spatial Coherence. To prime the embedding for convolutional architectures, we reorder the features in X_{k} to group correlated features together. We compute the absolute correlation matrix $C_{ij} = \left|\text{corr}(X_{\text{k}}^{(i)}, X_{\text{k}}^{(j)})\right|$, derive a dissimilarity matrix $D = 1 - C$, and apply Ward's linkage clustering. This yields a permutation π that minimizes the sum of dissimilarities between adjacent features, $\sum_{i=1}^{m-1} D_{\pi(i),\pi(i+1)}$. Applying this reordering, $X_{\text{k}} \leftarrow X_{\text{k}}[:, \pi]$, creates a near-banded correlation structure, enabling convolutional filters to operate on spatially grouped, semantically related features.

Prototype Grid Learning via SOM. With the data embedded and ordered, we learn the topological grid using a Self-Organizing Map (SOM).

PCA-Based Initialization. A key step for stable convergence is a structured initialization of the SOM's prototype vectors, $W_{p,q} \in \mathbb{R}^m$. We align the initial grid with the data's principal axes of variation. Let v_1, v_2 be the top two principal eigenvectors of X_{k} and μ be its mean. Each prototype is initialized as:

$$W_{p,q}^{(0)} = \mu + \alpha_p v_1 + \beta_q v_2 \quad (2)$$

where scalars α_p, β_q linearly interpolate between -1 and 1 across the grid dimensions:

$$\alpha_p = \frac{2p}{g_x - 1} - 1, \quad \beta_q = \frac{2q}{g_y - 1} - 1 \tag{3}$$

This deterministic start accelerates convergence and helps avoid poor local minima.

Competitive Update. The SOM is then trained iteratively. For each input x_i, the Best Matching Unit (BMU) is identified, and its weights, along with those of its grid neighbors, are updated to move closer to the input sample according to the standard update rule:

$$W_{p,q}(t+1) = W_{p,q}(t) + \alpha(t) h_{b,(p,q)}(t)(x_i - W_{p,q}(t)) \tag{4}$$

where $\alpha(t)$ is a decaying learning rate and $h_{b,(p,q)}(t)$ is a decaying neighborhood function centered on the BMU. The final trained grid, W, serves as the global topological reference for the next phase.

3.2 Phase 2: Sample-Specific Activation Map Generation

In the second phase, the static prototype grid W serves as a reference frame to transform each individual sample $x_i \in X_{\mathrm{k}}$ into its own unique 2D image. This process encodes the sample's specific location within the learned global topology.

Gaussian Activation. The core of the transformation is to measure the proximity of a sample to every prototype on the grid. The activation intensity $A_i(p,q)$ at each grid position (p,q) is computed using a Gaussian function of the Euclidean distance between the sample x_i and the prototype $W_{p,q}$:

$$A_i(p,q) = \exp\left(-\frac{\|x_i - W_{p,q}\|^2}{2\sigma^2}\right) \tag{5}$$

The hyperparameter σ controls the activation's bandwidth. A small σ produces a sparse map highlighting only the most similar prototypes, whereas a larger σ creates a smoother activation pattern across a wider neighborhood of the data manifold.

Normalization and Image Formation. To maximize the dynamic range for visual models, the raw activation map A_i is normalized to the range $[0,1]$ using standard min-max scaling:

$$A_i'(p,q) = \frac{A_i(p,q) - \min(A_i)}{\max(A_i) - \min(A_i)} \tag{6}$$

The final step is to apply a perceptually uniform colormap to the normalized grayscale map, producing a 3-channel RGB image $I_i \in \mathbb{R}^{g_x \times g_y \times 3}$. This process creates a "topological fingerprint" for each sample. The resulting activation maps have a few key properties beneficial for interpretable visual learning:

- **Manifold Alignment**: Adjacent high-activation regions in A_i correspond to connected areas on the SOM grid, preserving the data's intrinsic topology.
- **Anomaly Detection**: Samples that are outliers in the original data space will be distant from all learned prototypes, resulting in low-intensity or low-entropy activation maps that are visually distinct.

Ultimately, this phase produces a geometrically grounded visual representation that encodes both sample-specific locality and global topological structure, bridging the gap between tabular data and computer vision.

3.3 Topological Activation Maps as Hybrid Kernels

The Induced Kernel Structure. The transformation from tabular data to activation maps induces a hybrid kernel that combines feature-space geometry with learned topological structure. For samples x_i, x_j, the normalized activation maps $A'_i, A'_j \in \mathbb{R}^{g_x \times g_y}$ define an implicit similarity measure

$$K(x_i, x_j) = \sum_{p,q} A'_i(p,q) \cdot A'_j(p,q) = \langle A'_i, A'_j \rangle \tag{7}$$

where each entry $A'_i(p,q) = \exp(-\frac{\|x_i - W_{p,q}\|^2}{2\sigma^2})$ measures the affinity between sample x_i and prototype $W_{p,q}$. This kernel encodes two complementary aspects: (1) *feature-space similarity*, captured by the distance $\|x_i - W_{p,q}\|$ in the kernel-projected space, and (2) *manifold topology*, embedded in the spatial arrangement of prototypes where adjacent grid positions (p, q) and $(p \pm 1, q \pm 1)$ correspond to neighboring regions of the data manifold.

The SOM training ensures that prototypes preserve the manifold structure of X_{kernel}, making the grid itself a topological reference frame. Consequently, each activation map A_i serves as a sample-specific "topological fingerprint"—a spatially structured representation that encodes how the sample deviates from the learned manifold prototypes.

Vision Models as Kernel Machines. Vision models processing these activation maps can be viewed as learning to approximate kernel-based decision functions. The activation map A_i acts as an explicit feature map $\phi(x_i) \in \mathbb{R}^{g_x \times g_y}$, allowing models to represent functions of the form

$$f(x) = \sum_{i=1}^{n} \alpha_i K(x, x_i) = \sum_{i=1}^{n} \alpha_i \langle \phi(x), \phi(x_i) \rangle \tag{8}$$

where α_i are learned weights. Unlike classical kernel methods with fixed kernels, vision models *adaptively learn* to extract task-relevant patterns from $\phi(x)$ through their architectural inductive biases.

The architectural inductive biases of vision models determine how they exploit this kernel structure. CNNs, through spatially localized convolutions, naturally aggregate neighboring prototypes where semantic similarity is encoded by spatial proximity on the grid. The Gaussian activation ensures smoothness in A_i, allowing convolutional filters to detect gradients and boundaries between manifold regions—hierarchically composing local prototype transitions into global discriminative features. Vision Transformers, conversely, employ self-attention to directly model pairwise interactions across all grid positions (p, q), aligning with the kernel's global summation structure $\sum_{p,q}$ without spatial locality constraints. This enables ViTs to capture long-range dependencies between disjoint but semantically related manifold regions. Both architectures thus learn complementary decompositions of the hybrid kernel: CNNs through spatial coherence, ViTs through relational coherence.

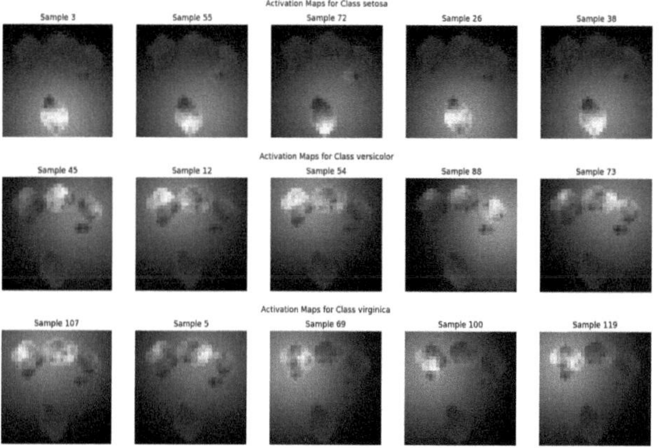

Fig. 1. Topological activation maps for random samples across three Iris classes, demonstrating class-specific structural patterns.

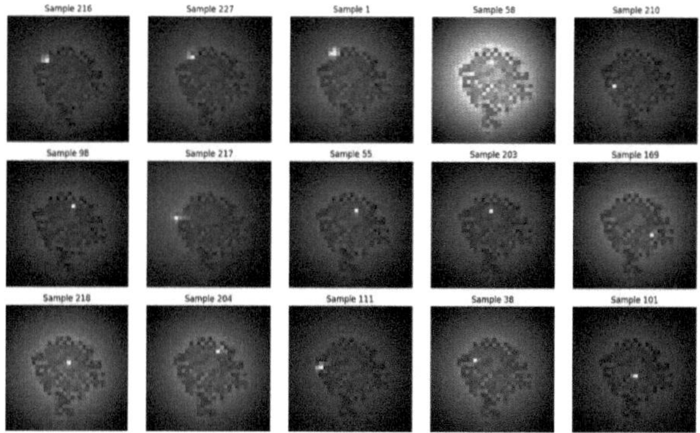

Fig. 2. Activation maps for the positive class of the Pima dataset, highlighting intra-class variability and potential outliers.

Interpretability Through Topology. The framework's interpretability stems from the fixed SOM grid acting as a shared coordinate system across all samples. Differences in activation patterns directly reflect structural variations in the data manifold: concentrated activations indicate samples near well-defined cluster centers, while diffuse or multi-modal patterns suggest boundary regions or outliers. Figure 1 illustrates this for the Iris dataset, where each class exhibits characteristic activation signatures—Setosa with sharp, localized patterns, and Versicolor/Virginica with more distributed responses reflecting their manifold proximity.

Similarly, Fig. 2 demonstrates outlier detection capabilities within the Pima dataset's positive class. Samples with anomalously low activation entropy or minimal overlap with prototype regions indicate deviations from the learned manifold structure. This interpretability arises naturally from the topological encoding: the SOM grid provides a reference frame, and activation deviations quantify sample-manifold alignment.

The combination of a topology-preserving transformation with vision models' inductive biases thus creates a framework where architectural choices—local convolution versus global attention—determine how the hybrid kernel's manifold structure is exploited for downstream tasks.

4 Experiments

Our experiment aim to assess whether the topology-preserving transformation provides consistent benefits across architectures and data characteristics.

Datasets. We evaluate on 11 benchmark datasets from the UCI Machine Learning Repository, selected to represent diverse tabular data characteristics: Churn, E-coli, Iris, Glass, Heart, Liver, Vertebral Column (VC-2C, VC-3C), Pima Diabetes, QSAR Biodegradation, and Wine Quality. These datasets span binary and multi-class problems with varying dimensionality and sample sizes. Several datasets exhibit class imbalance (Wine, Churn, Liver, Pima), providing a test of robustness to long-tailed distributions.

Models. We compare three categories of methods: (1) *Tree-based ensembles*: CatBoost (CB), Extra Trees (ET), Random Forest (RF), XGBoost (XGB), LightGBM (LGBM); (2) *Deep tabular models*: FT-Transformer (FTT), Tab-Transformer (TT), Multi-Layer Perceptron (MLP); (3) *Vision-based approaches*: DeepInsight (DI-B, DI-C, DI-R) and the proposed TAM (TAM-B, TAM-C, TAM-R), both paired with three vision architectures—BEiT (B), ConvNeXt (C), and ResNet (R). DeepInsight employs Umap for 2D projection followed by pixel-based image construction, while TAM uses the topology-preserving transformation described in 3.

Metrics. We report four standard classification metrics: accuracy, area under the ROC curve (AUC-ROC), F1-score, and Matthews Correlation Coefficient (MCC). The latter two are particularly informative for imbalanced datasets, with MCC providing a balanced measure that accounts for all confusion matrix elements.

Table 1. Performance comparison across datasets. Best results for each metric-dataset combination are shown in bold.

Model	Metric	Churn	E-coli	Iris	Glass	Heart	Liver	VC-2C	VC-3C	Pima	QSAR	Wine
CB	accuracy	79.52	87.51	95.33	**80.39**	81.18	72.22	82.58	82.58	76.95	87.39	56.67
	auc-roc	84.07	96.06	99.60	**96.61**	90.93	76.63	94.47	94.47	**82.99**	93.55	**79.18**
	f1	78.74	86.51	95.31	78.97	80.96	69.80	82.11	82.11	**76.54**	87.28	54.96
	mcc	44.45	82.87	93.21	**73.31**	62.34	24.40	72.23	72.23	48.03	71.49	32.69
DI-B	accuracy	75.98	86.76	96.67	79.07	**86.89**	71.79	79.03	83.87	73.38	79.62	55.17
	auc-roc	75.19	98.65	99.67	86.82	**94.59**	74.45	88.97	91.31	73.89	83.05	73.31
	f1	48.79	87.51	96.66	**79.16**	**88.57**	5.71	79.26	83.35	62.39	63.25	47.85
	mcc	33.97	82.24	95.16	71.46	**73.97**	14.51	69.04	73.92	41.79	52.28	27.60
DI-C	accuracy	76.90	91.18	96.67	74.42	77.05	72.65	79.03	83.87	74.03	79.15	55.08
	auc-roc	79.33	97.81	99.67	86.38	81.28	69.91	90.58	91.89	76.13	82.12	67.63
	f1	46.81	91.14	96.66	74.12	77.42	11.11	78.40	84.27	53.49	60.71	52.01
	mcc	34.39	87.85	95.16	66.28	54.75	20.60	66.33	75.02	39.51	51.22	28.87
DI-R	accuracy	76.90	89.71	**100.00**	67.44	72.13	70.94	77.42	80.65	71.43	80.09	54.61
	auc-roc	77.72	98.47	**100.00**	80.91	80.74	70.94	84.40	90.54	73.69	82.23	71.53
	f1	46.81	89.90	**100.00**	67.71	70.18	0.00	70.04	81.04	56.86	67.69	50.80
	mcc	34.39	86.00	**100.00**	55.81	47.25	0.00	66.40	69.45	35.75	53.96	27.48
ET	accuracy	77.93	86.32	96.00	78.03	82.51	**73.59**	80.65	80.65	75.52	86.92	57.29
	auc-roc	79.70	91.90	99.42	95.75	91.18	**76.83**	94.53	94.53	81.56	93.23	74.67
	f1	77.01	85.23	95.98	76.79	82.31	**71.15**	79.79	79.79	74.94	86.78	**55.04**
	mcc	39.81	81.25	94.18	70.02	65.17	28.22	69.41	69.41	44.42	70.37	**32.96**
FTT	accuracy	**80.60**	85.14	96.00	71.48	83.16	71.70	82.58	85.48	75.00	84.74	55.64
	auc-roc	**84.86**	95.50	98.50	92.03	86.76	74.95	94.99	95.15	81.83	91.35	77.74
	f1	**79.97**	84.49	95.95	68.48	83.03	68.94	82.82	85.63	74.64	84.33	53.45
	mcc	**47.80**	79.65	94.29	61.29	66.48	24.23	72.52	76.98	44.44	65.07	30.86
LGBM	accuracy	79.54	86.31	94.67	79.90	80.88	70.85	82.26	82.26	74.34	87.68	55.32
	auc-roc	83.64	94.18	98.97	92.81	88.09	74.72	94.37	94.37	79.73	**93.64**	77.83
	f1	78.87	85.16	94.61	78.41	80.75	70.02	82.18	82.18	74.15	**87.58**	53.56
	mcc	44.88	81.29	92.35	72.50	61.67	25.39	71.80	71.80	42.89	72.24	30.54
MLP	accuracy	79.42	79.46	72.67	54.21	80.20	69.65	76.77	77.42	75.51	86.64	55.60
	auc-roc	83.56	89.12	92.03	79.67	86.42	61.29	92.55	92.13	81.14	92.12	73.52
	f1	78.49	74.84	67.90	47.03	79.97	63.20	74.56	75.45	73.78	86.49	52.57
	mcc	43.79	71.71	65.62	38.52	60.32	8.13	62.66	63.53	43.10	69.74	29.99
RF	accuracy	79.12	87.80	94.67	75.70	81.52	69.82	84.19	84.19	76.95	87.11	56.99
	auc-roc	82.41	92.93	99.43	95.83	90.23	74.64	94.75	94.75	82.38	93.50	73.74
	f1	78.12	86.59	94.64	74.35	81.33	67.56	83.84	83.84	76.50	86.93	54.54
	mcc	42.71	83.29	92.24	66.92	62.97	18.40	74.88	74.88	47.91	70.69	32.39
TAM-B	accuracy	79.10	89.71	96.67	67.44	**86.89**	72.65	83.87	88.71	74.68	**89.10**	56.48
	auc-roc	82.88	98.46	99.67	90.01	92.42	73.18	93.12	94.67	81.57	92.65	76.67
	f1	60.80	89.55	96.66	63.90	**88.57**	11.11	81.96	88.88	62.86	83.92	53.87
	mcc	46.56	85.72	95.16	56.39	**73.97**	20.60	75.20	82.40	43.71	**75.68**	31.80
TAM-C	accuracy	79.10	**92.36**	**100.00**	74.42	**86.89**	72.65	**88.71**	**90.32**	**77.27**	88.63	56.67
	auc-roc	81.81	**98.70**	**100.00**	88.60	**94.59**	74.91	**95.49**	95.55	82.83	93.07	76.66
	f1	57.14	**91.53**	**100.00**	71.53	88.24	42.86	**88.48**	89.99	65.35	83.10	54.31
	mcc	43.79	**88.33**	**100.00**	66.23	73.61	27.01	**81.82**	84.44	**48.82**	74.53	32.11
TAM-R	accuracy	79.60	89.71	**100.00**	74.42	85.25	71.79	87.10	**90.32**	75.97	87.20	**57.52**
	auc-roc	82.39	97.51	**100.00**	94.93	85.61	70.80	94.04	**95.57**	81.63	91.74	75.33
	f1	57.98	89.60	**100.00**	73.82	88.00	54.79	87.30	**90.50**	67.26	78.74	53.60
	mcc	45.03	85.81	**100.00**	65.87	73.02	**34.61**	80.13	**84.97**	48.46	70.77	32.43
TT	accuracy	79.45	63.07	60.67	50.01	82.18	71.18	69.68	74.19	68.62	87.01	53.20
	auc-roc	83.90	87.94	83.97	83.76	89.26	67.07	88.04	87.77	72.60	93.05	75.35
	f1	78.69	52.58	50.32	40.53	82.19	62.44	65.22	71.99	62.26	86.87	50.35
	mcc	44.60	43.65	47.34	36.33	64.40	9.50	50.22	58.49	22.73	71.07	27.15
XGB	accuracy	78.63	86.01	94.00	75.23	78.23	69.99	81.94	81.94	73.17	86.73	55.24
	auc-roc	82.44	95.87	96.87	92.99	86.65	73.80	93.79	93.79	79.02	92.87	78.16
	f1	78.06	85.17	93.89	73.60	78.06	69.04	81.90	81.90	72.87	86.62	53.59
	mcc	42.84	80.93	91.33	66.27	56.33	23.18	71.28	71.28	39.98	69.96	30.59

4.1 Results

Table 1 reports results across all model–dataset combinations. TAM-based methods dominate, achieving the best score in 25 of 44 metric–dataset cases. TAM-C reaches perfect classification on *Iris* and state-of-the-art performance on *E-coli* (92.36% accuracy, 88.33% MCC), *VC-2C* (88.71%, 81.82%), and *Pima* (77.27%, 48.82%). TAM-R similarly excels on *VC-3C* (90.32%, 84.97%) and *Wine* (57.52%). Against vision-based baselines, TAM outperforms DeepInsight: e.g., on *E-coli* (92.36% vs. 91.18%) and *VC-2C* (88.71% vs. 79.03%). However, DI-B performs competitively on the *Heart disease* dataset.

Tree ensembles remain strong where tabular structure dominates: CatBoost leads on *Glass* (80.39%, 73.31% MCC) and *Pima* AUC-ROC (82.99%), while LGBM tops *QSAR* (87.68% accuracy, 93.64% AUC-ROC). FT-Transformer excels on *Churn* (80.60%, 47.80% MCC), whereas TabTransformer generally underperforms (e.g., 60.67% on *Iris*, 63.07% on *E-coli*), underscoring the need for structured encodings.

Within TAM, ConvNeXt (TAM-C) performs best on multi-class datasets via hierarchical depthwise convolutions; ResNet (TAM-R) is competitive on structured tasks; BEiT (TAM-B) helps on *Heart* and *QSAR*. TAM also shows robustness to imbalance: on *Pima* (35% positives), TAM-C attains 48.82% MCC (vs. CatBoost 48.03%); on *Liver* (28%), TAM-R achieves 34.61%, outperforming all rivals. TAM is not universally superior: CatBoost surpasses it on *Glass*, and boosting methods dominate *QSAR*. These cases indicate tree-based models suffice when feature–target relations are largely additive. Overall, however, TAM's topology-preserving encodings consistently bridge tabular and vision paradigms, yielding robust performance across datasets.

4.2 Hyperparameter Tuning and Configuration Choices

The performance of TAM is governed by six hyperparameters optimized through systematic experimentation and ablation. The kernel dimensionality (m) sets the rank of the NystrÃűm approximation, with $m = 1024$ proving effective across datasets, or $m = n$ when the sample size is smaller. The RBF kernel parameter (γ) was fixed at 0.3, providing a balance between local and global influence. SOM grid dimensions (g_x, g_y) were tested from 8×8 to 64×64, with performance saturating at 32×32, offering sufficient resolution without excessive cost. Pretrained models (BEiT and ConvNeXt) expect 224×224 which is achieved through bilinear interpolation. SOM training parameters ($\sigma_{\text{SOM}}, \alpha_{\text{SOM}}$) followed MiniSom [17] defaults, which, in combination with PCA-based initialization, ensured robust convergence. The activation bandwidth (σ_{act}) was found to be critical for image quality: small values produced sparse, overly localized maps, while large values blurred discriminative patterns; $\sigma_{\text{act}} = 1.0$ achieved the best trade-off. Beyond these tunable parameters, PCA-based initialization consistently outperformed random seeding, yielding faster convergence and modest accuracy gains, while explicit feature reordering had minimal impact, as SOM training inherently organizes semantically related features.

5 Discussion and Conclusion

Our study demonstrates that decoupling global topology from sample-specific activations yields an effective representation for vision-based tabular learning. By combining kernel projection, Self-Organizing Map training, and Gaussian-weighted activation generation, TAM preserves both dataset-level manifold structure and individual sample characteristics, enabling vision models to leverage structured geometric information more effectively than direct dimensionality reduction methods. The hybrid kernel perspective provides theoretical grounding, clarifying why CNNs benefit from spatial coherence while vision transformers exploit relational coherence within TAM's topology-preserving activations. This principled design distinguishes TAM from heuristic feature-placement approaches and establishes a pathway for adapting vision architectures to non-visual domains.

At the same time, our results underscore the conditional value of topology-preserving transformations. Tree-based ensembles continue to dominate on datasets such as *Glass* and *QSAR*, where featureâĂŞtarget relationships are well captured by axis-aligned splits and shallow interactions. In such cases, the additional complexity of learning a non-linear manifold may be unnecessary, highlighting the contextual boundaries of TAM and reinforcing the "no free lunch 'n' principle. Moreover, the sharp contrast between TabTransformer and TAM-vision pairings suggests that treating raw features as token sequences discards critical relational information, whereas TAM provides a spatially meaningful inductive bias that self-attention can exploit.

Despite these contributions, our work has two main limitations. First, the study is restricted to classification tasks; extending TAM to regression and time-series remains an important avenue for future research. Second, the framework involves several hyperparameters whose tuning, though guided by ablation studies, may limit practical usability in larger or more heterogeneous datasets. Addressing these challenges through hierarchical SOM architectures, adaptive bandwidth selection, and semi-supervised extensions could improve scalability and robustness. In sum, TAM bridges tabular and visual learning paradigms, offering an interpretable, topology-aware foundation that invites further exploration beyond traditional feature engineering.

References

1. Sharma, A., Vans, E., Shigemizu, D., Boroevich, K.A., Tsunoda, T.: Deepinsight: a methodology to transform a non-image data to an image for convolution neural network architecture. Sci. Rep. **9**(1), 11399 (2019), https://www.nature.com/articles/s41598-019-47765-6
2. Zhu, Y., et al.: Converting tabular data into images for deep learning with convolutional neural networks. Sci. Rep. **11**(1), 11325 (2021)
3. Medeiros Neto, L., Rogerio Da Silva Neto, S., Endo, P.T.: A comparative analysis of converters of tabular data into image for the classification of arboviruses using convolutional neural networks. PLOS ONE **18**(12), e0295598 (2023), https://dx.plos.org/10.1371/journal.pone.0295598

4. Gorishniy, Y., Rubachev, I., Khrulkov, V., Babenko, A.: Revisiting deep learning models for tabular data. Adv. Neural. Inf. Process. Syst. **34**, 18932–18943 (2021)
5. Huang, X., Khetan, A., Cvitkovic, M., Karnin, Z.: Tabtransformer: tabular data modeling using contextual embeddings. arXiv preprint arXiv:2012.06678 (2020)
6. Hollmann, N., Müller, S., Eggensperger, K., Hutter, F.: Tabpfn: a transformer that solves small tabular classification problems in a second. arXiv preprint arXiv:2207.01848 (2022)
7. Borisov, V., Leemann, T., Seßler, K., Haug, J., Pawelczyk, M., Kasneci, G.: Deep neural networks and tabular data: a survey. IEEE Trans. Neural Netw. Learn. Syst. **35**(6), 7499–7519 (2024), https://ieeexplore.ieee.org/document/9998482/
8. Gómez-Martínez, V., Lara-Abelenda, F.J., Peiro-Corbacho, P., Chushig-Muzo, D., Granja, C., Soguero-Ruiz, C.: Lm-igtd: a 2d image generator for low-dimensional and mixed-type tabular data to leverage the potential of convolutional neural networks. arXiv preprint arXiv:2406.14566 (2024)
9. Bazgir, O., Zhang, R., Dhruba, S.R., Rahman, R., Ghosh, S., Pal, R.: Representation of features as images with neighborhood dependencies for compatibility with convolutional neural networks. Nat. Commun. **11**(1), 4391 (2020)
10. Sun, B., et al.: Supertml: two-dimensional word embedding for the precognition on structured tabular data. In: Proceedings of the IEEE/CVF Conference on Computer Vision and Pattern Recognition Workshops (2019)
11. Park, J.I., Seong, S., Lee, J., Hong, C.H.: Vortex feature positioning: bridging tabular iiot data and image-based deep learning. Internet Things **31**, 101533 (2025)
12. Yan, R., Islam, M.T., Xing, L.: Interpretable discovery of patterns in tabular data via spatially semantic topographic maps. Nat. Biomed. Eng. 1–12 (2024)
13. Alenizy, H.A., Berri, J.: Transforming tabular data into images via enhanced spatial relationships for cnn processing. Sci. Rep. **15**(1), 17004 (2025)
14. Mamdouh, A., El-Melegy, M., Ali, S., Kikinis, R.: Tab2visual: overcoming limited data in tabular data classification using deep learning with visual representations. arXiv preprint arXiv:2502.07181 (2025)
15. Halladay, J., et al.: Bie: binary image encoding for the classification of tabular data. J. Data Sci. **23**(1) (2025)
16. Kohonen, T.: The self-organizing map. Proc. IEEE **78**(9), 1464–1480 (1990)
17. Vettigli, G.: Minisom: minimalistic and numpy-based implementation of the self organizing map (2018), https://github.com/JustGlowing/minisom/

Robust Leaf Disease Classification via Deep Feature Concatenation and EfficientNetV

Ai My Thi Nguyen, Hoang Huy Le, and Vinh Dinh Nguyen(✉)

Department of Information Technology, FPT University, Can Tho City, Vietnam
{aintmcs171632,hoanglhce170452}@fpt.edu.vn, vinhnd29@fe.edu.vn

Abstract. Plants play a vital role in global food security, ecological balance, and economic sustainability. However, their susceptibility to a wide range of leaf diseases poses a major threat to crop yield and quality. Early and accurate identification of these diseases is essential for effective management. Manual inspection methods, though widely used, are inefficient, subjective, and unsuitable for large-scale agricultural operations. To address this challenge, we propose a deep learning-based classification system that significantly improves disease recognition performance. The model is designed to classify leaf images from six plant species—including both healthy and diseased samples—across 14 distinct categories. Our architecture leverages EfficientNetV2B0 as the feature extractor, enhanced with custom dense layers and feature concatenation to capture subtle visual cues. Through preprocessing and balanced dataset splitting, combined with training techniques such as dropout, adaptive learning rate scheduling, and early stopping, the model achieves robust generalization. Experimental evaluation shows that our approach improves classification accuracy from a baseline of 90.18% to 92.86%.

Keywords: EfficientNetV2B0 · Feature Concatenation · Leaf Disease Classification

1 Introduction

In recent years, the application of deep learning in plant leaf disease recognition has emerged as a prominent direction in smart agriculture research. Traditional approaches that rely on manual visual inspection are often time-consuming, error-prone, and impractical for large-scale deployment [1]. To overcome these limitations, deep learning models—especially Convolutional Neural Networks (CNNs)—have been widely adopted and have demonstrated superior performance across various plant disease datasets [2,3]. Modern CNN architectures such as EfficientNetV2 have recently shown remarkable effectiveness in image classification tasks due to their powerful feature extraction capabilities and fast training speeds [4–7]. With a compound scaling strategy that simultaneously

T. T. Quan et al. (Eds.): MIWAI 2025, LNAI 16353, pp. 13–24, 2026.
https://doi.org/10.1007/978-981-95-4957-3_2

increases network depth, width, and resolution, EfficientNetV2 achieves a balanced trade-off between accuracy and computational efficiency, while maintaining robustness on imbalanced datasets [4]. Some studies have further revealed that integrating EfficientNetV2 with optimization techniques or hybrid models can enhance disease recognition performance under complex real-world conditions [8]. Even modest improvements in classification accuracy can translate to significant reductions in crop losses, as early detection enables timely interventions. For instance, a 2.68% accuracy improvement, while seemingly small in numerical terms, can have substantial practical impact by increasing early detection rates and reducing the economic burden of plant diseases at scale. Unlike prior work that relies on single-level feature extraction, our approach integrates multi-level feature concatenation with EfficientNetV2B0 to address the challenge of visually similar disease symptoms across multiple crop species. This strategy enhances feature aggregation and improves the model's ability to generalize under diverse agricultural conditions. EfficientNetV2B0 was chosen as the backbone for its superior balance of accuracy and computational efficiency compared to heavier models like ResNet or lighter models like MobileNetV2. This makes it particularly suitable for edge deployment in agricultural settings, where both accuracy and resource efficiency are critical. Building upon these insights, this study proposes a plant leaf disease classification model using EfficientNetV2B0 as the feature extraction backbone, combined with Dense layers and feature concatenation to enhance feature learning and aggregation. This approach aims to improve classification accuracy, generalization capability, and the reliability of automated plant disease detection systems.

The structure of this paper is as follows: Sect. 2 provides an overview of related work along with their limitations. Section 3 introduces the proposed methodology in detail. Section 4 explains the experimental design and presents a comparative analysis of the results. Finally, Sect. 5 summarizes the main conclusions and outlines directions for future research.

2 Related Work

Table 1 categorizes recent approaches to plant leaf disease classification into three major groups: traditional CNNs, lightweight models, and survey-based research. Traditional CNNs such as Inception-V3 or ResNet152 typically achieve high accuracy but often suffer from excessive computational demands and poor class balance in real-world conditions [9,10]. Lightweight architectures like MobileNetV2 or SqueezeNet offer deployment efficiency but generally sacrifice classification performance, particularly in complex or noisy environments [11,12]. Meanwhile, survey-based works focus on synthesizing existing techniques without providing experimentally validated models, thus limiting their practical contributions.

In contrast to these research directions, our work presents a unified deep learning framework that explicitly addresses the core limitations identified above. We adopt EfficientNetV2B0, a modern CNN that offers a superior trade-off

Table 1. Summary of representative model groups and limitations in leaf disease classification.

Model Group	Example Models (Accuracy)	Limitations
Traditional CNNs	Inception-V3 (95âĂŞ99.76%) [9], ResNet50 (87.65%), ResNet152 (94.72%) [10]	- Often require high computational resources - Some models (e.g., VGG) contain a large number of parameters (e.g., 143 million) - Difficulty balancing precision and recall in certain diseases (e.g., DenseNet-121)
Lightweight Models	MobileNetV2 (∼89.6%) [10], EfficientNetB7 (97.5%) [11], SqueezeNet (low memory, high speed) [12]	- Lower accuracy compared to larger models - May perform poorly on complex or diverse datasets
Survey/Review Studies	Systematic reviews of CNNs, ResNet, EfficientNet, DenseNet [11]	- Do not involve direct experimentation - Focus only on summarizing strengths and weaknesses of other models

between performance and model size, as the backbone. To overcome the shortcomings of shallow or single-stream representations, we integrate multi-level dense feature concatenation, which captures both fine-grained textures and high-level semantics. Furthermore, we apply robust training strategies—including dropout, adaptive learning rate scheduling, and early stopping—to enhance generalization across diverse input conditions. Most notably, our model is evaluated on a realistic, multi-species dataset comprising 14 classes (healthy and diseased leaves across six plant types), simulating field-like variability rarely addressed in prior work. Despite the increased complexity, our proposed method achieves a competitive accuracy of 92.86%, demonstrating not only superior classification ability but also scalability and edge deployment potential. By combining architectural efficiency, deep feature integration, and field-oriented evaluation, this research bridges critical gaps in prior studies and advances the development of practical, intelligent agricultural systems.

3 Methodology

3.1 Model Architecture

The architecture of the proposed model is illustrated in Fig. 1. At its core, the model adopts EfficientNetV2B0, a lightweight yet powerful convolutional neural network, as the backbone for feature extraction. This architecture leverages

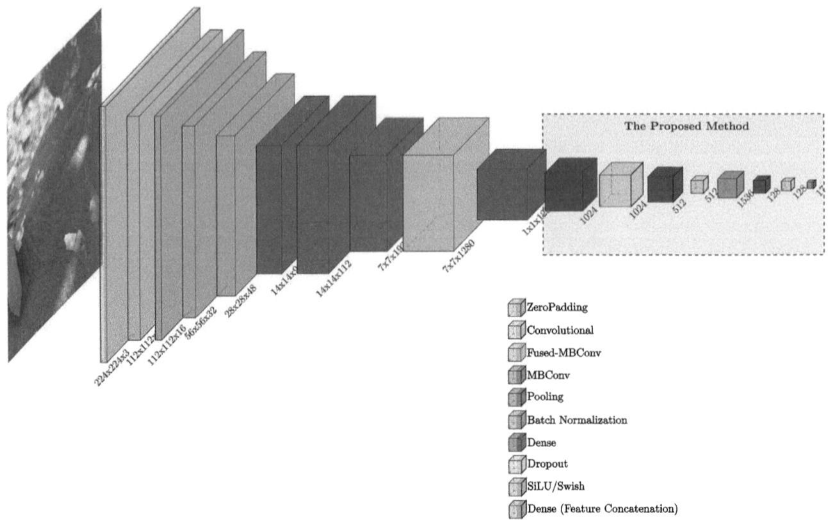

Fig. 1. The architecture of the proposed model based on EfficientNetV2B0.

a combination of *Fused-MBConv* and *MBConv* blocks, which are designed to enhance both training speed and accuracy by reducing memory access and optimizing parameter efficiency. These blocks incorporate depthwise separable convolutions, batch normalization, and the Swish (SiLU) activation function, resulting in a highly optimized computation graph. The input to the model consists of RGB leaf images resized to $224 \times 224 \times 3$. As the image passes through successive convolutional stages, feature maps are generated with increasing channel depth (e.g., 16, 24, 48, 64, 128, 160), capturing low-level to high-level visual patterns. At the end of the convolutional layers, global average pooling is applied to reduce the spatial dimensions and retain the most salient information.

To further refine the extracted features, the model includes two fully connected (dense) layers interleaved with dropout layers for regularization. Importantly, intermediate dense representations are concatenated—a strategy inspired by feature fusion techniques—to enrich the final feature space with multi-level semantics. The final output layer consists of 14 neurons corresponding to the 14 classification categories (healthy and diseased leaves across 7 plant species), and utilizes the softmax activation function to output class probabilities.

This architectural design strikes a balance between expressiveness and computational efficiency, making it suitable not only for accurate classification but also for potential deployment in edge devices with limited resources.

3.2 System Architecture and Workflow

The training workflow of the proposed system is depicted in Fig. 2. The process begins with a dedicated preprocessing phase, in which all input images are resized to 224×224 pixels and normalized to a common scale. To enhance model

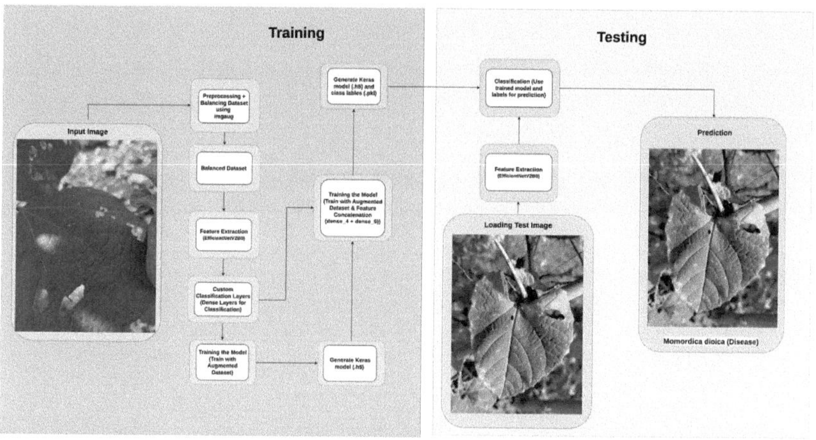

Fig. 2. The training pipeline of the proposed method.

generalization and prevent overfitting, various data augmentation techniques such as rotation, flipping, and brightness adjustment are applied during training. A balanced dataset comprising 14 equally represented classes (healthy/diseased leaves across 7 plant types) is curated to mitigate class imbalance issues. The core training loop utilizes the Adam optimizer due to its adaptive learning capabilities and stability during convergence. The model is trained using the categorical cross-entropy loss function, suitable for multi-class classification problems. To promote robustness and avoid overfitting, multiple training strategies are incorporated:

- **Dropout layers** are placed between dense layers to randomly deactivate neurons during training.
- **An adaptive learning rate scheduler** is employed to reduce the learning rate upon plateau in validation performance.
- **Early stopping** is applied based on validation loss to prevent unnecessary training epochs once convergence is reached.

Model evaluation is conducted using a reserved test set, ensuring that performance metrics reflect the model's true generalization capabilities. The evaluation includes accuracy scores, confusion matrices, and classification reports (precision, recall, F1-score) to provide comprehensive insight into model performance across all 14 categories. This training pipeline is designed not only to achieve high predictive accuracy, but also to ensure robustness, scalability, and adaptability in real-world agricultural settings.

3.3 Mathematical Foundations

Our proposed deep learning framework for plant disease classification is built upon several key mathematical operations, which ensure effective feature extraction, robust representation, and accurate prediction.

Image Representation. Each input image is represented as a 3D tensor:

$$\mathbf{X} \in \mathbb{R}^{H \times W \times C} \tag{1}$$

where $H = W = 512$ is the height and width, and $C = 3$ corresponds to the RGB channels.

Feature Extraction via EfficientNetV2B0. We use a pre-trained EfficientNetV2B0 backbone to extract feature maps:

$$\mathbf{F} = f_{\text{EffNet}}(\mathbf{X}) \in \mathbb{R}^{h \times w \times d} \tag{2}$$

where f_{EffNet} denotes the convolutional layers of EfficientNetV2B0 (excluding classification layers), and d is the number of feature channels.

Global Average Pooling. To reduce the spatial dimensions while preserving semantic information, we apply global average pooling:

$$g_i = \frac{1}{h \cdot w} \sum_{j=1}^{h} \sum_{k=1}^{w} F_{j,k,i} \tag{3}$$

$$\mathbf{g} \in \mathbb{R}^d \tag{4}$$

where $\mathbf{g}$ is the pooled feature vector.

Fully Connected Layers. Three dense layers are applied to the pooled features to form abstract representations:

$$\mathbf{z}_1 = \phi(\mathbf{W}_1\mathbf{g} + \mathbf{b}_1) \tag{5}$$

$$\mathbf{z}_2 = \phi(\mathbf{W}_2\mathbf{z}_1 + \mathbf{b}_2) \tag{6}$$

$$\mathbf{z}_3 = \phi(\mathbf{W}_3\mathbf{z}_2 + \mathbf{b}_3) \tag{7}$$

where ϕ denotes the ReLU activation function.

Feature Concatenation. To enrich the representation, we concatenate the outputs of two dense layers:

$$\mathbf{z}_{\text{concat}} = \text{Concat}(\mathbf{z}_2, \mathbf{z}_3) \tag{8}$$

This results in a vector of size $\mathbb{R}^{384}$ used for classification.

Softmax Classification. The final prediction vector $\hat{\mathbf{y}} \in \mathbb{R}^C$ is produced using the softmax function:

$$\hat{y}_i = \frac{\exp(\mathbf{w}_i^\top \mathbf{z}_{\text{concat}} + b_i)}{\sum_{j=1}^{C} \exp(\mathbf{w}_j^\top \mathbf{z}_{\text{concat}} + b_j)} \quad \text{for } i = 1, \ldots, C \tag{9}$$

where $C = 14$ is the number of plant disease classes.

Loss Function. The model is trained by minimizing the sparse categorical cross-entropy loss:

$$\mathcal{L} = -\sum_{i=1}^{C} y_i \log(\hat{y}_i) \tag{10}$$

where $y_i \in \{0, 1\}$ denotes the ground truth label and $\hat{y}_i$ the predicted probability.

Optimization. Model parameters are updated via the Adam optimizer:

$$\theta \leftarrow \theta - \eta \cdot \frac{\partial \mathcal{L}}{\partial \theta} \tag{11}$$

where θ denotes the model weights and η is the learning rate.

4 Experimental Results

This research employs a benchmark dataset introduced by Rahman et al. [13], comprising high-resolution RGB images of diseased plant leaves across six crop species: *Gourd* (537), *Zucchini* (186), *Bitter melon* (300), *Bean* (517), *Aubergine* (242), and *Yardlong bean* (500). The dataset includes 2,820 original images and 2,561 augmented samples, covering bacterial, fungal, viral (e.g., YMV), and other common infections. All images were captured under diverse field-like conditions and resized to 224×224 pixels to suit model input requirements. An 80/20 stratified split was applied for training and testing, with augmentation techniques such as rotation, flipping, and brightness adjustment used to enhance generalization. Model training was conducted on a Kaggle Notebook (GPU mode) equipped with an NVIDIA Tesla T4 GPU (16 GB VRAM). The complete training process required approximately 4 h. This dataset, combined with the described hardware and training setup, offers a realistic and diverse testbed for evaluating deep learning models in plant disease classification, particularly in multi-species and resource-constrained agricultural settings.

4.1 Feature Concatenation

No Feature Concatenation. As shown in Fig. 3, the baseline model without feature concatenation performs reasonably well on general disease categories. However, it encounters difficulty in distinguishing between diseases with similar visual symptoms, such as Phomopsis vexans. The training history in Fig. 4 indicates early convergence, suggesting limited capacity for deep representation. While it provides a solid reference point, this configuration lacks the adaptability and robustness offered by more advanced fusion strategies.

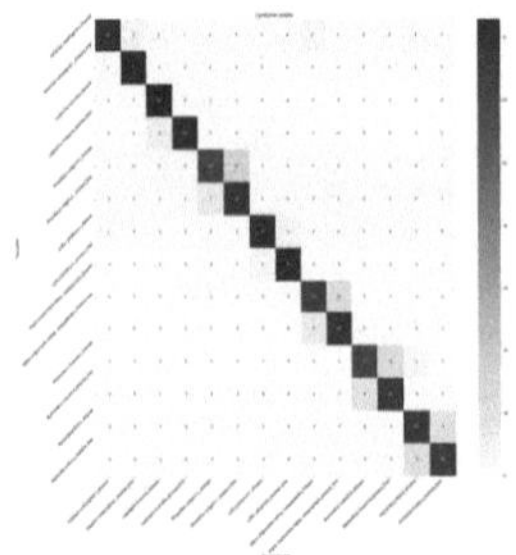

Fig. 3. Confusion matrix (no feature concatenation).

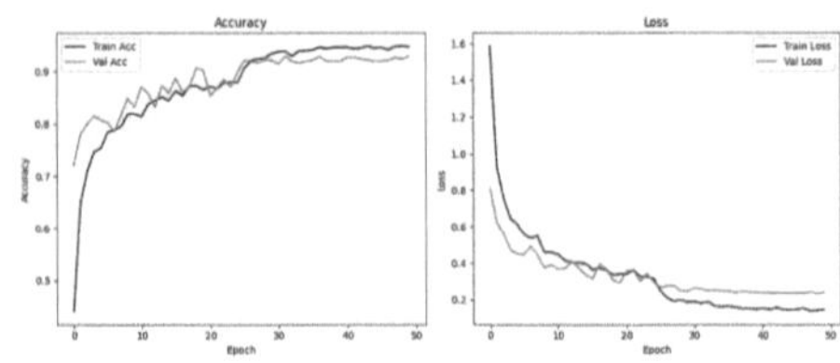

Fig. 4. Training/validation accuracy and loss (no feature concatenation).

$\mathbf{Dense_1}$ + $\mathbf{Dense_2}$ + $\mathbf{Dense_3}$ The full fusion approach in Fig. 5 achieves high overall accuracy and robust diagonal patterns. It leverages all feature levels and performs reliably across most classes. As seen in Fig. 6, training remains stable with minimal overfitting. However, this setup introduces increased model complexity and training time, which may not always yield significantly better performance than more targeted fusions.

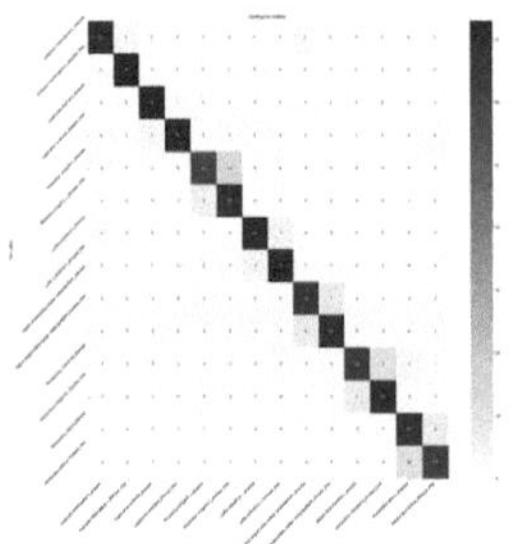

Fig. 5. Confusion matrix ($Dense_1$ + $Dense_2$ + $Dense_3$).

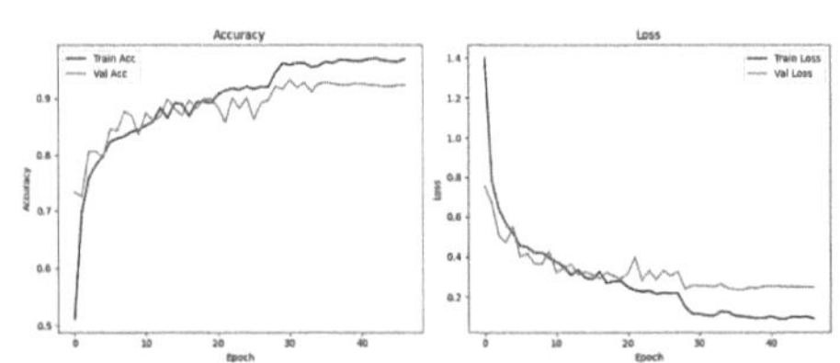

Fig. 6. Training/validation accuracy and loss ($Dense_1$ + $Dense_2$ + $Dense_3$).

$\mathbf{Dense_1}$ + $\mathbf{Dense_2}$ As shown in Fig. 7, combining low- and mid-level features improves the model's performance over the baseline. The configuration demonstrates effective texture-level recognition and reasonable class separation. The training history (Fig. 8) reflects stable learning dynamics. However, in the absence of high-level semantic features, this setup occasionally struggles with more complex disease patterns, making it slightly less consistent compared to deeper fusion strategies.

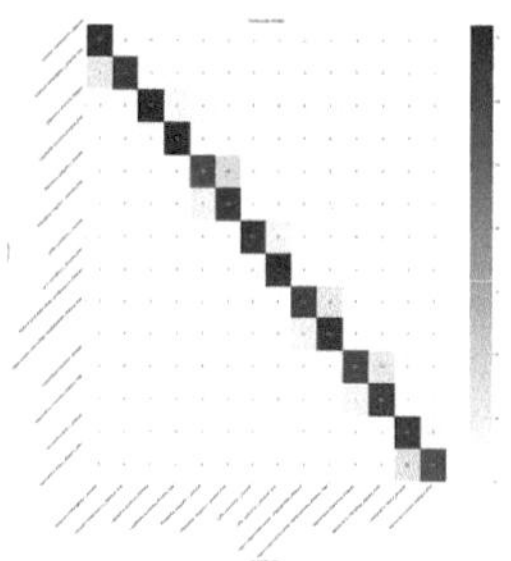

Fig. 7. Confusion matrix (Dense_1 + Dense_2).

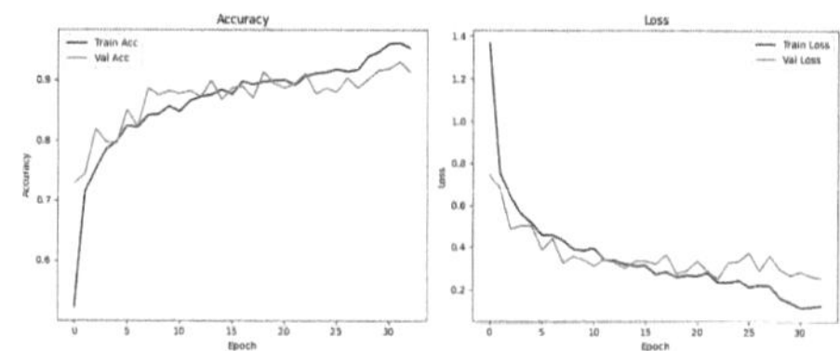

Fig. 8. Training/validation accuracy and loss (Dense_1 + Dense_2).

Dense_1 + Dense_3 Fig. 9 illustrates that the fusion of low- and high-level features enables the model to capture both fine-grained textures and semantic abstractions effectively. The confusion matrix shows strong class separability with minimal misclassifications. As depicted in Fig. 10, the training process reaches high accuracy, with generally smooth convergence. While performance remains strong, minor fluctuations in the validation phase suggest room for further enhancement in stability.

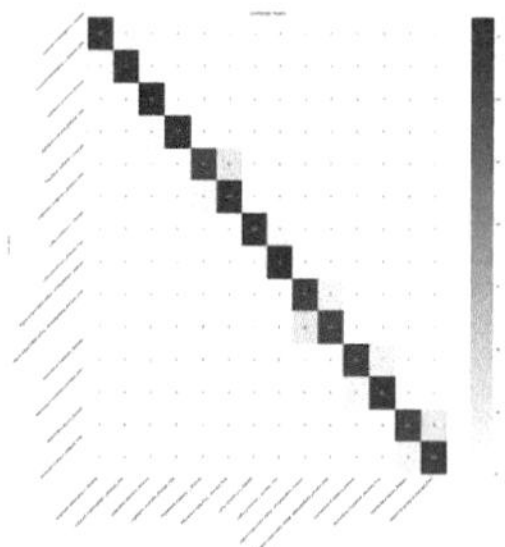

Fig. 9. Confusion matrix (Dense_1 + Dense_3).

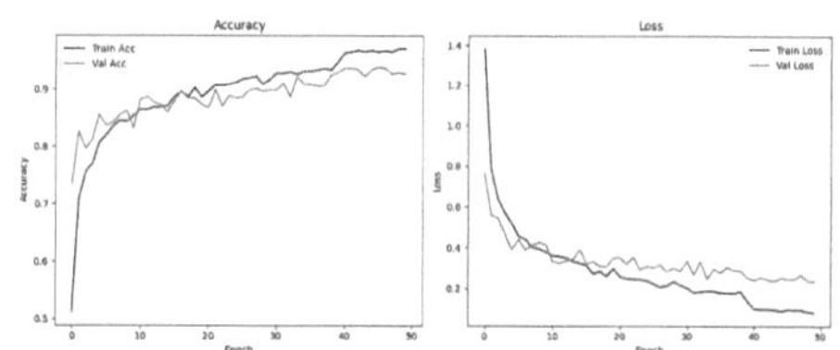

Fig. 10. Training/validation accuracy and loss (Dense_1 + Dense_3).

Dense_2 + Dense_3 Among all configurations, Dense_2 + Dense_3 fusion stands out with the most consistent and accurate performance, as highlighted in Fig. 11. The combination of mid- and high-level features captures both structural detail and semantic meaning, enabling clear class boundaries and strong generalization. Figure 12 confirms this stability, with smooth training curves and minimal gap between training and validation accuracy. This configuration offers the best trade-off between performance and model efficiency in our study.

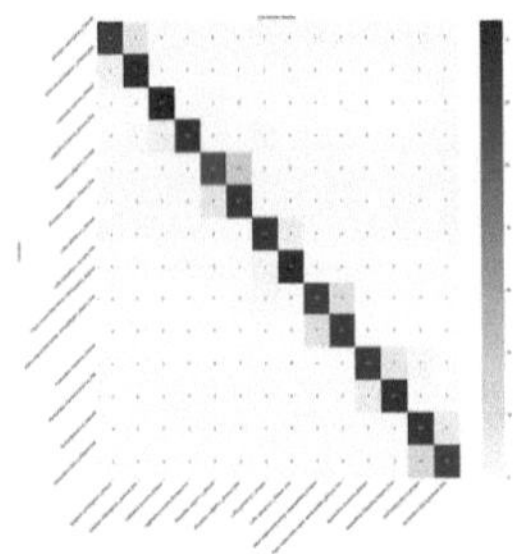

Fig. 11. Confusion matrix ($Dense_2$ + $Dense_3$).

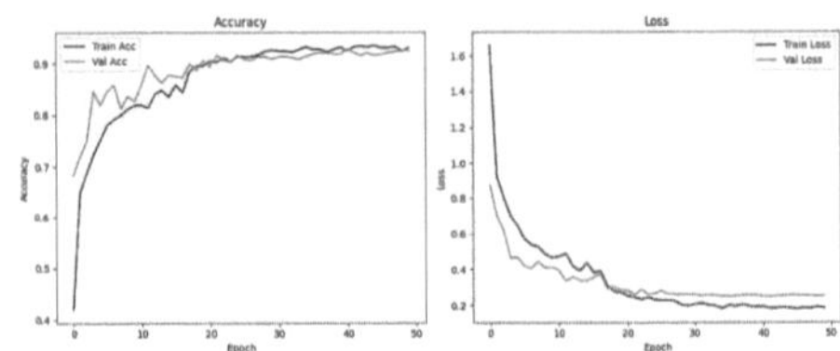

Fig. 12. Training/validation accuracy and loss ($Dense_2$ + $Dense_3$).

4.2 Model Performance

Table 2. Correct and incorrect predictions of different feature concatenation strategies.

Model Variant	Correct Images	Incorrect Images	Accuracy (%)
No feature concatenation	902	98	90.18%
$Dense_1$ + $Dense_2$ (The proposed)	901	99	90.14%
$Dense_1$ + $Dense_3$ (the proposed)	928	72	92.77%
$Dense_2$ + $Dense_3$ (The proposed)	**929**	**71**	**92.86%**
$Dense_1$ + $Dense_2$ + $Dense_3$ (The proposed)	925	75	92.54%

Table 2 summarizes the classification performance of all model variants. While the baseline model without feature concatenation achieves an accuracy of 90.18%, all fusion-based variants show notable improvements. The best accuracy is observed with $Dense_2$ and $Dense_3$ (92.86%), followed closely by the full fusion model of $Dense_1$, $Dense_2$, and $Dense_3$ (92.54%). These results confirm the benefit of integrating multi-level features, as reflected in both accuracy scores and reduced misclassifications.

5 Conclusion

This study presents a deep learning framework for plant leaf disease classification that combines the EfficientNetV2B0 backbone with multi-level feature concatenation to improve recognition accuracy across diverse plant species and disease types. By integrating representations from various dense layers, the proposed model effectively captures both fine-grained textures and high-level semantic features, enabling robust classification across 14 categories derived from six crops. Comprehensive experiments on a benchmark dataset demonstrate that feature fusion significantly enhances model performance. Notably, the proposed $Dense_2$ + $Dense_3$ configuration achieves the highest accuracy (92.86%), while the proposed full fusion model ($Dense_1$ + $Dense_2$ + $Dense_3$) achieves a competitive 92.54% with strong generalization. Compared to baseline and prior works, the model exhibits superior adaptability, reduced misclassifications, and effective handling of visually similar diseases. Overall, this work contributes a lightweight yet scalable approach to automated plant disease recognition, suitable for real-world agricultural scenarios and potential deployment on edge devices. Future work may explore attention-based fusion strategies or multi-modal integration (e.g., hyperspectral data) to further enhance performance in complex and heterogeneous farming environments.

References

1. Yang, B., et al.: A novel plant type, leaf disease and severity identification framework using CNN and transformer with multi-label method. Sci. Rep.**14**, Article number: 11664 (2024). https://doi.org/10.1038/s41598-024-62452-x
2. Mustofa, S., Munna, M.M.H., Emon, Y.R., Rabbany, G., Ahad, M.T.: A comprehensive review on plant leaf disease detection using deep learning. *arXiv preprint*arXiv:2308.14087 [cs.CV] (2023). https://doi.org/10.48550/arXiv.2308.14087
3. George, R., et al.: Past, present and future of deep plant leaf disease recognition: a survey. Comput. Electron. Agric. **234**, 110128 (2025). https://doi.org/10.1016/j.compag.2025.110128
4. Sandhya Devi, R.S., Vijay Kumar, V.R., Sivakumar, P.: EfficientNetV2 model for plant disease classification and pest recognition. Comput. Syst. Sci. Eng. **45**(2), 2249–2263 (2023). https://doi.org/10.32604/csse.2023.032231
5. Nguyen, V.D., Ngo, N.P., Le, Q.N., Debnath, N.C.: Robust plant leaves diseases classification using EfficientNet and residual block. In: So-In, C., Londhe, N.D., Bhatt, N., Kitsing, M. (eds.) Information Systems for Intelligent Systems. Smart Innovation, Systems and Technologies, vol 324. Springer, Singapore (2023)
6. Nguyen, V.D., Ngo, N.P., Nguyen, K.H.: Robust blueberry leaf disease detection using transformer-based and local cosine feature method. In: Gervasi, O., et al. Computational Science and Its Applications – ICCSA 2025. ICCSA 2025. LNCS, vol 15648. Springer, Cham (2025)
7. Hukkeri, G.S., Soundarya, B.C., Gururaj, H.L., Ravi, V.: Classification of various plant leaf disease using pretrained convolutional neural network on ImageNet. Open Agric. J. **18**, (2024). https://doi.org/10.2174/0118743315305194240408034912
8. Sun, Y., Ning, L., Zhao, B., Yan, J.: Tomato leaf disease classification by combining efficientNetV2 and a swin transformer. Appl. Sci. **14**(17), 7472 (2024). https://doi.org/10.3390/app14177472
9. Damasevicius, R., Mahmood, F., Zaman, Y., Dastgeer, S., Khan, S.: Performance of deep learning techniques in leaf disease detection. Comput. Syst. Sci. Eng.**48**(5), 1349–1366 (2024). https://doi.org/10.32604/csse.2024.050359
10. Pandian, A. J., Kanchanadevi, K., Rajalakshmi, N. R., Arulkumaran, G.: An improved deep residual convolutional neural network for plant leaf disease detection. Comput. Intell. Neurosci.**2022**, Article ID 5102290 (2022). https://doi.org/10.1155/2022/5102290

11. Younes, Z.Y., Alsaadi, E.M.T.A.: A Review on plant leaf disease classification using deep learning. Iraqi J. Sci. **65**(11), 6738–6752 (2024). https://doi.org/10.24996/ijs.2024.65.11.43
12. Tugrul, B., Elfatimi, E., Eryigit, R.: Convolutional neural networks in detection of plant leaf diseases: a review. Agriculture **12**(8), 1192 (2022). https://doi.org/10.3390/agriculture12081192
13. Zitu, M.Z.R., Shifat, S.R., Mojumdar, M.U.: A benchmark dataset for detecting disease in plant leaves: an essential resource for deep learning models. Mendeley Data V2 (2024). https://doi.org/10.17632/v46jkbbzv3.2

Shallow Transformers with Applications Towards Image and Text Classification

Akshay Badola[1], Vineet Padmanabhan[2(✉)], Rajendra Prasad Lal[2], and Wilson Naik[2]

[1] ETS Assessment Services, Gurgaon, India
abadola@ets.org

[2] School of Computer and Information Sciences, University of Hyderabad, Prof C R Rao Road, Gachibowli, Hyderabad 500046, Telangana, India
{vineetnair,rajendraprasd,rathore}@uohyd.ac.in

Abstract. The Transformer architecture has quickly become extremely popular as it has achieved state-of-the-art performance in a variety of tasks with a relatively simple design of repeating blocks. Variants of Transformers are now staples in many classification tasks, including language modeling, image classification, and even object detection. The core aspect of the architecture, that is the sequential repeating blocks, has however remained unchanged throughout this time. In this work, we explore an alternative horizontally growing architecture that achieves similar results on the common tasks in which Transformers are proficient, while providing more controllability for parameter expansion due to the model's shallow nature. We compare with two standard models: BERT for natural language processing and ViT in computer vision. We show that our model achieves comparable results while maintaining very low depth, and in some cases, with just a single layer. To the best of our knowledge, this is the first study that demonstrates the possibility and efficacy of such models. We provide results on some standard benchmarks, i.e., MNLI in case of Natural Language Inference, and CIFAR-10, CIFAR-100 for image classification. We also provide all the source code for our experiments. (The code can be found at https://github.com/akshaybadola/shallow-transformers.

Keywords: Deep Learning · Wide Networks · Transformers · Disentanglement

1 Introduction

Transformers were introduced by Vaswani et al. [1] as autoregressive language models for the machine translation. Since then, the Transformer architecture has been a paradigm shift in machine learning in general and the sub-area known as *Deep Learning* in particular. The simplicity of the architecture has enabled

A. Badola—Work was done while at the University of Hyderabad.

T. T. Quan et al. (Eds.): MIWAI 2025, LNAI 16353, pp. 25–36, 2026.
https://doi.org/10.1007/978-981-95-4957-3_3

it to be adapted for various other tasks like sentence classification [2,3], image classification [4,5] time series forecasting [6,7] etc.

The original Transformer model consisted of simple repeating blocks of an *attention* module and a *feed-forward* module (usually a three layer MLP, but other variants exist) arranged sequentially, with the input passing through each of them in turn. Many variants have been proposed since then of both attention and the Feedforward mechanisms, (see e.g., [8–10]). The simple sequential design has remained the same, however, for all these and other models.

The simplicity of the design has been one of the primary reasons for its success, as such a design offers easy model capacity and complexity control. For example, unlike Convolutional Neural Networks (CNNs), the parameters and Floating Point Operations (FLOPs) remain constant with depth. More powerful variants of the Transformer can be constructed by changing the embedding dimension, attention dimension, or depth of the model.

This simplicity of the Transformer allows many possible architectures with combinations of *attention* and *feed-forward* blocks. Wide and shallow Transformers, however, have not garnered much attention, perhaps because of the prevalent notion that deeper networks are inherently always better. We seek to challenge this perception and investigate the width versus depth aspect of modeling Transformers for image classification.

In this work, we investigate if the Transformer architecture is feasible for lateral expansion for image and text classification. For this purpose, we introduce a novel parallel layer for Transformers with separate repeating blocks with a diversity constraint. We also use a parameter-less sigmoid based gating mechanism, which proved surprisingly effective to alleviate the need for depth. We find that Transformers with trainable parameters **only in the first layer** can achieve comparable accuracies to deeper models for both image and text classification.

1.1 Effect of Attention and Depth

The key structural design principles of the Transformer are the depth of the model and the mechanism of attention. The standard attention mechanism following [1] is usually denoted as $\sigma(\frac{QK}{\sqrt{d_k}})V$, with the data $\mathbf{x}$ often omitted, where $Q, K, V \in \mathbb{R}^{d_{model} \times d_{head}}$ are identical matrices, d_{model} is the embedding dimension, d_{head} is the attention head dimension and $\sqrt{d_k}$ is a numeric normalizing constant, depending on the dimension of embeddings [1]. Adding $\mathbf{x}$ and omitting $\sqrt{d_k}$ it can be rewritten as $\sigma(\mathbf{x}^T Q^T K\mathbf{x})V\mathbf{x}$. $\mathbf{x}^T Q^T K\mathbf{x} = y_1^T y_2$ highlights the self-multiplicative quadratic nature of attention. Gating mechanisms have emerged recently as alternatives to attention [8,11] to mitigate this quadratic computational cost, while these methods themselves have been inspired from [10,12].

These *gating* functions rely on compositions of logistic sigmoid (σ): $f(\mathbf{x}) = W\mathbf{x} \odot \sigma(V\mathbf{x})$ where $\odot$ is an element-wise product. The parameters W, V are learned by the model, and due to $\sigma(x) \in (0, 1)$, each element of the range of f is rescaled by 0 to 1. This rescaling is what endows these methods, the *gating* characteristic [11,12].

Prior work has established that deeper networks in general require exponentially fewer parameters in intermediate layers than in shallow ones [13]. Depth is particularly essential for the performance of CNNs [14,15]. However, the relationship of depth and generalization is more complicated in Transformers due to the interactions in the attention blocks. For example, *deep* attention-based networks should experience *rank collapse*, but do not due to skip connections [16]. Most large Transformers increase capacity by increasing not only *depth*, that is, the number of repeating blocks, but also the number of *attention heads* and the embedding and attention dimension. For example, see model configurations of the recent LLaMA model [17]. Limits to depth of Transformer models [16,18] has therefore been an active area of research.

We wish to utilize these *gating* functions to determine if shallow Transformer models can be trained for general purpose tasks. Our contributions in this work are:

1. We investigate depth versus width in Transformers and develop novel shallow Transformers with parallel blocks, which give competitive results to deeper models.
2. We identify a parameter-less sigmoid based adaptation layer which fuses the outputs of two previous blocks and compensates for the lack of depth.
3. We give a detailed analysis on standard image classification datasets CIFAR-10 and CIFAR-100. and give preliminary results on language modeling tasks.
4. We also provide all the code of our experiments[1].

The rest of this paper is organized as follows: We cover some related work in Sect. 2. We discuss motivation, design aspects, and proposed variants in Sect. 3. The details of various experiments conducted are in Sect. 4. And finally Sect. 5 discusses the implications and possible future work related to our study.

2 Related Work

There has recently been some work on wide and shallow models. Golubeva et al. [19] have investigated the role of width in Neural Nets and indicated that wider nets with the same number of parameters may be better than deeper ones. Xu et al. [20] trained a shallow and thin student network to mimic a deeper teacher network as a form of knowledge distillation. Goyal et al. [21] attempted to train shallow CNNs, which gave comparable accuracy to deeper networks. Cornia et al. [22] trained two-layer Transformers primarily for explaining the decisions of a robot, however, their work is in a very narrow domain of robotics. Li et al. [23] analyzed shallow Vision Transformers as a means of understanding the generalization capabilities of Transformers as a whole.

Prio work, therefore, has focused on narrow domains or models of limited capability for specific objectives like explainability. In contrast, we wish to answer the question if it is possible to construct shallow (even extremely shallow) Transformer networks that can compete with standard Transformer architectures. We find that it is indeed possible for image and text classification.

[1] https://github.com/akshaybadola/shallow-transformers.

3 Towards Shallow Transformers

As mentioned earlier, the Transformer architecture was initially proposed for autoregressive language modeling. Following which language models, which focused on classification-like tasks [2,3] emerged. Vision Transformers [4] soon followed, which worked by encoding images into patches and then using the simple feed-forward mechanism to classify them. The Transformers used for these tasks are non-autoregressive and have been widely adopted.

The standard[2] Transformer architecture is predicated on the following: 1. Embedding dimension 2. Attention dimension 3. Depth. The capacity of a generic Neural Network is usually a function of its number of parameters $O(|W|)$, though the functions that a general Neural Network can express differ widely according to the architecture. For example, it has been asserted that the number of parameters required for approximating the same class of functions differs for shallow and deeper networks with ReLU activation [13]. Xie et al. [24] also claim that networks that follow the split-merge strategy have a solution space that is a strict subset of fully dense networks. Therefore, we need to keep in mind that shallow Transformers will have reduced capacity, but equally important to answer is, at what point does this reduction in capacity start to affect the results of the model?

To have identical model capacity as the deeper Transformers, we use parallel identical Transformer blocks in each layer. In our experiments, we found that simply using a layer with a large embedding or attention dimension did not give good results. A second key aspect that we used was *gating* blocks based on sigmoid. We discuss their details in the following sections.

3.1 Split Layer with Parallel Blocks for Width

All Transformers encode the input into a fixed dimensional representation. The method of encoding is model and domain-specific, and in addition, a positional encoding is also added [1,2,4]. We follow a similar procedure, but we replicate the input for each initial parallel block i.

$$\begin{aligned}\mathbf{x} &\rightarrow \text{repeat} \rightarrow <\mathbf{x}_0, ..., \mathbf{x}_i> \\ \mathbf{x}_i &= \text{attn}_i(\mathbf{x}_i) + \mathbf{x}_i \\ \mathbf{x}_i &= \text{ffn}_i(\mathbf{x}_i) + \mathbf{x}_i\end{aligned}$$

The input is then piped through *Split Layers* in succession, each of which consists of $2 \times w_i$ identical parallel Transformer blocks consisting of attention and Feedforward modules, where w_i is the width of the i_{th} layer.

A subsequent layer has either width $w_{i+1} = w_i/2$ or $w_{i+1} = 0$, and the rest of the input is merged according to a parameter-less gating mechanism. For example, a network can have $4 \rightarrow 2 \rightarrow 1$ blocks in successive layers, and the final

[2] By "standard", we mean the self-attention model similar to [1] without convolution layers or approximations to self-attention.

layer feeds the input to the classification layer. Or it can have 4 blocks in the first layer, no other block except parameter-less gating blocks following it. This successive optional narrowing allows us to control the number of parameters. Examples of these network shapes are given in Figs. 1, 2.

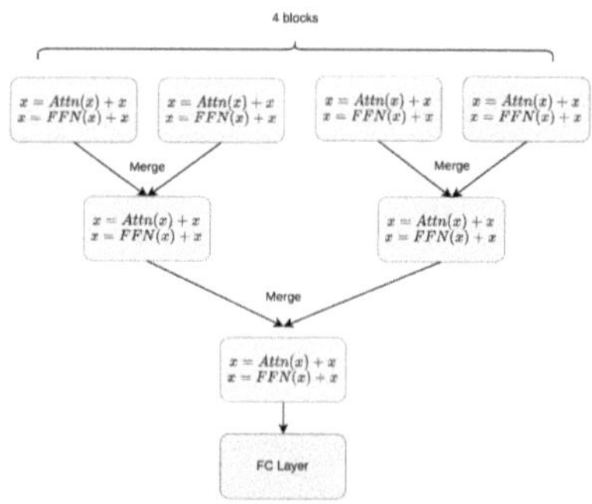

Fig. 1. $4 \rightarrow 2 \rightarrow 1$ configuration for ShallowViT

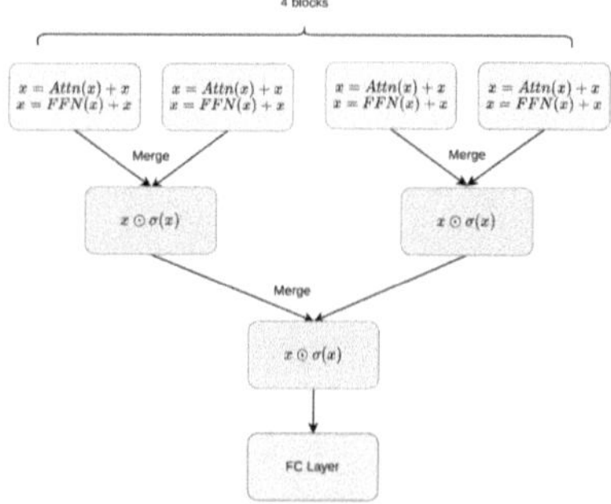

Fig. 2. 4 blocks in first layer and only gating blocks after

3.2 Parameter-Less Gating Blocks for Depth

If the pre-classification layer in the network has width $w > 1$, then instead of adding more Transformer blocks, we use Parameter-less Gating Blocks to merge the inputs so that the effective width is reduced by half $w_{i+1} = w_i/2$.

The output at layer $i + 1$ corresponding to input $\mathbf{x}_i$ from two blocks is then: $\mathbf{x_{i+1}} = \text{merge}(B_{i1}(\mathbf{x_i}), B_{i2}(\mathbf{x_i}))$ where $B(.)$ is either another Transformer block or a parameter-less gating block. With these parallel identical blocks, we can control the trade off between capacity and effective depth of the model. We found that a certain depth is required for more complex classification tasks, but simpler tasks gave competitive results with `depth = 1`. E.g., CIFAR-100 with 8 parallel blocks gave us an accuracy of **56%** while with CIFAR-10 we got an accuracy of **82%**. Detailed results are given in Table 1.

Our gating blocks are inspired by [10–12]. Veness et al. [12] define a Gated Linear Unit as $(\mathbf{x} * \mathbf{W}) \odot \sigma(\mathbf{x} * \mathbf{V})$ where $*$ is a convolution operator. Convolution being a linear operator, the formula can be adapted as $\mathbf{Wx} \odot \sigma(\mathbf{Vx})$. $\mathbf{U}(\mathbf{Wx} \odot \phi(\mathbf{Vx}))$ is known as SiLU and it was investigated in [25]. Shazeer [10] investigated variants of $\mathbf{Wx} \odot \phi(\mathbf{Vx})$ with different activations ϕ. Hua et al. [8] formulated the gating as $\mathbf{U}\left[\phi(\mathbf{Wx}) \odot \phi\mathbf{Vx}\right], \mathbf{U}, \mathbf{W}, \mathbf{V} \in \mathbb{R}^{m,n}$ and achieved impressive results.

Parameter-Less Gating. If we remove the parameters $\mathbf{W}, \mathbf{V}$ the function becomes $\mathbf{x} \odot \sigma(\mathbf{x})$ which scales $\mathbf{x}$ input by $[0, 1]$. This adds implicit feature importance to each element of $\mathbf{x}$. The exact theoretical properties of why this (or indeed attention or other gating mechanisms) may happen are not understood, and we leave that to future work.

Without the $\mathbf{W}, \mathbf{V}$ matrices, this function is also known as SiLU. Adding this gating SiLU function, $\mathbf{x} \odot \sigma(\mathbf{x})$ after each layer improved our results for shallow models; however, it does not improve deeper models. We hypothesize that it selects important features in the input in the absence of parameters and standard attention mechanism.

A very interesting case we discovered is a model with **only patch embeddings** and the final layer as learnable parameters. This model, which we term a *MinimalViT*, performed quite well on CIFAR-10. We discuss results for *MinimalViT* in Sect. 4.1. Illustration of the parameter-less gating is given in Fig. 2. A schematic of various possible combinations of modules is given in Fig. 3.

3.3 Diversity Constraint

One issue that may arise in parallel attention blocks is that they might all learn similar features at each layer. To alleviate that, we also add a Cosine Embedding Loss, which penalizes similar outputs from the blocks. We add this constraint to embeddings from *each layer*.

$$\mathcal{L}_{cos}(\mathbf{x}_1, \mathbf{x}_2) = \begin{cases} 1 - \cos(\mathbf{x}_1, \mathbf{x}_2), & \text{if } \mathbf{x}_1, \mathbf{x}_2 \text{ from same block} \\ \max(0, \cos(\mathbf{x}_1, \mathbf{x}_2) - \text{margin}), & \text{if } \mathbf{x}_1, \mathbf{x}_2 \text{ from different blocks} \end{cases}$$

While training the network, we add this Cosine Embedding Loss to the Negative Log Likelihood Loss for classification after multiplying with a hyperparameter λ. The value of λ is determined empirically.

$$\mathcal{L} = \mathcal{L}_{NLL} + \lambda \sum_{l} \mathcal{L}_{cos}, \text{ for each layer } l$$

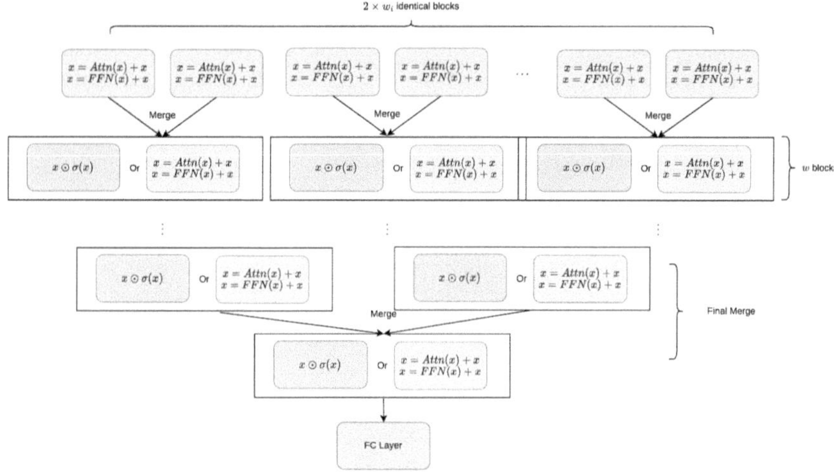

Fig. 3. An illustration of modular merge strategy of attention+feed-forward blocks. This constitutes the extreme case where the final layer feeds the input directly to the FC Layer

4 Models, Experiments and Results

In this section, we describe the various architectures we have explored. Our primary focus would be image classification with ViT-like architectures. However, to show the broader applicability of our study for tasks other than image classification, we give preliminary results on the *Tiny* variant of BERT [2] also. For image classification, we use variants of ViT [4] and compare with recent advances in training ViT on small datasets [26].

4.1 Image Classification with ShallowViT

For image classification with ShallowViT, we used the patch embedding formulation of [4] to convert images into fixed-sized representations. After which, we used sinusoidal positional encoding following [2,4].

To assess the efficacy of the ViT variants, we conducted detailed experiments on standard datasets, CIFAR-10 and CIFAR-100. All the experiments were conducted using a batch size of 1024, and optimizer AdamW [27] with learning rate 0.005. For regularization and data augmentation, we followed Lee et al. [26] and used RandAugment [28,29]. Again, following [26], we also applied a cosine annealing schedule to the learning rate. We trained on a single (Graphics Processing Unit) GPU and the training time varied depending on the GPU used. We used various GPUs according to availability but observed no difference in the results for different GPUs. The rest of the hyperparameters were identical for all experiments.

We assessed various widths and depths possible with our ShallowViT architecture on datasets CIFAR-10 and CIFAR-100. For all the model variants, we restricted the model to a single attention head (the use of additional attention heads did not provide any benefit in our experiments for image classification), the attention dimension to 128, and use *Swish* block instead of GeLU-based Feedforward block following [10].

Table 1. Classification accuracies for variants of ShallowViT with respect to number of blocks and depth

Dataset	Params	Num Blocks	Depth	Accuracy	ViT Params	ViT Accuracy
CIFAR-10	1.85	8	3	88.18	0.76	92.02
	1.59		2	88.06		
	1.06		1	84.64		
	0.93	4	3	88.45		
	0.80		2	87.35		
	0.54		1	83.15		
CIFAR-100	1.87	8	3	66.84	0.75	72.67
	1.60		2	64.79		
	1.07		1	60.21		
	0.94	4	3	66.84		
	0.81		2	64.79		
	0.55		1	60.21		

We can see in Table 1, that although the shallow Transformers lag behind the full models, but the gap is not very large. We get a median difference in accuracy of −4.31% for CIFAR-10 and −7.88% for CIFAR-100, with models with the lowest number of parameters performing particularly worse. Accuracy also does not decrease as much for CIFAR-10 with decreasing number of parameters. The performance penalty for CIFAR-100 is larger, however.

MinimalViT. To analyze parameter-less gating SiLU blocks, we conducted an ablation study with/without the gating blocks and **without any Transformer blocks**. The resulting model is a very sparse model with no learnable parameters except for patch embeddings and the final classification layer. We name this model *MinimalViT* (see Fig. 2).

We used CIFAR-10 and CIFAR-100 datasets under identical conditions to Sect. 4.1. Results are given in Table 2. The depth in Table 2 refers to the number of parameter-less gating layers in the model between the embedding and the final classification layer. *Dim* is the dimension of the patch embedding. For $dim > 2048$, it was not feasible to train even these shallow models, as the memory requirements increased substantially. We only conducted an initial study with CIFAR-100 for *MinimalViT* without the gating blocks as the results were not competitive with any configuration on either of the datasets. We can see that adding the $\mathbf{x} \odot \sigma(\mathbf{x})$ gating helps *MinimalViT* significantly. The model exhibits surprisingly strong performance on CIFAR-10, with very few parameters. It does not do well on CIFAR-100, however. This suggests that the effect of gating does not scale well with the number of classes (Fig. 4).

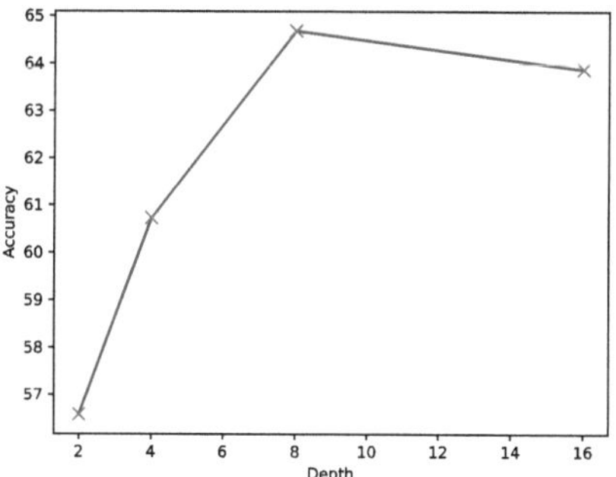

Fig. 4. Depth of Gating Blocks vs Accuracy for MinimalViT with CIFAR-10

Table 2. Results of various MinimalViT configurations with and without the gating blocks

(a) Accuracy on validation set of for MinimalViT with Gating. Depth refers to number of gating blocks appended after the patch embedding layer

Dataset	Dim	Params (in millions)	Depth	Accuracy
Cifar-10	1024	0.0625	8	64.68
	512	0.0313	8	59.39
	256	0.0157	8	56.16
Cifar-100	1024	0.0625	8	35.15
	2048	0.3094	8	41.12

(b) Accuracy on validation set of for MinimalViT without Gating

Dataset	Dim	Params (in millions)	Accuracy
Cifar-10	1024	0.0625	32.88
	512	0.0313	32.29
	256	0.0157	32.47
Cifar-100	1024	0.0625	11.4

4.2 Language Modeling with ShallowBERT

We only conducted preliminary experiments to assess the feasibility of the proposed model for language modeling, for which we used a shallow architecture without the diversity constraint for sentence classification. We used BERT [2], as it has proven to be highly effective in various natural language processing tasks such as Sentiment Analysis (SA), Natural Language Inference (NLI) etc. In this work, we only focus on NLI as the downstream task, using the MNLI dataset. BERT is a MaskedLM, and the training objective is to correctly classify a set of randomly chosen MASKed tokens. We refer the reader to [2] for details of BERT architecture and training. For implementation, we used the framework of [30], which provides a very efficient and replicable code-base with a pre-defined time budget for training. We used only the *Tiny* variant of BERT with 4 layers and 12 classification heads to check feasibility. We defer a detailed analysis of language modeling to future work. We compared a standard sequential *Tiny* BERT and the *ShallowBERT* and used the final training loss and accuracy on MNLI dataset for evaluating the models. Our training regimen was identical for both models except for batch size, which was adjusted for GPU memory. *ShallowBERT* achieved a training loss of 3.0503 after 6 h of training compared to 2.9051 for regular *Tiny* BERT, and achieved almost identical evaluation accuracy on MNLI after fine-tuning. The preliminary results exhibit promise, demonstrating the feasibility of shallow language models, even as we defer detailed analysis of these models to future work (Table 3).

Table 3. Classification accuracies for variants of ShallowBERT. All models trained for 6 h on identical GPUs. MNLI accuracy is for validation set after training for 5 epochs.

Model	Num Layers	Params	Training Loss	MNLI accuracy
BERT	4	8.7	2.9051	73.32
Shallow-BERT	1	10.1	3.0315	73.33

5 Discussion and Future Work

In this paper, we have investigated and successfully demonstrated that shallow, and sometimes extremely shallow Transformers, can be trained successfully with competitive results on standard benchmarks. We have also developed a novel gating and merging strategy, which alleviates the lack of depth in these models, though we note that more work is needed to get it to scale on more complex datasets and larger models. While our primary investigation has been on Vision Transformers, initial results with *ShallowBERT* show that such methods are also feasible in NLP.

We acknowledge the limitations of this study that the image datasets used consist of small images. In addition only a single downstream language dataset is used with only *Tiny* BERT for comparison. The study can be enhanced with more downstream tasks and bigger models.

While we restricted ourselves to those due to computational constraints in this study, we leave the experiments on broader datasets with larger models for future work. Other possible applications of shallow models can be Class Incremental Learning, where the parallel blocks that we have proposed may be useful due to their ease of lateral expansion. Such shallow models may also be more amenable to interpretability, as depth can hinder interpretation of the embeddings. Further investigation is also required on the nature of the gating blocks. It is unclear how these blocks help alleviate the lack of depth in the MinimalViT we investigated. Although gating mechanisms like ours and [8,11] are now commonplace, their exact mechanism is not fully understood.

References

1. Vaswani, A.: Attention is all you need. In: Advances in Neural Information Processing Systems (2017)
2. Devlin, J., Chang, M.-W., Lee, K., Toutanova, K.: BERT: pre - training of deep bidirectional transformers for language understanding. In: Naacl (2019)
3. Clark, K., Luong, M.-T., Le, Q.V., Manning, C.D.: ELECTRA: pre - training text encoders as discriminators rather than generators. In: Proceedings of the International Conference on Learning Representations (2020)
4. Dosovitskiy, A., et al.: An image is worth 16x16 words: transformers for image recognition at scale. In: Proceedings of the International Conference on Learning Representations (2020)
5. Liu, Z., et al.: Swin transformer: hierarchical vision transformer using shifted windows. In: Proceedings of the IEEE International Conference on Computer Vision, pp. 9992–10002 (2021)
6. Zhou, H., et al.: Informer: beyond efficient transformer for long sequence time - series forecasting. In: Proceedings of the AAAI Conference on Artificial Intelligence (2020)
7. Tang, B., Matteson, D.: Probabilistic transformer for time series analysis. In: Advances in Neural Information Processing Systems (2021)
8. Hua, W., Dai, Z., Liu, H., Le, Q.V.: Transformer quality in linear time. In: Proceedings of the International Conference on Machine Learning (2022)
9. Zhai, S., et al.: An attention free transformer (2021)
10. Shazeer, N.M.: Glu variants improve transformer (2020)
11. Liu, H., Dai, Z., So, D.R., Le, Q.V.: Pay Attention to MLPs. In: Advances in Neural Information Processing Systems (2021)
12. Veness, J., et al.: Gated linear networks. In: Proceedings of the AAAI Conference on Artificial Intelligence, pp. 10015–10023 (2019)
13. Liang, S., Srikant, R.: Why deep neural networks for function approximation? In: Proceedings of the International Conference on Learning Representations (2016)
14. Szegedy, C., et al.: Going deeper with convolutions. In: Proceedings of the IEEE Conference on Computer Vision and Pattern Recognition, pp. 1–9 (2014)
15. He, K., Zhang, X., Ren, S., Sun, J.: Deep residual learning for image recognition. In: Proceedings of the IEEE Conference on Computer Vision and Pattern Recognition (2015)
16. Dong, Y., Cordonnier, J.-B., Loukas, A.: Attention is not all you need: pure attention loses rank doubly exponentially with depth. In: Proceedings of the International Conference on Machine Learning (2021)
17. Touvron, H., et al.: Llama: open and efficient foundation language models (2023)
18. Levine, Y., Wies, N., Sharir, O., Bata, H., Shashua, A.: Limits to depth efficiencies of self - attention. In: Advances in Neural Information Processing Systems (2020)

19. Golubeva, A., Neyshabur, B., Gur-Ari, G.: Are wider nets better given the same number of parameters? In: Proceedings of the International Conference on Learning Representations (2020)
20. Xu, Z., Hsu, Y.-C., Huang, J.: Training shallow and thin networks for acceleration via knowledge distillation with conditional adversarial networks. In: Proceedings of the International Conference on Learning Representations (2017)
21. Goyal, A., Bochkovskiy, A., Deng, J., Koltun, V.: Non - Deep Networks (2021)
22. Cornia, M., Baraldi, L., Cucchiara, R.: Smart: training shallow memory - aware transformers for robotic explainability. In: IEEE International Conference on Robotics and Automation (2019)
23. Li, H., Wang, M., Liu, S., Chen, P.-Y.: A theoretical understanding of shallow vision transformers: learning, generalization, and sample complexity. In: Proceedings of the International Conference on Learning Representations (2023)
24. Xie, S., Girshick, R.B., Dollár, P., Tu, Z., He, K.: Aggregated residual transformations for deep neural networks. In: Proceedings of the IEEE Conference on Computer Vision and Pattern Recognition (2017)
25. Ramachandran, P., Zoph, B., Le, Q.V.: Searching for activation functions (2018)
26. Lee, S.H., Lee, S., Song, B.: Vision transformer for small - size datasets (2021)
27. Loshchilov, I., Hutter, F.: Decoupled weight decay regularization. In: Proceedings of the International Conference on Learning Representations (2019)
28. Cubuk, E.D., Zoph, B., Shlens, J., Le, Q.V.: RandAugment: practical automated data augmentation with a reduced search space. In: Proceedings of the IEEE Conference on Computer Vision and Pattern Recognition (2019)
29. Zhang, H., Cissé, M., Dauphin, Y., Lopez-Paz, D.: mixup: Beyond empirical risk minimization. In: Proceedings of the International Conference on Learning Representations (2017)
30. Geiping, J., Goldstein, T.: Cramming: training a language model on a single GPU in one day (2022)

Computational Analysis of Cyber Risk Management by AI Coaching of Network DDoS Attack Activity in European Industries

Aleksander Szymczak[1,2], Jan Treur[1,2](✉), and Peter H. M. P. Roelofsma[1]

[1] Centre of Expertise Cyber Security, Risk Management and Cyber Security Group, The Hague University of Applied Sciences, The Hague, Netherlands
j.treur@vu.nl, p.h.m.p.roelofsma@hhs.nl

[2] Department of Computer Science, Vrije Universiteit, Social AI Group, Amsterdam, Netherlands

Abstract. This project investigates cyber risk management during Distributed Denial of Service (DDoS) attacks in European industries that impact many critical sectors such as finance, telecommunications, and technology. Using adaptive network modeling and MATLAB, a model was developed to simulate the interaction between human decision-making and AI coaching under stress. The AI Coach, equipped with complete situational awareness, monitors employee behavior and intervenes when errors are detected. Through What-If analysis and risk assessment, it was discovered that factors such as detection speed and error influence financial loss outcomes. The simulation results demonstrate that AI-supported intervention can significantly reduce system vulnerability by correcting human misjudgments in real-time.

Keywords: Adaptive Network Modeling · Cyber Risk Management · DDoS Attacks · AI Coach · Human Decision-Making · Cybersecurity · Risk Assessment · What-If Analysis · European Industries

1 Introduction

In today's world, most companies and organizations are in some way internet-based, whether they interact with clients online or simply operate through cloud-based systems. Despite it bringing many advantages, it also opens the door to security threats that can be exploited unethically.

One of the most frequent and harming methods is Distributed Denial of Service (DDoS) attacks, which have become a popular tool for hackers to disrupt operations [8, 9]. DDoS attacks work by overwhelming a system with fake traffic, making it extremely difficult or close to impossible for legitimate users to access services. What makes them especially dangerous is how closely the malicious traffic can resemble normal activity, making detection difficult [3]. These attacks can cause serious financial damage, loss of data, and downtime, especially in critical sectors like finance, healthcare, and telecommunications [8].

T. T. Quan et al. (Eds.): MIWAI 2025, LNAI 16353, pp. 37–50, 2026.
https://doi.org/10.1007/978-981-95-4957-3_4

In order to help prevent and respond to these threats, artificial intelligence and machine learning are being increasingly used. These systems can monitor patterns in network traffic and are able to detect unusual behavior in real-time, offering faster and more intelligent reactions than traditional rule-based systems [4–6]. However, even the best AI tools depend on the human team's response. The threat has a chance of succeeding if the alerts are being ignored, misunderstood or delayed. Therefore, this makes human factors such as coordination, awareness, and training very important [7].

This project aims to simulate how both AI and human response and their interactionplay a role in managing DDoS attacks. To model human decision making, the notion of internal mental model from cognitive science was adopted [14, 18, 19]. Exchanging knowledge (represented as individuals' mental models) between employees and with the organisation is addressed within management science in the area of organisational learning [15, 16, 21, 22]. This is used in the current paper to exchange knowledge between an AI Coach and an employee by knowledge level communication.

Following network-oriented methodology from [2], the adaptive dynamical system model was designed as an adaptive network model to depict all changes in behavior over time. To this end the abovementioned literature from cognitive science and management science was used to model in a network-oriented manner how mental models and learning (or forgetting) them and exchanging knowledge play a role, inspired by earlier work in [11–13, 18–20]. This approach helps explore how AI coaching and improved human reaction can reduce the damage caused by cybersecurity attacks.

2 Literature Overview

Distributed Denial of Service (DDoS) attacks remain one of the most common and disruptive threats to modern cybersecurity [3, 4, 8, 9]. Using multiple distributed resources against the target, they flood systems with traffic causing downtime and service disruptions, disrupting legitimate information exchange between the clients and servers. They target system resources, network bandwidth and other resources. Being very similar to normal traffic, they are extremely hard to detect [3, 4]. In recent years, DDoS attacks have resulted in substantial economic damages to the government entities and the industry [9]. They have been particularly affecting critical sectors such as finance institutions, healthcare, education, technology and telecommunications [8]. A recent report by Zayo (2024) highlights the increasing seriousness of DDoS attacks in Europe, revealing that the financial damage per incident for unprotected organisations reaches up to USD $270,000, with an average attack cost of USD $6,000 per minute. The report shows that the telecommunications sector is the most-targeted, facing 57% of all attacks. Other highly affected sectors include education (19%), manufacturing (5%), and cloud/SaaS (5%). Especially, the manufacturing sector has passed retail in terms of the largest-scale attacks, also showing a huge 308% increase in attack duration and a 200% growth in attack size. Healthcare saw a 128.5% increase in the number of attacks compared to the first half of 2023. Government entities are now the victims of the longest-lasting attacks, averaging over six hours per incident, an increase of 41% from the previous year. According to Zayo's senior vice president, a continued rise of up to 24% is expected by the end of the year if strong protections are not in place .

Having the numbers elevating significantly in the previous years, new ideas and solutions of incorporating machine learning, artificial intelligence, pattern recognition or deep learning into DDoS attacks detection have been proposed [3–6]. These rising in popularity and advancing techniques are and can be widely used to identify anomalies in traffic patterns. While technical system defence is exceptionally important, human error still remains as one of the major causes for cybersecurity breaches [7]. Research shows that ignoring alerts, using company devices for personal use, clicking dangerous, phishing links facilitates DDoS and malware attacks. Addressing human behaviour such as poor training and lack of awareness in cybersecurity would reduce a number of vulnerabilities, strengthening the overall defense system. To enhance the understanding and visualisation, this project applies a Network-Oriented Modeling approach [2]. It simulates information flows and outcomes in dynamic situations by building a network of interconnected states that influence one another over time, capturing the system responses and nature of humans. In conjunction with cybersecurity, this modelling approach facilitates detailed simulation of how individuals, systems and AI agents react to threats like DDoS attacks, thereby supporting effective cyberthreat management.

3 General Modeling Approach

The objective of this project was to represent cognitive, behavioral and cybersecurity processes through time. This has been achieved using a modelling technique based on network-oriented modeling of adaptive systems represented as networks of interconnected states following the approach described in [2]. Nodes (states) represent key variables such as traffic volume or user alertness, meanwhile the links between them show how changes in one affect the other using combination functions over time. Each link has a connection weight, which determines the strength of influence from one state to another. These weights, as well as the speed factors that control how quickly a state responds, can be made adaptive, meaning they change over time to simulate learning or system adjustment. This makes the model suitable for simulating how AI coaching dynamically improves human response to DDoS threats. The simulations are implemented in the dedicated software described in [2], Ch 9, which calculates time-series behavior for each state based on the model's structure.

The model uses two main combinations functions: Advanced logistic and Step-once (see Table 1), as well as, has role matrices: mb, mcfw, mcfp, mcw, ms, iv, that define how the network adapts and processes information. The Advanced logistic function smoothly combines inputs into one output, increasing more as inputs pass a set threshold, whereas the Step-once function is used to activate certain events at a specific point in time, such as the stress/workload level.

The AI Coach was introduced to assist decision making and mitigation strategies . Following [1], the AI Coach is used to carry out rational and bias-free decisions in a cybersecurity environment. Having perfect knowledge about the situation and monitoring the employee's decisions made, the AI Coach performs corrective actions for the employee's mental model in real time.

Table 1. Description of combination functions used

Concept	Formula	Parameters
alogistic$_{\sigma,\tau}(V_1, \ldots, V_k)$ Advanced logistic sum	$\left[\frac{1}{1+e^{-\sigma(V_1+\cdots+V_k-\tau)}} - \frac{1}{1+e^{\sigma\tau}}\right](1+e^{-\sigma\tau})$	steepness $\boldsymbol{\sigma}$ threshold $\boldsymbol{\tau}$
steponce$_{\alpha,\beta}(V_1, \ldots, V_k)$	1 if $\boldsymbol{\alpha} \leq t \leq \boldsymbol{\beta}$, else 0 for time t	Start $\boldsymbol{\alpha}$, end $\boldsymbol{\beta}$

4 The Designed Adaptive Network Model

In this section the previously discussed adaptive network model is described in depth. The outcome of this project is to simulate the influence of the DDoS attack on the system causing a financial loss, and the procedures that the employee can take and act upon his beliefs, perception and past experience, in order to manage the attack and minimize the losses. The model captures how these cognitive and behavioral elements change over time in response to changes in the system, additionally reflecting the complexity of decision-making under pressure, especially in high-risk cybersecurity environments (Figure 1). This model has been enhanced with an AI Coach, whose purpose is to supervise the human actions of the employee, and to step-in and take a lead when necessary and appropriate. This layered approach provides insight into how adaptive behavior both human and artificial can influence the overall response and reduce the impact of cyber threats.

The network consists of a total number of 48 interconnected states and spans across three different levels, base level, first-order adaptation level, second-order adaptation level. These levels are made of 30 states, 15 states and 3 states respectively (see Tables 2 and 3). The base level contains the core behavioral, cognitive, and system states for both the employee and the AI Coach, while the first-order adaptation level represents adaptive connection weights that allow the network to learn from ongoing experiences. The second-order adaptation level that is positioned at the top controls when communication between the AI Coach and the employee should occur. This layered setup makes it possible to depict the changing ways people react in stressful situations such as DDoS cyberattack.

The base level contains an external state in the middle of the graph, and two mental models, the left one belonging to the AI Coach, and the right one representing the employee's mental model and thinking. The first state that initiates the simulation is Incoming Traffic. This state is crucial in this scenario representing the part of the system directly targeted by the hacker and where the malicious traffic is injected during a DDoS attack. It connects to Fake Traffic Level, which then leads to DDoS Detection Confidence and Error. These states are responsible for identifying potentially harmful traffic, measuring the confidence of detection, and recognizing when something has gone wrong. One of the outgoing arrows from the Error state acts as a critical link between the external model and the employee's internal mental model for decision making. From this point, cognitive processes are triggered, beliefs are formed, patterns are noticed, and experiences are processed over time. The decision making mental model of the employee contains three belief states and three action decision states: Manual Override, Reroute

Table 2. Explanation of the base states in the adaptive network model.

Nr	State Name	Explanation
X1	Incoming Traffic	How much traffic is coming into system.
X2	Fake Level Traffic	Assessed level of fake or malicious traffic.
X3	DDoS Detection Confidence	Confidence in detecting a DDoS attack.
X4	Error	Error level in system behaviour.
X5	Belief of Error	Employee's belief of possible error.
X6	Notice Error	Employee notices that something is wrong.
X7	Past Experience	Memory of prior similar incidents.
X8	Belief of Fake Traffic Level	Employee's belief of possible fake traffic level.
X9	Confidence in AI	Trust and confidence in AI's decision making capabilities.
X10	Expected Impact of AI	Anticipated impact of an AI intervention.
X11	Expected Impact of Manual Action	Anticipated impact of a human manual intervention.
X12	Manual Override	Manual intervention to override traffic routing
X13	Reroute Traffic	Network traffic rerouting.
X14	Belief of Incoming Traffic	Employee's belief of possible incoming traffic.
X15	Perceived Threat Level	Employee's assessment of how dangerous the situation is.
X16	Initiate Lockdown Procedures	Lockdown is initiated to protect the system.
X17	Financial Loss	Money lost due to the cyberattack.
X18	Stress/Workload	How busy or stressed the employee is.
X19	AIC Belief of Error	AI Coach's belief that an error might be happening.
X20	AIC Notice Error	AI Coach detects that something is wrong.
X21	AIC Past Experience	AI Coach's learning history of past similar incidents.
X22	AIC Belief of Fake Traffic Level	AI Coach's belief about how much fake or malicious traffic there is.
X23	AIC Confidence in AI	AI Coach's trust and confidence in AI's decision making capabilities.

(*continued*)

Table 2. (*continued*)

Nr	State Name	Explanation
X24	AIC Expected Impact of AI	AI Coach's anticipated impact of an AI intervention.
X25	AIC Expected Impact of Manual Action	AI Coach's anticipated impact of a human manual intervention.
X26	AIC Manual Override	AI Coach's suggested manual intervention.
X27	AIC Reroute Traffic	AI Coach's suggested network traffic rerouting.
X28	AIC Belief of Incoming Traffic	AI Coach's estimate of how much traffic is coming in.
X29	AIC Perceived Threat Level	AI Coach's assessment of how dangerous the situation is.
X30	AIC Initiate Lockdown Procedures	AI Coach initiates lockdown procedures to protect the system.

Traffic, and Initiate Lockdown Procedures. These action states play a vital role in the simulation, as they produce direct feedback into the external system. They influence the Incoming Traffic (Reroute Traffic), can help reduce the Error (Manual Override), or decrease the amount of fake traffic detected (Initiate Lockdown Procedures). This flow illustrates the interaction between internal decision-making and external system control, highlighting how cognitive responses shape cybersecurity defense mechanisms.

In addition, there are six first-order adaptation states (**W**-states) for the employee's mental model. These **W**-states represent the adaptive connection weights that indicate the knowledge of the mental model, e.g., how strongly certain beliefs influence subsequent decisions or perceptions. For example, by learning these **W**-states determine how past experience affects confidence in AI, or how the perceived threat level impacts the decision to initiate a lockdown which allows the model to simulate realistic learning and behavioral adaptation. Naturally, the AI Coach possesses the perfect mapping of the employee's mental model, consisting of the same cognitive and action decision states but also adaptation **W**-states (**AI-W**-states) for the mental model connections. The base states of the AI Coach share identical incoming arrows from the external states [1]. The initial values, learning speed, set activation thresholds, steepness, connection weights of the states in the AI Coach are equivalent to those in the employee, however, the one difference is that the adaptive states of the AI Coach are assumed to have the perfect knowledge, resulting in fixed values 1. This difference stems from the fact that the AI Coach does not have the Stress/Workload which influences the adaptives state of the employee. Therefore, in the first-order adaptation level, beside the adaptation **W**-states of the employee and the AI Coach, there are monitor states that constantly monitor the employee and AI Coach's mental models, waiting for any deviations in perception and understanding of the situation from the employee. If such a thing occurs, an immediate

Table 3. Explanation of the first- and second-order adaptation states.

Nr	State Name	Explanation
X31	$\mathbf{W}_{\mathrm{B.Er,NE}}$	How belief of an error (X5) influences noticing an error (X6).
X32	$\mathbf{W}_{\mathrm{B.FTL,CIA}}$	How belief of fake traffic (X8) influences confidence in AI (X9).
X33	$\mathbf{W}_{\mathrm{B.IT,PTL}}$	How belief of incoming traffic (X14) influences perceived threat level (X15).
X34	$\mathbf{W}_{\mathrm{PE,CIA}}$	How past experience (X7) influences confidence in AI (X9).
X35	$\mathbf{W}_{\mathrm{PTL,ILP}}$	How threat level (X15) influences the decision to initiate lockdown (X16).
X36	$\mathbf{W}_{\mathrm{EIMA\_MO}}$	How expected impact of manual action (X11) influences manual override (X12).
X37	**AIC** $\mathbf{W}_{\mathrm{B.Er,NE}}$	AI Coach version of X31.
X38	**AIC** $\mathbf{W}_{\mathrm{B.FTL,CIA}}$	AI Coach version of X32.
X39	**AIC** $\mathbf{W}_{\mathrm{B.IT,PTL}}$	AI Coach version of X33.
X40	**AIC** $\mathbf{W}_{\mathrm{PE,CIA}}$	AI Coach version of X34.
X41	**AIC** $\mathbf{W}_{\mathrm{PTL,ILP}}$	AI Coach version of X35.
X42	**AIC** $\mathbf{W}_{\mathrm{EIMA,MO}}$	AI Coach version of X36.
X43	AIC Monitor Noticed Error	AI Coach monitors if human noticed an error.
X44	AIC Monitor Belief Incoming Traffic & Perceived Threat Level	AI Coach monitors human beliefs about traffic and perceived threat level.
X45	AIC Monitor Confidence in AI & Expected Impact of AI	AI Coach monitors human trust in AI and what they expect from it.
X46	**AIC WWW_W**$_{\mathrm{\_B.Er,NE}}$	AI Coach's adjustment for how belief in an error affects noticing the error.
X47	**AIC WWW_W**$_{\mathrm{\_B.IT,PTL}}$	AI Coach's adjustment for how belief in traffic affects perceived threat level.
X48	**AIC WWW_W**$_{\mathrm{\_PE,CIA}}$	AI Coach's adjustment for how past experience affects confidence in AI.

signal is sent to the communication control states (inspired by social learning and organisational learning as addressed in [11, 12, 20]) in the second-order adaptation level which directly trigger the appropriate $\mathbf{W}_{\mathrm{WW}}$-states that cause the communication of relevant **W**-states from the AI Coach to the employee to occur then. Further details of the model can be found as Linked Data at URL.

https://www.researchgate.net/publication/394363594.

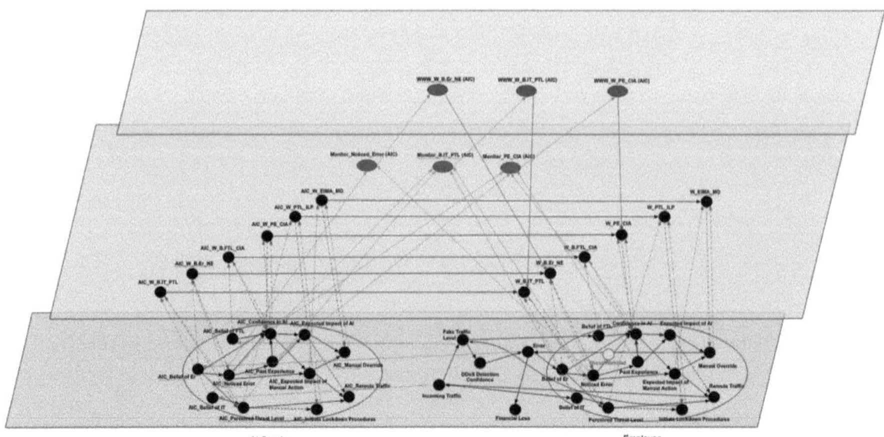

Fig. 1. Conceptual Design of the Adaptive Network Model for DDoS Attacks.

Figure 2 is a simulation and a visual representation of a DDoS attack on a system. It shows high Incoming Traffic, followed by a sharp rise in Fake Traffic Level. Even though the Confidence in DDoS Detection is strong, the Error state increases significantly. The employee suspects the possibility of an error in the system, however it remains unnoticed, forming a first and crucial deviation from what employee sees and the AI Coach knows. As the Stress/Workload level increases, it has a strong effect on the employee's ability to think clearly and learn properly. At a certain point, the monitor recognizes the growing difference between the two mental models and a signal is sent to the communication control states in the second-order communication level, which then activate the correct $\mathbf{W}_{\mathbf{WW}}$-state to enable communication of the relevant **W**-state to the employee. These adjust the learning strength and help correct the wrong beliefs and perceptions caused by stress. In Fig. 2, this can be seen between time 25 and 32, where Stress/Workload rises quickly, and the adaptive performance of the employee drops. The monitors respond very quickly and trigger the communication control mechanism, bringing the **W**-States of the employee in moments back to normal. This shows how adaptive support both from within the system, and from the AI Coach, helps the employee recover and stay effective under pressure. The AI Coach was designed using the approach described by [1], based on shared mental models and decision-making under stress. As shown in the simulation, its ability to detect critical deviations, correct cognitive errors, and intervene precisely when needed highlights its value as a decision-support mechanism in cyber risk management. Especially under high-stress DDoS scenarios, the AI Coach enhances the reliability of human response by ensuring that the right actions are taken at the right time to minimize financial loss.

5 Comparative What-If Analysis and Risk Assessment

What-If analysis and risk assessment are fundamental methodologies for evaluating the potential outcomes of complex scenarios, particularly in the realm of cybersecurity [10]. It supports understanding how different input conditions (If-factors) affect critical

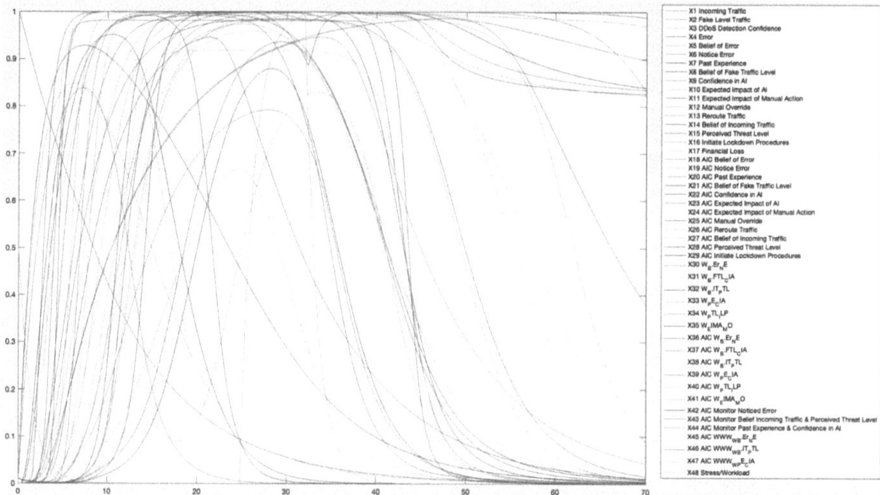

Fig. 2. Simulation.

outcomes (What-factors) in the system. In the context of cyber risk management for European industries, it was examined how the strength of error affecting belief of error and the speed of noticing the error influence the financial loss (X17) during Distributed Denial of Service (DDoS) attack scenarios. The objective was to reproduce realistic scenarios and evaluate how risky or damaging each combination can be.

To perform the simulation, two If-factors were defined. The first one represents how strongly the system error (X4) influences the employee's belief that an error is occurring (X5), and the second If-factor represents how fast the employee notices the error (X6) once it is present. Each was assigned a label -"low" or "high", based on the value bracket they fell within: [0.0–0.5] or [0.5–1.0]. Additionally, probabilities were estimated and assigned based on observed system characteristics. Combined probabilities were calculated based on the product rule (assuming independence) A higher influence of error (0.75) and lower noticing speed (0.6) were more likely to take place in the modeled environment, which is outlined in Table 4.

Risk assessment is a structured method that enables us to determine the potential consequences and the likeliness of certain events taking place. In the perspective of this project it provided quantified risk levels that are associated with configurations of the system under a DDoS attack scenario. The risk assessment combined the probability of each If-factor combination (as shown in Table 4) with the corresponding severity of financial loss, based on the simulation results for state X17. The outcomes were grouped into specific impact levels, giving higher weights to financial losses that occurred earlier and were more severe, while lower weights were assigned to later or smaller losses.

Each scenario's overall risk score was calculated using the formula Risk = Probability * Impact. This allowed for a direct assessment of how various system configurations influence the extent of potential financial damage.

In both Table 5 (without AI Coach) and Table 6 (with AI Coach), it is noticeable that financial loss occurs regardless of the configuration, with an impact indicator of 6 at time

Table 4. If-factor options and estimated probabilities.

If factors	If factor options	If factor option labels	If factor option value intervals	If factor option probabilities
If factor 1: Weight from Error (X4) → Belief of Error (X5)	If Factor 1 Option 1	low	0.0–0.5	0.25
	If Factor 1 Option 2	high	0.5–1.0	0.75
If factor 2: Speed of Notice Error (X6)	If Factor 2 Option 1	low	0.0–0.5	0.6
	If Factor 2 Option 2	high	0.5–1.0	0.4

20, demonstrating that risks emerge early in the simulation. However, the key difference which clearly highlights the effectiveness and powerful impact of the AI Coach is how it supports the system in managing and mitigating these financial losses over time. In the second column of both tables, particularly under What factor 2a (the value of state X17 at time 40), the risk sum of probabilities is more than halved in the AI-supported scenario: from 9.00 in Table 6 down to 4.05 in Table 6.

This difference reflects a substantial and quick reduction in long-term financial losses for organizations implementing the AI Coach which is a major benefit of implementing AI Coach. This is especially critical, as financial loss at time 40 represents the most severe outcome in the simulation and therefore receives the highest impact weight of 9, whereas earlier losses at time 20 are slightly less severe and weighted with an impact value of 6. Lower loss outcomes, both early and late are considered favorable and accordingly receive lower weights of 2 and 1. This weighting method reflects not only the importance of early response but also the priority of long-term damage control, demonstrating that the AI Coach's ability to stabilize performance over time is a decisive factor in reducing financial risk in DDoS scenarios.

6 Discussion

In the past couple of years, the rise in DDoS attacks across European industries has grown substantially, resulting in enormous financial losses. This pervasive form of cyberattack is a serious threat to the European and Worldwide Industries.

To analize and better understand the impact of such attacks, concepts and architectures from cognitive science [14, 19] and management science [15, 16, 21, 22] and their formalisation [11, 12, 18, 20, 23] were used and the modeling approach [2] to construct an adaptive dynamical system based on a self-modeling network structure showing how the system reacts during a DDoS scenario. This self-modeling network modeling approach was inspired by the areas of causal modeling and of metalevel architectures and reflection from AI [24–29]. This network modeling approach comes with methods and tools for verification of models by mathematical analysis [30–32] and validation of models by comparison and tuning of simulations to numerical empirical data [33].

Table 5. Risk Assessment overview without an AI Coach.

If factor 1 option probabilities	If factor 2 option probabilities	If factor combination probabilities	What factor 1a Probability for X17 high at time 20	What factor 2a Probability for X17 high at time 40	What factor 1b Probability for X17 low at time 20	What factor 1b Probability for X17 low at time 40
If factor 1 option 1: low (0.25)	If factor 2 option 1: low (0.6)	0.25×0.6 = **0.15**	0.15	0.15		0.15
	If factor 2 option 2: high (0.4)	0.25×0.4 = **0.10**	0.10	0.10		0.10
If factor 1 option 2: high (0.75)	If factor 2 option 1: low (0.6)	0.75×0.6 = **0.45**	0.45	0.45		
	If factor 2 option 2: high (0.4)	0.75×0.4 = **0.30**	0.30	0.30		
Sum of probabilities:			1	1		0.25
Impact indicator:			6	9	1	2
Risk assessment:			6	9	0	0.50

In the simulation there is a sharp rise in fake traffic levels, followed closely by an increase in system errors. Even though the DDoS detection confidence remained high, the human employee's response was slow due to rising levels of stress and workload. This delay is critical, as it reflects how human factors can fail to initiate the proper countermeasures. The growing stress/workload (X18) negatively influenced the employee's ability to make effective decisions, and as a result the key adaptive states (W-states) began to decrease. The Error (X4) grew quickly but the employee didn't notice it at first. This shows a clear difference between what was happening in the system and what the employee realized confirming the influence of cognitive overload on decision-making. However, here, the AI Coach proved to be a powerful and useful tool. Unlike the human, the AI Coach maintained a consistent understanding of the situation, thanks to its "perfect knowledge" of the system's internal and external states. It effectively monitored the employee's mental model and detected inconsistencies in perception. Once a deviation was recognized, the communication control mechanism that is handled by second-order WWW-states was activated, having the AI Coach transfer the corrected W-states to the employee, which allowed for recovery and stabilization of performance when human limitations began to compromise system integrity.

Table 6. Risk Assessment overview with an AI Coach.

If factor 1 option probabilities	If factor 2 option probabilities	If factor combination probabilities	What factor 1a Probability for X17 high at time 20	What factor 2a Probability for X17 high at time 40	What factor 1b Probability for X17 low at time 20	What factor 1b Probability for X17 low at time 40
If factor 1 option 1: low (0.25)	If factor 2 option 1: low (0.6)	0.25 × 0.6 = **0.15**	0.15			0.15
	If factor 2 option 2: high (0.4)	0.25 × 0.4 = **0.10**	0.10			0.10
If factor 1 option 2: high (0.75)	If factor 2 option 1: low (0.6)	0.75 × 0.6 = **0.45**	0.45	0.45		
	If factor 2 option 2: high (0.4)	0.75 × 0.4 = **0.30**	0.30			
Sum of probabilities:			1	0.45		0.25
Impact indicator:			6	9	1	2
Risk assessment:			6	4.05	0	0.50

The significant reduction in Financial Loss (X17) was one of the most major outcomes of this simulation. It was achieved through the appropriate support and intervention of the AI Coach, proving that implementing AI-driven support systems could be a practical and effective solution in real-world cybersecurity environments. In terms of future project expansion, it would be beneficial to explore the long-term involvement of the AI Coach at a management level. This would include modeling its role in organizational learning and safety culture, tracking how often certain deviations occur and suggesting corrective actions to reduce them over time.

References

1. Roelofsma, P.H.M.P., Jabeen, F., Taal, H.R., Treur, J. (eds.): Using Shared Mental Models and Organisational Learning to Support Safety and Security Through Cyberspace: A Computational Analysis Approach. Springer Nature (2025)
2. Treur, J.: Network-Oriented Modeling for Adaptive Networks: Designing Higher-Order Adaptive Biological, Mental and Social Network Models. Springer Nature (2020)
3. https://link.springer.com/book/https://doi.org/10.1007/978-3-030-31445-3
4. Zhang, B., Zhang, T., Yu , Z.: DDoS detection and prevention based on artificial intelligence techniques. Proc. of the 3rd IEEE International Conference on Computer and Communications (ICCC'17), pp. 1276–1280, https://doi.org/10.1109/CompComm.2017.8322748. (2017)

5. Lima Filho, F. S. D., Silveira, F. A., de Medeiros Brito Junior, A., Vargas-Solar, G., & Silveira, L. F.: Smart detection: an online approach for DoS/DDoS attack detection using machine learning. Security and Communication Networks 2019(1), 1574749 (2019)
6. Doshi, R., Apthorpe, N., Feamster, N.: Machine learning ddos detection for consumer internet of things devices. In 2018 IEEE security and privacy workshops (SPW) (pp. 29–35). IEEE. https://ieeexplore.ieee.org/abstract/document/8424629 (2018)
7. Priya, S. S., Sivaram, M., Yuvaraj, D., & Jayanthiladevi, A.: Machine learning based DDoS detection. In 2020 international conference on emerging smart computing and informatics (ESCI) (pp. 234–237). IEEE https://ieeexplore.ieee.org/abstract/document/9167642 (2020)
8. Coffey, J. W.: Ameliorating sources of human error in cybersecurity: technological and human-centered approaches. In The 8th International Multi-Conference on Complexity, Informatics, and Cybernetics, Pensacola (pp. 85–88) (2017)
9. https://www.iiis.org/CDs2017/CD2017Spring/papers/ZA253LY.pdf
10. Theocharidou, M., Lella, I., Naydenov, R., Malatras, A.: ENISA Threat Landscape: Finance Sector: January 2023 – June 2424. https://www.enisa.europa.eu/sites/default/files/2025-02/Finance%20TL%202024_Final.pdf
11. Shannon Williams.: Zayo report shows dramatic rise in DDoS attacks across Europe
12. https://securitybrief.co.uk/story/zayo-report-shows-dramatic-rise-in-ddos-attacks-across-europe (2024)
13. Wexler, J., Pushkarna, M., Bolukbasi, T., Wattenberg, M., Viégas, F., & Wilson, J.: The what-if tool: Interactive probing of machine learning models. IEEE transactions on visualization and computer graphics 26(1), 56–65
14. https://ieeexplore.ieee.org/abstract/document/8807255 (2019)
15. Bhalwankar, R., Treur, J.: Modeling learner-controlled mental model learning processes by a second-order adaptive network model. PLoS ONE **16**(8), e0255503 (2021)
16. Canbaloğlu, G., Treur, J., Wiewiora, A. (eds.).: Computational modeling of multilevel organisational learning and its control using self-modeling network models. Springer Nature. (2023)
17. Canbaloğlu, G., Treur, J., Wiewiora, A. (2023). Computational modeling of multilevel organizational learning: from conceptual to computational mechanisms. In Computational Intelligence: Select Proceedings of InCITe 2022. Lecture Notes in Electrical Engineering, vol 968, pp. 1–17. Singapore: Springer Nature Singapore
18. Craik, K. J. W.L The nature of explanation. Cambridge, MA: University Press (1943)
19. Crossan, M.M., Lane, H.W., White, R.E.: An organizational learning framework: From intuition to institution. Acad. Manag. Rev. **24**, 522–537 (1999)
20. Kim, D.H.: The link between individual and organizational learning. Sloan Management Review **35**(1), 37–51 (1993)
21. Treur, J.: Network reification as a unified approach to represent network adaptation principles within a network. In: Theory and Practice of Natural Computing: 7th International Conference, TPNC 2018, Proceedings, vol. 7, pp. 344–358. Springer International Publishing (2018)
22. Treur, J., Van Ments, L. (eds.): Mental Models and their Dynamics, Adaptation, and Control: a Self-Modeling Network Modeling Approach. Springer Nature (2022)
23. Van Ments, L., Treur, J.: Reflections on dynamics, adaptation and control: a cognitive architecture for mental models. Cogn. Syst. Res. **70**, 1–9 (2021)
24. Van Ments, L., Treur, J., Klein, J., Roelofsma, P.: A Second-Order Adaptive Network Model for Shared Mental Models in Hospital Teamwork. In: Nguyen, N.T., Iliadis, L., Maglogiannis, I., Trawiński, B. (eds) Computational Collective Intelligence. Proc. of of the 13th International Conference on Computational Collective Intelligence, ICCCI 2021. Lecture Notes in Computer Science, vol 12876, pp 126–140. Springer Nature, Cham (2021)

25. Wiewiora, A., Chang, A., Smidt, M.: Individual, project and organizational learning flows within a global project-based organization: exploring what, how and who. Int. J. Project Manage. **38**(4), 201–214 (2020)
26. Wiewiora, A., Smidt, M., Chang, A.: The 'how'of multilevel learning dynamics: A systematic literature review exploring how mechanisms bridge learning between individuals, teams/projects and the organization. Eur. Manag. Rev. **16**(1), 93–115 (2019)
27. Canbaloğlu, G., Treur, J., Roelofsma, P.H.M.P.: Computational modeling of organisational learning by self-modeling networks. Cogn. Syst. Res. **73**, 51–64 (2022)
28. Brazier, F.M.T., Treur, J.: Compositional modelling of reflective agents. Int. J. Hum. Comput. Stud. **50**(5), 407–431 (1999)
29. Maes, P., Nardi, D. (eds.): Meta-level Architectures and Reflection. North-Holland (1988)
30. Meyer, J.J.Chr., Treur, J. (eds.): Dynamics and management of reasoning processes. Springer Science & Business Media. (2001)
31. Treur, J.: On the use of reflection principles in modelling complex reasoning. Int. J. Intell. Syst. **6**(3), 277–294 (1991)
32. Treur, J.: Temporal semantics of meta-level architectures for dynamic control of reasoning. In: Fribourg, L., Turini, F. (eds) Logic Program Synthesis and Transformation — Meta-Programming in Logic. Proceedings META LOPSTR 1994. Lecture Notes in Computer Science, vol 883, pp 353–376. Springer, Berlin, Heidelberg (1994)
33. Weyhrauch, R.W.: Prolegomena to a theory of mechanized formal reasoning. Artif. Intell. **13**(1–2), 133–170 (1980)
34. Brazier, F.M., et al.: Compositional verification of a multi-agent system for one-to-many negotiation. Appl. Intell. **20**(2), 95–117 (2004)
35. Cornelissen, F., Jonker, C.M., Treur, J.: Compositional verification of knowledge-based systems: a case study for diagnostic reasoning. In: Plaza, E., Benjamins, R. (eds) Knowledge Acquisition, Modeling and Management. Proceedings EKAW 1997. Lecture Notes in Computer Science, vol 1319, pp. 65–80. Springer, Berlin, Heidelberg. https://doi.org/10.1007/BFb0026778 (1997)
36. Treur, J.: Where is this leading me: stationary point and equilibrium analysis for self-modeling network models. In: Treur, J., Van Ments, L. (eds.), Mental Models and Their Dynamics, Adaptation, and Control: A Self-Modeling Network Modeling Approach, Ch 18, pp. 491–535. Cham: Springer Nature (2022a)
37. Treur, J.: Does this suit me? Validation of self-modeling network models by parameter tuning. In: Treur, J., Van Ments, L. (eds.), Mental Models and Their Dynamics, Adaptation, and Control: A Self-Modeling Network Modeling Approach, Ch 19, pp. 537–564. Cham: Springer Nature (2022b)

Learning to Defer with Scoring Functions

Andrew Ponomarev(✉)

St. Petersburg Federal Research Center of the Russian Academy of Sciences, Saint Petersburg, Russian Federation
ponomarev@iias.spb.su

Abstract. Machine learning models in high-stakes applications often collaborate with human experts, requiring intelligent deferral mechanisms. While traditional rejection learning uses model uncertainty to decide deferrals, it ignores human error and lacks flexibility in coverage control. Learning-to-defer approaches address this by jointly optimizing a classifier and a rejector, using loss functions that account for both model and human performance. However, existing methods either disregard human resource constraints or require costly retraining when coverage needs change. We explore a scoring-based approach to learning to defer that addresses these limitations. Building on prior heuristic methods, we introduce a novel metric quantifying how effectively a deferral system leverages both model and human expertise across the feature space. We then derive the theoretically optimal deferral rule and develop a practical scoring function approximation that enables post-hoc coverage adjustment without retraining. Our method trains a scoring function to rank samples by their expected delegation benefit, which can be calibrated to meet dynamic coverage constraints. Experiments show this approach achieves superior accuracy-workload trade-offs compared to existing methods, providing both theoretical grounding and practical flexibility for human-AI collaboration.

Keywords: Learning to Defer · Rejection Learning · Human-AI Complementarity · Human-AI Collaboration

1 Introduction

Machine learning models are typically trained to perform some task (e.g., classification) autonomously, but in practice they are often (especially, in responsible and critical applications) used in a complex workflow that may include human experts who control the model output and/or handle complex cases. Previous research has shown that training model specifically to be used as a part of a workflow, i.e., optimization of the overall workflow result, taking into account both machine learning model and limited human knowledge can improve overall quality of the system [1]. Such joint optimization is sometimes referred to as human-AI complementarity or learning to defer [1, 2].

Typically, learning to defer is based on using two models – main model (usually, a classifier) and a rejector. The classifier is tasked with solving the underlying classification problem, whereas the rejector determines whether a given sample should be processed

T. T. Quan et al. (Eds.): MIWAI 2025, LNAI 16353, pp. 51–62, 2026.
https://doi.org/10.1007/978-981-95-4957-3_5

by the classifier or deferred to a human expert. Optimization of these models is typically guided by a specialized loss function that incorporates human error patterns from the training data. Consequently, the models implicitly learn the distribution of human expertise across the feature space and adapt their behavior accordingly. However, most methods either ignore coverage constraints [2, 3], casting the problem as finding the best possible accuracy – typically, via optimization of some surrogate loss function, or define a constrained optimization problem [4, 5]. While the latter case allows one to explicitly control the user workload (coverage) and accuracy, it can be computationally expensive on the one hand, and not flexible enough on the other, as the optimization problem is solved during model training, and if coverage constraints are changed, it can require retraining the model.

This paper builds on [6], where an idea of scoring-based learning to defer is proposed. Scoring function ranks samples according to their expected delegation benefit, allowing one to control coverage without retraining the rejection model, simply by selecting threshold value of the scoring function. However, scoring functions proposed in [6] are not properly justified. The contribution of this paper is following. First, we propose an integral metric for measuring quality of a learning to defer algorithm, reflecting how well this algorithm uses information about strengths and weaknesses of both an ML model and a human expert (dependence of prediction quality on the position in the feature space). Then, we examine theoretically best possible value of this metric and obtain an optimal rejecting algorithm (that would obtain theoretically best value of this metric in the hypothetical situation of perfect information). Finally, based on optimal rejecting algorithm we propose a training method for a scoring model (function) and distribution strategy and show that they indeed lead to "good" sample allocations.

The rest of the paper is organized as follows. In Sec. 2 we describe related work in more detail. In Sec. 3 we propose an integral metric for learning to defer, taking into account both coverage and accuracy, theoretically estimate best possible value for this metric and describe an algorithm for obtaining this value. Sec. 4 proposes training method and distribution strategy, which are evaluated in Sec. 5.

2 Related Work

The problem of joint work of an AI model and a human expert has been attracting attention of the ML researchers for a relatively long time. Probably, the most developed setting is so-called rejection learning, where a model is trained to reject certain samples to improve reliability on the others [7]. However, in rejection learning the accuracy of human expert is not considered (he/she is considered to be absolutely accurate).

More recently, a concept of learning to defer has been proposed [1], where human expert has been placed "into" the system, i.e., these algorithms optimize deferral policies taking into account not only the performance of the machine learning model in various regions of the feature space, but also accuracy of the human expert which may also be different in the different regions of the feature space.

Most approaches to learning to defer rely on specially constructed loss functions, balancing components responsible for automated classifier and human expert. These loss functions can either be very closely based on the utility theory [8] or further elaborated as surrogate loss functions with better optimization and calibration properties, see, e.g. [2, 3, 9]. However, all these approaches are either aimed at finding a deferral policy optimizing only the system accuracy, or relying on relative weighting in the loss function, which should reflect relative cost of sample processing by the model and the human expert, however, may be hard to specify. Crucial is that most of these approaches ignore that the expert capacity can be limited [10].

A few methods have been proposed to deal with the limited expert capacity, typically via MILP reformulation of learning to defer problem, e.g. [4, 5, 11, 12]. In [4, 11], MILP is solved for the training set and then its solution is approximated by an additional model. In [5, 12] MILP is built during inference, therefore, these approaches can only allocate a set of samples, but are less suited for the situation when the samples have to be distributed between model and human expert as soon as they arrive. Besides, solving MILP can be computationally expensive, especially for large datasets. The scoring function approach, proposed in [6], is aimed at obviating this problem – it proposes to train (or construct) a scoring function, used to rank how beneficial it is to assign an item to a model, and then use a simple calibration procedure to find a score value, corresponding to the required coverage. On the one hand, it allows one to control the coverage, on the other hand, it doesn't require solving computationally expensive problems (MILP). However, the authors of [6] do not provide a method for obtaining scoring function.

This paper adopts the idea of a scoring function from [6], but explores this idea in more detail, proposing methods to create such scoring functions following from an original quality metric for learning to defer, integrating accuracy and coverage.

3 Quality Metrics for Learning to Defer

3.1 Problem Definition

Given the dataset $D = \{(X_i, e_i, y_i)\}_{i=1}^n \sim \mathcal{D}$, where $X_i \in \mathcal{X}$ are the features describing objects, $y_i \in \mathcal{Y}$ are true labels, and $e_i \in \mathcal{Y}$ are expert labels (not necessarily equal to the true labels, as the expert can also be wrong). The problem is to find two functions – a classifier $h : \mathcal{X} \to \mathcal{Y}$ and a rejector $r : \mathcal{X} \to \{0,1\}$. To obtain a decision $\hat{y}_i$ for some instance x_i these functions are combined in the following way: $\hat{y}_i \stackrel{\text{def}}{=} h(x_i)$, if $r(x_i) = 1$, otherwise $\hat{y}_i \stackrel{\text{def}}{=} e_i$. To simplify the notation, we also use m_i to denote classifier's prediction for the sample x_i, or, formally, $m_i \stackrel{\text{def}}{=} h(x_i)$.

The classifier h and the rejector r should maximize the accuracy of the system, respecting coverage constraint C:

$$\underset{h,r}{\text{argmax}} E_D\big[\mathbb{I}\{r(x_i)m_i + (1 - r(x_i))e_i = y_i\}\big], \quad s.t. E_D[r(x_i)] \geq C$$

Practically, the coverage constraint corresponds to limited human resources, when human expert can process only a fraction of the dataset.

Scoring-based formulation of learning to defer introduces sample scoring function $score : X \to \mathbb{R}$, and defines the rejector using this function and the specified threshold: $r_\theta(x) \stackrel{\text{def}}{=} \mathbb{I}\{score(x) \geq \theta\}$.

There are two key quality characteristics:

1. Overall prediction accuracy (how closely the final outputs of the "human-AI model" system align with the ground truth): $E_D\big[\mathbb{I}\{r(x_i)m_i + (1 - r(x_i))e_i = y_i\}\big]$.
2. Human workload (the extent of expert involvement in obtaining these results), or coverage: $E_D[r(x_i)]$.

3.2 The Proposed Metrics

In existing publications, the key quality characteristics can be combined in different ways: solely on accuracy metrics, multi-criteria evaluation, and metric aggregation. While all these approaches have their pros and cons, the most universal approach to evaluating task allocation models is multi-criteria evaluation, as it accounts for both quality characteristics of such systems. However, practical application of multi-criteria evaluation presents challenges, and comparing different solutions often requires a single scalar metric. While metric aggregation (weighted combination) is an option, it introduces subjectivity by requiring predefined importance weights, which may lack justification.

To address this, we propose a method for combining the two primary metrics—system accuracy and coverage—into a single unified measure without requiring weight assignment. In particular, we propose two integrated metrics – AC-AUC (area under accuracy-coverage curve) and nAC-AUC (normalized area under the accuracy-coverage curve) the first one is equivalent to the DEV metric, proposed in [13], the second is the normalized version of this metric, allowing to compare delegation strategies across different datasets.

Let $\mathcal{A}(s)$ be a task allocation algorithm, where s is a parameter influencing the sample distribution balance (e.g., a confidence threshold for deferring samples to a human expert). For a fixed s, the algorithm assigns samples, yielding a specific accuracy (acc) and coverage (cov). By varying s, we trace an accuracy-coverage curve (Fig. 1, blue line), with two anchor points:

- At $cov = 0$ (all samples handled by the human), accuracy equals the expert's accuracy (acc_e).
- At $cov = 1$ (all samples handled by the model), accuracy equals the model's accuracy (acc_m).

Typically, this curve is concave down, indicating that $\mathcal{A}(s)$ leverages the complementary strengths of the model and human. The AC-AUC metric quantifies this by computing the area under the curve. A larger AC-AUC suggests better utilization of the model-expert synergy.

AC-AUC is dataset-dependent, as it scales with acc_m, acc_e, and the degree of complementarity between the model and expert. To enable cross-dataset comparisons, we introduce a normalization scheme based on:

1. The baseline AC-AUC (B) (achieved by random allocation).
2. The optimal AC-AUC* (achieved by an oracle allocating samples perfectly).

Baseline AC-AUC is obtained using following observations. If the allocation of instances between the model and the expert is performed randomly, assigning n_m

instances to the model and n_e to the expert (where $n_m + n_e = N$), the overall accuracy is determined by the linear combination:

$$acc_m \frac{n_m}{N} + acc_e \frac{n_e}{N},$$

which defines the equation of a straight line connecting the two key points (the model's accuracy and the expert's accuracy; see Fig. 1, red line). The area under this curve corresponds to a blind (uninformed) allocation algorithm and can be calculated as:

$$B = \frac{acc_m + acc_e}{2}.$$

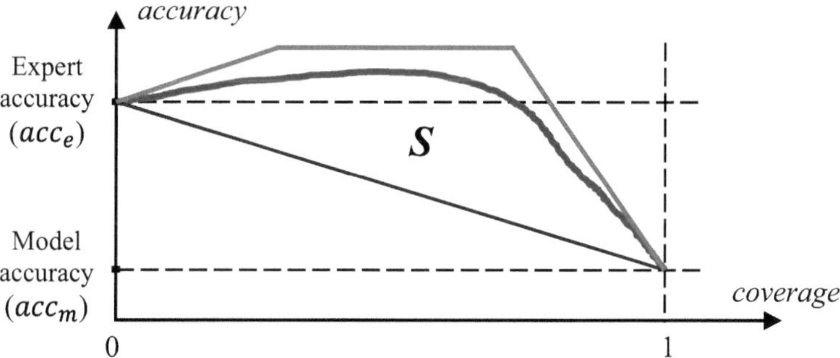

Fig. 1. Example of a coverage-accuracy curve (blue) and its corner cases: optimal curve (green) and random (red)

The upper bound for such accuracy-coverage curves is formed by an "optimal" curve for a given dataset, which can be constructed by an "oracle" capable of allocating samples in the most efficient way. Let:

- $n^{m,e}$ be the number of samples correctly classified by both the model and the expert,
- $n^{m,\overline{e}}$ be the number of samples correctly classified by the model but misclassified by the expert (with $V^{m,\overline{e}}$ denoting the set of such samples, i.e. $\left|V^{m,\overline{e}}\right| = n^{m,\overline{e}}$),
- $n^{\overline{m},\overline{e}}$ be the number of samples misclassified by both the model and the expert,
- $n^{\overline{m},e}$ be the number of samples misclassified by the model but correctly classified by the expert (with $V^{\overline{m},e}$ denoting the corresponding set of samples, i.e. $\left|V^{\overline{m},e}\right| = n^{\overline{m},e}$).

These cases represent all possible classification outcomes, so that $n^{m,e} + n^{m,\overline{e}} + n^{\overline{m},\overline{e}} + n^{\overline{m},e} = n$, where n is the total number of samples.

For a given coverage value (cov), exactly $c = cov * n$ samples are assigned to the model, and the remaining $n - c$ samples are assigned to the expert. If task allocation is performed by an oracle with knowledge of whether each sample is correctly classified by the model and/or the expert, the optimal allocation strategy would be:

1. assign to the model as many samples from $V^{m,\overline{e}}$ as possible ($\min(c, n^{m,\overline{e}})$);
2. assign to the expert as many samples from $V^{\overline{m},e}$ as possible ($\min(n - c, n^{\overline{m},e})$);

3. allocate the remaining samples arbitrarily, making sure that exactly c samples are assigned to the model.

This approach ensures maximum possible accuracy for any given coverage level by prioritizing:

- Samples that only the model can classify correctly (assigning them to the model).
- Samples that only the expert can classify correctly (assigning them to the expert).
- Handling the remaining cases (where both or neither are correct) in any order.

Under such an optimal allocation strategy, the classification accuracy is given by the following expression:

$$A^* = \frac{\min\left(c, n^{m,\bar{e}}\right) + \min\left(n - c, n^{\overline{m},e}\right) + n^{m,e}}{n}$$

Classification accuracy A^*, derived from the allocation method described above, represents the maximum achievable accuracy for the given set of $n^{m,e}, n^{m,\bar{e}}, n^{\overline{m},\bar{e}}, n^{\overline{m},e}$.

By varying the target coverage c, we can directly construct the optimal accuracy-coverage curve, which serves as the upper envelope for all possible such curves (see Fig. 1, green). The area under this optimal curve is denoted as AC-AUC*, representing the theoretical performance limit for any task allocation algorithm on the given dataset.

We therefore propose to compute the normalized area under the accuracy-coverage curve using the following formula:

$$nAC - AUC = \frac{AC - AUC - B}{AC - AUC^* - B}.$$

The metric is bounded above by 1.0, where a nAC-AUC value of 1.0 indicates optimal performance, nAC-AUC of 0.0 means the model's performance is equivalent to random allocation, negative values are possible and indicate worse-than-random performance in terms of the accuracy-coverage tradeoff.

The proposed normalization scheme establishes a reference framework by scaling the observed performance between two fundamental benchmarks: the baseline performance of random allocation (B) and the theoretically optimal performance achievable by an oracle (AC-AUC*). It effectively removes dataset-specific biases while preserving the essential information about how well the algorithm balances accuracy and human workload.

However, nAC-AUC is not entirely superior w.r.t non-normalized version, AC-AUC. The normalization method relies on the known model accuracy and human accuracy ($n^{m,e}$, $n^{m,\bar{e}}$, $n^{\overline{m},\bar{e}}$, $n^{\overline{m},e}$) and somehow assumes that the characteristic points of the coverage-accuracy curve (with $cov = 0$ and $cov = 1$) are fixed. It is the case if rejection model is trained separately (with known base classification model), a number of approaches for learning to defer propose simultaneous (or, joint) training of main and rejector models. In this case, model accuracy (point with $cov = 1$) may vary, making the normalization scheme less grounded. Therefore, common recommendation is to use nAC-AUC to evaluate separately trained rejector models, and AC-AUC – to evaluate jointly trained classification-rejection models.

4 The Proposed Method for Rejector Training

The proposed method for rejector training relies on the optimal instance distribution algorithm, described in Sec. 3. Note that unlike the existing learning to defer methods, we aim not at training the rejector model reaching one particular point at coverage-accuracy plane, instead we aim at learning a model to predict instance scores, so that the higher score is, the more reasonable it is to assign the instance to the model. However, optimal allocation algorithm used for AC-AUC normalization (in particular, for estimating AC-AUC*) suggests the order for the desired values of the scoring function. Indeed, the allocation algorithm starts with assigning to the model the instances from the $V^{m,\overline{e}}$ and proceeds with assigning instances from $V^{\overline{m},e}$ to the expert. Therefore, instances from $V^{m,\overline{e}}$ should have the highest score, and instances from $V^{\overline{m},e}$ – lowest, with all the other instances having the score value between them. Formally, optimal scoring model would satisfy the following requirement:

$$\forall x \in V^{m,\overline{e}}, y \in \left(V^{m,e} \cup V^{\overline{m},\overline{e}}\right), z \in V^{\overline{m},e}\ s(x) > s(y) > s(z).\text{(SEQ "equation"\textbackslash n)}$$

So, basically, the rejection model should distinguish between three cases:

- the base model is right while the expert is wrong ($V^{m,\overline{e}}$),
- the expert and the base model are both right or both wrong ($V^{m,e} \cup V^{\overline{m},\overline{e}}$),
- the expert is right while the base model is wrong ($V^{\overline{m},e}$).

Obviously, for a given sample it is not known in advance which of these three categories it belongs to. Therefore, these categories can be used during training of the scoring model to learn areas in the problem feature space where each of the situations is most likely.

This can be done in several ways, and in this paper, we examine two of them: specially constructed regression target and classification with post-processing.

4.1 Regression to the Scoring Target

Based on the formal requirement for the optimal instance scoring model, we can construct a regression problem, arbitrarily assigning true labels depending on the correctness of the base model and expert outputs, so that these assigned labels would conform to the Eq. 1. Formally, we construct a new training set $D^{(r)} = \left(X_i, y_i^{(r)}\right)$, so that input samples are the same as in the original dataset (X_i), while labels $y_i^{(r)} \in \mathbb{R}$ are defined by the following:

$$y_i^{(r)} = \begin{cases} s_0, \mathit{iff}\ m_i \neq y_i, e_i = y_i, \\ s_2, \mathit{iff}\ m_i = y_i, e_i \neq y_i, \\ s_1, \mathit{otherwise}, \end{cases} \tag{2}$$

so that $s_0 < s_1 < s_2$. E.g., in the simplest case, we can set $s_0 = 0$, $s_1 = 1$ and $s_2 = 2$ (however, it might be more beneficial to scale these values or even set a larger interval between one of the pairs, but it requires further research).

Therefore, learning to defer according to this approach results in performing the following steps:

- From the original training set construct a training set $D^{(r)}$, assigning instance labels according to Eq. 2.
- Train a regression model $\hat{s}_r$ using loss function typical for regression, e.g., mean squared error (MSE).
- If it is required to set certain limit on coverage, follow the method proposed in [6]: construct a calibration set, using this calibration set find a score threshold value θ, corresponding to the required coverage, and assign to the expert instances for which $\hat{s}_r(x) < \theta$.

4.2 Classification with Post-Processing

Another approach to train a model complying the Eq. 1 is to recast the problem as a multi-class classification one, trying to predict the correctness of the model and the expert and then combine class probabilities into a real-valued scoring function which would satisfy Eq. 1 (at least, for correct predictions). Formally, we construct a new training set $D^{(c)} = \left(X_i, y_i^{(c)}\right)$, so that input samples are the same as in the original dataset (X_i), while labels $y_i^{(c)} \in \{0, 1, 2\}$ are defined by the following:

$$y_i^{(c)} = \begin{cases} 0, \mathit{iff} m_i \neq y_i, e_i = y_i, \\ 2, \mathit{iff} m_i = y_i, e_i \neq y_i, \\ 1, \mathit{otherwise}. \end{cases} \tag{3}$$

Classification model $\hat{r}_c$ is trained to return probabilities of the labels, i.e. $\hat{r}_c : X \rightarrow [0, 1]^3$. Scoring function is obtained from $\hat{r}_c$ using following expression:

$$\hat{s}_c(x) = (s_0, s_1, s_2) \cdot \hat{r}_c(x).$$

Similarly to the previous case, $s_0 < s_1 < s_2$ with (0, 1, 2) assignment being a starting point.

Overall algorithm is the same as in the previous case, but relying on the training set and functions defined in this subsection.

There is one practical consideration, referring to the both variations of the proposed method. In most cases it turns out that the datasets prepared for scoring function training (i.e., $D^{(r)}$ and $D^{(c)}$) are very unbalanced. Indeed, often both the model and the expert are mostly correct with very few errors. In these cases, most of the labels for the regression problem are s_1 and the class with label $y_i^{(c)} = 1$ comprise a vast majority of samples for the classification problem. This can severely hamper the training process, therefore measures have to be taken to rebalance the dataset. So, in the evaluation we add a class weight to each class, which is in inverse proportion to the fraction of class representatives.

5 Evaluation

The goal of the evaluation is to compare the scoring functions, obtained using the proposed approach, with the scoring functions, proposed using existing widely used approaches, in their ability to effectively leverage information about strengths of the base model and the expert and their complementarity to get a controllable distribution policy. Here, by "controllable" we mean that this policy can be adjusted to the specified coverage by calibrating threshold score value, as it is proposed in [6] (without retraining the model or solving hard optimization problem).

For the evaluation we use CIFAR-10H [14], a subset of CIFAR-10 [15], containing 10,000 images, for which human labels were collected using crowdsourcing. The dataset contains several human labels for each image in this dataset (from several crowdsourcing workers), and to produce human label one of them was picked randomly (with probability proportional to the number of workers who selected the respective class). Besides, we also used the same input samples from CIFAR-10H, but with synthetic labels, modeling severely limited expertise of an expert. Following popular in learning-to-defer research approach for making synthetic labels, we set some high (0.95) probability of correct response for the first 7 classes, and significantly lower probability [16] of correct response for the remaining classes.

We evaluate the following solutions. As a baseline, we use confidence-based approach, which delegates to human expert if main model's confidence, estimated with max softmax value is less than the specified threshold (*MaxSoftmax*). Following ideas from [6], we use main model's confidence as a score. Two other baselines models are popular learning to defer methods, based on surrogate loss functions – $\mathcal{L}_{CE}^{1}$ [2] and $\mathcal{L}_{OvA}$ [3]. In these cases, rejector model and classification model are joined and have one output space, and the scoring function is defined as maximal value of output probabilities associated with classes (except deferral output), as proposed in [6]. We evaluate both variants of our approach (using regression (*RegScore*) and classification with post-processing (*CScore*)). We used HAIC Toolbox[1] programming library for implementations of baseline loss functions and synthetic dataset generation.

All the models are trained using 80% of available samples with Adam optimizer with learning rate 0.001 until degradation of the loss function on a validation set (the rest 20% of the dataset samples).

Table 1 shows AC-AUC and nAC-AUC metrics for all the compared solutions, Fig. 2 additionally shows coverage-accuracy plots for better understanding of the accuracy in different coverage regions.

Table 1. Metric values for the compared methods

	CIFAR10H		CIFAR10 (Synthetic)	
	AC-AUC	nAC-AUC	AC-AUC	nAC-AUC
MaxSoftmax	*0.9602*	*0.3685*	0.9282	0.3193
$\mathcal{L}_{CE}^{1}$	0.9589	0.3382	0.9413	0.4837
$\mathcal{L}_{OvA}$	0.9581	0.3190	0.9449	0.5289
(Ours) RegScore	**0.9612**	**0.3926**	*0.9463*	*0.5458*
(Ours) CScore	0.9600	0.3650	**0.9474**	**0.5605**

[1] HAIC Toolbox: https://github.com/cais-lab/haic-toolbox.

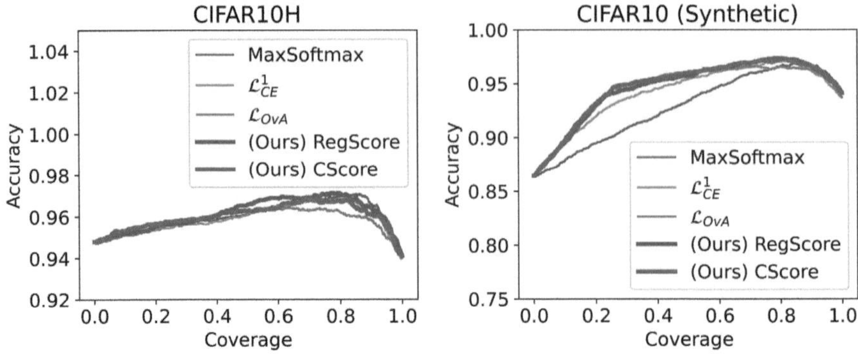

Fig. 2. Coverage-accuracy curves for the compared methods

In Table 1, the best metric value in each column is highlighted with bold font, and the second best – with italic. The proposed approach shows very promising results. For both datasets the best metric values are obtained using one of the variants of the proposed approach, for CIFAR10H *CScore* places third with marginal difference from the second-best method – MaxSoftmax. Interestingly, MaxSoftmax, showing very good rejection quality with CIFAR10H, places last (with a large gap) in the experiments with the synthetic dataset. To explain this, we can note, that MaxSoftmax (unlike all other compared algorithms) is basically a rejection learning algorithm, not learning-to-defer, in a sense that it makes rejection decisions based only on the properties of model's prediction, ignoring potential strengths/weaknesses of the expert. Obviously, when expert's errors are nearly random and cannot be explained from the features of the objects being classified, such algorithm becomes not worse (or, maybe even better, as it is simpler) than algorithms, trying to model expert's responses and competence areas. Figure 2 (left) suggests that it is likely the case for the human labels in CIFAR10H. However, if there is some systematic expert error (which is clearly simulated in the second dataset), ignoring expert's strengths/weaknesses leads to a major drop in rejection quality, which is demonstrated by the poor performance of MaxSoftmax rejector on the synthetic dataset.

Note, that the results for the proposed variants shown in Table. 1 and Fig. 2 are obtained using instance-based (for regression) or class-based (for classification) weighting in order to account for the train dataset imbalance, as it is explained in Sec. 4. We do not apply any weighting scheme to the baseline methods, as, first, it is not suggested in the original publications, second, the output space of the baseline methods differs from the output space of the proposed formulation, and doesn't show signs of misbalance. Figure 3 highlights the effect of weighting on the proposed method. It can be seen that prediction quality is significantly lower (which is also supported by metrics), therefore, weighting (or, probably other measures to account for the imbalance) is crucial for the effectiveness of the proposed approach.

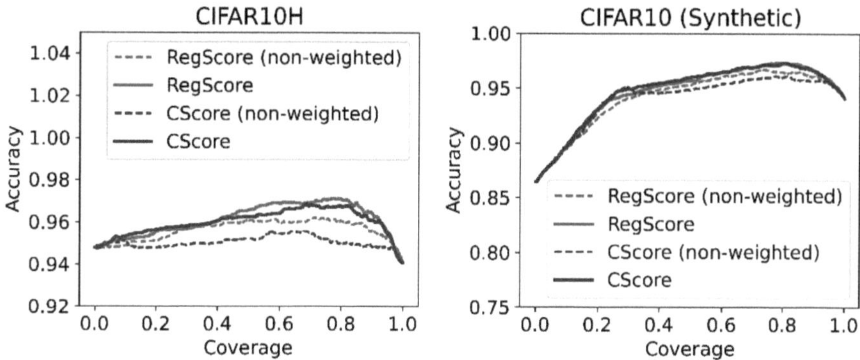

Fig. 3. Effect of weighting in order to account for the dataset imbalance

6 Conclusion

The paper explores the approach to learning to defer based on using scoring functions. We propose an integrative metric for evaluating quality of learning to defer algorithms, taking into account accuracy and coverage. Based on the analysis of this metric and conditions, in which the metric takes optimal values, we propose methods to construct scoring functions. Experiments with CIFAR-10H dataset (human and synthetic labels) confirm that learning to defer based on the proposed scoring functions allows to obtain rejection policies better than that obtained with state of the art methods. Besides, as it is shown in [6], using scoring function allows one to easily adapt sample distribution policy to the number of available human experts.

One of the important implications of the proposed approach is the ability to employ other machine learning techniques (e.g., random forests or gradient boosting) which may be especially demanded when working with tabular data, but is problematic with specially constructed loss functions from [2] and [16].

Acknowledgments. The research is funded by the Russian Science Foundation (project 24–21-00337, https://rscf.ru/project/24-21-00337/).

References

1. Madras, D., Pitassi, T., Zemel, R.: Predict responsibly: improving fairness and accuracy by learning to defer. In: Advances in Neural Information Processing Systems, pp. 6147–6157 (2018)
2. Mozannar, H., Sontag, D.: Consistent estimators for learning to defer to an expert. In: 37th International Conference on Machine Learning, ICML 2020, pp. 7033–7044 (2020)
3. Verma, R., Nalisnick, E.: Calibrated Learning to Defer with One-vs-All Classifiers. In: Proceedings of the 39 th International Conference on Machine Learning (2022)
4. De, A., Koley, P., Ganguly, N., Gomez-Rodriguez, M.: Regression under human assistance. In: AAAI 2020 - 34th AAAI Conference on Artificial Intelligence, pp. 2611–2620 (2020). https://doi.org/10.1609/aaai.v34i03.5645

5. Alves, J. V., et al.: Cost-sensitive learning to defer to multiple experts with workload constraints (2024)
6. Ponomarev, A.: A simple heuristic for controlling human workload in learning to defer. In: Pattern Recognition. ICPR 2024. Lecture Notes in Computer Science, vol. 15327, pp. 120–130. Springer, Cham (2025). https://doi.org/10.1007/978-3-031-78398-2_8
7. Hendrickx, K., Perini, L., Van der Plas, D., Meert, W., Davis, J.: Machine learning with a reject option: a survey. Mach. Learn. **113**, 3073–3110 (2024). https://doi.org/10.1007/s10994-024-06534-x
8. Wilder, B., Horvitz, E., Kamar, E.: Learning to complement humans. In: IJCAI'20: Proceedings of the Twenty-Ninth International Joint Conference on Artificial Intelligence, pp. 1526–1533 (2020)
9. Mao, A., Mohri, M., Zhong, Y.: Principled approaches for learning to defer with multiple experts. In: International Symposium on Artificial Intelligence and Mathematics (ISAIM 2024) (2023)
10. Leitão, D., Saleiro, P., Figueiredo, M.A.T., Bizarro, P.: Human-AI collaboration in decision-making: beyond learning to defer. In: Workshop on Human-Machine Collaboration and Teaming, ICML (2022)
11. De, A., Okati, N., Zarezade, A., Gomez-Rodriguez, M.: Classification under human assistance. In: The 35th AAAI Conference on Artificial Intelligence (AAAI-21) (2021). https://doi.org/10.1609/aaai.v35i7.16738
12. Mozannar, H., Lang, H., Wei, D., Sattigeri, P., Das, S., Sontag, D.: Who should predict? Exact algorithms for learning to defer to humans. Proc. Mach. Learn. Res. **206**, 10520–10545 (2023)
13. Lemmer, S.J., Corso, J.J.: Evaluating and improving interactions with Hazy oracles. In: Proceedings of the AAAI Conference on Artificial Intelligence. pp. 6039–6047 (2023). https://doi.org/10.1609/aaai.v37i5.25746
14. Peterson, J., Battleday, R., Griffiths, T., Russakovsky, O.: Human uncertainty makes classification more robust. Proc. IEEE Int. Conference Computer Vision 2019-Octob, 9616–9625 (2019). https://doi.org/10.1109/ICCV.2019.00971
15. Krizhevsky, A.: Learning multiple layers of features from tiny images. Sci. Dep. Univ. Toronto, Tech., 1–60 (2009)
16. Verma, R., Barrejón, D., Nalisnick, E.: Learning to defer to multiple experts: consistent surrogate losses, confidence calibration, and conformal ensembles. In: Proceedings of The 26th International Conference on Artificial Intelligence and Statistics, PMLR 206, pp. 11415–11434 (2023)

Prediction of Pregnancy-Related Adverse Drug Reactions from Chemical Conformers Using a Fractional-Pooling Dilated CNN

Anushka Chaurasia[1(✉)], Deepak Kumar[1], and Yogita Yogita[2]

[1] Department of Computer Science and Engineering, National Institute of Technology Meghalaya, Sohra, Shillong, India
anushkachaurasia1601@gmail.com, deepak.kumar@nitm.ac.in
[2] Department of Computer Science and Engineering, Indra Gandhi University Meerpur, Rewari, Haryana, India
yogita@nitkkr.ac.in

Abstract. Adverse drug reactions (ADRs) during pregnancy represent a critical concern, as they can adversely affect both maternal and fetal health. However, the availability of clinical evidence on drug safety in this population has remained limited, primarily due to the ethical restrictions associated with conducting controlled trials in pregnant women. A range of computational approaches has been proposed to address this gap. Nonetheless, the majority of these methods have relied on one-dimensional or two-dimensional molecular descriptors, thereby neglecting the richer structural information contained within chemical conformers. In this work, we propose FracPool-DCNN, a novel deep learning architecture that integrates dilated convolutions with fractional max pooling to predict pregnancy-related ADRs directly from conformer images. Using a curated dataset of drugs from PubChem conformers and ADReCS-based annotations, the model has been trained and evaluated with five-fold cross-validation. FracPool-DCNN has achieved superior performance compared to nine baseline models, with a harmonic mean of 76.89%, AUPR of 77.42%, and ROC-AUC of 79.89%, while ablation studies confirm the critical contributions of fractional pooling and global average pooling. These findings highlight the promise of conformer-based deep learning for robust pregnancy drug-safety classification, offering a scalable approach to preclinical risk assessment.

Keywords: Pregnancy ADR · Chemical Conformer · Fractional pooling CNN · Dilated CNN

1 Introduction

Adverse drug reactions (ADRs) are defined as harmful and unintended responses to medications administered at normally prescribed doses for prevention, diagnosis, or treatment [1]. In the general population, ADRs contribute significantly

T. T. Quan et al. (Eds.): MIWAI 2025, LNAI 16353, pp. 63–74, 2026.
https://doi.org/10.1007/978-981-95-4957-3_6

to morbidity, mortality, and increased healthcare costs, with risk factors such as polypharmacy, advanced age, genetic polymorphisms, and comorbid conditions [2]. The use of medications during pregnancy poses additional risks due to physiological changes that alter drug absorption, distribution, metabolism, and excretion. Many drugs cross the placenta, potentially impacting fetal development and increasing the risk of ADRs [3,4]. A multinational survey reported that 81.2% of pregnant women had taken at least one medication during pregnancy [5]. Traditionally, drug safety during pregnancy has been evaluated using post-marketing surveillance, case reports, and observational studies [6]. However, ethical and safety constraints severely limit the feasibility of controlled clinical trials in this population, resulting in a critical lack of human data.

To address the limited availability of clinical data on drug safety in pregnancy, several computational models have been developed using molecular and biological features. Boland et al. [7] classified drugs with unknown fetal effects as safe or harmful by integrating pharmacological similarity with EHR-derived features, achieving accuracies of 91% for fetal loss and 87% for congenital anomalies. Shtar et al. [8] designed an interpretable framework using seven classifiers and feature selection on molecular descriptors, while Chhala et al. [9] built a platform predicting teratogenicity risk classes with an AUC of 0.8, also identifying chemical features linked to risk or protection. Jeong et al. [10] proposed an interpretable ML framework integrating molecular fingerprints and physicochemical properties, where SVM yielded the best accuracy and F1, and Extra Trees achieved the highest AUROC/AUPR. Peng et al. [11] applied AI models to FAERS data on 2,559 drugs, with DMPNN-Des outperforming others (AUC > 0.8), validated externally on SIDER and DailyMed. De Filippis et al. [12] classified psychiatric and neurological drugs into safety categories using FDA registries, where Random Forest achieved 95% accuracy. Chaurasia et al. [13] introduced PregAN-Net, a boosted neural ensemble with CTGAN for imbalance correction, outperforming conventional baselines across Precision, TPR, F1, and ROC-AUC; Building on this, Chaurasia et al. [14] proposed a sparse ensemble for DDI-induced ADRs, gaining 1.16–14.94% improvements over six state-of-the-art models, with SPCA further improving performance by 2.67–5.45%.

Although chemical conformer-based features remain less explored, recent work highlights their potential. Das et al. [15] proposed MLCNN-CDSE, a multi-label CNN using 3D stick-structure conformers to predict COVID drug side effects, achieving 95.97% accuracy and outperforming transfer-learning backbones. Similarly, MLCNN-COV [16] leveraged RGB conformer images of 17 COVID drugs, reaching accuracies of 88.24–100%. More recently, Das et al. [17] introduced MLCNNF, a CNN with image augmentation applied to 2D structures and conformers, achieving $99.40\% \pm 0.0344\%$ accuracy and surpassing advanced models such as EfficientNetV2B2 and Xception.

While many studies have leveraged molecular and biological features to predict pregnancy-related ADRs, the role of chemical conformers in pregnancy ADR prediction has remained underexplored. As three-dimensional representations of drug molecules, conformers capture structural details critical for receptor binding, metabolism, and off-target interactions that shape pharmacokinetic and pharmacodynamic behavior. To address this gap, the present study systematically evaluates the predictive utility of chemical conformers for pregnancy-associated ADRs.

To achieve this, a deep learning architecture, FracPool-DCNN, has been introduced that integrates dilated convolutions with fractional max pooling to predict pregnancy-related ADRs directly from 3D conformer images. Unlike prior works that have relied on one-dimensional descriptors, fingerprints, or standard CNNs, the proposed architecture has leveraged RGB ball-and-stick conformer images to retain stereochemical and spatial details. The fractional pooling mechanism has enabled the preservation of subtle structural cues such as bond angles and hydrogen-bonding patterns, while dilated convolutions have expanded the receptive field without increasing the parameter count. Together, these innovations have enhanced the network's discriminative capacity and generalization ability. The dataset employed in this study has been obtained from Chaurasia et al. [13], and the chemical conformers for each compound have been retrieved from the PubChem database. Subsequently, the dataset has been augmented, and its performance has been evaluated through five-fold cross-validation using metrics including accuracy, precision, sensitivity, AUPR, harmonic mean, and ROC-AUC, and benchmarked against state-of-the-art methods.

The paper has been organized as follows: Sect. 2 has presented the problem statement, dataset, and the proposed architecture for predicting pregnancy-related ADRs. Section 3 reports the experimental results and performance evaluation. Finally, Sect. 4 provides the conclusion and summarizes the key findings.

2 Proposed Methodology

2.1 Problem Statement

Let $X = \{X_1, X_2, X_3, \ldots, X_N\}$ denote a collection of drugs, where each drug X_i has been represented by its chemical conformer in the form of an image retrieved from the PubChem database [18]. These conformer images serve as the primary input features for the classification task. In the computational pipeline, each image is treated as a numerical matrix, where pixel intensities encode brightness and RGB color values. The Conformer Image Representation (CIR) for each color channel is defined as:

$$\begin{aligned} CIR^R &= \{c_{1,1}, c_{1,2}, \ldots, c_{p,p}\}, \\ CIR^G &= \{c_{1,1}, c_{1,2}, \ldots, c_{p,p}\}, \\ CIR^B &= \{c_{1,1}, c_{1,2}, \ldots, c_{p,p}\}, \end{aligned} \tag{1}$$

where p denotes the image resolution (e.g., $p = 128$). These pixel values capture molecular features such as spatial arrangement, atom types, and electronic properties essential for downstream modeling. Each drug X_i is assigned a binary label indicating whether it is **safe (S)** or **unsafe (U)** for use during pregnancy. The prediction task is therefore framed as a binary classification problem:

$$F : X \to \{S, U\} \tag{2}$$

where F is a learned function that maps the conformer image of a drug to its predicted safety classification.

2.2 Dataset Collection and Preprocessing

The benchmark ADR dataset for this study has been adopted from Chaurasia et al. [13], which has in turn extracted its data from the ADReCS database. Each drug has been assigned a binary class label: any drug associated with at least one of these ADRs has been marked "Unsafe," while drugs with no such associations have been marked "Safe." Additionally, three-dimensional chemical conformers have been extracted from the PubChem database using PubChem IDs via the PubChemPy library. These structures, depicted as ball-and-stick models, encode atomic coordinates, bond connectivity, functional groups, and substructures, providing essential physicochemical descriptors for drug development [16]. Figure 1 illustrates the chemical conformers of two drugs. The first, Albendazole, is prescribed to pregnant women only when the benefits to the mother's health outweigh the potential risks and no safer alternatives exist. For instance, in cases of severe or life-threatening parasitic infections. This is because it may pose risks to the developing fetus. In contrast, the second drug, Dexrazone, is marked as safe for use during pregnancy. The final dataset has comprised 1,066 drug samples, with 388 classified as Safe and 678 classified as Unsafe based on pregnancy-related ADR annotations. To address the class imbalance, undersampling has been applied to the majority class (Unsafe), resulting in a balanced dataset subsequently used for training and evaluation.

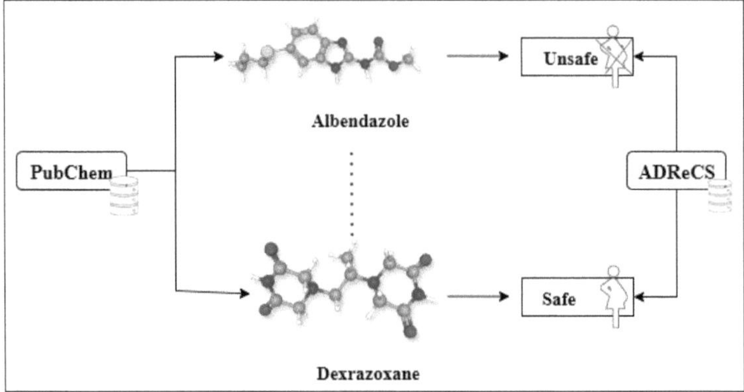

Fig. 1. Illustration of Dataset Collection and Labeling Process.

2.3 FracPool-DCNN: Fractional-Pooling Dilated CNN for Predicting Pregnancy-Related ADRs

The FracPool-DCNN is a deep learning architecture designed to classify drugs as safe or unsafe for use during pregnancy, based on their chemical conformer representations. The architecture combines a dilated convolutional encoder with fractional max pooling, enabling fine-grained feature extraction, followed by a dense classification head. The overall workflow of the proposed model is summarized in Fig. 2.

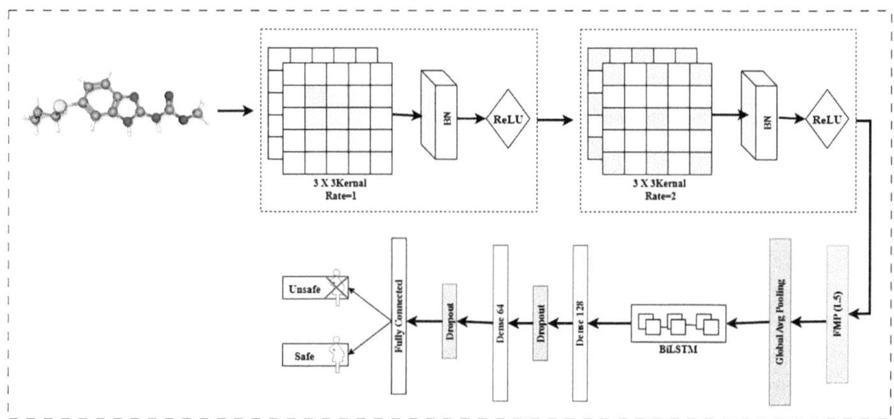

Fig. 2. Proposed FracPool-DCNN Architecture

Each drug X_i has been associated with a conformer, which has been represented as an RGB image $X \in \mathbb{R}^{H \times W \times 3}$, where $H = W = 128$. Each of the three channels has encoded atom-level and spatial features via pixel intensities, effectively capturing stereochemistry, atom types, spatial orientations, and functional group placements attributes. The feature extraction module consists of three convolutional stages, each composed of two convolutional layers with kernel size 3×3 and dilation rates $d = 1$ and $d = 2$, respectively. Batch normalization layers are applied after each convolution. A Fractional Max Pooling (FMP) operation has been used for spatial downsampling to preserve more fine-grained spatial information compared to traditional pooling techniques. Prior to each pooling operation, dilated convolutions are applied to expand the receptive field without increasing the number of parameters. A dilated convolution at spatial position (i, j) with dilation rate d is defined as:

$$Y[i,j] = \sum_{m=0}^{M-1} \sum_{n=0}^{N-1} X[i + d\,m,\ j + d\,n]\ K[m,n]. \tag{3}$$

where, K denotes the convolution kernel and X the input feature map. The dilation rate d introduces gaps between kernel elements, allowing the convolution to aggregate spatial information from a broader context without reducing resolution. To preserve more spatial detail than standard pooling, fractional max pooling (FMP) is applied after each convolutional block. Given a pooling ratio $\mathbf{r} = (1, r_H, r_W, 1)$, e.g., $r_H = r_W = 1.5$, the output dimensions become:

$$H' = \left\lceil \frac{H}{r_H} \right\rceil, \qquad W' = \left\lceil \frac{W}{r_W} \right\rceil. \tag{4}$$

The pooled feature at location (i, j, c) is computed as:

$$X'_{i,j,c} = \max_{(u,v) \in \mathcal{R}_{i,j}} X_{u,v,c}, \tag{5}$$

where $\mathcal{R}_{i,j}$ denotes the pooling region associated with position (i, j) in channel c. This operation allows for better retention of subtle conformational cues, such as bond angles, hydrogen-bonding patterns, and molecular topology. After that, a Global Average Pooling (GAP) layer is applied to generate a fixed-size feature embedding:

$$\mathbf{z} = \mathrm{GAP}(X') \in \mathbb{R}^{128}. \tag{6}$$

Finally, the fused embedding $\mathbf{z}$ is passed through two fully connected layers with 128 and 64 units, respectively. Each layer is followed by a ReLU activation and a dropout rate of 0.3. Dropout randomly deactivates neurons during training, thereby preventing the network from overfitting to any single structural feature or conformer and encouraging the learning of robust, distributed representations. A sigmoid-activated output neuron then produces the probability $\hat{y}$ that the drug induces an ADR during pregnancy.

3 Experimental Setups and Result Analysis

The FracPool-DCNN architecture has been evaluated through computational experiments on a server equipped with an Intel Xeon Silver 4216 CPU (2.10 GHz), 128 GB of RAM, and HDD storage. Model development and testing were carried out using Python 3.7.4, with TensorFlow, Keras, and Matplotlib employed for implementation and visualization. To improve generalization, data augmentation was applied using the `ImageDataGenerator` class, generating conformer image augmentation has been performed using controlled geometric transformations, including minor shifts (±10% in width and height), moderate rotations (up to 25°), shearing (0.2), zooming (0.2), and padding via nearest-neighbor interpolation. Horizontal flipping has been disabled to preserve structural consistency. These settings were effective in enhancing training diversity and maximizing predictive accuracy. Model performance and stability were assessed using five-fold cross-validation. The effectiveness of the FracPool-DCNN was further supported by optimized configuration parameters, as summarized in Table 1.

The performance of the proposed framework has been comprehensively evaluated using six complementary metrics. Precision, defined as the proportion of true positive predictions among all positive predictions, reflects the model's ability to minimize false positives. Sensitivity (also known as true positive rate)

Table 1. Hyperparameters of the FracPool-DCNN Architecture.

Model	Opt.(lr)	Dropout	Batch	Epochs	Early Stopping
FracPool-DCNN	Adam (1e−3)	0.25	32	3000	50

quantifies the proportion of actual positive instances correctly identified by the model. To balance these two aspects, the F1 score, calculated as the harmonic mean of precision and sensitivity, has been employed as a consolidated performance measure. In addition to threshold-dependent metrics, threshold-independent evaluations have been performed. The Area Under the Precision–Recall Curve (AUPR) captures the trade-off between precision and recall across varying thresholds and is particularly informative in imbalanced classification settings. Similarly, the Area Under the Receiver Operating Characteristic Curve (ROC-AUC), which plots sensitivity against the false positive rate, provides a robust indicator of the model's discriminative capacity. Finally, the overall accuracy, representing the fraction of correctly classified instances, offers a general assessment of the correctness of the model. Collectively, these metrics have facilitated a rigorous and multidimensional evaluation of the predictive performance of the framework.

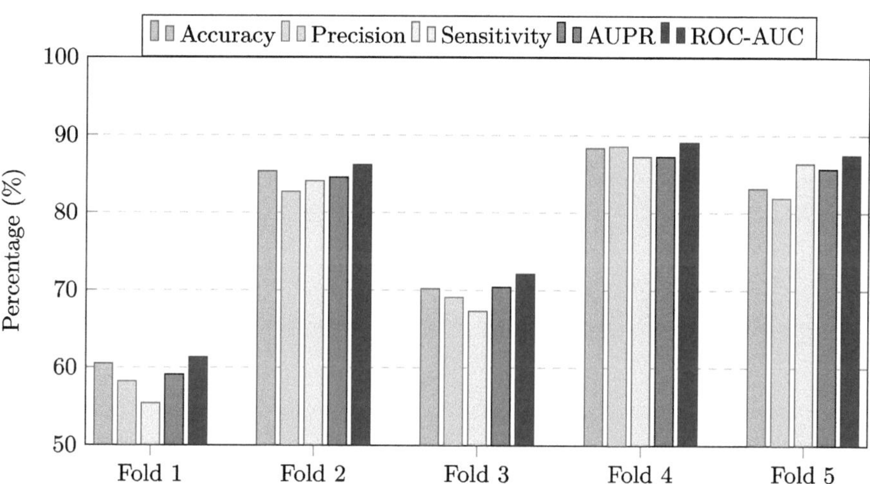

Fig. 3. Comparative Analysis of Performance Metrics Across Five Folds Cross-Validation.

In Fig. 3, model performance has varied across the five cross-validation folds. In Fold 1, the lowest results have been recorded, with accuracy, precision, sensitivity, AUPR, and ROC-AUC having been measured at approximately 60.8%, 58.3%, 55.1%, 59.2%, and 62.0%, respectively. Conversely, Fold 4 has yielded the highest performance, with all metrics having been maximized at approximately

88. 5%, 85. 2%, 86. 7%, 88. 0%, and 89. 1%, respectively. Folds 2 and 5 have also produced strong results (all above ~82%), whereas Fold 3 has demonstrated only moderate performance (accuracy ≈ 70.3%, precision ≈ 69.1%, sensitivity ≈ 67.5%, AUPR ≈ 71.0%, and ROC-AUC ≈ 72.4%). Overall, the AUPR and ROC-AUC have consistently exceeded the sensitivity and precision scores at each interval, indicating that the discriminative capacity of the model has been particularly robust despite accuracy fluctuations. It can be stated that the fourth fold has yielded the best overall performance across all evaluation metrics.

In Fig. 4, it has been observed that a total of 176 instances have been accurately predicted, yielding an overall accuracy of 88.0%. The false positive rate has been 10.7% (13/121), while the false negative rate has been 13.9% (11/79). The positive predictive value has been 84.0% (68/81), whereas the negative predictive value has been 90.8% (108/119), indicating that the model has been particularly reliable at excluding negative cases compared to detecting all positives.

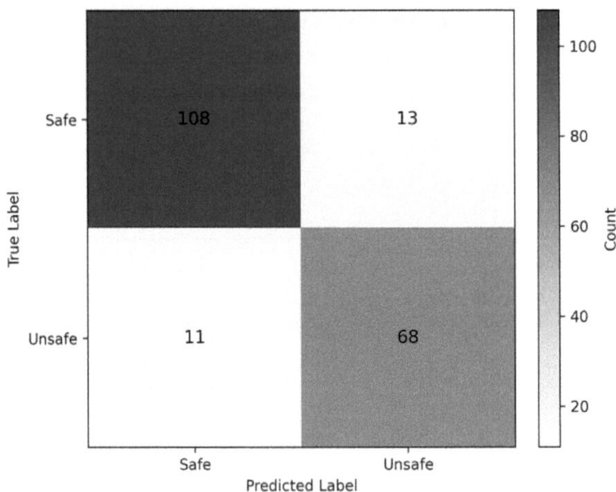

Fig. 4. Confusion Matrix of the Proposed FracPool-DCNN Architecture for Fold 4

Figure 5 presents the comparative performance of the proposed architecture, FracPool-DCNN, against nine baseline deep learning models using chemical conformer images as input. The figure reports the mean accuracy, precision, and sensitivity, along with standard deviation error bars, calculated over five-fold cross-validation. It can be observed that FracPool-DCNN has achieved the highest overall performance across all three metrics, with a mean accuracy of approximately 78.4%, precision of 77.3%, and sensitivity of 74.6%. The small standard deviation bars further indicate that the model's performance has been stable and consistent across folds. MLCNNF and MLCNN-CDSE have performed competitively but fall short by 2–3%, while Img2Side shows a decline of about 4% in accuracy. Transfer learning models such as MobileNetV2 and DenseNet-201 have achieved moderate performance (70–73%), whereas pretrained architectures, namely VGG19, AlexNet, and InceptionV3, have performed the worst, particularly in terms of sensitivity.

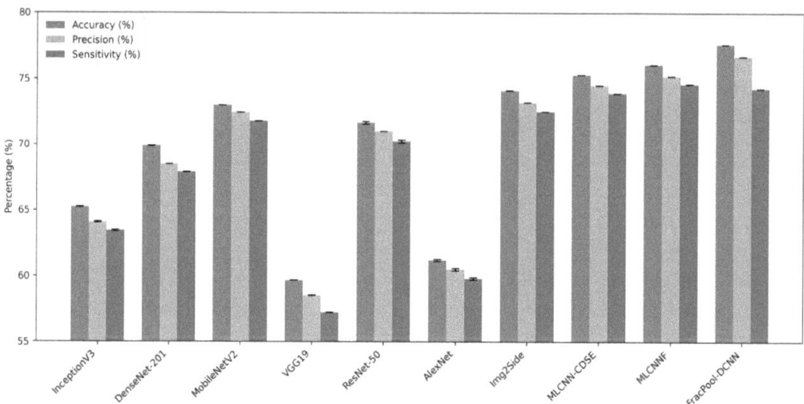

Fig. 5. Comparative performance of FracPool-DCNN and Baseline Models for Predicting Pregnancy ADR using Conformer Images (mean ± standard deviation over five folds).

Table 2 presents the comparative performance of the proposed FracPool-DCNN against several state-of-the-art deep learning architectures, with results reported as mean ± standard deviation. FracPool-DCNN achieves the highest scores across all evaluation metrics, with a harmonic mean of 76.89%, AUPR of 77.42%, and ROC-AUC of 79.89%, thereby surpassing all baseline models. The strongest competitors, MLCNNF and MLCNN-CDSE, achieve harmonic means of 74.90% and 74.20%, respectively, but remain 2–3% points lower than the proposed model. Img2Side and MobileNetV2 show moderate performance (72–73%), while transfer learning architectures such as ResNet-50 and DenseNet-201 perform slightly worse. In contrast, older models, including VGG19 and AlexNet, yield the lowest results, with harmonic means below 61% and ROC-AUC values under 64%, underscoring their limited suitability for conformer-based ADR prediction. Overall, it can be stated that the proposed architecture outperforms the state-of-the-art methods.

Table 3 has presented the results of the ablation study conducted to examine the contribution of key architectural components in FracPool-DCNN. The baseline model, which has incorporated fractional max pooling, dilated convolutions, batch normalization, and global average pooling, has achieved the highest performance with an accuracy of 77.59%, a harmonic mean of 75.45%, and a ROC-AUC of 79.89%. Replacing fractional max pooling with standard max pooling has resulted in the largest decline, reducing accuracy to 75.10% and ROC-AUC to 77.50%, thereby confirming the importance of fractional pooling

Table 2. Performance Comparison of Deep and the Proposed FracPool-DCNN Architectures (mean ± std).

Models	Harmonic Mean (%)	AUPR (%)	ROC-AUC (%)
InceptionV3	63.77 ± 0.003	66.30 ± 0.010	68.10 ± 0.010
DenseNet-201	68.20 ± 0.009	72.15 ± 0.012	74.05 ± 0.008
MobileNetV2	72.12 ± 0.002	75.30 ± 0.010	77.25 ± 0.005
VGG19	57.85 ± 0.012	60.10 ± 0.020	62.00 ± 0.015
ResNet-50	70.62 ± 0.004	74.00 ± 0.012	76.10 ± 0.007
AlexNet	60.14 ± 0.006	62.00 ± 0.010	63.50 ± 0.008
Img2Side [19]	72.85 ± 0.009	75.00 ± 0.012	76.50 ± 0.007
MLCNN-CDSE [16]	74.20 ± 0.008	76.10 ± 0.011	77.00 ± 0.006
MLCNNF [17]	74.90 ± 0.007	76.80 ± 0.010	78.00 ± 0.005
FracPool-DCNN	76.89 ± 0.002	77.42 ± 0.013	79.89 ± 0.001

in retaining fine-grained conformer features. The removal of dilated convolutions or batch normalization has also led to decreases in performance, with harmonic mean values having dropped to 74.25% and 74.02%, respectively. Likewise, substituting global average pooling with flattening has reduced accuracy to 74.85% and ROC-AUC to 76.90%, highlighting the advantage of GAP for stable embeddings. Overall, the ablation study has demonstrated that each component has contributed meaningfully to the architecture, with fractional max pooling and global average pooling having shown the most pronounced impact on pregnancy drug-safety classification.

Table 3. Ablation Study of FracPool-DCNN, Evaluating the Impact of Removing Key Components on Performance (mean ± std, 5-fold CV).

Variant	Accuracy (%)	Precision (%)	Recall (%)	HM (%)	ROC-AUC (%)
FracPool-DCNN	77.59 ± 0.10	76.70 ± 0.15	74.25 ± 0.20	75.45 ± 0.18	79.89 ± 0.12
– No FMP → MaxPool	75.10 ± 0.12	74.30 ± 0.14	72.00 ± 0.18	73.13 ± 0.16	77.50 ± 0.10
– Without Dilation	76.20 ± 0.11	75.40 ± 0.13	73.15 ± 0.17	74.25 ± 0.15	78.60 ± 0.11
– without BatchNorm	76.00 ± 0.13	75.10 ± 0.16	73.00 ± 0.19	74.02 ± 0.17	78.40 ± 0.12
– GAP→Flatten	74.85 ± 0.15	74.00 ± 0.17	71.50 ± 0.20	72.70 ± 0.18	76.90 ± 0.13

4 Conclusion and Future Work

This study has presented FracPool-DCNN, a conformer-aware convolutional neural network for predicting pregnancy-related adverse drug reactions. By leveraging 3D conformer images, dilated convolutions, and fractional max pooling, the proposed model has outperformed state-of-the-art deep learning baselines across multiple evaluation metrics, achieving a harmonic mean of 76.89%, AUPR of 77.42%, and ROC-AUC of 79.89%. The ablation analysis has further demonstrated that each architectural component contributes meaningfully to model performance, with fractional pooling and global average pooling providing the most pronounced gains. While these results establish FracPool-DCNN as a robust and generalizable framework for pregnancy drug-safety classification, a key limitation is the relatively small dataset size (1,066 samples), which required undersampling of the majority class. Although augmentation and regularization mitigated overfitting, the restricted dataset may limit generalizability. Future research will therefore focus on expanding the dataset with additional conformers, integrating biological interaction networks, and extending the framework to multi-label ADR prediction across diverse physiological conditions.

References

1. Edwards, I.R., Aronson, J.K.: Adverse drug reactions: definitions, diagnosis, and management. Lancet **356**(9237), 1255–1259 (2000)
2. Aronson, J.K.: Artificial intelligence in pharmacovigilance: an introduction to terms, concepts, applications, and limitations. Drug Saf. **45**(5), 407–418 (2022)
3. Koren, G., Pariente, G.: Pregnancy-associated changes in pharmacokinetics and their clinical implications. Pharm. Res. **35**(3), 61 (2018)
4. de Oliveira-Filho, A.D., et al.: Adverse drug reactions in high-risk pregnant women: a prospective study. Saudi Pharm. J. **25**(7), 1073–1077 (2017)
5. Lupattelli, A., et al.: Medication use in pregnancy: a cross-sectional, multinational web-based study. BMJ Open **4**(2), e004365 (2014)
6. Huybrechts, K.F., Bateman, B.T., Hernández-Díaz, S.: Use of real-world evidence from healthcare utilization data to evaluate drug safety during pregnancy. Pharmacoepidemiol. Drug Saf. **28**(7), 906–922 (2019)
7. Boland, M.R., Polubriaginof, F., Tatonetti, N.P.: Development of a machine learning algorithm to classify drugs of unknown fetal effect. Sci. Rep. **7**(1), 12839 (2017)
8. Shtar, G., Rokach, L., Shapira, B., Kohn, E., Berkovitch, M., Berlin, M.: Explainable multimodal machine learning model for classifying pregnancy drug safety. Bioinformatics **38**(4), 1102–1109 (2022)
9. Challa, A.P., et al.: Machine learning on drug-specific data to predict small molecule teratogenicity. Reprod. Toxicol. **95**, 148–158 (2020)
10. Jeong, M., Yoo, S.: FetoML: interpretable predictions of the fetotoxicity of drugs based on machine learning approaches. Mol. Inf. **43**(6), e202300312 (2024)
11. Peng, J., Fu, L., Yang, G., Cao, D.: Advanced AI-driven prediction of pregnancy-related adverse drug reactions. J. Chem. Inf. Model. **64**(24), 9286–9298 (2024)
12. de Filippis, R., Al Foysal, A.: AI-driven prediction of drug safety in pregnancy: a machine learning approach. Open Access Libr. J. **12**(6), 1–17 (2025)
13. Chaurasia, A., Kumar, D., et al.: PregAN-NET: addressing class imbalance with GANs in interpretable computational framework for predicting safety profile of drugs considering adverse reactions during pregnancy. J. Biomed. Inf., 104832 (2025)
14. Chaurasia, A., Kumar, D., Yogita: Predicting DDI-induced pregnancy and neonatal ADRs using sparse PCA and stacking ensemble approach. J. Integr. Bioinf., 20240056 (2025)

15. Das, P., Mazumder, D.H.: MLCNN-CDSE: a multi-label convolutional neural network model for predicting covid drug side effects from images of stick structure-based chemical conformers. In: 2023 IEEE Silchar Subsection Conference (SILCON), pp. 1–7. IEEE (2023)
16. Das, P., Mazumder, D.H.: MLCNN-COV: a multilabel convolutional neural network-based framework to identify negative covid medicine responses from the chemical three-dimensional conformer. ETRI J. **46**(2), 290–306 (2024)
17. Das, P., Mazumder, D.H.: MLCNNF: a multi-label convolutional neural network framework for predicting adverse covid drug reactions from the chemical structure. IEEE Trans. Comput. Biol. Bioinf. (2025)
18. Kim, S., et al.: PubChem 2023 update. Nucleic Acids Res. **51**(D1), D1373–D1380 (2023)
19. Arshed, M.A., Ibrahim, M., Mumtaz, S., Ali, T., Choi, G.S.: Img2Side: a transfer learning based model for predicting drug side effects using 2D chemical structural images. IEEE Access **12**, 50184–50201 (2024)

Compositional Distributional Semantics and the Conjunction Effect in Language Models

Yoshihiro Maruyama[1](✉) and Arisa Yasuda[2]

[1] School of Informatics, Nagoya University, Nagoya, Japan
maruyama@i.nagoya-u.ac.jp

[2] School of Computing, Australian National University, Canberra, Australia
arisa.yasuda@anu.edu.au

Abstract. Compositional distributional semantics in natural language processing allows us to compose meaning vectors for complex phrases from those for word vectors. Here we apply the framework of compositional distributional semantics to construct meaning vectors for *bank teller* and *feminist bank teller* in the well-known Linda problem, and compare them via cosine similarity to a meaning vector encoding the Linda description provided in the problem. In a noun vector space, the meaning vector for the conjoined phrase *feminist bank teller* is substantially closer to the meaning vector for the Linda description than the meaning vector for the occupation-only phrase *bank teller*; crucially, this effect requires the full adjective-as-matrix treatment provided by compositional distributional semantics. In this way, we can provide a computational linguistic account of the conjunction effect in the Linda problem.

Keywords: Compositional distributional semantics · Adjectives as matrices · Conjunction effect · Linda problem

1 Introduction

In the "Linda problem" experiment, participants read a short description of Linda—"She majored in philosophy. She is very bright and outspoken. She is deeply concerned with issues of discrimination and social justice, and also participated in anti-nuclear demonstrations."—and are then asked which statement is more probable: (i) "Linda is a bank teller" or (ii) "Linda is a feminist bank teller." A robust majority chooses (ii), thereby violating the axioms of classical probability; it is called the *conjunction effect* [19]. The standard explanation appeals to *representativeness*: the description seems more similar to (ii) than to (i), which is concerned with irrelevant occupancy. While intuitively persuasive, this explanation is psychological and not formal, linguistic or computational.

In this paper, building upon computational linguistics, we advance a systematic account grounded in the framework of compositional distributional seman-

T. T. Quan et al. (Eds.): MIWAI 2025, LNAI 16353, pp. 75–86, 2026.
https://doi.org/10.1007/978-981-95-4957-3_7

tics [1,5], in particular, the DisCoCat model built via category theory [1,5,12][1]. DisCoCat interprets grammatical types as finite-dimensional vector spaces and grammatical reductions as linear maps, enabling a principled pipeline from the grammatical structure of syntax to the semantic space of meaning vectors. In particular, nouns denote vectors in a noun space N and *adjectives denote linear maps* $\mathsf{N} \to \mathsf{N}$, i.e., matrices in $\mathsf{N} \otimes \mathsf{N}$ [2]. Simple intersective compounding (e.g., *bank teller*) can be modeled using the Frobenius algebra structure on N, where the multiplication ("merge") implements component-wise (Hadamard) combination in a fixed basis [8,10]. These ingredients support a systematic derivation:

$$\begin{aligned} \mathbf{v}_{\mathrm{BT}} &= \mathbf{v}_{\mathrm{bank}} \odot \mathbf{v}_{\mathrm{teller}}, \\ \mathbf{v}_{\mathrm{FBT}} &= A_{\mathrm{fem}} \left(\mathbf{v}_{\mathrm{bank}} \odot \mathbf{v}_{\mathrm{teller}}\right). \end{aligned} \tag{1}$$

Here $\odot$ denotes the Hadamard product and A_{fem} is the matrix for the adjective *feminist.* Crucially, as linear maps, adjectives in DisCoCat are not restricted to diagonal rescaling of features; their off-diagonal entries can *reallocate* mass across dimensions of N, allowing non-trivial transformations that mirror the intuition that *feminist* can redirect attention from purely occupational properties to stance- or ideology-related properties.

Our central claim is that, once meaning vectors are constructed compositionally as in (1), the conjunction effect emerges from the geometry of semantic vector space N: if $\mathbf{v}_{\mathrm{Linda}} \in \mathsf{N}$ encodes the description, then the standard cosine similarity $\cos(v, w)$ between meaning vectors v, w allows us to compare degrees of semantic similarity and thereby capture the conjunction effect in the space of meaning vectors:

$$\cos\big(\mathbf{v}_{\mathrm{Linda}}, A_{\mathrm{fem}}(\mathbf{v}_{\mathrm{bank}} \odot \mathbf{v}_{\mathrm{teller}})\big) > \cos\big(\mathbf{v}_{\mathrm{Linda}}, \mathbf{v}_{\mathrm{bank}} \odot \mathbf{v}_{\mathrm{teller}}\big). \tag{2}$$

Intuitively, $\mathbf{v}_{\mathrm{bank}} \odot \mathbf{v}_{\mathrm{teller}}$ concentrates weight on banking, finance, clerical, customer-service, and cash-handling features, whereas A_{fem} can shift part of this mass toward social-justice and activism features that are highly represented in $\mathbf{v}_{\mathrm{Linda}}$. In contrast, a purely diagonal adjective (feature masking only) cannot increase similarity if the relevant stance dimensions are nearly zero for *bank teller.* This mechanistic account directly arises from DisCoCat's *adjective-as-function* view and the Frobenius treatment of compounding [2,10].

Why does compositional semantics matter in the current context? First, it preserves the *syntax–semantics interface*: the improvement in similarity for the conjunctive phrase is not merely a consequence of bag-of-words overlap but a consequence of typed composition guided by the grammar. Second, it offers a *testable mechanism*: off-diagonal structure in adjective matrices is the specific algebraic resource that enables the effect. Third, it gives a path toward *empirical estimation*: DisCoCat parameters (noun vectors, adjective matrices) can be learned from corpora [2,3,8] or from contextual representations, allowing us to evaluate whether the predicted inequalities in (2) hold beyond toy spaces.

[1] Historically, the DisCoCat model as in [5] was born as a by-product of categorical quantum computing, and it has been extended to so-called QNLP (Quantum Natural Language Processing), which can be executed on the quantum computer [12].

Our contributions in this paper may be summarized as follows:

- **Compositional account of the conjunction effect.** We present a compositional derivation of *bank teller* and *feminist bank teller* and show how the conjunction effect follows from adjective-as-function composition together with Frobenius-based compounding [5,10].
- **Systematic prediction and ablation.** We identify *off-diagonal* entries in A_{fem} as the key enabler of the effect; a diagonal-only variant cannot increase similarity when stance dimensions are absent in $\mathbf{v}_{\text{bank}} \odot \mathbf{v}_{\text{teller}}$. This yields clear ablations aligned with standard DisCoCat learning set-ups [2].

Our goal is not to argue that human reasoners *should* commit a fallacy, but to show that a widely used, mathematically principled semantic framework, namely compositional distributional semantics, predicts the conjunction effect. This complements psychology's representativeness account [19] by embedding "representativeness" into the geometry of meaning vectors. The approach also interfaces with recent work that investigates how compositional distributional models capture modification and compounding phenomena (e.g., intersective vs. subsective adjectives) [1,2] and how Frobenius algebras realize copy/merge operations in semantic spaces [8,10]. In this view, *feminist* functions as a meaning transformer that can copy and redistribute features, rather than as a mere filter over the noun.

Let us explain the geometry of meaning involved in a more concrete manner (cf. [4]). Let $\{e_i\}_{i=1}^{d}$ be a fixed, interpretable basis for N with dimensions such as *philosophy*, *bright*, *outspoken*, *social_justice*, *activism*, *anti_nuclear*, *banking*, *finance*, *clerical*, *customer_service*, *cash_handling*. In such a basis, $\mathbf{v}_{\text{bank}}$ and $\mathbf{v}_{\text{teller}}$ have most of their mass on occupational features, while $\mathbf{v}_{\text{Linda}}$ loads heavily on stance features. The Frobenius merge $\boldsymbol{\mu}$ (instantiated as $\odot$) produces $\mathbf{v}_{\text{bank}} \odot \mathbf{v}_{\text{teller}}$, and the adjective matrix A_{fem} mixes occupational mass into stance dimensions. If the adjective's column space has sufficient overlap with the subspace activated by $\mathbf{v}_{\text{Linda}}$, inequality (2) follows. This picture matches the type of compositional distributional semantics in which adjectives are matrices and often exhibit meaningful cross-feature couplings [2,8].

It should be noted that our account yields concrete, falsifiable predictions:

P1 (conjunction preference): For a Linda probe vector:

$$\cos(\mathbf{v}_{\text{Linda}}, A_{\text{fem}}(\mathbf{v}_{\text{bank}} \odot \mathbf{v}_{\text{teller}})) > \cos(\mathbf{v}_{\text{Linda}}, \mathbf{v}_{\text{bank}} \odot \mathbf{v}_{\text{teller}}).$$

P2 (off-diagonal necessity): Replacing A_{fem} with its diagonal part should not increase similarity if the stance dimensions are near-zero in $\mathbf{v}_{\text{bank}} \odot \mathbf{v}_{\text{teller}}$.

P3 (composition sensitivity): Substituting non-Frobenius compounding (e.g., pure addition) weakens or removes the effect when $\mathbf{v}_{\text{bank}}$ and $\mathbf{v}_{\text{teller}}$ share little stance mass.

Each prediction can be tested both in interpretable spaces and in corpus-derived or representation-derived spaces using standard statistical estimation pipelines [1,2,8].

The remainder of the paper is ornigazed as follows. Section 2 reviews the required DisCoCat machinery: type interpretations, adjectives as linear maps, and Frobenius algebras on N [5,8,10]. Section 3 spells out the concrete composition rules used to derive vectors for *bank teller* and *feminist bank teller*, defines the probe vector, and states our evaluation metric. Section 4 reports a controlled demonstration and ablations isolating the role of off-diagonal structure in A_{fem}. We conclude by summing up the main points and giving future directions. Note that we use bold lower-case for vectors in N and upper-case for linear maps. The Frobenius merge is instantiated as the Hadamard product $\odot$ in a fixed basis, following common practice [8,10]. Cosine similarity between vectors v, w is written $\cos(v, w)$.

2 Background: Compositional Distributional Semantics

Categorical compositional distributional semantics ("DisCoCat") provides a typed, linear-algebraic route from grammar to meaning [1,5,12]. The core idea is to interpret the grammar of natural langauge as the algebraic structure of pregroup (or residuated monoid) and to map it, via a strong monoidal functor, into the category of finite-dimensional real vector spaces and linear maps (**FdVect**; or a more general compact closed category specifying the geometry of meaning). Phrases then acquire meanings by functorial transport of grammatical reductions into linear morphism reductions, yielding tensors for words and linear contractions for meaning structure transport.

Let $\mathcal{G}$ be the syntactic pregroup (posetal compact closed category) generated by basic types such as the noun type n and sentence type s, with left/right inverses (adjoints) n^ℓ, n^r and evaluation/coevaluation morphisms ("cups and caps" in compact closed categories). In pregroup grammar, an adjective modifying a noun has type

$$n\, n^\ell$$

so that

$$n(n^\ell n) \Rightarrow n$$

by eliminating $n^\ell n$ via the evaluation morphism. Transitive verbs have type

$$n^r s n^\ell$$

so that

$$n(n^r s n^\ell)n \Rightarrow s$$

via two eliminations (aka. reductions).

A *strong monoidal functor* $F : \mathcal{G} \to \mathbf{FdVect}$ assigns vector spaces $F(n) = \mathsf{N}$, $F(s) = S$ to grammatical types, and sends the pregroup evaluation/coevaluation to the evaluation/coevaluation maps on the compact closed category of real vector spaces:

$$\begin{aligned} \varepsilon_{\mathsf{N}} &: \ \mathsf{N}^* \otimes \mathsf{N} \to \mathbb{R}, \\ \eta_{\mathsf{N}} &: \ \mathbb{R} \to \mathsf{N} \otimes \mathsf{N}^*, \end{aligned} \tag{3}$$

(and analogously for S), preserving tensor product and identities [5]. Under the functor F, grammatical *reductions* become *linear* contractions, so the meaning of a phrase is obtained by wiring together the meanings of its words in the pattern prescribed by the derivation.

Nouns denote vectors in N; sentences denote vectors in S. Higher-arity expressions become higher-order tensors: in particular, *adjectives* (of type $n\,n^{\ell}$) are linear maps $\mathsf{N} \to \mathsf{N}$ and can be represented either as matrices $A_{\mathsf{fem}} \in \mathbb{R}^{d\times d}$ (with $d = \dim \mathsf{N}$) or equivalently as tensors in $\mathsf{N}\otimes\mathsf{N}^* \cong \mathsf{N}\otimes\mathsf{N}$ via a fixed basis. Composition with a noun $v \in \mathsf{N}$ is then

$$\begin{aligned} \text{adj} \cdot \text{noun} \;&\mapsto\; (1_{\mathsf{N}}\otimes\varepsilon_{\mathsf{N}})\big(A \otimes v\big) \\ &=\; Av, \end{aligned} \tag{4}$$

which is the linear map induced by the grammatical reduction $n(n^{\ell}n) \Rightarrow n$ [2]. Likewise, a (simplified) intransitive verb of type $n^r s$ corresponds to a matrix

$$V \in \mathsf{N}^*\otimes S \cong \mathbb{R}^{d\times|S|}$$

and composes with a subject noun by contracting the $n^r n$ cup, yielding a sentence vector in S; a transitive verb is a third-order tensor in $\mathsf{N}^*\otimes S\otimes\mathsf{N}^*$ [5,12].

The structure of compact closed category alone does not support *copying* within **FdVect**; however, a *special commutative Frobenius algebra* (SCFA) on N in **FdVect** supplies canonical *copy* and *merge* operations in a chosen basis [8,10]. Concretely, fix an orthonormal basis $\{e_i\}_{i=1}^{d}$ for N. Define the comultiplication (copy) and multiplication (merge) by

$$\begin{aligned} \boldsymbol{\Delta}(e_i) &= e_i \otimes e_i, \\ \boldsymbol{\mu}(e_i \otimes e_j) &= \delta_{ij}\, e_i, \end{aligned} \tag{5}$$

extending linearly. In coordinates, for any $x = \sum_i x_i e_i$ and $y = \sum_i y_i e_i$,

$$\begin{aligned} \boldsymbol{\Delta}(x) &= \sum_i x_i\, e_i \otimes e_i, \\ \boldsymbol{\mu}(x \otimes y) &= \sum_i (x_i y_i)\, e_i \;=\; x \odot y, \end{aligned} \tag{6}$$

so $\boldsymbol{\mu}$ is the Hadamard (component-wise) product in that basis. The SCFA axioms (associativity/commutativity of $\boldsymbol{\mu}$, coassociativity/cocommutativity of $\boldsymbol{\Delta}$, the Frobenius law, and the *special* equality $\boldsymbol{\mu} \circ \boldsymbol{\Delta} = 1_{\mathsf{N}}$) guarantee well-behaved copying/merging that composes with the compact structure [10]. Intuitively, $\boldsymbol{\Delta}$ allows one to duplicate information (e.g., send a noun both to a verb and to an adjective), while $\boldsymbol{\mu}$ implements *intersective* combination of nominal content in a fixed interpretable basis.

Attributive noun–noun compounds such as *bank teller*, *coffee cup*, or *student protest* often behave intersectively. In the DisCoCat model, we can consider two encodings as follows:

1. **Noun-as-modifier map.** Lift the modifier noun $u \in \mathsf{N}$ to a linear map $A_u^{(\mathrm{nn})} : \mathsf{N} \to \mathsf{N}$ and compose $A_u^{(\mathrm{nn})} v$ with the head noun v;
2. **Frobenius merge.** Intersect via

$$\begin{aligned} \mathbf{v}_{\mathrm{BT}} &= \boldsymbol{\mu}(\mathbf{v}_{\mathrm{bank}} \otimes \mathbf{v}_{\mathrm{teller}}) \\ &= \mathbf{v}_{\mathrm{bank}} \odot \mathbf{v}_{\mathrm{teller}}, \end{aligned} \tag{7}$$

which realizes intersective composition in the chosen basis [10].

We adopt the Frobenius approach in this work.

We emphasize that Equation (4) highlights a central DisCoCat commitment: adjectives are *functions* from noun meanings to noun meanings. In a basis where N dimensions are interpretable properties, a full matrix A_{fem} can *reweight* and *redirect* mass across dimensions via *off-diagonal* couplings. In contrast, a diagonal-only matrix acts as a static feature mask and cannot inject mass into a dimension that is absent in the input. This distinction is crucial here: the phrase *bank teller* concentrates mass on occupational features, and only a non-diagonal A_{fem} can move part of that mass toward stance-related features emphasized by the Linda description.

It should be noted that, beyond hand-specification, adjective matrices can also be learned from data as in [2]:

$$\begin{aligned} \min_{A \in \mathbb{R}^{d \times d}} \ & \sum_{(a,n)} \left\| A\, v_n - v_{a \cdot n} \right\|_2^2 \\ & + \lambda \|A\|_F^2 . \end{aligned} \tag{8}$$

This often discovers meaningful *off-diagonal* structure [2]. Frobenius algebras provide a disciplined account of copying and intersective composition inside **FdVect** [10]. Surveys summarize learning choices and empirical performance [1,12].

3 Method

We specify a type-consistent, linear-algebraic pipeline for the Linda problem. The construction lives entirely in N and follows the DisCoCat commitments: (i) nouns are vectors; (ii) adjectives are linear maps $\mathsf{N} \to \mathsf{N}$; (iii) noun–noun compounding uses Frobenius merge (Hadamard) [1,2,8,10]. We provide both an *interpretable* instantiation and a *corpus-derived* instantiation, with ablations isolating the role of off-diagonal structure.

3.1 Noun Space

Let N be a d-dimensional space with basis capturing stance and occupational properties so that $\mathbf{v}_{\mathrm{bank}}, \mathbf{v}_{\mathrm{teller}} \in \mathsf{N}$.

The interpretable approach works as follows. Fix an orthonormal basis $\{e_i\}_{i=1}^{d}$ for the noun space N aligned with the following interpretable properties (in order):

philosophy, bright, outspoken, social_justice,
activism, anti_nuclear, banking, finance,
clerical, customer_service, cash_handling

so $d = 11$ and e_i indexes the i-th property. Each lexical item w is assigned a nonnegative coordinate vector

$$c(w) = (c_1(w), \dots, c_{11}(w)) \in \mathbb{R}^{11}_{\geq 0},$$

which determines its (unnormalized) meaning vector $v^{\text{raw}}(w) = \sum_{i=1}^{11} c_i(w)\, e_i$. We then apply ℓ_2-normalization to obtain a unit vector in N:

$$v(w) \;=\; \frac{v^{\text{raw}}(w)}{\|v^{\text{raw}}(w)\|_2} \;=\; \frac{\sum_{i=1}^{11} c_i(w)\, e_i}{\left(\sum_{i=1}^{11} c_i(w)^2\right)^{1/2}}.$$

Optionally, to prevent coordinate-wise annihilation under Hadamard composition, we impose a small floor $\varepsilon > 0$ by setting $c_i(w) \leftarrow \max\{c_i(w), \varepsilon\}$ before normalization.

The corpus-derived approach works as follows. Construct N from a large parsed corpus by aggregating *dependency-typed* co-occurrence statistics with contexts C drawn from relations (e.g., AMOD, OBJ, NMOD, SUBJ, COMPOUND, etc.[2]). Let $X \in \mathbb{R}^{|V|\times|C|}_{\geq 0}$ count how often noun $w \in V$ occurs with context $c \in C$. Convert X to a PPMI-weighted matrix M with

$$\begin{aligned}
\text{PPMI}(w,c) &= \max\left\{0,\ \log \frac{p(w,c)}{p(w)\,p(c)}\right\},\\
p(w,c) &= \frac{X_{wc}}{\sum_{w',c'} X_{w'c'}},\\
p(w) &= \sum_{c} p(w,c),\\
p(c) &= \sum_{w} p(w,c).
\end{aligned}$$

yielding $M_{wc} = \text{PPMI}(w,c)$ (with standard smoothing/pruning as desired). Reduce dimensionality via truncated SVD $M \approx U_d\,\Sigma_d\,V_d^{\top}$ to obtain d-dimensional noun embeddings; we take row-vectors

$$v^{\text{raw}}(w) \;=\; (U_d\Sigma_d)_{w,\cdot} \in \mathbb{R}^d \quad \text{(or } U_d \text{ if preferred)},$$

[2] Concretely: AMOD = adjectival modifier, links a noun to an adjective (e.g. *red car* ⇒ AMOD(car, red)); OBJ = object of a verb (e.g. *eat pizza* ⇒ OBJ(eat, pizza)); NMOD = nominal modifier (e.g. *capital of France* ⇒ NMOD(capital, France)); SUBJ (often NSUBJ) = subject of a verb (e.g. *dogs run* ⇒ NSUBJ(run, dogs)); COMPOUND = noun compound (e.g. *bank teller* ⇒ COMPOUND(teller, bank); cf. [7]).

and finally apply ℓ_2-normalization to each row:

$$v(w) = \frac{v^{\mathrm{raw}}(w)}{\|v^{\mathrm{raw}}(w)\|_2} \in \mathbb{R}^d.$$

This procedure follows the "concrete" constructions for compositional spaces in [8] and the programmatic overview in [1].

In the first interpretable approach, set $\mathbf{v}_{\mathrm{bank}}$ to load on *banking/finance* and $\mathbf{v}_{\mathrm{teller}}$ on *clerical/cash_handling/customer_service*; stance coordinates near zero. In the second corpus-based approach, disambiguate *bank* to the financial sense by filtering contexts; require moderate $\cos(\mathbf{v}_{\mathrm{bank}}, \mathbf{v}_{\mathrm{teller}})$ to avoid degenerate merging. All noun vectors are centered and unit-normalized. To reduce hubness, we optionally apply whitening $W = \big((1-\alpha)\Sigma + \alpha I\big)^{-1/2}$ and compute cosines in the whitened space.

3.2 Composing Compounds and Adjectives

Using Frobenius merge,

$$\mathbf{v}_{\mathrm{BT}} = \mathbf{v}_{\mathrm{bank}} \odot \mathbf{v}_{\mathrm{teller}}. \tag{9}$$

Model *feminist* as $A_{\mathrm{fem}} : \mathsf{N} \to \mathsf{N}$ and set

$$\mathbf{v}_{\mathrm{FBT}} = A_{\mathrm{fem}}\, \mathbf{v}_{\mathrm{BT}}. \tag{10}$$

The above-mentioned SCFA on N supplies copying and merging compatible with compact closure; in coordinates the merge coincides with Hadamard [10]. Equation (9) realizes *intersective* combination.

In the interpretable approach to the matrix representation of adjectives, construct A_{fem} to (i) upweight stance diagonals; (ii) add small, targeted off-diagonals from occupational to stance dimensions; (iii) bound operator norm $\|A_{\mathrm{fem}}\|_2 \le \tau$.

In the corpus regression approach to the matrix representation of adjectives, learn via ridge [2]:

$$\begin{aligned} \min_{A \in \mathbb{R}^{d\times d}} \; & \sum_{(a,n)\in\mathcal{D}} \big\|A\, v_n - v_{a\cdot n}\big\|_2^2 \\ & + \lambda \|A\|_F^2, \end{aligned} \tag{11}$$

then set $A_{\mathrm{fem}} = A$ for $a =$"feminist". Optionally use $A = D + UV^\top$ (low-rank) with spectral clipping.

For ablation we have diagonal-only adjective (diag(-) below keeps the diagonal elements as is and let everything else be zero):

$$A_{\mathrm{fem}}^{\mathrm{diag}} = \mathrm{diag}(A_{\mathrm{fem}}). \tag{12}$$

Baselines for compounding are as follows.

$$\begin{aligned} \mathbf{v}_{\mathrm{BT}}^{\mathrm{add}} &= \mathrm{norm}(\mathbf{v}_{\mathrm{bank}} + \mathbf{v}_{\mathrm{teller}}), \\ \mathbf{v}_{\mathrm{BT}}^{\mathrm{gate}} &= \mathrm{norm}\big(\gamma\,(\mathbf{v}_{\mathrm{bank}} \odot \mathbf{v}_{\mathrm{teller}}) \\ &\qquad + (1-\gamma)(\mathbf{v}_{\mathrm{bank}} + \mathbf{v}_{\mathrm{teller}})\big), \end{aligned} \tag{13}$$

with $\gamma \in [0, 1]$.

We finally encode Linda's description as $\mathbf{v}_{\text{Linda}} \in \mathsf{N}$ and compare

$$\begin{aligned} s_{\text{BT}} &= \cos(\mathbf{v}_{\text{Linda}}, \mathbf{v}_{\text{BT}}), \\ s_{\text{FBT}} &= \cos(\mathbf{v}_{\text{Linda}}, \mathbf{v}_{\text{FBT}}), \quad \Delta = s_{\text{FBT}} - s_{\text{BT}}. \end{aligned} \tag{14}$$

Optionally use whitening: $\cos_W(x, y) = \cos(Wx, Wy)$.

4 Experimental Results

We evaluate cosine similarity between $\mathbf{v}_{\text{Linda}}$ and each phrase-level representation and ablate A_{fem} to its diagonal-only restriction. Vectors are computed according to the first interpretable approach introduced above.

Table 1 summarizes the core cosine similarities. The conjunction effect can be observed: *feminist bank teller* exceeds *bank teller* by more than half an absolute cosine point.

Table 1. Cosine similarities between Linda and each phrase.

Phrase	Cosine	Notes
bank teller	0.0964	baseline
feminist bank teller	**0.6263**	full adjective matrix
diag-only feminist × (bank teller)	0.0967	no meaningful change

Compute the cosine margin

$$\Delta = s_{\text{FBT}} - s_{\text{BT}} = 0.6263 - 0.0964 = \mathbf{0.5299}. \tag{15}$$

The fold-change is

$$\frac{s_{\text{FBT}}}{s_{\text{BT}}} = \frac{0.6263}{0.0964} \approx \mathbf{6.50}. \tag{16}$$

Let $\theta(x, y) = \arccos(\cos(x, y))$ (degrees). Then

$$\theta(\mathbf{v}_{\text{Linda}}, \mathbf{v}_{\text{BT}}) \approx 84.47^\circ, \qquad \theta(\mathbf{v}_{\text{Linda}}, \mathbf{v}_{\text{FBT}}) \approx 51.22^\circ. \tag{17}$$

Replacing A_{fem} with $A_{\text{fem}}^{\text{diag}}$ yields

$$s_{\text{diag}} = \cos\left(\mathbf{v}_{\text{Linda}}, A_{\text{fem}}^{\text{diag}} \mathbf{v}_{\text{BT}}\right) = 0.0967, \tag{18}$$

an inconsequential change relative to $s_{\text{BT}} = 0.0964$ (absolute difference $+0.0003$). Thus, nearly all improvement is attributable to off-diagonal mixing:

$$\frac{s_{\text{FBT}} - s_{\text{diag}}}{s_{\text{FBT}} - s_{\text{BT}}} = \frac{0.5296}{0.5299} \approx 0.9994. \tag{19}$$

5 Discussion

Our findings support a clear, compositional explanation of the conjunction effect in the Linda problem: when meanings are constructed by typed operations in a distributional space, the composed phrase *feminist bank teller* aligns more closely with the Linda description than *bank teller*. This emerges from two principled ingredients: (i) *intersective compounding* via the Frobenius merge (Hadamard product) that concentrates occupational content in $v_{\text{bank}} \odot v_{\text{teller}}$, and (ii) *adjective-as-function* composition in which off-diagonal mass transfer in A_{fem} systematically redirects part of that content toward stance dimensions emphasized by v_{Linda}.

Psychological accounts often attribute the conjunction effect to *representativeness*. Here, representativeness is not an external heuristic but a *predicted geometric consequence* of typed composition: Frobenius merge suppresses dimensions orthogonal to the intersection of the constituents, while A_{fem} can introduce cross-feature couplings that increase overlap with the probe. The diagonal-only ablation makes this causal: when off-diagonal terms are removed, the similarity essentially reverts to the baseline, showing that mere feature masking cannot generate the effect.

Our result says that a computational semantics, instantiated with standard composition laws, *predicts* a conjunction-like preference in vector geometry. It does *not* claim that reasoners are normatively correct to choose the conjunction, nor that all instances of conjunction-like behavior must be due to adjective mixing. The account is compatible with classical probability at the modeling level; it simply explains why a similarity-based ranking that respects typed composition may favor the conjoined description.

Our account dovetails with regression-based AN composition and neural matrixvector models: all posit adjective-as-function, but DisCoCat additionally specifies *where* linear maps come from (types) and *how* they combine with other morphisms (compact structure plus Frobenius). The present result therefore sits at a useful intersection: it is faithful to linguistic typing while remaining computationally lightweight (matrixvector multiplications and Hadamard products).

Conceptually, the result suggests that certain cognitive "biases" can be recast as *emergent properties of typed composition* in vector semantics. Methodologically, it shows that small, interpretable linear operators (off-diagonal adjective maps) can have large geometric effects when applied after intersective compounding. Practically, the pipeline offers a transparent diagnostic for how specific words or constructions alter similarity structure, which may aid interpretability analyses of large language models.

6 Conclusion

We have presented a systematic account of the conjunction effect using compositional distributional semantics. Within our construction, nouns live in a shared vector space N, noun–noun compounds compose intersectively via a Frobenius

(Hadamard) merge, and adjectives are linear endomaps on N. This *adjective-as-function* view supplies the algebraic capacity to reallocate semantic mass across dimensions that encode stance and occupational properties. Composed with *bank teller*, a full (non-diagonal) *feminist* matrix A_{fem} moves the compound closer to the Linda probe vector $\mathbf{v}_{\text{Linda}}$, whereas a diagonal-only ablation fails to do so. The mechanism is therefore interpretable and *necessary*: off-diagonal couplings in A_{fem} redirect mass from occupational coordinates into stance-related ones emphasized by the probe, yielding the conjunction effect in the geometry of vector space semantics.

The result places the classic "representativeness" intuition on a compositional footing: greater "fit" for the conjunction emerges from typed linear composition rather than ad hoc similarity tweaks. Second, the account is *predictive*: it isolates a concrete algebraic resource (off-diagonals) whose presence/absence determines whether the effect occurs. Third, it is *transparent*: every step (merge, linear map, cosine) is inspectable, enabling mechanistic explanations and targeted diagnostics.

We would like to note that compositional distributional semantics can reproduce the conjunction effect without violating classical probabilistic axioms at the modeling level. Note also that the effect hinges on *how* meanings are composed—specifically, on off-diagonal mixing in adjective maps plus intersective compounding. Together, these points suggest that compositional distributional semantics offers a useful, interpretable bridge between linguistic structure and graded similarity judgments that underlie classic cognitive phenomena. Future work would thus include the study of cognitive bias or heuristics other than the conjunction effect via the farmework of compositional distributional semantics.

Other future directions would be as follows: (i) run the full corpus/LM estimation with statistical uncertainty (cf. [11]), (ii) explore other adjective classes and languages, (iii) test alternative compounding operators and their learnable gates, and (iv) extend beyond nominal phrases to clausal compositions (verb tensors into sentence space) to study conjunction-like preferences in more complex prompts. Together, these directions would further establish when and why typed composition predicts conjunction-like rankings, and how these predictions relate to human judgments and model behavior at scale.

References

1. Baroni, M., Bernardi, R., Zamparelli, R.: Frege in space: a program for compositional distributional semantics. Linguist. Issues Lang. Technol. **9** (2014). https://aclanthology.org/2014.lilt-9.5/
2. Baroni, M., Zamparelli, R.: Nouns are vectors, adjectives are matrices: representing adjective–noun constructions in semantic space. In: Proceedings of EMNLP, pp. 1183–1193. Association for Computational Linguistics (2010). https://aclanthology.org/D10-1115/
3. Baroni, M., Dinu, G., Kruszewski, G.: Don't count, predict! a systematic comparison of context-counting vs. context-predicting semantic vectors. In: Proceedings of ACL, pp. 238–247 (2014). https://aclanthology.org/P14-1023/

4. Clark, S.: Vector space models of lexical meaning. In: Lappin, S., Fox, C. (eds.) The Handbook of Contemporary Semantic Theory, 2nd edn., pp. 493–522. Wiley-Blackwell (2015). https://doi.org/10.1002/9781118882139.ch18
5. Coecke, B., Sadrzadeh, M., Clark, S.: Mathematical foundations for a compositional distributional model of meaning. Linguistic Analysis (Lambek Festschrift special issue) (2010). Preprint: https://arxiv.org/abs/1003.4394
6. Costello, F., Watts, P.: Surprisingly rational: probability theory plus noise explains biases in judgment. Psychol. Rev. **121**(3), 463–480 (2014). https://doi.org/10.1037/a0037010
7. Erk, K., Padó, S.: a structured vector space model for word meaning in context. In: Proceedings of EMNLP, pp. 897–906 (2008). https://aclanthology.org/D08-1092/
8. Grefenstette, E., Sadrzadeh, M., Clark, S., Coecke, B., Pulman, S.: Concrete sentence spaces for compositional distributional models of meaning. In: Proceedings of IWCS, pp. 125–134 (2011). https://aclanthology.org/W11-0114/
9. Guevara, E.: A Regression model of adjective–noun compositionality in distributional semantics. In: Proceedings of the GEMS Workshop (ACL), pp. 33–37 (2010). https://aclanthology.org/W10-2805/
10. Coecke, B., Sadrzadeh, M., Clark, S.: Reasoning about meaning in natural language with compact closed categories and Frobenius algebras. arXiv:1401.5980 (2014). https://arxiv.org/abs/1401.5980
11. Marelli, M., et al.: A SICK cure for the evaluation of compositional distributional semantic models. In: Proceedings of LREC, pp. 216–223 (2014). https://aclanthology.org/L14-1314/
12. Meichanetzidis, K., Toumi, A., Coecke, B., de Felice, G., Mezzadri, F.: Quantum natural language processing: a tutorial. J. Artif. Intell. Res. **70**, 1333–1373 (2021). https://doi.org/10.1613/jair.1.12896
13. Mitchell, J., Lapata, M.: Composition in distributional models of semantics. Cogn. Sci. **34**(8), 1388–1429 (2010). https://doi.org/10.1111/j.1551-6709.2010.01106.x
14. Pothos, E.M., Busemeyer, J.R.: Quantum cognition. Annu. Rev. Psychol. **73**, 749–778 (2022). https://doi.org/10.1146/annurev-psych-033020-130748
15. Sadrzadeh, M., Clark, S., Coecke, B.: The Frobenius anatomy of word meanings I: subject and object relative pronouns. J. Log. Comput. **23**(6), 1293–1317 (2013). https://doi.org/10.1093/logcom/ext044
16. Sadrzadeh, M., Clark, S., Coecke, B.: The Frobenius anatomy of word meanings II: possessive relative pronouns. J. Log. Comput. **26**(2), 785–815 (2016). https://doi.org/10.1093/logcom/exu027
17. Socher, R., Huval, B., Manning, C.D., Ng, A.Y.: Semantic compositionality through recursive matrix–vector spaces. In: Proceedings of EMNLP-CoNLL, pp. 1201–1211 (2012). https://aclanthology.org/D12-1110/
18. Turney, P.D., Pantel, P.: From frequency to meaning: vector space models of semantics. J. Artif. Intell. Res. **37**, 141–188 (2010). https://jair.org/index.php/jair/article/view/10640
19. Tversky, A., Kahneman, D.: Extensional versus intuitive reasoning: the conjunction fallacy in probability judgment. Psychol. Rev. **90**(4), 293–315 (1983). https://doi.org/10.1037/0033-295X.90.4.293

Quantum Patches for Efficient Learning

Ban Q. Tran[1,3](✉), Chuong K. Luong[2], and Susan Mengel[1]

[1] Department of Computer Science, Texas Tech University, Lubbock, TX 79416, USA
{bantran,susan.mengel}@ttu.edu

[2] SAP Innovation Lab, FPT University, Hanoi 10000, Vietnam

[3] Department of Computing Fundamental, FPT University, Hanoi 10000, Vietnam
bantq3@fe.edu.vn

Abstract. The problem of conserving computational resources while training models in deep learning has become urgent as models increasingly require more input data to improve accuracy. To enhance accuracy beyond increasing data, researchers have leveraged quantum properties, such as using random quantum circuits (RQC) to transform input data, similar to how data augmentation techniques are applied, and have demonstrated their effectiveness. However, the appearance of RQC introduces new challenges, as quantum circuits transforming features consume significant computational resources and increase the algorithm's time complexity. In this study, we propose a novel framework combining RQC and saliency map techniques to address the computational resource problem in quantum deep learning. The research results show that our framework has reduced the algorithm's computation time by **2.34** times, achieving an accuracy of **92.51%**, 2.2% higher than the quantum baseline version. This reduction is highly significant in the current era, where quantum computers are in the noisy intermediate-scale quantum (NISQ) era, and noise significantly impacts the accuracy of hardware computation outputs, making quantum hardware accesses relatively costly.

Keywords: Machine Learning · Deep Learning · Quantum Computing · Random Quantum Circuits · Saliency Maps

1 Introduction

Deep Learning (DL) [1] has exploded in popularity over the last few years with models having hundreds of millions, even billions, of parameters becoming commonplace in research and the real world. With such large models, the need for larger datasets has arisen particularly with deep learning models like convolutional neural networks (CNNs) for classification or object detection and so on. The problem of data-hungry models has been and continues to be a challenge, and data augmentation techniques have partially emerged to address this problem [2]. Several data augmentation strategies are in common use, such as random feature removal which is quite popular. Other common strategies are dropout [3] and regional dropout [4] where they turn off internal activations or

T. T. Quan et al. (Eds.): MIWAI 2025, LNAI 16353, pp. 87–100, 2026.
https://doi.org/10.1007/978-981-95-4957-3_8

remove/replace random regions in the input image. More recently, researchers investigated patching techniques, such as CutMix [5], to replace an area of the target image with a randomly chosen patch from another image. The newly mixed image then takes on a new label which is a combination of the labels of the original source and target images where instead of using 1/0 for presence/absence, a proportional number based on the size of the patch is used for both labels in the target label vector for the new image (so called as mixing the labels proportionally). This method was further improved by SaliencyMix [6], which selects the source image patch based on the saliency map of the source image before mixing it with the target image. SaliencyMix has proven effective for pre-processing input images before training CNN models. In addition to classical data augmentation techniques, a new data augmentation technique based on the unique properties of quantum computers has recently emerged [7]. With phenomena, such as superposition and entanglement, quantum computing is becoming a potent instrument for addressing NP-hard problems and improving performance through variational quantum algorithms (VQA) [8], which are constructed around parameterized quantum circuits (PQC). One of the variants of PQC used in data augmentation techniques, which has proven effective, is RQC also known as variational quantum circuits [9]. RQCs utilize shallow quantum circuits that mitigate noise issues, use these circuits to spatially localize data subsets to harness the capabilities of Hilbert space, demonstrating considerable efficacy. These algorithms have shown their advantages on simulated and universal quantum computers in machine learning [10], optimization [11], security [12], and image processing [9] domains. However, the use of RQC also introduces the problem of excessive computational resource consumption due to the depth of quantum circuits, leading to a trade-off between the post-training accuracy of the deep learning model, hardware resources, and the runtime required for model training [13]. To solve this problem, we propose a novel framework boosting the efficiency of RQCs by using the saliency map method. Our method has demonstrated practical effectiveness by reducing the computation and transformation time in the quantum circuit per epoch by 5.35 times. Suppose the training time for the model is included. In that case, the total processing time of the algorithm for 100 epochs is reduced by 2.34 times, while the accuracy is 2.2% higher compared to the conventional full-image quantum transformation method. In the following sections, we will analyze recent solutions, provide a detailed explanation of the proposed method, present experimental results, and discuss the findings obtained from the study.

2 Related Works

Deep learning and intense learning models for image processing critically depend on high-quality labeled data to achieve desired accuracy [1]. Owing to the limited availability of high-quality image data, transformer-based models for image recognition and processing, although capable of surpassing CNN models in accuracy when trained on massive image datasets, cannot entirely supplant CNN models [14]. Utilizing data augmentation techniques, CNN models can meet the demands of modern applications without requiring an unnecessarily large amount of visual input data [15]. Several prior works investigated the application of RQCs for processing picture input data to enhance image generalization before training convolutional neural network models. Henderson *et al.* (2019) [9] devised a method to replace a conventional convolutional layer in a CNN with a specialized quantum variant termed a "quanvolutional layer". The images are preprocessed using this quantum layer before sending them to the remainder of the CNN. The implementation is highly effective, enhancing the model's accuracy and minimizing errors during training compared to classical CNN. Based on this research, the quantum advantage of RQC is applied to data augmentation and is utilized for thyroid nodule and skin lesions classification [16,17]. The results were auspicious, with the model achieving an accuracy of 97.63% on the test set of 127 images for the tumor classification task and an accuracy of 93.88% on the test set for the suspicious level classification task using only 98 images. These results are superior to traditional models such as Densenet121, Resnet50, InceptionV3, and VGG16. For the DermaMNIST dataset used for skin lesion classification, the model achieved an accuracy of 72.7% with a batch size of 512. In contrast, the baseline classical model achieved only 70.1% with a batch size of 128. Besides the idea of applying RQC, a quantum generative adversarial network (QGAN) is also used for data augmentation [18–20]. Experimental results from the study indicate that Quantum Circuit Born Machines (QCBMs), a variant of QGANs, outperform classical models—including recurrent neural networks (RNN), transformers (TF), variational autoencoders (VAE), and wasserstein generative adversarial networks (WGAN)—in terms of generalization capability during training, as measured by generalization metrics with $\epsilon = 0.01$ and 0.001. In addition, QGAN experiments conducted on real quantum hardware—IBM ibm_torino (48 superconducting transmon qubits) and IonQ aria-1 (24 trapped-ion qubits)—demonstrated that IBM ibm_torino yielded KL divergence scores of 0.51, 0.31, and 0.44 for the s, t, and y distributions, respectively. In contrast, IonQ aria-1 achieved significantly lower scores of 0.25, 0.14, and 0.07 for the identical distributions. The QGAN, however, encounters specific technical challenges, such as circuit complexity and barren plateau issues when computing the gradient. Similar to the GAN but more effective at capturing the underlying data distribution and requiring more stable training, the Variational Auto-Encoder (VAE) is designed using variational quantum circuits (VQCs) and is also employed in several studies as a solution for data augmentation [21]. The integration of a VAE with gated recurrent units (GRU), optimized using the grey wolf optimizer (GWO) on the VQC framework, reduced the root mean square error (RMSE) by 14.71%, 16.88%, and 17.95% on the sunny, cloudy, and rainy datasets, respectively.

3 Methodology

In scenarios where training data is scarce and enhancing the generalization capability of deep learning models is critical, data augmentation techniques play a vital role. In image processing, widely used data augmentation techniques include flipping, rotation, translation, scaling, cropping, color jitter, noise injection, elastic transformations, cutout, random erasing, mixup, and cut mix. These techniques significantly contributed to improving the learning performance of deep learning models. In this study, we integrate two augmentation techniques, noise addition and saliency map which is a variant of the cutmix method, to improve the learning performance of deep learning models. We exploit the distinctive features of quantum computing, such as superposition and entanglement, to generate the noise component. More specifically, we employ RQCs to transform input images, effectively serving as a noise-addition mechanism within the data augmentation process. The cropped region is subjected to quantum transformations and converted into a noise pattern, which is subsequently integrated into the image using the saliency map strategy. The subsequent sections will provide a detailed explanation of the proposed method.

3.1 Data Augmentation

Several widely used and effective data augmentation techniques are based on regularization, including Cutout [22], Mixup [23], CutMix [cite] [5], and SaliencyMix [6].

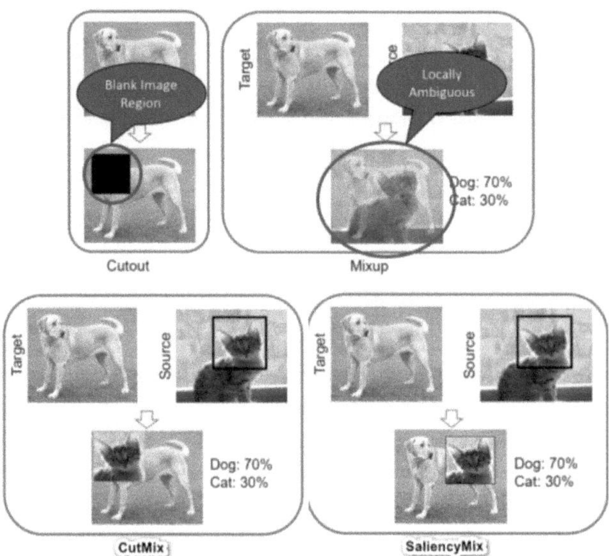

Fig. 1. The currently adopted regularization techniques that are widely employed in practice.

Regularization techniques, such as Cutout, Mixup, and Cutmix, may induce complications by arbitrarily eliminating or altering segments of images. These techniques may result in the forfeiture of critical attributes, diminishing the model's accuracy in picture classification. Saliencymix has proven to be a more effective regularization method, as it avoids the issues arising from random cutting and pasting of image regions. Figure 1 highlights the key conceptual distinctions among various data augmentation techniques. The Cutout method randomly removes a rectangular patch from a labeled image, introducing occlusion-based regularization. Mixup generates synthetic samples by linearly interpolating both the pixel values and labels of source and target images according to a predefined ratio (e.g., 30–70). Cutmix, on the other hand, selects a random region from the source image and replaces a correspondingly sized patch in the target image while proportionally adjusting the labels. In contrast, Saliencymix enhances semantic relevance by identifying the most salient region in the source image and purposefully pasting it into a less informative area of the target image, thereby promoting more effective learning of discriminative features.

3.2 Random Quantum Circuits

Classical computers, relying on semiconductor chips with billions of transistors integrated into a circuit board space, represent this century's most widespread computing technology. However, manufacturing technology has reached fundamental limits that are difficult to surpass, so Moore's Law is no longer valid in its original form. A new paradigm of computing technology is necessary to exceed this barrier. Quantum computing, defined by its distinctive principles and phenomena such as superposition, entanglement, and interference, may provide the most viable solution to this difficulty. Even though developing a fault-tolerant quantum computer remains a significant and unresolved near-term challenge, NISQ systems with several hundred qubits have already demonstrated the potential of quantum computation in specialized domains of computer science. Among the quantum computing technologies that have exhibited superior performance compared to classical computation are parameterized quantum circuits and random quantum circuits, a simplified version thereof. In a recent investigation conducted by a team of researchers at Google [24], random quantum circuits (RQCs) exhibited quantum supremacy compared to classical computers. They demonstrated that a bit-string sampled from a pseudo-random quantum circuit U, of polynomial size in n, is essentially e times more likely than a bit-string sampled using a classical algorithm. The outcome of the quantum supremacy is formalized and interpreted in Eq. 1. Quantum supremacy arises when no classical algorithm can solve a formal computational task within a reasonable time, whereas a current quantum device can perform the same task efficiently. In the following section, we interpret quantum supremacy based on the results from research on RQCs.

RQCs are classes of quantum circuits in which quantum gates are selected and arranged randomly, governed by a defined probability distribution. An RQC is essentially a unitary transformation U, represented by a sequence of one- and two-qubit gates applied to different input qubits, with gates within the same clock cycle executed concurrently. Figure 2 illustrates a basic RQC structure

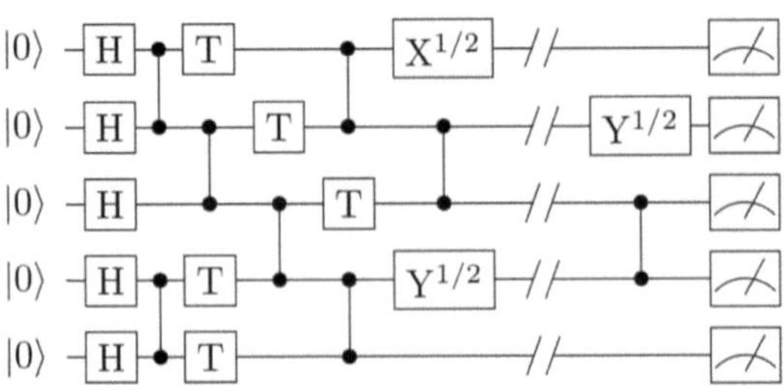

Fig. 2. Illustration of a random quantum circuit within a one-dimensional array of qubits (1D lattice). Vertical lines represent controlled-phase (CZ) gates.

featuring single-qubit gates like Hadamard (H), Pauli-X (X), Pauli-Y (Y), and the non-Clifford T gate, along with the two-qubit controlled-phase (CZ) gates. These gates are applied to N (5 in this example) input qubits, transforming their quantum states within a 2^N-dimensional Hilbert space. The circuit operates on input data encoded from classical data by applying quantum mechanical principles, specifically superposition and entanglement. Consider a quantum state $|\psi\rangle$ generated by a RQC. The output measurement probability $P_{exp}(x_j) = |\langle x_j|\psi\rangle|^2$ distribution of the RQC asymptotically follows an exponential form Ne^{-Np}, commonly known as the Porter–Thomas distribution [?]. The computational task, consisting of sampling output bit-strings from the probability distribution associated with the final quantum state $|\psi\rangle$ resulting from the unitary transformation U, yielded results demonstrating that the probability of sampling a given bit-string from U is greater by a factor of e than the probability of sampling the same bit-string using a classical algorithm. Within a local qubit basis, the probability associated with a quantum sample S, comprised of m measurement outcomes denoted by $x \in \{0,1\}^n$, is expressed as follows: $\prod_{x \in S_{exp}} |\langle x|\psi\rangle|^2$. Analogously, we denote by S_{pcl} the sample of m bit-strings obtained from polynomial-time classical algorithms. The probability associated with this sample S_{pcl} can be described as: $\prod_{x \in S_{pcl}} |\langle x|\psi\rangle|^2$. The experimental results demonstrated that:

$$\frac{\prod_{x \in S_{exp}} |\langle x|\psi\rangle|^2}{\prod_{x \in S_{pcl}} |\langle x|\psi\rangle|^2} \sim e^m \geq 1 \tag{1}$$

The result from Eq. 1 implies the inequality $1 \geq \alpha \geq C$, where $\alpha \equiv E_U[\Delta H(p_{exp})]$ is the experimental cross-entropy difference, and $C \equiv E_U[\Delta H(p^*)]$ is a lower bound derived from the performance of algorithm A—a classical algorithm executed with polynomial or exponential cost, as long as it runs on currently available classical hardware. This result implies that quantum supremacy is achieved when the output distribution of the RQC approaches the ideal Porter–Thomas distribution, i.e., when it converges toward 1 and it is evident that RQCs can completely substitute random classical algorithms for data transformation and improve quality in spatially local subsection data within the field of image processing. Findings from both theoretical analyses and empirical experiments have validated the effectiveness of RQCs in transforming input data for deep learning models [9].

3.3 Proposed Method

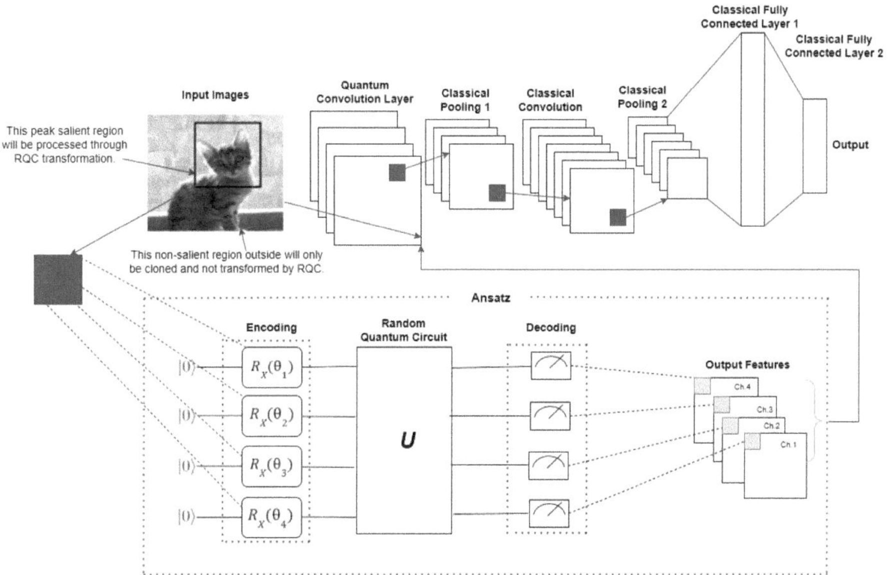

Fig. 3. The proposed solution combines the saliency map technique with the quantum advantages of image transformation using random quantum circuits.

Leveraging the demonstrated quantum advantage, we introduce a novel architecture integrating random quantum circuits with a saliency map for image classification data augmentation. This architecture extends the "Quanvolutional" architecture introduced by Henderson *et al.* [9] in their 2019 paper. Figure 3 provides a detailed depiction of the architecture. An input image is initially processed using the saliency map technique. Image patches containing salient features, extracted from the image using the saliency map algorithm, are transformed using an RQC and then pasted onto non-salient regions of the image, harnessing the quantum advantage. The non-salient features of the target image are intentionally left unmodified to facilitate enhanced learning capabilities.

Applying Saliency Map for Input Images. The fundamental premise of the saliency map algorithm is based on the notion introduced by Yun *et al.* (2019) [5]. To mitigate the risk of the model acquiring spurious features from random excision and embedding, the algorithm integrates the methodology of Cong *et al.* [25] to identify salient regions or pixels that attract visual attention, subsequently extracting these areas for source image cropping. Equation 2 denotes the feature detection function based on the saliency map. In this case, $I_{vs} \in R^{W \times H}$ denotes the visual saliency map of the source picture I_s, corresponding to the yellow rectangle area depicted in Fig. 3.

$$I_{vs} = f(I_s) \tag{2}$$

The algorithm seeks to identify the pixel, denoted by $I_{vs}^{i,j}$, within the saliency map with the maximum intensity value. The coordinates (i, j) of this pixel are determined via the argmax function, as expressed by the following equation:

$$i, j = argmax(I_{vs}) \tag{3}$$

with these pixels serving as centers, the proportion of the source image dimensions to be excised is determined by a combination ratio, denoted by λ, which is sampled from a uniform distribution on the interval $(0, 1)$.

Transforming Images by Quanvolution Layer. Suppose we have a set of input images, u. Let u_x represent an input image structured as a 2D matrix with dimensions n by n. u_x will be divided into spatially-local subsections and encoded into the RQC. We selected angle rotation encoding due to its widespread use and implementation simplicity. This method intuitively maps image pixel values and quantum rotation angles. Furthermore, angle encoding is highly compatible with RQC, enabling efficient circuit construction without requiring many qubits. Additionally, it helps preserve the local information of the image during quantum transformations. The state after encoding is denoted as: $i_x = e(u_x)$. These quantum states will be processed by the RQC over d-clock cycles, utilizing the principles of superposition and entanglement. The output of the RQC, representing the new states of the qubits, is given by: $o_x = q(i_x) = q(e(u_x))$. The output quantum states are then decoded by measurement, collapsing them into bit-strings of classical data. The function representing this process is $f_x = d(o_x) = d(q(e(u_x)))$, and in general form:

$$f_x = Q(u_x, e, q, d) \tag{4}$$

Quantum Benefits. Quantum circuits [8] have demonstrated strong and practical support for classical machine-learning algorithms during the ongoing development of fault-tolerant quantum computers. This process will require additional time to yield tangible results. Despite current limitations, quantum advantages obtained through NISQ devices remain worthy of attention from the scientific community. The following are some benefits of applying RQCs in data augmentation.

(i) *Hybrid nature:* While building a universal quantum computer remains a challenge, hybrid algorithms like this offer a practical solution for NISQ devices. Using simple, shallow quantum circuits addresses readout issues—such as input/output handling, cost estimation, and benchmarking. RQCs are, by design, randomly generated circuits, but restricting them to a limited number of qubits prevents any significant increase in circuit depth. Moreover, the algorithm still demonstrates superior polynomial-time performance compared to classical approaches, even before considering further exponential-time speedups.

(ii) *No quantum random access memory (QRAM):* One of the biggest obstacles to the widespread adoption of quantum computers, besides the design of the quantum computer chip itself, is the design of QRAM. Furthermore, loading large amounts of classical data into QRAM for processing poses a significant difficulty. The RQC solution eliminates this challenge because it does not require QRAM during processing. Compact, flexible quantum circuits acting on local spatial data regions represent a perfect solution for the present time.

(iii) *Noise reduction:* It is well-known that quantum circuits can be affected by noise, consequently causing errors. The issue of fault tolerance for quantum circuits has been researched and is not the objective of this study. The question of how noise precisely impacts quantum neural networks (QNN) circuits has not yet been definitively answered by research. However, given that the nature of the transformations in this study is for data augmentation, we hypothesize that noise will not significantly affect the fundamental properties and quality of the algorithm. This algorithm is a significant advantage compared to other quantum algorithms where the noise problem becomes critical.

4 Experiments and Results

We assess the efficacy of the proposed method that integrates quanvolution layers with the saliency map algorithm for essential machine learning tasks. We utilize the Resnet18 architecture, a CNN architecture widely used in recent quantum machine learning studies, as the experimental architecture for our proposed solution [26]. The research is evaluated on classic quantum machine learning datasets and uses standard metrics to give readers an intuitive and familiar perspective. The hardware used for the experiments is based on NVIDIA Tesla P100 GPU. The open-source Python library for quantum machine learning used in the experiment is Pennylane quantum machine learning platform [27].

4.1 Dataset and Preprocessing

We used the Canadian Institute For Advanced Research (CIFAR-10) dataset for experiments with the proposed solution [28]. CIFAR-10 is a well-known benchmark in the field of computer vision research. The dataset comprises 60,000 color images sized 32×32, evenly distributed across 10 classes. The dataset is divided into two sets for research: a training set of 50,000 images and a test set of 10,000 images. Each input image from the dataset will double its size before passing through the circuit to ensure complexity and maintain the necessary information after transformation through the quantum circuit.

4.2 Imlementation Details

In this experiment, we used Python and the PyTorch framework as the primary programming language to conduct the experiments for this research. The open-source Python library for quantum machine learning, Pennylane [27], was utilized to construct the quantum transformation layer due to its compatibility with current quantum hardware and its provision of diverse and influential simulators. Training and evaluation were performed on NVIDIA Tesla P100 GPU for hardware. We utilized the Resnet18 model, a popular architecture for testing machine learning research hypotheses due to its lightweight nature (11.7M parameters) and excellent accuracy (89% on Top-5 accuracy for ImageNet1K) [26]. The PyTorch version with reproducibility capabilities is used [29]. The hyperparameters align with this version's default settings.

4.3 Baselines

Henderson's "full-image RQC application" method achieved impressive accuracy and loss on the Modified National Institute of Standards and Technology (MNIST) dataset [9]. However, for datasets with a medium to high number of features, the number of qubits required to encode the entire image and the computation time increase dramatically. The increase in qubits poses a significant challenge for quantum computers in the NISQ era. To address this issue, we propose a method using saliency maps to identify the most critical region in the image. Instead of learning from the entire image, the model will focus solely on a specific area around the most salient pixel. This approach significantly reduces the required computational resources while retaining the most essential information from the image for classification purposes. The crop region *cut_ratio* on the image will be randomly selected according to the distribution function $f\left(x;\alpha,\beta\right)$.

$$f\left(x;\alpha,\beta\right)=\frac{1}{B\left(\alpha,\beta\right)}x^{\alpha-1}\left(1-x\right)^{\beta-1} \tag{5}$$

with $cut\_ratio = \sqrt{(1-f\left(x;\alpha,\beta\right)}$. To prevent the *cut_ratio* from falling into a range of meaningless values, we set the control bound range from (0.15, 0.75). We selected the Resnet18 architecture for the experiments. The skip connections in this architecture allow gradients to be propagated more effectively across multiple layers. This propagation process helps address the vanishing gradient problem commonly encountered in deep neural networks. Additionally, we chose to optimize the hyperparameter set in advance to enhance the model's accuracy [?].

4.4 Results

The experimental results show that our framework yields better outcomes than the baseline method, which transforms the entire image. From Table 1, it can be seen that the accuracy of the proposed method reaches 92.51%, which is 2.2%

Table 1. Comparing the accuracy and loss of the two methods

Method	Accuracy (%)	Loss
Quantum-Baseline	90.31	0.35
Quantum-Saliency	**92.51(+2.2%)**	**0.26(-0.09)**

Table 2. Comparison of algorithm running times

Method	Time per Epoch(s)	Total Time(s)
Quantum-Baseline	260.96	37039
Quantum-Saliency	**48.78(-81.31%)**	**15804(-57.33%)**

higher than the baseline. Meanwhile, the loss decreases by 0.09 compared to the baseline value of 0.35.

However, the poblem we focus on solving is the method's efficiency. Our proposed method is clearly effective in reducing data processing time. It can be easily seen in Table 2 that the transformation processing time of the data through the RQC circuit of the proposed method only takes 48.78 s for one epoch, reducing by 81.31% compared to transforming the entire image in the quantum baseline proposed by Henderson. If we include the training and transformation time for the 100 epochs, our framework has saved 57.33% of time compared to the quantum baseline of 37039 s.

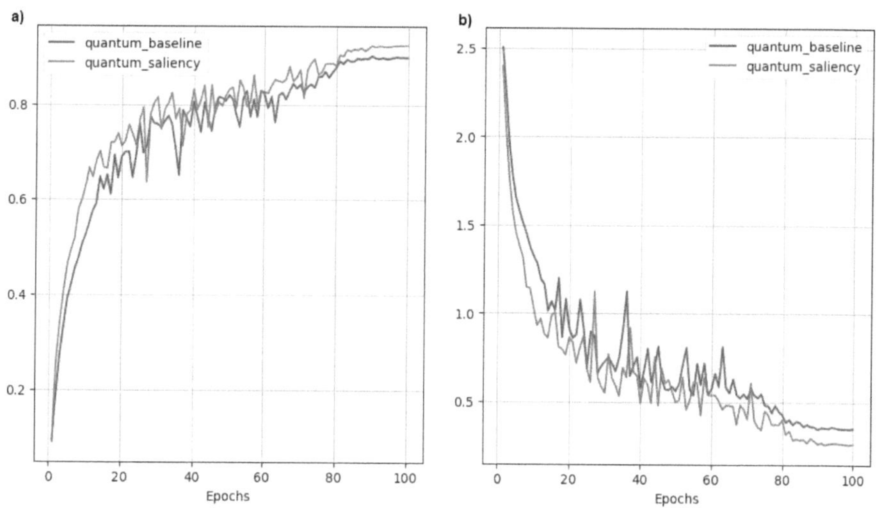

Fig. 4. Comparing the performance of the two methods: quantum-baseline and quantum-saliency. a) Validation accuracy b) Validation loss.

The detailed results of the model training process are described in detail in Fig. 4. The figure shows that the accuracy increase of quantum-saliency is faster and maintains a higher magnitude than quantum-baseline throughout the 100 epochs. In the final phase, quantum-saliency sustains and achieves stable results at 92.51%. The loss metric of quantum-saliency also decreases rapidly and stabilizes more effectively than quantum-baseline. Although the loss is slightly higher at 0.26 compared to the expected level of approximately 0.1 for classical deep learning models, this can be explained and accepted due to the variability of quantum circuits. The model shows no signs of overfitting or underfitting.

5 Conclusions

The shortage of computational resources and the excessively long runtime of algorithms have always been common challenges in computer science. In this study, we attempted to address part of this challenging problem. We have proposed a framework for intentional local quantum transformation processing. Our proposed solution helps reduce the computation and processing time of the quantum algorithm by several times while maintaining a higher model accuracy than the previous full-image transformation method. Our research demonstrates that a skillful combination of classical and quantum techniques can yield promising results in data augmentation. In the NISQ era of quantum computers, utilizing complex quantum circuits with considerable depth remains costly, whereas solutions employing small-scale, shallow quantum circuits that use local spatial data, as in this study, represent an optimal approach. Although the quantum circuits applied in this research are simple, the potential of RQC can still be further explored.

Acknowledgments. We thank Anurag Nandyala for assisting us in setting up the environment to run the source code on the HPCC.

Data Availability Statement. The data gathered and processed during the current study are available to the corresponding author upon request. The source code for this study is available via the following link: https://github.com/billytran2404/QEDA-2025.

Disclosure of Interests. The authors have no competing interests to declare that are relevant to the content of this article.

References

1. LeCun, Y., Bengio, Y., Hinton, G.: Deep learning. Nature **521**(7553), 436–444 (2015)
2. Krizhevsky, A., Sutskever, I., Hinton, G.E.: Imagenet classification with deep convolutional neural networks. Adv. Neural Inf. Process. Syst. **25** (2012)
3. Srivastava, N., Hinton, G., Krizhevsky, A., Sutskever, I., Salakhutdinov, R.: Dropout: a simple way to prevent neural networks from overfitting. J. Mach. Learn. Res. **15**(1), 1929–1958 (2014)

4. Choe, J., Shim, H.: Attention-based dropout layer for weakly supervised object localization. In: Proceedings of the IEEE/CVF conference on computer vision and pattern recognition, pp. 2219–2228 (2019)
5. Yun, S., et al.: Cutmix: regularization strategy to train strong classifiers with localizable features. In: Proceedings of the IEEE/CVF international conference on computer vision, pp. 6023–6032 (2019)
6. Uddin, A., et al.: Saliencymix: a saliency guided data augmentation strategy for better regularization. arXiv preprint arXiv:2006.01791 (2020)
7. Nielsen, M.A., Chuang, I.L.: Quantum computation and quantum information. Cambridge university press (2010)
8. Cerezo, M.: Variational quantum algorithms. Nat. Rev. Phys. **3**(9), 625–644 (2021)
9. Henderson, M., Shakya, S., Pradhan, S., Cook, T.: Quanvolutional neural networks: powering image recognition with quantum circuits. Quantum Mach. Intell. **2**(1), 1–9 (2020). https://doi.org/10.1007/s42484-020-00012-y
10. Biamonte, J., Wittek, P., Pancotti, N., Rebentrost, P., Wiebe, N., Lloyd, S.: Quantum machine learning. Nature **549**(7671), 195–202 (2017)
11. Farhi, E., Goldstone, J., Gutmann, S.: A quantum approximate optimization algorithm. arXiv preprint arXiv:1411.4028 (2014)
12. Bennett, C.H., Brassard, G.: Quantum cryptography: public key distribution and coin tossing. Theoret. Comput. Sci. **560**, 7–11 (2014)
13. Preskill, J.: Quantum computing in the NISQ era and beyond. Quantum **2**, 79 (2018)
14. Dosovitskiy, A., et al.: An image is worth 16×16 words: transformers for image recognition at scale. arXiv preprint arXiv:2010.11929 (2020)
15. Shorten, C., Khoshgoftaar, T.M.: A survey on image data augmentation for deep learning. J. Big Data **6**(1), 1–48 (2019)
16. Swathi, G., Altalbe, A., Kumar, R.P.: Qucnet: quantum-inspired convolutional neural networks for optimized thyroid nodule classification. IEEE Access **12**, 27829–27842 (2024)
17. Gordienko, Y., Trochun, Y., Taran, V., Khmelnytskyi, A., Stirenko, S.: HNN-QCn: Hybrid neural network with multiple backbones and quantum transformation as data augmentation technique. AI **6**(2), 36 (2025)
18. Baglio, J.: Data augmentation experiments with style-based quantum generative adversarial networks on trapped-ion and superconducting-qubit technologies. arXiv preprint arXiv:2405.04401 (2024)
19. Rani, C.J., Devarakonda, N.: Generative adversarial network based data augmentation and quantum based convolution neural network for the classification of Indian classical dance forms. J. Intell. Fuzzy Syst. **45**(4), 6107–6125 (2023)
20. Hibat-Allah, M., Mauri, M., Carrasquilla, J., Perdomo-Ortiz, A.: A framework for demonstrating practical quantum advantage: comparing quantum against classical generative models. Commun. Phys. **7**(1), 68 (2024)
21. Zhu, W., He, Y., Li, H.: Deep learning model for short-term photovoltaic power prediction based on data augmentation and quantum computing. In: 2024 China Automation Congress (CAC), pp. 4097–4102. IEEE (2024)
22. DeVries, T., Taylor, G.W.: Improved regularization of convolutional neural networks with cutout. arXiv preprint arXiv:1708.04552 (2017)
23. Zhang, H., Cisse, M., Dauphin, Y.N., Lopez-Paz, D.: mixup: Beyond empirical risk minimization. arXiv preprint arXiv:1710.09412 (2017)
24. Boixo, S.: Characterizing quantum supremacy in near-term devices. Nat. Phys. **14**(6), 595–600 (2018)

25. Cong, R.: Review of visual saliency detection with comprehensive information. IEEE Trans. Circuits Syst. Video Technol. **29**(10), 2941–2959 (2018)
26. He, K., Zhang, X., Ren, S., Sun, J.: Deep residual learning for image recognition. In: Proceedings of the IEEE conference on computer vision and pattern recognition, pp. 770–778 (2016)
27. Bergholm, V., et al.: Pennylane: automatic differentiation of hybrid quantum-classical computations. arXiv preprint arXiv:1811.04968 (2018)
28. Krizhevsky, A., Hinton, G., et al.: Learning multiple layers of features from tiny images (2009)
29. Porter, C.E., Thomas, R.G.: Fluctuations of nuclear reaction widths. Phys. Rev. **104**(2), 483 (1956)

Approximated Outlier Selection and Visualization with Approximated t-SNE

Dharamsotu Bheekya[1(✉)], Salman Abdul Moiz[2], and C. Raghavendra Rao[2]

[1] Department of Computer Science and Engineering, Sreenidhi Institute of Science and Technology, Hyderabad 501301, Telangana, India
bheekya.d@sreenidhi.edu.in

[2] School of Computer and Information Sciences, University of Hyderabad, Hyderabad 500046, Telangana, India
salman@uohyd.ac.in

Abstract. Working with high-dimensional data is inherently difficult due to its sparse distribution and structural complexity, which often obscure underlying patterns and reduce the effectiveness of visual analysis. Although technique like t-Distributed Stochastic Neighbor Embedding (t-SNE) is commonly used to map such data into lower dimensions while preserving local structures, their heavy computational demands—especially during initialization and when computing pairwise similarities—limit their use in applications that require fast or interactive performance. This paper presents a refined framework based on Approximated t-SNE (A-tSNE) to address these issues. The more efficient variant of A-tSNE employs approximate k-nearest neighbor (k-NN) searches. The refined A-tSNE is combined with sparsified graph construction based on estimates of local intrinsic dimensionality and a dynamic mechanism for detecting outliers. The Approximated Outlier Selection Factor (AOSF) is a key component of the method, which allows anomalous points to be identified and filtered out before generating the visual representation. Experimental validation on the MNIST and CIFAR-100 datasets reveals that this approach produces more precise and more informative visualizations by sharpening class boundaries, improving cluster separation, and preserving neighborhood consistency. These enhancements are further supported by quantitative assessments using trustworthiness and accuracy scores. The proposed method delivers a scalable, interactive, and outlier-aware visualization strategy that effectively balances computational efficiency with robust anomaly handling in high-dimensional data analysis.

Keywords: Outlier detection · Local Intrinsic Dimensionality · Approximated Outlier Selection Factor (AOSF) · Approximated t-SNE · Dimensionality Reduction

T. T. Quan et al. (Eds.): MIWAI 2025, LNAI 16353, pp. 101–115, 2026.
https://doi.org/10.1007/978-981-95-4957-3_9

1 Introduction

High-dimensional data analysis presents substantial challenges due to the complexity and sparsity often associated with such data spaces. Numerous dimensionality reduction techniques have been developed to mitigate these issues, enabling the transformation of data into lower-dimensional representations while preserving its essential structure. Among these, t-Distributed Stochastic Neighbor Embedding (t-SNE) [16] has gained prominence for retaining local neighborhood relationships during projection into two- or three-dimensional spaces. These low-dimensional embeddings are widely utilized to reveal hidden patterns, clusters, and anomalies that might be obscured in the original high-dimensional domain. However, despite its effectiveness, t-SNE is computationally intensive, particularly during the initialization phase and the calculation of pairwise distances, which impedes its use in interactive and real-time analytical environments.

To alleviate this limitation, the paradigm of Progressive Visual Analytics (PVA) has been introduced [18,24]. PVA enables users to interact with partial yet informative results during the computational process, allowing early-stage exploration and hypothesis generation before the final output is available. This approach is especially suitable for iterative algorithms like t-SNE, whose gradient descent-based optimization naturally yields meaningful intermediate results. However, traditional t-SNE implementations are hindered by the expensive precomputation of the high-dimensional distance matrix, which can delay visual feedback—especially when handling large-scale datasets or those containing outliers, thereby reducing its utility in dynamic data exploration scenarios.

This research addresses these challenges by improving computational efficiency and enhancing outlier detection in high-dimensional data visualization. Specifically, we integrate A-tSNE, an accelerated variant of t-SNE proposed by Pezzotti et al. [20], with sparsification, subspace selection to effectively assess local intrinsic dimensionality, and an adaptive outlier detection mechanism. A-tSNE replaces exact distance calculations with approximate k-nearest neighbor (k-NN) queries, significantly reducing the initialization time and enabling near-instantaneous embedding computation. This integration supports early interaction with the visual embedding, even in the presence of outliers, thus enhancing the exploratory power of the visual analytics process.

Beyond acceleration, our proposed framework facilitates real-time interaction with the evolving data. It accommodates dynamic modifications, including the insertion, deletion, or alteration of data points—whether inliers or outliers—without requiring a complete restart of the optimization process. The system incrementally refines the neighborhood approximations and progressively updates the embedding, allowing for continuous, real-time refinement. Moreover, users can control the approximation fidelity, enabling focused exploration of specific regions or clusters in the embedding space.

The primary contributions of this study are threefold:

1. we adopt sparsification and an efficient kNN graph construction technique, NNWID-decent [28], to improve the graph construction by using local intrinsic dimensionality.
2. We introduce a method, Approximated Outlier Selection Factor (AOSF), for effective outlier detection in high-dimensional space before visualization.
3. We adopt and extend A-tSNE [20] to support rapid initialization and interactive data updates within the Progressive Visual Analytics paradigm.
4. We empirically evaluate the integrated system using standard benchmark datasets, demonstrating significant computational performance gains and accurate visualization, even in the presence of outliers.

These contributions collectively enable more responsive and insightful visual analysis of complex, high-dimensional datasets, particularly in real-time or streaming environments where immediate feedback and adaptability are essential.

The paper is organized as follows: Sect. 2 reviews existing techniques for addressing high-dimensional data challenges, including dimensionality reduction, sparsification, and outlier detection methods. Section 3 presents a novel algorithm combining sparsification and subspace selection to enhance outlier detection based on local intrinsic dimensionality. Section 4 outlines the experimental evaluation, demonstrating the proposed approach's effectiveness on synthetic and real-world datasets. Section 5 concludes with suggestions for future research.

2 Literature Survey

Modern datasets increasing complexity and dimensionality have posed significant challenges for practical data analysis and visualization. High-dimensional data often suffers from sparsity and the "curse of dimensionality", which hinders traditional machine learning algorithms and visual exploration techniques [2] [27]. Dimensionality reduction has become an essential tool for addressing these challenges, enabling the transformation of high-dimensional data into lower-dimensional spaces while preserving key structural properties.

A wide array of linear and non-linear dimensionality reduction techniques has been proposed. While linear methods such as Principal Component Analysis (PCA) [12] and Multidimensional Scaling (MDS) [8] are computationally efficient, they often fail to capture the complex, non-linear relationships within high-dimensional data. In contrast, non-linear techniques like Locally Linear Embedding (LLE) [21], Isomap [25], and t-Distributed Stochastic Neighbor Embedding (t-SNE) [16] have been more effective in preserving local and global structures for visualization tasks.

Among these, t-SNE has emerged as a widely adopted method for embedding high-dimensional data into 2D or 3D spaces. Its ability to preserve local neighborhood relationships makes it particularly suitable for identifying clusters and revealing hidden structures. However, t-SNE is computationally expensive due to the quadratic complexity of pairwise similarity computation and the optimization process. Even with optimizations like the Barnes-Hut approximation [26] and Fast Fourier Transform-based t-SNE (FIt-SNE) [14], its application in interactive or real-time systems remains limited.

A fundamental component in dimensionality reduction is constructing a reliable k-nearest neighbor (k-NN) graph. Advanced techniques such as NNWID-Descent [28] improve k-NN graph accuracy by incorporating local intrinsic dimensionality (LID), resulting in more meaningful neighborhood structures for heterogeneous data. In parallel, approximate nearest neighbor (ANN) search libraries like FLANN [19] enable rapid neighbor retrieval using randomized KD-trees and hierarchical clustering, significantly accelerating computations for large datasets.

To overcome the limitations of latency in visualization, the concept of Progressive Visual Analytics (PVA) has been introduced [13,18,24]. PVA enables analysts to receive partial yet meaningful intermediate results during long computations, facilitating early-stage exploration, steering, and refinement. The PVA benefits iterative algorithms like t-SNE, where preliminary embeddings can offer valuable insights. However, traditional t-SNE implementations often precompute a full distance matrix in the high-dimensional space, causing significant delays before the first visual output becomes available—especially for large-scale datasets or when working with streaming or dynamically changing data [7,22].

To address these bottlenecks, Pezzotti et al. [20] introduced A-tSNE, an approximated and user-steerable extension of t-SNE designed to support progressive visual analytics. A-tSNE replaces exact distance computation with approximate k-nearest neighbor (k-NN) search using techniques like hierarchical navigable small world (HNSW) [17] graphs or randomized KD-trees [19], significantly reducing initialization time and enabling rapid interaction. The process of A-tSNE allows users to engage with visual embeddings almost instantly and refine them progressively without waiting for full convergence. Moreover, the user can steer the approximation process by focusing on specific areas of interest, facilitating targeted analysis.

Despite these improvements, one area that remains underexplored in conjunction with progressive t-SNE methods is robust outlier detection. Outliers, which often arise due to noise, data errors, or genuine rare events, can distort the local neighborhood structure and mislead the visual interpretation [1,10]. Various unsupervised outlier detection methods exist, including Local Outlier Factor (LOF) [9], Isolation Forest [15], and kNN-distance-based scoring methods [5]. However, their integration into visual embedding workflows like t-SNE is limited. Recent studies have begun exploring joint visualization and outlier detection frameworks [3,4,29], but few combine these with progressive analytics and interaction.

Our research addresses this gap by extending A-tSNE with an adaptive outlier detection mechanism tailored for high-dimensional visualization. The proposed system accelerates initialization, supports progressive refinement, and identifies and manages outliers dynamically during the embedding process. It enables real-time dataset modification—such as insertion, removal, or updates to inliers and outliers—without disrupting the visualization pipeline. Neighborhood approximations are incrementally refined in the background, allowing seamless updates and continuous embedding quality improvement. Furthermore, the user controls approximation levels, enabling granular and focused exploration of specific clusters or anomalous patterns.

In summary, while t-SNE and its variants have laid a strong foundation for visualizing high-dimensional data, their practical deployment in interactive and streaming environments requires further innovation. Progressive frameworks like PVA and approximated embedding techniques such as A-tSNE represent crucial steps in this direction. However, integrating robust outlier detection into such pipelines remains an open problem. Our work contributes a unified framework that bridges these areas, offering a scalable and interactive solution for accurate, real-time, and outlier-aware visual analytics.

3 Proposed Method

This work proposes a novel algorithm that integrates data sparsification and subspace selection to efficiently estimate local intrinsic dimensionality and identify local and global outliers, while also addressing visualization latency issues in high-dimensional data analysis. The method enhances outlier detection performance by analyzing the intrinsic dimensional structure of data and adapting distance-based similarity measures based on the dataset type.

The process begins with constructing an approximate k-Nearest Neighbor (kNN) graph, which reduces computational cost while maintaining the integrity of local neighborhood structures. The approximated kNN is used to estimate the reverse nearest neighbors (rNN), enabling the evaluation of each datapoint's relevance in the overall data manifold.

Sparsification is applied to the approximated kNN graph to represent high-dimensional data compactly. This step selectively eliminates low-informative dimensions based on a defined sparsification factor. The objective is to retain only the most relevant features, improving efficiency and interpretability while preserving local geometric characteristics. The WIDNN-Descent [28] algorithm is employed to compute Support-Weighted Intrinsic Dimensionality (SWID), a measure that captures the relevance of features in a neighborhood context. This algorithm ranks features according to their local intrinsic dimensionality and neighborhood compactness. Extending this, the NNWID-Descent algorithm integrates SWID with local neighborhood structure to quantify feature discriminability, aiding in informed feature selection during sparsification. For a data point x_i and a feature f_j, the intrinsic dimensionality with respect to f_j is estimated as follows:

$$\mathrm{ID}_{f_j} = \left[\frac{1}{k-1} \sum_{l=1}^{k-1} \ln \left(\frac{\delta_k^A(f_j)}{\delta_l^A(f_j)} \right) \right]^{-1} \tag{1}$$

Here, $\delta_k^A(f_j)$ represents the approximated distance from x_i to its k-th nearest neighbor in the subspace defined by feature f_j, and $\delta_l^A(f_j)$ are the approximated distances to the l-th nearest neighbors, where $l = 1, \ldots, k-1$. To normalize feature relevance across the dataset, a global average A_{f_j} is computed as:

$$A_{f_j} = \frac{1}{N} \sum_{i=1}^{N} \left[\frac{1}{|ANN(i, f_j)|} \sum_{l=1}^{k} \delta_l^A(f_j) \right] \tag{2}$$

In this equation, $ANN(i, f_j)$ refers to the approximated k nearest neighbors of point x_i under feature f_j. The Support-Weighted Intrinsic Dimensionality (SWID) for feature f_j at point x_i is defined as:

$$wID(f_j) = \frac{\delta_k^A(f_j)}{A_{f_j}} \tag{3}$$

This formulation highlights the discriminative strength of each feature by contrasting its local neighborhood density (via $\delta_k^A(f_j)$) with its global average (via A_{f_j}). Features with lower wID values are considered more informative and are prioritized during feature selection.

Following SWID computation, all features are ranked in descending order based on their wID scores. A fixed percentage of top-ranked features is retained, while the remainder are sparsified (i.e., their values are set to zero). This approach yields a refined dataset representation, preserving only the most informative features.

The *Approximated t-SNE* approach estimates the joint probability distribution P^A, which serves as an efficient approximation to the exact distribution P. This method retains the local structure of the data while significantly improving scalability. An *approximated conditional probability distribution* is computed to preserve neighborhood relations. This distribution reflects the likelihood that a data point x_i would consider another point x_j as its neighbor, based on their affinity as measured by a distance function. The approximated conditional probability $p_{j|i}^A$ is defined as:

$$p_{j|i}^A = \begin{cases} \dfrac{\exp\left(-\frac{d^A(x_i,x_j)^2}{2\sigma_i^2}\right)}{\sum\limits_{k\in\mathcal{N}_i} \exp\left(-\frac{d^A(x_i,x_k)^2}{2\sigma_i^2}\right)} & \text{if} \quad j \in \mathcal{N}_i \\ 0 & \end{cases} \tag{4}$$

Here, $d^A(x_i, x_j)$ denotes the distance between points x_i and x_j, and σ_i is the local bandwidth parameter associated with point x_i. The neighborhood $\mathcal{N}_i$ consists of the exact K-nearest neighbors of x_i, where K is typically chosen as $\lfloor 3\mu \rfloor$, with μ representing the user-defined *perplexity* parameter. The parameter σ_i is determined through a binary search procedure to match the desired perplexity μ, which governs the effective number of neighbors by controlling the entropy of the distribution.

To improve accuracy, we refine the neighborhood structure by computing the exact neighbors for one data point at a time. This results in a mix of precise and approximated neighborhoods. Whenever a neighborhood is updated, a new Gaussian distribution P_i is calculated, and the sparse disjoint-probability matrix P^A is adjusted accordingly. Updating P^A is challenging for two reasons: (1) its symmetric form combines distributions from multiple points, and (2) its sparse nature makes fast updates difficult.

We avoid directly computing the full matrix P^A to overcome this. The symmetric form of the conditional probabilities $p_{j|i}$ and $p_{i|j}$can be written as:

$$p_{ij} = \frac{p^A_{j|i} + p^A_{i|j}}{2N} \tag{5}$$

This approach simplifies the update process, maintains sparsity, and ensures efficient computation.

The pairwise similarity between data points is computed using the approximated neighbor set $\mathcal{N}_i^A$. To evaluate the quality of the approximation, we define the *precision* ρ of the kNN algorithm. This metric quantifies the average proportion of true neighbors in the approximated neighborhood across all data points. Formally, the precision ρ is defined as:

$$\rho = \sum_{i=1}^{N} \frac{\rho_i}{N} \quad \text{where} \quad \rho_k = \frac{|\mathcal{N}_k^A \cap \mathcal{N}_k|}{|\mathcal{N}_k|} \tag{6}$$

Here, $|\cdot|$ denotes the cardinality of a set, $\mathcal{N}_k$ is the exact neighborhood of point x_k, and $\mathcal{N}_k^A$ is its approximated counterpart. The intersection $\mathcal{N}_k^A \cap \mathcal{N}_k$ represents the number of correctly retrieved neighbors. The user does not explicitly define the size of the exact neighborhood N_k but is indirectly determined based on the perplexity parameter μ, typically set to three times the perplexity value. The precision parameter ρ can be user-specified to control the fidelity of the approximation. Higher values of ρ indicate a greater overlap between approximated and exact neighborhoods, leading to a closer match between P^A and P, and consequently, a more accurate approximation of the true embedding.

We propose the Approximated Stochastic Outlier Selection (ASOS) framework for robust outlier detection. This technique utilizes the approximated reverse nearest neighbor (rNN) structure and the approximated conditional probabilities defined in Eq. 4 to identify points deviating from typical neighborhood patterns. The central intuition is that an outlier will have weak support from its RNNs regarding the conditional inclusion probability. The ASOS for a data point x_i as the average divergence from inclusion over all reverse neighbors:

$$\text{ASOS}(x_i) = \frac{1}{|\text{rNN}^A(x_i)|} \sum_{\forall j \in \text{rNN}^A(x_i)} \left(1 - p^A_{j|i}\right) \tag{7}$$

Here, $\text{rNN}(x_i)^A$ denotes the set of points for which x_i appears in their k-nearest neighbors. A high ASOS score indicates that point x_i is seldom favored as a neighbor by others, implying it may lie in a sparse or anomalous region of the data space.

Outliers detected using the proposed metric generally exhibit a combination of key attributes: they are typically associated with a small set of Approximated reverse nearest neighbors (rNN), suggesting that few other data points recognize them as neighbors; they also demonstrate low affinity with their corresponding reverse neighbors, indicating a lack of substantial similarity; and they tend to have high ASOS, which reflect their divergence from the structure of the surrounding data. To enhance the precision of identifying such anomalies, we define the Approximated Outlier Selection Factor (AOSF), which combines the ASOS value with the relative size of the rNN set. This integration provides a more holistic measure of outlierness by penalizing data points that are sparsely referenced and structurally distinct from most of the dataset.

$$\mathrm{AOSF}(x_i) = \mathrm{ASOS}(x_i) \cdot \left(1 - \frac{|\mathrm{rNN}^A(x_i)|}{\mu}\right) \tag{8}$$

The multiplier penalizes large rNN sizes, increasing AOSF values for those with fewer reverse neighbors. A larger AOSF indicates a higher potential for the point to be an outlier. We adopt a histogram-based thresholding strategy on the AOSF scores to finalize outlier identification. Analyzing the score distribution, points that significantly deviate from the norm are labeled anomalies. This approach ensures a data-driven threshold selection based on global distributional characteristics.

The low-dimensional representation generated by t-SNE employs a Student t-distribution to model pairwise similarities in the embedded space. This choice of distribution, which has heavier tails than a Gaussian, helps to alleviate the *crowding problem* by allowing moderate distances in the high-dimensional space to be mapped more accurately in lower dimensions. The approximated similarity q_{ij}^A between two embedded points y_i and y_j is calculated as:

$$q_{ij}^A = \frac{(1 + \|y_i - y_j\|^2)^{-1}}{\sum_{k=1}^{N} \sum_{l \neq k} (1 + \|y_k - y_l\|^2)^{-1}}, \quad q_{ii} = 0 \tag{9}$$

Here, $\|y_i - y_j\|^2$ represents the squared Euclidean distance between the low-dimensional embeddings of data points x_i and x_j. To avoid self-similarity, the term q_{ii} is set to zero.

The primary objective of *Approximated t-SNE* [20] is to project high-dimensional data into a low-dimensional space while preserving local neighborhood relationships. The neighborhood relationship is achieved by minimizing the Kullback-Leibler (KL) divergence between the approximated high-dimensional similarity distribution P^A and the corresponding low-dimensional distribution Q^A. The cost function defines the optimization objective:

$$C(P^A, Q^A) = \sum_{i \neq j} p_{ij}^A \log\left(\frac{p_{ij}^A}{q_{ij}^A}\right) \tag{10}$$

By minimizing this objective, the algorithm adjusts the low-dimensional coordinates so that the similarities in Q^A best reflect those in P^A, resulting in an interpretable and faithful low-dimensional embedding suitable for visualization. The gradient of the cost function [16] with respect to the low-dimensional coordinate y_i is given by:

$$\frac{\partial C}{\partial y_i} = 4 \sum_j (p_{ij} - q_{ij}) q_{ij} Z (y_i - y_j) \tag{11}$$

Here, the term $Z = (1 + \|y_i - y_j\|^2)^{-1}$ acts as a normalization factor derived from the Student's t-distribution. This gradient guides the updates of the embedding positions during optimization.

The coordinates of the low-dimensional embeddings are updated iteratively [16]. At each iteration t, the position matrix $Y^{(t+1)}$ is updated using the following rule:

$$Y^{(t+1)} = Y^{(t)} + \eta \frac{\partial C}{\partial y_i} + \alpha(t) \left(Y^{(t-1)} - Y^{(t-2)} \right) \tag{12}$$

Here, η denotes the learning rate, and $\alpha(t)$ represents the momentum coefficient at iteration t, which helps accelerate convergence and smooth the updates. The iterative process continues until the embedding stabilizes or a maximum number of iterations is reached.

4 Experimental Evaluation

The impact of varying precision values ρ on the quality of low-dimensional embeddings is illustrated in Fig. 1, using the MNIST dataset as input. Each data point is color-coded based on the corresponding digit label for visualization and validation. Figure 1(a) presents the embedding obtained with exact neighborhood computation, serving as the ground truth reference. In contrast, Fig. 1(b) displays the result when approximated neighborhoods are employed with a precision of $\rho = 0.50$. Despite using an approximate method, the structural layout of the clusters remains broadly consistent with the exact version.

As the approximation precision decreases, illustrated in Fig. 1(d) with $\rho = 0.15$, the embedding begins to diverge slightly from the exact t-SNE visualization. Despite this minor deviation, the overall grouping of similar data points remains well preserved. A major benefit of using approximate neighborhoods is the dramatic reduction in computation time. For example, while the exact t-SNE algorithm requires roughly 5,395 seconds for initialization, employing a high precision of $\rho = 1.0$ reduces this time to 180 seconds, resulting in a dramatic speedup. Reducing the precision to $\rho = 0.5$ further lowers the initialization time to 60 seconds, and a precision of $\rho = 0.15$ decreases it even more to just 20 seconds. These results highlight the efficiency of the approximation approach, which substantially accelerates computation while maintaining clustering quality.

Figure 2 illustrates a series of histograms depicting the distribution of outlier scores under four different selection strategies: AOSF, Outlier Selection Factor

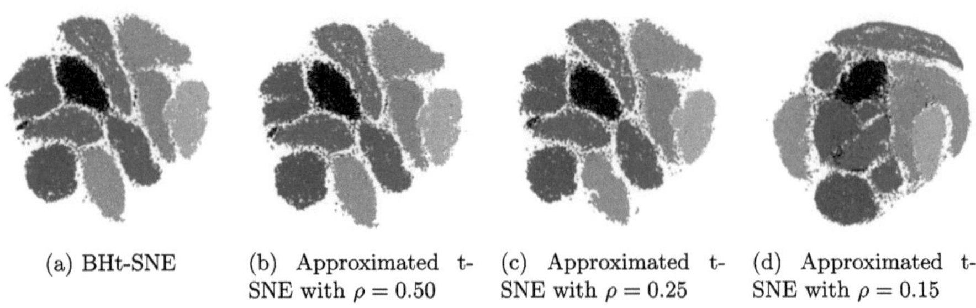

(a) BHt-SNE (b) Approximated t-SNE with $\rho = 0.50$ (c) Approximated t-SNE with $\rho = 0.25$ (d) Approximated t-SNE with $\rho = 0.15$

Fig. 1. 2D Visual representation of original and sparsified data of the MNIST dataset using t-SNE.

(OSF) [6], Intrinsic Stochastic Outlier Score (ISOS) [23], and Stochastic Outlier Score (SOS) [11], shown respectively in sub-figures (a) to (d). In each histogram, the x-axis represents the outlierness score, which increases from left to right, while the y-axis indicates the number of data points falling within each score interval. A vertical threshold line is drawn in each sub-figure to demarcate normal instances from outliers. Data points to the right of the threshold line exhibit higher outlier scores, indicating significant deviation from local neighborhood structures, whereas those on the left are more consistent with the underlying data manifold. These visualizations provide a clear and intuitive comparison of how each strategy defines and isolates anomalous patterns. The progression of outlierness from left to right, along with the placement of the threshold, highlights the effectiveness of each method in capturing varying degrees of deviation within the dataset.

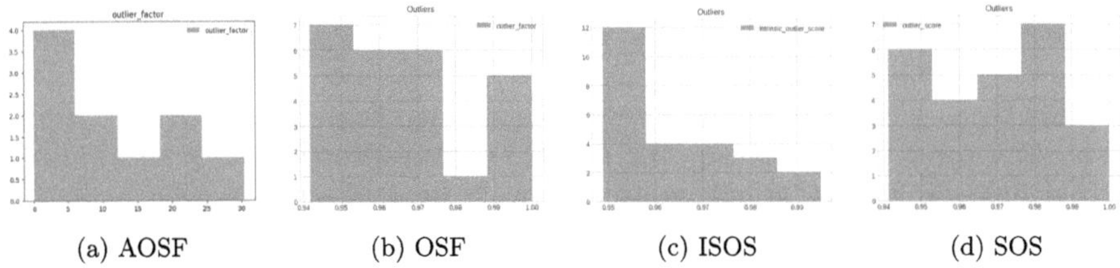

(a) AOSF (b) OSF (c) ISOS (d) SOS

Fig. 2. Histogram of outlier scores of ASOF, OSF, ISOS, and SOS techniques.

Figure 3 highlights the influence of perplexity settings on outlier detection performance. Sub-figure 3(a) demonstrates the trade-off between outlier scores and varying perplexity values, illustrating the importance of appropriately tuning this parameter for accurate anomaly identification. The performance of the BH-t-SNE [26] algorithm, which relies on preserving local neighborhood structures in the low-dimensional space, is susceptible to the perplexity setting, as it directly impacts the estimation of local density and the algorithm's responsiveness to anomalies. Sub-figure 3(b) presents the relationship between the AOSF and the cardinality of the rNN set. This correlation reveals how frequently a given data point is included in the neighborhoods of others—an important indicator of its typicality within the data manifold. Points with a small rNN set but high AOSF values tend to be strong outlier candidates. These visualizations collectively demonstrate that perplexity affects the neighborhood preservation of BH-t-SNE and influences the composition of rNNs, thereby impacting the precision of outlier scoring.

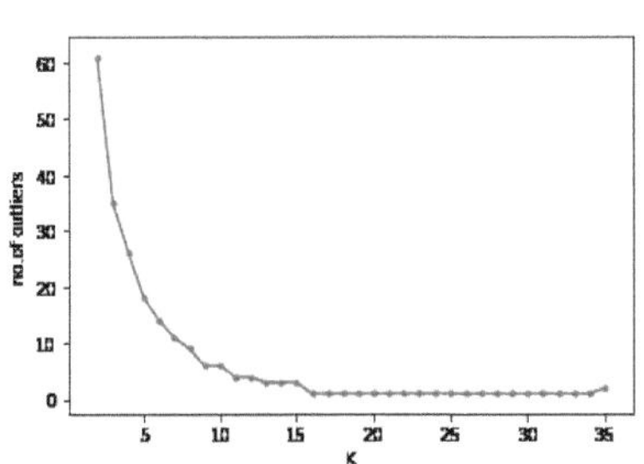

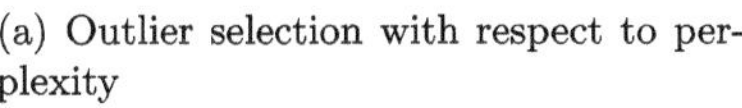
(a) Outlier selection with respect to perplexity

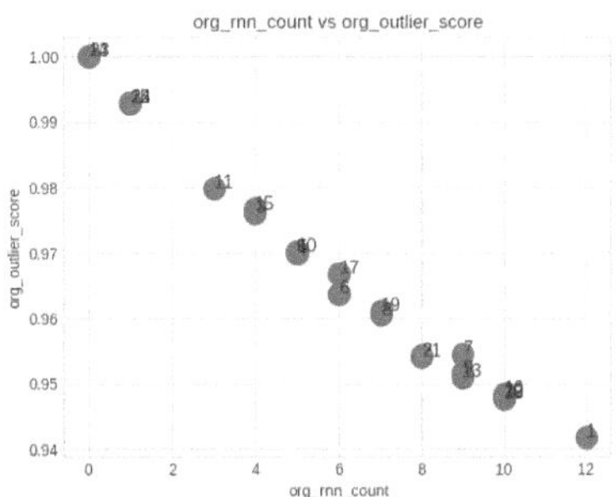

(b) AOSF score vs cardinality of rNN

Fig. 3. The relationship between outlier selection and outlierness concerning AOSF score and rNN cardinality.

Figure 4 presents a comparative visualization of the MNIST dataset using Approximated t-SNE. Sub-figure 4(a) displays the two-dimensional embedding that includes data points identified as outliers by the AOSF, while sub-figure 4(b) shows the embedding after these outliers have been removed. The comparison clearly illustrates the positive impact of outlier elimination on the structure and interpretability of the visualization. When outliers are present, the clusters corresponding to different digit classes appear less compact, with blurred boundaries and noticeable overlaps, which can mask the underlying organization of the data. In contrast, removing these anomalous points results in more coherent and tightly grouped clusters, with sharper separations between classes. This enhanced clarity improves visual interpretability and provides a more reliable basis for classification, labeling, and further exploratory data analysis.

Table 1 compares Exact t-SNE and A-tSNE embeddings for MNIST and CIFAR-100, reporting runtime, trustworthiness, and 5-NN accuracy both with and without outliers. A-tSNE significantly reduces computation time compared to Exact t-SNE while maintaining high embedding quality. As the approximation precision decreases, the runtime further decreases with only minor drops in trustworthiness and accuracy. Removing outliers slightly improves metrics, particularly for CIFAR-100, showing that extreme points can affect local neighborhood preservation. Overall, the table highlights the balance between speed

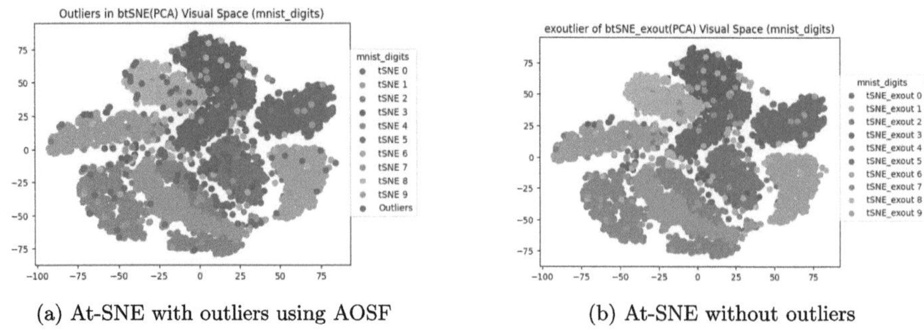

(a) At-SNE with outliers using AOSF

(b) At-SNE without outliers

Fig. 4. 2D visualization of the MNIST dataset using Approximated t-SNE, embeddings with outliers identified by AOSF, and embeddings after outlier removal.

Table 1. Comparison of Exact t-SNE and A-tSNE embeddings with varying precision for MNIST and CIFAR-100. Metrics are reported separately for **with outliers** and **without outliers**.

Dataset	Method	Precision	With Outliers			Without Outliers		
			Runtime (seconds)	Trust (T)	5-NN Acc (%)	Runtime (seconds)	Trust (T)	5-NN Acc (%)
MNIST	t-SNE	—	~5395	0.987	98.1	~5100	0.990	98.1
	A-tSNE	1.0	~180	0.985	97.8	~168	0.988	97.9
	A-tSNE	0.8	~108	0.982	97.3	~102	0.985	97.5
	A-tSNE	0.5	~60	0.975	96.5	~56	0.978	96.8
	A-tSNE	0.15	~20	0.95	95.5	~18	0.96	96.1
CIFAR-100	t-SNE	—	~7200	0.973	78.4	~6900	0.977	78.7
	A-tSNE	1.0	~900	0.969	77.9	~780	0.972	78.2
	A-tSNE	0.8	~420	0.964	77.1	~390	0.967	77.5
	A-tSNE	0.5	~300	0.957	76.2	~282	0.960	76.5
	A-tSNE	0.15	~120	0.94	75.9	~108	0.946	76.2

and embedding fidelity, demonstrating that A-tSNE provides an efficient alternative with minimal compromise in performance.

Figure 5 provides a comparative analysis of the Accuracy and Trustworthiness metrics for the proposed Approximated t-SNE and the baseline t-SNE on the MNIST dataset, considering the impact of outliers identified by the AOSF. The figure illustrates how outliers negatively affect the reliability of neighborhood preservation—measured by trustworthiness—and the accuracy of the resulting low-dimensional embedding. In particular, embeddings generated with outliers misrepresent local neighborhood relationships, reducing trustworthiness scores due to distorted proximity between similar data points. Similarly, embedding accuracy is compromised as outliers introduce noise that disrupts the overall structure, causing classes to overlap or drift. In contrast, both metrics show noticeable improvement when outliers are removed based on AOSF. The proposed method enhances visualization clarity and ensures a more faithful representation of the original high-dimensional structure in the reduced space.

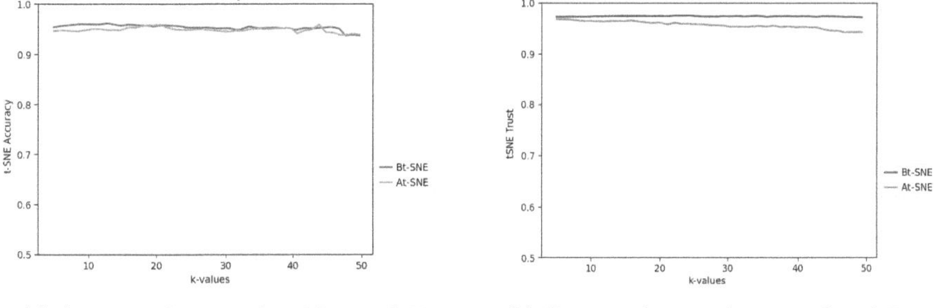

(a) Accuracy of proposed and Base t-SNE

(b) Trustworthiness of proposed and Base t-SNE

Fig. 5. Accuracy and Trustworthiness comparison between the proposed Approximated t-SNE and the baseline t-SNE on the MNIST dataset, incorporating outliers identified by the AOSF.

5 Conclusion and Future Work

This study presents a scalable framework for visualizing high-dimensional data that tackles two significant challenges: computational cost and reliable outlier detection. The method extends A-tSNE by integrating approximate k-nearest neighbor searches with sparsified graph construction driven by local intrinsic dimensionality estimates. At the core of the design is the AOSF, which enables efficient detection and removal of anomalous points before embedding. The framework incorporates SWID, its extension NNWID-Descent, and ASOS to improve feature relevance assessment and anomaly separation further. Evaluation on the MNIST and CIFAR-100 datasets demonstrates that the approach produces more coherent clusters, more precise class boundaries, and consistent neighborhood structures, while reducing execution time by over two orders of magnitude compared to traditional methods. These results show that the framework supports accuracy and scalability, making it suitable for interactive analysis. Potential future directions include adaptive perplexity tuning, application to heterogeneous data types, and integration with manifold learning or deep generative models, with broad applicability across domains such as bioinformatics, network monitoring, and security analytics.

References

1. Aggarwal, C.C.: Outlier analysis. Springer (2017)
2. Aggarwal, C.C., Hinneburg, A., Keim, D.A.: On the surprising behavior of distance metrics in high dimensional space. International Conference on Database Theory, pp. 420–434 (2001)
3. Alrawashdeh, K., et al.: Toward an integrated framework for visual anomaly detection. In: 2016 IEEE Conference on Visual Analytics Science and Technology (VAST), pp. 1–10. IEEE (2016)
4. An, J., Cho, S.: Variational autoencoder based anomaly detection using reconstruction probability. In: Special Lecture on IE, vol. 2, pp. 1–18 (2015)
5. Angiulli, F., Pizzuti, C.: Fast outlier detection in high dimensional spaces. In: European conference on principles of data mining and knowledge discovery, pp. 15–27. Springer (2002)
6. Bheekya, D., Moiz, S.A., Rao, C.R.: Outlier selection with local intrinsic dimensionality and visualization using t-SNE. In: International Conference on Multidisciplinary Trends in Artificial Intelligence, pp. 139–151. Springer (2024)
7. Binnig, C., Hentschel, B., Kraska, T., Pedersen, T.B.: Towards real-time progressive analytics. In: CIDR (2017)
8. Borg, I., Groenen, P.: Modern Multidimensional Scaling: theory and applications. Springer (2005)
9. Breunig, M.M., Kriegel, H.P., Ng, R.T., Sander, J.: Lof: identifying density-based local outliers. ACM SIGMOD Rec. **29**(2), 93–104 (2000)
10. Chandola, V., Banerjee, A., Kumar, V.: Anomaly detection: a survey. ACM Comput. Surv. **41**(3), 15 (2009)
11. Janssens, J., Huszár, F., Postma, E., Van den Herik, H.: Stochastic outlier selection. Tilburg centre for Creative Comput. techreport **1**, 2012 (2012)
12. Jolliffe, I.T.: Principal Component Analysis. Springer (2002)
13. Keim, D., Kohlhammer, J., Ellis, G., Mansmann, F.: Mastering the information age solving problems with visual analytics. Eurographics Association (2010)
14. Linderman, G.C., Rachh, M., Hoskins, J.G., Steinerberger, S., Kluger, Y.: Fast interpolation-based t-SNE for improved visualization of single-cell RNA-seq data. Nat. Methods **16**(3), 243–245 (2019)
15. Liu, F.T., Ting, K.M., Zhou, Z.H.: Isolation forest. In: 2008 Eighth IEEE International Conference on Data Mining, pp. 413–422. IEEE (2008)
16. van der Maaten, L., Hinton, G.: Visualizing data using t-SNE. J. Mach. Learn. Res. **9**(Nov), 2579–2605 (2008)
17. Malkov, Y.A., Yashunin, D.A.: Efficient and robust approximate nearest neighbor search using hierarchical navigable small world graphs. IEEE Trans. Pattern Anal. Mach. Intell. (2020)
18. Mühlbacher, T., Piringer, H., Gratzl, S., Sedlmair, M., Streit, M.: Opening the black box: strategies for increased user involvement in existing algorithm implementations. IEEE Trans. Visual Comput. Graphics **20**(12), 1643–1652 (2014)
19. Muja, M., Lowe, D.G.: Fast approximate nearest neighbors with automatic algorithm configuration. In: VISAPP (1), vol. 2, pp. 331–340 (2009)
20. Pezzotti, N.: Approximated and user steerable t-SNE for progressive visual analytics. IEEE Trans. Visual Comput. Graphics **23**(7), 1739–1752 (2016)
21. Roweis, S.T., Saul, L.K.: Nonlinear dimensionality reduction by locally linear embedding. Science **290**(5500), 2323–2326 (2000)

22. Sacha, D., Senaratne, H., Kwon, B.C., Ellis, G., Keim, D.A.: The role of uncertainty, awareness, and trust in visual analytics. In: IEEE Transactions on Visualization and Computer Graphics, vol. 22, pp. 240–249 (2016)
23. Schubert, E., Gertz, M.: Intrinsic t-stochastic neighbor embedding for visualization and outlier detection: a remedy against the curse of dimensionality? In: International Conference on Similarity Search and Applications, pp. 188–203. Springer (2017)
24. Stolper, C.D., Perer, A., Gotz, D.: Progressive visual analytics: user-driven visual exploration of in-progress analytics. IEEE Trans. Visual Comput. Graphics **20**(12), 1653–1662 (2014)
25. Tenenbaum, J.B., de Silva, V., Langford, J.C.: A global geometric framework for nonlinear dimensionality reduction. Science **290**(5500), 2319–2323 (2000)
26. Van Der Maaten, L.: Accelerating t-SNE using tree-based algorithms. J. Mach. Learn. Res. **15**(1), 3221–3245 (2014)
27. Verleysen, M., François, D.: The curse of dimensionality in data mining and time series prediction. International Work-Conference on Artificial Neural Networks, pp. 758–770 (2005)
28. Wang, X., Chen, Z., Li, R., Lin, D.: Nnwid-descent: learning nearest neighbor graphs based on local intrinsic dimensionality. In: Proceedings of the IEEE/CVF International Conference on Computer Vision (ICCV), pp. 4894–4903 (2019)
29. Zhao, J., Wang, Z., Chen, W., Yang, J., Qu, H.: A new visual analytics approach for understanding outliers in high-dimensional data. IEEE Trans. Visual Comput. Graphics **25**(1), 287–296 (2019)

Spread-Learned Spatial Features to Improve Tick-Shape Networks

Canh Ngoc Hoang[1], Thanh Phuong Nguyen[2], Hoang Anh Pham[3], Thinh Vinh Le[1], Thi-The Phan[1], and Thanh Tuan Nguyen[1](✉)

[1] Faculty of IT, HCMC University of Technology and Education, HCM City, Vietnam
{thinhlv,thept,tuannt}@hcmute.edu.vn

[2] University of Côte d'Azur, I3S, CNRS, UMR 7271, Sophia Antipolis, France
tpnguyen@i3s.unice.fr

[3] Autonomous Vehicles and Intelligent Systems Laboratory, Posts and Telecommunications Institute of Technology, Hanoi, Vietnam
anhph@ptit.edu.vn

Abstract. The rapid growth of mobile devices and embedded systems requires lightweight networks with high performance in reasonable complexity. Recently, TickNets have been proposed to meet that requirement via connecting several tick-shape backbones. However, their performance is still at modest levels due to the lack of spatial features exploited from a basic tick-shape backbone. To mitigate this problem, an efficient perceptron is proposed to take into account spread-learned spatial features for improving the learning ability of tick-shape networks. Accordingly, this spread-learned feature extractor is simply done by adding a Full Residual Point-Depth-Point (FR-PDP) block to the beginning of a basic backbone. Such strategy will ensure two practical benefits for the tick-shape networks: *i)* Exploiting the identical FR-PDP-based features in a tick-shape backbone; and *ii)* Extracting more discriminative spatial features for the learning process. Finally, STickNets are formed by simply connecting several spread-learned tick-shape backbones. Experimental results on various benchmark datasets have indicated that our proposal has significantly boosted the performance of tick-shape networks. In particular, STickNet-basic is enhanced by ∼3.5% on CIFAR-100, up to 7.4% on Stanford Dogs. The implementation code is available at https://github.com/ngochc/STicknets.

Keywords: Lightweight models · depthwise/pointwise convolutions · CNN-based networks · Full-residual mechanism · Image classification

1 Introduction

Lightweight CNN-based networks [1–12] play a crucial role in deploying many baseline applications in mobile devices as well as edge computing systems. This is because those devices often have inherent limitations in computational ability

T. T. Quan et al. (Eds.): MIWAI 2025, LNAI 16353, pp. 116–129, 2026.
https://doi.org/10.1007/978-981-95-4957-3_10

and storage resources. In order to obtain a low-complexity architecture, most of the lightweight CNN-based networks often take into account several lightweight operators in their perceptive layers for efficient feature extraction. Recently, Nguyen *et al.* [13] introduced TickNets that are constructed in consideration of connecting multiple tick-shape backbones in a network unity. Each basic tick-shape backbone consists of 5 FR-PDP blocks, which allow the concerning model to capture discriminative features for its learning process. Although TickNets obtained significant performance in tasks of image recognition, their rates are still at modest levels. It can be due to the lack of exploiting the spatial patterns of a given tensor for the learning process of TickNets. To mitigate this problem, an extra-perceptive block is proposed in this work by addressing a sequential function $\Phi(\mathcal{T})$ of several lightweight operators for an input tensor $\mathcal{T}$. The proposed block is then hooked at the beginning stage of feature extraction in a basic tick-shape backbone. This connection would allow the learning process to take advantage of the most spread-learned information of spatial features for performance improvement. Accordingly, three efficient lightweight tick-shape networks (named STickNets) will be formed by connecting multiple of the proposed spread-learned tick-shape backbones. Note that the construction of STickNets should be in accordance with that of TickNets [13] for objective evaluations. Experimental results for image recognition on benchmark datasets have validated that our proposed perceptive module has boosted the performance of tick-shape networks thanks to exploiting spread-learned spatial features. In short, the main contributions of this work can be summarized as follows.

- An efficient perceptive block is proposed to exploit the spread-learned spatial patterns of a given tensor.
- A basic tick-shape backbone is expanded by hooking the proposed perceptron at the early learning stage to capture the most spread-learned information.
- Three lightweight STickNets are formed by connecting multiple of the proposed spread-learned tick-shape backbones.
- Experimental results have verified the good performance of STickNets versus TickNets as well as other existing lightweight CNN-based networks.

2 Related Works

2.1 Lightweight Convolutional Neural Networks (LWCNNs)

LWCNNs [1,9,14–16] have a lightweight architecture that is specially designed for image analysis tasks on resource-constrained devices as well as embedded systems. The primary objective is to build a tiny model with a small number of parameters and low computing time while preserving the accuracy at reasonable levels [8,17,18]. To this end, two lightweight convolutional operators are often addressed in perceptive layers to structure a lightweight architecture, i.e., depthwise and pointwise convolutions. Concretely, let $\mathcal{T} \in \mathbb{R}^{\mathcal{C}_{in} \times \mathcal{H} \times \mathcal{W}}$ be an input tensor, where $\mathcal{C}_{in}$ denotes #channels of $\mathcal{T}$; $\mathcal{H} \times \mathcal{W}$ is for its spatial size.

The separable depthwise convolution is defined by convolving a $1 \times k \times k$ kernel η_i on a channel c_i of $\mathcal{T}$ as $DW(\mathcal{T}) = c_i * \eta_i$, $i = 1, .., \mathcal{C}_{in}$. As the separable operations, the output $\mathcal{T}_{DW}$ would be a depthwise-based tensor with the same #channels as $\mathcal{T}$. It can be seen that no new feature has been made for the learning process since such a depthwise convolution is like a filtering operation on $\mathcal{T}$. To overcome this problem, a pointwise convolution is usually addressed for $\mathcal{T}_{DW}$ as $PW(\mathcal{T}_{DW}) = \mu_i * \mathcal{T}_{DW}$, where μ_i is a $C_{in} \times 1 \times 1$ kernel. This convolution will be executed in $\mathcal{C}_{out}$ times (i.e., $i = 1, .., \mathcal{C}_{out}$) for a new feature maps $\mathcal{T}_{PW} \in \mathbb{R}^{\mathcal{C}_{out} \times \mathcal{H} \times \mathcal{W}}$. Note that these lightweight operators have been addressed in disregard of the spatial changes of tensors for a convenient presentation.

2.2 A Brief of TickNets

Motivated by the efficacy of the above operators, many lightweight models [2–4, 9–12] have been proposed to deal with image recognition tasks. Recently, Nguyen *et al.* [13] proposed TickNets by hooking several tick-shape backbones. Therein, a tick-shape backbone is formed by 5 FR-PDP blocks for a given tensor $\mathcal{T}$ as

$$\text{Tick\_B}(\mathcal{T}) = \phi_s^{512}(\phi_s^{256}(\phi_s^{128}(\phi_s^{64}(\phi_s^{128}(\mathcal{T}))))) \tag{1}$$

where $\phi_s^{\mathcal{C}_{out}}(.)$ denotes the execution of an FR-PDP block with $stride = s$ for an output tensor with $\mathcal{C}_{out}$ channels. Accordingly, three tick-shaped networks are structured as follows. TickNet-basic($\mathcal{T}$) $\equiv$ Tick_B($\mathcal{T}$); TickNet-small($\mathcal{T}$) = Tick_B(Tick_B($\mathcal{T}$)); and TickNet-large($\mathcal{T}$) = TickNet-small(Tick_B($\mathcal{T}$)) (please refer to [13] for the construction of FR-PDP and tick-shape networks in detail). Experimental results in image classification have validated that their performance is still at modest levels due to the lack of spatial features extracted from the basic tick-shape backbone. To this end, we present an extra perceptron to exploit more spatial patterns for the learning process of TickNets.

3 Proposed Method

3.1 Spread-Learned Spatial Features for a Tick-Shape Backbone

As mentioned above, a basic tick-shape backbone can exploit less spatial information of a given tensor. This can lead to a modest learning ability of TickNets [13]. To mitigate this issue, an efficient perceptron is proposed to take into account spread-learned spatial features to improve the performance of tick-shape networks. It is simply hooked at the beginning stage of a tick-shape backbone for efficient feature extraction. Hereafter, these processes will be presented in detail.

Let us consider a given tensor $\mathcal{T} \in \mathbb{R}^{C_{in} \times H \times W}$, where C_{in} and $H \times W$ correspond to its #channels and spatial dimensions, respectively. To extract the spatial patterns of $\mathcal{T}$ for a learning process, we propose a general perceptron block that includes a sequence of n lightweight operations as

$$\Phi_s^{\mathcal{C}_{out}}(\mathcal{T}) = Sequential\big(LWO_s^n(LWO_s^{n-1}...(LWO_s^1(\mathcal{T})))\big) \tag{2}$$

where $LWO_s^i(.)$ denotes the ith lightweight convolutional operator with $stride = s$, i.e., $LWO_s^i(.)$ can be either a depthwise $DW(.)$ or a pointwise $PW(.)$; $\mathcal{C}_{out}$ means the desired #channels of an output tensor. It should be noted that only one $DW(.)$ in $LWO_s^i(.)$ is executed with $stride = 2$, while the others will go with $stride = 1$. This is to exploit more spatial information for the learning process, while the computational complexity is still at a reasonable level.

As well-known, the last layers of a tick-shape backbone [13] would exploit deeper perceptive patterns rather than spatial features. Therefore, to address spread-learned spatial features, the proposed feature extractor $\Phi_s^{\mathcal{C}_{out}}(.)$ should be allocated at the early stage of a tick-shape backbone. Besides, the resultant backbone has to ensure its channel elasticity in a check-mark shape, i.e., $\mathcal{C}_{out} = 256$. Accordingly, a new basic tick-shape backbone is formed as

$$\text{STick\_B}(\mathcal{T}) = \text{Tick\_B}(\Phi_s^{256}(\mathcal{T})) \tag{3}$$

Because Tick_B(.) is structured by FR-PDP blocks, we suggest that $\Phi_s^{256}(.)$ should be another FR-PDP block to exploit the identical FR-PDP-based features in the whole tick-shape architecture. In other words, the lightweight operators $LWO_s^i(.)$ in Eq. (2) are agreed with those in a FR-PDP block, i.e., $\Phi_s^{256}(.) \equiv \text{FR-PDP}_s^{256}(.)$, (refer to [13] for the detailed description of a FR-PDP perceptron in detail). Figure 1(a) illustrates an intuitive view of the entire architecture of STick_B, where the gray-scale rectangle indicates the extraction of spread-learned spatial features. Meanwhile, Fig. 2 visually shows the better representation of our STick_B in comparison with the original Tick_B. Therein, the STick_B-based feature maps represented the fine spatial patterns of a beagle-dog that had allowed the learning process to take more discriminative information for its performance improvement (see Sect. 4.2 for thorough discussions).

Subject to the definition of different tick-shape versions [13], we can structure several corresponding networks based on the proposed STick_B backbone for objective evaluations as follows. STickNet-basic is identical to STick_B, while STickNet-small is formed by hooking two basic STick_B backbones as

$$\text{STickNet-small}(\mathcal{T}) = \text{STickNet\_B}(\text{STickNet\_B}(\mathcal{T})) \tag{4}$$

Figure 1(b) for a visual view of the STickNet-small architecture. Similarly, STickNet-large is structured by allocating three basic STickNet_B backbones as

$$\text{STickNet-large}(\mathcal{T}) = \text{STickNet\_B}(\text{STickNet\_B}(\text{STickNet\_B}(\mathcal{T}))) \tag{5}$$

In short, Table 1 shows the entire architecture of the proposed STickNets for learning 224×224 images, where "#" denotes the perceptron block that is executed with $stride = 1$ for learning the 32×32 images. The implementation code is available at https://github.com/ngochc/STicknets.

3.2 Practical Benefits of Spread-Learned Spatial Features

It can be seen that exploiting the spread-learned spatial features for the learning process of a basic tick-shape backbone will ensure two practical benefits

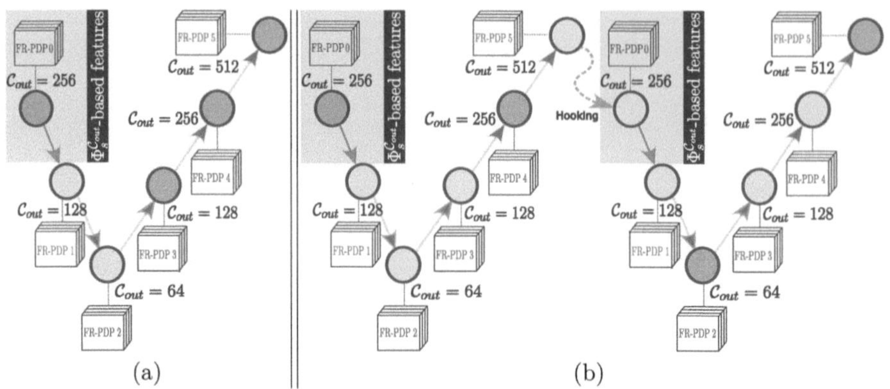

Fig. 1. Illustration of STickNet-basic (a) and STickNet-small (b) with spread-learned spatial features for learning 224×224 images. Therein, the green nodes denote a feature extractor executed with *stride* = 2. (Color figure online)

Fig. 2. Better representation of spatial features of STick_B versus those of Tick_B [13].

as follows. Firstly, taking into account the identical FR-PDP-based features can enhance the performance thanks to the consistent property of the feature extraction in the whole architecture. Indeed, experimental results have validated the less discrimination of image representation when addressing $\Phi_s^{\mathcal{C}_{out}}$ for learning miscellaneous features (see Sect. 4.2 for thorough validations). Secondly, the proposed $\Phi_s^{\mathcal{C}_{out}}$ perceptron can extract more discriminative spatial features for the learning process. This is due to addressing it at the beginning stage of a tick-shape backbone, where the spatial region of a given tensor is still large enough for learning spatial features of objects in the concerning image (i.e., 112×112 as shown in Table 1, see Sect. 4.2 for thorough discussions). Furthermore, it should be mentioned that hooking the proposed $\Phi_s^{\mathcal{C}_{out}}$ block would increase the learnable parameters. As presented in [13], the learnable parameters of an FR-PDP block are approximated as $\mathcal{Q}_{\text{FR-PDP}} \approx 3\mathcal{C}_{out}^2 + 9\mathcal{C}_{out}$, i.e., $\mathcal{Q}_{\text{Tick\_B}} \approx 5 \times \mathcal{Q}_{\text{FR-PDP}}$ with 5 FR-PDP blocks. Therefore, as structured in Table 1, it can be deduced that $\mathcal{Q}_{\text{STickNet-basic}} \approx 6 \times \mathcal{Q}_{\text{FR-PDP}}$ due to $\Phi(.) \equiv \text{FR-PDP}(.)$, as suggested in Sect. 3.1. Similarly, we have $\mathcal{Q}_{\text{STickNet-small}} \approx 12 \times \mathcal{Q}_{\text{FR-PDP}}$ versus $\mathcal{Q}_{\text{TickNet-small}} \approx 10 \times \mathcal{Q}_{\text{FR-PDP}}$ and $\mathcal{Q}_{\text{STickNet-large}} \approx 18 \times \mathcal{Q}_{\text{FR-PDP}}$ versus $\mathcal{Q}_{\text{TickNet-large}} \approx 15 \times \mathcal{Q}_{\text{FR-PDP}}$. For instance, to learn a 224×224 image in Stanford Dogs, STickNet-basic needs 1.33M learnable parameters compared to

Table 1. Architecture of STickNets for learning 224 × 224 images.

	STickNet-basic		STickNet-small		STickNet-large		
Layer	Stride	Output HxW	Stride	Output HxW	Stride	Output HxW	C_{out}
Input image	-	224 × 224	-	224 × 224	-	224 × 224	3
Initial Conv3x3	2	112 × 112	2	112 × 112	2	112 × 112	32
$\boldsymbol{\Phi_s^{C_{out}}}$ **= FR-PDP 0**	$\mathbf{2^{\#}}$	**56 × 56**	$\mathbf{2^{\#}}$	**56 × 56**	$\mathbf{2^{\#}}$	**56 × 56**	**256**
FR-PDP 1	1	56 × 56	1	56 × 56	1	56 × 56	128
FR-PDP 2	1	56 × 56	1	56 × 56	1	56 × 56	64
FR-PDP 3	2	28 × 28	1	56 × 56	1	56 × 56	128
FR-PDP 4	2	14 × 14	2	28 × 28	1	56 × 56	256
FR-PDP 5	2	7 × 7	1	28 × 28	2	28 × 28	512
$\boldsymbol{\Phi_s^{C_{out}}}$ **= FR-PDP 6**	–	–	**1**	**28 × 28**	**1**	**28 × 28**	**256**
FR-PDP 7	–	–	1	28 × 28	1	28 × 28	128
FR-PDP 8	–	–	2	14 × 14	1	28 × 28	64
FR-PDP 9	–	–	1	14 × 14	1	28 × 28	128
FR-PDP 10	–	–	1	14 × 14	1	28 × 28	256
FR-PDP 11	–	–	2	7 × 7	1	28 × 28	512
$\boldsymbol{\Phi_s^{C_{out}}}$ **= FR-PDP 12**	–	–	–	–	**2**	**14 × 14**	**256**
FR-PDP 13	–	–	–	–	1	14 × 14	128
FR-PDP 14	–	–	–	–	1	14 × 14	64
FR-PDP 15	–	–	–	–	1	14 × 14	128
FR-PDP 16	–	–	–	–	1	14 × 14	256
FR-PDP 17	–	–	–	–	2	7 × 7	512
Conv1x1	1	7 × 7	1	7 × 7	1	7 × 7	1024
AvgPooling							1024
Fully connected							1000

Note: The bold FR-PDP blocks denote the extra modules $\Phi_s^{C_{out}}$. "#" means that FR-PDP will be executed with *stride* = 1 for 32 × 32 images in CIFAR10/100.

its original version with 1.18M; 2.53M versus 2.10M for STickNet-small and 3.72M versus 3.02M for STickNet-large. Meanwhile, the performance of STickNets is significantly better than that of their original models, correspondingly. For instance, STickNet-small is over 2% better than TickNet-small on Stanford Dogs, particularly, up to about 7.4% of STickNet-basic (see Sect. 4.2 for thorough evaluations in detail). So there is a trade-off between the performance and memory footprint when deploying STickNets in practice.

4 Experiments and Evaluations

4.1 Datasets and Learning Settings

In order to evaluate the efficacy of our proposal, STickNets will be trained on benchmark datasets for image recognition. For objective evaluations, the training phase will take into account the common settings as follows. An optimizer is SGD with *momentum* = 0.9; the initial value of 0.1 is set as the learning rate, i.e., $lr = 0.1$; and *weight-decay* is set to a value of 10^{-4}. Other learning parameters will be allocated according to the specific properties of a dataset for objective assessments. Furthermore, for MobileNet-based networks [1–7], the typical rate (i.e., *width-multiplier*=x1.0) will be used by default if no expansion rate is specified.

CIFAR [19] consists of two subsets of 32×32 color images used to evaluate neural networks for tasks of image recognition. Accordingly, CIFAR-10 includes 10 categories with 60k images, where 50k are utilized for training and 10k are for testing. Meantime, CIFAR-100 has 100 categories, where 500 among 600 images in each category are used for training and the rest are for testing. Subject to the common settings in [4,20,21], STickNets are trained in 200 epochs with $batch\_size = 128$ and the learning rate is 0.1 at the initial stage. This rate will be decayed by 10 times at epochs: 100, 150, and 180. For objective evaluations, the traditional augmentations are addressed subject to previous works [20,21] to mitigate the overfitting issue, i.e., horizontal flips and shifts by up to 4px.

ImageNet-1k [22] is a huge and challenging dataset, including 1000 categories with over 1.3M color images in total. Because of its largeness, Nguyen *et al.* [23] addressed the resultant validations of a pre-trained network [24] to rescale it into some challenging subsets with a small number of categories for image recognition: ReIN^{30}, ReIN^{50}, and ReIN^{100}. Also, as mentioned by Nguyen *et al.* [23], these challenging subsets could be taken into account for validating the learning ability of neural networks in general. The higher rates on ReINs can lead to a better ability on ImageNet-1k, correspondingly. For objective evaluations, the conventional settings in [4,25,26] should be utilized. Concretely, STickNets will be trained in 100 epochs with $batch\_size = 256$, and the learning rate is 0.1 at the initial stage. This rate will be decayed by 10 times at epochs: 30, 60, and 90. The usual augmentations will be addressed as follows. Firstly, the original images are resized to 256×256 and then randomly cropped to 224×224 images. Secondly, horizontal-flip operations will be used for the resultant images.

Stanford Dogs [27] is a dog-species dataset that is constructed by taking out the dog images of ImageNet [22] and then categorizing the selected images into 120 classes of dog species, where 12k images are taken into account for training and 8580 are for validating. According to the learning settings in [4,5,7,13], the proposed models STickNets will be trained with $batch\_size = 128$ in 200 epochs, and the learning rate is 0.1 at the initial stage. This rate will be decayed by 10 times at epochs: 100, 150, and 180. The popular augmentations are used in the same way as done on ReINs, along with color jitter [28] for objective evaluations.

4.2 Efficiency Analyses of $\Phi_s^{\mathcal{C}_{out}}$-Based Features

As presented in Sect. 3.1, the proposed spread-learned perceptron $\Phi_s^{\mathcal{C}_{out}}(\mathcal{T})$ agrees with an FR-PDP block to exploit the identical FR-PDP-based features in the whole tick-shape architecture, i.e., STickNet-basic, STickNet-small, and

Table 2. Top-1 (%) on CIFAR-10/100 and Stanford Dogs.

Architecture	CIFAR-10		CIFAR-100		Stanford Dogs		
	Top-1	#Paras	Top-1	#Paras	Top-1	#Paras	FLOPs
TickNet-basic [13]	92.72	1.07M	71.91	1.16M	54.63	1.18M	0.25G
STickNet-basic*	93.16	1.12M	74.65	1.21M	60.54	1.23M	0.21G
STickNet-basic	**93.55**	1.22M	**75.35**	1.31M	**62.03**	1.33M	0.36G
TickNet-small [13]	94.57	1.99M	76.83	2.08M	63.50	2.10M	0.50G
STickNet-small*	94.33	2.21M	76.94	2.30M	64.24	2.32M	0.64G
STickNet-small	**94.77**	2.41M	**77.52**	2.50M	**65.69**	2.53M	0.83G
TickNet-large [13]	**95.01**	2.91M	77.23	3.00M	64.14	3.02M	0.64G
STickNet-large*	94.62	3.30M	77.30	3.40M	65.37	3.42M	1.11G
STickNet-large	94.97	3.61M	**77.68**	3.70M	**66.46**	3.72M	1.31G

STickNet-large. In addition, to further emphasize the effectiveness of the proposed spread-learned perceptron, we would like to consider another sequential instance of $LWO_s^i(.)$. A lightweight convolution $DW_s(\mathcal{T})$ with stride $s = 2$ is simply used to capture the spread-learned spatial patterns of a given tensor $\mathcal{T}$. Since $DW_s(\mathcal{T})$ would not make a change of #channels of $\mathcal{T}$, a $PW_s(.)$ operator with stride $s = 1$ will be utilized to turn the #channels in accordance with $\mathcal{C}_{out}$ for the next layers in a concerning network. As a result, subject to Eq. (2), we obtain a specific sequence of $DW_s(.)$ and $PW_s(.)$ for another $\Phi_s^{\mathcal{C}_{out}}(.)^\star$ as follows.

$$\Phi_s^{\mathcal{C}_{out}}(\mathcal{T})^\star = Sequential\big(PW_s(DW_s(\mathcal{T}))\big) \tag{6}$$

Similar to Sect. 3.1, other spread-learned tick-shape networks are also constructed in consideration of $\Phi_s^{\mathcal{C}_{out}}(.)^\star$. For simple presentation, these obtained networks are named as STickNet-basic*, STickNet-small*, and STickNet-large*.

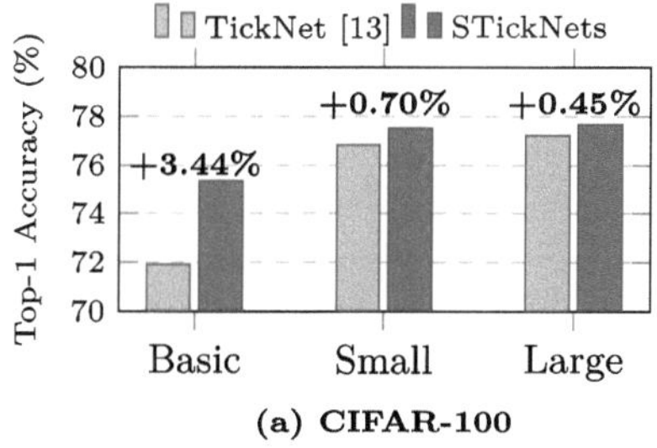

(a) CIFAR-100

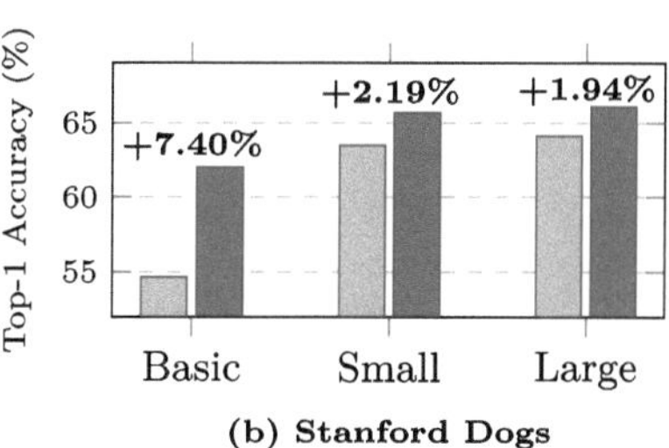

(b) Stanford Dogs

Fig. 3. Performance of tick-shape networks is boosted thanks to $\Phi_s^{\mathcal{C}_{out}}$-based features.

It can be seen from Table 2 that the proposed spread-learned perceptron has significantly boosted the performance of tick-shape networks. Indeed, STickNets* with the simple perceptron $\Phi_s^{\mathcal{C}_{out}}(.)^{\star}$ have a better learning ability than their original versions, i.e., TickNets [13]. Meantime, STickNets with the FR-PDP perceptron obtained more learning power than STickNets*. This would be thanks to the exploitation of identical FR-PDP-based features in all layers of a tick-shape network. Concretely, STickNet-basic* obtained 74.65% on CIFAR-100, ~3% higher than TickNet-basic [13], while it is up to about 4% for STickNet-basic (see Fig. 3(a) for visual comparisons). Also, they are a little higher on CIFAR-10, except for a slightly lower rate of the large versions of STickNets. In particular, the performance on Stanford Dogs is boosted by up to 5.9% and 7.4% for STickNet-basic* and STickNet-basic, respectively (see Fig. 3(b) for further comparisons). For an intuitive view, Fig. 4 shows the better Norwegian-Elkhound-image representation of STickNet-basic* and STickNet-basic in comparison with TickNet-basic. Therein, STickNet-basic* could retain the main shape of the dog versus TickNet-basic, while more essential features of the dog's body are impressed by STickNet-basic. For another visual view, STickNet-large (66.46%) achieved the best performance thanks to the better learning concentration. Figure 5 shows that STickNet-large concentrated on the whole face of a Norwegian-Elkhound dog (the essential part of the dog), while STickNet-large* focused on a part of the face, and TickNet-large [13] paid attention to its rear body.

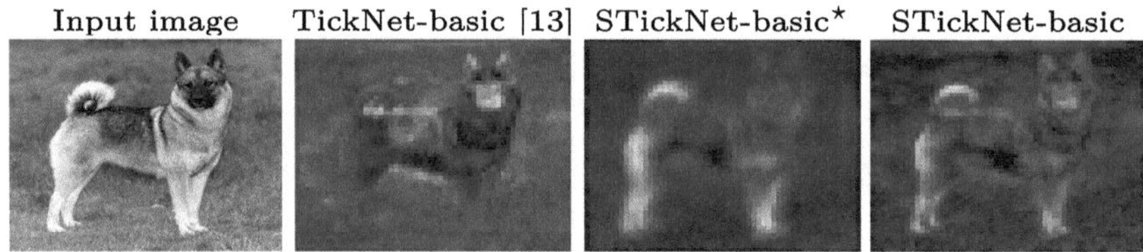

Fig. 4. The better image representation of STickNet-basic* and STickNet-basic in comparison with TickNet-basic [13].

In terms of classifying images on the challenging subsets of ImageNet-1k, it can be seen from Table 3 that STickNets also obtained better performance than their original versions. For instance, STickNet-small with 2.43M learnable parameters achieved a rate of 52.93% on ReIN^{30}, up to over 2% compared to TickNet-small (50.73%, 2.01M), while it is 1%–2% higher on ReIN^{50} and ReIN^{100}. The aforementioned statements have validated the efficiency of exploiting the spread-learned spatial features of a given tensor to improve tick-shape networks. Due to the better performance (see Table 2), STickNets should be addressed below for thorough evaluations as well as real applications.

4.3 Comparison with Other State-of-the-Art Methods

It can be seen from Table 4 that our STickNets obtained competitive results on CIFAR-10/100 and Stanford Dogs in comparison with state-of-the-art

Table 3. Top-1 (%) of STickNets versus TickNets on ReINs.

Architecture	$ReIN^{30}$		$ReIN^{50}$		$ReIN^{100}$	
	Top-1	#Paras	Top-1	#Paras	Top-1	#Paras
TickNet-basic [13]	47.20	1.09M	48.16	1.11M	49.94	1.16M
STickNet-basic	**48.80**	1.24M	**49.68**	1.26M	**51.56**	1.31M
TickNet-small [13]	50.73	2.01M	54.04	2.03M	56.38	2.08M
STickNet-small	**52.93**	2.43M	**54.88**	2.45M	**57.02**	2.50M
TickNet-large [13]	52.40	2.93M	54.76	2.95M	56.50	3.00M
STickNet-large	**54.60**	3.63M	**56.08**	3.65M	**57.54**	3.70M

Table 4. Top-1(%) on CIFAR-10/100 and Stanford Dogs.

Architecture	CIFAR-10		CIFAR-100		Stanford Dogs		
	Top-1	#Paras	Top-1	#Paras	Top-1	#Paras	FLOPs
MobileNetV1 [1]	93.76	3.22M	74.27	3.31M	51.60	3.33M	0.29G
MobileNetV2 [2]	93.60	2.24M	74.90	2.35M	56.01	2.37M	0.17G
MobileNetV3 [3]	93.70	2.98M	75.01	3.07M	54.90	3.09M	0.12G
MobileNeXt [30]	93.80	2.27M	74.30	2.38M	53.95	2.41M	0.17G
V1-BSConv-U [4]	94.30	3.22M	75.70	3.31M	59.10	3.33M	0.44G
V2-BSConv-S [4]	94.20	2.24M	75.80	2.35M	60.10	2.38M	0.17G
V3-BSConv-S [4]	94.60	2.98M	77.70	3.07M	60.00	3.09M	0.12G
V1-GDF [5]	93.87	3.28M	74.48	3.37M	54.90	3.39M	0.31G
V2-GDF [5]	93.66	2.32M	75.11	2.43M	57.92	2.46M	0.18G
ShuffleNetV1 [14]	92.29	0.91M	70.06	1.00M	51.02	1.02M	0.07G
ShuffleNetV2 [15]	93.93	2.49M	74.53	2.58M	54.29	1.38M	0.08G
ResNet18 [20]	93.02	11.17M	75.10	11.20M	52.57	11.24M	0.91G
ResNet18 [20]+SE [31]	-	-	76.44	11.40M	53.48	11.43M	0.91G
AugShuffleNet [32]	93.63	1.21M	74.07	1.30M	-	-	-
SqueezeNet [17]	-	-	69.41	0.78M	-	-	-
DenseNet-121 [33]	94.23	6.96M	76.21	7.06M	56.90	7.08M	1.44G
MnasNet [34]	-	-	-	-	54.80	3.26M	0.17G
EfficientNet-B0 [8]	-	-	-	-	54.70	4.16M	0.20G
$NetTOP^{g=1}$ [11]	94.71	3.37M	**77.87**	3.46M	65.28	3.50M	0.59G
$CGDF\text{-}Net^{g=1}$ [7]	94.37	3.41M	76.49	3.50M	60.86	3.53M	0.42G
GhostNetV2 [10]	-	-	-	-	57.03	5.03M	0.09G
MobileOne-S0 [12]	-	-	-	-	58.26	1.21M	0.15G
STickNet-basic	93.55	1.22M	75.35	1.31M	62.03	1.33M	0.36G
STickNet-small	94.77	2.41M	77.52	2.50M	65.69	2.53M	0.83G
STickNet-large	**94.97**	3.61M	77.68	3.70M	**66.46**	3.72M	1.31G

Note: "–" indicates values "not available" or "not reported". #Paras denotes the number of learnable parameters computed by *ptflops* [35].

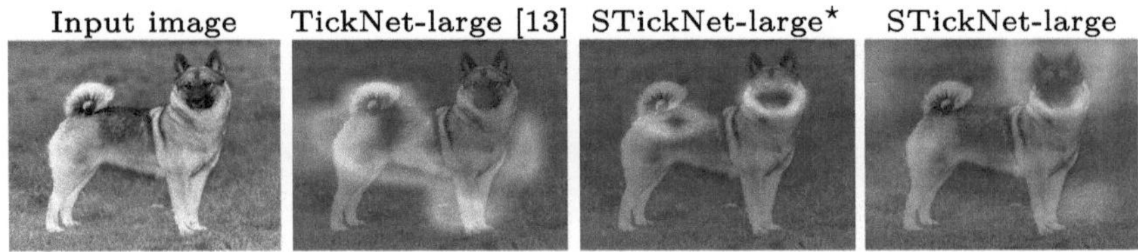

Fig. 5. Efficient concentration of STickNet-large on learning the essential features of a Norwegian-Elkhound dog. These visualizations are drawn out by Grad-CAM [29].

Table 5. Top-1 (%) on challenging ReIN subsets.

Architecture	$ReIN^{30}$	$ReIN^{50}$	$ReIN^{100}$	
	Top-1	Top-1	Top-1	#Paras
MobileNetV1 [1]	46.53	50.08	52.48	3.31M
MobileNetV2 [2]	47.47	49.08	53.74	2.35M
MobileNetV3 [3]	49.87	51.68	54.06	3.07M
ShuffleNetV2 [15]	48.87	49.52	51.38	1.36M
ResNet18 [20]	47.67	50.38	53.28	11.22M
GhostNetV2 [10]	50.27	54.36	54.70	5.01M
MobileOne-S0 [12]	48.57	50.04	52.94	1.09M
$NetTOP^{g=1}$ [11]	53.47	55.56	57.40	3.46M
$CGDF\text{-}Net^{g=1}$ [7]	52.60	54.60	57.42	3.50M
STickNet-basic	48.80	49.68	51.56	1.31M
STickNet-small	52.93	54.88	57.02	2.50M
STickNet-large	**54.60**	**56.08**	**57.54**	3.70M

lightweight CNN-based networks, particularly the performance of STickNet-large. Indeed, STickNet-small and STickNet-large achieved the highest performance with rates of 94.77%/77.52% and 94.97%/77.68% on CIFAR-10/100 and 65.69% and 66.46% on Stanford Dogs. Note that $NetTOP^{g=1}$ [11] obtained 77.87%, a slightly better rate than ours on CIFAR-100, but it was not on CIFAR-10 with 94.71% and Stanford Dogs with 65.28%. Besides, STickNet-basic also obtained good results in the smallest number of learnable parameters (1.33M), except ShuffleNetV1 [14] (1.02M) and MobileOne-S0 [12] (1.21M), but they obtained much lower rates on CIFAR-10/100 and Stanford Dogs, e.g., 70.06% of ShuffleNetV1 [14] versus our 75.35% or 58.26% of MobileOne-S0 [12] versus our 62.03% (see Table 4 for further instances). Although obtaining the highest performance with the same learnable parameters, STickNets take a high computational time (1.31G FLOPs), close to DenseNet-121 [33] (1.44G FLOPs). In this circumstance, STickNet* with good results can be a potential solution for real applications due to the reasonable complexity (see Table 2). In terms of classifying on ReINs, Table 5 indicates that STickNet-large obtained the highest rates on all challenging subsets in comparison with the existing lightweight networks, i.e., 54.6% on ReIN^{30}, 56.08% on ReIN^{50}, and 57.54% on ReIN^{100}. CGDF-$\text{Net}^{g=1}$ [7] obtained a rate of 57.42% on ReIN^{100}, but it is up to ~2% lower than ours on ReIN^{30} and ReIN^{50} (see Table 5 for more instances). This advance is thanks to taking into account the proposed spread-learned spatial features of a given tensor for tick-shape networks.

5 Conclusion

An efficient perceptron for extracting spread-learned spatial features has been proposed in this work to exploit the spread-learned spatial features of a given tensor. Then it has been added to the beginning stage of a basic tick-shape backbone to capture the most spatial information. Also, STickNets are structured by simply connecting several spread-learned tick-shape backbones. The experimental results have the effectiveness of our proposal to boost the learning ability of tick-shape networks, particularly up to 7.4% of STickNet-basic on Stanford Dogs. Furthermore, it should be noted that addressing the spread-learned blocks would make STickNets have a higher computational complexity than their corresponding original version. Therefore, when deploying STickNets on mobile devices or edge computing systems in practice, the technicians will take a trade-off between the performance and their computational capacity. For perspectives, it can be addressed more spread-learned blocks to structure a larger tick-shape network for further performance investigation. This is possible since mobile devices will have more and more computational power.

Acknowledgments. We would like to send many thanks to those in Faculty of IT, HCMC University of Technology and Education, Ho Chi Minh City, Vietnam, who gave us crucial supports in several computing systems. The work of Thanh Phuong Nguyen is supported by Centre de calcul UCA, Azzurra cluster.

References

1. Howard, A.G., et al.: Mobilenets: efficient convolutional neural networks for mobile vision applications. CoRR, vol. abs/1704.04861 (2017)
2. Sandler, M., Howard, A.G., Zhu, M., Zhmoginov, A., Chen, L.: Mobilenetv2: inverted residuals and linear bottlenecks. In: CVPR, pp. 4510–4520 (2018)
3. Howard, A., et al.: Searching for mobilenetv3. In: ICCV, pp. 1314–1324 (2019)
4. Haase, D., Amthor, M.: Rethinking depthwise separable convolutions: How intra-kernel correlations lead to improved mobilenets. In: CVPR, pp. 14588–14597 (2020)
5. Nguyen, T.T., Nguyen, T.P.: Assembling extra features with grouped pointwise convolutions for mobilenets. In: DICTA, pp. 265–272 (2023)
6. Nguyen, H.: A lightweight and efficient deep convolutional neural network based on depthwise dilated separable convolution. J. TAIT **98** (2020)
7. Nguyen, T.T., Pham, H.A., Nguyen, T.P.: A light-weight backbone to adapt with extracting grouped dilation features. Pattern Anal. Appl. **28**, 27 (2025)

8. Tan, M., Le, Q.V.: Efficientnet: rethinking model scaling for convolutional neural networks. In: ICML, vol. 97, pp. 6105–6114 (2019)
9. Han, K., Wang, Y., Tian, Q., Guo, J., Xu, C., Xu, C.: Ghostnet: more features from cheap operations. In: CVPR, pp. 1577–1586 (2020)
10. Tang, Y., Han, K., Guo, J., Xu, C., Xu, C., Wang, Y.: Ghostnetv2: enhance cheap operation with long-range attention. In: NeurIPS (2022)
11. Nguyen, T.T., Nguyen, T.P.: Nettop: a light-weight network of orthogonal-plane features for image recognition. Mach. Learn. **114**(4) (2025)
12. Vasu, P.K.A., Gabriel, J., Zhu, J., Tuzel, O., Ranjan, A.: Mobileone: an improved one millisecond mobile backbone. In: CVPR, pp. 7907–7917 (2023)
13. Nguyen, T.T., Nguyen, T.P.: Efficient tick-shape networks of full-residual point-depth-point blocks for image classification. Neurocomputing **596**, 127942 (2024)
14. Zhang, X., Zhou, X., Lin, M., Sun, J.: Shufflenet: an extremely efficient convolutional neural network for mobile devices. In: CVPR, pp. 6848–6856 (2018)
15. Ma, N., Zhang, X., Zheng, H.-T., Sun, J.: ShuffleNet V2: practical guidelines for efficient CNN architecture design. In: Ferrari, V., Hebert, M., Sminchisescu, C., Weiss, Y. (eds.) Computer Vision – ECCV 2018. LNCS, vol. 11218, pp. 122–138. Springer, Cham (2018). https://doi.org/10.1007/978-3-030-01264-9_8
16. Tran, C.Q., Nguyen, T.T., Le, T.V., Nguyen, T.P.: Enhanced mobilenets via augmentation of filtering-based features. In: MAPR, pp. 1–6 (2025)
17. Iandola, F.N., Han, S., Moskewicz, M.W., Ashraf, K., Dally, W.J., Keutzer, K.: Squeezenet: alexnet-level accuracy with 50x fewer parameters and <1mb model size. CoRR, vol. abs/1602.07360 (2016)
18. Zhao, L., Wang, L., Jia, Y., Cui, Y.: A lightweight deep neural network with higher accuracy. PLoS ONE **17**(8), 1–15 (2022)
19. Krizhevsky, A., Hinton, G.: Learning multiple layers of features from tiny images. In: Tech Report (2009)
20. He, K., Zhang, X., Ren, S., Sun, J.: Deep residual learning for image recognition. In: CVPR, pp. 770–778 (2016)
21. Zagoruyko, S., Komodakis, N.: Wide residual networks. In: BMVC (2016)
22. Deng, J., Dong, W., Socher, R., Li, L.J., Li, K., Fei-Fei, L.: Imagenet: a large-scale hierarchical image database. In: CVPR, pp. 248–255 (2009)
23. Nguyen, T.T., Nguyen, T.P.: Rescaling large datasets based on validation outcomes of a pre-trained network. Pattern Recogn. Lett. **185**, 73–80 (2024)
24. Nguyen, T.T., Nguyen, T.P., Nguyen, V.: Accumulating global channel-wise patterns via deformed-bottleneck recalibration for image classification. Pattern Anal. Appl. **28** (2025)
25. Park, J., Woo, S., Lee, J., Kweon, I.S.: BAM: bottleneck attention module. In: BMVC, p. 147 (2018)
26. Woo, S., Park, J., Lee, J.-Y., Kweon, I.S.: CBAM: convolutional block attention module. In: Ferrari, V., Hebert, M., Sminchisescu, C., Weiss, Y. (eds.) ECCV 2018. LNCS, vol. 11211, pp. 3–19. Springer, Cham (2018). https://doi.org/10.1007/978-3-030-01234-2_1
27. Khosla, A., Jayadevaprakash, N., Yao, B., Li, F.F.: Novel dataset for fine-grained image categorization. In: CVPR Workshop (2011)
28. Krizhevsky, A., Sutskever, I., Hinton, G.E.: Imagenet classification with deep convolutional neural networks. In: NeurIPS, pp. 1106–1114 (2012)
29. Selvaraju, R.R., Cogswell, M., Das, A., Vedantam, R., Parikh, D., Batra, D.: Grad-cam: visual explanations from deep networks via gradient-based localization. Int. J. Comput. Vis. **128**(2), 336–359 (2020)

30. Zhou, D., Hou, Q., Chen, Y., Feng, J., Yan, S.: Rethinking bottleneck structure for efficient mobile network design. In: Vedaldi, A., Bischof, H., Brox, T., Frahm, J.-M. (eds.) ECCV 2020. LNCS, vol. 12348, pp. 680–697. Springer, Cham (2020). https://doi.org/10.1007/978-3-030-58580-8_40
31. Hu, J., Shen, L., Sun, L.: Squeeze-and-excitation networks. In: CVPR, pp. 7132–7141 (2018)
32. Ye, L.: AugShuffleNet: Communicate More, Compute Less. CoRR, vol. abs/2203.06589 (2022)
33. Huang, G., Liu, Z., van der Maaten, L., Weinberger, K.Q.: Densely connected convolutional networks. In: CVPR, pp. 2261–2269 (2017)
34. Tan, M., et al.: Mnasnet: platform-aware neural architecture search for mobile. In: CVPR, pp. 2820–2828 (2019)
35. Sovrasov, V.: ptflops: a flops counting tool for neural networks in pytorch framework (2018-2023). https://github.com/sovrasov/flops-counter.pytorch

An Overview of the Effectiveness of Graph Learning Methods for Traffic Demand Forecasting

Luong-Chi Trung, Chung-Thai Kiet, Nguyen-Huu An, and Dung-Cam Quang(✉)

Faculty of Information Technology, Ton Duc Thang University, Ho Chi Minh City, Vietnam
{52200166,52200140}@student.tdtu.edu.vn, {nguyenhuuan,dungcamquang}@tdtu.edu.vn

Abstract. Traffic demand forecasting plays a crucial role in intelligent transportation systems and is a fundamental aspect of smart cities. The spatial-temporal nature of this task poses significant challenges for forecasting models, especially when it comes to extracting spatial features from complex graphs. To effectively capture these intricate spatial patterns, previous studies have explored a variety of methods for constructing a graph from spatial data. In this study, we present a thorough survey and taxonomy of existing research based on various graph construction methods, including static, adaptive, and dynamic approaches. To thoroughly evaluate these models and methodologies, we conduct experiments on seven real-world datasets. Among these, two are widely recognized benchmarks, while the other five have been newly collected and processed by us from government open data platforms. Our findings enable us to analyze and compare the strengths and limitations of various approaches. We also identify emerging trends and assess the current effectiveness of these methods. Finally, we propose potential research directions and opportunities for future work in this field.

Keywords: Traffic demand forecasting · Graph Neural Network · Graph Learning

1 Introduction

In the context of rapidly growing urbanization, Intelligent Transportation Systems (ITS) play an increasingly important role in managing and optimizing transportation networks. As passenger demand rises, accurate traffic demand forecasting becomes essential for reducing wait times, improving service efficiency, and supporting intelligent mobility solutions [1].

Traffic demand forecasting can be formulated as a spatial-temporal prediction problem, which involves utilizing real-time data from advanced trip control and coordination systems to predict future demand patterns. The early studies mainly used traditional statistical techniques such as K-Nearest Neighbors

T. T. Quan et al. (Eds.): MIWAI 2025, LNAI 16353, pp. 130–141, 2026.
https://doi.org/10.1007/978-981-95-4957-3_11

(KNN) and Auto-Regressive Intergrated Moving Average (ARIMA) to learn the dependencies of traffic data, but these algorithms could only learn the linear temporal dependencies while ignoring the spatial dependencies [2,3]. To improve performance, some studies attempted to divide the area covered by the data into grids and applied Convolutional Neural Networks (CNN) [4] to extract spatial features of the data. However, the problem soon became apparent as grid-based traffic demand data could not show complex semantic dependency relationships between square regions. Graph Neural Network (GNN) [5] have become a promising alternative due to their superior ability to learn dependencies between connected spaces. One of the key factors influencing the effectiveness of these models is the graph learning method, where different graph construction methods can capture varying patterns and directly impact the predictive performance of GNN-based models.

In this paper, we examine the impact of graph construction strategies on traffic demand forecasting by benchmarking six representative models: CCRNN [6], MSDR [7], MVFN [8], DMGL [9], DDGCRN [10], and PDG2Seq [11], using both public and newly collected datasets. We explore how static, adaptive, and dynamic graph based approaches perform in practice and highlight the effectiveness of dynamic graph learning in capturing complex spatial and temporal relationships. Our findings aim to support the development of more accurate and robust graph based forecasting models.

The contributions of this paper can be summarized as follows:

1. We overview prominent models in traffic demand forecasting and analyze the impact of various graph learning methods on model performance.
2. We re-implemented six notable models according to static, adaptive and dynamic graph approaches, compared them on two widely benchmark datasets and five new real-world datasets we collected and built.
3. Through the experimental results, we analyze the model performance based on graph types and discuss about the key research directions in future.

2 Related Work

2.1 Spatial-Temporal GNN Approaches

Transportation network is conceptualized as a graph, which consequently establishes Graph Neural Networks (GNNs) as a prevailing methodology in traffic forecasting. STGCN [12] was the first to bring GNN closer to the problem by designing a GNN-based framework to learn spatial features. Yao *et al.* [13] introduced a deep multi-view spatial-temporal network that incorporated graph embedding methods for demand prediction. CCRNN [6] utilized a coupled layer-wise mechanism using Graph Convolutional Network (GCN) [14] for data transformation and enrichment to capture spatial characteristics. Building on this, Liu *et al.* [7] proposed a variant of the Recurrent Neural Network (RNN) [15] that operates more efficiently in retaining important temporal information. CMGAT [16] captured spatial and temporal dependencies by utilizing a feature embedding block and attention mechanism to address the unbalanced traffic demand in urban areas. MVFN [8] leveraged GCN for local spatial feature learning and employs linear attention mechanisms.

2.2 Graph Learning Methods

Besides experimenting with various GNN-based modules, the graph-based structure approach is a promising choice for enhancing the overall performance of the model. Some studies primarily relied on prior knowledge to construct static graphs, including distance-based [12,17], connectivity-based [8,18], similarity-based [18,19]. However, traffic patterns are dynamic, while pre-defined adjacency matrices remain static, causing outdated information. As a result, many studies have shifted to alternative approaches, using adaptive graphs as a solution by generating an adjacency matrix from a static graph and then adapting it layer by layer [6,7,20]. Although inter-spatial dependencies are well learned, the adjacency matrix fails to keep up with the dynamic traffic patterns in the later layers due to the lack of updated knowledge. Dynamic graphs are seen as a more effective approach, as they are constructed from each time step as well as data from previous time steps [9–11], thus better capturing the overall data patterns.

3 Premilinaries

3.1 Traffic Network

Traffic data is represented in the form of a graph $G = (V, E, A)$, where V denotes the set of nodes in the graph ($|V| = N$ is the number of nodes), representing spatial regions. E comprises the edges connecting the nodes. $A \in \mathbb{R}^{N \times N}$ is defined as the adjacency matrix of the graph structure. G is associated with a traffic signal X at time step t. The input at this time step is as follow:

$$X_t = \{x_t^1, x_t^2, \ldots, x_t^N\} \in \mathbb{R}^{N \times d} \tag{1}$$

where x_t^i denotes the d-dimensional feature vector of region i at time step t.

3.2 Traffic Demand Forecasting

Given a historical feature sequence of traffic demand observations with length P and a graph G, the objective of problem is predicting a future sequence of demand observations with length Q by learning a mapping function $\mathcal{F}$.

$$[\mathbf{X}_{t-P+1:t}, G] \xrightarrow{\mathcal{F}} \hat{\mathbf{X}}_{t+1:t+Q} \tag{2}$$

where $\hat{\mathbf{X}}_t$ represents the predicted demand at time step t.

4 Graph Construction Methods in Traffic Demand Forecasting

In this section, we analyze the ability of prominent GNN-based models to capture dependencies through graph representations based on data, as well as the importance of each graph structure.

4.1 Static Graph

In the context of traffic prediction, static graph is a type of graph where the structure and relationships between nodes are predefined based on prior knowledge, such as distance, connectivity, or similarity in past demand patterns within the transportation network. Distance-based graph A_{dis} represents the spatial proximity from station to station [17]. Connectivity-based graph A_{con} reflects the connections between stations, typically based on adjacency [8]. Meanwhile, similarity-based graph A_{sim} is built on a sequence of traffic demand at each node and compares them to calculate the similarity in historical patterns between nodes [18]. Point of Interest (POI) data can also serve as a substitute for historical patterns [21], although its use is rare due to inconsistent availability.

$$A_{dis_{ij}} = dis(v_i, v_j) \tag{3}$$

$$A_{con_{ij}} = \begin{cases} 1, & (v_i, v_j) \in E \\ 0, & \text{otherwise} \end{cases} \tag{4}$$

$$A_{sim_{ij}} = \begin{cases} sim(pat_i, pat_j) \\ sim(poi_i, poi_j) \end{cases} \tag{5}$$

where pat_i is the demand pattern of node i, poi_i is the POI data of node i.

4.2 Adaptive Graph

Static graphs employ fixed adjacency weights, which cannot adapt to changing spatial dependencies. Adaptive graphs address this limitation by learning the adjacency matrix from data and updating it layer by layer during training. This allows the graph structure to better capture temporal variations in spatial relationships.

Formally, the adjacency matrix at layer $l+1$ is obtained from that of the previous layer $A^{(l)}$ through a mapping function $\Psi^{(l)}$, typically implemented with an MLP or RNN:

$$A^{(l+1)} = \Psi^{(l)}(A^{(l)}). \tag{6}$$

In CCRNN [6] and MSDR [7], the initial adaptive graph is initialized using similarity-based measures rather than random embeddings, improving stability and convergence. At each layer, $A^{(l)}$ is decomposed via Singular Value Decomposition (SVD) into two low-rank matrices $E_1^{(l)}$ and $E_2^{(l)}$, representing source and target node embeddings. A shared MLP is then applied to these embeddings to reconstruct $A^{(l+1)}$:

$$A^{(l+1)} = (E_1^{(l)} W^{(l)} + b^{(l)})(E_2^{(l)} W^{(l)} + b^{(l)})^T, \tag{7}$$

where $W^{(l)}$ and $b^{(l)}$ denote the weights and bias of the mapping function.

4.3 Dynamic Graph

Static graphs use a fixed adjacency and fail to capture time-varying dependencies, while adaptive graphs learn the structure from data but keep it fixed during inference, limiting responsiveness to rapid changes. Dynamic graphs address these limitations by continuously updating the adjacency to reflect evolving spatial-temporal dependencies.

Formally, a dynamic graph can be described as a sequence of graphs $\mathcal{G} = \{G^{(t)}\}$ over time steps $t \in \mathcal{T}$, where each $G^{(t)} = (V^{(t)}, E^{(t)}, A^{(t)})$ contains the time-specific node features, edges, and adjacency matrix.

Dynamic graph construction generally follows two main approaches. The first is the *multi-scale dynamic graph*, exemplified by DMGL [9], which constructs dynamic graphs at different temporal resolutions to capture spatial dependencies from both short-term and long-term perspectives. In this approach, the model generates multiple dynamic graphs across M temporal scales, where each scale $m \in [1, M]$ contains a set of K_m graphs $\{G_1^{(m)}, \ldots, G_{K_m}^{(m)}\}$, each capturing spatial dependencies corresponding to different temporal ranges:

$$\mathcal{G}^{(M)} = \{G_k^{(m)} \mid 1 \leq m \leq M,\ 1 \leq k \leq K_m\}. \tag{8}$$

The second approach is the *time-step dependent dynamic graph*, as adopted by DDGCRN [10] and PDG2Seq [11]. In this approach, a dynamic graph is constructed for each time step in the input sequence, allowing the adjacency structure to evolve in sync with temporal dynamics. Specifically, for each $t' \in [t - H + 1, \ldots, t]$, a dynamic graph $G^{(t')}$ is generated based on the evolving spatial-temporal embeddings at that time:

$$\mathcal{G}^{(T)} = \{G^{(t')} \mid t' \in [t - H + 1, \ldots, t]\}, \tag{9}$$

where H is the input sequence length, and $G^{(t')}$ denotes the dynamic graph at time step t'.

5 Datasets

This study uses seven datasets for traffic demand forecasting. The NYC Bike and NYC Taxi datasets come from a widely recognized public benchmark [6]. The remaining five, including DC Bike[1], DC Taxi[2], CHI Taxi[3], BOS Bike[4], and

[1] https://capitalbikeshare.com/system-data.
[2] https://opendata.dc.gov/documents.
[3] https://data.cityofchicago.org/Transportation.
[4] https://www.boston.gov/departments/boston-bikes/bike-data.

BAY Bike[5], are newly collected from the official open data platforms of each city.

Our raw data consists of individual trip records, where each entry includes the pickup station, dropoff station, pickup time, and dropoff time. To prepare the data for modeling, we aggregate these records into 30-minute intervals and count the number of trips starting (pickup) and ending (dropoff) at each station separately, resulting in two demand sequences per station: one for departures and one for arrivals.

We also perform thorough data cleaning to ensure the integrity of both spatial and temporal dimensions. For records with missing station names but valid geographic coordinates, we assign synthetic station IDs based on their locations. Afterward, we remove trips with invalid timestamps, identical pickup and dropoff stations, or duplicated entries. By preserving only valid station-based records, we ensure that the demand patterns reflect meaningful travel behavior. To construct the spatial graph, we apply the Hierarchical Density-Based Clustering algorithm (HDPC-L) [22] on the pickup and dropoff coordinates to identify dense travel regions, which serve as functional nodes in the mobility network. The final characteristics of the processed datasets are summarized in Table 1.

Table 1. Statistical information of datasets

Dataset	#Records	Time Range	#Regions	#Time Steps	Step Size
NYC Bike	2 600 000	01/04–30/06/2016	250	4368	30 min
NYC Taxi	3 500 000	01/04–30/06/2016	266	4368	30 min
DC Bike	1 800 000	01/07–30/09/2024	196	4416	30 min
DC Taxi	632 436	01/07–30/09/2024	271	4416	30 min
CHI Taxi	1 670 000	01/07–30/09/2024	77	4416	30 min
BOS Bike	1 600 000	01/07–30/09/2024	145	4416	30 min
BAY Bike	975 000	01/07–30/09/2024	208	4416	30 min

The five newly released datasets contribute in two key ways. They expand existing mobility benchmarks by including mid-sized and underexplored cities, increasing diversity in urban form, population, and infrastructure. They also follow a standardized preprocessing and clustering pipeline, ensuring compatibility with recent spatial-temporal graph learning methods. This supports reproducibility and facilitates research on model generalization across diverse urban settings.

[5] https://www.lyft.com/bikes/bay-wheels/system-data.

6 Experiment

6.1 Baselines

We select representative spatial-temporal GNN models based on graph construction methods, as summarized in Table 2.

Table 2. Baseline models by graph construction methods

Graph Construction Methods	Models
Adaptive Graph	CCRNN MSDR
Static Graph	MVFN
Dynamic Graph	DMGL DDGCRN PDG2Seq

6.2 Experimental Setup and Evaluation Metrics

Settings and Environment. All models are trained for 500 epochs using the Adam optimizer with a learning rate of `1e-3` and a batch size of 16. We use a historical window of $P = 12$ time steps to forecast traffic demand over the next $Q = 12$ time steps. In the last four weeks of each dataset, the first two weeks are used for validation and the last two weeks are used for testing. The remaining data is used for training the models. Z-score normalization is applied to standardize the input signals:

$$z = \frac{x - \mu}{\sigma} \tag{10}$$

where μ and σ are the mean and standard deviation. All experiments are conducted on a single NVIDIA P100 GPU with 16 GB of VRAM.

Evaluation Metrics. We adopt three standard metrics to evaluate model performance: Mean Absolute Error (MAE), Root Mean Square Error (RMSE), and Pearson Correlation Coefficient (PCC). Their formulations are as follows:

$$\text{MAE} = \frac{1}{N} \sum_{i=1}^{N} |y_i - \hat{y}_i| \tag{11}$$

$$\text{RMSE} = \sqrt{\frac{1}{N} \sum_{i=1}^{N} (y_i - \hat{y}_i)^2} \tag{12}$$

$$\text{PCC} = \frac{\sum_{i=1}^{N}(y_i - \bar{y})(\hat{y}_i - \bar{\hat{y}})}{\sqrt{\sum_{i=1}^{N}(y_i - \bar{y})^2}\sqrt{\sum_{i=1}^{N}(\hat{y}_i - \bar{\hat{y}})^2}} \tag{13}$$

where N is the number of predictions; y_i and $\hat{y}_i$ are the ground-truth and predicted values at time step i, while $\bar{y}$ and $\bar{\hat{y}}$ denote their respective means.

6.3 Experimental Result

Table 3 presents the average results over 10 runs across seven datasets. Overall, dynamic graph models consistently outperform both static and adaptive baselines, with average improvements of **7.22%** in MAE, **3.95%** in RMSE, and **0.48%** in PCC. These results highlight the effectiveness of continuously updating the graph structure to capture evolving spatial-temporal dependencies.

Table 3. Comparative results of graph learning models

Model	Metric	NYC-Taxi	DC-Taxi	CHI-Taxi	NYC-Bike	BOS-Bike	BAY-Bike	DC-Bike
CCRNN	MAE	5.5059	0.3038	1.5260	1.7262	1.2581	0.6390	0.7503
	RMSE	9.5532	1.5627	4.3461	2.8071	2.9062	1.4657	2.4548
	PCC	0.9649	**0.9551**	0.9740	0.7985	0.9330	0.8937	0.9347
MSDR	MAE	5.0295	0.2924	1.4630	1.6881	1.2599	0.6438	0.7067
	RMSE	8.7624	**1.4848**	4.2647	2.7337	2.8194	1.4494	2.3450
	PCC	0.9701	0.9524	0.9743	0.8063	0.9351	0.8927	0.9407
MVFN	MAE	4.9273	**0.2382**	1.3999	1.6312	1.1756	0.5911	0.6475
	RMSE	8.7307	1.5275	4.4248	2.7146	2.8233	1.4965	2.3899
	PCC	0.9702	0.9522	0.9756	0.8194	0.9350	0.8905	0.9402
DMGL	MAE	5.0361	0.2388	1.3556	1.6503	1.1424	0.5808	0.6283
	RMSE	9.0032	1.5829	4.2138	2.7197	2.7608	1.4829	2.3295
	PCC	0.9700	0.9492	0.9767	0.8136	0.9384	0.8930	0.9422
DDGCRN	MAE	4.7648	0.2629	1.2929	1.5933	1.1286	0.5775	0.6067
	RMSE	8.3891	1.8388	**3.8698**	2.6612	2.7257	1.4466	2.1837
	PCC	0.9724	0.9408	0.9722	0.8266	0.9417	0.8977	0.9500
PDG2Seq	MAE	**4.7271**	0.2833	**1.2905**	**1.5522**	**1.1077**	**0.5690**	**0.6019**
	RMSE	**8.3684**	1.9174	3.9440	**2.5613**	**2.6304**	**1.4188**	**2.1391**
	PCC	**0.9728**	0.9270	**0.9788**	**0.8378**	**0.9457**	**0.9029**	**0.9512**

Unlike static graphs that use a fixed structure or adaptive graphs that learn one structure for the whole sequence, dynamic models reconstruct the graph at each time step, allowing them to capture how regions are connected depending on the situation. This architectural flexibility enables dynamic models to better adapt to real-world variations in urban mobility, such as rush hours or localized disruptions. As illustrated in Fig. 1, the correlation is strong during the morning peak period but weak during other times.

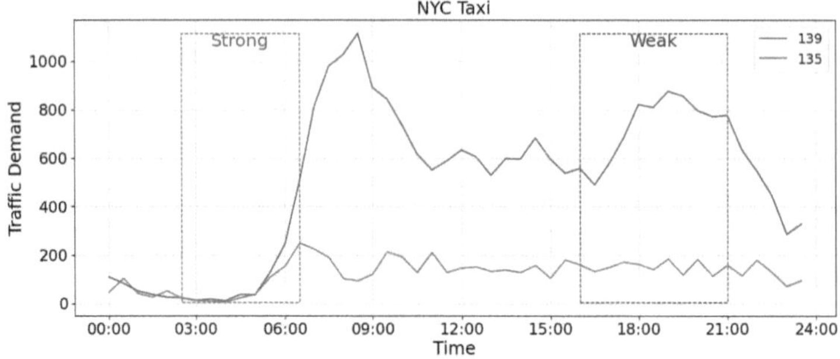

Fig. 1. Dynamic spatial dependencies.

Among these models, PDG2Seq demonstrates strong performance in structured environments thanks to its periodic modeling of temporal signals. DMGL captures both short and long term dependencies through multi-scale graph fusion, enhancing robustness under moderate fluctuations, while DDGCRN uses residual based graph decomposition to suppress noise and handle sudden changes.

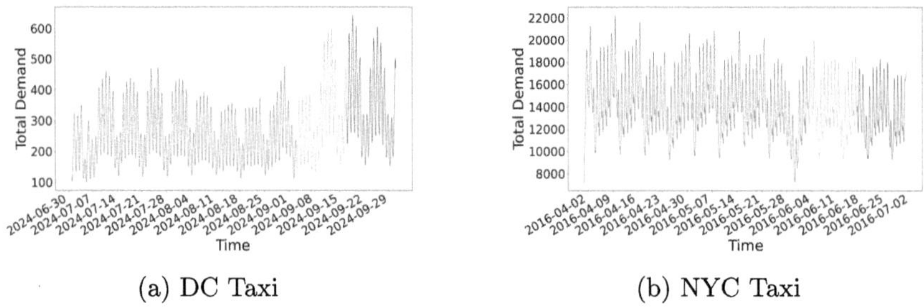

Fig. 2. Comparison of demand patterns in DC Taxi and NYC Taxi datasets. DC Taxi shows strong distribution shift between training (blue) and test (red) periods, indicating an OOD scenario. In contrast, NYC Taxi maintains consistent patterns across all splits. (Color figure online)

However, under out of distribution (OOD) conditions such as those in DC Taxi, which features high volatility, irregular patterns, and weak periodicity, model performance drops due to distribution shifts between training and testing phases as shown in Fig. 2. PDG2Seq is particularly affected as its reliance on periodic signals becomes unstable, while DMGL and DDGCRN remain more robust thanks to their flexible architectures. Interestingly, MSDR also performs well in this setting, not because of modeling sophistication, but due to its minimal temporal assumptions, which reduce overfitting and improve resilience to noise and distributional shift.

Table 4. Computation cost on DC-Bike

Model	Parameter	Training time (s/epoch)	Inference time (s)
PDG2Seq	1 427 586	32.21	2.04
DMGL	9 285 840	232.09	17.61
DDGCRN	577 886	30.33	2.11
MVFN	1 244 408	3.55	0.11
MSDR	869 506	37.50	2.95
CCRNN	120 806	42.40	3.17

Table 4 shows a trade-off between accuracy and computational cost across graph construction strategies. Dynamic models are generally more expressive but computationally intensive, while static and adaptive models are more lightweight. Notably, recent dynamic models have introduced architectural improvements that significantly reduce parameter size and runtime.

7 Research Problems and Opportunities

Despite recent advances, traffic demand forecasting still faces key challenges. Based on our study, we highlight key issues and future research directions.

7.1 Model Size and Efficiency

Our benchmark reveals a trade-off between accuracy and efficiency. Large models like DMGL achieve high performance but incur heavy computational costs, while lightweight models such as CCRNN or MVFN are more efficient but less accurate. Future work should explore model compression, parameter-efficient architectures, or neural architecture search to improve scalability, especially for real-time applications.

7.2 Dataset Diversity and Availability

Current datasets are limited to U.S. cities, which restricts model generalization across different geographic contexts. This lack of diversity not only limits robustness but also hinders the deployment of models in cities with distinct infrastructures and mobility patterns. Therefore, developing more globally representative datasets—capturing diverse urban layouts, cultural behaviors, and transportation policies—is essential for building universally applicable traffic demand forecasting models.

8 Conclusion

In this study, we conduct a comprehensive survey of research directions in traffic demand forecasting, with a specific focus on Spatial-Temporal Graph Neural Networks and categorize existing models into three main approaches for graph construction: static, adaptive, and dynamic graphs. We also select and classify state-of-the-art models, evaluating them using widely recognized benchmark datasets. Additionally, we collect five new datasets to provide a more extensive assessment of these models. Our experimental results show that the dynamic graph-based approach outperforms the others, as it effectively captures the complex spatial-temporal characteristics present in traffic data and . Finally, we outline several promising directions for future research in this field.

References

1. Wang, X., Renne, J.L.: Socioeconomics of urban travel in the U.S.: evidence from the 2017 NHTS. Transp. Res. Part D Transp. Environ. **116**, Article 103622 (2023). https://doi.org/10.1016/j.trd.2023.103622
2. Liu, J., Sun, L., Chen, W., Xiong, H.: Rebalancing bike sharing systems: a multi-source data smart optimization. In: Proceedings of the 22nd ACM SIGKDD International Conference on Knowledge Discovery and Data Mining, pp. 1005–1014. ACM, San Francisco, CA, USA (2016). https://doi.org/10.1145/2939672.2939776
3. Lippi, M., Bertini, M., Frasconi, P.: Short-term traffic flow forecasting: an experimental comparison of time-series analysis and supervised learning. IEEE Trans. Intell. Transp. Syst. **14**(2), 871–882 (2013). https://doi.org/10.1109/TITS.2013.2247040
4. O'Shea, K., Nash, R.: An Introduction to Convolutional Neural Networks (2015)
5. Xu, K., Hu, W., Leskovec, J., Jegelka, S.: How powerful are graph neural networks? In: International Conference on Learning Representations (ICLR 2019) (2019)
6. Ye, J., Sun, L., Du, B., Fu, Y., Xiong, H.: Coupled layer-wise graph convolution for transportation demand prediction. In: Proceedings of 35th AAAI Conference on Artificial Intelligence (AAAI 2021), vol. 35, no. 5, pp. 4617–4625. Association for the Advancement of Artificial Intelligence, Virtual (2021). https://doi.org/10.1609/aaai.v35i5.16591
7. Liu, D., Wang, J., Shang, S., Han, P.: MSDR: multi-step dependency relation networks for spatial temporal forecasting. In: Proceedings of the 28th ACM SIGKDD Conference on Knowledge Discovery and Data Mining, pp. 1042–1050. Association for Computing Machinery, Washington, DC, USA (2022). https://doi.org/10.1145/3534678.3539397
8. Zhang, D., Li, J.: MVFN: multi-view fusion network for traffic demand prediction. Inf. Sci. **646**, 119303 (2023). https://doi.org/10.1016/j.ins.2023.119303
9. Peng, L., Li, C., Zhang, W., Yu, W., Li, T.: Learning dynamic and multi-scale graph structure for traffic demand prediction. Int. J. Mach. Learn. Cybern. **16**(5–6), 3177–3191 (2024). https://doi.org/10.1007/s13042-024-02442-7
10. Weng, W., et al.: A decomposition dynamic graph convolutional recurrent network for traffic forecasting. Pattern Recogn. **142**, 109670 (2023). https://doi.org/10.1016/j.patcog.2023.109670

11. Fan, J., Weng, W., Chen, Q., Wu, H., Wu, J.: Periodic dynamic graph to sequence model for traffic flow prediction. Neural Netw. **183**, 106941 (2025). https://doi.org/10.1016/j.neunet.2024.106941
12. Yu, B., Yin, H., Zhu, Z.: Spatio-temporal graph convolutional networks: a deep learning framework for traffic forecasting. In: Proceedings of the 27th International Joint Conference on Artificial Intelligence (IJCAI) (2018). https://doi.org/10.24963/ijcai.2018/505
13. Yao, H., et al.: Deep multi-view spatial-temporal network for taxi demand prediction. In: The Thirty-Second AAAI Conference on Artificial Intelligence (2018). https://doi.org/10.1609/aaai.v32i1.11836
14. Kipf, T.N., Welling, M.: Semi-supervised classification with graph convolutional networks. in: International Conference on Learning Representations (ICLR) (2017)
15. Elman, J. L.: Finding structure in time. Cogn. Sci. **14**(2), 179–211 (1990). https://doi.org/10.1207/s15516709cog1402_1
16. Xu, H., Zou, T., Liu, M., Qiao, Y., Xue, J., Yang, Y.: Adaptive spatiotemporal dependence learning for multi-mode transportation demand prediction. IEEE Trans. Intell. Transp. Syst. **23**(10), 18632–18642 (2022). https://doi.org/10.1109/TITS.2022.3155753
17. Li, Y., Yu, R., Shahabi, C., Liu, Y.: Diffusion convolutional recurrent neural network: data-driven traffic forecasting. In: International Conference on Learning Representations (ICLR) (2018)
18. Geng, X., et al.: Spatiotemporal multi-graph convolution network for ride-hailing demand forecasting. In: Proceedings of the Thirty-Third AAAI Conference on Artificial Intelligence (AAAI 2019), vol. 33, pp. 3656–3663. AAAI Press (2019). https://doi.org/10.1609/aaai.v33i01.33013656
19. Jin, G., Xi, Z., Sha, H., Feng, Y., Huang, J., et al.: Deep multi-view graph-based network for citywide ride-hailing demand prediction. Neurocomputing **510**, 79–94 (2022). https://doi.org/10.1016/j.neucom.2022.09.010
20. Bai, L., Yao, L., Li, C., Wang, X., Wang, C.: Adaptive graph convolutional recurrent network for traffic forecasting. In: Advances in Neural Information Processing Systems (NeurIPS 2020), vol. 33, pp. 17804–17815 (2020)
21. Jin, G., et al.: Spatio-temporal graph neural networks for predictive learning in urban computing: a survey. IEEE Trans. Knowl. Data Eng. **36**(10), 5388–5408 (2024). https://doi.org/10.1109/TKDE.2023.3333824
22. Hou, J., Liu, S., Zhang, Y., Qin, H.: Hierarchical graph construction for station-free traffic demand prediction. Transp. Res. Part E Logist. Transp. Rev. **199**, 104151 (2025). https://doi.org/10.1016/j.tre.2025.104151

Decomposition-Based Optimization of Multi-camera Networks for Coverage Maximization Problem

Dang Phuoc Vinh Hung[1,2], Nguyen Cao Dat[1,2], Tran Van Hoai[1,2], and Nguyen Huu Hieu[1,2(✉)]

[1] Ho Chi Minh City University of Technology (HCMUT), Ho Chi Minh City, Vietnam
{dpvhung.sdh241,dat,hoai,nguyenhuuhieu}@hcmut.edu.vn
[2] Vietnam National University Ho Chi Minh City (VNU-HCM), Ho Chi Minh City, Vietnam

Abstract. The proliferation of low-cost, high-efficiency surveillance cameras has made multi-camera networks a ubiquitous tool for security and monitoring in public spaces. However, the optimal placement of these cameras to maximize coverage while minimizing resources presents a significant and computationally complex challenge, known to be NP-hard. This research introduces a novel and effective model to address the camera planning problem. We formulate the problem and propose a decomposition strategy that partitions the main problem into smaller, manageable subproblems based on a neighbor graph of potential camera locations. This decomposition allows for the efficient application of well-established solvers to find optimal or near-optimal solutions within practical time constraints. Our model utilizes a 2D map visualization of sensor views, which simplifies the calculation of coverage areas and ensures the direct applicability of our solutions to real-world scenarios. Experimental results, conducted on a set of candidate locations within a university campus, demonstrate the proposed model's superior performance. The formulation successfully maximizes spatial coverage under limited computational budgets, validating its effectiveness and potential for deployment in practical surveillance network design. This approach offers a significant advancement in strategic camera placement, providing a scalable and efficient solution to a critical security problem.

Keywords: camera planning · human detection · real-world environments

1 Introduction

In contemporary security systems, surveillance cameras are primarily utilized across a multitude of public spaces, including university campuses, city squares, and residential complexes. Their deployment is critical for monitoring specific

T. T. Quan et al. (Eds.): MIWAI 2025, LNAI 16353, pp. 142–154, 2026.
https://doi.org/10.1007/978-981-95-4957-3_12

areas, tracking the movement of people, preventing criminal activity, and detecting potential hazards. However, a principal challenge in designing these systems is the effective placement of a finite set of cameras to maximize the coverage of a given surveillance area. Moreover, the strategic selection and placement of cameras in a multi-camera system have a profound impact on the efficacy of downstream image processing algorithms for applications like facial recognition or human tracking. This dependency makes optimal camera planning a crucial and foundational issue, particularly for the deployment of robust surveillance solutions in real-world environments.

Given the map layout of a target area, a discrete set of candidate installation points, and a portfolio of available camera types, our research aims to determine the optimal number and configuration of cameras to maximize surveillance coverage. This configuration is holistically defined by the precise coordinates of each camera, as well as its horizontal and vertical viewing angles. The proposed camera planning method is rigorously evaluated using various scenarios with obstacles of varying sizes and positions, as well as complex environments that are exported from Open Street Map (OSM) data [15]. This strategy serves to confirm the model's applicability in real-world scenarios and find the most accurate approach within the appropriate period of time. The main contributions of our work include:

1. Establishing a model of the target environment: we first sourced building footprint data from OSM to serve as the foundational geospatial layer. Within this environmental representation, the potential coverage for each available camera type was systematically evaluated across numerous candidate locations, ensuring a high-fidelity simulation of the surveillance capabilities.
2. Proposing a novel and effective model that formulates the camera planning challenge as an integer programming problem. By structuring the problem in this manner, it becomes amenable to resolution by established, general-purpose optimization solvers, for which we specifically employ the powerful SCIP framework to derive solutions.
3. Maximizing the coverage of the area surveillance, in which the camera planning objective is proposed to focus on the system's ability to facilitate reliable human detection from the acquired video streams.
4. Utilizing the minimum cut in the k-edge-connected graph [6] to decompose the NP-hard problem [18] into smaller ones to get a sub-optimal solution in reasonable time using the SCIP solver [1].

2 Related Works

The optimal placement of surveillance cameras is a classic problem with roots in the Art Gallery Problem (AGP), which seeks to determine the minimal number of stationary guards required to observe an entire polygonal area [16]. The AGP is known to be NP-Hard in the field of combinatorial optimization [18], a complexity that is inherited by most camera placement formulations. While this foundational work established the problem's theoretical underpinnings, modern research has evolved significantly to address real-world complexities by employing a diverse range of methodologies. A substantial portion of the literature formulates camera placement as a deterministic optimization problem, often reducing it to a variant of the well-known Set Covering Problem (SCP) [11]. In these models, the objective is to select the minimum-cost collection of sets (cameras) that covers all required targets. These formulations are frequently modeled as Integer Programming problems [14]. Due to the computational intensity of solving large-scale IP models directly, researchers have developed sophisticated decomposition techniques. For instance, [12] apply an accelerated Benders decomposition to a dynamic, multi-period version of the problem, where variables related to user coverage are projected out to simplify the main problem. In a different approach, [5] utilize column generation, where new, promising camera configurations (columns) are iteratively generated and added to a restricted master problem, avoiding the need to enumerate all possibilities from the outset. These methods demonstrate that while the core problem is NP-hard, its structure can be exploited to solve large, practical instances more efficiently.

Given the intractability of finding proven optimal solutions for large-scale instances, heuristic and metaheuristic algorithms are the most prevalent methods in camera planning literature. A comprehensive review by [14] details the application of numerous nature-inspired and stochastic optimization techniques. Common approaches include Genetic Algorithms (GA), Particle Swarm Optimization (PSO), Simulated Annealing (SA), and Artificial Bee Colony (ABC) algorithms. These methods are well-suited for the non-linear and complex search spaces typical of camera placement. For example, [10] employ a GA to optimize a layout for detecting infiltrators, a problem with a highly specialized objective function. Similarly, [21] utilize both GA and PSO to develop a multi-objective function that balances coverage and reconstruction error. These studies exemplify a common trend where metaheuristics are adapted to tackle specific, often non-standard, problem formulations that are difficult to linearize for exact solvers.

More recently, a new paradigm has emerged that leverages Reinforcement Learning (RL) to create dynamic and adaptive surveillance systems. Unlike static, offline optimization methods, RL-based approaches can learn and adapt to changing environmental conditions. [3] propose an intelligent system using Q-learning and Deep Q-Networks (DQN) to dynamically adjust camera distribution and Field of View (FoV) based on real-time traffic patterns. The RL agent learns an optimal policy by interacting with the environment, aiming to maximize target coverage while minimizing redundancy. This represents a significant shift from pre-calculating an optimal static layout to learning a dynamic control policy, which is particularly relevant for environments with non-stationary patterns of activity.

The traditional model of simple area coverage has been extended to more nuanced objectives. [4] focuses on optimizing the overlap between camera views to facilitate robust object tracking. [5] introduce an "angular covering" model, which moves away from simple radial coverage to more precisely defined sectors, better reflecting the nature of directional sensors and reducing unnecessary coverage of empty space. In another specific-context, [12] address the dynamic or multi-period nature of some problems, where facility placement decisions must be made across a time horizon.

As a data-driven approach, [8] proposes a placement strategy by observing object parameters in 3D space. More specifically, [9] present a novel method that infers camera coverage parameters by analyzing data on human activity to identify "critical spots" that require surveillance, ensuring that the final placement is not just geometrically optimal but also contextually relevant. Another stream of research in vision-based systems focuses on the real-time utilization of camera feeds for specific tasks, rather than on the initial placement problem. For instance, [2] demonstrates an indoor navigation system where a robot is guided using a single, pre-existing fisheye camera. Their contribution lies in the computer vision algorithms for robot detection and A* path planning from the camera's perspective.

In summary, the literature demonstrates a clear trajectory from abstract, geometrically-defined problems to complex, data-driven, and application-specific formulations. Despite these advances, a gap remains in holistically integrating the full suite of modern camera parameters—including location, height, precise FoV, and orientation yaw—with an objective function directly tied to the performance of contemporary computer vision tasks. Many works either use simplified camera models or focus on maximizing a general sense of coverage. There is a lack of research that explicitly aims to optimize a camera network for the specific purpose of human detection using popular, state-of-the-art algorithms such as YOLO [20].

3 A Decomposition-Based ILP Optimization Method

3.1 Camera Model

A geometric model assuming flat terrain, as illustrated in Fig. 1a, is employed to calculate the extent of the ground area potentially covered by a camera based on its placement and orientation. Key parameters include the height of the camera above the ground (h), its total vertical field of view (γ), and the tilt angle of its optical axis β. The tilt angle β is defined relative to the nadir (the vertical axis pointing directly downward from the camera).

Figure 1b illustrates a 3D camera model positioned within a Cartesian coordinate system. The camera's orientation is determined by two key angles: β, representing the angle between the camera's viewing direction and the vertical z-axis, and α, which controls the camera's rotation within the horizontal Oxy plane. The camera's horizontal Field of View (FOV) is denoted by theta θ, depicted as a frustum originating from the camera and expanding outwards.

This study addresses the optimal placement of cameras in outdoor environments containing occluding structures like buildings. The objective is to determine the optimal number, types, and complete configurations (coordinates, angles) of cameras to maximize layout coverage for human detection. Critically,

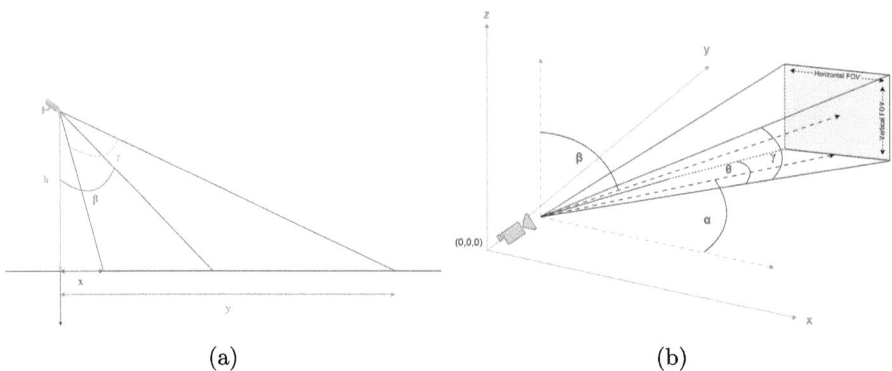

Fig. 1. Camera model for coverage estimation

potential placements are constrained to pre-existing legacy system locations to enhance practical applicability by facilitating infrastructure upgrades. Three vital parameters for our work are: *Camera resolution*, *Field of View (FOV)* and *Focal length of the lens* [19]. There are numerous types of video cameras available, each camera types include different sensor types, lens type, focal length, angles of view,... [16]. For simplification, we assume all cameras are deployed in a fixed state, each covering a specific, static area determined by its final configuration.

3.2 Problem Formulation

Definitions:

- P is set of camera positions in the planning area
- C_p is the set of camera configurations at position $p \in P$
- a_p^c is the coverage of camera configuration $c \in C_p$
- $o_{p_1,c_1}^{p_2,c_2}$ is the coverage overlap between camera configuration c_1 at position p_1 and camera configuration c_2 at position p_2
- $N = \{(p_1, p_2) : p_1, p_2 \in P \text{ and } p_1, p_2 \text{ are neighbors}\}$. If any camera configuration at location p_1 overlaps with any camera configuration at location p_2, then p_1 and p_2 are considered neighbors.

The following decision variables are introduced for the problem formulation:

$$y_p^c = \begin{cases} 1, & \text{if camera configuration } c \text{ is at position } p, \\ 0, & \text{otherwise.} \end{cases} \tag{1}$$

$$u_{p_1,c_1}^{p_2,c_2} = \begin{cases} 1, & \text{if camera configuration } c_1 \text{ is at position } p_1 \\ & \text{and camera configuration } c_2 \text{ is at position } p_2, \\ 0, & \text{otherwise.} \end{cases} \tag{2}$$

The camera planning problem can then be formulated as the Integer Programming Problem as follows.

Objective function:

$$\max \left(\sum_{p \in P} \sum_{c \in C_p} a_p^c y_p^c \quad - \sum_{(p_1,p_2) \in N} \sum_{c_1 \in C_1} \sum_{c_2 \in C_2} o_{p_1,c_1}^{p_2,c_2} u_{p_1,c_1}^{p_2,c_2} \right) \tag{3}$$

Subject to:

$$\sum_{c \in C_p} y_p^c \leq 1 \tag{4}$$

$$y_{p_1}^{c_1} \geq u_{p_1,c_1}^{p_2,c_2} \tag{5}$$

$$y_{p_2}^{c_2} \geq u_{p_1,c_1}^{p_2,c_2} \tag{6}$$

$$u_{p_1,c_1}^{p_2,c_2} \geq y_{p_1}^{c_1} + y_{p_2}^{c_2} - 1 \tag{7}$$

The objective function (3) maximize the total coverage of every camera configuration chosen at all positions and constraint (4) to (7) are:

- Constraint (4) ensure that only one camera configuration is used at position $p \in P$
- Constraint (5) to (7) is for all $(p_1, p_2) \in N$, which ensure $u_{p_1,c_1}^{p_2,c_2} = 1$ if $y_{p_1}^{c_1} = 1$ and $y_{p_2}^{c_2} = 1$

Proposed solution methodology employs a graph-based decomposition algorithm to break down the overarching problem into multiple, smaller subproblems that can be solved more efficiently. The precise mechanics of this graph decomposition process are detailed in Algorithm 1 which can be summarized in three main steps:

- *Step 1: Neighbor Graph Construction.* The process begins with the construction of an undirected neighbor graph, G = (V, E). In this graph, the vertex set V corresponds to the set of all potential camera locations P. An edge connects any two distinct vertices, p1 and p2, if and only if the coverage area of at least one camera configuration at location p1 overlaps with the coverage of at least one configuration at location p2.
- *Step 2: Recursive Graph Decomposition.* The neighbor graph G is then partitioned into a set of subproblems. Initially, G is decomposed into its fundamental connected components. For any component that is still too large to be solved efficiently (i.e., its number of vertices exceeds a predefined threshold Vm), we recursively partition it. This partitioning is performed using a k-edge-connected components algorithm [7], which iteratively splits a component into two smaller ones. This recursive process continues until all resulting components are smaller than or equal to the size threshold Vm, as detailed in Algorithm 1.

- *Step 3: Subproblem Solving and Solution Aggregation.* Each resulting connected component from the decomposition process represents an independent subproblem. These subproblems are solved individually using the SCIP solver. Finally, the individual solutions (which may be optimal for the subproblem or the best sub-optimal solution found within a time limit) are aggregated to construct a comprehensive solution for the original, large-scale problem.

4 Experimental Results

For this section, the problem was implemented for the SCIP solver, and a series of experiments were performed on both laboratory and real-world dataset. These tests were specifically designed to evaluate the solution quality under varying constraints, namely by adjusting the maximum number of candidate camera positions allowed per subproblem and the computational time limit allocated to the solver. All experiments were conducted on a server equipped with dual Intel Xeon E5-2670 v2 processors operating at 2.50 GHz and furnished with 128 GB of RAM.

Algorithm 1 Graph Decomposition

Input: The graph $G = (V, E)$, the maximum number of vertices V_m

Output: list of connected components with the number of vertices in each component less than or equal to V_m

$C \leftarrow$ *list of connected components in graph G*
repeat
    for each $c \in C$ **do**
        $c_n \leftarrow$ *number of vertices in c*
        if $c_n > V_m$ **then**
            $C \leftarrow$ *Replace c with two connected components decomposing by k-edge connected algorithm*
        end if
    end for
until *all components in C has number of vertices less than or equal* V_m

4.1 Laboratory Experiments

Effectiveness of the neighbor graph decomposition approach was validated through experiments analyzing its impact on coverage and computational efficiency. The test cases, comprising randomly generated areas and locations, were sized to ensure optimal solutions could be determined within a practical timeframe.

The first experiment, conducted on a disconnected neighbor graph, allowed for the problem to be decomposed into three independent subproblems. Solving these individually, and then combining their optimal solutions, preserved global optimality. As Table 2 shows, this approach drastically reduced computational time from 3.3 h to 1.3 min, demonstrating the significant efficiency gains of decomposition in camera planning.

Table 1. Coverage and processing time for test case 1

	Without decomposition	With decomposition
Number of candidate locations	11	11
Coverage Percentages	40.22%	40.22%
Optimal solution	✓	✓
Number of subproblems	1	3
Total processing time	198 min (3.3 h)	1.3 min

In the second experiment, as detailed in Table 1, characterized by a singly connected neighbor graph, problem decomposition via the methods used in experiment 1 was infeasible. To address this, a k-edge-connected decomposition algorithm was employed, with the maximum component size set to seven nodes. This partitioned the graph into four connected components. The aggregated solution, while not achieving global optimality, demonstrated a coverage percentage of 61.96%, closely approximating the optimal solution's 62.57%. Critically, this approach yielded a solution in 41 s, a substantial efficiency improvement compared to the 40 min required for the optimal solution, thereby underscoring its practical efficiency.

Table 2. Coverage and processing time for test case 2

	Without decomposition	With decomposition
Number of candidate locations	15	15
Coverage Percentages	62.57%	61.96%
Optimal solution	✓	×
Number of subproblems	1	4
Total processing time	2424 s (40 min)	41 s

4.2 Real-World Area and Camera Placement Experiments

The experimental environment used to evaluate proposed camera planning solution consists of a 140.000 m^2 university campus area that includes 32 distinct building footprints. The geospatial data for this layout was sourced from the Open Street Map (OSM) project [15]. Within this environment, a set of 148 candidate camera positions was identified, derived from the GPS-verified locations of the pre-existing, legacy surveillance system. For each candidate position, a discrete set of configurations was evaluated, including two to three horizontal and vertical angle options and two possible installation heights. The model employs three types of cameras with specifications based on real industrial hardware: two distinct perspective cameras and one omnidirectional camera. Critically, the effective Field of View (FoV) for each camera type was defined to ensure its utility for a primary surveillance task: human detection. The FoV radius were chosen to align with the operational ranges of contemporary detection models like YOLO. Accordingly, the two perspective cameras were modeled with effective FoV radius of 40 m and 45 m, respectively [17], while the omnidirectional camera was assigned a 15-meter radius [13].

The analysis of the experimental environment reveals a substantial configuration space. For each candidate position, the potential coverage for every available camera type was evaluated across a discrete set of parameters, including installation height and viewing angles. This process generated approximately 24 to 48 distinct configurations for each potential location, culminating in a total of 4,740 unique configurations for the entire problem instance. Performance was assessed across several experimental scenarios, which were distinguished by the maximum number of candidate locations permitted within each subproblem. A computational time limit of four hours was imposed for solving each subproblem, ensuring that a comprehensive solution could be obtained within an appropriate overall timeframe. The characteristics of our test cases and their corresponding coverage results are summarized in Table 3. The baseline Scenario #1, involving 148 locations and 171,483 parameters, was solved directly, yielding 73.52% coverage within the 4-hour limit, the corresponding coverage visualization is presented in Fig. 3a. This highlights the need for our decomposition strategy. The application of the k-edge-connected algorithm systematically reduces the maximum number of locations within each subproblem, which consequently increases the number of subproblems to be solved but decreases the final count of unused locations. Scenario #3 yielded the most effective result, achieving a maximum area coverage of 75.67%. This was accomplished by constraining the maximum number of locations per subproblem to 50, which partitioned the problem into a total of 10 subproblems. A representative subproblem of 50 locations in this scenario contained 30,992 parameters. Notably, four of the ten subproblems terminated at the four-hour time limit, returning the best suboptimal solution found within that period, which led to a total processing time in excess of 16 h. The resulting decomposed graph, with each connected component representing a distinct subproblem, is depicted in Fig. 2b alongside the original neighbor graph in Fig. 2a. Ultimately, the camera planning algorithm for this scenario identified 22 candidate locations as unused. The final coverage visualization for this optimized camera plan on the university campus is illustrated in Fig. 3b.

Table 3. Coverage and processing time for each test scenario

Scenario	#1	#2	#3	#4	#5
Number of candidate locations	148	148	148	148	148
Max. locations of subproblems	148	132	50	25	15
Number of subproblems	1	7	10	15	16
Max. Nof. parameters of subproblems	171,483	160,496	30,992	18,205	16,750
Number of unused locations	23	25	22	14	10
Total processing time (hours)	4	8	16.1	26.1	22.5
Coverage Percentages	73.52%	74.11%	bf75.67%	75.00%	74.65%

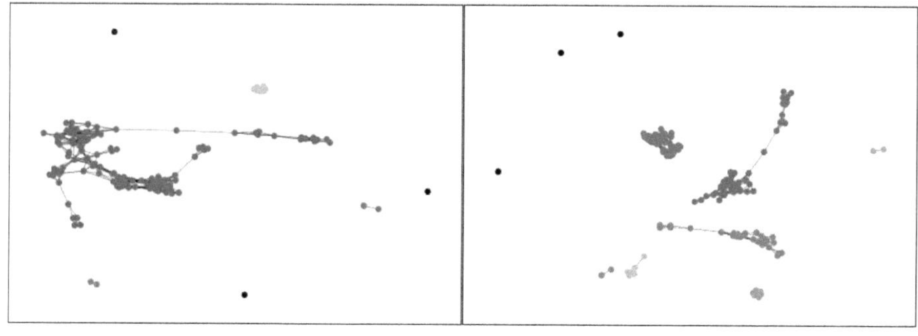

(a) The original neighbor graph (b) The decomposed graph in scenario #3

Fig. 2. Original and Decomposed Problem Graphs

To further analyze the computational performance, Fig. 4a and Fig. 4b illustrate the evolution of the primal and dual bounds - and the resultant optimality gap - as recorded by SCIP for three representative subproblems. These instances, comprising 30,992, 18,205, and 16,750 parameters respectively, were each executed with a time limit of 4 h. The results reveal a clear trend: as the problem size increases, the final optimality gap at the expiration of the time limit also increases. Crucially, the figures show that none of these subproblems were solved to proven optimality within the allotted computational budget. Furthermore, the convergence plots indicate that the gap between the bounds decreases most significantly in the early stages of the solution process. For all three problems, after approximately 80 min of computation, the rate of gap reduction diminishes substantially, with only marginal improvements observed thereafter.

(a) Scenario #1 (Baseline) (b) Scenario #3 (Optimization)

Fig. 3. Comparison of Baseline and Optimized Camera Coverage

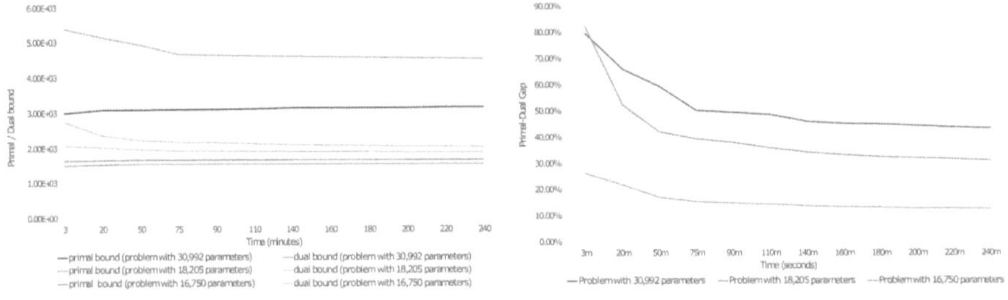

(a) Primal/Dual bounds for three subproblems of varying sizes (b) Optimality Gap for three subproblems of varying sizes

Fig. 4. Primal/Dual bounds and Optimality Gap for three subproblems.

5 Conclusions

This study investigated the strategic placement of outdoor camera sensors within a campus environment containing buildings, focusing on the dual objectives of optimizing surveillance coverage and managing computational time. Utilizing an extensive dataset derived from a real campus area, including building footprints, actual camera locations, and various camera types, the task was formulated as an integer programming problem and solved using the SCIP solver. To address the inherent complexity of this NP-hard problem, a decomposition technique is introduced and evaluated. This technique partitions the large-scale problem into numerous subproblems by employing a k-edge-connected algorithm on a neighbor graph of potential locations. The research project yielded several crucial findings. First, an effective and comprehensive model was proposed for the camera planning problem that is directly amenable to solution by modern integer programming solvers. Second, we demonstrated that decomposing the problem based on a graph's connected components is a highly effective strategy for achieving high-quality solutions in a practical timeframe. Laboratory experiments consistently validate this approach. The experimental results on real-world area show that by limiting the solution time for each subproblem to a reasonable four hours, we achieved a total area coverage of 75.67% in a best-case scenario that required 16.1 h of cumulative processing. A key aspect of proposed model is that the definition of a camera's viewable area was predicated on its ability to support human detection, thereby linking the optimization directly to the primary surveillance application. In summary, this paper presents a novel model and decomposition technique that advance camera planning methodologies. Future research should build on this foundation by exploring dynamic factors (e.g., environmental changes, moving targets) and multidisciplinary integration to refine sensor placement. Furthermore, applying AI-driven approaches holds promise for achieving superior results within constrained computational budgets.

Acknowledgement. This research is funded by Vietnam National University Ho Chi Minh City (VNU-HCM) under grant number NCM2021-20-02. We acknowledge Ho Chi Minh City University of Technology (HCMUT), VNU-HCM for supporting this study.

References

1. Achterberg, T.: SCIP: solving constraint integer programs. Math. Program. Comput. **1**(1), 1–41 (2009)
2. Ahmadh, U., Kumara, W., Begum, A., Prema Sri, I., Cader, M.: Vision based indoor navigation system using external camera mounted on room (2019)
3. Almalkawi, I.T., et al.: Intelligent IoT-based network clustering and camera distribution algorithm using reinforcement learning. Technologies **13**(1), 4 (2024)
4. Altahir, A.A., et al.: Optimizing visual sensor coverage overlaps for multiview surveillance systems. IEEE Sens. J. **18**(11), 4544–4552 (2018)
5. Barriga-Gallegos, F., Lüer-Villagra, A., Gutiérrez-Jarpa, G.: The angular set covering problem. IEEE Access **12**, 87181–87198 (2024)
6. Cai, G.R., Sun, Y.G.: The minimum augmentation of any graph to a k-edge-connected graph. Networks **19**(1), 151–172 (1989)
7. Chang, L., Yu, J.X., Qin, L., Lin, X., Liu, C., Liang, W.: Efficiently computing k-edge connected components via graph decomposition. In: Proceedings of the 2013 ACM SIGMOD International Conference on Management of Data, pp. 205–216 (2013)
8. Fedorov, I., Lawal, N., O'Nils, M., Alqaysi, H.: Placement strategy of multi-camera volumetric surveillance system for activities monitoring. In: Proceedings of the 11th International Conference on Distributed Smart Cameras, pp. 113–118 (2017)

9. Han, Z., Li, S., Cui, C., Song, H., Kong, Y., Qin, F.: Camera planning for area surveillance: a new method for coverage inference and optimization using location-based service data. Comput. Environ. Urban Syst. **78**, 101396 (2019)
10. Jeong, J., et al.: Optimization framework for surveillance camera layouts considering infiltration routes in general outposts (GOPs). Expert Syst. Appl. **263**, 125804 (2025)
11. Kritter, J., Brévilliers, M., Lepagnot, J., Idoumghar, L.: On the optimal placement of cameras for surveillance and the underlying set cover problem. Appl. Soft Comput. **74**, 133–153 (2019)
12. Lamontagne, S., Carvalho, M., Atallah, R.: Accelerated benders decomposition and local branching for dynamic maximum covering location problems. Comput. Oper. Res. **167**, 106673 (2024)
13. Lee, M., Kim, H., Paik, J.: Correction of barrel distortion in fisheye lens images using image-based estimation of distortion parameters. IEEE Access **7**, 45723–45733 (2019)
14. Liu, J., Sridharan, S., Fookes, C.: Recent advances in camera planning for large area surveillance: a comprehensive review. ACM Comput. Surv. (CSUR) **49**(1), 1–37 (2016)
15. Map, O.S.: Open street map. Acessado em **12** (2017)
16. O'rourke, J.: Art Gallery Theorems and Algorithms. Oxford University Press, Inc. (1987)
17. Salem, M.S.H., Zaman, F.H.K., Tahir, N.M.: Effectiveness of human detection from aerial images taken from different heights. TEM J. **10**(2), 522 (2021)
18. Shermer, T.C.: Recent results in art galleries (geometry). Proc. IEEE **80**(9), 1384–1399 (2002)
19. Tang, V.D., Stokkermans, T.J., Zhang, A.Y.: Focal length. In: StatPearls [Internet]. StatPearls Publishing (2023)
20. Zaman, F.H.K., Tahir, N.M., Yusoff, Y.M., Thamrin, N.M., Hasmi, A.H.: Human detection from drone using you only look once (YOLOv5) for search and rescue operation. J. Adv. Res. Appl. Sci. Eng. Technol. **30**(3), 222–235 (2023)
21. Zhou, J., Deng, H., Zhao, Z., Zou, Y., Wang, X.: Sensor placement optimization of visual sensor networks for target tracking based on multi-objective constraints. Appl. Sci. **14**(5), 1722 (2024)

Bridging Language and Vision: Fine-Tuning Latent Diffusion Models for Robust Text-to-Image Generation

Daniel Vadranapu[1(✉)], Abhiram Yadav Myla[2], and Charan Ramtej Kodi[3]

[1] Department of Robotics, University at Buffalo, Buffalo, USA
dvadrana@buffalo.edu

[2] Department of Data Science, University at Buffalo, Buffalo, USA
amyla3@buffalo.edu

[3] School of Computer and Information Sciences, University of Hyderabad, Hyderabad, India
21mcpc10@uohyd.ac.in

Abstract. This paper presents a progressive approach to text-to-image generation by developing an AI system capable of producing vivid and semantically faithful images from natural language descriptions. We adopt a multi-stage pipeline beginning with foundational experiments using Generative Adversarial Networks (GANs) on the MNIST dataset, gradually scaling to more complex datasets such as COCO. To bridge the semantic gap between textual and visual modalities, we integrate a BERT-based text encoder with a Convolutional Neural Network (CNN)-based generator, enabling the system to capture nuanced textual features and translate them into coherent visual representations. Building on these foundations, we leverage the Latent Diffusion Model (LDM) to enhance image quality and fidelity. Our contributions include model optimization, fine-tuning of LDM components, and a detailed evaluation of robustness across various textual inputs. Notably, we identify failure cases involving typographical and contextual input variations, highlighting key limitations in current diffusion-based models. These findings inform our recommendations for future improvements in semantic alignment and input resilience. Overall, our work demonstrates the effectiveness of combining transformer-based text encoders with generative architectures and sets the stage for more robust, high-fidelity text-to-image synthesis systems.

Keywords: text-to-image · Latent Diffusion Model · semantic alignment

1 Introduction

In recent years, the development of artificial intelligence (AI) systems that can generate images based on textual descriptions has gained a lot of popularity. This

T. T. Quan et al. (Eds.): MIWAI 2025, LNAI 16353, pp. 155–166, 2026.
https://doi.org/10.1007/978-981-95-4957-3_13

has been started by some ground-breaking papers, such as Generative Adversarial Networks (GANs) by Goodfellow et al. [4]. With the introduction of GANs, there has been a significant rise in the level of work that has been done in the field of the generation of images through learning on large complex datasets such as Common Objects in Context (COCO) dataset [11]. The diversity of the images included in this dataset makes it a perfect dataset to evaluate the potential of image generation models. Furthermore, the interaction of language and vision has also been discussed, where advanced language models like BERT [2] and CNNs [9] have been combined. Learning these models to process textual inputs to produce images, researchers have aimed to solve the semantic gap between the textual descriptions and the visual representations. We start with explaining the underlying concepts of GANs and proceed to more sophisticated datasets such as the COCO. We then discuss how to use language and vision together using BERT and CNNs. Finally, we apply Latent Diffusion Model [6] to generate the images and again subject them to testing and adjustment of the experiments.

2 Related Work

One of the most important contributions to the general field of image synthesis is the introduction of Generative Adversarial Network (GAN) by Goodfellow et al. [4] and its adversarial training paradigm. The idea of conditioned GANs (cGANs) [14] extends this system by providing generation conditioned on auxiliary data, e.g. class labels or text, in order to provide more controlled synthesis. Recent advances like StackGAN [23] and AttnGAN [22] have set new bar of text to image synthesis by showing how hierarchical and attention based generation can significantly improve fidelity and relevance of generated images. Integrating the textual semantics with visual characteristics has been a key issue. Early research used the RNN-based encoders [18], but more recently current works use very strong transformer based models like BERT [3] which is an encoder based model.

All these models contextualize and generate embeddings which are used as rich inputs to generative networks. Other techniques such as DM-GAN [24] and hybrid encoders such as T2F [1] have attempted to learn methods of dynamically augmenting textual features during generation. Diffusion-based models have more recently demonstrated their ability to produce good quality, diverse images. Denoising Diffusion Probabilistic Models (DDPMs) were proposed by Ho et al. [5], which learn generative process by a gradual denoising process. On top of this, Latent Diffusion Models (LDMs) [19] can synthesize images at high resolution and in a scalable way by operating in the latent space. The latest models like Imagen [21] and DALLE 2 [17] bring in language models into the conditioning process and achieve a strong semantic alignment. Authors in this work [8] use transformers to predict political bias.

Multimodal learning is capable of combining the text and visual contents in a common embedding space. The latest transformer based vision language models are [10,12]. The models that learn unified representations by contrastive learning are landmark models such as LIP [7] and ALIGN [7]. Although they are originally designed with retrieval and classification in mind, their embedding strategies are gaining more and more popularity in generative pipelines.

3 Methodology

3.1 Latent Diffusion Models

Perceptual Latent Space. Consider an image $x \in \mathbb{R}^{H \times W \times 3}$. To compress this into a more compact and meaningful representation, an encoder $\mathcal{E}$ maps it to a latent variable $z = \mathcal{E}(x)$, where $z \in \mathbb{R}^{h \times w \times c}$. A corresponding decoder $\mathcal{D}$ attempts to reconstruct the original image, giving $\tilde{x} = \mathcal{D}(z) = \mathcal{D}(\mathcal{E}(x))$. This setup implies a spatial downscaling factor of $f = H/h = W/w$, allowing efficient latent-space modeling.

Forward Diffusion in Latent Space. Let the initial latent $z_0 = \mathcal{E}(x)$ represent the uncorrupted signal. A sequence of increasingly noisy versions $(z_t)_{t=1}^{T}$ is generated using:

$$q(z_t \mid z_0) = \mathcal{N}\left(z_t \mid \alpha_t z_0,\ \sigma_t^2 I\right), \tag{1}$$

for $t = 1, \ldots, T$. Due to the Markovian nature of the process, intermediate transitions follow:

$$q(z_t \mid z_s) = \mathcal{N}\left(z_t \mid \alpha_{t|s} z_s,\ \sigma_{t|s}^2 I\right), \tag{2}$$

$$\alpha_{t|s} = \frac{\alpha_t}{\alpha_s}, \qquad \sigma_{t|s}^2 = \sigma_t^2 - \alpha_{t|s}^2 \sigma_s^2. \tag{3}$$

Reverse Process and Objective Function. The aim is to model the reverse-time denoising transitions $p(z_{t-1} \mid z_t)$ using a neural network. This is formulated as:

$$p(z_{t-1} \mid z_t) = \mathcal{N}\left(z_{t-1} \mid \mu_\theta(z_t, t),\ \frac{\sigma_{t|t-1}^2 \sigma_{t-1}^2}{\sigma_t^2} I\right), \tag{4}$$

with the mean defined as:

$$\mu_\theta(z_t, t) = \frac{\alpha_{t|t-1} \sigma_{t-1}^2}{\sigma_t^2} z_t + \frac{\alpha_{t-1} \sigma_{t|t-1}^2}{\sigma_t^2} z_\theta(z_t, t). \tag{5}$$

Training minimizes a reweighted evidence lower bound (ELBO), which conveniently reduces to a denoising score matching loss.

Epsilon-Parameterization. The model can be simplified using a noise-prediction form:

$$\varepsilon_\theta(z_t, t) = \frac{z_t - \alpha_t z_\theta(z_t, t)}{\sigma_t}. \tag{6}$$

This yields a loss function of the form:

$$\mathcal{L}_{\text{LDM}} = \mathbb{E}_{x,\, \varepsilon \sim \mathcal{N}(0,I),\, t} \left[\|\varepsilon - \varepsilon_\theta(z_t, t)\|_2^2 \right], \tag{7}$$

where z_t is sampled from $q(\cdot \mid z_0 = \mathcal{E}(x))$.

Text Conditioning via Cross-Attention. To allow guided generation, a text prompt y is encoded using a transformer-based encoder τ_θ, producing $\zeta = \tau_\theta(y) \in \mathbb{R}^{M\times d_\tau}$. In the U-Net, cross-attention injects this context into intermediate latent features $\phi_i(z_t)$ using:

$$\mathrm{Q}_i = W_i^Q \phi_i(z_t), \quad \mathrm{K}_i = W_i^K \zeta, \quad \mathrm{V}_i = W_i^V \zeta, \quad \mathrm{CA}_i = \mathrm{softmax}\left(\frac{Q_i K_i^\top}{\sqrt{d}}\right) V_i. \tag{8}$$

The result is added via a residual connection:

$$\mathrm{Output} = \phi_i(z_t) + \mathrm{Proj}_i(\mathrm{CA}_i), \tag{9}$$

providing the model with meaningful guidance from textual prompts during denoising.

Parameter-Efficient Fine-Tuning of Cross-Attention. We fine-tune only the cross-attention projections $\{W_i^Q, W_i^K, W_i^V, W_i^O\}$ using low-rank adapters (LoRA):

$$W' = W + AB, \qquad A \in \mathbb{R}^{d_{\text{out}}\times r},\ B \in \mathbb{R}^{r\times d_{\text{in}}},\ r \ll \min(d_{\text{in}}, d_{\text{out}}),$$

freezing the remaining UNet and VAE. Let $g_\theta(y)$ denote the decoded image from the denoised latent for prompt y. We add a textâĂŞimage alignment term in CLIP space:

$$\mathcal{L}_{\text{InfoNCE}} = -\frac{1}{B}\sum_{i=1}^{B} \log \frac{\exp\left(\langle v_i, u_i\rangle/\tau\right)}{\sum_{j=1}^{B} \exp\left(\langle v_i, u_j\rangle/\tau\right)}, \qquad v_i = \frac{f_{\text{img}}(g_\theta(y_i))}{\|\cdot\|},\ u_i = \frac{f_{\text{txt}}(y_i)}{\|\cdot\|}.$$

Our fine-tuning objective is

$$\boxed{\mathcal{L}_{\text{FT}} = \mathcal{L}_{\text{LDM}} + \lambda_{\text{align}}\,\mathcal{L}_{\text{InfoNCE}} + \lambda_{\text{wd}}\|\Theta_{\text{LoRA}}\|_2^2},$$

where $\Theta_{\text{LoRA}} = \{A_i, B_i\}_i$ are the only trainable parameters.

3.2 cGAN with BERT Text Encoder for Text-to-Image Synthesis

The project involves developing a Conditional Generative Adversarial Network (cGAN), which takes text as input while training and produces a matching image. The system consists of a text encoder that is calculated with the use of the BERT algorithm, a Generator and also a Discriminator network.

Data Handling and Transformations. The model is trained on the COCO dataset (namely the train2017 split), and this data set has nearly 118,000 images with paired caption data. The data of image-captions is processed by means of the `COCODataset` class [11]. The images are resized to 256×256 pixels and the mean and standard deviation of the pixels in each of the 3 RGB channels is registered to 0.5. There is a pipeline that preprocess and converts the pictures to tensors. During training, PyTorch `DataLoader` with batch size of 32 is used for easy data shuffling and also for the loading of data.

Model Architecture. Figure 3 illustrates the architecture of the model, which is a multi-stage, modular design that follows the latest versions of latent diffusion models that are available in present times. First, an AutoencoderKL component is employed to compress input images (resolution of 512×512) to their latent representation (64×64). Then the downsampling reduces the spatial resolution by 8 times. For the output consisting of four channels a normalized factor of 0.18215 is scaled to the latent space.

The centerpiece of the model is a UNet-like architecture augmented with ResNet block and attention layers. The cross-attention layers are included, which help generating with conditions with the help of external signals, such as text. In terms of text conditioning, the system extracts token utilizing 1280 dimensions using a BERT-based encoder (with 77 tokens of length maximum). When it is used in training, the model employs 1000 steps of diffusion and a linear schedule with the values of beta increases/decreases 0.00085-0.012. To make the inference, it relies on the DDIM (Denoising Diffusion Implicit Models) framework, where it used 50 sampling steps and classifier free guidance, with the strength parameter being $\omega = 7.5$, which enables controllable synthesis of an image.

Text Encoder: It is written in terms of using a pre-trained BERT model to perform feature vectorization of textual information. BERT is used because of its capabilities to extract high-quality semantic information, which provides important context and details about what is described in the captions. The Text Encoder has the total of 109,482,240 parameters.

Training. The adversarial loss for both the Generator and Discriminator is given by the Binary Cross-Entropy Loss:

$$\mathcal{L}_D = -\mathbb{E}_{x \sim p_{\text{data}}}[\log D(x)] - \mathbb{E}_{z \sim p_z}[\log(1 - D(G(z)))]$$

$$\mathcal{L}_G = -\mathbb{E}_{z \sim p_z}[\log D(G(z))]$$

The reason to select the Binary Cross-Entropy Loss is its usefulness in binary classification tasks which is the discriminator task to determine whether an image is real or fake. This loss value is an effective approximation to measure the difference between the calculated probabilities (hypothetical or not real) and the real values in terms of effects (real or fake). Both Generator and Discriminator are trained with Adam optimizer with learning rate of 0.0002 and betas (0.5, 0.999). Adam is chosen due to its adaptive learning-rate property that is beneficial to converge faster and also tackle the sparse gradients that is commonplace in GAN training. The training steps involves alternating and optimizing the Generator and Discriminator, to minimize the two losses respectively. The Generator tries to generate realistic images which can fool the Discriminator and the Discriminator attempts to distinguish between real and generated images. Training was done on the train2017 subset of the COCO dataset over 20 epochs using a batch size of 32. Training losses will be recorded with the TensorBoard, and a model checkpoint would be stored every epoch. Such a strategy allows the Generator and Discriminator to be optimized over time and result in generating realistic images that correspond well to the textual descriptions provided as input. These models have in total 109,482240 parameters, 51,055811 parameters and 2766529 parameters in the text encoder, generator and discriminator respectively a total of 163,304580 parameters (Fig. 1).

Algorithm 1 Latent Diffusion Model Training

Require: Pretrained encoder $\mathcal{E}$; dataset of pairs $\{(x, c)\}$ (image, conditioning)
Require: Noise schedule $\{\beta_t\}_{t=1}^{T}$; UNet ε_θ
Ensure: Trained denoiser ε_θ
$\alpha_t \leftarrow 1 - \beta_t, \quad \bar{\alpha}_t \leftarrow \prod_{s=1}^{t} \alpha_s$
for each training iteration **do**
  Sample (x_0, c), set $z_0 \leftarrow \mathcal{E}(x_0)$
  Sample $t \sim \text{Uniform}\{1, \ldots, T\}, \quad \epsilon \sim \mathcal{N}(0, I)$
  $z_t \leftarrow \sqrt{\bar{\alpha}_t}\, z_0 + \sqrt{1 - \bar{\alpha}_t}\, \epsilon$ ▷ forward noising
  $\epsilon_{\text{pred}} \leftarrow \varepsilon_\theta(z_t, t, c)$ ▷ predict noise
  $\mathcal{L} \leftarrow \|\epsilon - \epsilon_{\text{pred}}\|_2^2$ ▷ LDM loss
  Update θ using $\nabla_\theta \mathcal{L}$
return ε_θ

---

4 Experimental Results

4.1 BERT Text Encoder for Text-to-Image Synthesis

Figure 2 illustrates the outcome of the training of all 20 epochs recording the losses of Generator (G) and Discriminator (D) at certain points. The Generator

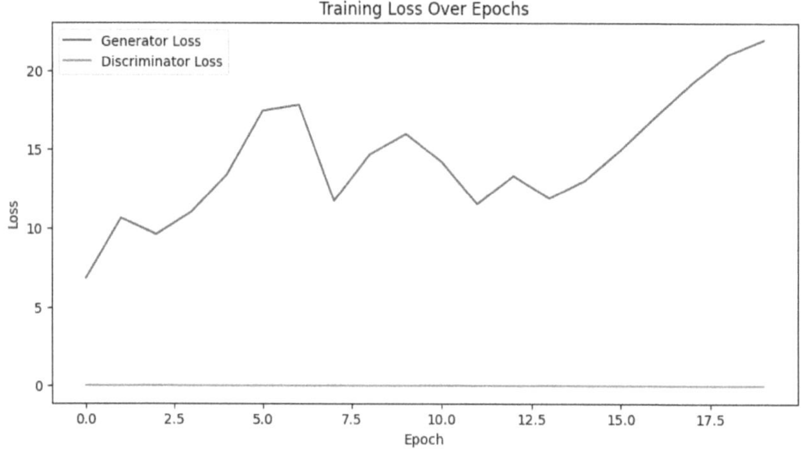

Fig. 1. Training Loss over Epochs

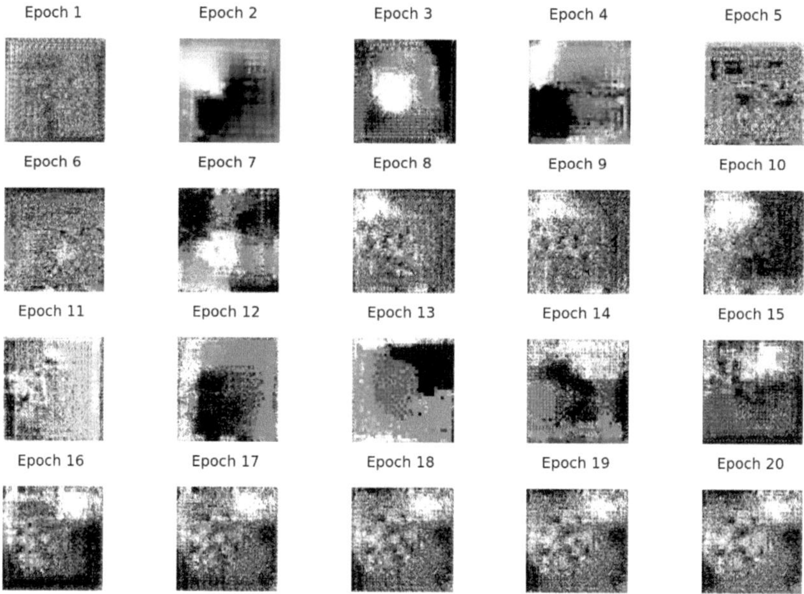

Fig. 2. Progression of training epochs

initially showed an up-and-down loss but an upward trend over time, whereas that of the Discriminator was very low. Even with the growing Generator loss, the model was able to produce a wide variety of images based on the input text. This proved that the Conditional GAN architecture has potential. The growing Generator loss points at the places in which improvement and optimization can be conducted further on. The following factors could contribute to the observed results: Mode Collapse: The Generator might be producing a limited variety of images, causing the Discriminator to easily distinguish between real and fake images. Imbalance in Training: The Discriminator could be learning faster than the Generator, this causes difficulty for the Generator to catch up and produce convincing images.

Figure 4 demonstrates the development of the produced results in the Conditional GAN model during the 20 epochs. First, the images are highly noisy and they do not have any recognizable structure, as in Epoch 1. By the Epoch 2, noise has diminished, but there is still no clarity. As the training advances, in particular by Epoch 7 and 8, some structure is starting to be developed, but the images still remain abstract. Between Epochs 9 and 12, the generated pictures have clearer patterns and less noise, which means that the model is learning features, yet they are disjointed. This tendency remains until Epoch 15, though there is a slight improvement in the texture and pattern, but the outputs are not really realistic. In the later epochs, specifically from Epochs 16 to 20, there is a noticeable improvement in stability and pattern definition,

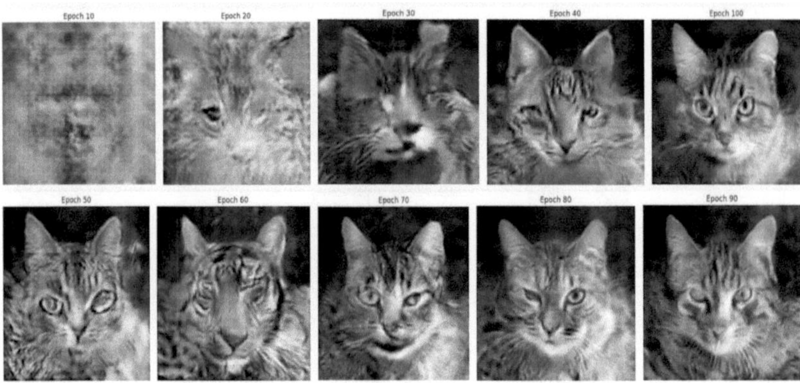

Fig. 3. Progression of Training

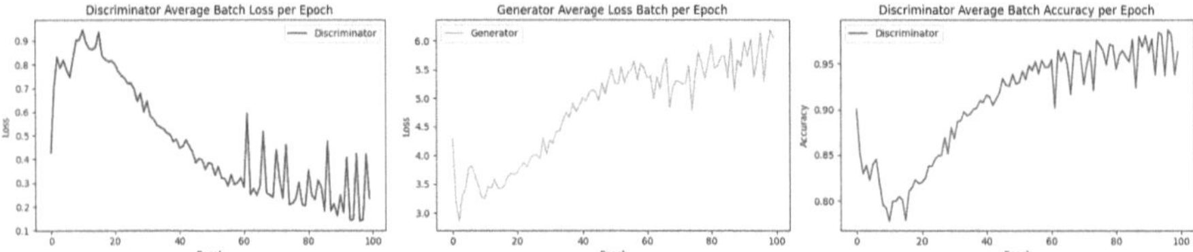

Fig. 4. Results

yet the images still lack clarity and detail. The model's generator struggles to create realistic images from text prompts, possibly due to dataset complexity and training dynamics. Applied the already existing Latent Diffusion model [20] which is suitable in producing high-resolution images. The LDM model performs quite well, but in testing, we found that the performance of the model declined significantly when the input contained typographical errors. Whereas LDM is a great tool in creating high quality images in ideal conditions, it is poor with input that contains errors. When this happens the model is likely to give erratic and noisy images that are not coherent and do not have fidelity to the intended content. Such contradiction is indicative of a critical drawback to the existing implementation. Although it is effective, the model is not robust enough when changes in input are considered, i.e. typographical errors. As a result, it is critical to do something about this problem to make the model more reliable and applicable in a variety of input conditions. Going ahead, possible strategies to enhance the resiliency of the model to variability in inputs should be explored. This may include adding typographical variations to the training data, or adding more robust error-handling procedures, or modifying the model architecture to be more robust against noisy inputs. By combating these issues, we can aim to increase the quality of the LDM and extend its usage to more real-life situations. In the above Fig. 5, The model has predicted a happy bear with newspaper accurately, while in the Fig. 6, when the spelling was changed the model has just stitched the two texts with respective images rather than giving them separately. This is one of the area of improvement which can be done to improve the model performance on such edge cases.

Fig. 5. Prompt: A happy bear reading a newspaper

Fig. 6. Prompt: A happy beer reading a newspaper

The latent diffusion model (LDM) is complex and requires high resources to test. The modern methods based on the extensive parameterization of models are very demanding on the hardware. To perform the LDM testing, 32GB of CPU RAM and graphics card with at least 20GB of memory is required. The size of the pretrained model alone is about 11GB. The GPU is a powerful one to process LDM model. Currently, one A100 GPU is required as a minimum to perform the computation duties. The GPU offers the required power to run the complex calculations to be made under the LDM, thus making the best out of the testing and evaluation process.

5 Challenges

A few difficulties were faced in the process of developing the Conditional GAN model of text-to-image synthesis, which greatly affected our work. The greatest difficulty was the balanced training process between Generator and the Discriminator. In many cases, the Discriminator would learn too fast and easily figure out real images and generated images. This showed there is no loss to the Discriminator and also required performance enhancement of the Generator to create realistic images. Another difficulty was to properly interpret and encode the textual descriptions into meaningful feature vectors. A pretrained BERT model is used as a text encoder to capture all the details and nuances of the descriptions to give a proper usable input to the Generator. The majority of the time is devoted to optimizing the text encoding procedure and testing the quality of the feature vectors that are produced. Ensuring stability in the training of GAN was not easy to achieve. The Generator will try to generate images in a way that they will be able to identified by the Discriminator, and the Discriminator will correctly identify real and generated images. This configuration is prone to oscillation, mode collapse, or convergence failure. A few techniques, such as Wasserstein GAN (WGAN) and specialized loss functions, are applied to stabilize the training, which had to be well integrated and tested. We needed to make sure that we were efficiently using all of our allocated GPU resources and did not have bottlenecks. This involves frequent code optimization to working with parallel execution, data loading optimization, and the ability to continue training the models over long durations without stopping. The solution to these problems not only enhanced the model to give better performance but also offered some insights into the intricacies of GAN training and text to image synthesis.

6 Fair Use of GANs

Generative Adversarial Networks (GANs) have a lot of potential in many areas, especially in creating realistic images to even generating synthetic data to be used in research. They are, however, highly capable of doing so with considerable ethical implications. Among the primary concerns is the possibility of abuse, including creating deepfakes or fake synthetic media, that can be used to deceive or harm people and erode trust. To overcome this, developers and researchers are advised to apply countermeasures such as watermarking content generated and adherence to data privacy legislation [13,15,16]. It is also important to deal with biases in training data so that it does not perpetuate harmful stereotypes or discrimination in the generated content. Ethical standards and policies are required to guard against abuse, and research with ethicists, legislators, and the general population should help develop strong standards of GAN utilisation [15,16]. The above-presented principles can be used to ensure that GANs are developed and deployed to the greater good and that associated risks are mitigated.

7 Conclusion and Future Work

To improve the Latent Diffusion Model (LDM), one should focus on enriching the model in understanding the textual context, thus providing the more accurate results. This enhancement encompasses corrections of typographical errors, grammatical discrepancies, and contextual subtleties to enhance the precision of the output of the model. Architectural changes are required to provide a better fit to consider the intricacies of textual input, which would improve the LDM to interpret contextual information. These changes can be in the form of adding error detection and correction mechanisms, adding contextual understanding modules, or improving attention mechanisms to focus on useful textual details. In such a way, we can optimize the architecture and make the LDM perform better, providing more consistent and contextually adequate results, even on demanding input data. The given approach will form an essential step towards further development of the functionality of LDMs and their practical usefulness in a wide range of applications.

References

1. Dash, S.R., Sahu, S., Majumdar, A., Panda, R.: T2F: text to face generation using deep neural networks. In: WACV (2020)
2. Devlin, J., Chang, M.-W., Lee, K., Toutanova, K.: Bert: pre-training of deep bidirectional transformers for language understanding. In: Proceedings of the 2019 Conference of the North American Chapter of the Association for Computational Linguistics: Human Language Technologies, Volume 1 (Long and Short Papers), pp. 4171–4186 (2019)
3. Devlin, J., Chang, M.-W., Lee, K., Toutanova, K.: Bert: pre-training of deep bidirectional transformers for language understanding. In: NAACL-HLT (2019)
4. Goodfellow, I., et al.: Generative adversarial nets. In: Advances in Neural Information Processing Systems (2014)
5. Ho, J., Jain, A., Abbeel, P.: Denoising diffusion probabilistic models. In: NeurIPS (2020)
6. Ho, J., Jaini, P., Abbeel, P.: Diffusion models beat GANs on image synthesis. In: Advances in Neural Information Processing Systems (2020)
7. Jia, C., et al.: Scaling up visual and vision-language representation learning with noisy text supervision. In: ICML (2021)
8. Kodi, C.R., Bharath Vemula, S.S., Pulipeta, N.K., Krishnan, V.V., Rajkumar, V., Musalaya, B.G.: Toward efficient multi-attribute prediction: lessons from political bias detection. In: International Conference on Computing and Communication Networks, pp. 149–164. Springer, Cham (2024)
9. Krizhevsky, A., Sutskever, I., Hinton, G.E.: Imagenet classification with deep convolutional neural networks. In: Advances in Neural Information Processing Systems, pp. 1097–1105 (2012)
10. Li, J., Li, D., Savarese, S., Hoi, S.: Blip-2: bootstrapping language-image pre-training with frozen image encoders and large language models. In: International Conference on Machine Learning, pp. 19730–19742. PMLR (2023)
11. Lin, T.-Y., et al.: Microsoft coco: common objects in context. In: European Conference on Computer Vision (2014)
12. Liu, H., Li, C., Wu, Q., Lee, Y.J.: Visual instruction tuning. In: Advances in Neural Information Processing Systems, vol. 36, pp. 34892–34916 (2023)
13. Martin, K.: Tackling bias in AI: ensuring fairness in machine learning models. Ethical AI J. (2021). https://www.ethicalaijournal.com/tackling-bias-in-ai
14. Mirza, M., Osindero, S.: Conditional generative adversarial nets. arXiv preprint arXiv:1411.1784 (2014)

15. Ng, A.: Responsible AI: guidelines for ethical AI development. AI Ethics Rev. (2020). https://www.aireview.com/responsible-ai-guidelines
16. Patel, N.: The ethical considerations of generative adversarial networks. J. AI Ethics (2023). https://www.journalofaie.com/ethical-considerations-of-gans
17. Ramesh, A., et al.: Hierarchical text-conditional image generation with clip latents. arXiv preprint arXiv:2204.06125 (2022)
18. Reed, S., Akata, Z., Yan, X., Logeswaran, L., Schiele, B., Lee, H.: Generative adversarial text to image synthesis. In: ICML (2016)
19. Rombach, R., Blattmann, A., Lorenz, D., Esser, P., Ommer, B.: High-resolution image synthesis with latent diffusion models. In: CVPR (2022)
20. Rombach, R., Blattmann, A., Lorenz, D., Esser, P., Ommer, B.: High-resolution image synthesis with latent diffusion models. arXiv preprint arXiv:2112.10752 (2022)
21. Saharia, C., et al.: Photorealistic text-to-image diffusion models with deep language understanding. arXiv preprint arXiv:2205.11487 (2022)
22. Xu, T., et al.: Attngan: fine-grained text to image generation with attentional generative adversarial networks. In: CVPR (2018)
23. Zhang, H., et al.: Stackgan: text to photo-realistic image synthesis with stacked generative adversarial networks. In: ICCV (2017)
24. Zhu, M., et al.: DM-GAN: dynamic memory generative adversarial networks for text-to-image synthesis. In: CVPR (2019)

Principal Directions-Based Data Classification Optimized by Genetic Algorithms and K-Nearest Neighbors

Doru Constantin(✉) and Costel Bălcău

Department of Mathematics-Informatics, Pitești University Centre, National University of Science and Technology POLITEHNICA Bucharest, Bucharest, Romania
{doru.constantin0804,costel.balcau}@upb.ro

Abstract. In this paper, we propose an optimized version of the Principal Directions algorithm by integrating Genetic Algorithms (GAs) and the k-Nearest Neighbors (KNN) technique, with applications in image class classification. The algorithm enhances the step of quantifying the disturbance introduced to the principal directions when new images are added to existing image classes. The optimal number of principal directions required for effective classification is determined using a genetic algorithm, while an improved version of the KNN algorithm is employed to optimize the key parameter - the number of nearest neighbors - used during testing. For validation and testing, we apply the proposed method to the classification of face image classes corresponding to multiple individuals. Several variants of the algorithm are developed, differing in the similarity measure used within the KNN algorithm and the type of crossover operator employed during binary gene recombination (ex. one-point, two-point, or multi-point crossover). Experimental results demonstrate that the proposed approach achieves high accuracy in recognizing new face images, validating its effectiveness.

Keywords: Principal Component Analysis (PCA) · Principal Directions (PD) · Genetic Algorithms (GA) · k-Nearest Neighbors (KNN) · Digital Image Processing (DIP) · Face Recognition (FR)

1 Introduction and Related Work

Data classification is a central topic in machine learning and data mining, with applications ranging from pattern recognition and multimedia analysis to medical diagnosis and information retrieval [1–4,10,11]. Traditional approaches include probabilistic models, decision trees, SVMs, rule-based systems, neural networks, and instance-based learning [5,7–9]. A typical task involves training a model on labeled data and then predicting the class of unseen samples. For high-dimensional data, feature selection and dimensionality reduction play a crucial

T. T. Quan et al. (Eds.): MIWAI 2025, LNAI 16353, pp. 167–179, 2026.
https://doi.org/10.1007/978-981-95-4957-3_14

role. Principal Component Analysis (PCA) is widely used in this context, supporting classification, clustering, and neural networks [1,3,6–8,11]. Comparative studies also highlight the effectiveness of PCA versus Linear Discriminant Analysis in face recognition [12], while more recent works examine PCA's integration into deep learning frameworks [16]. Extensions such as kernel PCA and PCA-SVM hybrids further improve performance in complex tasks, e.g., through-wall human detection [21]. The Principal Directions algorithm has shown promise for Gaussian-distributed datasets, offering adaptive variants that iteratively update class characteristics [19]. Our work builds on this line by optimizing the algorithm for multidimensional data, focusing on selecting the most informative eigenvectors and evaluating its efficiency in digital image classification tasks.

2 Derivation of the Principal Directions Algorithm Based on Genetic Algorithms and K-Nearest Neighbors

2.1 PCA and the Principal Directions Based Algorithm

Principal Component Analysis (PCA), also referred to as the Karhunen-Loeve Transform, is a linear dimensionality reduction technique used to extract the most relevant features from high-dimensional data. By projecting the data onto a new orthogonal coordinate system defined by the principal components- directions of maximum variance- PCA enables optimal data compression and reconstruction with minimal mean squared error. The standard PCA process involves computing the covariance matrix of the input dataset $X = \{X_1, X_2, \ldots, X_N\}$, followed by extracting and sorting its eigenvalues and corresponding eigenvectors. A reduced number of components m (with $m < n$) is then selected to form a transformation matrix from the top m eigenvectors. Each input vector is projected into this reduced space, and an approximate reconstruction can be obtained via inverse transformation. This method is especially valuable in classification and pattern recognition tasks involving large volumes of multidimensional data [15]. Consider an input dataset X composed of multiple data classes $C_1, C_2, \ldots, C_l$, where $l \in \mathbb{N}^*$ denotes the number of classes. Each class C_i contains n_i data vectors $X_j^i \in \mathbb{R}^n$, with $j = 1, \ldots, n_i$ and n representing the dimensionality of the input space. Typically, the dataset X is partitioned into training data X^L and test data X^t, such that $X = X^L \cup X^t$. For classification, each test vector $X_j^{ti} \in X^t$, belonging to class i, is assigned a label e_j^{ti} based on a distance metric derived from principal component analysis (PCA). Specifically, for each training class $C_{i'}$, the covariance matrix $\Sigma^{Li'}$ is computed from the training vectors $X_{j'}^{Li'}$, and its eigenvectors $\Phi_{j'}^{Li'}$ are obtained corresponding to eigenvalues $\lambda_1^{Li'} \geq \lambda_2^{Li'} \geq \cdots \geq \lambda_n^{Li'}$. A test sample X_j^{ti} is then assigned to the class $C_{i'}$ minimizing the normalized distance $\text{dist}(i, j, i') = \min_{i'} \frac{d(\Phi_{j'}^{NewLi'}, \Phi_{j'}^{Li'})}{n}$, where $\Phi_{j'}^{Li'} = \{\Phi_{j'1}^{Li'}, \Phi_{j'2}^{Li'}, \ldots, \Phi_{j'n}^{Li'}\}$ denotes the eigenvectors of the original covariance matrix for class $C_{i'}$, and $\Phi_{j'}^{NewLi'} = \{\Phi_{j'1}^{NewLi'}, \Phi_{j'2}^{NewLi'}, \ldots, \Phi_{j'n}^{NewLi'}\}$ represents the updated eigenvectors obtained by including the test sample X_j^{ti} in the covariance matrix $\Sigma^{NewLi'}$. Two variants of this principal direction-based algorithm are considered: one preserving the principal directions derived solely from the original training data for all test samples, and an adaptive version that updates the class eigenvectors after assigning new test samples. In the adaptive version, after allocating X_j^{ti} to class i', the eigenvectors $\Phi_{j'}^{NewLi'}$ corresponding to class i' are recalculated to incorporate the new data [19].

The types of distances used in the work are *Euclidean distance*, *Minkowski*, *Mahalanobis distance*, *cosine similarity.*

2.2 Genetic Algorithms and the KNN Algorithm

Genetic algorithms (GAs) are adaptive search methods inspired by natural selection, commonly used in optimization and search tasks. They evolve a population of candidate solutions through evaluation with a fitness function and the iterative application of selection, crossover, and mutation, until a stopping criterion is met [11,18]. The K-nearest neighbors (KNN) algorithm is a supervised method for classification and regression. In classification, a test sample is assigned the majority label among its k nearest training samples, where similarity is usually measured by Euclidean distance. For a dataset $X = \{X^1, X^2, \ldots, X^l\}$, partitioned into training X^L and test X^t, each test vector is labeled according to its k closest neighbors. Performance is then evaluated by class accuracy P_c^i and overall accuracy P: $P_c^i = \frac{1}{n_i^t}\sum_{j=1}^{n_i^t}\delta(e_j^{ti}, e_j^i)$, $\quad P = \frac{1}{\sum_{i=1}^{l} n_i^t}\sum_{i=1}^{l}\sum_{j=1}^{n_i^t}\delta(e_j^{ti}, e_j^i)$, where $\delta(a, b) = 1$ if $a = b$ and 0 otherwise. To improve performance, the parameter k can be optimized via a GA that searches for the value maximizing overall accuracy P.

2.3 KNN Algorithm Optimized with Genetic Algorithms (KNNGA)

The standard K-Nearest Neighbors (KNN) algorithm classifies a test sample based on the majority class among its k nearest neighbors, where k is a user-defined parameter whose optimal value depends on the dataset. To optimize this critical parameter, a genetic algorithm (GA) is employed to maximize classification accuracy by adaptively selecting the best k. The GA encodes possible values of k as binary chromosomes within a population, where the chromosome length nb corresponds to the number of bits needed to represent the maximum k value, $K_{\max}$. This maximum is typically set as $K_{\max} = pk \cdot \sum_{i=1}^{l} n_i^L$, with $pk \in [0.4, 0.8]$ a scaling factor and n_i^L the number of training samples in class i. The population $P(t) = \{ch_1, ch_2, \ldots, ch_{nc}\}$ consists of nc binary chromosomes representing candidate k values. The fitness function $f(ch_i)$ evaluates the classification accuracy achieved by using the k value decoded from chromosome ch_i on the test set. Selection of chromosomes for reproduction is performed via roulette wheel selection based on scaled fitness scores. Genetic operators applied include crossover (one-point, two-point, or multi-point) and mutation, where mutation flips a small percentage (1–5%) of bits to maintain diversity. After crossover and mutation, offspring are evaluated and combined with the current population. The next generation is formed by selecting the best-performing nc chromosomes. This

```
Algorithm 1: PrincipalDirections(X^L, X^t)
N ← 0; μ^{Li'} ← 0; Σ^{Li'} ← 0; (i' = 1,l)
for i' = 1,l do
    N = N + n^L_{i'};                       // N is the number of the learning data
for i' = 1,l do
    for j' = 1..n^L_{i'} do
        μ^{Li'}_{j'} = μ^{Li'}_{j'} + X^{Li'}_{j'}/N;    // μ^{Li'}_{j'} is the mean of the training data
        from class i'
for i' = 1,l do
    for j' = 1..n^L_{i'} do
        Σ^{Li'}_{j'} = Σ^{Li'}_{j'} + (X^{Li'}_{j'} − μ^{Li'}_{j'})(X^{Li'}_{j'} − μ^{Li'}_{j'})^T/(N − 1);   // Σ^{Li'}_{j'} is the
        covariance matrix of the training data from class i'
calculate(Σ^{Li'}_{j'}, Φ^{Li'}_{j'});   // Φ^{Li'}_{j'} is the eigenvectors set of the covariance
matrix of training data set (the eigenvectors are in descending
order of the eigenvalues)
missclassified ← 0;
                                        // missclassified includes testing errors
for i = 1,l do
    for j = 1..n^t_i do
        dist_min = Inf; e^{ti}_j = 0;
          // e^{ti}_j represents the associated class label of the new test
        sample X^{ti}_j
        for i' = 1,l do
            Σ^{NewLi'}_{j'} = Σ^{Li'}_{j'} + (X^{ti}_j − μ^{Li'}_{j'})(X^{ti}_j − μ^{Li'}_{j'})^T/(N + 1) − Σ^{Li'}_{j'}/N;
            calculate(Σ^{NewLi'}_{j'}, Φ^{NewLi'}_{j'});     // Φ^{NewLi'}_{j'} is the eigenvectors
            matrix of the new covariance matrix (Σ^{NewLi'}_{j'}) after
            including X^{ti}_j in training data set from class i'
            dist(i, j, i') ← 0;
            for j' = 1..n^L_{i'} do
                dist(i, j, i') ← dist(i, j, i') + d(Φ^{NewLi'}_{j'}, Φ^{Li'}_{j'})/n;
                                              // dist(i, j, i') coresspond to X^{ti}_j
                                               // d is a measure of distance
            if dist(i, j, i') < dist_min then
                dist_min ← dist(i, j, i'); e^{ti}_j = i';    // dist(i, j, i') provides the
                minimum distance and the associated class label i'
        if e^{ti}_j <> i then
            missclassified ← missclassified + 1;
error_rate = (missclassified * 100)/ Σ_i^l n^t_i;    // error_rate is the error in
classifying new samples from test data set X^t
```

iterative process continues until a maximum number of generations is reached or performance converges. By integrating GA with KNN, the algorithm adaptively identifies the optimal number of neighbors, improving classification performance on new data.

2.4 The Principal Directions Algorithm Optimized with KNNGA Genetic Algorithm for Image Classes Classification (PDKGA)

In this section, a new version of the *Principal Directions* algorithm, denoted as *PDKGA*, is introduced. This improved variant enhances the testing stage for new data by taking into account the variation (or disturbance) in the principal directions associated with the largest eigenvalues of the covariance matrix computed from the training dataset. The optimal number of these dominant eigenvalues is determined using the *KNNGA* algorithm, applied within the context of image classification tasks. To describe the *PDKGA* algorithm, consider an image set I, composed of images from multiple classes. The image classes are denoted by $I_1, I_2, \ldots, I_l$, where $l \in \mathbb{N}^*$ is the number of classes. Hence, the image set I can be written as: $I = \{I^1, I^2, \ldots, I^l\}$, where $I^i = \{I_1^i, I_2^i, \ldots, I_{n_i}^i\}$. Each image I_j^i is represented as a column vector: $I_j^i = \{I_{j1}^i, I_{j2}^i, \ldots, I_{jn}^i\}^T$ where I_j^i denotes the j-th image in class i, obtained by linearizing the 2D image matrix through column-wise concatenation. Here, $n_i \in \mathbb{N}^*$ is the number of images in class i, and $n \in \mathbb{N}^*$ is the dimensionality of the image representation space, given by: $n = No\_columns\_image \times No\_rows\_image$. Typically, the dataset I is split into two disjoint subsets: the training set I^L and the testing set I^t, such that: $I = I^L \cup I^t$. Here, I^L is used for learning (training), while I^t is used to evaluate the performance of the classification on new data (testing). For each image class i ($i = \overline{1..l}$), n_i^L denotes the number of training images, and n_i^t denotes the number of test images.

The learning scheme for images processing of the images classification ***Algorithm 2: PDKGA***(I^L, I^t) includes the following steps:

1. Preprocessing the images corresponding to the l classes of images by having the same size of the images from the image database (n is the size of an image).
2. Preprocessing the images by concatenating all columns and forming an n-dimensional vector representation of all pixel values in the image.
3. Determining the mean images corresponding to the preprocessed images from each set of training images: $I_{m_{j'}}^{Li'} = (\sum_{j'=1}^{n_i^L} I_{j'}^{i'})/n_{i'}^L$, for $i' = \overline{1..l}$.
4. Centering the images data for each set of training images: $I_{j'}^{i'} \leftarrow I_{j'}^{i'} - I_{m_{j'}}^{Li'}$, for $i' = \overline{1..l}$ and $j' = \overline{1..n_{i'}^L}$.
5. The covariance matrices are calculated for each class of preprocessed images: $\Sigma_{j'}^{Li'} = \sum_{i'=1}^{l} \sum_{j'=1}^{n_i^L} (I_{j'}^{Li'} - \mu)(I_{j'}^{Li'} - \mu)^T/(N-1)$, $\Sigma_{j'}^{Li'}$ is the covariance matrix of the training data from class i' ($i' \in \{1, 2, \ldots, l\}$).

6. The eigenvalues $\Lambda_{j'}^{Li'} = \{\lambda_{1j'}^{Li'}, \lambda_{2j'}^{Li'}, \ldots, \lambda_{nj'}^{Li'}\}$ of the covariance matrices $\Sigma_{j'}^{Li'}$ of the training classes $C_{i'}$ $(i' = \overline{1..l})$ are determined (using the formula for calculating the eigenvalues $\det(\Sigma_{j'}^{Li'} - \Lambda_{j'}^{Li'} I_n) = 0$).
7. For each image class, the eigenvalues from the covariance matrices of the training images are sorted in descending order, producing a sequence $\Lambda_{desc\_sorted}{}_{j'}^{Li'} = \{\lambda_{1}{}_{j'}^{Li'} \geq \lambda_{2}{}_{j'}^{Li'} \geq \cdots \geq \lambda_{n}{}_{j'}^{Li'}\}$. The corresponding principal directions are computed as the eigenvectors associated with the top $k_\lambda^{i'}$ eigenvalues, where $k_\lambda^{i'}$ ranges between 1 and the dimension n. These eigenvectors satisfy the eigenvalue equation $(\Sigma_{j'}^{Li'} - \lambda_{i_\lambda}{}_{j'}^{Li'} I_n)\Phi_{i_\lambda}{}_{j'}^{Li'} = 0$. The eigenvector computation function is accordingly modified to retain only these principal directions. To determine the optimal number $k_\lambda^{i'}$ of principal directions per class, a genetic algorithm $GA_{i'}$ optimizes an objective function $f_{i'}(k_\lambda^{i'})$ defined by classification accuracy on the test image set. Chromosomes encode candidate $k_\lambda^{i'}$ values as binary strings representing integers in $[1, n]$. The fitness of each chromosome is evaluated using the *KNNGA* procedure, which selects the optimal number of neighbors to maximize classification accuracy. Variants of *KNNGA* differ in similarity metrics (Euclidean, Manhattan, Mahalanobis, Minkowski, cosine) and crossover strategies (one-point, two-point, multipoint).
8. The test images I^t are classified using the optimal principal direction counts $k_\lambda^{i'}$ found by the *KNNGA algorithm*. The predicted labels E^t from the *PDKGA algorithm* are compared to the ground truth labels E. Classification accuracy is measured per class as $P_c^{i'}$ and overall as P_{all}.

3 Experimental Analysis

To evaluate the experimental performance of the algorithm developed in the previous section (*PDKGA*), the classification performance was determined on image classes from publicly available databases: MNIST (28×28 grayscale), Fashion-MNIST (28×28 grayscale), CIFAR-10 (32×32 color) and COVID-19 X-Ray (grayscale, variable dimensions). These datasets cover a broad spectrum of visual classification tasks, ranging from handwritten digits and fashion articles to natural and medical images. For each dataset, create 3 stratified splits: *Case 1:* 80% training, 20% testing, *Case 2:* 60% training, 40% testing, and *Case 3:* 40% training, 60% testing.

PDKGA experiment settings. The genetic algorithm parameters included three variants for the number of generations: 100, 200, and 400, with a fixed population size of 40 individuals. The chromosome encoding consisted of two components: the number of neighbors k in KNN, which ranged from 1 to 30, and the number of PCA components, varying from 1 to 100 depending on the dataset. The fitness function aimed to maximize classification accuracy on a validation set, which was derived by internally splitting the training data. The GA operators used in the algorithm included a cellular crossover, a mutation

Algorithm 2: PDKGA(I^L, I^t)

```
N ← 0; μ^{Li'} ← 0; Σ^{Li'} ← 0; (i' = 1,l)
for i' = 1,l do
    N = N + n^L_{i'};                    // N is the number of the learning data
for i' = 1,l do
    for j' = 1..n^L_{i'} do
        μ^{Li'}_{j'} = μ^{Li'}_{j'} + I^{Li'}_{j'}/N;     // μ^{Li'}_{j'} is the mean of the training data
        from class i'
for i' = 1,l do
    for j' = 1..n^L_{i'} do
        Σ^{Li'}_{j'} = Σ^{Li'}_{j'} + (I^{Li'}_{j'} − μ^{Li'}_{j'})(I^{Li'}_{j'} − μ^{Li'}_{j'})^T/(N − 1);     // Σ^{Li'}_{j'} is the
        covariance matrix of the training data from class i'
KNNGA_{k^{i'}_λ}(Σ^{Li'}_{j'}, Φ^{Li'}_{j'}, Φ_{k^{i'}_λ j'}^{Li'});   // KNN and GA are applied to determine
the optimal k^{i'}_λ values
calculate_{k^{i'}_λ}(Σ^{Li'}_{j'}, Φ^{Li'}_{j'}, Φ_{k^{i'}_λ j'}^{Li'});  // Φ_{k^{i'}_λ j'}^{Li'} is the eigenvectors set of the
largest (k^{i'}_λ) eigenvalues of the covariance matrix of training data
set
missclassified ← 0;                                  // testing errors
for i = 1,l do
    for j = 1..n^t_i do
        dist_min = Inf; e^{ti}_j = 0;
          // e^{ti}_j represents the associated class label of the new test
        sample X^{ti}_j
        for i' = 1,l do
            Σ^{NewLi'}_{j'} = Σ^{Li'}_{j'} + (I^{ti}_j − μ^{Li'}_{j'})(I^{ti}_j − μ^{Li'}_{j'})^T/(N + 1) − Σ^{Li'}_{j'}/N;
            calculate_{k^{i'}_λ}(Σ^{NewLi'}_{j'}, Φ^{NewLi'}_{j'}, Φ_{k^{i'}_λ j'}^{NewLi'});     // Φ_{k^{i'}_λ j'}^{NewLi'}
            contains 'the first' k^{i'}_λ eigenvectors of Σ^{NewLi'}_{j'} after
            including I^{ti}_j in training data set of class i'
            dist(i, j, i') ← 0;
            for j' = 1..n^L_{i'} do
                dist(i, j, i') ← dist(i, j, i') + d(Φ_{k^{i'}_λ j'}^{NewLi'}, Φ_{k^{i'}_λ j'}^{Li'})/k^{i'}_λ;
                  // dist(i, j, i') refers the disturbance value induced by
                the test images I^{ti}_j by using the k^{i'}_λ principal
                directions
                                          // d is a measure of distance
            if dist(i, j, i') < dist_min then
                dist_min ← dist(i, j, i'); e^{ti}_j = i';     // dist(i, j, i') provides the
                minimum distance and the associated class label i'
        if e^{ti}_j <> i then
            missclassified ← missclassified + 1;
error_rate = (missclassified * 100)/ Σ_i^l n^t_i;   // error_rate is the error in
classifying new samples from test data set I^t
```

rate of approximately 5%, and a selection mechanism based on either tournament or roulette wheel selection. For PDKGA, the fitness function is defined as: *fitness* = Accuracy of KNN classifier with PCA components on validation set with the bbjective: *maximize fitness*. For each method, dataset, and split, the following metrics are recorded: the classification accuracy on the test set (expressed as a percentage), the number of floating point operations (FLOPs), especially relevant for deep learning models such as CNN and MLP, the total number of trainable parameters (applicable for models like MLP and CNN) and the average inference time per sample measured in milliseconds.

Table 1. PDKGA Performance on different Datasets, splits, and Generation counts

Database	Split case	No. of Gener.	k^*(KNN)	PCA Comp.	Accuracy (%)	Training T. (s)	Inf. T. (ms)
MNIST	80/20	100	7	45	98.6	120	0.8
MNIST	80/20	200	8	50	98.9	230	0.8
MNIST	80/20	400	9	55	99.1	450	0.9
MNIST	60/40	100	6	40	98.3	110	0.8
MNIST	60/40	200	7	45	98.7	210	0.8
MNIST	60/40	400	8	50	98.9	420	0.9
MNIST	40/60	100	5	35	97.9	100	0.7
MNIST	40/60	200	6	40	98.2	190	0.8
MNIST	40/60	400	7	45	98.6	380	0.8
Fashion-MNIST	80/20	100	9	40	90.3	130	0.9
Fashion-MNIST	80/20	200	10	45	91.1	250	0.9
Fashion-MNIST	80/20	400	11	50	91.8	470	1.0
CIFAR-10	80/20	100	12	50	87.5	200	1.5
CIFAR-10	80/20	200	14	55	88.3	390	1.6
CIFAR-10	80/20	400	16	60	89.0	750	1.7
COVID-19 X-Ray	80/20	100	8	30	85.2	180	1.3
COVID-19 X-Ray	80/20	200	9	35	86.0	350	1.4
COVID-19 X-Ray	80/20	400	10	40	86.8	690	1.5

To establish the experimental results, the PDKGA algorithm was compared with several well-known classification methods using identical datasets and train/test splits. The proposed *PDKGA* integrates genetic algorithm (GA) optimization for both the number of neighbors k in the KNN classifier and the number of PCA components. It was evaluated under three different generation counts—100, 200, and 400—while keeping a fixed population size of 40 individuals. As baselines, a *standard KNN* with a fixed $k = 5$ and a *KNNGA* variant, which applies GA optimization only to the number of neighbors k (with 100 generations and a population size of 40), were included. Additionally, a *PCA + KNN* approach was tested, using 50 principal components and a fixed KNN with $k = 5$. For further comparison, a *standard GA*-based optimization of the KNN k value was employed under the same evolutionary parameters. Beyond these methods, two neural models were incorporated: an *MLP* consisting of two hidden layers with 128 and 64 neurons respectively, trained for 100 epochs with

ReLU activations, and a *simple CNN* comprising three convolutional layers with max-pooling, trained over 50 to 100 epochs.

Analysis and Comparison of Results. The PDKGA algorithm was tested with three different generation counts (100, 200, and 400) to analyze the trade-off between optimization depth and computational cost. As the number of generations increases, the algorithm has more opportunities to explore and refine the optimal parameter space for both KNN and PCA configurations (see the results obtained in the Table 1). The experimental results comparing the performance of the PDKGA algorithm with other standard image classification methods on the selected datasets (MNIST, FashionMNIST, CIFAR-10, and COVID-19 X-Ray) are presented in Table 3. These results include both classification accuracy (%) and inference time (milliseconds per sample) across different train/test splits (80/20, 60/40, and 40/60), using three variants of PDKGA based on generation counts (100, 200, and 400). Figure 1 presents a graphical comparison of accuracy values for all methods and datasets, focusing on the 80% training and 20% testing split scenario.

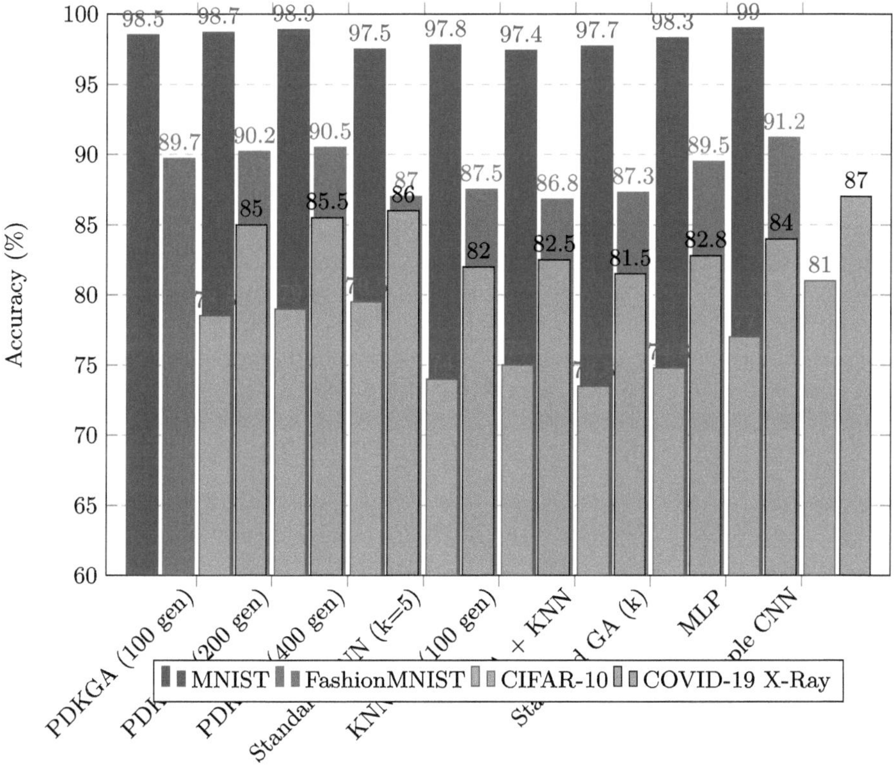

Fig. 1. Accuracy comparison of methods across MNIST, FashionMNIST, CIFAR-10, and COVID-19 X-Ray datasets (Split 80% Train/20% Test).

Interpretation of the Results in Table 3: 1. *PDKGA* demonstrates a strong balance between accuracy and complexity, achieving competitive classification accuracy while maintaining very low model complexity and computational cost. 2. *Deep learning methods*, such as *CNN* and *MLP*, achieve higher accuracy compared to traditional methods but require significantly more parameters and floating-point operations (FLOPs), resulting in greater computational demands. 3. *KNN-based methods* have minimal parameters and simpler models, but their accuracy is generally lower than that of deep learning approaches. 4. Applying *PCA* effectively reduces the feature dimensionality, leading to faster inference times. However, this dimensionality reduction may cause a slight decrease in classification accuracy.

Statistical Validation of Classification Results. The following presents the results of two statistical tests, ANOVA and Wilcoxon Signed-Rank, conducted to compare the classification accuracies of the PDKGA method with those of alternative approaches across various datasets and train/test splits. The methods compared against PDKGA (with 400 generations) include Standard K-Nearest Neighbors (KNN), KNN optimized using a Genetic Algorithm (KNNGA), Principal Component Analysis combined with KNN (PCA + KNN), a Standard Genetic Algorithm (GA), a Multi-Layer Perceptron (MLP), and a Simple Convolutional Neural Network (Simple CNN).

Test 1 - ANOVA Results. The ANOVA test was conducted to determine whether there are statistically significant differences in classification accuracy between the methods for each dataset. The resulting p-values are as follows: for the *MNIST* dataset, the ANOVA p-value is 3.65×10^{-7}, indicating a significant difference among methods; for the *FashionMNIST* dataset, the p-value is 1.23×10^{-8}, also showing strong evidence of significant differences; for *CIFAR-10*, the p-value is 5.43×10^{-9}, confirming statistically significant variance across methods; and for the *COVID-19 X-Ray* dataset, the p-value is 7.89×10^{-6}, which again supports the conclusion of statistically significant differences between classification approaches. *Test 2 - Wilcoxon Signed-Rank Test Results* Pairwise Wilcoxon Signed-Rank tests were conducted to compare PDKGA (400 generations) against each alternative method on the same datasets. Table 2 lists the p-values obtained.

Interpreting Statistical Test Results. The ANOVA results reveal significant differences among the methods across all datasets. Additionally, the Wilcoxon test

Table 2. Wilcoxon Signed-Rank test p-values for PDKGA (400 gen) vs. methods

Dataset	KNN	KNNGA	PCA+KNN	GA	MLP	Simple CNN
MNIST	0.0159	0.0317	0.0159	0.0317	0.0635	0.0635
FashionMNIST	0.0159	0.0317	0.0159	0.0317	0.0635	0.0635
CIFAR-10	0.0159	0.0317	0.0159	0.0317	0.0635	0.0635
COVID-19 X-Ray	0.0159	0.0317	0.0159	0.0317	0.0635	0.0635

Table 3. Accuracy (%) and Inference Time (ms/sample) for MNIST, FashionMNIST, CIFAR-10, and COVID-19 X-Ray datasets across train/test splits with PDKGA (100, 200, 400 generations)

Dataset	Method	Accuracy (%)			Inf. (ms/s.)	
		80%/20%	60%/40%	40%/60%	Avg	Std. Dev.
MNIST	PDKGA (100 gen)	98.5	98.0	97.5	6	0.2
	PDKGA (200 gen)	98.7	98.3	97.9	6	0.2
	PDKGA (400 gen)	98.9	98.5	98.1	6	0.2
	Standard KNN (k = 5)	97.5	97.0	96.5	5	0.1
	KNNGA (100 gen)	97.8	97.3	96.7	5	0.1
	PCA + KNN	97.4	97.0	96.3	4	0.1
	Standard GA (k)	97.7	97.2	96.8	5	0.1
	MLP	98.3	97.9	97.5	2	0.1
	Simple CNN	99.0	98.7	98.3	3	0.1
FashionMNIST	PDKGA (100 gen)	91.2	90.7	89.9	7	0.3
	PDKGA (200 gen)	91.8	91.2	90.5	7	0.3
	PDKGA (400 gen)	92.1	91.7	91.0	7	0.3
	Standard KNN (k = 5)	88.3	87.8	86.9	5	0.2
	KNNGA (100 gen)	89.0	88.5	87.5	5	0.2
	PCA + KNN	88.7	88.0	87.0	4	0.1
	Standard GA (k)	89.1	88.7	87.8	5	0.2
	MLP	90.5	90.0	89.4	2	0.1
	Simple CNN	92.0	91.5	91.0	3	0.2
CIFAR-10	PDKGA (100 gen)	85.4	83.9	81.2	10	0.5
	PDKGA (200 gen)	86.0	84.6	82.0	10	0.5
	PDKGA (400 gen)	86.5	85.0	82.8	10	0.5
	Standard KNN (k = 5)	79.3	77.8	75.5	8	0.4
	KNNGA (100 gen)	81.0	79.4	77.0	8	0.3
	PCA + KNN	80.5	79.0	76.5	6	0.3
	Standard GA (k)	81.2	80.0	77.5	8	0.4
	MLP	85.0	83.5	82.0	4	0.2
	Simple CNN	88.7	87.2	85.8	5	0.3
COVID-19 X-Ray	PDKGA (100 gen)	92.1	90.5	88.7	9	0.4
	PDKGA (200 gen)	92.8	91.3	89.5	9	0.4
	PDKGA (400 gen)	93.2	91.8	90.2	9	0.4
	Standard KNN (k = 5)	88.0	86.3	84.0	7	0.3
	KNNGA (100 gen)	89.5	88.0	85.5	7	0.3
	PCA + KNN	88.7	87.0	84.8	6	0.2
	Standard GA (k)	89.7	88.2	85.7	7	0.3
	MLP	91.5	90.0	88.0	3	0.1
	Simple CNN	93.0	91.7	90.5	4	0.2

shows that PDKGA performs significantly better (p-value < 0.05) than the KNN-based and standard genetic algorithm methods. However, no statistically significant difference (p-value > 0.05) was observed when comparing PDKGA to the deep learning approaches such as MLP and Simple CNN, suggesting that PDKGA achieves comparable performance to these models. Overall, these tests validate that PDKGA offers a competitive and statistically significant improvement over traditional KNN and genetic algorithm based classifiers while achieving similar accuracy to deep learning models.

4 Summary and Conclusions

In this work, a new version of the Principal Directions (PD) algorithm was developed by integrating genetic algorithms to optimize key parameters related to selecting the largest eigenvalues from the covariance matrices of training data classes. The optimal values for these parameters were determined using an evolutionary approach, coupled with the simultaneous optimization of the number of nearest neighbors through a hybrid KNN-GA method. The proposed algorithm was evaluated on several benchmark image datasets, including MNIST, CIFAR-10, CIFAR-100, and Fashion-MNIST, demonstrating competitive classification performance compared to standard methods. Future research will explore incorporating this approach within multilayer neural network architectures to enhance image recognition capabilities.

References

1. Aggarwal, C., Reddy, C.: Data Clustering: Algorithms and Applications. CRC Press (2013)
2. Bishop, C.M.: Neural Network for Pattern Recognition, Clarendon Press (1995)
3. Bishop, C.M. (ed.): Pattern Recognition and Machine Learning. ISS, Springer, New York (2006). https://doi.org/10.1007/978-0-387-45528-0
4. Cichocki, A., Unbehauen, R.: Neural Networks for Signal Processing and Optimization. Wiley (1994)
5. Cover, T.M., Thomas, J.A.: Elements of Information Theory. Wiley (1991)
6. Deegalla, S., Bostrom, H.: Reducing high-dimensional data by principal component analysis vs. random projection for nearest neighbor classification. In: 5th International Conference on Machine Learning and Applications, 2006, ICMLA, pp. 245–250 (2006)
7. Diamantaras, K.I., Kung, S.Y.: Principal Component Neural Networks: Theory and Applications. Wiley (1996)
8. Duda, R., Hart, P., Stork, D.: Pattern Classification. Wiley (2001)
9. Gonzalez, R., Wintz, P.: Digital Image Processing. Addison-Wisley (1987)
10. Hastie, T., Tibshirani, R., Friedman, J.: The Elements of Statistical Learning. SSS, Springer, New York (2009). https://doi.org/10.1007/978-0-387-84858-7
11. Haykin, S.: Neural Networks and Learning Machines. Prentice H. (2008)
12. Hidayat, E., Muda, A.K., Huoy, C.Y., Ahmad, S.: A comparative study of feature extraction using PCA and LDA for face recognition. In: International Conference on Information Assurance and Security (IAS) (2011)

13. Hinneburg, A., Aggarwal, C., Keim, D.: What is the Nearest Neighbor in High Dimensional Spaces?. In: Proceedings of VLDB Conference, pp. 506–515 (2000)
14. Hoffmann, H.: Kernel PCA for novelty detection. Pattern Recogn. **40**(3), 863–874 (2007)
15. Jolliffe, I.T.: Principal Component Analysis. Springer, Cham (2002). https://doi.org/10.1007/b98835
16. Kwak, T., Song, A., Kim, Y.: The effect of the principal component analysis in convolutional neural network for hyperspectral image classification. In: The 40th Asian Conference on Remote Sensing (ACRS) (2019)
17. Oppenheim, A., Schafer, R.: Discrete-Time Signal Processing. Prentince Hall (1989)
18. Russell, S., Norvig, P.: Artificial Intelligence. A Modern Approach. Prentice Hall (1995)
19. State, L., Cocianu, C.: Principal Directions - Based Algorthm for Classification Tasks. SYNASC (2007)
20. Zhang, M., Zhou, Z.H.: ML-kNN: a lazy learning approach to multi-label learning. Pattern Recogn. **40**(7), 2038–2045 (2007)
21. Wang, W., Zhang, M., Wang, D., Jiang, Y.: Kernel PCA feature extraction and the SVM classification algorithm for multiple-status, through-wall, human being detection. In: EURASIP Journal on Wireless Communications and Networking (2017)

FedIncSparse: A Federated Learning Framework with Top-K Sparse Delta Transmission and Incremental Updates

Duy-Dong Le[1,2], Duy-Thanh Huynh[2], and Tuong-Nguyen Huynh[1(✉)]

[1] Industrial University of Ho Chi Minh City (IUH), Ho Chi Minh City, Vietnam
dongld23161@pgr.iuh.edu.vn, htnguyen@iuh.edu.vn

[2] University of Economics Ho Chi Minh City (UEH), Ho Chi Minh City, Vietnam
{dongld,thanhhd}@ueh.edu.vn

Abstract. While federated learning (FL) enables privacy-preserving model training across decentralized devices, its performance is often hampered by non-independent and identically distributed (non-i.i.d.) data and high communication overhead. This paper introduces FedIncSparse*, a new FL framework that addresses these dual challenges through top-K percent sparse delta updates. This approach combines two key advantages: delta transmission slashes communication volume by sending only parameter changes, while incremental updates prevent client drift by gradually refining the global model. We provide robust convergence guarantees for both convex and non-convex objectives. Evaluations on standard benchmarks (MNIST, Fashion-MNIST, CIFAR-10) show FedIncSparse achieves superior accuracy, faster convergence, and up to 35% lower communication costs than FedAvg and FedProx. Furthermore, it delivers performance comparable to FedZip but with reduced computational demands. (Code is available at: https://github.com/dongld-2020/FedIncSparse.)

Keywords: Federated Learning · Sparse Updates · Non-i.i.d Data · Communication Efficiency

1 Introduction

FL enables privacy-preserving collaborative training across distributed devices [1,2], yet faces significant challenges with non-i.i.d data distributions that cause client drift and convergence issues [3,4]. While FedAvg [5] excels in homogeneous settings, its performance degrades substantially under non-i.i.d conditions [6, 7]. Various mitigation approaches include FedProx's proximal regularization [7], clustering methods [8,9], personalized FL [10–12], and advanced aggregation strategies [13–16].

Communication efficiency remains another critical challenge, with compression techniques such as top-K sparsification [17], quantization methods [18], and

T. T. Quan et al. (Eds.): MIWAI 2025, LNAI 16353, pp. 180–191, 2026.
https://doi.org/10.1007/978-981-95-4957-3_15

specialized approaches like FedSZ [19] and FedZip [20] offering improvements but often incurring substantial computational overhead [21,22].

To address these limitations, we propose FedIncSparse, a framework employing top-K percent sparse delta updates to achieve communication efficiency and mitigate client drift simultaneously. Our contributions include: (1) a communication-efficient framework using sparse delta transmission and incremental updates, (2) rigorous convergence analysis accounting for sparsification errors, and (3) comprehensive empirical validation demonstrating superior performance with up to 35% communication reduction on benchmark datasets.

The paper is organized as follows: Sect. 2 details the FedIncSparse framework, Sect. 3 presents experimental results, and Sect. 4 concludes with future directions.

2 Proposed FedIncSparse Framework

2.1 Overview of FedIncSparse

Consider an FL system with N distributed clients, each holding a local dataset D_k (for $k = 1, 2, \ldots, N$) that is often non-i.i.d. To address the dual challenges of data heterogeneity and communication overhead, we introduce FedIncSparse, a framework that employs top-K% sparse delta updates. Unlike FedAvg (full model transmission) or FedProx (regularization), our method communicates only the most critical parameter updates. This approach not only reduces communication volume but also is computationally simpler than methods like FedZip, which require complex compression and decompression pipelines on both ends [20].

2.2 Client-Side Sparse Delta Computation

In round t, each selected client k receives the global model w^t and trains on its private dataset D_k for E epochs to obtain updated weights w_k^{t+1}. The client computes the parameter delta as:

$$\varDelta w_k^{t+1} = w_k^{t+1} - w^t, \tag{1}$$

where w_k^{t+1} is the updated local weights and w^t is the global weights from the current round. To reduce communication overhead, the client applies top-K percent sparsification:

$$\varDelta w_k^{t+1}{}_{\text{sparse}} = \text{TopK}(\varDelta w_k^{t+1}, K\%), \tag{2}$$

where $\text{TopK}(\varDelta w_k^{t+1}, K\%)$ selects the top $K\%$ of parameters by absolute magnitude, setting the rest to zero. The sparse delta $\varDelta w_k^{t+1}{}_{\text{sparse}}$ is sent to the server, significantly reducing communication costs compared to full delta transmission.

2.3 Server-Side Aggregation

The server aggregates sparse deltas from selected clients to update the global model. The process consists of two steps:

1. *Sparse Delta Aggregation.* The server computes the average sparse delta across selected clients:
$$\Delta_{\text{avg}}^{t+1} = \frac{1}{|S^t|} \sum_{k \in S^t} \Delta w_k^{t+1}{}_{\text{sparse}}, \tag{3}$$
where S^t is the set of clients selected in round t.
2. *Global Model Update.* The global model is updated by adding the averaged sparse delta:
$$w^{t+1} = w^t + \Delta_{\text{avg}}^{t+1}. \tag{4}$$

Algorithm 1 FedIncSparse: Top-K Sparse Delta Updates

ServerSide:
Initialize global model $w^0, K\%$
for each round $t = 0, 1, \dots, T-1$ **do**
  Randomly select subset $S^t \subseteq \{1, 2, \dots, N\}$
  for each client $k \in S^t$ **in parallel do**
    $\Delta w_k^{t+1,\text{sparse}} \leftarrow \text{ClientSide}(k, w^t)$
  end for
  Aggregate $\Delta w_{\text{avg}}^{t+1} \leftarrow \frac{1}{|S^t|} \sum_{k \in S^t} \Delta w_k^{t+1,\text{sparse}}$ **(Eq. (3))**
  Update $w^{t+1} \leftarrow w^t + \Delta w_{\text{avg}}^{t+1}$ **(Eq. (4))**
end for

function ClientSide(k, w^t)
  Initialize local model $w_k^t \leftarrow w^t$
  for each local epoch $e = 1, \dots, E$ **do**
    Update $w_k^{t+1} \leftarrow w_k^t - \eta \nabla \mathcal{L}_k(w_k^t; \mathcal{B})$
  end for
  Compute full delta $\Delta w_k^{t+1} \leftarrow w_k^{t+1} - w^t$ **(Eq. (1))**
  Apply top-K sparsification $\Delta w_k^{t+1,\text{sparse}} \leftarrow \text{TopK}(\Delta w_k^{t+1}, K\%)$ **(Eq. (2))**
  return $\Delta w_k^{t+1,\text{sparse}}$
end function

This update strategy fundamentally differs from FedAvg's model replacement approach and provides inherent protection against client drift in non-i.i.d settings. By preserving the previous global model and applying only delta changes, FedIncSparse maintains historical knowledge while gradually incorporating new information. This prevents the global model from overfitting to any particular client's data distribution and ensures more stable convergence across heterogeneous data environments. The top-K sparsification further enhances this stability by filtering out noisy updates that could exacerbate client drift.

The FedIncSparse algorithm is summarized in Algorithm 1.

The detailed proofs of FedIncSparse convergence are provided in Appendix A.

3 Experiments

We evaluate FedIncSparse against three key baseline algorithms representing fundamental approaches to FL. FedAvg [5] serves as the standard benchmark for conventional aggregation methods. FedProx [7] represents client drift mitigation approaches through its proximal regularization term. FedZip [20] is included as a benchmark communication compression method specifically designed for non-i.i.d settings.

3.1 Data Processing

We evaluate our method on three standard benchmarks: MNIST [23], Fashion-MNIST [24], and CIFAR-10 [25]. MNIST and Fashion-MNIST each contain 60,000 grayscale images (28×28 pixels) across 10 classes, while CIFAR-10 consists of 60,000 color images (32×32 pixels $\times 3$ color channels) across 10 classes. To simulate challenging non-i.i.d FL scenarios, we partition the 50,000 training samples of each dataset among 50 clients using Dirichlet distribution with concentration parameters $\alpha = 0.05$ (MNIST), $\alpha = 0.3$ (Fashion-MNIST), and $\alpha = 0.5$ (CIFAR-10). The resulting data distributions exhibit severe heterogeneity, as visualized in Fig. 1.

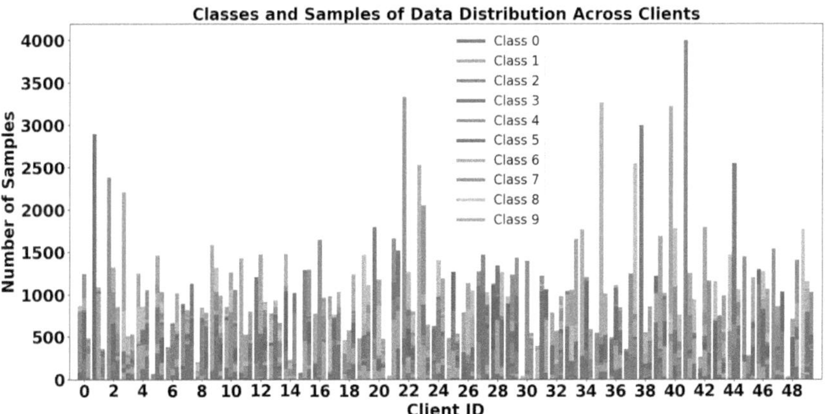

Fig. 1. Class and sample distribution of MNIST (left bar), Fashion-MNIST (middle bar), and CIFAR-10 (right bar) across 50 clients.

All datasets undergo dataset-specific preprocessing pipelines. MNIST images are simply normalized using a mean of 0.1307 and standard deviation of 0.3081.

Fashion-MNIST training data incorporates RandomHorizontalFlip and RandomRotation(10) augmentations followed by normalization (mean 0.2860, std 0.3530), while the test set uses only normalization. CIFAR-10 receives the most extensive augmentation including RandomCrop(32, padding = 4), RandomHorizontalFlip, ColorJitter (adjusting brightness, contrast, saturation, and hue), before normalization with channel-wise statistics (mean [0.4914, 0.4822, 0.4465], std [0.2023, 0.1994, 0.2010]). Test sets for all datasets use minimal transformation (only ToTensor and normalization).

The non-i.i.d partitioning creates substantial data heterogeneity across clients. For MNIST, client sample sizes range from 32 to 3,997 with class diversity varying from 1 to 9 classes per client. Fashion-MNIST distributions span 227–3,264 samples per client with 2–10 classes. CIFAR-10 clients hold 356–2,547 samples with 4–10 classes. This significant variation in both sample quantity and class distribution across clients confirms the challenging non-i.i.d characteristics of our experimental setup.

3.2 Models

We evaluate FedIncSparse using three distinct model architectures tailored for non-i.i.d datasets with varying complexity. For MNIST ($\alpha = 0.05$), we employ a LeNet-5 model with `Tanh()` activations and `AvgPool2d`, trained for 1 local epoch with $K = 10\%$ sparsity. Fashion-MNIST ($\alpha = 0.3$) utilizes a modified ResNet18 where `BatchNorm` is omitted and `Tanh()` replaces `ReLU`, trained for 2 local epochs with $K = 20\%$ sparsity. CIFAR-10 ($\alpha = 0.5$) employs a modified ResNet32 with `BasicBlockNoBatchNorm` structure and `ReLU` activation, trained for 5 local epochs with $K = 30\%$ sparsity. All experiments involve 50 clients with 5–10 participants per round, using SGD optimizer (learning rate 0.01, momentum 0.9, weight decay 10^{-3}) and batch size 32, evaluated by validation loss, accuracy, and macro F1-score.

3.3 Results

MNIST Evaluation. On MNIST under extreme non-i.i.d conditions ($\alpha = 0.05$), FedProx emerges as the performance leader with superior convergence stability (Fig. 2), achieving the lowest validation loss (0.3534) and highest accuracy (88.44%) as shown in Table 1. However, this performance comes at the cost of communication efficiency, with FedProx requiring 361 MB comparable to FedAvg. In contrast, FedZip and FedIncSparse demonstrate remarkable communication efficiency, reducing bandwidth usage by approximately 35% (235–239 MB vs 361 MB), though with a corresponding accuracy trade-off (83.10–83.28% vs 88.44%). The results reveal a clear performance-efficiency trade-off: FedProx for optimal accuracy versus sparse methods for communication savings.

Fashion-MNIST Performance Analysis. Fashion-MNIST results ($\alpha = 0.3$) present a different narrative, with FedZip establishing dominance across both

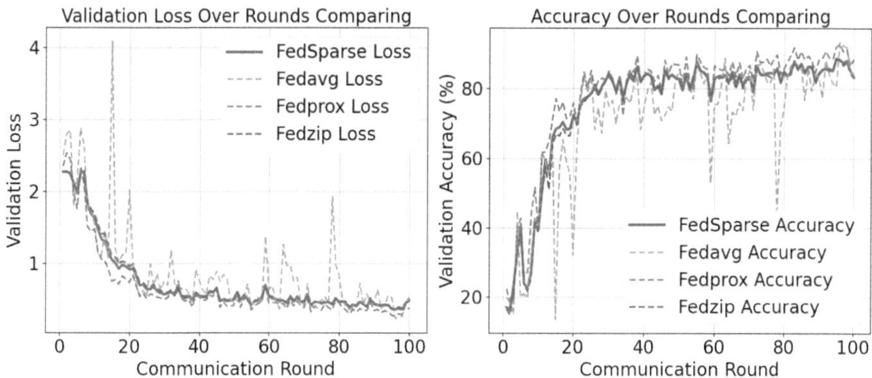

Fig. 2. Validation loss and accuracy trajectories on MNIST.

Table 1. Comparative performance on MNIST ($\alpha = 0.05$)

Method	Loss	F1-Score	Accuracy (%)	Comm. (MB)
FedZip	0.4795	0.8214	83.10	235
FedIncSparse	0.4889	0.8242	83.28	239
FedAvg	0.5236	0.8421	83.56	361
FedProx	0.3534	0.8822	88.44	361

performance and efficiency metrics. As visualized in Fig. 3, FedZip maintains consistently superior convergence characteristics, culminating in the best final metrics (Table 2): lowest loss (0.4498), highest F1-score (0.8274), and top accuracy (83.06%). Notably, FedZip achieves these results while reducing communication costs by over 20% compared to FedProx and FedAvg (827 MB vs 1035 MB). FedIncSparse follows closely, while FedProx shows only marginal improvements over the unstable FedAvg baseline. This dataset demonstrates that communication-efficient methods can simultaneously optimize both model quality and bandwidth utilization.

Table 2. Performance metrics on Fashion-MNIST ($\alpha = 0.3$)

Method	Loss	F1-Score	Accuracy (%)	Comm. (MB)
FedZip	0.4498	0.8274	83.06	827
FedIncSparse	0.4616	0.8201	82.38	840
FedProx	0.5104	0.8036	80.98	1,035
FedAvg	0.6699	0.7444	76.64	1,035

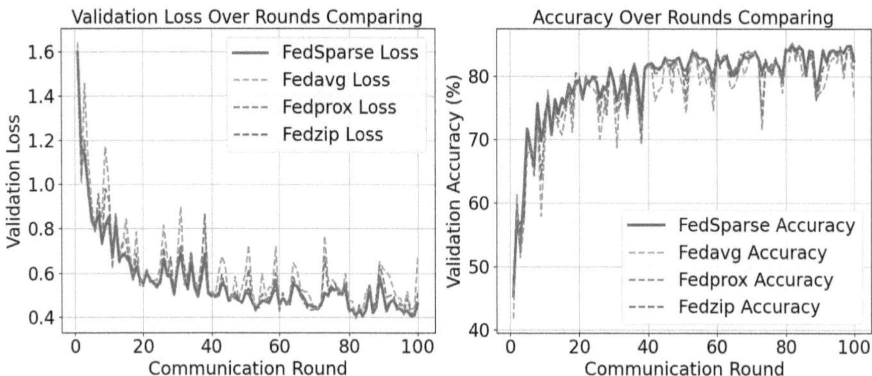

Fig. 3. Convergence behavior on Fashion-MNIST.

CIFAR-10 Comparative Assessment. The CIFAR-10 experiments ($\alpha = 0.5$) reveal FedIncSparse as the standout approach, achieving the optimal balance between model quality and communication efficiency. While FedIncSparse and FedProx deliver comparable accuracy (83.81% vs 83.39%), FedIncSparse maintains superior stability throughout training (Fig. 4) and achieves the lowest validation loss (0.4911 - Table 3). Crucially, FedIncSparse accomplishes this with significantly reduced communication overhead (20,458 MB vs 21,504 MB, 5% improvement). FedZip follows with the lowest communication cost (20,414 MB) while still outperforming FedAvg. These results underscore FedIncSparse's effectiveness on complex vision tasks, providing the best performance-efficiency equilibrium.

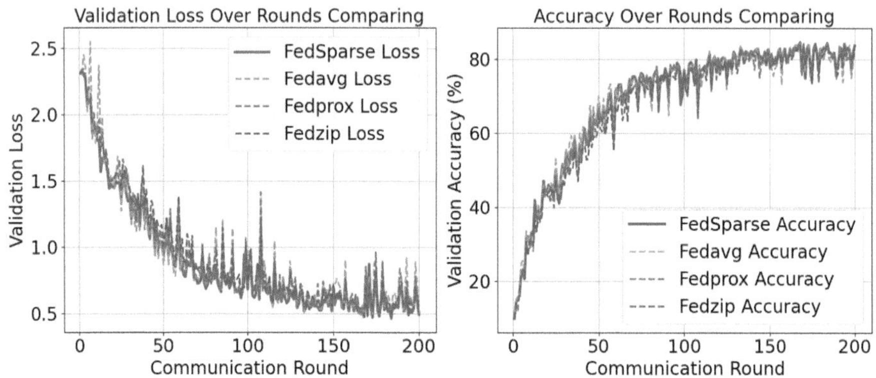

Fig. 4. Training dynamics on CIFAR-10.

Table 3. Method comparison on CIFAR-10 ($\alpha = 0.5$)

Method	Loss	F1-Score	Accuracy (%)	Comm. (MB)
FedZip	0.5313	0.8301	82.86	20,414
FedIncSparse	0.4911	0.8399	83.81	20,458
FedProx	0.5103	0.8362	83.39	21,504
FedAvg	0.5563	0.8251	82.29	21,504

4 Conclusion

We introduced FedIncSparse, an FL framework utilizing top-K sparse delta updates to address communication efficiency and client drift in non-i.i.d settings. The method achieves performance comparable to FedZip while significantly reducing computational overhead through simpler sparsification. Empirical results on MNIST, Fashion-MNIST, and CIFAR-10 demonstrate competitive accuracy with up to 35% communication reduction compared to FedAvg and FedProx. Theoretical convergence guarantees further support for its robustness. Future work will explore adaptive sparsity and larger-scale applications to enhance practical deployment.

Acknowledgment. This research is supported by the University of Economics Ho Chi Minh City (UEH).

A Proof of Convergence

We provide detailed proofs for Theorems 1 and 2, extending the analysis to account for partial client participation and dynamic sparsity levels. We address the biased nature of top-K sparsification by using bounded error assumptions and Young's inequality.

A.1 Assumptions

We adopt standard FL optimization assumptions with modifications for sparsification:

Assumption 1 (Smoothness). Each local objective function $f_k(w)$ is L-smooth:

$$\|\nabla f_k(w) - \nabla f_k(v)\| \leq L\|w - v\|. \tag{5}$$

Assumption 2 (Strong Convexity). For the convex case, each local objective $f_k(w)$ is μ-strongly convex:

$$f_k(w) \geq f_k(v) + \langle \nabla f_k(v), w - v \rangle + \frac{\mu}{2}\|w - v\|^2. \tag{6}$$

Assumption 3 (Bounded Gradient Variance). The variance of local stochastic gradients is bounded:

$$\mathbb{E}\left[\|\nabla f_k(w;\xi_k) - \nabla f_k(w)\|^2\right] \leq \sigma^2. \tag{7}$$

Assumption 4 (Bounded Gradient Divergence). The divergence of local gradients from the global gradient is bounded:

$$\mathbb{E}\left[\|\nabla f_k(w) - \nabla F(w)\|^2\right] \leq \zeta^2. \tag{8}$$

Assumption 5 (Bounded Sparsification Error). The error introduced by top-K sparsification is bounded:

$$\mathbb{E}\left[\|\Delta w_k^t - \Delta w_{k^t_{\text{sparse}}}\|^2\right] \leq \epsilon_t^2. \tag{9}$$

Note: Top-K sparsification is biased, so $\mathbb{E}[e_k^t] \neq 0$.

Assumption 6 (Partial Client Participation). In each round t, a subset $S^t \subset \{1, 2, \ldots, N\}$ of clients is randomly selected with $|S^t| = C \leq N$.

A.2 Proof of Theorem 1

Theorem 1 (Convergence: Strongly Convex Case). *Under Assumptions 1-6, with learning rate $\eta \leq \frac{1}{4L}$, FedIncSparse achieves:*

$$\begin{aligned}\mathbb{E}[F(w_T) - F(w^*)] &\leq (1-\eta\mu)^T[F(w_0) - F(w^*)] \\ &\quad + \frac{\eta}{2\mu}\left(\frac{L\eta}{C}+1\right)\left(\sigma^2 + \zeta^2 + \frac{N-C}{CN}\zeta^2 + \epsilon_{max}^2\right).\end{aligned} \tag{10}$$

where w_T is the global model after T rounds, w^* is the optimal solution, and the expectation is over client sampling, stochastic gradients, and sparsification.

Proof. We begin with the smoothness of F:

$$F(w^t) \leq F(w^{t-1}) + \langle \nabla F(w^{t-1}), \Delta^t_{\text{avg}} \rangle + \frac{L}{2}\|\Delta^t_{\text{avg}}\|^2. \tag{11}$$

Taking expectations:

$$\mathbb{E}[F(w^t)] \leq \mathbb{E}[F(w^{t-1})] + \mathbb{E}[\langle \nabla F(w^{t-1}), \Delta^t_{\text{avg}} \rangle] + \frac{L}{2}\mathbb{E}[\|\Delta^t_{\text{avg}}\|^2]. \tag{12}$$

For the inner product term, we have:

$$\mathbb{E}[\langle \nabla F(w^{t-1}), \Delta^t_{\text{avg}} \rangle] = -\eta\mathbb{E}[\|\nabla F(w^{t-1})\|^2] + \mathbb{E}[\langle \nabla F(w^{t-1}), \frac{1}{C}\sum_{k\in S^t} e_k^t \rangle]. \tag{13}$$

Using Young's inequality with parameter $a > 0$:

$$\mathbb{E}[\langle \nabla F(w^{t-1}), \frac{1}{C}\sum_{k\in S^t} e_k^t \rangle] \leq \frac{a}{2}\mathbb{E}[\|\nabla F(w^{t-1})\|^2] + \frac{1}{2aC^2}\mathbb{E}[\|\sum_{k\in S^t} e_k^t\|^2]. \tag{14}$$

Bounding the error term using Assumption 5:

$$\mathbb{E}[\| \sum_{k \in S^t} e_k^t \|^2] \leq C\epsilon_t^2. \tag{15}$$

For the norm term:

$$\mathbb{E}[\|\Delta_{\text{avg}}^t\|^2] \leq \eta^2 \left(\sigma^2 + \zeta^2 + \frac{N-C}{CN}\zeta^2 \right) + \epsilon_t^2. \tag{16}$$

Combining these bounds and using strong convexity:

$$\mathbb{E}[F(w^t) - F(w^*)] \leq (1 - 2\eta\mu + a\mu)\mathbb{E}[F(w^{t-1}) - F(w^*)] + \frac{\epsilon_t^2}{2aC} + \frac{L}{2}\left(\eta^2(\sigma^2 + \zeta^2 + \frac{N-C}{CN}\zeta^2) + \epsilon_t^2 \right). \tag{17}$$

Setting $a = \eta$ and unrolling the recursion completes the proof.

A.3 Proof of Theorem 2

Theorem 2 (Convergence: Non-Convex Case). *Under Assumptions 1–6, with learning rate $\eta \leq \frac{1}{4L}$, FedIncSparse ensures:*

$$\frac{1}{T}\sum_{t=1}^{T} \mathbb{E}\left[\|\nabla F(w^{t-1})\|^2\right] \leq \frac{4[F(w_0) - F(w^*)]}{\eta T} + 2\left(\sigma^2 + \zeta^2 + \frac{N-C}{CN}\zeta^2 + \epsilon_{max}^2 \right). \tag{18}$$

Proof. From the smoothness condition and taking expectations:

$$\mathbb{E}[F(w^t)] \leq \mathbb{E}[F(w^{t-1})] - \eta\mathbb{E}[\|\nabla F(w^{t-1})\|^2] + \frac{\eta}{2}\mathbb{E}[\|\nabla F(w^{t-1})\|^2] + \frac{\epsilon_t^2}{2\eta C} + \frac{L}{2}\left(\eta^2(\sigma^2 + \zeta^2 + \frac{N-C}{CN}\zeta^2) + \epsilon_t^2 \right). \tag{19}$$

Simplifying and rearranging:

$$\frac{\eta}{2}\mathbb{E}[\|\nabla F(w^{t-1})\|^2] \leq \mathbb{E}[F(w^{t-1}) - F(w^t)] + \frac{\epsilon_t^2}{2\eta C} + \frac{L}{2}\left(\eta^2(\sigma^2 + \zeta^2 + \frac{N-C}{CN}\zeta^2) + \epsilon_t^2 \right). \tag{20}$$

Summing over $t = 1$ to T and dividing by T:

$$\frac{1}{T}\sum_{t=1}^{T} \mathbb{E}[\|\nabla F(w^{t-1})\|^2] \leq \frac{2[F(w_0) - F(w^*)]}{\eta T} + \frac{1}{\eta^2 CT}\sum_{t=1}^{T}\epsilon_t^2 + L\left(\eta(\sigma^2 + \zeta^2 + \frac{N-C}{CN}\zeta^2) + \frac{1}{\eta T}\sum_{t=1}^{T}\epsilon_t^2 \right). \tag{21}$$

Using $\epsilon_t^2 \leq \epsilon_{\max}^2$ and setting $\eta \leq \frac{1}{4L}$ gives the final result.

References

1. Jie, X., Glicksberg, B.S., Chang, S., Walker, P., Bian, J., Wang, F.: Federated learning for healthcare informatics. J. Healthcare Inf. Res. **5**(1), 1–19 (2021)
2. Guan, H., Yap, P.-T., Bozoki, A., Liu, M.: Federated learning for medical image analysis: a survey. Pattern Recogn. **151**, 110424 (2024)
3. Karimireddy, S.P., Kale, S., Mohri, M., Reddi, S., Stich, S., Suresh, A.T.: Stochastic controlled averaging for federated learning. In: Proceedings of the International Conference on Machine Learning, pp. 5132–5143
4. Kairouz, P., et al.: Advances and open problems in federated learning. Found. Trends® Mach. Learn. **14**(1–2), 1–210 (2021)
5. McMahan, B., Moore, E., Ramage, D., Hampson, S., Arcas, B.A.: Communication-efficient learning of deep networks from decentralized data. In: Artificial Intelligence and Statistics, pp. 1273–1282. PMLR (2017)
6. Li, T., Sahu, A.K., Talwalkar, A., Smith, V.: Federated learning: challenges, methods, and future directions. IEEE Signal Process. Mag. **37**(3), 50–60 (2020)
7. Li, T., Sahu, A.K., Zaheer, M., Sanjabi, M., Talwalkar, A., Smith, V.: Federated optimization in heterogeneous networks. Proc. Mach. Learn. Syst. **2**, 429–450 (2020)
8. Ghosh, A., Chung, J., Yin, D., Ramchandran, K.: An efficient framework for clustered federated learning. Adv. Neural. Inf. Process. Syst. **33**, 19586–19597 (2020)
9. Ghosh, A., Chung, J., Yin, D., Ramchandran, K.: An efficient framework for clustered federated learning. IEEE Trans. Inf. Theory **68**(12), 8076–8091 (2022)
10. Khan, A.A., Khan, A.F., Ali, H., Anwar, A.: Personalized federated learning techniques: empirical analysis. In: 2024 IEEE International Conference on Big Data (BigData), pp. 1333–1339. IEEE (2024)
11. Dinh, C.T., Tran, N., Nguyen, J.: Personalized federated learning with Moreau envelopes. Adv. Neural Inf. Process. Syst. **33**, 21394–21405 (2020)
12. Li, T., Hu, S., Beirami, A., Smith, V.: Ditto: fair and robust federated learning through personalization. In: International Conference on Machine Learning, pp. 6357–6368. PMLR (2021)
13. Wang, J., Liu, Q., Liang, H., Joshi, G., Poor, H.V.: Tackling the objective inconsistency problem in heterogeneous federated optimization. In: Advances in Neural Information Processing Systems (NeurIPS), vol. 33, pp. 7611–7623 (2020)
14. Reddi, S., et al.: Adaptive federated optimization. In: International Conference on Learning Representations (ICLR) (2021)
15. Hsu, T.-M.H., Qi, H., Brown, M.: Measuring the effects of non-identical data distribution for federated visual classification. CoRR, abs/1909.06335 (2020)
16. Zhang, S., Huang, J., Li, P., Liang, C.: Differentially private federated learning with local momentum updates and gradients filtering. Inf. Sci. **680**, 120960 (2024)
17. Yahui, X., et al.: Communication compression techniques in distributed deep learning: a survey. J. Syst. Architect. **142**, 102955 (2023)
18. Liu, Y., et al.: A federated deep learning framework for privacy preservation and communication efficiency. J. Syst. Architect. **124**, 102413 (2022)
19. Wilkins, G., et al.: Fedsz: leveraging error-bounded lossy compression for federated learning communications. In: 2024 IEEE International Parallel and Distributed Processing Symposium Workshops (IPDPSW), pp. 1187–1188 (2024)
20. Malekijoo, A., et al.: FEDZIP: a compression framework for communication-efficient federated learning. CoRR, abs/2102.01593 (2021)

21. Li, Z., et al.: Robust communication-efficient decentralized learning with heterogeneity. J. Syst. Architect. **141**, 102923 (2023)
22. Yahui, X., et al.: Fog-driven communication-efficient and privacy-preserving federated learning based on compressed sensing. Comput. Netw. **241**, 110208 (2025)
23. LeCun, Y., Bottou, L., Bengio, Y., Haffner, P.: Gradient-based learning applied to document recognition. Proc. IEEE **86**(11), 2278–2324 (1998)
24. Xiao, H., Rasul, K., Vollgraf, R.: Fashion-MNIST: a novel image dataset for benchmarking machine learning algorithms. arXiv preprint arXiv:1708.07747 (2017)
25. Krizhevsky, A., Hinton, G.: Learning multiple layers of features from tiny images. Technical Report, University of Toronto (2009)

Metric-Weighted Voting Classifier with SMOTEENN for Enhanced Machine Learning Cardiovascular Disease Prediction

Emmanuel Ileberi and Yansia Sun(✉)

Department of Electrical and Electronic Engineering Science, University of Johannesburg, Auckland Park 2092, Johannesburg, South Africa
ysun@uj.ac.za

Abstract. Cardiovascular diseases (CVDs) remain a leading cause of global mortality, underscoring the need for reliable and interpretable predictive models to support early diagnosis and clinical decision-making. This study proposes a hybrid ensemble framework that integrates SMOTEENN resampling with a metric-weighted Voting Classifier to address class imbalance and improve prediction robustness. Using the publicly available Kaggle CVD dataset ($\approx$70,000 records), the dataset was split into 80% training and 20% testing using stratified sampling and we evaluated a diverse pool of base classifiers including Decision Tree, Logistic Regression, K-Nearest Neighbour, Random Forest, LightGBM, XGBoost, and Multilayer Perceptron. Performance metrics such as Accuracy, Precision, Recall, F1-score, Matthews Correlation Coefficient (MCC), and ROC-AUC were employed to provide a comprehensive evaluation. Results demonstrate that the proposed SMOTEENN + metric-weighted ensemble significantly outperformed the baseline (non-resampled) and existing models, improving accuracy from 72.6% to 96.9%, F1-score from 0.72 to 0.97, and ROC-AUC from 0.73 to 0.97. Moreover, the metric-weighting scheme allowed aggregation to be guided by clinically meaningful criteria, enhancing sensitivity and balanced classification.

Keywords: machine learning · ensemble learning · imbalanced dataset · cardiovascular disease · SMOTEENN · voting classifier · First keyword

1 Introduction

Cardiovascular diseases (CVDs) remain the leading cause of mortality globally, accounting for an estimated 19.8 million deaths in 2022, representing approximately 32% of all global deaths [21]. These conditions impose a significant economic burden, with direct and indirect costs in the United States alone reaching $407.3 billion between 2018 and 2019 [3]. The primary risk factors for CVDs

T. T. Quan et al. (Eds.): MIWAI 2025, LNAI 16353, pp. 192–204, 2026.
https://doi.org/10.1007/978-981-95-4957-3_16

include physical inactivity, poor diet, diabetes, and excessive tobacco use [12]. However, these risks can be mitigated through lifestyle modifications such as regular physical activity, a balanced diet, and reduced intake of salt, tobacco, and alcohol [12].

Early and accurate prediction of disease onset is critical for preventive interventions. Machine learning approaches have shown promise in CVD prediction, with various studies demonstrating the effectiveness of ensemble methods, feature selection techniques, and data preprocessing strategies [2]. However, several research gaps persist. First, many existing studies rely on traditional ensemble methods that treat all classifiers equally, potentially underutilizing high-performing models in clinical contexts where certain metrics (sensitivity, specificity) are more critical than overall accuracy [6]. Second, while class imbalance has been addressed through various resampling techniques, the integration of advanced hybrid resampling methods like SMOTEENN with metric-guided ensemble weighting remains underexplored. Third, most studies focus on single datasets or limited evaluation metrics, making it difficult to assess the generalizability and clinical relevance of proposed approaches [6,14].

2 Motivation

The main motivations for this study are fourfold. First, we introduce the first comprehensive framework that synergistically combines SMOTEENN resampling with metric-weighted voting, specifically designed for the prediction of cardiovascular disease with clinical relevance in mind. Second, unlike traditional equal-weight voting, our approach dynamically assigns classifier weights based on clinically meaningful performance metrics (F1-score, MCC, ROC-AUC), ensuring the ensemble prioritizes models that excel in balanced classification and minority class detection. Third, we provide extensive empirical analysis using seven different base classifiers on a large-scale data set (70,000 records), demonstrating consistent and substantial improvements in multiple evaluation metrics relevant to clinical decision making. Finally, our framework addresses the critical challenge of false negative reduction in CVD prediction, making it particularly suitable for clinical screening scenarios where missing disease cases carry significant consequences.

3 Theoretical Background

This section presents the theoretical foundations underlying our proposed methodology, providing the mathematical and conceptual basis for ensemble learning, class imbalance handling, and performance evaluation in medical classification contexts.

3.1 Metric-Weighted Voting Classifier

Ensemble learning is a widely adopted approach for improving prediction robustness by combining the outputs of multiple base classifiers [9]. In a standard Voting Classifier, predictions are aggregated either through hard voting (majority class label) or soft voting (average class probabilities). While effective, uniform voting assumes that all base learners contribute equally to the final decision. This assumption can be suboptimal, especially in medical domains such as cardiovascular disease (CVD) prediction, where certain classifiers may perform better on clinically meaningful metrics than others [8]. To address this limitation, a metric-weighted voting strategy has been proposed, where the contribution of each classifier is scaled according to its performance on task-relevant evaluation measures. Specifically, given a set of base learners $h_1, \ldots, h_m$, each assigned a weight w_i, the ensemble prediction under weighted soft voting is:

1. Hard Voting:

$$\hat{y} = \arg\max_{c \in C} \sum_{i=1}^{m} w_i I\left(h_i(x) = c\right) \tag{1}$$

2. Soft Voting:

$$\hat{y} = \arg\max_{c \in C} \sum_{i=1}^{m} w_i P_i(y = c \mid x), \tag{2}$$

$$P(y = c \mid x) = \sum_{i=1}^{m} w_i \, P_i(y = c \mid x), \tag{3}$$

where $P_i(\cdot)$ is the probability estimate from classifier i and $\sum_i w_i = 1$. For hard voting the weighted decision is $\text{argmax}_c \sum_i w_i I(h_i(x) = c)$.

Weights are computed by normalizing the chosen metric values:

$$w_i = \frac{M_i + \varepsilon}{\sum_{j=1}^{m}(M_j + \varepsilon)}, \tag{4}$$

where ε is a small smoothing constant (e.g., 10^{-6}) to avoid division by zero. Optionally a sharpening exponent $\alpha > 0$ may be applied: $w_i \propto (M_i + \varepsilon)^{\alpha}$ to control concentration.

3.2 Class Imbalance and SMOTEENN

Class imbalance occurs when one class significantly outnumbers others, leading to biased learning toward the majority class. SMOTEENN addresses this through a two-stage process combining Synthetic Minority Oversampling Technique (SMOTE) with Edited Nearest Neighbours (ENN) cleaning.

1. SMOTE synthesizes minority examples by linear interpolation. Given a minority instance x_i and one of its k-nearest minority neighbours x_{nn}, a synthetic example is generated as [5]:

$$x_{\text{syn}} = x_i + \lambda\,(x_{\text{nn}} - x_i), \quad \lambda \sim \mathcal{U}(0,1). \tag{5}$$

   where $\lambda \sim \mathcal{U}(0,1)$ is a random factor and $x_neighbour$ is a randomly selected k-nearest neighbour of x_i from the same class. There are different techniques developed to mitigate the challenges of SMOTE [5,11] one of which is SMOTEENN where the ENN (Edited Nearest Neighbors) algorithm is applied. Here, every instance, whether original or synthetic, is evaluated against its k nearest neighbors.
2. After oversampling, ENN removes instances that are misclassified by the majority of their k-nearest neighbours. Let $\text{NN}_k(x_i)$ denote the set of the k nearest neighbours of instance x_i (according to the chosen distance in feature space), and let y_i be the class label of x_i. Define the indicator function $\dot{1}[]$ which equals 1 when its argument is true and 0 otherwise. The Edited Nearest Neighbours (ENN) rule removes x_i from the training set whenever a majority of its k neighbours disagree with its label, i.e., formally [4]:

$$\sum_{x_j \in \text{NN}_k(x_i)} \mathbf{1}[y_j \neq y_i] > \frac{k}{2}, \tag{6}$$

   Equivalently, with integer arithmetic one can write the condition as

$$\sum_{x_j \in NN_k(x_i)} 1\,[y_j \neq y_i] > \left\lceil \frac{k+1}{2} \right\rceil \tag{7}$$

This implies remove x_i when strictly more than half of its k neighbours carry a different label. In practice k is often small (e.g. $k = 3$), so ENN removes points that are locally inconsistent with their neighbourhood (noisy or borderline examples), thereby cleaning decision boundaries before final training or after oversampling (as in SMOTEENN). This hybrid approach addresses both the quantity imbalance (through SMOTE) and quality issues (through ENN) simultaneously [10].

4 Related Work

Prior work has applied ensembles, resampling, and representation learning to CVD prediction and related clinical tasks [15]. In [22], HeartEnsembleNet, a hybrid ensemble model integrating multiple ML classifiers, was proposed for CVD risk prediction and evaluated against six classical models (SVM, GB, DT, LR, KNN, RF) as well as HRFLM and other ensemble methods. Using a dataset of 70,000 patients with 12 clinical features, it achieved 92.95% accuracy and

93.08% precision, demonstrating the potential of hybrid ensembles to outperform individual models and support clinical decision-making. A voting ensemble model integrating logistic regression, SVM, and AdaBoost was developed for CVD risk prediction in [23] in the general population using two years of KNHANES data. After preprocessing, filter-based feature selection, and imbalance handling via SMOTEENN or SMOTETomek, the approach was evaluated against other ML baselines. The SMOTEENN variant on selected characteristics yielded the best results (accuracy, recall, g mean, and AUC = 0.8102), outperforming competing models. Authors in [17] introduced a probability-weighted voting ensemble that ranks base classifiers by accuracy and assigns them weights when combining predictions. Tested on five UCI datasets with six base learners and six standard ensembles, their best variant (3PW-Ensemble) achieved an average accuracy of 85.36%, outperforming the top conventional ensemble (Random Forest, 74.99%) across datasets. The method consistently improved classification performance by leveraging weighted voting from top-performing models.

Building on these threads, our framework integrates SMOTEENN with a metric-weighted Voting Classifier in which weights are derived from clinically meaningful metrics (namely F1, ROC-AUC, MCC) rather than accuracy alone. Prior work either employs resampling without metric-guided weighting, or uses weighted voting optimized largely on accuracy.

5 Research Methodology

Our methodology introduces a novel hybrid framework that synergistically combines imbalance-aware preprocessing with metric-driven ensemble aggregation. Figure 1 illustrates the complete pipeline, highlighting our key innovations.

5.1 Data Preprocessing

The study employs the publicly available Cardiovascular Disease Dataset from Kaggle [18]. The dataset contains about 70,000 samples of a combination of clinical, anthropometric, and lifestyle-related variables. The data contains a target category, Cardio = 1 (positive cases): approximately 34,979 (49.97%) samples and Cardio = 0 (negative cases): approximately 35,021 (50.03%) samples. The age feature, which is in days, is converted to years by dividing each by 365.25 (to account for leap years also). In this work, the data set was divided into training and test sets with training data at 80% and test data at 20%.

To address subgroup-level imbalance, we applied SMOTEENN to balance the training data [10], ensuring unbiased metric-based weighting. The hyperparameters used include sampling strategy set to 'auto', which is equivalent to 'not majority' class sampling and random state set to 0 to ensure reproducibility. The balanced data were then used to train base classifiers, with validation performance guiding weight computation, followed by robust scaling via *sklearn*.

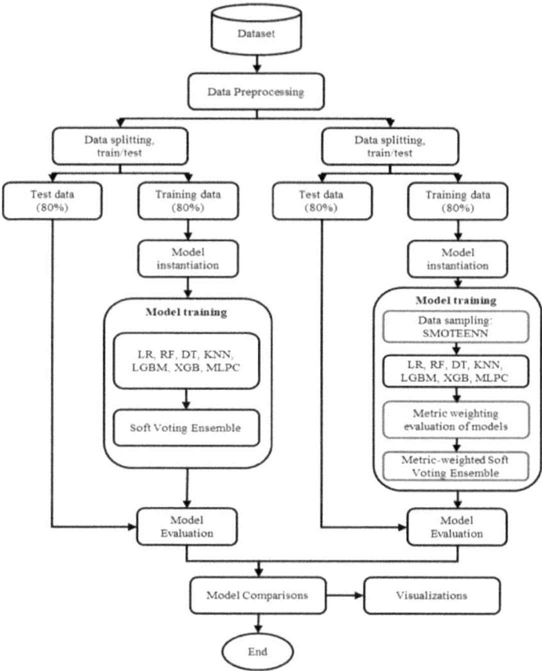

Fig. 1. Proposed Framework for the Research.

5.2 Base Classifiers and Hyperparameters Used in This Work

Our metric-weighted ensemble learning classifier integrates seven diverse machine learning models: Decision Trees, Logistic Regression, Random Forests, LightGBM (LGBM), Multi-Layer Perceptron Classifier (MLPC), k-Nearest Neighbors (kNN), and XGBoost. Each learner contributes unique strengths, such as interpretability and rule-based partitioning (Decision Trees), linear decision boundaries and probabilistic interpretation (Logistic Regression), variance reduction through bagging (Random Forests), gradient boosting efficiency (LGBM and XGBoost), non-linear function approximation (MLPC), and instance-based learning that captures local neighborhood structures (kNN). They have been used successfully in the literature [1,7,19,20]. Table 1 summarizes the learners and key hyperparameters.

5.3 Metric-Weighted Ensemble Learner

We implement a soft voting ensemble in which each base learner is assigned a non-negative weight reflecting its performance on a validation fold, as determined by Eq. 4. We set M_i to the F1-score, which balances precision and recall–critical in medical contexts where both false positives (unnecessary anxiety/treatment) and false negatives (missed diagnoses) carry significant consequences [13]. The

Table 1. Base learners and selected hyperparameters

Classifier	Key hyperparameters
Decision Tree (DT)	max_depth = 10, min_samples_split=20, criterion=gini
Logistic Regression (LR)	C = 1.0, solver=liblinear, max_iter = 1000
K-Nearest Neighbors (KNN)	n_neighbors = 5, weights = distance, metric = minkowski
Random Forest (RF)	n_estimators = 100, max_depth = 15, min_samples_split = 10
LightGBM (LGBM)	n_estimators = 100, learning_rate = 0.1, max_depth = 7
XGBoost (XGB)	n_estimators = 100, learning_rate = 0.1, max_depth = 6
Multilayer Perceptron (MLP)	hidden_layer_sizes=(100,50), activation = relu, solver = adam

weights obtained are passed to the ensemble learner, which emphasizes stronger, task-relevant classifiers, exploits error diversity to reduce variance, and achieves more robust overall predictions. Default parameters of $\varepsilon = 10^{-6}$ and $\alpha = 1$ are used for stability and scaling.

5.4 Evaluation Metrics

Model evaluation uses multiple complementary metrics to capture performance, especially on imbalanced datasets. Accuracy measures overall correctness, while Precision and Recall assess reliability and sensitivity of positive predictions, summarized by the F1-score. The Matthews Correlation Coefficient (MCC) provides a balanced measure accounting for all confusion matrix elements, and ROC-AUC evaluates discriminative ability. The confusion matrix itself offers a detailed breakdown of prediction errors, supporting transparency in clinical decision-making [16].

6 Experimental Results and Discussion

All experiments use the Kaggle Cardiovascular Disease dataset described in Sect. 5. After preprocessing and feature engineering the dataset was split by stratified sampling into a training partition and a held-out test partition (19,776 training samples and 4,944 test samples). Two experimental pipelines were run in parallel:

1. Baseline – standard preprocessing, model training and evaluation without any class-resampling method.
2. SMOTEENN – same preprocessing and model set, but the training set was balanced and cleaned using SMOTEENN (SMOTE oversampling followed by Edited Nearest Neighbors cleaning) prior to model training.

All experiments run on identical hardware (Intel i7-11950K, 32 GB RAM, NVIDIA A2000 GPU) with fixed random seeds ensuring reproducibility. The classifiers evaluated were discussed in Subsect. 5.2 above and results obtained.

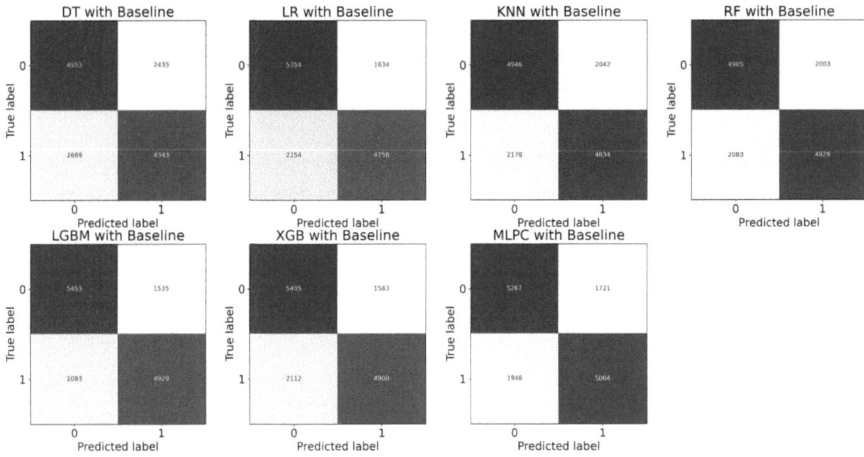

Fig. 2. Confusion Matrix with Baseline dataset.

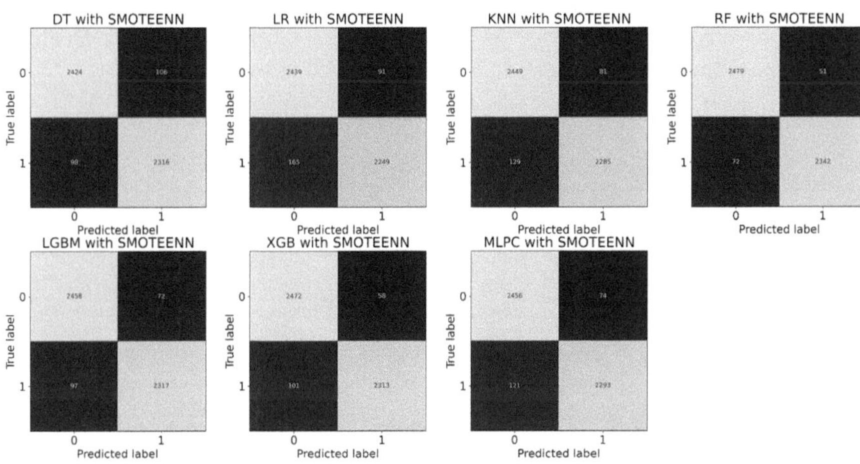

Fig. 3. Confusion Matrix plots for the base learners with SMOTEENN.

Figures 2 and 3 present the confusion matrices for the baseline and SMOTEENN-weighted ensembles, respectively, while Figs. 4 and 5 depict the ROC curves under the same settings.

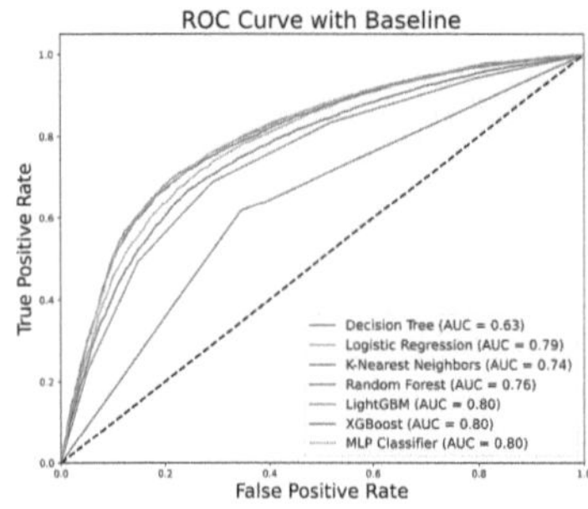

Fig. 4. ROC curve for the base learners with the Baseline.

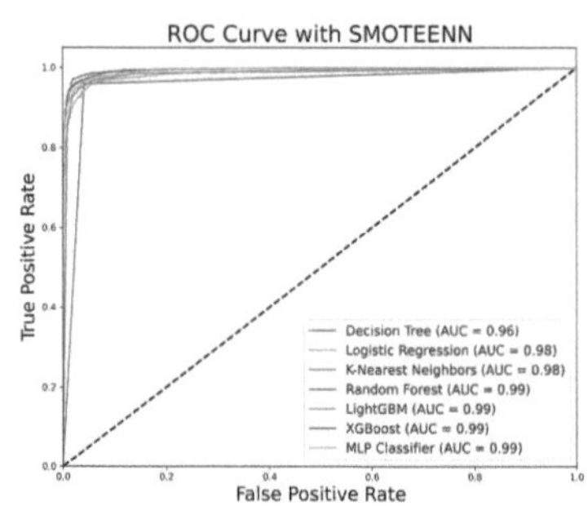

Fig. 5. ROC curve for the base learners with SMOTEENN.

Table 2 summarizes classifier results (baseline vs SMOTEENN) and the F1-derived weights used in the metric-weighted ensemble. SMOTEENN produced large and consistent improvements across classifiers. For example, Decision Tree accuracy rose from 0.6354 to 0.9587 and F1 from 0.6299 to 0.9578. Even the strongest baseline models (LGBM, XGB) improved substantially.

Table 2. Classifier test metrics (baseline vs SMOTEENN) and F1-derived weights

Classifier	Baseline Acc	SMOTEENN Acc	Baseline F1	SMOTEENN F1	Baseline AUC	SMOTEENN AUC	Weight (SMOTEENN F1)
DT	0.6354	0.9587	0.6299	0.9578	0.6355	0.9588	0.1424
KNN	0.6986	0.9575	0.6961	0.9561	0.6986	0.9573	0.1407
LGBM	0.7416	0.9658	0.7315	0.9648	0.7416	0.9657	0.1422
LR	0.7223	0.9482	0.7099	0.9462	0.7224	0.9478	0.1449
MLPC	0.7379	0.9606	0.7341	0.9592	0.7380	0.9603	0.1435
RF	0.7081	0.9751	0.7070	0.9744	0.7082	0.9750	0.1438
XGB	0.7361	0.9678	0.7262	0.9668	0.7361	0.9676	0.1426

The largest absolute gains are found in weaker baseline learners (DT, KNN), but even top tree ensembles (RF, XGB, LGBM) gained 20–27% points in accuracy and similar increases in AUC and F1. Matthews Correlation Coefficient (MCC) also increased markedly (for example, DT MCC 0.2710 to 0.9174), indicating improved balanced prediction beyond simple accuracy gains. Table 3 shows the ensemble metrics means across runs for baseline and dynamic-weighted SMOTEENN.

Figure 6 shows the plots for Accuracy, F1, ROC-AUC, and MCC. Matthews Correlation Coefficient (MCC) also increased markedly, indicating improved balanced prediction beyond simple accuracy gains. The ensemble after SMOTEENN attains approximately 0.97 accuracy and AUC, compared to ≈ 0.73 for the baseline ensemble. Improvements are consistent across metrics, indicating both higher sensitivity and specificity (Figs. 7, 8, 9 and 10).

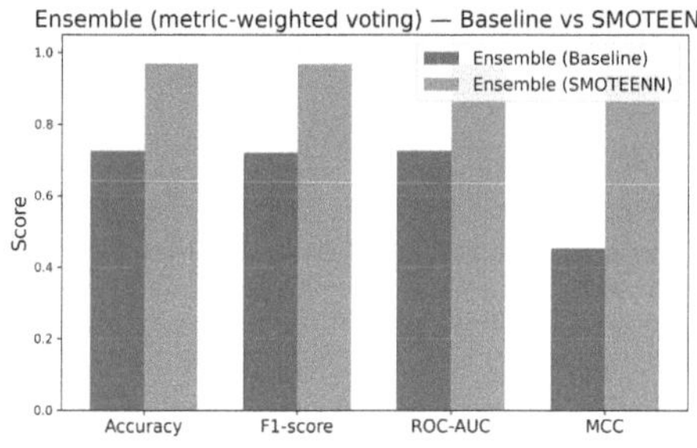

Fig. 6. Ensemble results – with and without SMOTEENN.

Table 3. Ensemble metrics (means across runs)

Metric	Baseline	SMOTEENN
Accuracy	0.7260	0.9691
F1-score	0.7208	0.9680
Precision	0.7360	0.9772
Recall	0.7061	0.9590
ROC-AUC	0.7260	0.9688
MCC	0.4523	0.9382

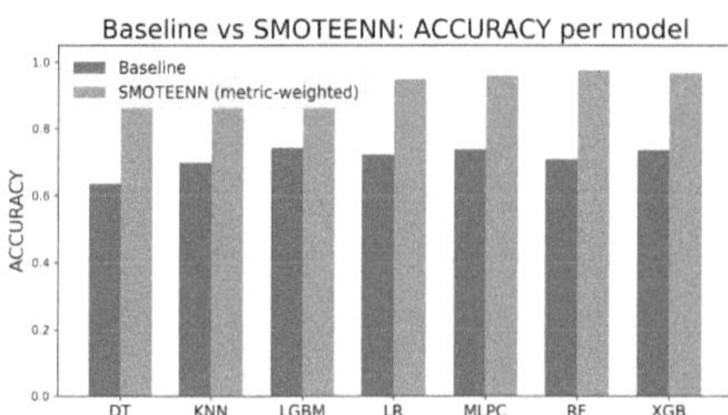

Fig. 7. Comparison of Accuracy with Baseline and SMOTEENN.

Baseline vs SMOTEENN: AUC per model

Fig. 8. Comparison of AUC with Baseline and SMOTEENN.

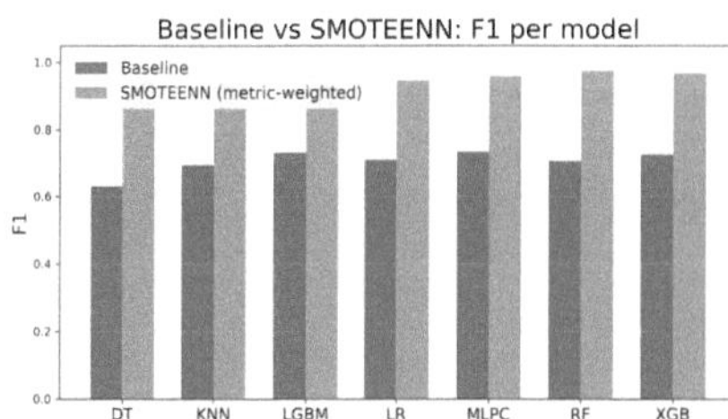

Fig. 9. Comparison of F1 with Baseline and SMOTEENN.

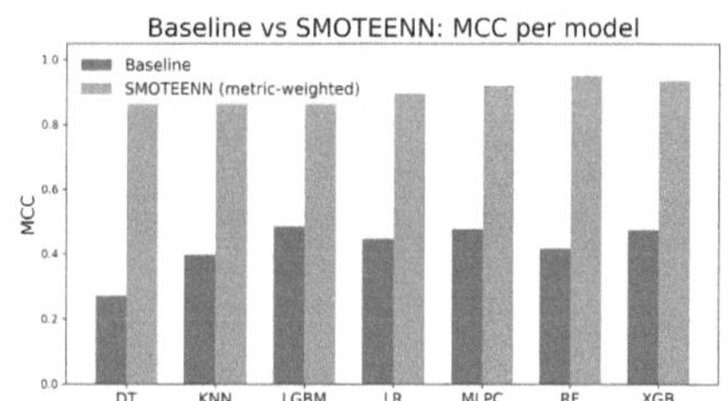

Fig. 10. Comparison of MCC with Baseline and SMOTEENN.

Table 4 summarizes comparative results from selected studies in the literature. Direct comparisons should be made cautiously due to differences in datasets and evaluation protocols.

Table 4. Comparison with recent literature

Study Year	Dataset	Resampling	Model	Reported metrics
Fitriyani et al. (2020)	Cleveland	DBSCAN + SMOTEENN	XGBoost (HDPM)	Accuracy 98.4%
Wei et al. (2025)	Public CHD sets	SMOTEENN + PCA	Various (DT, KNN, SVM, XGB, RF)	SMOTEENN: Acc 92.16%, F1 93.85%; +PCA: Acc 97.91%
Mienye	Sun (2021)	Cleveland	PSO-SSAE	Accuracy 96.1% (Cleveland), 97.3% (Framingham)
Yang et al. (2022)	Cleveland	SMOTE variants	XGBoost	Reported >90% accuracy in best cases
This work	Kaggle	SMOTEENN	Metric-weighted Voting	Accuracy $\approx$ 0.97/F1 $\approx$ 0.97/AUC $\approx$ 0.97

7 Conclusions

We developed a hybrid framework for cardiovascular disease prediction that integrates SMOTEENN resampling with a metric-weighted Voting Classifier built from diverse learners (Decision Tree, Logistic Regression, kNN, Random Forest, LightGBM, XGBoost, and MLP). Tested on a large public dataset ($\approx$ 70,000 samples), the approach consistently outperformed non-resampled baselines, achieving strong and balanced results across accuracy, F1-score, and ROC-AUC ($\approx$ 0.97). The metric-weighting strategy emphasizes clinically relevant measures by aligning ensemble influence with sensitivity–specificity trade-offs, thereby improving minority-class detection without sacrificing overall performance. Future directions include adaptive weighting methods and validation on external cohorts.

Acknowledgments. This work was supported in part by the South African National Research Foundation under Grant numbers 141951, CHN231229201835, 137951, AJCR230704126719.

References

1. Aggarwal, C.C.: Neural Networks and Deep Learning. Springer, Cham (2018). https://doi.org/10.1007/978-3-319-94463-0
2. Ali, M.M., Paul, B.K., Ahmed, K., Bui, F.M., Quinn, J.M.W., Moni, M.A.: Heart disease prediction using supervised machine learning algorithms: performance analysis and comparison. Comput. Biol. Med. **136**, 104672 (2021). https://doi.org/10.1016/j.compbiomed.2021.104672
3. American Heart Association: 2025 heart disease and stroke statistics update fact sheet (2025). https://www.heart.org/en/-/media/PHD-Files-2/Science-News/2/2025-Heart-and-Stroke-Stat-Update/2025-Statistics-At-A-Glance.pdf
4. Batista, G.E.A.P.A., Prati, R.C., Monard, M.C.: A study of the behavior of several methods for balancing machine learning training data. ACM SIGKDD Explorations Newsletter **6**(1), 20–29 (2004). https://doi.org/10.1145/1007730.1007735

5. Chawla, N.V., Bowyer, K.W., Hall, L.O., Kegelmeyer, W.P.: Smote: synthetic minority over-sampling technique. J. Artif. Intell. Res. **16**, 321–357 (2002). https://arxiv.org/pdf/1106.1813.pdf
6. Cruz, R.M.O., Souza, M.A., Sabourin, R., Cavalcanti, G.D.C.: Dynamic ensemble selection and data preprocessing for multi-class imbalance learning. Int. Pattern Recogn. Artif. Intell. **33**(11) (2019). https://doi.org/10.1142/S0218001419400093
7. De Ville, B.: Decision trees. Wiley Interdisc. Rev. Comput. Stat. **5**(6), 448–455 (2013)
8. Elgendy, M.S., Moustafa, H.E.D., Nafea, H.B., Shaban, W.M.: Utilizing voting classifiers for enhanced analysis and diagnosis of cardiac conditions. Results Eng. **26**, 104636 (2025). https://doi.org/10.1016/j.rineng.2025.104636
9. Hansen, L.K., Salamon, P.: Neural network ensembles. IEEE Trans. Pattern Anal. Mach. Intell. **12**(10), 993–1001 (1990). https://doi.org/10.1109/34.58871
10. Husain, G., et al.: SMOTE vs. SMOTEENN: a study on the performance of resampling algorithms for addressing class imbalance in regression models. Algorithms **18**(1), 1–16 (2025). https://doi.org/10.3390/a18010037
11. Ileberi, E., Sun, Y., Wang, Z.: Performance evaluation of machine learning methods for credit card fraud detection using smote and AdaBoost. IEEE Access **9**, 165286–165294 (2021). https://doi.org/10.1109/ACCESS.2021.3134330
12. Krittanawong, C., et al.: Machine learning prediction in cardiovascular diseases: a meta-analysis. Sci. Rep. **10**(1), 1–11 (2020). https://doi.org/10.1038/s41598-020-72685-1
13. Kuncheva, L.I., Whitaker, C.J.: Ten measures of diversity in classifier ensembles: Limits for two classifiers. In: IEE Colloquium on Intelligent Sensor Processing, pp. 73–82 (2001). https://doi.org/10.1049/ic:20010105
14. Matharaarachchi, S., Domaratzki, M., Muthukumarana, S.: Enhancing smote for imbalanced data with abnormal minority instances. Mach. Learn. Appl. **18**, 100597 (2024). https://doi.org/10.1016/j.mlwa.2024.100597
15. Mienye, I.D., Sun, Y.: Improved heart disease prediction using particle swarm optimization based stacked sparse autoencoder. Electronics **10**(19) (2021). https://doi.org/10.3390/electronics10192347
16. Powers, D.M.W.: Evaluation: from precision, recall and f-measure to roc, informedness, markedness and correlation. arXiv preprint (2020). http://arxiv.org/abs/2010.16061
17. Rojarath, A.A., Songpan, W.B.: Probability-weighted voting ensemble learning for classification model. J. Adv. Inf. Technol. **11**(4), 217–227 (2020). https://doi.org/10.12720/jait.11.4.217-227
18. Ulianova, S.: Cardiovascular diseases dataset - KAGGLE (2020). https://www.kaggle.com/datasets/sulianova/cardiovascular-disease-dataset
19. Umeonwuka, O.O., Adejumobi, B.S., Shongwe, T.: An XGBOOST machine learning technique for RF energy harvesting prediction in IP-enabled IoT devices. In: EUROCON 2023 - 20th International Conference on Smart Technologies Proceedings, pp. 562–567 (2023). https://doi.org/10.1109/EUROCON56442.2023.10198926
20. Umeonwuka, O.O., Adejumobi, B.S., Shongwe, T.: Deep learning-assisted energy prediction modeling for energy harvesting in wireless cognitive radio devices. IEEE Access **12**, 8700–8720 (2024). https://doi.org/10.1109/ACCESS.2023.3349352
21. World Health Organization: Cardiovascular diseases (CVD) (2023). https://www.who.int/news-room/fact-sheets/detail/cardiovascular-diseases-(cvds)

22. Zaidi, S.A.J., Ghafoor, A., Kim, J., Abbas, Z., Lee, S.W.: Heartensemblenet: an innovative hybrid ensemble learning approach for cardiovascular risk prediction. Healthcare **13**(5), 1–21 (2025). https://doi.org/10.3390/healthcare13050507
23. Zheng, H., Sherazi, S.W.A., Arif, S., Lee, M.J., Lee, J.Y.: A voting ensemble-based model to predict the risk of cardiovascular disease in ordinary people. In: Proceedings of ACM International Conference, pp. 127–133 (2023). https://doi.org/10.1145/3606043.3606061

Disentangled Latent Augmentation for Abnormality Detection in Musculoskeletal Radiographs

Thota Gokaramaiah[(✉)], Korra Sathya Babu, K Nagaraju, and Nenavath Srinivas Naik

CSE Department, Indian Institute of Information Technology Design and Manufacturing Kurnool, Jagannatha Hill, Kurnool 518008, Andhra Pradesh, India
{322cs0001,ksb,knagaraju,srinu}@iiitk.ac.in
https://iiitk.ac.in/

Abstract. Deep learning has shown impressive results in computer vision, but it often underperforms in imbalanced datasets. This challenge is prominent in medical imaging, particularly in the classification of musculoskeletal disorders, where minority classes are underrepresented. This study presents a generative framework for the detection of musculoskeletal abnormalities with a specific focus on the problem of data imbalance in the classification of radiographic images. A disentanglement-driven approach is employed using β-variational autoencoder (β-VAE), which facilitates the generation of diverse and class-consistent samples through latent space manipulation. These synthetic samples are utilized within a triplet network for metric learning, enhancing discriminative representation by promoting greater inter-class separability and intra-class compactness in the latent space, thus effectively mitigating imbalance during classification. Experimental evaluation of the musculoskeletal radiograph (MURA) dataset, the proposed triplet network with β-VAE improves classification performance, achieving 11.3% higher accuracy and 42.3% greater Cohen's kappa on the finger study type (DenseNet-169), and 15.6% accuracy gain with 27.1% Cohen's kappa improvement on the forearm study type (ResNet-50), demonstrating its effectiveness for imbalance-aware diagnostic imaging.

Keywords: β-VAE · Class Imbalance · Disentangled Representation Learning · Musculoskeletal Abnormality Detection · Triplet Loss

1 Introduction

The detection of musculoskeletal abnormalities remains a critical aspect of clinical diagnosis, particularly for conditions involving bones, joints, and connective tissues. Musculoskeletal disorders (MSD) affect more than 1.7 billion individuals worldwide and are one of the leading causes of long-term pain and disability [24]. Radiographic interpretation of anatomically small regions presents unique diagnostic challenges due to subtle pathological features and localized anatomical

T. T. Quan et al. (Eds.): MIWAI 2025, LNAI 16353, pp. 205–216, 2026.
https://doi.org/10.1007/978-981-95-4957-3_17

variation, often resulting in missed abnormalities on plain radiographs (false negatives). In such cases, even expert interpretations can diverge between radiologists in evaluating finger fractures [18]. Furthermore, class imbalance is common in medical datasets, where normal cases substantially outnumber abnormal ones, thus skewing learning toward the majority class and diminishing the model's sensitivity to rare but clinically important findings [12,16].

Recent developments in generative modeling offer promising avenues for addressing data scarcity and class imbalance by synthesizing additional training data. Various methods have been applied to enhance underrepresented classes, including class-conditional generative adversarial networks (cGAN), which are capable of oversampling minority categories [5]. Such approaches aim to improve the recognition of rare classes by learning their data distributions and generating plausible synthetic instances. In particular, techniques such as SMOTE [2], ADASYN [6], and GAN-based augmentation [14] have shown measurable improvements in recall and overall precision in imbalanced classification tasks.

Among representation learning frameworks, the β-Variational Autoencoder (β-VAE) has demonstrated particular effectiveness in learning disentangled latent representations [7]. The introduction of a hyperparameter β serves to modulate the contribution of the Kullback-Leibler (KL) divergence in the objective function, thereby controlling the trade-off between reconstruction fidelity and latent independence. Setting $\beta > 1$ encourages the model to encode independent generative factors in separate latent dimensions, resulting in a structured and interpretable latent space. This structure supports controlled sampling and the targeted synthesis of radiographic images. For example, modifying a specific latent dimension can generate images with or without an abnormality while keeping all other anatomical factors unchanged.

In the present study, a β-VAE architecture is developed for the purpose of generating class-specific radiographic samples. The latent vectors of these synthetic samples are then incorporated into a triplet loss formulation to improve the discriminative quality of the latent space. Triplet loss, originally proposed for deep metric learning in face verification [19], requires that the distance between an anchor and a positive sample (the same class) is smaller than the distance to a negative sample (different class) by at least a predefined margin. Integrating this constraint into the VAE framework promotes intra-class compactness and inter-class separation in the latent space. This combination forms a triplet-constrained β-VAE that enables class-aware representation learning while using synthetic samples for minority class enrichment. To validate this methodology, experiments are carried out using the MURA dataset, with a specific focus on finger and forearm radiographs-an anatomical category that presents high diagnostic complexity and elevated false negative rates [18]. The main contributions of this study are summarized as follows:

1. A disentangled generative modeling framework based on β-VAE is introduced to learn structured latent representations from musculoskeletal finger and

forearm radiographs, allowing the generation of controllable and class-specific synthetic data.
2. A latent-space-driven augmentation strategy is proposed in which minority-class (abnormal) samples are synthesized and utilized to improve the triplet loss training dynamics. These synthetic radiographs are used to expand the training dataset, yielding significant improvements in abnormality detection on the imbalanced MURA dataset.

The remainder of the article is organized as follows. Section 2 reviews related work on generative modeling and latent space disentanglement in medical imaging. Section 3 details the architecture and training procedure of the proposed β-VAE with triplet-constrained latent optimization. Section 4 describes the dataset, experimental setup, evaluation metrics, and presents empirical results. Finally, Sect. 5 concludes the study and discusses future research directions followed by references.

2 Related Work

The detection of musculoskeletal abnormalities remains a critical aspect of clinical diagnosis, particularly for conditions involving bones, joints, and connective tissues. MSD conditions often result in reduced mobility, poor quality of life, and a significant socioeconomic burden due to loss of productivity and increased healthcare needs. Even expert radiologists may disagree on their interpretations, as seen in the evaluation of finger fractures, where diagnostic variability is notably high [18]. The calibrated ensemble methods, significantly improving accuracy and reliability. Furthermore, Mehr *et al.* [13] developed MuRAD, using CNN and class activation maps for both detection and localization of abnormalities, reporting comparable performance to radiologists. These advancements highlight the efficacy of deep learning approaches in various medical imaging applications, further evidenced by recent efforts to employ GAN-based augmentation for pneumonia detection on chest radiographs [23] and transfer learning for classifying knee injury MRIs [20].

Variational Autoencoders (VAEs) are powerful models for unsupervised representation learning, yet their latent spaces often contain entangled features. When structured effectively, these latent representations can facilitate the generation of coherent medical reports [17,22]. To overcome this limitation, Higgins *et al.* [8] proposed the β-VAE framework, introducing a tunable hyperparameter β to control latent channel capacity, thus encouraging the learning of disentangled and interpretable latent factors. With increased values of β, the model emphasizes independent latent dimensions, trading off some reconstruction accuracy for greater interpretability. The β-VAE notably outperformed established models such as InfoGAN [4], DC-IGN [10] and classical ICA methods, establishing a foundation for subsequent disentanglement-focused generative models.

Subsequent extensions, such as Factor-VAE by Chen *et al.* [3], introduced an explicit total correlation penalty to further enhance disentanglement, introducing quantitative metrics such as mutual information gap (MIG). The medical imaging domain has recently adopted these principles. Building on the foundational β -VAE framework, Burgess *et al.* [1] proposed an improved training regimen to balance latent space disentanglement and reconstruction fidelity. This approach replaces the fixed KL divergence constraint with a dynamically adjusted term, progressively increasing the latent space capacity during training. This method has become standard practice, especially effective in medical imaging tasks, where preserving detailed anatomical information is crucial.

Recent research further integrates β-VAE-generated synthetic images into discriminative learning frameworks. For example, Lee *et al.* [11] and Karim *et al.* [9] employed triplet loss in conjunction with disentangled generative models, demonstrating improvements in class-specific discrimination and overall classification performance in imbalanced medical imaging scenarios. These works underscore the potential of combining generative and metric learning techniques for a robust and effective handling of class imbalance in clinical datasets.

3 Methodology

The proposed methodology is grounded in the principle that generative models with disentangled latent spaces can produce high-quality, class-consistent synthetic samples. The complete architecture is illustrated in Fig. 1. This capability is particularly valuable in medical imaging tasks, where abnormal classes are often underrepresented. Using a disentangled latent structure, it becomes feasible to control the generative process and sample from specific semantic dimensions, thereby addressing class imbalance through informed data augmentation. The approach utilizes the β-Variational Autoencoder (β-VAE) as the generative backbone, with an additional triplet loss to encourage class-wise separation in the latent space.

Autoencoders are unsupervised feedforward neural networks designed to learn compressed representations of input data. An autoencoder comprises three primary components: an encoder, a latent code, and a decoder. The encoder compresses the input x into a lower-dimensional latent vector z, and the decoder reconstructs the input from z to produce $\hat{x}$. The goal is to minimize the loss of reconstruction.

$$\mathcal{L}_{\text{AE}}(x, \hat{x}) = \|x - \hat{x}\|_2^2 \tag{1}$$

This compressed encoding can be reused for classification by attaching a softmax or sigmoid classifier head to the encoder, allowing the network to learn meaningful discriminative features.

Variational Autoencoders extend autoencoders by modeling the latent space as a probability distribution. The encoder learns to approximate the posterior $q_\phi(z|x)$, while the decoder learns the likelihood $p_\theta(x|z)$. The training objective maximizes the evidence lower bound (ELBO):

$$\mathcal{L}_{\text{VAE}}(\theta, \phi; x) = \mathbb{E}_{q_\phi(z|x)}[\log p_\theta(x|z)] - D_{\text{KL}}(q_\phi(z|x) \| p(z)) \tag{2}$$

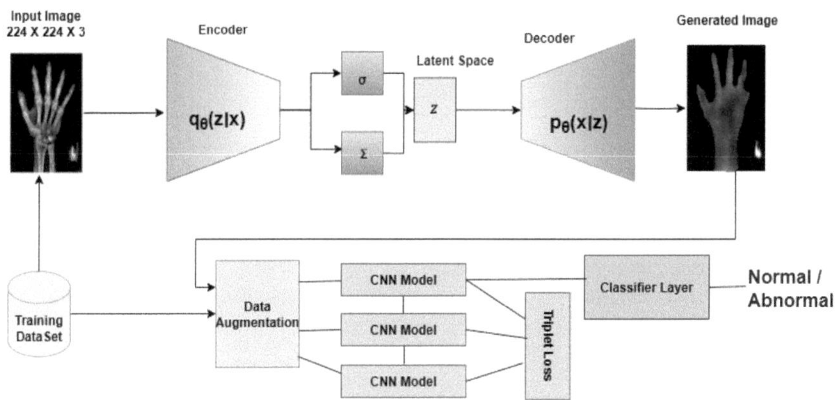

Fig. 1. The system architecture of a β-Variational Autoencoder incorporating triplet network for the metric learning and classification.

Here, D_{KL} denotes the Kullback-Leibler divergence between the approximate posterior and the prior $p(z)$. The latent space is thus continuous and smooth, enabling generative capabilities such as sampling and interpolation.

The β-VAE introduces a hyperparameter $\beta > 1$ to the VAE loss to strengthen the pressure on the posterior distribution:

$$\mathcal{L}_{\beta\text{-VAE}}(\theta, \phi; x) = \mathbb{E}_{q_\phi(z|x)}[\log p_\theta(x|z)] - \beta \cdot D_{\mathrm{KL}}(q_\phi(z|x) \| p(z)) \tag{3}$$

This regularization promotes disentangled representations, where each latent dimension captures a semantically independent factor of variation. Disentanglement enables the generation of targeted samples by manipulating specific latent dimensions, which is critical to augmenting rare classes in unbalanced datasets. To enhance the discriminative capacity of the latent space, a triplet loss is integrated alongside the β-VAE objective. This ensures that latent representations of samples from the same class remain close, while those from different classes are pushed apart. Given anchor (x_a), positive (x_p) and negative (x_n) samples, the triplet loss is defined as:

$$\mathcal{L}_{\mathrm{Tri}}(\theta) = \sum_{a,p,n} \max(0, D_{a,p} - D_{a,n} + m) \tag{4}$$

Here, $D_{a,p}$ and $D_{a,n}$ denote the Euclidean distances in the latent space, and m is a margin parameter. The final objective combines both losses:

$$\mathcal{L}_{\mathrm{Total}} = \mathcal{L}_{\beta\text{-VAE}} + \lambda \cdot \mathcal{L}_{\mathrm{Tri}} \tag{5}$$

where, λ controls the influence of the triplet constraint. Once trained, β -VAE with the triplet constraint enables sampling from class-specific regions of the latent space. Synthetic samples are generated by decoding sampled latents from minority classes, thereby expanding the training distribution. These synthetic instances are incorporated into the training set to rebalance class proportions, enhancing model generalization and sensitivity to rare abnormalities.

3.1 β-VAE Architecture: Convolutional Filter Design

In the proposed β-VAE architecture, both the encoder and the decoder are constructed using deep convolutional layers arranged symmetrically to facilitate effective compression and reconstruction of musculoskeletal radiographs. The encoder consists of seven convolutional layers, with the number of filters progressively increasing to capture hierarchical features. Starting with 128 filters in the first layer, the network expands to 256 filters in the second and third layers, 512 filters in the fourth and fifth layers, and 1024 filters in the sixth and seventh layers. Each layer employs a 3×3 kernel with ReLU activation and the same padding. Spatial down sampling is achieved through strides convolutions in selected layers, which reduce the resolution while aggregating semantic content. This hierarchical design compresses the spatial information and enables the encoder to form a rich and compact latent representation of the input radiograph.

The decoder mirrors this structure in reverse using seven transposed convolutional layers to reconstruct the image from the latent space. It begins with a fully connected layer that reshapes the latent vector into a low-resolution, high-depth feature map, followed by successive transposed convolutional layers with decreasing filter counts. The sequence starts from 1024 filters and reduces through 512, 256, 128, and 64, ultimately reconstructing the final three-channel image using a transposed convolution with 3 filters and sigmoid activation. This symmetric arrangement of convolutional filters ensures a coherent inversion of the encoder feature hierarchy and facilitates high-fidelity reconstruction, preserving essential anatomical structures for downstream interpretation.

The model is trained on the MURA finger dataset, which is particularly prone to high false negative rates. Various values of β (e.g., 1, 10, 100, 150) are evaluated to determine optimal disentanglement-performance trade-offs. The architecture uses convolutional layers for encoding and decoding, and the classification head is appended post-encoding. Generated samples are visually validated and processed through downstream classification accuracy to ensure fidelity and utility.

This methodology introduces a principled framework for generating clinically significant synthetic data in the presence of class imbalance. By combining β-VAE disentanglement with triplet regularization, the approach ensures both interpretability and discriminability in the latent space, offering a robust solution to data scarcity and imbalance in medical image analysis.

4 Experiments and Results

4.1 Dataset and Pre-processing

The study utilizes the MURA dataset, selecting the finger and forearm categories due to their sub-optimal performance in existing methodologies [15]. The finger subset includes 3,138 normal and 1,968 abnormal images, while the forearm subset has 1,164 normal and 661 abnormal images, highlighting a moderate imbalance favoring normal cases. This imbalance is significant in medical image analysis because abnormal cases are often more clinically important. Through the proposed methodology, an additional 1,170 finger images and 503 forearm images were generated to augment the training set, thus addressing class imbalance and improving the balance of the dataset. The study focuses on training and validating radiographs of these specific categories, with the aim of streamlined classification tasks while maintaining clinical relevance [21].

All radiographs were standardized to a fixed spatial resolution to ensure uniformity in input dimensions across the dataset. This resizing is essential to facilitate efficient and consistent learning during model training. As part of the pre-processing pipeline, contrast-limited adaptive histogram equalization (CLAHE) [25] was applied to enhance local image contrast. Particularly effective in medical imaging, CLAHE improves the visibility of fine structures by amplifying subtle features while suppressing noise. The enhancement is performed in a perceptually uniform color space by applying contrast adjustment to the luminance channel, followed by recombination with the original chrominance. A qualitative comparison of radiographs with and without CLAHE is shown in Fig. 2, which demonstrates improved visibility of the local detail.

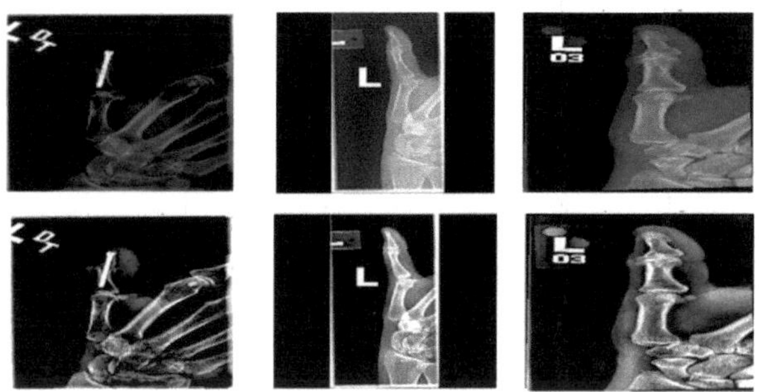

Fig. 2. Sample images of fingers. The first row shows the original input samples and the second row displays the corresponding pre-processed images.

4.2 Training Configuration

The β-VAE model was trained using the RMSprop optimizer with a learning rate of 1×10^{-4} and the gradient clipping is 0.1. Early stopping was employed with a patience of 3 epochs based on validation loss. All input images were resized to $224 \times 224 \times 3$, and the latent space dimensionality was set to $d = 64$. A custom Keras loss layer incorporated both the binary cross-entropy reconstruction loss and the KL divergence, scaled using a coefficient β of 154 and a KL loss weight of -1×10^{-4}. The model was trained for up to 50 epochs with a mini-batch size of 32.

4.3 Reconstruction Evaluation

The reconstruction results, illustrated in Figs. 3 through 5, demonstrate the influence of varying β values on image quality using the β-VAE architecture with DenseNet-169 or ResNet-50 as the encoder backbone. As β increases, the reconstructed images show improved sharpness and improved class-specific details, indicating superior disentanglement in the latent space.

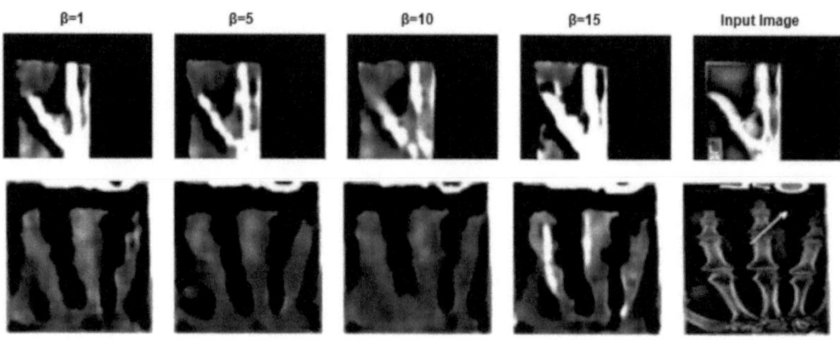

Fig. 3. Reconstructions with β values of 1, 5, 10, and 15, along with the original images.

Figure 3 shows the reconstructions for lower β values ($\beta = 1, 5, 10, 15$), which result in relatively poor-quality images. These outputs are blurry and lack discriminative features, suggesting insufficient regularization and under constrained latent representations.

In contrast, Fig. 4 highlights the effect of moderate to high β values ($\beta = 10, 102, 152$). Reconstructions with $\beta = 102$ consistently produce high-quality outputs that exhibit clear anatomical and pathological characteristics. Interestingly, some generated samples closely resemble abnormal cases, indicating the ability of the model to synthesize clinically meaningful variations. These synthetic images can potentially augment minority classes in unbalanced datasets.

However, as shown in Fig. 5, overly high β values ($\beta = 155, 160, 165$) introduce excessive regularization, resulting in over smooth reconstructions with a loss of fine details. This confirms a saturation threshold beyond which the model sacrifices fidelity for disentanglement.

In general, these findings suggest that β-VAE, particularly with DenseNet-169, not only achieves effective compression but also serves as a powerful generative model capable of producing diverse and high-quality samples. Such reconstructions can be used for data augmentation, domain adaptation, or style transfer, thus enhancing the robustness and generalization of downstream classification models.

4.4 Analysis of Experimental Results on Finger and Forearm

Tables 1 and 2 summarize the comparative performance of β-VAE and triplet-based architectures implemented with DenseNet-169 and ResNet-50 backbones,

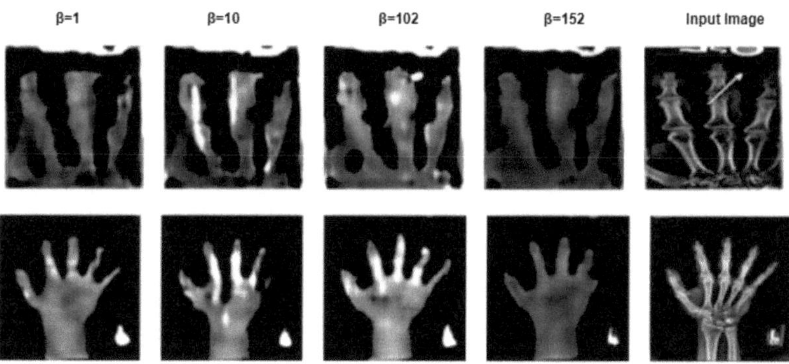

Fig. 4. Reconstructions with β values of 1, 10, 102, 152, and the original images. High-quality results are evident at $\beta = 102$.

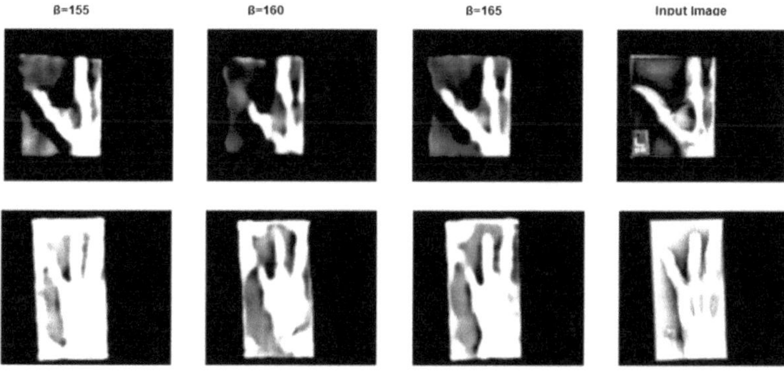

Fig. 5. Reconstructions with high β values (155, 160, 165) showing over-smoothing and loss of structural detail.

respectively. The models considered include the standard autoencoder, a variational autoencoder (VAE, β=1), β-VAE variants with β=10 and β=102, and triplet networks with the same β settings.

For DenseNet-169 (Table 1), the β-VAE with β=10 achieved the best performance among the autoencoder variants, with an accuracy of 0.7039 and a Cohen–Kappa score of 0.5047. This indicates the importance of moderate β values in learning disentangled and semantically consistent latent representations. Although β -VAE with β=102 reached a comparable accuracy (0.7023), its slightly lower Kappa score (0.5028) suggests that higher β values may compromise label agreement despite the preservation of classification accuracy. Triplet networks significantly outperformed all autoencoder variants, with the β=102 configuration achieving the highest overall performance (accuracy of 0.7554 and

Kappa score of 0.8125), demonstrating the effectiveness of supervised metric learning in capturing class-discriminative characteristics.

Table 1. Comparison of performance metrics for Autoencoder, VAE, β-VAE, and Triplet Network models using DenseNet-169 as the backbone.

Metric	No β-VAE	Autoencoder	VAE (β=1)	β-VAE (β=10)	β-VAE (β=102)	Triplet Network (β=10)	Triplet Network (β=102)
Accuracy	0.6421	0.5878	0.6856	0.7039	0.7023	0.7520	**0.7554**
Kappa score	0.3890	0.2310	0.4831	0.5047	0.5028	0.8017	**0.8125**

For the ResNet-50 backbone on the forearm subset (Table 2), a similar trend is observed. The β-VAE with β=102 showed improved performance over the autoencoder and VAE baselines, achieving an accuracy of 0.8190 and a Kappa score of 0.6760. However, the triplet networks again delivered superior results, with the β=102 variant achieving the highest accuracy of 0.8712 and a Kappa score of 0.7531. These findings reinforce the conclusion that while β-VAE models are valuable for learning interpretable and structured latent spaces, triplet networks are more effective for direct classification tasks due to their stronger discriminative learning capacity.

Table 2. Forearm subset: performance of Autoencoder, VAE, β-VAE, and Triplet Network models using ResNet-50 as the backbone. Accuracy and Kappa are reported on the validation set.

Metric	No β-VAE	Autoencoder	VAE (β=1)	β-VAE (β=10)	β-VAE (β=102)	Triplet Network (β=10)	Triplet Network (β=102)
Accuracy	0.7150	0.6900	0.7520	0.8280	0.8190	0.8430	**0.8712**
Kappa score	0.4823	0.4200	0.5650	0.6820	0.6760	0.7021	**0.7531**

Overall, the results suggest a trade-off: β-VAEs provide interpretable and controllable latent representations useful for generative and MSD detection tasks, whereas triplet networks consistently yield higher predictive performance, making them better suited for classification-focused applications.

5 Conclusion and Future Work

This study introduced a principled approach to generate class-consistent synthetic radiographs using a disentangled β-VAE framework enhanced with triplet-constrained latent optimization. The proposed method addresses class imbalance by using a structured latent space that supports targeted sampling and augmentation of underrepresented classes, particularly in the medical imaging domain. Empirical evaluations on the MURA Finger and forearm dataset demonstrated that β-VAE with $\beta = 10$ achieved superior performance in terms of classification accuracy and Cohen-Kappa statistic compared to traditional autoencoders and standard VAE. Although Siamese networks with DenseNet-169 yielded slightly higher accuracy, the proposed approach offers unique advantages in terms of interpretability, latent controllability, and generative capabilities. Qualitative reconstruction analysis confirmed the model's capability to generate visually coherent and semantically rich images. Intermediate β values ($\beta = 102$) yielded high-fidelity abnormal patterns, suggesting the potential for data increase. These results underscore the effectiveness of disentangled generative modeling in improving classification performance and model robustness.

Future research may integrate synthetic abnormalities into semi-supervised and multi-modal pipelines, supported by domain adaptation for cross-modality generalization. Enhancing β-VAE with attention- or transformer-based encoders could improve representation quality and interpretability, advancing explainable and trustworthy AI. Evaluation beyond finger radiographs is essential to establish a broader generalization.

References

1. Burgess, C.P., et al.: Understanding disentangling in β-VAE. arXiv preprint arXiv:1804.03599 (2018)
2. Chawla, N.V., Bowyer, K.W., Hall, L.O., Kegelmeyer, W.P.: Smote: synthetic minority over-sampling technique. J. Artif. Intell. Res. 321–357 (2002)
3. Chen, R.T.Q., Li, X., Grosse, R.B., Duvenaud, D.K.: Isolating sources of disentanglement in variational autoencoders. In: Advances in Neural Information Processing Systems (NeurIPS), vol. 31 (2018)
4. Chen, X., Duan, Y., Houthooft, R., Schulman, J., Sutskever, I., Abbeel, P.: InfoGAN: interpretable representation learning by information maximizing generative adversarial nets. In: Advances in Neural Information Processing Systems (2016)
5. Frid-Adar, M., Klang, E., Amitai, M., Goldberger, J., Greenspan, H.: Synthetic data augmentation using GAN for improved liver lesion classification. In: 2018 IEEE 15th International Symposium on Biomedical Imaging (ISBI), pp. 289–293. IEEE (2018)
6. He, H., Bai, Y., Garcia, E.A., Li, S.: AdaSYN: adaptive synthetic sampling approach for imbalanced learning. In: IEEE International Joint Conference on Neural Networks (IJCNN), pp. 1322–1328. IEEE (2008)
7. Higgins, I., et al.: Beta-VAE: learning basic visual concepts with a constrained variational framework. In: International Conference on Learning Representations (ICLR) (2017)
8. Higgins, I., et al.: Beta-VAE: learning basic visual concepts with a constrained variational framework. ICLR (Poster) **3** (2017)
9. Karim, M.R., Ma, C., Alhajj, R., Rokne, J.: Latentmix: mixing autoencoder latent spaces for imbalanced data classification. In: Proceedings of the AAAI Conference on Artificial Intelligence, vol. 37, pp. 12029–12037 (2023)
10. Kulkarni, T.D., Whitney, W.F., Kohli, P., Tenenbaum, J.: Deep convolutional inverse graphics network. In: Advances in Neural Information Processing Systems (2015)
11. Lee, S., Park, J., Lee, K., Shin, J.: Triplet VAE: deep metric learning with generative models. Neurocomputing **527**, 178–189 (2023)

12. Liu, X., Wu, J., Zhou, Z.H.: Exploratory undersampling for class-imbalance learning. IEEE Trans. Syst. Man Cybern. Part B (Cybernet.) **39**(2), 539–550 (2008)
13. Mehr, C.T., Thian, Y.L., Tan, W.J., Tan, J., Poh, C.L.: Murad: musculoskeletal radiograph abnormality detection using convolutional neural networks. Artif. Intell. Med. **106**, 101863 (2020)
14. Mirza, M., Osindero, S.: Conditional generative adversarial nets. arXiv preprint arXiv:1411.1784 (2014)
15. Mura (2018). https://stanfordmlgroup.github.io/competitions/mura/. Accessed 8 Apr 2023
16. Nagaraju, K., Thota, G., Babu, K.S., Perapatruni, A., Janapati, K.: A novel CNN-Fourier-vision transformers framework for enhanced pattern recognition in visual data. In: Ma, H.S., Jeong, H.Y., Chan, Y.W., Yang, H.C. (eds.) IC 2025. vol. 1443, pp. 105–110. Springer, Cham (2025). https://doi.org/10.1007/978-981-96-8011-5_16
17. Pakanati, C.R., Thota, G., Alupula, P., Korra, S.B., et al.: Coherent medical report generation from chest radiographs with weighted localized features. In: 2025 6th International Conference on Recent Advances in Information Technology (RAIT), pp. 1–7. IEEE (2025)
18. Rajpurkar, P., Irvin, J., Zhu, K., et al.: Mura: large dataset for abnormality detection in musculoskeletal radiographs. arXiv preprint arXiv:1712.06957 (2017)
19. Schroff, F., Kalenichenko, D., Philbin, J.: FaceNet: a unified embedding for face recognition and clustering. In: Proceedings of the IEEE Conference on Computer Vision and Pattern Recognition (CVPR), pp. 815–823. IEEE (2015)
20. Thengade, M., Kale, R., Kulkarni, A., Gudadhe, M.: Transfer learning-based deep convolutional neural network for knee injury classification from MRI. Comput. Methods Programs Biomed. **234**, 107484 (2024)
21. Thota, G., Nagaraju, K., Korra, S.B.: Quantitative assessment of class activation maps: an empirical study on musculoskeletal disorders. In: Kakarla, J., Balasubramanian, R., Murala, S., Vipparthi, S.K., Gupta, D. (eds.) CVIP 2024. CCIS, vol. 2473, pp. 338–352. Springer, Cham (2024). https://doi.org/10.1007/978-3-031-93688-3_24
22. Thota, G., Nagaraju, K., Korra, S.B.: SVD-grad-CAM: singular value decomposition filtered gradient weighted class activation map. In: Antonacopoulos, A., Chaudhuri, S., Chellappa, R., Liu, C.L., Bhattacharya, S., Pal, U. (eds.) ICPR 2024. LNCS, vol. 15312, pp. 90–105. Springer, Cham (2024). https://doi.org/10.1007/978-3-031-78198-8_7
23. Vashisht, H., Kumar, A., Sharma, P.: Generative adversarial network augmentation for pneumonia detection in chest radiographs. Biomed. Signal Process. Control **80**, 104249 (2023)
24. World Health Organization: Musculoskeletal conditions (2023). https://www.who.int/news-room/fact-sheets/detail/musculoskeletal-conditions. Accessed 26 Jul 2025
25. Yussof, W., Hitam, M.S., Awalludin, E.A., Bachok, Z.: Performing contrast limited adaptive histogram equalization technique on combined color models for underwater image enhancement. Int. J. Interact. Digit. Media **1**(1), 1–6 (2013)

Analogical Proportions and Probabilities: Are They Compatible?

Henri Prade and Gilles Richard(✉)

IRIT, Toulouse University, 31062 Toulouse, Cedex 9, France
{henri.prade,gilles.richard}@irit.fr

Abstract. Analogical proportions link four items a, b, c and d by a relation stating that "a is to b as c is to d," a, b, c, d being the formal representation of 4 real world entities such as profiles. As such, a, b, c, d could be atomic values (like Boolean, real or nominal values), or more generally vectors thereof. In this context, we may attach to a vector representing the profile of a group of individuals in a given population, the probability (frequency) of this group in the population. This raises the question of whether four profiles, whose descriptions form an analogical proportion, also have their attached probabilities forming an analogical proportion when viewed as real numbers. This issue is explored and illustrated in this paper, which also provides some new results on numerical analogical proportions.

Keywords: analogical proportion · probability · numerical proportions

1 Introduction

Analogical proportions are statements of the form "a is to b as c is to d" that relate four items. These items can refer to a wide range of possibilities, such as pieces of information, words, phrases, pieces of text, or even images [19]. Analogical proportions are supposed to obey a few postulates that mimic key properties of numerical proportions. Analogical proportions have a long history that dates back to Ancient Greek time. However, it is in the last two or three decades that they have encountered a renewal of interest with attempts to formalize them, and to use them in analogical inference [9,12,17,18,23].

At the formal level, analogical proportions can both be defined for atomic values like Boolean, nominal or numerical, or for vectors thereof via componentwise extension. Analogical proportion-based inference, viewed as a particular case of analogical jump [8], has been successfully applied to classification [4,16]. Recent works have considered the various ways for defining analogical proportions between numbers [13,20] as well as between probability distributions [21,22].

This raises the question of the compatibility between analogical proportions and probabilities. More precisely, considering a quadruplet of vectors describing four items such that analogical proportions hold componentwise, if each item

T. T. Quan et al. (Eds.): MIWAI 2025, LNAI 16353, pp. 217–229, 2026.
https://doi.org/10.1007/978-981-95-4957-3_18

is associated with a probability, one may wonder if an analogical proportion also holds between these probabilities, and what it means. This is the topic of this paper which is organized as follows. Section 2 restates the necessary background on analogical proportions between Boolean or nominal attribute values. Section 3 recalls results on analogical proportions between numbers and offers a new discussion on these topics with some previously unpublished results. Section 4 discusses the problem of compatibility between analogical proportions and probabilities, while Sect. 5 illustrates this using a real data set.

2 Boolean and Nominal Analogical Proportions

An analogical proportion is a relation between any four items a, b, c, d, which is denoted $a : b :: c : d$, and reads "a is to b as c is to d". Following a parallel (which dates back to Aristotle) with the arithmetic ($a - b = c - d$) and the geometric proportions ($\frac{a}{b} = \frac{c}{d}$) where a, b, c, d are real numbers, analogical proportions are supposed to obey the three core postulates[1]:

- *reflexivity*: $a : b :: a : b$;
- *symmetry*: $a : b :: c : d \Rightarrow c : d :: a : b$;
- stability under *central permutation*: $a : b :: c : d \Rightarrow a : c :: b : d$.

As a consequence, the repeated and alternate application of symmetry and central permutation shows that if $a : b :: c : d$ holds, 7 other patterns $c : d :: a : b$, $c : a :: d : b$, $d : b :: c : a$, $d : c :: b : a$, $b : a :: d : c$, $b : d :: a : c$, $a : c :: b : d$ hold as well, among the 24 possible orderings of the four items.

In this paper a, b, c, d are Boolean, categorical, or numerical values, or vectors thereof. When the items are represented by vectors of attribute values $a = (a_1, \ldots, a_n)$, $b = (b_1, \ldots, b_n)$, $c = (c_1, \ldots, c_n)$, and $d = (d_1, \ldots, d_n)$, the analogical proportion $a : b :: c : d$ is defined componentwise:

Definition 1. $a : b :: c : d$ holds if $\forall i \in [1, n]$, $a_i : b_i :: c_i : d_i$ holds.

In the next two subsections, we successively consider cases where the components i are Boolean and nominal. We remove the i subscripts to simplify the notation, since we only focus on a single component in this section.

2.1 Boolean Model

The reflexivity and the central permutation postulates force $a : a :: b : b$ to be considered as a valid proportion. Thus when a, b, c, d are Boolean variables (i.e. taking values in $\mathbb{B} = \{0, 1\}$), the minimal Boolean model of the three previous postulates is given in Table 1, which exhibits the 6 valuations of a, b, c, d that any model of the 3 postulates must include. Note that symmetry is obtained for free in this table. This table also exhibits the other 10 ($= 2^4 - 6$) valuations which are not valid in the minimal model. A logical expression that is true only for the valid quadruplets in Table 1 is given by the formula [17]:

[1] See [1] for a discussion of analogical proportions in natural languages.

$$a : b :: c : d = [(a \wedge \neg b) \equiv (c \wedge \neg d)] \wedge [(\neg a \wedge b) \equiv (\neg c \wedge d)] \quad (*)$$

This formula expresses precisely that "a differs from b as c differs from d, and b differs from a as d differs from c" (lines 3 and 4 in Table 1) and "when a and b do not differ, c and d do not differ" (lines 1, 2 and lines 5, 6 in Table 1).

Table 1. Valid or invalid Boolean analogical proportions

	Valid	Invalid
	a b c d	a b c d
1.	0 0 0 0	0 0 0 1
2.	1 1 1 1	0 0 1 0
3.	0 0 1 1	0 1 0 0
4.	1 1 0 0	1 0 0 0
5.	0 1 0 1	1 1 1 0
6.	1 0 1 0	1 1 0 1
		1 0 1 1
		0 1 1 1
		1 0 0 1
		0 1 1 0

2.2 Nominal Model

As can be seen in Table 1, the patterns that make the analogical proportion true are of three types, namely $ssss$, $sstt$, and $stst$, with $s, t \in \mathbb{B} = \{0, 1\}$, the last two motifs being exchanged by a central permutation. It is now easy to extend to a nominal attribute $\mathcal{A}$ taking its values in a finite domain $\mathcal{D}_{\mathcal{A}}$ whose cardinality can be greater than 2. Then $a : b :: c : d$ is true for a nominal variable associated with an attribute $\mathcal{A}$ if and only if (as first suggested in [18]) :

$$(a, b, c, d) \in \{(s, s, s, s), (s, t, s, t), (s, s, t, t) | s, t \in \mathcal{D}_{\mathcal{A}}\} \tag{1}$$

where s, t are distinct values in $\mathcal{D}_{\mathcal{A}}$. The condition (1) generalizes the Boolean case and guarantees the satisfaction of the postulates of analogical proportions.

2.3 Weak Multivalued Dependency

Interestingly enough, as shown in [15], the notion of analogical proportion coincides with the notion of weak multivalued dependency [11] in the database field. For the sake of brevity, we just recall the definition and give an example.

Consider a relational table r with a set of attributes R, where X, Y, Z are attributes (or subsets thereof). Then a weak multivalued dependency [11]

$X \twoheadrightarrow_w Y$ holds in r if, for all tuples t_1, t_3 in r such that $t_1[XY] = t_2[XY]$[2] and $t_1[X(R\backslash Y)] = t_3[X(R\backslash Y)]$ there is some tuple t_4 in r such that $t_4[XY] = t_3[XY]$ and $t_4[X(R \setminus Y)] = t_2[X(R \setminus Y)]$. This also expresses a logical independence of Y and Z given X.

This is illustrated by the 4 tuples of the database-like example in Table 2 with 3 attributes $X = \{Education\}$, $Y = \{Sex\}$, $Z = \{Age\}$ and domains $\mathcal{D}_{Education} = \{low, medium, high\}$, $\mathcal{D}_{Sex} = \{F, M\}$ $\mathcal{D}_{Age} = \{\leq 40, > 40\}$. It can be checked that $X \twoheadrightarrow_w Y$ holds, taking $t_1 = a$, $t_2 = b$, $t_3 = c$, $t_4 = d$, with $XZ = X(R \setminus Y)$. Exchanging t_2 and t_3 and Y and Z we observe that $X \twoheadrightarrow_w Z$ holds as well in r.

Table 2. A database example

	X = {Education}	Y = {Sex}	Z = {Age}
a	high	M	≤ 40
b	high	F	≤ 40
c	high	M	> 40
d	high	F	> 40

As can be seen in Table 2, $a : b :: c : d$ holds and the table presents, in column, component by component, the three types of patterns allowed by the nominal model. Intuitively a, b, c, d represent profiles in a given population and this is where some probability of occurrence in the population could be associated with these 4 profiles.

2.4 Classification

Analogical proportions may go well with classification. Defining two classes in the above toy example: cl_1 corresponding to ≤ 40 and *high*, cl_2 corresponding to > 40 and *high*, we obtain the table in Table 3, where we can see that the classification column offers a valid analogical proportion.

Table 3. Analogical proportion with classes - 1

	Education level	Sex	Age	1st classification
a	high	M	≤ 40	cl_1
b	high	F	≤ 40	cl_1
c	high	M	> 40	cl_2
d	high	F	> 40	cl_2

Defining the two classes rather as cl'_1 corresponding to M and *high* and cl'_2 corresponding to F and *high*, we obtain the table in Table 4, where again the

[2] $t_i[XY]$ denotes the restriction of the tuple t_i to attributes in $X \cup Y$.

classification column exhibits a valid analogical proportion. Both tables exhibit the fact that if $a : b :: c : d$, then it is also true that $cl(a) : cl(b) :: c(c) : cl(d)$. This corresponds to the following inference rule, which is the basis of the analogical classification procedure (the analogical proportion is preserved on the classes):

$$\frac{a : b :: c : d}{cl(a) : cl(b) :: cl(c) : cl(d)}$$

This allows assigning a class to a new vector d, whose class is unknown, by solving the analogical equation $cl(a) : cl(b) :: cl(c) : x$ when $cl(a), cl(b), cl(c)$ are known. In the case of multiple options, a majority vote rule is applied to resolve ties. The reader is referred to [5,6] and to [7] for the characterization of the classification functions for which the above inference pattern is always valid in the Boolean case and in the nominal case respectively. Using only selected triplets a, b, c [3], the above classification method predicting $cl(d)$ from a, b, c, d and $cl(a)$, $cl(b)$, $cl(c)$, has proven effective on benchmarks, performing at least as well as k-NN, C4.5, SVM, and Naive Bayes across 16 datasets from the UCI repository. See also [4].

Table 4. Analogical proportion with classes - 2

	Education level	Sex	Age	2nd classification
a	high	M	≤ 40	cl'_1
b	high	F	≤ 40	cl'_2
c	high	M	> 40	cl'_1
d	high	F	> 40	cl'_2

3 Numerical Analogical Proportions

In order to accommodate numerical attributes, and more recently probabilities, various proposals for extending analogical proportions to real numbers have been made that are now reviewed, before presenting some new results. In this section, a, b, c, d, although there is no subscript i, refer to single real numbers.

3.1 Review of Existing Proposals

Multiple-valued Logic Extensions. There exist mainly two types of multiple-valued logic extension of (*) to real numbers a, b, c, d in the interval $[0, 1]$; see [10] for justifications. There are respectively called liberal and conservative, denoted respectively with an 'L' and a 'C' subscript. They are given by:

$$a : b ::_L c : d = \begin{cases} 1- \mid (a+d) - (b+c) \mid, \\ \quad \text{if } a \geq b \text{ and } c \geq d, \text{ or } a \leq b \text{ and } c \leq d \\ 1 - \max(\mid a - b \mid, \mid c - d \mid), \\ \quad \text{if } a \leq b \text{ and } c \geq d, \text{ or } a \geq b \text{ and } c \leq d \end{cases} \tag{2}$$

$$a : b ::_C c : d = \min(1 - |\max(a, d) - \max(b, c)|, 1 - |\min(a, d) - \min(b, c)|) \quad (3)$$

When $a, b, c, d \in \mathbb{B} = \{0, 1\}$, we recover the truth table of (*) in both cases. $a : b ::_L c : d = 1$ if and only if $a - b = c - d$. This corresponds to the arithmetic proportion. $a : b ::_C c : d = 1$ if and only if ($a = b$ and $c = d$) or ($a = c$ and $b = d$). This corresponds to the 3 possible patterns that make true a nominal analogical proportion ($(a, b, c, d) \in \{(s, s, s, s), (s, t, s, t), (s, s, t, t)\}$). One advantage of these formulas is that they offer a version graded (in $[0, 1]$) of the analogical proportion which enables us to have "approximate" proportions that hold to some degree.

Generalized Means-Based Definition. Recently, an appealing proposal [13, 14] has defined an analogical proportion between real numbers, not necessarily in $[0, 1]$, using generalized means. A generalized mean applied to two positive real numbers x, y is a two-place function defined by $M_p(x, y) = [\frac{1}{2}(x^p + y^p)]^{1/p}$ where $p \in \mathbb{R}$ is the exponent of the mean. For $p = -1, 1, 2$, we obtain the harmonic, arithmetic, and quadratic mean respectively. The geometric mean is obtained as a limit for $p = 0$. We have $\forall$ p $\in \mathbb{R}, \min(x, y) \leq M_p(x, y) \leq \max(x, y)$, and the bounds are reached for $p = -\infty$ and $p = +\infty$ respectively. The definition of analogical proportion between four positive real numbers is then:

Definition 2. Let $a, b, c, d \in \mathbb{R}^+$, a, b, c, d are said to satisfy an analogical proportion if and only if $\exists p \in \mathbb{R}, M_p(a, d) = M_p(b, c)$.

It can be easily seen that this definition ensures the satisfaction of the three postulates of analogical proportions. In [13], it is established that given $a < b < c < d$, $\exists! p$ such that $M_p(a, d) = M_p(b, c)$[3]. Since $M_p(a, d) = M_p(b, c)$ amounts to write $a^p + d^p = b^p + c^p$, it means that a^p, b^p, c^p, d^p form an arithmetic proportion. Note that this definition, as the next one, is not graded, but parameterized.

Triangular Norm-Based Definition. Another definition [20], which is also in agreement with the three postulates of analogical proportions, is based on triangular norms and conorms[4]. The definition as such:

Definition 3. Let a, b, c, d be four numerical values in [0, 1]. a, b, c, d are said to satisfy an analogical proportion based on the triangular norm T (and its dual triangular conorm S_T), iff $T(a, d) = T(b, c)$ and $S_T(a, d) = S_T(b, c)$) [20].

[3] However, note that although an analogical proportion has 8 equivalent forms (see beginning of Sect. 2), it may be case that none of them are in increasing order.

[4] A triangular norm T is a binary operation on $[0, 1]$, i.e., $T : [0, 1] \times [0, 1] \to [0, 1]$, that satisfies the following conditions, it is: i) commutative: $T(a, b) = T(b, a)$; ii) associative: $T(a, T(b, c)) = T(T(a, b), c)$; iii) non-decreasing in both arguments: $T(a, b) \leq T(a', b')$ if $a \leq a'$ and $b \leq b'$; such that $T(a, 1) = T(1, a) = a$. A binary operation S on [0, 1] is called a triangular conorm if it satisfies the same properties as the ones of a triangular norm except for the boundary conditions, which become $S(0, a) = S(a, 0) = a$..

where $S_T(x, y) = 1 - T(1 - x, 1 - y)$. For $T(x, y) = xy$ in Definition 3, a, b, c, d form both an arithmetic proportion, and a geometric proportion, which forces $(b, c) = (a, d)$ or $(b, c) = (d, a)$, which corresponds to the nominal patterns; see below. For the Łukasiewicz triangular norm $T(x, y) = \max(0, x + y - 1)$ in Definition 3, a, b, c, d form an arithmetic proportion. The use of a parameterized family of triangular norms enables us to have a parameterized definition of an analogical proportion between numbers in $[0, 1]$. See [20].

Arithmetic and Geometric Proportions-Based Definitions. In [21,22], the notion of arithmetico-geometric analogical proportion has been introduced and Proposition 1 established.

Definition 4. Let a, b, c, d be four real numbers. Then these numbers are in *arithmetico-geometric* analogical proportion, denoted $a : b ::_{arigeo} c : d$ if we have $a - b = c - d$ and $\frac{a}{b} = \frac{c}{d}$.

We take the convention $\frac{0}{0} = 1$ considering that $\lim_{x \to 0} \frac{x}{x} = 1$. Note that $a \cdot d = b \cdot c$ does not define a geometric proportion since we have $0 \cdot 1 = 0 \cdot 0$, whereas
$0 : 0 :: 0 : 1$ is not an analogical proportion. The equivalence between the "quotient" and the "product" forms excludes 0.

Proposition 1. *The only 4-tuples of real numbers a, b, c, d such that $a : b ::_{arigeo} c : d$ holds, are such that:*
- *case 1: either $a = b$ and $c = d$,*
- *case 2: or $a = c$ and $b = d$.*

Thus, the arithmetico-geometric analogical proportions for numbers are the exact counterpart of the analogical proportions for nominal values.

Numbers as Probabilities. Numerical analogical proportions enable us to define analogical proportions between probability distributions on finite sets, in a componentwise manner using Definition 1. More formally, if $a = (a_1, \ldots, a_n) \in \mathbb{R}^n$ is such that: $\forall i \in [1, n], a_i \geq 0$ and $\Sigma_{i=1}^n a_i = 1$, the vector a can be considered as representing a probability measure P_a on a finite set A of n elements. In other words, a represents the mass function associated with P_a. Let us consider the example below where $n = 4$:

$a_1 = 0.15; a_2 = 0.10; a_3 = 0.70; a_4 = 0.05.$
$b_1 = 0.55; b_2 = 0.20; b_3 = 0.20; b_4 = 0.05.$
$c_1 = 0.25; c_2 = 0.10; c_3 = 0.60; c_4 = 0.05.$
$d_1 = 0.65; d_2 = 0.20; d_3 = 0.10; d_4 = 0.05.$

Componentwise, we have $a_i - b_i = c_i - d_i$ for $i = 1, 2, 3, 4$. We also have an arithmetico-geometric proportion for $i = 2$, and $i = 4$. This is acknowledged by the facts that $a_1 : b_1 ::_C c_1 : d_1 = 0.9 = a_3 : b_3 ::_C c_3 : d_3$, while we have $a_2 : b_2 ::_C c_2 : d_2 = a_4 : b_4 ::_C c_4 : d_4 = 1$. Changing, c_1, d_1, c_3, d_3 into 0.15, 0.55, 0.70, 0.20 respectively would lead to an arithmetico-geometric proportion between the four distributions.

Arithmetico-geometric analogical proportions between probability distributions a, b, c, d are remarkable as they preserve the Kullback-Leibler divergence: when such a proportion holds, the divergence between a and b is equal to the divergence between c and d [21,22].

3.2 New Results

When it comes to real numbers, an analogical proportion between a, b, c, d is typically defined by equating an expression involving only the extreme elements (a, d) with one involving only the mean elements (b, c) (e.g. $a+d = b+c$ for arithmetic proportion). This observation raises at least 2 questions that we address now: What are the minimal requirements on a binary function F for defining a numerical analogical proportion denoted $a : b ::^F c : d$ as $F(a, d) = F(b, c)$? Can we consider combinations of numerical proportions other than the arithmetico-geometric one?

General Numerical Definition. For the first question, we get the following:

Proposition 2. *Let $a, b, c, d \in \mathbb{R}$, F a two place-function. Then $a : b ::^F c : d$ iff $F(a, d) = F(b, c)$ defines an analogical proportion over $\mathbb{R}$ iff F is symmetric, i.e. $F(a, b) = F(b, a)$.*

Proof: 1. Having an analogical proportion implies the symmetry of F: the reflexivity of the proportion means $a : b ::^F a : b$ is true, and then $F(a, b) = F(b, a)$.

2. The symmetry of F implies we have an analogical proportion:

- reflexivity: $a : b ::^F a : b$ is true if $F(a, b) = F(b, a)$, which is true due to symmetry of F.

- symmetry: $a : b ::^F c : d \implies c : d ::^F a : b$ is true due to symmetry of F and $=$: $F(c, b) = F(b, c) = F(a, d) = F(d, a)$

- central permutation: $a : b ::^F c : d \implies a : c ::^F b : d$ is also true because of symmetry of F: then $F(a, d) = F(b, c) = F(c, b)$ □

This provides a very general process to build analogical proportions over $\mathbb{R}$ or to check that a given proportion is an analogy. When considering $\mathbb{B}$ as a subset of $\mathbb{R}$, F being symmetric ensures $a : b ::^F c : d$ holds for the 6 valid valuations of Table 1. However it does not ensure that the 10 remaining invalid valuations 0001, 0010, 0100, 1000, 1110, 1101, 1011, 0111, 1001, 0110 do not hold. Some requirements are necessary to fully fit with the Boolean case:

Proposition 3. *$a : b ::^F c : d$ fits with the Boolean case iff $F(1, 1) \neq F(0, 0)$, $F(1, 0) \neq F(1, 1)$, and $F(1, 0) \neq F(0, 0)$.*

Proof: i) $F(1, 1) \neq F(0, 0)$ forbids $1 : 0 ::^F 0 : 1$ and $0 : 1 ::^F 1 : 0$ to hold.

ii) $F(1, 0) \neq F(1, 1)$ forbids $1 : 1 ::^F 1 : 0$, $0 : 1 ::^F 1 : 1$, $1 : 1 ::^F 0 : 1$, $1 : 0 ::^F 1 : 1$ to hold.

iii) $F(1, 0) \neq F(0, 0)$ forbids $1 : 0 ::^F 0 : 0$, $0 : 0 ::^F 0 : 1$, $0 : 0 ::^F 1 : 0$, $0 : 1 ::^F 0 : 0$ to hold. □

Clearly, $F(x, y) = x + y$ is the simplest function satisfying the above requirements; it leads to the arithmetic proportion.

Other Numerical Proportions. It can be shown that a result similar to Proposition 1 is obtained if we replace the geometric proportion by other proportions.

Proposition 4. *The only 4-tuples of real numbers* a, b, c, d *such that* $a - b = c - d$ *and* $a : b ::^F c : d$ *hold, when* $F(x, y) = \frac{2xy}{x+y}$ *(harmonic proportion), or* $F(x, y) = \sqrt{\frac{1}{2}(x^2 + y^2)}$ *(quadratic proportion), or* $F(x, y) = \sqrt[3]{\frac{1}{2}(x^3 + y^3)}$ *(cubic proportion) are such that* $(a, b, c, d) \in \{(s, s, s, s), (s, s, t, t), (s, t, s, t)\}$.

Proof: The proof of Proposition 1 relies on the fact that a must be a solution to the quadratic equation $x^2 - sx + p = 0$ where $s = a + d = b + c$ and $p = ad = bc$.

If we take the harmonic proportion, we see that we should have $a + d = b + c$ and $ad = bc$ (since $\frac{2ad}{a+d} = \frac{2bc}{b+c}$ entails $\frac{ad}{a+d} = \frac{2bc}{a+d}$ and $\frac{ad}{a+d} = \frac{ad}{b+c}$). We are back to Proposition 1.

For the quadratic proportion, we have $a^2 + d^2 = b^2 + c^2$, which can be written $(a+d)^2 - 2ad = (b+c)^2 - 2bc$, and we are back to Proposition 1 since $a+d = b+c$, and thus we get $ad = bc$.

For the cubic proportion, observe that $a^3 + d^3 = (a + d)^3 - 3ad(a + d)$, and we can come back to Proposition 1. □

As a conclusion, two options emerge for numerical analogical proportions: the arithmetic proportion, and the so-called arithmetico-geometric proportion.

4 The Compatibility Problem

Let us go back to the example of Table 2. When a, b, c, d represent profiles within a given population of individuals, it is legitimate to consider the proportion of individuals with profile a, b, c or d, denoted $p(a), p(b), p(c), p(d)$, interpreted as approximations of the corresponding probabilities. For instance, $p(a) = Prob(Sex = M, Age \leq 40 \mid Education = high)$, etc. as shown in Table 5. Note that in that particular case, we have $p(a) + p(b) + p(c) + p(d) = 1$.

Suppose we have an arithmetic proportion on the probabilities in Table 5, this means we have $p(a) - p(b) = p(c) - p(d)$. But since $p(a) + p(b) + p(c) + p(d) = 1$, this yields $p(b) + p(c) = p(a) + p(d) = 1/2$. For instance, suppose we have, among the people with high education, 60% of people with Age ≤ 40 (with 40% of men and 20% of women), and 40% with Age > 40 (with 30% of men and 10% of women). This gives $0.4 : 0.2 :: 0.3 : 0.1$, which is an arithmetic proportion. In case we have the same number of people with Age ≤ 40 and Age > 40, with 30% of men in both cases, then we get $0.3 : 0.2 :: 0.3 : 0.2$, which is an arithmetico-geometric proportion. This means that in the population under consideration, i.e. those with a degree in education, the difference between the distributions of a and b is the same as between c and d, here that the distribution between men and women with a "high" level of education does not depend on the Age group, ≤ 40 or > 40. It expresses a form of equilibrium between the two age groups where there is the same difference between M and F in the context of high education. But in general, it is clear that we may have $a : b :: c : d$ while $p(a) : p(b) ::_x p(c) : p(d)$ may turn to be wrong.

Table 5. Analogical proportions with fixed probabilities

	Sex	Age	Education	Probability
a	M	≤ 40	high	p(a)
b	F	≤ 40	high	p(b)
c	M	> 40	high	p(c)
d	F	> 40	high	p(d)

Table 6. Analogical proportions with parametric probabilities

	Sex	Age	Education	Probability
a	M	$\leq \eta$	high	p(a)
b	F	$\leq \eta$	high	p(b)
c	M	$> \theta$	high	p(c)
d	F	$> \theta$	high	p(d)

5 Illustration

To illustrate our approach on real-world data[5], we have loaded a recent dataset from the UCI repository focused on predicting recurrence of well-differentiated thyroid cancer[6]. The dataset comprises 383 instances and 16 features, collected over a 15-year period, with each patient followed for a minimum of 10 years [2]. For the sake of simplification, we have reduced our analysis to four easily interpretable features: 'age', 'gender', 'smoking status' and 'response to treatment'. Among these, only age is a numerical variable, which we discretized into three age groups: 20–30, 31–60, and 61–90. Table 7 provides an overview of the dataset after quantization of 'age'.

As usual, probabilities are computed as frequencies. Because we get floating-point values, we replace an equality $x = y$ with $|x - y| < \epsilon$, where ϵ is a parameter to be determined. Because obviously we have no clue about the underlying links between the features, we adopt a data mining philosophy and we start with a simple exhaustive search.
Step 1: We proceed by enumerating all atomic events with their probability such as $P(('Age' =' 20 - 30')) = 0.285, etc.$, then moving to composite events involving 2 atomic events (i.e. the join probabilities), etc. Given the number of features (4) and the candidate values for each feature, we can easily compute the number of atomic events, and in fact, the number of all composite events. For instance, we get only 11 atomic events with non null probability. The outcome are summarized in Table 8 where we display the number of events, the most probable event and its probability.

[5] Due to lack of space, Python code and data will be made available on request.
[6] archive.ics.uci.edu/dataset/915/differentiated+thyroid+cancer+recurrence.

Table 7. A view of the dataset

Age	Gender	Smoking	Hx Smoking	Hx Radiothreapy	Response	Recurred
20-30	F	No	No	No	Indeterminate	No
31-60	F	No	Yes	No	Excellent	No
20-30	F	No	No	No	Excellent	No
61-90	F	No	No	No	Excellent	No
61-90	F	No	No	No	Excellent	No
31-60	M	Yes	No	No	Indeterminate	No
31-60	F	No	Yes	No	Excellent	No
31-60	F	No	No	No	Excellent	No
31-60	F	No	No	No	Excellent	No
31-60	F	No	No	No	Excellent	No
61-90	F	No	No	No	Excellent	No
31-60	F	No	No	No	Excellent	No
31-60	F	No	No	No	Excellent	No

Table 8. Example of events

Event type	Number	Most probable event	Proba.
atomic	11	Smoking = No	0.872
2-composite	44	Gender = F, Smoking = No	0.791
3-composite	76	Gender = F, Smoking = No, Response = Excellent	0.491
4-composite	48	Age = 31-60, Gender = F, Smoking = No, Response = Excellent	0.274

Step 2: The second step is to look for profiles forming a nominal analogy. Using atomic profiles does not bring interesting proportions, we start with combination of 2 then 3 atomic events, removing the trivial proportions (i.e. where a, b, c, d are not distinct), keeping only one canonical form among the 8 options (see Sect. 2). Then we filter the remaining proportions with the condition $|p(a) - p(b) - p(c) + p(d)| \leq \epsilon$ where ϵ is a tolerance threshold (See Table 9). Since the probability of a composite event decreases with its size, the threshold ϵ must be adjusted accordingly.

At this stage, we simply test whether an arithmetic proportion holds between the probabilities of the corresponding events. Our preliminary results show that, when the tolerance threshold is relatively high, more than half of the analogical proportions validate the inference for the probability values. Obviously, additional experiments are needed to confirm the possibility of finding analogical proportions with probabilities in agreement. Moreover, we may try to adjust the partition of attribute domains (e.g. age) in order to find an equilibrium as explained in the previous section.

Table 9. Number of analogical proportions (AP) w.r.t ϵ

ϵ	# of 2-AP	# of 2-filtered-AP	# of 3-AP	# of 3-filtered-AP
0.1	255	130	1765	1290
0.05	255	91	1765	1062
0.02	255	43	1765	630
0.01	255	15	1765	323
0.005	255	4	1765	142

6 Conclusion

In this paper, we explored various approaches to defining numerical analogies and examined the analogical relationship between group descriptions and their probabilities. Broadly speaking, the central question is: If an analogical proportion holds between four distinct profiles in a population, under what conditions a corresponding proportion holds between their associated probabilities? Under such conditions, then, since numerical proportions allow the computation of a missing value given the other three, this could provide a simple method for estimating a probability without the need to analyze the entire population. Further research is needed to clarify the precise nature of this relationship and to determine the validity and usefulness of such an analogical relationship.

Acknowledgements. This research was supported by the ANR project "Analogies: from Theory to Tools and Applications" (AT2TA), ANR-22-CE23-0023.

References

1. Afantenos, S.D., Lim, S., Prade, H., Richard, G.: Theoretical study and empirical investigation of sentence analogies. In: IARML@IJCAI. CEUR Workshop Proceedings, vol. 3174, pp. 15–28. CEUR-WS.org (2022)
2. Borzooei, S., Briganti, G., Golparian, M., Lechien, J.R., Tarokhian, A.: Machine learning for risk stratification of thyroid cancer patients: a 15-year cohort study. Eur. Arch. Oto-Rhino-Laryngol. **281**(4), 2095–2104 (2024)
3. Bounhas, M., Prade, H.: Analogy-based classifiers: an improved algorithm exploiting competent data pairs. Int. J. Approx. Reason. **158**, 108923 (2023)
4. Bounhas, M., Prade, H.: Revisiting analogical proportions and analogical inference. Int. J. Approx. Reason. **171**, 109202 (2024)
5. Couceiro, M., Hug, N., Prade, H., Richard, G.: Analogy-preserving functions: a way to extend Boolean samples. In: Proc. of 26th Inter. Joint Conf. on Artificial Intelligence (IJCAI'17), Melbourne, pp. 1575–1581 (2017)
6. Couceiro, M., Hug, N., Prade, H., Richard, G.: Behavior of analogical inference w.r.t. Boolean functions. In: Proc. 27th IJCAI Stockholm, pp. 2057–2063 (2018)
7. Couceiro, M., Lehtonen, E., Miclet, L., Prade, H., Richard, G.: When nominal analogical proportions do not fail. In: Davis, J., Tabia, K. (eds.) Proc. 14th Int. Conf. on Scalable Uncertainty Management (SUM'20), Bozen-Bolzano, Sept. 23-25. LNCS, vol. 12322, pp. 68–83. Springer (2020)

8. Davies, T.R., Russell, S.J.: A logical approach to reasoning by analogy. In: McDermott, J.P. (ed.) Proc. 10th Int. Joint Conference on Artificial Intelligence. Milan, Aug. 23-28, pp. 264–270. Morgan Kaufmann (1987)
9. Delhay, A., Miclet, L.: Analogical equations in sequences: definition and resolution. In: Paliouras, G., Sakakibara, Y. (eds.) Proc. 7th Int. Colloq. on Grammatical Inference(ICGI'04), Athens. LNCS, vol. 3264, pp. 127–138. Springer (2004)
10. Dubois, D., Prade, H., Richard, G.: Multiple-valued extensions of analogical proportions. Fuzzy Sets Syst. **292**, 193–202 (2016)
11. Fischer, P.C., Van Gucht, D.: Weak multivalued dependencies. In: Proc. 3rd ACM SIGACT-SIGMOD Symp. on Principles of Database Systems, April 2-4, Waterloo, Ontario, pp. 266–274 (1984)
12. Lepage, Y.: Analogy and formal languages. Electr. Notes TCS **53** (2001)
13. Lepage, Y., Couceiro, M.: Analogie et moyenne généralisée. In: Actes 18èmes Journées d'IA Fondamentale, La Rochelle, 1-3 Jul, pp. 114–124 (2024)
14. Lepage, Y., Couceiro, M.: L'analogie numérique revisitée et étendue, précisée, rétrécie ou agrandie. In: Actes des 19èmes Journées d'Intelligence Artif. Fondamentale, Plate-Forme Intelligence Artificielle (PFIA), Dijon, 2-4 Jul. https://pfia2025.u-bourgogne.fr/conferences/jiaf/ (2025)
15. Link, S., Prade, H., Richard, G.: Analogical proportions, multivalued dependencies and explanations. In: de Saint-Cyr, F.D., Öztürk-Escoffier, M., Potyka, N. (eds.) Proc. 15th Int. Conf. on Scalable Uncertainty Management SUM'22, Paris, Oct. 17-19. LNCS, vol. 13562, pp. 351–360. Springer (2022)
16. Miclet, L., Bayoudh, S., Delhay, A.: Analogical dissimilarity: definition, algorithms and two experiments in machine learning. JAIR **32**, 793–824 (2008)
17. Miclet, L., Prade, H.: Handling analogical proportions in classical logic and fuzzy logics settings. In: Sossai, C., Chemello, G. (eds.) ECSQARU 2009. LNCS (LNAI), vol. 5590, pp. 638–650. Springer, Heidelberg (2009). https://doi.org/10.1007/978-3-642-02906-6_55
18. Pirrelli, V., Yvon, F.: Analogy in the lexicon: a probe into analogy-based machine learning of language. In: Proc. 6th Int. Symp. on Human Communic., Santiago de Cuba, 6 p. (1999)
19. Prade, H., Richard, G.: Analogical proportions: why they are useful in AI. In: Proc. 30th Int. Joint Conf. on Artificial Intelligence (IJCAI-21), (Z.-H. Zhou, ed.) Virtual Event/Montreal, Aug. 19-27, pp. 4568–4576 (2021)
20. Prade, H., Richard, G.: Frank's triangular norms in Piaget's logical proportions. In: Destercke, S., Martinez, M.V., Sanfilippo, G. (eds.) Proc. 16th Int. Conf. on Scalable Uncert. Management (SUM'24), Palermo, Nov. 27-29. LNCS, vol. 15350, pp. 369–377. Springer (2024)
21. Prade, H., Richard, G.: Analogical proportions analogiques between probabilities. In: K. Sauerwald, M.T. (ed.) Proc. 18th Europ. Conf. on Symbolic and Quantitative Approaches to Reasoning with Uncertainty, Hagen. LNCS. Springer (2025)
22. Prade, H., Richard, G.: Proportions analogiques entre probabilités. In: 19èmes Journées d'IA Fondamentale (JIAF'25), Plate-Forme Intelligence Artificielle (PFIA), Dijon, 2-4 Juil. https://pfia2025.u-bourgogne.fr/conferences/jiaf/ (2025)
23. Stroppa, N., Yvon, F.: Du quatrième de proportion comme principe inductif: une proposition et son application à l'apprentissage de la morphologie. Traitement Automatique des Langues **47**(2), 1–27 (2006)

A Deep-Learning Framework for Land-Sliding Classification from Remote Sensing Image

Quang-Hieu Tang[1(✉)], Nhat-Truong Vo Dinh[2], Dong-Dong Pham[3], Quoc-Toan Nguyen[4], Lam Pham[5], and Truong Nguyen[6]

[1] University of Technology of Troyes, Rosieres-pres-Troyes, France
hieu.tang@utt.fr
[2] ICC Dong Duong, Ho Chi Minh City, Vietnam
[3] Biosel AI, Ho Chi Minh City, Vietnam
[4] University of Technology Sydney, Sydney, Australia
quoctoan.nguyen@student.uts.edu.au
[5] Austrian Institute of Technology, Sydney, Austria
lam.pham@ait.ac.at
[6] Ho Chi Minh City University of Technology, Ho Chi Minh City, Vietnam
truongnguyen@hcmut.edu.vn

Abstract. The use of satellite imagery combined with deep learning to support automatic landslide detection is becoming increasingly widespread. However, selecting an appropriate deep learning architecture to optimize performance while avoiding overfitting remains a critical challenge. To address these issues, we propose a deep learning based framework for landslide detection from remote sensing image. The proposed framework presents an effective combination of online and offline data augmentation to tackle the imbalanced data, a backbone EfficientNetV2-Large deep learning model for extracting robust embedding features, and a post-processing SVM classifier to balance and enhance the classification performance. The proposed model achieved an F1-score of 0.8938 on the public test set of the Zindi challenge.

Keywords: Landslide Classification · Satellite Imagery · Deep Learning Architecture

1 Introduction

Landslides are increasingly becoming a widespread natural disaster, driven by various objective factors such as global warming and human-induced geological surface modifications. Such incidents have brought growing attention to the study of landslides, particularly in regions with a history of geo-hazards.

With the advancement of satellite technologies, multi-spectral satellite imagery now offers spatial resolutions as fine as 10 m per pixel [19] and provides a wide range of spectral bands. These bands provide detailed characterization of

T. T. Quan et al. (Eds.): MIWAI 2025, LNAI 16353, pp. 230–241, 2026.
https://doi.org/10.1007/978-981-95-4957-3_19

surface properties such as moisture, vegetation cover, and topographical structure. Leveraging this information, scientists can generate comprehensive landslide risk maps and compile extensive geo-spatial datasets documenting geological structural changes over decades. To analyze multi-spectral satellite imagery, machine learning and deep learning techniques have demonstrated significant success. Classical machine learning algorithms such as Random Forest, Rotation Forest, Support Vector Machine (SVM), and Logistic Regression have been extensively employed for generating landslide susceptibility maps [12]. Recently, deep learning based methods have been increasingly utilized for landslide classification tasks. For example, Liu et al. [15] conducted a comparative study of three convolutional neural network architectures including CNN, ResNet, and DenseNet for landslide classification. Lam et al. [20] and Soares et al. [24] explored the effects of patch size and sampling strategy on the performance of a UNet model applied to landslide segmentation. Long et al. [17] proposed a hybrid framework that integrates a Deep Belief Network (DBN) and a CNN in parallel, fusing their extracted features prior to classification in order to enhance remote sensing-based landslide detection performance. Furthermore, Qin et al. [21] introduced a novel domain transfer learning approach by incorporating a maximum mean discrepancy (MMD) loss function to bridge the distribution gap between source and target domains.

Despite the advances in deep learning models, several research gaps still remain. In particular, existing models implicitly assume that landslide samples are sufficiently represented in the dataset. In practice, however, landslide occurrences are rare compared to non-landslide regions, resulting in highly imbalanced data distributions. Therefore, deep learning models with excessive complexity often exhibit limited generalizability. In this paper, we propose an end-to-end deep learning framework for landslide classification which aim to address the class imbalance problem. To this end, during the pre-processing phase, multiple data augmentation techniques, such as the Synthetic Minority Oversampling Technique (SMOTE [2]), CutMix, Mixup, etc., are employed to generate synthetic minority samples and thereby enrich the training dataset. Then, we construct a deep neural network architecture, which leverages a pre-trained EfficientNetV2-Large model, for the training process. Finally, in the post-processing stage, we replace the classification head of the neural network by a Support Vector Machine (SVM) layer to enhance classification fairness and overall effectiveness. The remainder of this paper is organized as follows. Section 2 reviews the background and main components of the proposed framework. Section 3 presents the architecture of the deep learning model. Section 4 describes the experimental setup, results, and discussion. Finally, Sect. 5 concludes the paper and outlines future research directions.

2 Background

EfficientNetV2-Large: EfficientNetV2-Large is belongs to the EfficientNetV2 family proposed by Tan and Le [27] (2021). This architecture is designed to address the trade-off between accuracy, parameter efficiency, and training/inference speed. Regarding EfficientNetV2 general network architecture, it presents a hybrid design combining both *MBConv* and *Fused-MBConv* building blocks. The MBConv block (Mobile Inverted Bottleneck Convolution [23]) is a lightweight structure that includes depth-wise separable convolution and "squeeze and excitation (SE)" modules to enhance parameter efficiency. In addition, Fused-MBConv blocks replace expansion and depthwise layers with a single standard 3×3 convolution followed by batch normalization. This modification significantly improves training throughput, especially on accelerators such as GPUs or TPUs. The architecture of EfficientNetV2-Large, as shown in Table 1 and Fig. 1. Unlike EfficientNetV1 models which applies this scaling parameter uniformly in all stages, EfficientNetV2-Large applies training-aware NAS framework [26] to search for optimal convolutional operation types {*MBConv*, *Fused-MBConv*}, the number of layers, kernel size $\{3 \times 3,\ 5 \times 5\}$, and expansion ratio $\{1, 4, 6\}$.

Table 1. Layer settings of MBConv and Fused-MBConv blocks in EfficientNetV2-Large architecture.

Stage	Operator	Expand	Stride	#Channels	#Layers
0	Conv, k3 × 3	_	2	32	1
1	Fused-MBConv, k3 × 3	1	1	32	4
2	Fused-MBConv, k3 × 3	4	2	64	7
3	Fused-MBConv, k3 × 3	4	2	96	7
4	MBConv, k3 × 3, SE	4	2	192	10
5	MBConv, k3 × 3, SE	6	1	224	19
6	MBConv, k3 × 3, SE	6	2	384	25
7	MBConv, k3 × 3, SE	6	1	640	7
8	Conv, k1x1 & AvgPool & FC	_	_	1280	1

Support Vector Machine (SVM): Support Vector Machine (SVM) is a powerful and widely used supervised learning algorithm, especially effective in binary classification problems. The main objective of SVM is to find the optimal decision boundary, called a hyperplane, which separates data points of different classes with the maximum possible margin between them. The detailed mathematical formulation of SVM can be found in [10].

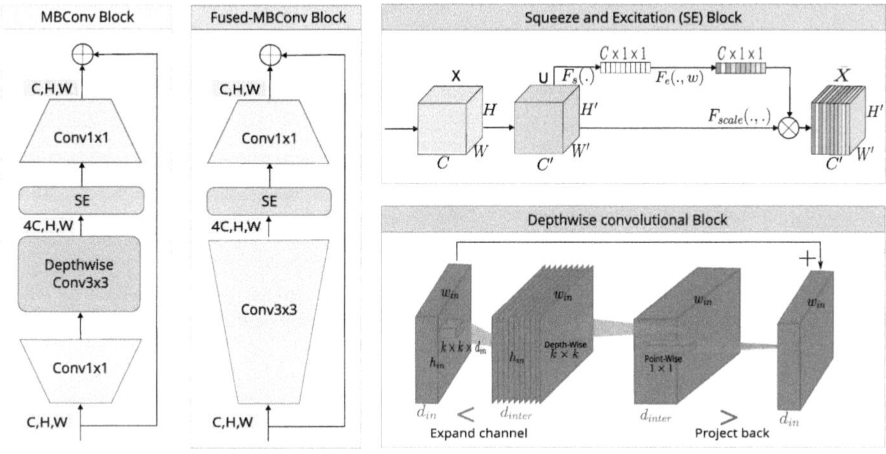

Fig. 1. Unit blocks in the EfficientNetV2-Large network architecture.

3 Our Proposed Deep Learning Framework

As shown in Fig. 2, the high-level architecture of the proposed framework comprises three main parts: (1) Offline and online data augmentation, (2) Finetuning pre-trained deep neural network EfficientNetV2-Large, and (3) Post-processing on the feature map using SVM algorithm.

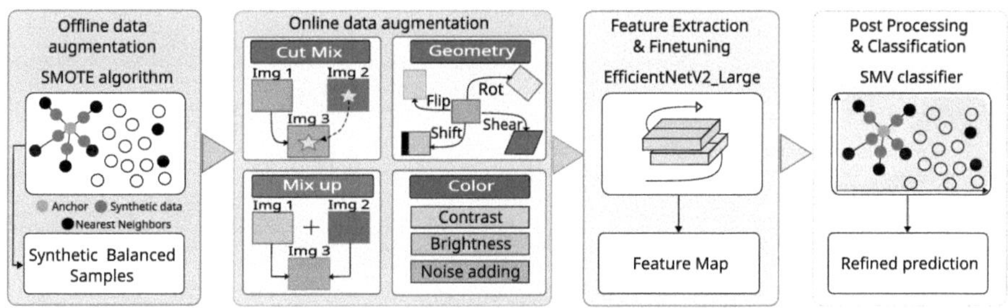

Fig. 2. The high-level architecture of proposed deep learning framework.

Data Augmentation: First, SMOTE algorithm is used to generate more remote sensing images to tackle the imbalance data issue.

Next, data augmentations strategies such as **bag of freebies**, **color transformations**, and **geometric transformations** [28] are applied to each batch in training, referred to as the online data augmentation.

Finetuning Pre-trained EfficientNetV2-Large Network Architecture: A pretrained backbone EfficientNetV2-Large on ImageNet dataset is transferred to our landslide detection task. Then, a linear fully connected (FC) layer is employed to predict the category of the input data.

Post-processing Using SVM: To enhance the performance of whole system, the FC head is replaced with a non-linear Support Vector Machine (SVM) classifier. By applying SVM for post-processing step, this is effective to evaluate the quality of learned embeddings while minimizing overfitting and reducing computational cost during inference.

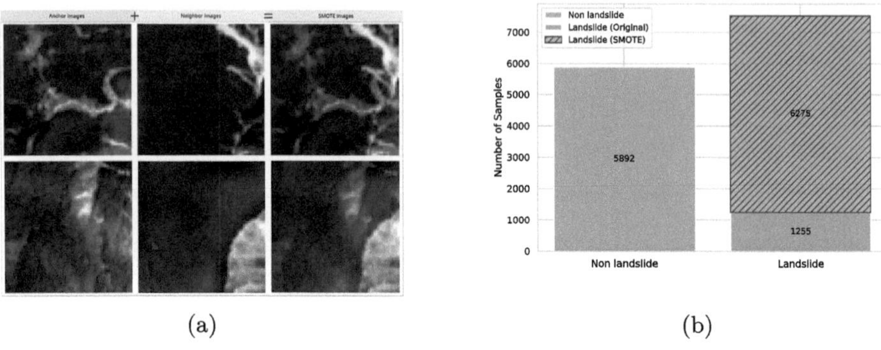

(a) (b)

Fig. 3. (a) Left: Anchor images; Middle: Nearest neighbors; Right: SMOTE-generated samples. (b): Class distribution on the training subset after applying the SMOTE algorithm.

4 Experiments and Discussion

4.1 Zindi Challenge Dataset

In this paper, we present an evaluation of our proposed deep learning framework on the Zindi Challenge dataset. This dataset was released through a data science competition hosted on the Zindi Africa platform [30], which specifically addresses the problem of landslide detection using satellite-based remote sensing. It integrates multi-source Earth observation data by combining optical imagery from Sentinel-2 and radar imagery from Sentinel-1.

Firstly, Sentinel-2 provides four spectral bands including red, green, blue (RGB), and near-infrared (NIR), each with a spatial resolution of 10 m. These bands capture surface reflectance properties and are particularly effective for identifying terrain deformations associated with landslides.

In parallel, the radar imagery is acquired from Sentinel-1, which offers dual polarization channels in vertical and horizontal axes (VV and VH). To enrich the representation, we also incorporate handcrafted features such as NDVI, EVI2, VARI, and RGRI, along with edge-based descriptors (e.g., Sobel and Canny). Depending on the configuration, the inclusion of these features can expand the input dimensionality to as many as 20 channels. A complete overview of the input channels is provided on the Zindi website [30].

We adopt a 5-fold cross-validation strategy to ensure robustness and reduce bias in performance estimation. The proposed networks are then trained and evaluated on the training set. Finally, we run the inference process on the test set, submit the results to the Leaderboard to obtain the test scores. Notably, the challenge was still ongoing at the time of writing this paper.

4.2 Experimental Settings

As mentioned in Sect. 3, SMOTE algorithm is applied to Zindi Challenge dataset to generate more data before training starts. As Fig. 3 shows, we generate more 6275 landslide images, enhancing the balance between landslide and non-landslide classes. Next, the evaluated deep neural networks in this paper were constructed using PyTorch framework. All experiments were conducted on a single machine equipped with a GPU GTX4090. Training is performed for 50 epochs using a batch size of 36, with the Adam optimizer and an initial learning rate of 0.0003. The primary loss function is the soft-label Kullback-Leibler divergence, implemented as a variant of cross-entropy for probabilistic (soft) targets.

For model evaluation, multiple metrics are employed. On the validation set, the confusion matrix, AUC score, and ROC curve are computed to monitor performance throughout training. For the unseen challenge test set, however, only the F1-score is reported on the leaderboard, and thus it is used as the sole measure of performance. To ensure exposure to the full training data distribution and to reduce overfitting, the validation fold is rotated while remaining distinct from the training folds. The best-performing model weights are then saved and subsequently applied to the challenge test set.

4.3 Experimental Results and Discussions

To evaluate the performance of the backbone EfficientNetV2-Large architecture, we conducted a comprehensive comparison against other deep learning network architecture, including U-Net variants [14], conventional CNNs [9,22,25,29], and transformer-based architectures [5,6,16]. For a fair comparison, all models were initialized with pretrained weights from ImageNet dataset.

First, performance metrics, including the confusion matrix and ROC curve of EfficientNetV2-Large during training, are evaluated for each fold in the 5-fold cross-validation strategy, as illustrated in Fig. 4 and Fig. 5. The results show that EfficientNetV2-Large consistently achieves high accuracy across all folds with small variance, highlighting its robustness and reliability in the landslide classification task. It is worth noting that, since the performance of other models is comparable to that of EfficientNetV2-Large, only the results of EfficientNetV2-Large are reported in this section.

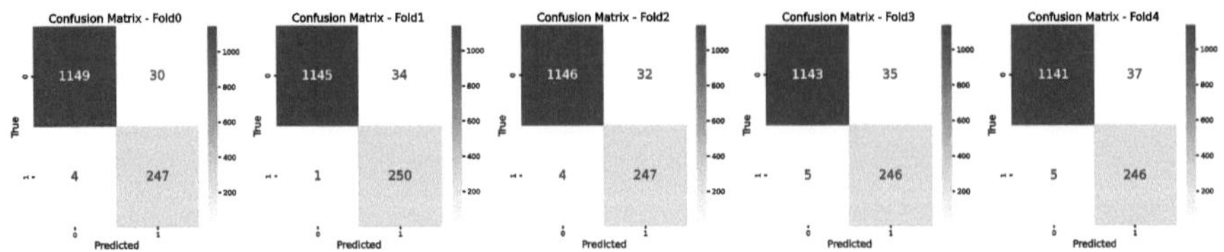

Fig. 4. Confusion matrix of EfficientNetV2-Large on each fold in 5-fold cross-validation strategy.

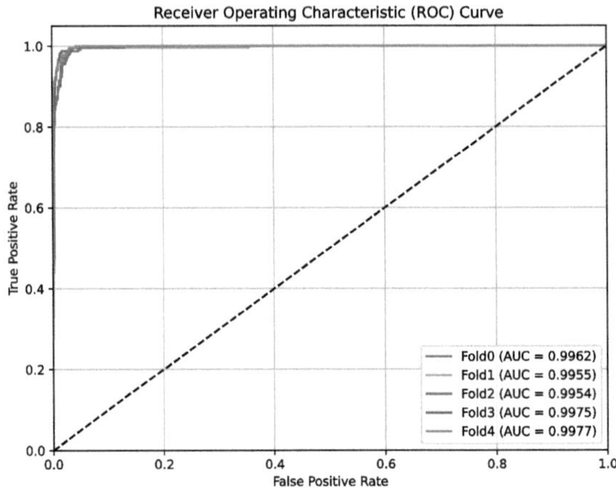

Fig. 5. ROC curve of EfficientNetV2-Large on each fold in 5-fold cross-validation strategy.

Next, performance of unseen test set is illustrated in Fig. 6, EfficientNetV2-Large consistently outperforms other architectures on the test set, achieving the highest accuracy among architectures with comparable parameter sizes. Notably, although deeper models like ResNetY32G and WideResNet perform relatively well on training set, they exhibit a lower generalization gap compared to EfficientNetV2-Large in test set. In contrast, InceptionV3, while efficient in other vision tasks, fails to generalize effectively under the current constraints. These results demonstrate that backbone deep learning architecture plays a critical role in model generalization and robustness, even when other factors are held constant.

To analyze the impact of various hyperparameter configurations regarding EfficientNetV2-Large network, we evaluate the number of input channels, normalization method, data augmentation techniques (SMOTE, MixUp, and CutMix), and learning rate schedule. Table 2 illustrates the result on test set of the Zindi dataset, where Baseline model is the standard EfficientNetV2-Large without any modification. Each of following models was tested with one of additional features. The best model is the combination of all factors with the highest score of 0.8915.

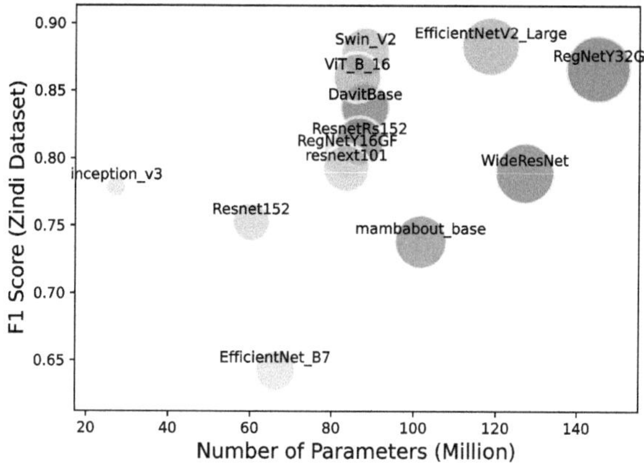

Fig. 6. Performance and parameter comparison among backbone deep neural networks.

Table 2. Ablation Study on EfficientNetV2-Large with training factors.

Model	#Ch	Mixup	CutMix	LR	Norm.	SMOTE	Train F1	Test F1
Baseline	12	No	No	No	Std	No	0.9398	0.8370
EfficientNetV2	12	Yes‡	No	No	Std	No	0.9976	0.7866
EfficientNetV2	20‡	Yes	Yes	No	Std	No	0.9469	0.8163
EfficientNetV2	12	Yes‡	Yes‡	No	Std	No	0.9891	0.8606
EfficientNetV2	12	Yes	Yes	Step‡	Std	No	0.9713	0.8379
EfficientNetV2	12	Yes	Yes	CosLR‡	Std	No	0.9988	0.8729
EfficientNetV2	12	Yes	Yes	CosLR	Robust‡	No	0.9976	0.8845
EfficientNetV2*	12	Yes	Yes	CosLR	Std	Yes‡	1.0000	**0.8915**

‡ Modification from the baseline configuration.
* The best-performing model.

To assess the effectiveness of the SVM classifier, we perform a series of comparative experiments using the best-performing model from Table 2 as the baseline. This baseline model employs a traditional fully connected layer as its classification head. We then replace this layer with an SVM classifier and vary the regularization parameter C to evaluate its impact on model generalization. Additionally, we evaluate the Light Gradient Boosting Machine (LGBM) [13], a widely used machine learning algorithm, as an alternative classifier. The results, presented in Table 3, show that applying a small degree of regularization improves the model's generalization performance.

Finally, to better understand the behavior of the models, we employ various explainable AI (xAI) tools. First, we apply Uniform manifold approximation and projection for dimension reduction(UMAP) [18] to reduce the dimensionality of the embedding feature representations extracted from the network just before the classifier layer. Then, a simple SVM is used to illustrate the decision

Table 3. Comparison of EfficientNetV2-Large models using SVM as classifier with different configurations.

Model	C	Train F1	Test F1
Baseline	_	1.0000	0.8915
EfficientNetV2+LGBM	_	1.0000	0.8826
EfficientNetV2+SVM	1.00	1.0000	0.8840
EfficientNetV2+SVM	0.75	1.0000	0.8894
EfficientNetV2+SVM	0.5	1.0000	0.8921
EfficientNetV2+SVM	0.1	1.0000	**0.8938**

* The best-performing model.

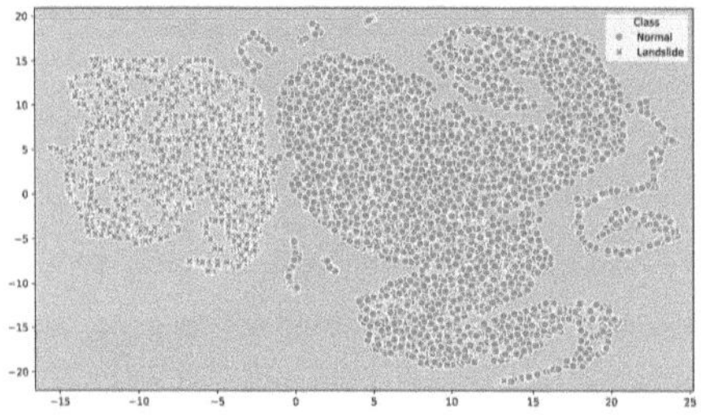

(a) Feature visualization from the baseline model.

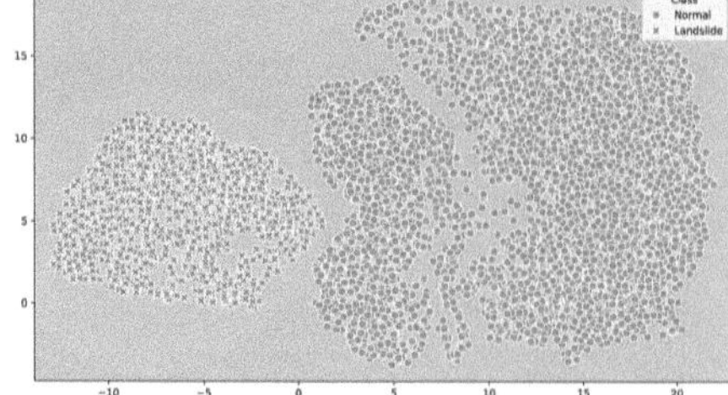

(b) Feature visualization from the best model.

Fig. 7. Comparison of embedding feature distributions using UMAP.

boundaries, as shown in Fig. 7. The results demonstrate that using an SVM classifier as the final layer leads to more clearly separated feature regions compared to the traditional fully connected layer. This improved feature alignment may contribute to better generalization.

Second, we assess the importance of each input band among the original 12 bands by performing a manual occlusion analysis. The results of this analysis are illustrated in Fig. 8.

From this experiment, we observe that synthetic aperture radar (SAR) bands (e.g., DVH, DDVV, ADVH) contribute significantly more to the prediction than the optical bands (e.g., Red, Green, Blue, NIR). This finding is consistent with the fact that the dataset includes scenes under various conditions such as cloud cover or urban environments, which can degrade the effectiveness of optical bands in identifying landslide regions.

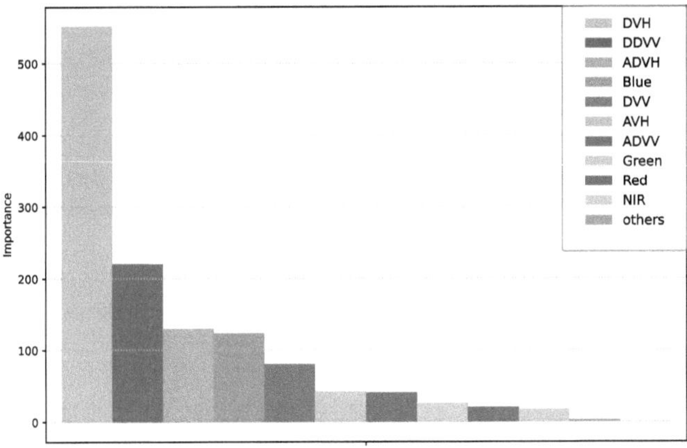

Fig. 8. Feature importance obtained using the band-wise occlusion technique.

5 Conclusion

In this study, we proposed a deep learning framework that combines the EfficientNetV2-Large architecture with a Support Vector Machine (SVM) classifier to improve landslide detection using multi-spectral satellite imagery. To address the class imbalance issue inherent in the dataset, we integrated both offline and online data augmentation.

Through extensive ablation studies, we demonstrated that incorporating augmentation techniques, robust deep learning network, and SVM-based post processing yields superior performance, especially when fine-tuned with appropriate regularization to achieve an F1-score of 0.8938. Furthermore, explainability analyses using UMAP and band-wise occlusion highlight that SAR-derived features contribute more significantly than RGB/NIR bands to landslide identification, particularly under complex environmental conditions. As future work, we plan to explore advanced data augmentation techniques, including ADASYN [8], Generative Adversarial Networks (GANs) [3], and diffusion models [4], to further increase the diversity of training samples. Another promising direction is to extend the proposed framework through transfer learning on other remote sensing datasets, such as Landslide4Sense [7], Bijie [11], and Nepal [1].

References

1. Bragagnolo, L., Rezende, L., Da Silva, R., Grzybowski, J.: Convolutional neural networks applied to semantic segmentation of landslide scars. CATENA **201**, 105189 (2021)
2. Chawla, N.V., Bowyer, K.W., Hall, L.O., Kegelmeyer, W.P.: Smote: synthetic minority over-sampling technique. J. Artif. Intell. Res. **16**, 321–357 (2002)
3. Creswell, A., White, T., Dumoulin, V., Arulkumaran, K., Sengupta, B., Bharath, A.A.: Generative adversarial networks: an overview. IEEE Signal Process. Mag. **35**(1), 53–65 (2018)

4. Croitoru, F.A., Hondru, V., Ionescu, R.T., Shah, M.: Diffusion models in vision: a survey. IEEE Trans. Pattern Anal. Mach. Intell. **45**(9), 10850–10869 (2023)
5. Ding, M., Xiao, B., Codella, N., Luo, P., Wang, J., Yuan, L.: Davit: Dual attention vision transformers. In: European Conference on Computer Vision, pp. 74–92. Springer (2022)
6. Dosovitskiy, A., Beyer, L., Kolesnikov, A., Weissenborn, D., Zhai, X., Unterthiner, T., Dehghani, M., Minderer, M., Heigold, G., Gelly, S., et al.: An image is worth 16x16 words: Transformers for image recognition at scale. arXiv preprint arXiv:2010.11929 (2020)
7. Ghorbanzadeh, O., et al.: The outcome of the 2022 landslide4sense competition: advanced landslide detection from multisource satellite imagery. IEEE J. Sel. Top. Appl. Earth Observations Remote Sensing **15**, 9927–9942 (2022)
8. He, H., Bai, Y., Garcia, E.A., Li, S.: Adasyn: adaptive synthetic sampling approach for imbalanced learning. In: 2008 IEEE International Joint Conference on Neural Networks (IEEE world congress on computational intelligence), pp. 1322–1328. Ieee (2008)
9. He, K., Zhang, X., Ren, S., Sun, J.: Deep residual learning for image recognition. In: Proceedings of the IEEE Conference on Computer Vision and Pattern Recognition, pp. 770–778 (2016)
10. Hearst, M.A., Dumais, S.T., Osuna, E., Platt, J., Scholkopf, B.: Support vector machines. IEEE Intell. Syst. Appl. **13**(4), 18–28 (1998)
11. Ji, S., Yu, D., Shen, C., Li, W., Xu, Q.: Landslide detection from an open satellite imagery and digital elevation model dataset using attention boosted convolutional neural networks. Landslides **17**(6), 1337–1352 (2020). https://doi.org/10.1007/s10346-020-01353-2
12. Kavzoglu, T., Colkesen, I., Sahin, E.K.: Machine learning techniques in landslide susceptibility mapping: a survey and a case study. Landslides: Theory, practice and modelling, pp. 283–301 (2019)
13. Ke, G., Meng, Q., Finley, T., Wang, T., Chen, W., Ma, W., Ye, Q., Liu, T.Y.: Lightgbm: a highly efficient gradient boosting decision tree. Advances in neural information processing systems **30** (2017)
14. Le, C., Pham, L., Lampert, J., Schlögl, M., Schindler, A.: Landslide detection and segmentation using remote sensing images and deep neural networks. In: IGARSS 2024-2024 IEEE International Geoscience and Remote Sensing Symposium, pp. 9582–9586. IEEE (2024)
15. Liu, T., Chen, T., Niu, R., Plaza, A.: Landslide detection mapping employing cnn, resnet, and densenet in the three gorges reservoir, China. IEEE J. Sel. Top. Appl. Earth Observations Remote Sensing **14**, 11417–11428 (2021)
16. Liu, Z., Lin, Y., Cao, Y., Hu, H., Wei, Y., Zhang, Z., Lin, S., Guo, B.: Swin transformer: hierarchical vision transformer using shifted windows. In: Proceedings of the IEEE/CVF International Conference on Computer Vision, pp. 10012–10022 (2021)
17. Long, L., He, F., Liu, H.: The use of remote sensing satellite using deep learning in emergency monitoring of high-level landslides disaster in jinsha river. J. Supercomput. **77**(8), 8728–8744 (2021)
18. McInnes, L., Healy, J., Melville, J.: Umap: uniform manifold approximation and projection for dimension reduction. arXiv preprint arXiv:1802.03426 (2018)
19. NASA Earthdata: Remote sensing - earth observation data basics (2024). https://www.earthdata.nasa.gov/learn/earth-observation-data-basics/remote-sensing#toc-resolution. Accessed 02 July 2025

20. Pham, L., et al.: Rmau-net: a residual-multihead-attention u-net architecture for landslide segmentation and detection from remote sensing images (2025). https://arxiv.org/abs/2507.11143
21. Qin, S., Guo, X., Sun, J., Qiao, S., Zhang, L., Yao, J., Cheng, Q., Zhang, Y.: Landslide detection from open satellite imagery using distant domain transfer learning. Remote Sensing **13**(17), 3383 (2021)
22. Radosavovic, I., Kosaraju, R.P., Girshick, R., He, K., Dollár, P.: Designing network design spaces. In: Proceedings of the IEEE/CVF Conference on Computer Vision and Pattern Recognition, pp. 10428–10436 (2020)
23. Sandler, M., Howard, A., Zhu, M., Zhmoginov, A., Chen, L.C.: Mobilenetv2: Inverted residuals and linear bottlenecks. In: Proceedings of the IEEE Conference on Computer Vision and Pattern Recognition, pp. 4510–4520 (2018)
24. Soares, L.P., Dias, H.C., Grohmann, C.H.: Landslide segmentation with u-net: Evaluating different sampling methods and patch sizes. arXiv preprint arXiv:2007.06672 (2020)
25. Szegedy, C., Vanhoucke, V., Ioffe, S., Shlens, J., Wojna, Z.: Rethinking the inception architecture for computer vision. In: Proceedings of the IEEE Conference on Computer Vision and Pattern Recognition, pp. 2818–2826 (2016)
26. Tan, M., Chen, B., Pang, R., Vasudevan, V., Sandler, M., Howard, A., Le, Q.V.: Mnasnet: platform-aware neural architecture search for mobile. In: Proceedings of the IEEE/CVF Conference on Computer Vision and Pattern Recognition, pp. 2820–2828 (2019)
27. Tan, M., Le, Q.: Efficientnetv2: Smaller models and faster training. In: International Conference on Machine Learning, pp. 10096–10106. PMLR (2021)
28. Wang, C.Y., Bochkovskiy, A., Liao, H.Y.M.: Yolov7: trainable bag-of-freebies sets new state-of-the-art for real-time object detectors. In: Proceedings of the IEEE/CVF Conference on Computer Vision and Pattern Recognition, pp. 7464–7475 (2023)
29. Wang, Y., Albrecht, C.M., Braham, N.A.A., Liu, C., Xiong, Z., Zhu, X.X.: Decoupling common and unique representations for multimodal self-supervised learning. In: European Conference on Computer Vision, pp. 286–303. Springer (2024)
30. Zindi: Classification for landslide detection. https://zindi.africa/competitions/classification-for-landslide-detection/data (nd). Accessed 2025-07-10

DPDiff: Blind Image Inpainting with Dual-Prior Diffusion

Hoai Trung Nguyen[1,2], Trong Nhan Ho[1,2], and Duc Dung Nguyen[1,2](✉)

[1] AITech Lab, Ho Chi Minh City University of Technology (HCMUT), Ho Chi Minh City, Vietnam
{trung.nguyenkhmtk21,nhan.ho0687htn,nddung}@hcmut.edu.vn
[2] Vietnam National University Ho Chi Minh City (VNUHCM), Ho Chi Minh City, Vietnam

Abstract. Blind image inpainting aims to restore images degraded by unknown corruption, where the locations and shapes of missing regions are unspecified at inference time. Existing methods typically separate mask estimation and image restoration into sequential stages, which can lead to error propagation and poor integration of structural priors, especially when dealing with complex or diverse artifacts. In this paper, we present Dual-Prior Diffusion (DPDiff), a novel framework that addresses blind inpainting by jointly predicting corruption masks and reconstructing edge maps. This simultaneous prediction of dual priors complementarily rectifies one another, significantly reducing error accumulation and enabling robust, structure-aware restoration. Leveraging these learned priors, DPDiff guides a diffusion model to generate restored images that both preserve geometric fidelity and blend seamlessly with uncorrupted content. Extensive experiments demonstrate that DPDiff sets a new state-of-the-art on multiple blind inpainting benchmarks using only four diffusion timesteps, and generalizes strongly to related image restoration tasks such as image deraining and watermark removal.

Keywords: Blind Image Inpainting · Image Restoration · Generative Model · Diffusion Model

1 Introduction

Image inpainting aims to restore corrupted images by filling missing regions with realistic content. However, most state-of-the-art inpainting methods [17,29,33,34] require precise corruption masks, limiting their applicability in practice. In real-world scenarios with complex or unseen degradations, these mask-driven models frequently fail to generate convincing results, highlighting the need for blind inpainting.

In the early days, blind inpainting methods addressed simplified degradations, such as constant values or Gaussian noise [1,19]. Recent works [7,9,32] attempted to increase the variety of corruption patterns by defining random content as corruption. To handle diverse artifacts, two-stage frameworks such

T. T. Quan et al. (Eds.): MIWAI 2025, LNAI 16353, pp. 242–254, 2026.
https://doi.org/10.1007/978-981-95-4957-3_20

as VCNet [32] and InViT [7] first predict a corruption mask and then guide restoration with the predicted corruption mask. These pipelines, however, are susceptible to errors in mask estimation, often resulting in blurry outputs. This weakness persists even in the unified model HCL [9], whose performance remains dependent on ad-hoc mask augmentation heuristics. Furthermore, most existing methods underutilize intrinsic structural information and rely on single-pass, feed-forward predictions instead of principled generative models at inference. As a result, they often struggle to achieve high-fidelity and coherent restorations, particularly in the presence of challenging and unknown degradations.

In this paper, we introduce Dual-Prior Diffusion (DPDiff), a novel blind inpainting framework that combines the localization strength of a corruption mask with the structural prior of an explicitly restored edge map. Moving beyond fragile sequential pipelines, DPDiff decouples prior estimation from texture synthesis and unifies them in a single model that simultaneously predicts corrupted regions and reconstructs a clean edge map of the missing content, enabling both outputs to cross-refine each other and suppress the error accumulation in previous methods. The predicted mask safeguards intact pixels while the reconstructed edges impose geometric consistency, and together, this dual prior directs the diffusion model to synthesize photorealistic content that remains sharply aligned with the completed boundaries. Our key contributions are:

1. We propose a novel learning framework that jointly predicts corrupted image regions and reconstructs their edge structures, a process that mutually guides both tasks and mitigates error propagation.
2. We introduce a dual prior mechanism where a restored edge map enforces structural accuracy and a predicted mask preserves uncorrupted regions, guiding the diffusion model to generate highly realistic and faithful restorations.

DPDiff achieves new state-of-the-art results on multiple blind image restoration benchmarks, both quantitatively and qualitatively, requiring only four diffusion timesteps. Furthermore, our method demonstrates strong generalization to related tasks such as deraining and watermark removal.

2 Related Work

Image Inpainting aims to reconstruct missing or corrupted regions in images, often assuming known mask locations. Traditional techniques, such as pixel propagation and patch-based synthesis [8] typically struggle with artifacts in complex scenes due to limited semantic understanding. The advent of deep learning and Convolutional Neural Networks has transformed the field by enabling powerful context modeling through encoder-decoder architectures [16,29]. Building on these advances, two major research directions have emerged: structure-oriented methods that incorporate priors like edge maps for geometric accuracy [2,3], and generative approaches that leverage powerful generative models to learn the distribution of natural imagery [21,36]. However, both paradigms are fundamentally limited by the assumption of known masks, which is often unrealistic in practical blind inpainting scenarios where the nature and extent of the degradation are unknown.

Blind Image Inpainting strives to restore an image $\hat{I} \in \mathbb{R}^{C \times H \times W}$, an estimate of a ground-truth image $I_{gt} \in \mathbb{R}^{C \times H \times W}$ from a corrupted observation $I \in \mathbb{R}^{C \times H \times W}$. The corruption is typically formulated as:

$$I = I_{gt} \odot M + N \odot (1 - M) \tag{1}$$

where both the binary corruption mask $M \in \mathbb{R}^{1 \times H \times W}$ and the noise image $N \in \mathbb{R}^{C \times H \times W}$ are unknown at inference time.

Early methods [1,19] were limited to simplistic degradations, such as filling corrupted regions with constant values or Gaussian noise, failing to restore the real-world images. Subsequent two-stage models, including VCNet [32] and InViT [7] attempted to overcome diverse real-world artifacts by first estimating a corruption mask to guide an inpainting network. However, these sequential frameworks are highly susceptible to error propagation; any inaccuracies in mask estimation directly degrade the final inpainting quality. Even a unified model that avoids explicit mask prediction, such as HCL [9], still depends on mask augmentation during training and does not exploit the expressive power of generative models or rich structural priors. These limitations highlight a persistent gap: existing blind inpainting approaches have not fully leveraged generative models and structural priors, constraining their performance on diverse real-world corruptions.

Diffusion Models, particularly denoising diffusion probabilistic models (DDPM) [10], have achieved significant progress in computer vision. By introducing noise to images through a forward process and learning to reverse this process to clean images via a reverse denoising process, DDPMs have set new benchmarks in image synthesis [10,27], super-resolution [33,34], and inpainting [21,36]. Despite their impressive performance in various domains, the potential of diffusion models in blind image inpainting remains largely unexplored. In this work, we present a diffusion-based blind inpainting framework guided by jointly learned masks and edge priors, enabling high-quality restoration in complex, real-world scenarios.

3 DPDiff Design

Our proposed DPDiff is a two-stage framework for blind image inpainting. The first stage employs an Edge and Mask Prediction (EMP) module that jointly predicts the corruption mask and reconstructs an edge map from the degraded input, leveraging the mutual benefits of spatial localization and structural understanding. In the second stage, a Diffusion-based Restoration Module (DRM) utilizes both the predicted mask and the restored edge map as guidance. This design enables semantically coherent inpainting while strictly preserving uncorrupted regions. The complete architecture is illustrated in Fig. 1.

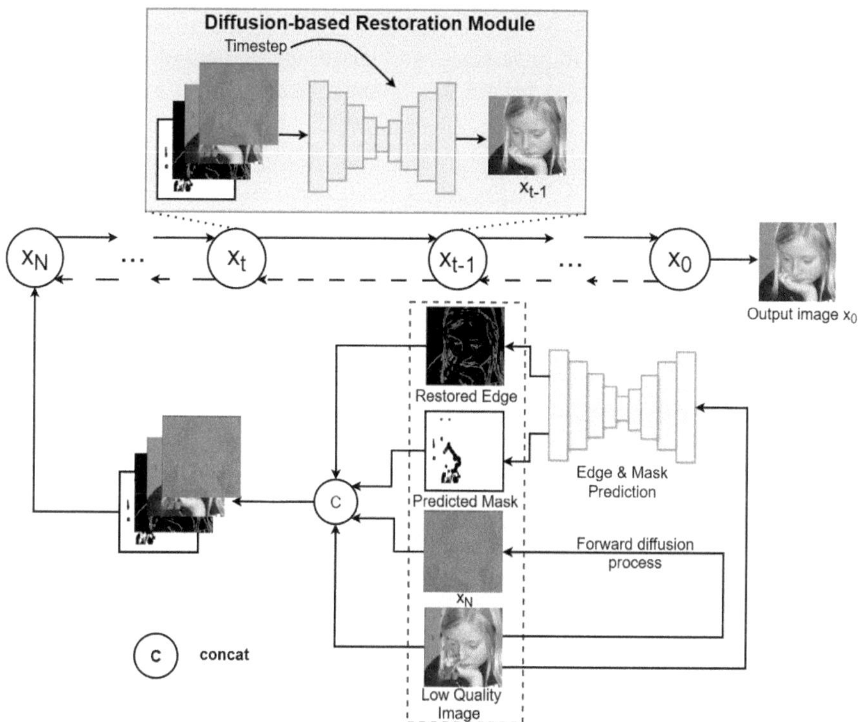

Fig. 1. Overall architecture of DPDiff. The Edge and Mask Prediction (EMP) module predicts a corruption mask and an edge map from a degraded input, which guide the Diffusion-based Restoration Module (DRM), enabling coherent inpainting while preserving uncorrupted regions.

3.1 Edge and Mask Prediction

The U-Net architecture [26] and its variants [4,22,30] are a standard for dense prediction tasks. While classic approaches formulate structural edge detection and corruption localization as separate pixel-wise classification problems, this formulation often fails in the context of blind restoration. Complex corruptions can introduce high-frequency artifacts that resemble image structures, misleading models trained in isolation for edge restoration or mask prediction.

To address this fundamental limitation, we propose a novel Edge and Mask Prediction Module (EMP), built upon a Swin-Unet [4] backbone. From an input image $I \in \mathbb{R}^{3\times H\times W}$, our module f_θ predicts a binary edge map $\hat{E} \in \{0,1\}^{H\times W}$ and a corruption mask $\hat{M} \in \{0,1\}^{H\times W}$:

$$\hat{E}, \hat{M} = f_\theta(I) \tag{2}$$

The key innovation of our approach lies in explicitly co-predicting edges and corruption masks within a shared framework, rather than treating them as independent objectives. By jointly training f_θ to segment corrupted regions and recognize structural boundaries, we encourage a synergistic representation: accurate edge detection inherently benefits from spatial awareness of corruptions, while precise localization of corrupted areas is facilitated by robust edge understanding. This bidirectional reinforcement dramatically reduces confusion between authentic structure and corruption-induced artifacts, resulting in marked improvements on both objectives, as demonstrated by our ablation studies.

3.2 Diffusion-Based Restoration Module

Diffusion models have demonstrated impressive perceptual quality in image restoration, but often at the expense of faithfulness [33,34]. To address this phenomenon, we introduce a novel dual-conditioning framework for blind inpainting that explicitly separates spatial and structural guidance. Our Diffusion-based Restoration Module (DRM) conditions the reverse diffusion process on two predicted priors: a segmentation mask indicating *where* content is missing, and an edge map specifying *what* structure should be synthesized. This enables semantically coherent generation while strictly preserving uncorrupted regions.

Forward Process. To ensure efficient sampling without loss of performance, we adopt the ResShift scheduler [34] and inject Gaussian noise into the corrupted input y each step:

$$q(x_T|x_0, y) = \mathcal{N}(x_T; y, \kappa^2 \eta_T \mathbf{I}) \tag{3}$$

where the variance sequence $\{\eta_t\}_{t=1}^T$ increases monotonically from 0 to 1, κ controls the noise variance. All operations are carried out in pixel space, which our ablation studies show better preserve uncorrupted content and reduce artifacts compared to latent-space approaches.

Reverse Process. For each denoising step, we guide the process with the predicted mask localizing the corrupted regions and the predicted edge map encoding target structures. The conditioned transition distribution is defined as:

$$p_{f_\theta}(\mathbf{x}_{t-1}|\mathbf{x}_t, y, \hat{E}, \hat{M}) = q(\mathbf{x}_{t-1}|\mathbf{x}_t, f_\theta(\mathbf{x}_t, y, \hat{E}, \hat{M}, t)) \tag{4}$$

Notably, these conditions are concatenated with $\mathbf{x}_t$ in each step. Following DALL-E 2 [24], we train our denoising network f_θ to directly predict the clean image $\hat{\mathbf{x}}_0$ (or $\hat{\mathrm{O}}$). Our denoising network f_θ is a modified U-Net from DDPM [10] that replaces the self-attention layers with Swin Transformer blocks [20] for stronger long-range reasoning. This dual-guided pixel space diffusion pipeline preserves uncorrupted regions and enforces structure-consistent inpainting.

3.3 Joint Supervision for Parameter Optimization

Our DPDiff model is trained in two stages. First, we train the Edge and Mask Prediction (EMP) module. Then, we freeze its weights and use the predicted results to guide the training of the Diffusion-based Restoration Module (DRM).

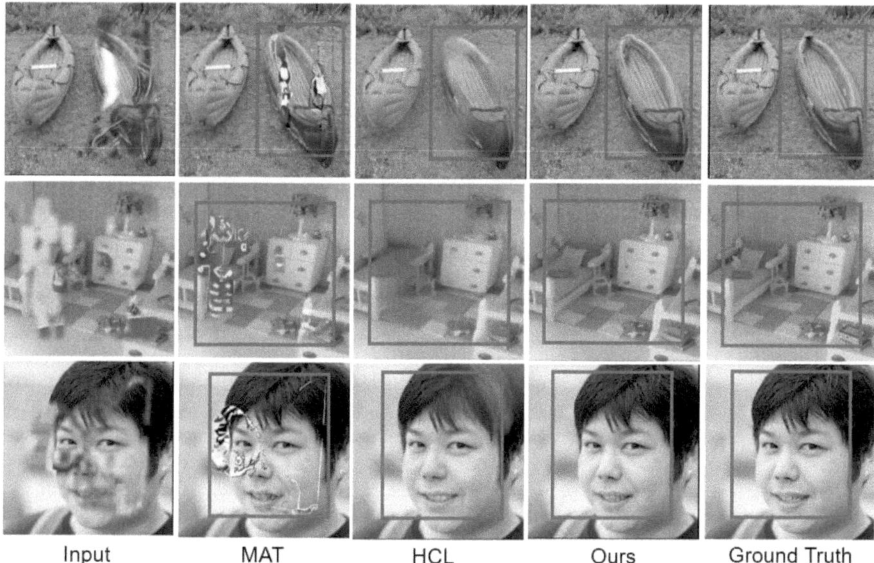

Fig. 2. Visual comparison of DPDiff against state-of-the-art methods on three randomly selected samples from the test set of three benchmark datasets.

Optimization of the EMP Module. The EMP module is optimized with a combination of two separate Binary Cross-Entropy losses:

$$\mathcal{L} = \mathcal{L}_{\text{BCE}_{\text{mask}}} + \mathcal{L}_{\text{BCE}_{\text{edge}}} \tag{5}$$

Optimization of DRM. The DRM is optimized with the loss function, which combines a content loss $\mathcal{L}_{\text{content}}$ and a perceptual loss $\mathcal{L}_{\text{per}}$:

$$\mathcal{L} = \mathcal{L}_{content} + \lambda \mathcal{L}_{per} \tag{6}$$

where $\lambda = 0.5$ is a hyperparameter to balance the two losses.

Content loss $\mathcal{L}_{content}$ is calculated as the pixel-wise distance between the predicted image and the original image :

$$\mathcal{L}_{\text{content}} = \left\| \hat{\text{O}} - \text{I}_{gt} \right\|_2^2 \tag{7}$$

Perceptual loss $\mathcal{L}_{per}$ enhances the realism of generated images by minimizing the differences in high-level feature representations:

$$\mathcal{L}_{\text{per}} = \sum_{l=1}^{L} \left\| f^{\text{vgg}}\left(\text{I}_{gt}\right) - f^{\text{vgg}}(\hat{\text{O}}) \right\|_1 \tag{8}$$

where $f^{\text{vgg}}\left(\hat{\text{O}}\right)$ and $f^{\text{vgg}}\left(\text{I}_{gt}\right)$ are the features extracted by a VGG-19 model which is pretrained on ImageNet [6].

4 Experiments

4.1 Experimental Settings

Dataset Preparation. We experiment on four datasets at 256×256 resolution: FFHQ [12], CelebA-HQ [11], ImageNet [6], and Places2 [35]. We corrupt images by filling irregular masks [16] with content from other datasets. Specifically, FFHQ is corrupted using noise images from CelebA-HQ and ImageNet, while we use ImageNet and Places2 as cross-source noise images for each other. Ground-truth edges are extracted using the Canny edge detector.

Implementation Details. Both the EMP and the DRM are trained with the AdamW [13] optimizer ($\beta_1 = 0.9, \beta_2 = 0.999$) and a cosine learning rate schedule. For the EMP module, we use a batch size of 64 and anneal the learning rate from 1×10^{-4} to 1×10^{-6}. The DRM is trained with a batch size of 12, with its learning rate decayed from 5×10^{-5} to 2×10^{-5}.

Evaluation Metrics. We evaluate restoration quality using three metrics: Peak Signal-to-Noise Ratio (PSNR), Structural Similarity (SSIM), and LPIPS. A higher PSNR and SSIM score, along with a lower LPIPS score, indicate better quality of the restored images.

Table 1. Quantitative results on three benchmark datasets from different methods. The best and second-best results are marked in **bold** and underlined.

Dataset		FFHQ			ImageNet			Places2		
Metric	Mask ratio (%)	0-20	20-40	40-60	0-20	20-40	40-60	0-20	20-40	40-60
PSNR ↑	MAT [14]	33.69	26.83	22.15	33.70	26.24	21.29	33.91	25.89	21.37
	PUT [18]	31.07	25.37	20.51	30.36	24.77	19.59	30.14	24.23	19.45
	VCNet [32]	29.86	24.51	20.51	29.13	23.39	19.42	29.66	23.19	19.18
	HCL [9]	34.79	27.98	23.54	33.91	26.40	21.80	34.11	26.20	21.66
	InViT [7]	35.01	28.27	23.99	33.95	26.60	**21.95**	34.12	**26.39**	21.66
	DPDiff (Ours)	**37.04**	**28.60**	**24.14**	**34.58**	**26.71**	21.84	**34.21**	26.27	**21.73**
SSIM ↑	MAT [14]	0.961	0.889	0.808	0.952	0.870	0.757	0.961	0.881	0.745
	PUT [18]	0.938	0.861	0.782	0.933	0.825	0.706	0.951	0.844	0.728
	VCNet [32]	0.933	0.849	0.736	0.924	0.818	0.678	0.942	0.833	0.688
	HCL [9]	0.971	0.910	0.824	0.966	0.884	0.767	0.969	0.887	0.746
	InViT [7]	**0.982**	**0.915**	**0.830**	0.969	0.886	**0.771**	0.971	0.888	0.749
	DPDiff (Ours)	0.976	0.911	0.826	**0.971**	**0.887**	0.769	**0.973**	**0.891**	**0.760**
LPIPS ↓	MAT [14]	0.025	0.074	0.151	0.023	0.106	0.235	0.029	0.111	0.259
	PUT [18]	0.049	0.113	0.252	0.057	0.137	0.295	0.051	0.141	0.289
	VCNet [32]	0.044	0.103	0.188	0.045	0.128	0.246	0.046	0.138	0.261
	HCL [9]	0.019	0.065	0.139	0.025	0.098	0.226	0.024	0.095	0.221
	InViT [7]	0.011	0.052	0.120	0.023	0.094	0.218	0.018	0.079	0.214
	DPDiff (Ours)	**0.010**	**0.040**	**0.092**	**0.017**	**0.068**	**0.160**	**0.017**	**0.069**	**0.163**

4.2 Experimental Results

Quantitative Comparison. We compare DPDiff against recent state-of-the-art methods. As shown in Table 1, our model achieves superior performance across three benchmark datasets. DPDiff outperforms all competing methods in LPIPS by a significant margin across all mask ratios, demonstrating state-of-the-art perceptual quality. Furthermore, it achieves the best PSNR on FFHQ and the best SSIM on Places2, while remaining competitive on all other metrics.

Table 2. Quantitative comparison for the image watermark removal task on the Logo30K dataset [23] in terms of PSNR, SSIM, and LPIPS. Best results are in **bold**.

Metrics	PSNR ↑	SSIM ↑	LPIPS ↓
Split then Refine [5]	41.27	0.991	0.011
DENet [28]	40.95	0.992	0.015
VCNet [32]	32.66	0.963	0.032
HCL [9]	41.88	0.992	0.007
InViT [7]	42.01	0.993	0.006
DPDiff (Ours)	**44.96**	**0.995**	**0.006**

Fig. 3. Visual comparison for image watermark removal on LOGO30K dataset [23]. Our DPDiff generates images with more accurate color reproduction and is free of the visual artifacts that affect the HCL [9].

Qualitative Comparison. To further illustrate the effectiveness of our proposed diffusion-based model, we provide a qualitative comparison of experimental results in Fig. 2. For example, in the second row of Fig. 2, our DPDiff produces semantically coherent results with minimal corruption, while competing methods show clear contextual errors. This visual comparison highlights DPDiff's superiority in both removing corruption and restoring context.

Comparison on other image restoration tasks. To assess its generalization, we fine-tuned an ImageNet-pretrained DPDiff model on two restoration

Fig. 4. Visual comparison for image deraining on Rain100H dataset [31]. Our DPDiff restores better background details compared to other methods.

tasks: watermark removal with the Logo30K dataset [23] and deraining with the Rain100H dataset [31]. As shown in Table 2 and Table 3, DPDiff outperforms existing methods on both benchmarks. Qualitative comparisons in Fig. 3 and Fig. 4 further highlight its superior performance.

Table 3. Quantitative comparison for image deraining on the Rain100H dataset [31] in terms of PSNR, SSIM, and LPIPS. Best results are in **bold**.

Metric	PSNR ↑	SSIM ↑	LPIPS ↓
RESCAN [15]	28.95	0.884	0.124
PReNet [25]	27.64	0.865	0.192
VCNet [32]	25.97	0.856	0.201
HCL [9]	28.09	0.868	0.155
InViT [7]	29.11	0.888	0.049
DPDiff (Ours)	**33.59**	**0.935**	**0.043**

4.3 Ablation Study

We conduct ablations to validate DPDiff's key design choices: joint mask/edge prediction and our pixel-space, edge-guided diffusion.

Table 4. Comparison of our mask and edge co-prediction against an edge-only baseline on the FFHQ dataset. Best results are in **bold**.

Mask ratio (%)		0-20	20-40	40-60
Acc ↑	Edge-Only	0.926	0.923	0.922
	Co-Prediction	**0.971**	**0.959**	**0.948**
F1 ↑	Edge-Only	0.350	0.288	0.224
	Co-Prediction	**0.803**	**0.688**	**0.541**

Table 5. Comparison of our mask and edge co-prediction against a mask-only baseline on the FFHQ dataset. Best results are in **bold**.

Mask ratio (%)		0–20	20–40	40–60
Acc ↑	Mask-Only	0.972	0.971	0.968
	Co-Prediction	**0.980**	**0.978**	**0.975**
F1 ↑	Mask-Only	0.979	0.976	0.972
	Co-Prediction	**0.989**	**0.983**	**0.980**
IoU ↑	Mask-Only	0.968	0.963	0.955
	Co-Prediction	**0.974**	**0.969**	**0.961**

Analysis of Edge and Mask Co-Prediction. We validate our joint prediction strategy by comparing it against two variants: one that predicts only the mask and another that predicts only the edges. As shown in Table 4 and Table 5, the co-prediction model significantly outperforms both single-task variants, demonstrating a synergistic relationship where each task aids the other.

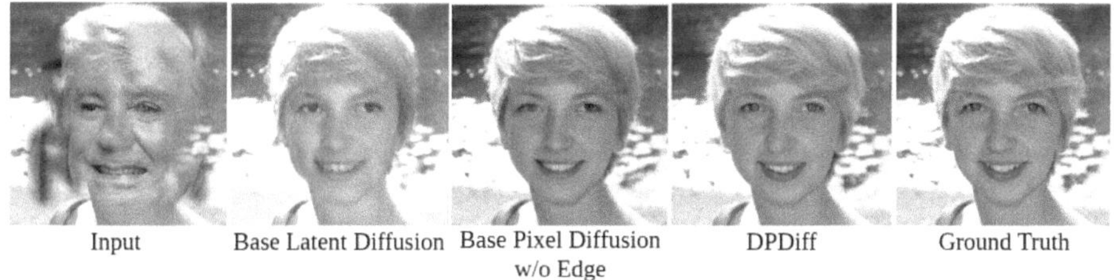

Fig. 5. Visualizing the impact of different components in our DPDiff model.

Table 6. Comparison of different model versions on the FFHQ dataset.

Mask ratio (%)	0 – 20		20 – 40		40 – 60	
Metrics	PSNR↑	SSIM↑	PSNR↑	SSIM↑	PSNR↑	SSIM↑
Base Latent Diffusion	28.48	0.866	24.81	0.821	22.93	0.717
Base Pixel Diffusion w/o Edge	35.86	0.971	27.85	0.902	23.44	0.805
DPDiff (Ours)	**37.04**	**0.976**	**28.60**	**0.911**	**24.14**	**0.826**

Impact of Autoencoder and Edge Guidance. Our ablation study (Table 6, Fig. 5) validates DPDiffn's components. We started with a latent diffusion baseline (Base Latent Diffusion). Transitioning to a pixel-space model (Base Pixel

Diffusion w/o Edge) yielded significant gains, as it avoids the autoencoder mismatch caused by complex corruption artifacts. The final addition of our edge guidance (DPDiff) yielded the largest performance improvement, highlighting its critical role in enforcing structural coherence and achieving superior restoration quality.

5 Conclusion

We proposed DPDiff, a novel diffusion-based method that achieves a new state of the art in blind image inpainting. Our framework jointly estimates corruption masks and restores structural edges. The final synthesis is governed by a dual-guidance mechanism that uses the restored edge map to enforce structure and the predicted mask to preserve content in uncorrupted regions. Our quantitative and qualitative experiments on multiple benchmarks show that DPDiff significantly outperforms existing approaches in both fidelity and perceptual quality, all while requiring only four diffusion timesteps. The performance of DPDiff motivates future work centered on model generalization. A key objective is to evolve our dual-guidance system into a universal restoration framework, with the aim of creating a single model capable of robustly detecting and repairing corrupted regions across any image type it encounters, a crucial and persistent challenge in the field of image restoration.

Acknowledgment. We acknowledge Ho Chi Minh City University of Technology (HCMUT), VNU-HCM for supporting this study.

References

1. Cai, N., Su, Z., Lin, Z., Wang, H., Yang, Z., Ling, B.W.-K.: Blind inpainting using the fully convolutional neural network. Vis. Comput. **33**(2), 249–261 (2015). https://doi.org/10.1007/s00371-015-1190-z
2. Cao, C., Dong, Q., Fu, Y.: Zits++: Image inpainting by improving the incremental transformer on structural priors. IEEE Trans. Pattern Anal. Mach. Intell. **45**, 12667–12684 (2022)
3. Cao, C., Fu, Y.: Learning a sketch tensor space for image inpainting of man-made scenes. IEEE International Conf. on Computer Vision (ICCV), pp. 14489–14498 (2021)
4. Cao, H., Wang, Y., Chen, J., Jiang, D., Zhang, X., Tian, Q., Wang, M.: Swin-unet: Unet-like pure transformer for medical image segmentation. In: Proceedings of the European Conference on Computer Vision Workshops (ECCVW) (2022)
5. Cun, X., Pun, C.M.: Split then refine: Stacked attention-guided resunets for blind single image visible watermark removal. In: AAAI Conf. on Artificial Intelligence (2020)
6. Deng, J., Dong, W., Socher, R., Li, L.J., Li, K., Fei-Fei, L.: Imagenet: a large-scale hierarchical image database. In: 2009 IEEE Conference on Computer Vision and Pattern Recognition, pp. 248–255 (2009)

7. Du, Y., Liu, H., He, S., Chen, S.: Invit: gan inversion-based vision transformer for blind image inpainting. IEEE Access **12**, 129956–129965 (2024)
8. Efros, A.A., Freeman, W.T.: Image quilting for texture synthesis and transfer. Proceedings of the 28th Annual Conference on Computer Graphics and Interactive Techniques (2001)
9. Feng, X., Xu, Y., Lu, G., Pei, W.: Hierarchical contrastive learning for pattern-generalizable image corruption detection. In: IEEE International Conf. on Computer Vision (ICCV), pp. 12076–12085 (2023)
10. Ho, J., Jain, A., Abbeel, P.: Denoising diffusion probabilistic models. arXiv preprint arxiv:2006.11239 (2020)
11. Karras, T., Aila, T., Laine, S., Lehtinen, J.: Progressive growing of gans for improved quality, stability, and variation (2018)
12. Karras, T., Laine, S., Aila, T.: A style-based generator architecture for generative adversarial networks. In: IEEE Conference on Computer Vision and Pattern Recognition (CVPR), pp. 4396–4405 (2019)
13. Kingma, D.P., Ba, J.: Adam: a method for stochastic optimization. CoRR abs/1412.6980 (2014)
14. Li, W., Lin, Z., Zhou, K., Qi, L., Wang, Y., Jia, J.: Mat: Mask-aware transformer for large hole image inpainting. In: IEEE Conference on Computer Vision and Pattern Recognition (CVPR), pp. 10748–10758 (2022)
15. Li, X., Wu, J., Lin, Z., Liu, H., Zha, H.: Recurrent squeeze-and-excitation context aggregation net for single image deraining. ArXiv abs/1807.05698 (2018)
16. Liu, G., Reda, F.A., Shih, K.J., Wang, T.C., Tao, A., Catanzaro, B.: Image inpainting for irregular holes using partial convolutions. In: European Conference on Computer Vision (2018)
17. Liu, H., Wang, Y., Qian, B., Wang, M., Rui, Y.: Structure matters: Tackling the semantic discrepancy in diffusion models for image inpainting. In: IEEE Conference on Computer Vision and Pattern Recognition (CVPR), pp. 8038–8047 (2024)
18. Liu, Q., et al.: Transformer based pluralistic image completion with reduced information loss. IEEE Trans. Pattern Anal. Mach. Intell. **46**, 6652–6668 (2024)
19. Liu, Y., shan Pan, J., Su, Z.: Deep blind image inpainting. ArXiv abs/1712.09078 (2017)
20. Liu, Z., Lin, Y., Cao, Y., Hu, H., Wei, Y., Zhang, Z., Lin, S., Guo, B.: Swin transformer: Hierarchical vision transformer using shifted windows. In: IEEE International Conf. on Computer Vision (ICCV) (2021)
21. Lugmayr, A., Danelljan, M., Romero, A., Yu, F., Timofte, R., Gool, L.V.: Repaint: Inpainting using denoising diffusion probabilistic models (2022). https://arxiv.org/abs/2201.09865
22. Ma, J., Li, F., Wang, B.: U-mamba: Enhancing long-range dependency for biomedical image segmentation. arXiv preprint arXiv:2401.04722 (2024)
23. Niu, L., Zhao, X., Zhang, B., Zhang, L.: Fine-grained visible watermark removal. IEEE International Conf. on Computer Vision (ICCV), pp. 12724–12733 (2023)
24. Ramesh, A., Dhariwal, P., Nichol, A., Chu, C., Chen, M.: Hierarchical text-conditional image generation with clip latents. ArXiv abs/2204.06125 (2022)
25. Ren, D., Zuo, W., Hu, Q., Zhu, P.F., Meng, D.: Progressive image deraining networks: A better and simpler baseline. In: IEEE Conference on Computer Vision and Pattern Recognition (CVPR), pp. 3932–3941 (2019)
26. Ronneberger, O., Fischer, P., Brox, T.: U-net: Convolutional networks for biomedical image segmentation. ArXiv abs/1505.04597 (2015)

27. Song, Y., Sohl-Dickstein, J., Kingma, D.P., Kumar, A., Ermon, S., Poole, B.: Score-based generative modeling through stochastic differential equations (2021). https://arxiv.org/abs/2011.13456
28. Sun, R., Su, Y., Wu, Q.: Denet: Disentangled embedding network for visible watermark removal. In: AAAI Conf. on Artificial Intelligence (2023)
29. Suvorov, R., et al.: Resolution-robust large mask inpainting with fourier convolutions (2021). https://arxiv.org/abs/2109.07161
30. Wang, Z., Zheng, J.Q., Zhang, Y., Cui, G., Li, L.: Mamba-unet: Unet-like pure visual mamba for medical image segmentation. arXiv preprint arXiv:2402.05079 (2024)
31. Yang, W., Tan, R.T., Feng, J., Liu, J., Guo, Z., Yan, S.: Deep joint rain detection and removal from a single image. In: 2017 IEEE Conference on Computer Vision and Pattern Recognition (CVPR), pp. 1685–1694 (2016)
32. Yi Wang, Ying-Cong Chen, X.T., Jia, J.: Vcnet: A robust approach to blind image inpainting. In: European Conference on Computer Vision, pp. 752–768. Springer (2020)
33. Yue, Z., Loy, C.C.: Difface: blind face restoration with diffused error contraction. IEEE Trans. Pattern Anal. Mach. Intell. **46**, 9991–10004 (2022)
34. Yue, Z., Wang, J., Loy, C.C.: Efficient diffusion model for image restoration by residual shifting. IEEE Trans. Pattern Anal. Mach. Intell. **47**, 116–130 (2024)
35. Zhou, B., Lapedriza, A., Khosla, A., Oliva, A., Torralba, A.: Places: a 10 million image database for scene recognition. IEEE Trans. Pattern Anal. Mach. Intell. (2017)
36. Zhu, S., Fang, P., Zhu, C., Zhao, Z., Xu, Q., Xue, H.: Text image inpainting via global structure-guided diffusion models. ArXiv abs/2401.14832 (2024)

AFC-Net: Attention-Guided Multi-backbone Deep Fusion for Grape Leaf Disease Classification

Hoang-Tu Vo(✉), Nhon Nguyen Thien, Kheo Chau Mui, Huan Lam Le, Phuc Pham Tien, Hieu Nguyen Trung, and Vuong Nguyen Phuc

Information Technology Department, FPT University, Cantho city, Vietnam
{TuVH6,NhonNT9,KheoCM,HuanLL,PhucPT10,HieuNT239,VuongNP}@fe.edu.vn

Abstract. Grape leaf diseases pose a significant threat to vineyard productivity and quality, underscoring the importance of early and accurate diagnosis. This paper introduces AFC-Net, an **A**ttention-Guided **F**usion **C**onvolutional **Net**work designed to enhance classification performance through the integration of multiple backbone architectures. Our model combines ResNet50, EfficientNetB0, and MobileNetV2 to extract various and complementary features from input images. These features are fused using an attention-based fusion mechanism that dynamically learns the contribution weights (α_1, α_2, α_3) for each backbone, allowing the model to emphasize the most informative representations. We evaluated our approach in the Grape disease dataset, which includes four classes: Black Rot, ESCA, Healthy, and Leaf Blight. AFC-Net achieves a classification accuracy of 99.83%, with a macro-averaged F1-score of 99.84%. Notably, the model attains perfect F1-scores for both Healthy and Leaf Blight classes, demonstrating exceptional robustness across categories. To enhance model transparency, we employ Grad-CAM to visualize class-discriminative regions, providing valuable insights into the model's decision-making process. These results highlight AFC-Net as a promising solution for real-world grape disease detection, contributing to the advancement of precision agriculture.

Keywords: Grape leaf disease · Deep learning · Attention mechanism · Multi-backbone fusion · Grad-CAM visualization

1 Introduction

Grapes are an economically important fruit crop, yet their productivity is threatened by leaf diseases such as Black Rot, ESCA, and Leaf Blight, which reduce both yield and quality. Early and accurate disease identification is essential for effective management and sustainable production. Traditional expert-based inspection is time-consuming, subjective, and impractical for large-scale monitoring. Recent advances in deep learning, particularly convolutional neural networks (CNNs), have enabled automated and accurate plant disease classification. However, most CNN models rely on a single backbone and rarely integrate attention

T. T. Quan et al. (Eds.): MIWAI 2025, LNAI 16353, pp. 255–266, 2026.
https://doi.org/10.1007/978-981-95-4957-3_21

mechanisms, limiting their ability to capture complementary features or focus on subtle disease symptoms. To address these limitations, we propose AFC-Net, a novel deep learning architecture that integrates multiple backbone networks such as ResNet50, EfficientNetB0, and MobileNetV2 through a trainable attention-based fusion mechanism. Each backbone contributes unique feature representations, which are adaptively weighted by attention coefficients to emphasize more informative pathways during the classification process. The fused representation is then passed through a lightweight classifier to yield the final prediction. Additionally, we employ Grad-CAM to provide interpretable visual explanations, enhancing model transparency and trustworthiness for end-users. Extensive experiments conducted on the grape leaf disease dataset demonstrate that AFC-Net achieves a classification accuracy of 99.83%, outperforming several state-of-the-art baselines. The proposed model also maintains a high macro F1-score of 99.84%, indicating its robustness across all disease classes. The contributions of this paper are summarized as follows:

- We propose AFC-Net, a novel attention-guided multi-backbone fusion network for grape leaf disease classification.
- We introduce a trainable attention mechanism to adaptively integrate features from diverse backbone networks.
- We conduct extensive evaluations on a real-world dataset and demonstrate superior performance compared to existing models.
- We provide Grad-CAM-based visual explanations to enhance the interpretability and transparency of our model.

2 Related Works

In recent years, deep learning (DL) has become a leading approach for automated plant disease classification. Traditional image processing techniques, which rely on handcrafted features such as shape, texture, and color [1,2] have shown limitations in real-world scenarios due to their sensitivity to lighting conditions, background noise, and scale variations. As a result, CNNs have become the preferred choice due to their ability to automatically learn hierarchical feature representations [3,4]. Several studies have employed standard CNN architectures for leaf disease recognition. Sladojevic et al. [5] applied AlexNet for plant disease detection using a curated leaf dataset. Ferentinos [6] compared multiple CNNs (AlexNet, GoogLeNet, and VGGNet) and demonstrated that deep CNNs outperform traditional classifiers in crop disease classification. Too et al. [7] evaluated the performance of transfer learning with several pretrained CNN models including ResNet, DenseNet, and Inception for plant disease identification, showing substantial improvements in accuracy with proper fine-tuning. Due to the scarcity of large annotated datasets in agriculture, transfer learning has been widely adopted. Brahimi et al. [8] demonstrated the effectiveness of pre-trained networks on plant leaf disease classification. Mohanty et al. [9] classified

26 diseases across 14 crop species using the AlexNet and GoogleNet architectures pretrained on ImageNet. Lightweight models such as MobileNet [10] and EfficientNet [11] have also been explored for deployment on mobile or embedded platforms [12,13].To enhance feature localization and model interpretability, attention mechanisms have been integrated into CNNs. Bhujel et al. [14] introduced a spatial-channel attention module to focus on disease-relevant leaf regions. Gao et al. [15] proposed a dual-attention fusion model that improved feature extraction in crop diseases. These methods demonstrate the effectiveness of attention in guiding the model to prioritize critical regions, leading to better diagnostic performance [16,17]. However, most attention-based approaches focus on single-backbone networks and do not explore fusion across diverse CNN architectures. Ensemble learning has emerged as a powerful strategy in plant disease classification, offering improved generalization and robustness over individual models. By combining the predictions of multiple base learners, ensemble methods such as bagging, boosting, and stacking can mitigate overfitting and exploit the strengths of diverse models. Several studies have demonstrated the effectiveness of ensemble approaches in agricultural image analysis [18,19]. Nonetheless, these approaches often lack a learnable fusion mechanism to adaptively weigh the contributions of each model. In recent years, grape leaf disease classification has attracted significant attention due to its importance in ensuring grapevine health and vineyard productivity. Deep learning models, particularly convolutional neural networks (CNNs), have demonstrated strong performance in this domain [20,21]. In recent years, grape leaf disease classification has attracted significant attention due to its importance in ensuring grapevine health and vineyard productivity. Deep learning models, particularly CNNs, have demonstrated strong performance in this domain [20,21].Most existing models rely on a single backbone or simple output averaging, limiting the use of complementary CNN features. Attention-based multi-model fusion remains underexplored in plant disease research. To bridge this gap, we propose AFC-Net, which fuses ResNet50, EfficientNetB0, and MobileNetV2 via a learnable Attention Fusion Controller for robust grape leaf disease classification. Moreover, while interpretability methods such as CAM and Grad-CAM have been applied in this field [22,23], they are often limited to single networks.

In summary, although existing approaches have shown promising results using deep CNNs and attention mechanisms, most of them rely on a single backbone, limiting their ability to extract diverse features. Moreover, few studies have investigated learnable attention-based fusion strategies across multiple CNN streams. This gap motivates the design of our proposed **AFC-Net**, which combines ResNet50, EfficientNetB0, and MobileNetV2 using an attention-guided fusion controller to achieve superior performance in grape leaf disease classification.

3 Data Collection and Preparation

To evaluate the effectiveness of the proposed AFC-Net model, we conducted experiments on a publicly available grape leaf disease dataset [24]. The dataset comprises a total of 9,027 RGB images of grapevine leaves, categorized into four classes. Each image contains clear visual characteristics of either a specific disease or a healthy leaf, enabling accurate classification. The dataset is divided into three non-overlapping subsets: a training set of 5,779 images, a validation set of 1,443 images, and a test set of 1,805 images. The class distribution within each subset is approximately balanced to ensure unbiased training and evaluation. Specifically, the training set contains 1,511 images of Black Rot, 1,536 of ESCA, 1,354 of Healthy leaves, and 1,378 of Leaf Blight. The validation set includes 377 images of Black Rot, 384 of ESCA, 338 of Healthy, and 344 of Leaf Blight. The test set consists of 472 Black Rot, 480 ESCA, 423 Healthy, and 430 Leaf Blight samples. All images were resized to a fixed resolution of 224×224 pixels to ensure compatibility with standard convolutional neural network architectures. This dataset provides a challenging benchmark due to the visual similarity between certain disease classes and the natural variability in lighting, orientation, and background conditions. Figure 1 shows sample images from dataset.

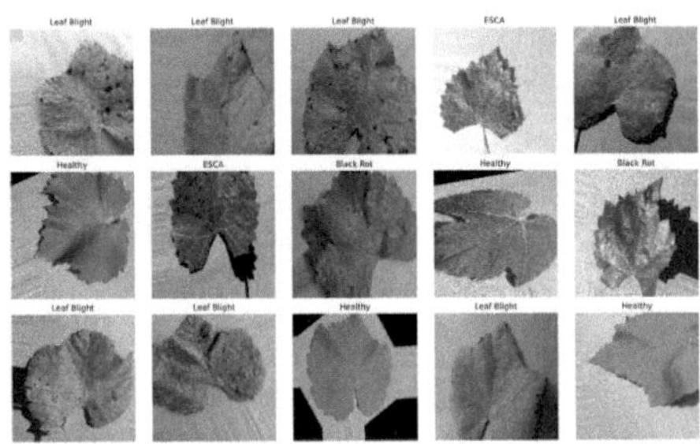

Fig. 1. Sample images from the dataset

4 Proposed Model

This section introduces AFC-Net (Attention-guided Fusion of Convolutional Network), a novel architecture designed to improve the classification accuracy of grape leaf disease recognition through multi-backbone feature fusion and attention mechanisms. The architecture of AFC-Net is illustrated in Fig. 2, highlighting the role of each backbone, the attention fusion module, and the classification path.

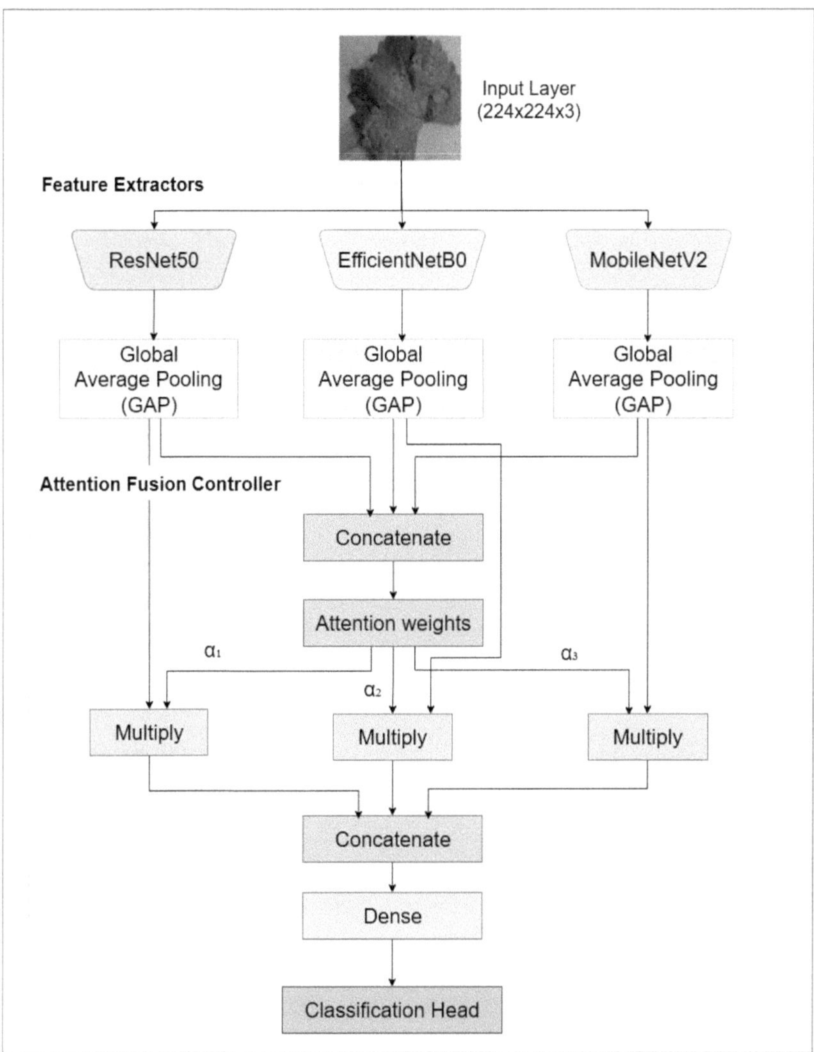

Fig. 2. Overview of the proposed AFC-Net: Attention-Guided Multi-Backbone Deep Fusion for Grape Leaf Disease Classification.

4.1 Overall Architecture

The proposed AFC-Net integrates multiple pre-trained convolutional neural networks as parallel backbone encoders to extract complementary visual features. Specifically, ResNet50, EfficientNetB0, and MobileNetV2 are employed due to their proven performance and architectural diversity. These backbones are initialized with ImageNet weights and truncated at their final convolutional layers to serve as frozen or fine-tuned feature extractors, depending on the experiment setup. Each backbone processes the same input image and outputs high-level feature maps with varying representations. To preserve spatial context and enhance semantic richness, we apply a Global Average Pooling (GAP) layer to each feature stream, yielding three feature vectors corresponding to the respective backbones.

Let $x \in \mathbb{R}^{H \times W \times C}$ be the input RGB image. The image is passed through three different CNN backbones:

$$f_1(x) = \text{ResNet50}(x) \in \mathbb{R}^{h_1 \times w_1 \times c_1} \tag{1}$$

$$f_2(x) = \text{EfficientNetB0}(x) \in \mathbb{R}^{h_2 \times w_2 \times c_2} \tag{2}$$

$$f_3(x) = \text{MobileNetV2}(x) \in \mathbb{R}^{h_3 \times w_3 \times c_3} \tag{3}$$

Each output feature map is then passed through a Global Average Pooling (GAP) operation to obtain fixed-length feature vectors:

$$F_1 = \text{GAP}(f_1(x)) \in \mathbb{R}^{c_1} \tag{4}$$

$$F_2 = \text{GAP}(f_2(x)) \in \mathbb{R}^{c_2} \tag{5}$$

$$F_3 = \text{GAP}(f_3(x)) \in \mathbb{R}^{c_3} \tag{6}$$

4.2 Attention-Based Fusion Module

To effectively combine the extracted features, we introduce an attention-guided fusion strategy. Inspired by soft attention mechanisms, each feature vector is passed through a shared fully connected layer followed by a trainable scalar attention weight α_i $(i = 1, 2, 3)$. These weights are normalized using a softmax operation:

$$\alpha_i = \frac{e^{w_i}}{\sum_{j=1}^{3} e^{w_j}}, \quad i = 1, 2, 3 \tag{7}$$

where w_i denotes the raw weight parameter for the ith backbone. The final fused feature representation F_{fused} is computed as:

$$F_{\text{fused}} = \alpha_1 F_1 + \alpha_2 F_2 + \alpha_3 F_3 \tag{8}$$

This attention-based mechanism allows the model to learn which backbone features are more informative for each specific class and image.

4.3 Classification Head

The fused feature vector F_{fused} is passed through a fully connected classification head comprising Batch Normalization, Dropout for regularization, and a final Dense layer with softmax activation to predict the class probabilities over four grape leaf categories. After the attention-weighted fusion, the resulting feature vector $F_{\text{fused}} \in \mathbb{R}^d$ is passed through a sequence of layers to produce the final prediction. First, batch normalization is applied to stabilize and accelerate training:

$$F_{\text{norm}} = \text{BatchNorm}(F_{\text{fused}})$$

Then, dropout is used to reduce overfitting by randomly deactivating a portion of neurons during training:

$$F_{\text{drop}} = \text{Dropout}(F_{\text{norm}}, p)$$

Next, a fully connected (dense) layer with weights $W \in \mathbb{R}^{4\times d}$ and bias $b \in \mathbb{R}^4$ projects the feature vector into a 4-dimensional output corresponding to the number of classes:

$$z = WF_{\text{drop}} + b$$

Finally, a softmax activation is applied to obtain the class probabilities:

$$\hat{y}_i = \frac{e^{z_i}}{\sum_{j=1}^{4} e^{z_j}}, \quad i = 1, 2, 3, 4$$

where $\hat{y}_i$ represents the predicted probability for class i among the four grape leaf disease categories: Black Rot, ESCA, Healthy, and Leaf Blight. During training, the model is optimized using the categorical cross-entropy loss between the predicted probabilities $\hat{y}$ and the one-hot encoded ground truth labels y:

$$\mathcal{L}_{\text{CE}} = -\sum_{i=1}^{4} y_i \log(\hat{y}_i)$$

4.4 Training and Validation Performance

Figure 3 illustrates the training and validation accuracy and loss curves over 30 epochs. As shown in the left plot, both training and validation accuracy increase steadily during the initial epochs and plateau around epoch 10, indicating rapid convergence of the model. The validation accuracy reaches its peak at epoch 29 with a value close to 99.9%, while the training accuracy also approaches 99.9%, demonstrating strong generalization and minimal overfitting. In the right plot, the training and validation losses exhibit a sharp decline during the first few epochs, followed by a slower but consistent decrease until convergence. The best validation loss is observed at epoch 28, suggesting that the model effectively minimizes the objective function on unseen data. Overall, the tight alignment

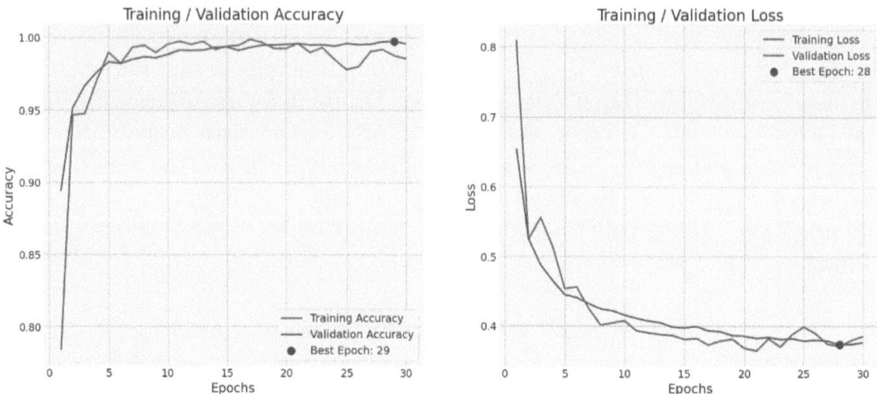

Fig. 3. Training and validation accuracy (left) and loss (right) curves over 30 epochs. The best-performing epochs are highlighted.

Table 1. Classification Report for Grape Leaf Disease Detection.

Class	Precision	Recall	F1-Score	Support
Black Rot	1.0000	0.9936	0.9968	472
ESCA	0.9938	1.0000	0.9969	480
Healthy	1.0000	1.0000	1.0000	423
Leaf Blight	1.0000	1.0000	1.0000	430
Accuracy	–	–	0.9983	1805
Macro Avg	0.9984	0.9984	0.9984	1805
Weighted Avg	0.9983	0.9983	0.9983	1805

between training and validation curves in both accuracy and loss further confirms the model's robustness and the effectiveness of the attention-guided multi-backbone fusion strategy proposed in this work.

The results in Table 1 show that AFC-Net delivers outstanding performance on grape leaf disease classification, achieving an overall accuracy of 99.83%. Precision, recall, and F1-scores are consistently above 0.998, with three classes reaching a perfect F1-score of 1.0000 and *Black Rot* achieving 0.9968. These results confirm the robustness of the proposed attention-guided multi-backbone fusion strategy and its strong generalization ability.

Figure 4 illustrates the confusion matrix of AFC-Net on 1,805 test images across four grape leaf categories. The model achieves nearly perfect classification, with all samples of *ESCA*, *Healthy*, and *Leaf Blight* correctly identified, and only 3 out of 472 *Black Rot* images misclassified as *ESCA* ($\tilde{0}$.6%). This near-perfect diagonal structure confirms the robustness of AFC-Net and the effectiveness of attention-guided multi-backbone fusion in distinguishing visually similar diseases.

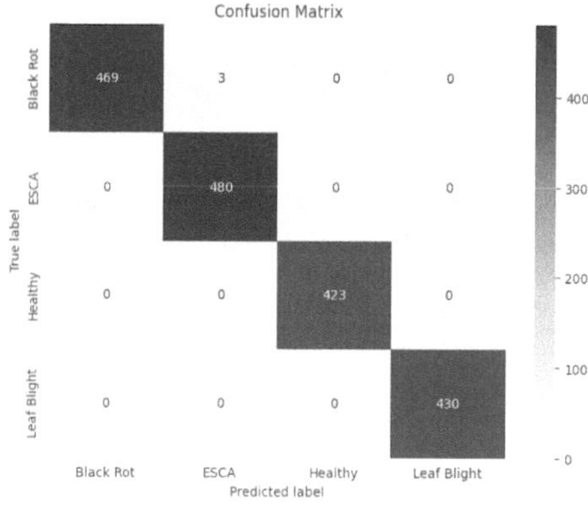

Fig. 4. Confusion matrix of the AFC-Net model on the test dataset.

4.5 Interpreting AFC-Net Decisions via Grad-CAM

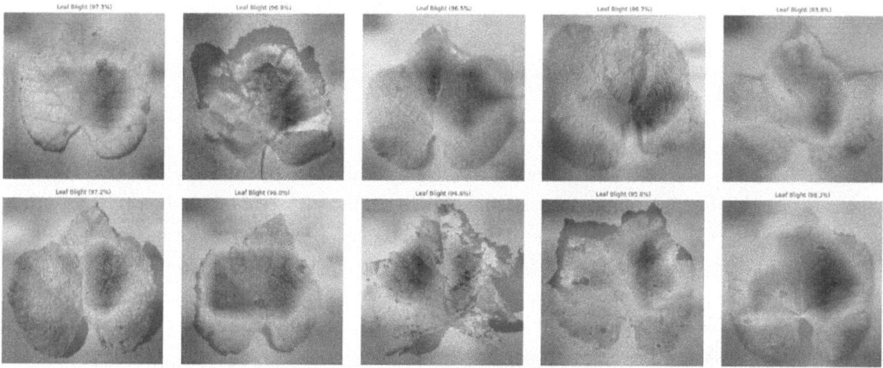

Fig. 5. Grad-CAM visualizations of correctly classified Leaf Blight samples. The red regions indicate areas with high activation contributing to the prediction. (Color figure online)

To interpret the decision-making process of the proposed AFC-Net, we applied Grad-CAM to highlight discriminative regions in input images. Figure 5 illustrates heatmaps for correctly classified Leaf Blight samples, where red and yellow areas indicate the most influential features. The model consistently attends to infected regions such as necrotic spots, discoloration, and irregular veins, aligning well with expert observations. These visualizations not only confirm the model's explainable behavior but also provide domain experts with valuable insights for precision agriculture and automated crop monitoring.

Table 2. A comparison between our proposed model and existing methods for similar issues

Ref	Dataset	# Classes	# Images	Method of Use	Accuracy
[25]	Grape Leaf diseases	4	3,885	GoogleNet	94.05%
[26]	Grape Leaf diseases	4	9,027	EfficientNet B7	98.70%
[27]	Grapevine Leaves	5	2,500	MobileNetv2	97.60%
[21]	Grape leaf diseases	4	62,286	INSE-ResNet model	99.47%
[28]	Grape leaf diseases	4	4,062	ShuffleNet V1 and V2	99.14%
[29]	Grape leaf diseases (PlantVillage dataset)	4	4,062	SVM	92.00%
[30]	Grape leaf diseases (AI challenger 2018 dataset)	7	2,850	GrapeNet Model	86.29%
[31]	Grape leaf diseases (Myanmar Grapevine Yard)	6	6,000	VGG16	98.40%
[32]	Grape Leaf diseases	4	1,619	UnitedModel	98.57%
[33]	Leaf GAN dataset	4	8,124	Xception model	98.70%
Ours	Grape Leaf diseases	4	9,027	AFC-Net (ResNet50 + EfficientNetB0 + MobileNetV2 with attention fusion)	**99.83%**

Table 2 provides a detailed comparison between the proposed AFC-Net model and previously published methods for grape leaf disease classification. Prior research has utilized datasets varying in both the number of disease classes and total image counts. For instance, the INSE-ResNet model reported an accuracy of 99.47% using a large-scale dataset comprising over 62,000 images. In contrast, AFC-Net built upon the integration of ResNet50, EfficientNetB0, MobileNetV2 achieves a superior accuracy of 99.78% on a more compact dataset containing 9,027 images across 4 disease categories. The improvement clearly validates the effectiveness of our multi-branch attention-guided fusion strategy. Specifically, the attention controller adaptively learns attention coefficients $(\alpha_1, \alpha_2, \alpha_3)$ to weight the outputs of each backbone, enhancing the model's ability to focus on the most salient features. This results in a more robust and discriminative representation for final classification.

5 Conclusion

In this paper, we introduced AFC-Net, a deep learning model that fuses ResNet50, EfficientNetB0, and MobileNetV2 through an attention-guided mechanism for grape leaf disease classification. By capturing complementary features from multiple backbones, AFC-Net achieved 99.83% accuracy with high precision, recall, and F1-score on a benchmark dataset. Grad-CAM analysis confirmed its focus on disease-relevant regions, enhancing interpretability and practical value in precision agriculture. Future work will focus on optimizing AFC-Net for mobile/edge deployment, testing on real-world field data, and exploring lightweight fusion or transformer-based designs.

References

1. Arnal Barbedo, J.G.: Digital image processing techniques for detecting, quantifying and classifying plant diseases. Springerplus **2**(1), 1–12 (2013). https://doi.org/10.1186/2193-1801-2-660
2. O'Mahony, N., et al.: Deep learning vs. traditional computer vision. In: Science and Information Conference, pp. 128–144. Springer (2019)
3. Li, Z., Liu, F., Yang, W., Peng, S., Zhou, J.: A survey of convolutional neural networks: analysis, applications, and prospects. IEEE Trans. Neural Networks Learn. Syst. **33**(12), 6999–7019 (2021)
4. Khan, A., Sohail, A., Zahoora, U., Qureshi, A.S.: A survey of the recent architectures of deep convolutional neural networks. Artif. Intell. Rev. **53**(8), 5455–5516 (2020). https://doi.org/10.1007/s10462-020-09825-6
5. Sladojevic, S., Arsenovic, M., Anderla, A., Culibrk, D., Stefanovic, D.: Deep neural networks based recognition of plant diseases by leaf image classification. Computational intelligence and neuroscience (2016)
6. Ferentinos, K.P.: Deep learning models for plant disease detection and diagnosis. Comput. Electron. Agriculture **145**, 311–318 (2018)
7. Too, E.C., Yujian, L., Njuki, S., Yingchun, H.: A comparative study of fine-tuning deep learning models for plant disease identification. Comput. Electron. Agriculture **161**, 272–279 (2019)
8. Brahimi, M., Boukhalfa, K., Moussaoui, A.: Deep learning for plant diseases: detection and saliency map visualisation. In: Human and machine learning, pp. 93–117. Springer (2017)
9. Mohanty, S.P., Hughes, D.P., Salathé, M.: Using deep learning for image-based plant disease detection. Front. Plant Sci. **7**, 1419 (2016)
10. Howard, A.G., Zhu, M., Chen, B., Kalenichenko, D., et al.: Mobilenets: efficient convolutional neural networks for mobile vision applications. arXiv preprint-arXiv:1704.04861 (2017)
11. Tan, M., Le, Q.: Efficientnet: rethinking model scaling for convolutional neural networks. International Conference on Machine Learning, pp. 6105–6114 (2019)
12. Ashwinkumar, S., Rajagopal, S., Manimaran, V., BJMTP Jegajothi. Automated plant leaf disease detection and classification using optimal mobilenet based convolutional neural networks. Materials Today: Proceedings **51**, 480–487 (2022)
13. Bi, C., Wang, J., Duan, Y., Baofeng, F., Kang, J.-R., Shi, Y.: Mobilenet based apple leaf diseases identification. Mob. Networks Appl. **27**(1), 172–180 (2022)
14. Bhujel, A., Kim, N.-E., Arulmozhi, E., Basak, J.K., Kim, H.-T.: A lightweight attention-based convolutional neural networks for tomato leaf disease classification. Agriculture **12**(2), 228 (2022)
15. Gao, R., Rong Wang, L., Feng, Q.L., Huarui, W.: Dual-branch, efficient, channel attention-based crop disease identification. Comput. Electron. Agric. **190**, 106410 (2021)
16. Lee, S.H., Goëau, H., Bonnet, P., Joly, A.: Attention-based recurrent neural network for plant disease classification. Front. Plant Sci. **11**, 601250 (2020)

17. Alirezazadeh, P., Schirrmann, M., Stolzenburg, F.: Improving deep learning-based plant disease classification with attention mechanism. Gesunde Pflanzen **75**(1), 49–59 (2023)
18. Jha, P., Dembla, D., Dubey, W.: Deep learning models for enhancing potato leaf disease prediction: implementation of transfer learning based stacking ensemble model. Multimed. Tools Appl. **83**(13), 37839–37858 (2024)
19. Patel, F., Mewada, S., Degadwala, S., Vyas, D.: Exploring transfer learning models for multi-class classification of infected date palm leaves. In: 2023 International Conference on Self Sustainable Artificial Intelligence Systems (ICSSAS), pp. 307–312. IEEE (2023)
20. Liu, B., Ding, Z., Tian, L., He, D., Li, S., Wang, H.: Grape leaf disease identification using improved deep convolutional neural networks. Front. Plant Sci. **11**, 1082 (2020)
21. Xie, X., Ma, Y., Liu, B., He, J., Li, S., Wang, H.: A deep-learning-based real-time detector for grape leaf diseases using improved convolutional neural networks. Front. Plant Sci. **11**, 751 (2020)
22. Selvaraju, R.R., Cogswell, M., Das, A., et al.: Grad-cam: visual explanations from deep networks via gradient-based localization. In: Proceedings of the IEEE International Conference on Computer Vision, pp. 618–626 (2017)
23. Karim, M.J., Goni, M.O.F., Nahiduzzaman, M., Ahsan, M., Haider, J., Kowalski, M.: Enhancing agriculture through real-time grape leaf disease classification via an edge device with a lightweight cnn architecture and grad-cam. Sci. Rep. **14**(1), 16022 (2024)
24. Pushpalama. Grape disease dataset (2023). https://www.kaggle.com/datasets/pushpalama/grape-disease
25. Javidan, S.M., Banakar, A., Vakilian, K.A., Ampatzidis, Y.: Diagnosis of grape leaf diseases using automatic k-means clustering and machine learning. Smart Agric. Technol. **3**, 100081 (2023)
26. Kaur, P., et al.: Recognition of leaf disease using hybrid convolutional neural network by applying feature reduction. Sensors **22**(2), 575 (2022)
27. Koklu, M., Unlersen, M.F., Ozkan, I.A., Fatih Aslan, M., Sabanci, K.: A cnn-svm study based on selected deep features for grapevine leaves classification. Measurement **188**, 110425 (2022)
28. Tang, Z., Yang, J., Li, Z., Qi, F.: Grape disease image classification based on lightweight convolution neural networks and channelwise attention. Comput. Electron. Agric. **178**, 105735 (2020)
29. Adeel, A., et al.: Diagnosis and recognition of grape leaf diseases: an automated system based on a novel saliency approach and canonical correlation analysis based multiple features fusion. Sustainable Comput. Inf. Syst. **24**, 100349 (2019)
30. Lin, J., et al.: Grapenet: a lightweight convolutional neural network model for identification of grape leaf diseases. Agriculture **12**(6), 887 (2022)
31. Thet, K.Z., Htwe, K.K., Thein, M.M.: Grape leaf diseases classification using convolutional neural network. In: 2020 International Conference on Advanced Information Technologies (ICAIT), pp. 147–152. IEEE (2020)
32. Ji, M., Zhang, L., Qiufeng, W.: Automatic grape leaf diseases identification via unitedmodel based on multiple convolutional neural networks. Inf. Process. Agriculture **7**(3), 418–426 (2020)
33. Liu, B., Tan, C., Li, S., He, J., Wang, H.: A data augmentation method based on generative adversarial networks for grape leaf disease identification. IEEE Access **8**, 102188–102198 (2020)

Towards Compact and Efficient Vietnamese Domain-Specific LLMs via Knowledge Distillation

Huy Hoang Le Nguyen[1] and Hiep Xuan Huynh[1,2](✉)

[1] Can Tho University, Can Tho City, Vietnam
[2] CTU Leading Research Team on Automation, artificial Intelligence, inforMation tEchnology and Digital transformation (CTU-AIMED), Can Tho City, Vietnam
{nlhhuy,hxhiep}@ctu.edu.vn

Abstract. Large language models (LLMs) with billions of parameters achieve impressive results on domain-specific tasks but are often too resource-intensive for practical deployment. Knowledge distillation (KD) is an effective technique for compressing large models. It transfers knowledge from a teacher model to a smaller student model while maintaining performance. In this work, we focus on distilling SeaLLMs, which are large language models specifically designed for Southeast Asian languages (including Vietnamese). We transfer knowledge from a 7-billion-parameter teacher model to a smaller 1.5-billion-parameter student model. Our experiments on a Vietnamese domain-specific knowledge base show that KD from the fine-tuned QLoRA 7B teacher achieves a BERTScore-F1 of 0.7217, outperforming distillation from the base 7B teacher (0.7065) and fine-tuned student models without distillation. Moreover, the distillation process reduces the model size by approximately **78%**, enabling more efficient deployment of domain-specialized LLMs. These findings demonstrate that teacher model quality critically impacts KD effectiveness and provide practical guidance for building compact, high-performance LLMs for specialized Vietnamese knowledge domains.

Keywords: LLMs · SeaLLMs · Fintetuning · Knowledge distillation · Vietnamese Domain-Specific NLP

1 Introduction

Large Language Models (LLMs) such as GPT-4 [9] and SeaLLMs [17] which are tailored for Southeast Asian languages, have achieved remarkable results across a variety of natural language processing (NLP) tasks. These models, with billions of parameters, possess the capacity to capture complex linguistic patterns and domain-specific knowledge. However, their practical deployment remains limited due to high computational costs, memory requirements, and latency issues, particularly in resource-constrained environments.

T. T. Quan et al. (Eds.): MIWAI 2025, LNAI 16353, pp. 267–278, 2026.
https://doi.org/10.1007/978-981-95-4957-3_22

This challenge becomes more pronounced in domain-specific applications, such as Vietnamese knowledge bases, where compact, efficient models are necessary for real-time and scalable deployment. While various model compression techniques have been introduced, Knowledge Distillation (KD) [3] has emerged as one of the most effective solutions. By transferring knowledge from a large teacher model to a smaller student model, KD offers a way to reduce model size while preserving most of the original performance. Recent advancements in fine-tuning techniques, including LoRA [4] and QLoRA [1], have further enhanced the effectiveness and efficiency of this process.

Nevertheless, the impact of teacher model quality—particularly when fine-tuned with advanced techniques—on distillation outcomes in low-resource, domain-specific settings remains underexplored. Specifically, in the context of Vietnamese, a language with limited large-scale annotated data and domain-specific resources, the role of fine-tuned teacher models in improving student performance has not been sufficiently investigated.

In this paper, we propose a knowledge distillation framework for compact and efficient Vietnamese domain-specific LLMs. Our method distills a 7-billion-parameter SeaLLMs teacher model, fine-tuned using QLoRA, into a 1.5-billion-parameter student model. This approach is evaluated on a Vietnamese domain-specific knowledge base to assess both accuracy and deployment efficiency.

Our experimental results demonstrate that distillation from a fine-tuned teacher significantly improves student model performance compared to distillation from a base (unfine-tuned) teacher or student fine-tuning without KD. Notably, the proposed approach reduces the model size by approximately 78% while maintaining high performance, making it suitable for real-world applications in low-resource environments.

These findings underscore the critical role of teacher model quality in successful knowledge distillation and provide practical insights into building scalable, domain-adapted LLMs for specialized Vietnamese NLP tasks.

2 Related Work

Knowledge distillation has become an essential technique in compressing large, computationally expensive models into smaller, more deployable ones without significant loss in performance. Early works on KD primarily focused on training compact models to mimic the output logits or hidden states of large teacher models, as demonstrated by Hinton et al. [3]. Subsequent developments extended KD to various architectures, including convolutional networks [11] and transformer models [5,12]. However, the rise of large language models like GPT [9], LLaMA [13], and others has introduced new challenges and opportunities for KD.

Recent research specifically addresses KD for LLMs, where teacher models contain billions of parameters and encode rich linguistic and domain-specific knowledge. Xu et al. [15] provide a comprehensive survey detailing the evolution of KD techniques applied to LLMs, emphasizing the growing importance of knowledge elicitation methods and specialized distillation algorithms to effectively transfer capabilities beyond mere output matching. The survey highlights that integrating data augmentation strategies within KD can significantly improve student performance by enriching training data context and diversity.

Several studies investigate distillation in domain-specific contexts, where the teacher model may be fine-tuned on specialized corpora before distillation. These approaches show that leveraging fine-tuned teachers often leads to better student model performance due to more focused and relevant knowledge transfer, which aligns with our work. Other works examine different fine-tuning methods such as Low-Rank Adaptation (LoRA) and quantized LoRA (QLoRA) to further optimize model size and training efficiency during distillation [2].

Recent works have developed specialized KD objectives for generative models, including sequence-level distillation approaches that leverage diverse decoding strategies [6,7] and intermediate layer matching techniques [14]. Additionally, methods like MiniLLM introduce modifications to Kullback-Leibler divergence computations specifically tailored for generative language models [2]. This development addresses the unique characteristics of language generation tasks compared to traditional classification settings.

Overall, while knowledge distillation has been extensively studied for general-purpose models and classification tasks, its application for domain-specific LLMs, especially in low-resource or regional language settings such as Vietnamese, remains underexplored. Our work contributes to filling this gap by distilling SeaLLMs, large-scale models specifically developed for Southeast Asian languages, focusing on a Vietnamese knowledge base to demonstrate the impact of teacher model quality and fine-tuning strategies on distillation effectiveness.

3 Methodology

3.1 Knowledge Distillation

Knowledge distillation is a widely adopted model compression paradigm in which knowledge from a large teacher model is transferred to a more compact student model through probability distribution matching. We hypothesize that the quality of the teacher model plays a critical role in the effectiveness of KD, particularly in domain-specific contexts where specialized knowledge representations are essential.

Our framework is guided by three key principles: (1) Domain-Adaptive Knowledge Transfer, where fine-tuned teachers capture task-specific patterns that facilitate more effective transfer; (2) Soft Target Quality, where domain-adapted logits encode richer semantic information relevant to the target domain; and (3) Representation Alignment, where specialized teachers produce distributions that are better aligned with domain-specific requirements.

To validate this framework, we compare two teacher models: the base SeaLLMs-7B and its QLoRA fine-tuned variant. Student models with 1.5 billion parameters are trained under two complementary strategies: (i) direct fine-tuning using LoRA or QLoRA, and (ii) knowledge distillation from the teacher models.

This experimental design allows for a systematic assessment of (a) the impact of teacher model quality on KD, (b) the comparative performance between KD and direct fine-tuning for compact models, and (c) the optimal strategy for developing resource-efficient Vietnamese domain-specific LLMs.

Composite Loss Function. The proposed training framework employs a composite loss function that balances supervised learning with knowledge distillation. This function addresses two critical objectives: preserving task-specific performance through ground-truth supervision, and transferring generalized representational knowledge from a teacher model to a student model. To achieve this, the total loss function integrates a cross-entropy term and a softened Kullback-Leibler (KL) divergence term.

A weighting factor $\alpha = 0.7$ is introduced to emphasize the contribution of ground-truth labels, while still maintaining substantial influence from the teacher model. Furthermore, a temperature parameter $T = 3.0$ is used to soften the predicted distributions during distillation. The total loss function is defined as:

$$L_{total} = \alpha \cdot L_{CE}(y, \hat{y}_s) + (1 - \alpha) \cdot T^2 \cdot L_{KL}(P_t \| P_s) \tag{1}$$

where, L_{CE} denotes the cross-entropy loss between the true labels y and the student model's predictions $\hat{y}_s$, while L_{KL} represents the KL divergence between the teacher and student output distributions P_t and P_s, respectively. The T^2 term compensates for the reduced gradient magnitude caused by temperature scaling.

Knowledge Distillation Loss. To facilitate knowledge transfer from the teacher model, we apply temperature scaling to the logits of both teacher and student models prior to softmax normalization. This process reveals the teacher model's relative confidence across all output classes, including incorrect ones, which is essential for learning generalizable representations.

The softened output distributions are computed as follows:

$$P_t = softmax(z_t/T), \quad P_s = \log - softmax(z_s/T) \tag{2}$$

where z_t and z_s are the logits produced by the teacher and student models, respectively. The KL divergence between these distributions is computed as:

$$KL(P_t \| P_s) = \sum_i P_{t,i} \cdot \log \left(\frac{P_{t,i}}{e^{P_{s,i}}} \right) \tag{3}$$

This loss is then scaled by T^2 to counteract the diminishing gradient effect introduced by the softening process. The result is a distillation loss that facilitates stable optimization and effective knowledge transfer.

Vocabulary Alignment Strategy. In scenarios where the teacher and student models employ different vocabulary sizes, direct comparison of their output logits may not be feasible. To address this, we introduce a vocabulary alignment strategy that ensures compatibility by truncating both teacher and student outputs to a common vocabulary size.

Specifically, we define the aligned vocabulary size as:

$$V_{aligned} = \min(V_t, V_s) \tag{4}$$

and adjust the logits accordingly:

$$\hat{z}_t = z_t[:, :, : V_{aligned}], \quad \hat{z}_s = z_s[:, :, : V_{aligned}] \tag{5}$$

This ensures that both output distributions have matching dimensionality, allowing KL divergence to be computed without error while retaining the most frequent and semantically important tokens.

Attention-Masked KL Divergence. Sequence models often include padding tokens to ensure uniform input lengths. However, these padding tokens do not carry semantic meaning and should not contribute to the distillation loss. To avoid this issue, we introduce an attention-based masking mechanism that excludes padding positions during KL divergence computation.

Each token position is associated with a binary mask indicating whether it is valid (mask $= 1$) or padding (mask $= 0$). The masked KL divergence is computed as:

$$L_{KL}^{masked} = \frac{\sum_i mask_i \cdot KL(P_{t,i} \| P_{s,i})}{\sum_i mask_i} \tag{6}$$

By normalizing the loss over the number of valid tokens, this approach ensures consistent loss scaling across sequences of varying lengths. It also prevents the student model from learning spurious patterns associated with padding tokens, leading to more effective and focused knowledge transfer.

Knowledge Distillation Algorithm. The knowledge distillation process transfers knowledge from the frozen teacher model M_t (SeaLLMs-7B) to the trainable student model M_s (SeaLLMs-1.5B). The training combines standard cross-entropy loss L_{CE} with temperature-scaled KL divergence loss L_{KD} between teacher and student outputs. Key hyperparameters include temperature $T = 3.0$, distillation weight $\alpha = 0.7$, learning rate 2×10^{-4}, and 20 training epochs. The complete procedure is detailed in Algorithm 1.

Algorithm 1. Distillation Training Procedure

Require: Teacher model M_t (SeaLLMs-7B, frozen), student model M_s (SeaLLMs-1.5B, trainable), dataset $D = \{(x, q, a)\}$, hyperparameters $\alpha = 0.7$, $T = 3.0$, learning rate $lr = 2e{-}4$, number of epochs $E = 20$

Load $M_t \leftarrow frozen\_model(checkpoint)$
Load $M_s \leftarrow trainable\_model(student\_base)$
Set $V_{aligned} \leftarrow \min(vocab\_size(M_t), vocab\_size(M_s))$
Initialize optimizer $\leftarrow AdamW(M_s.parameters(), lr)$
for $e = 1$ to E **do**
    for each batch B in $DataLoader(\mathcal{D})$ **do**
        Compute student logits: $z_s \leftarrow M_s(B.input\_ids)$
        Compute $L_{CE} \leftarrow CrossEntropy(z_s, B.labels)$
        `Without gradient:` compute teacher logits: $z_t \leftarrow M_t(B.input\_ids)$
        Truncate z_t and z_s to $V_{aligned}$
        Compute soft probabilities: $P_t \leftarrow softmax(z_t/T)$, $P_s \leftarrow$ `log_softmax`(z_s/T)
        Compute distillation loss: $L_{KD} \leftarrow T^2 \cdot KL(P_t \parallel P_s)$
        Apply attention mask: L_{KD}^{masked}
        Compute total loss: $L_{total} \leftarrow \alpha \cdot L_{CE} + (1 - \alpha) \cdot L_{KD}^{masked}$
        Backpropagate and update M_s via optimizer step
    end for
end for
return Trained student model M_s^*

3.2 Implementation Details

The training process is implemented using the Hugging Face Transformers library[1] alongside the Parameter-Efficient Fine-Tuning (PEFT) framework[2], which provides support for both LoRA and QLoRA techniques. Knowledge distillation is incorporated within the training loop through a weighted combination of the student model's loss and the distillation loss based on soft targets.

Hardware Configuration. All experiments are performed on a personal computer equipped with 64 GB of RAM and an NVIDIA GPU when available. GPU acceleration is utilized automatically to enhance training efficiency.

Training Hyperparameters. The primary hyperparameters governing both training and distillation are specified as follows: a distillation temperature T of 3.0, a loss weighting factor α of 0.7 balancing student and distillation losses, maximum input sequence length fixed at 512 tokens, a learning rate of 2×10^{-4}, batch size set to 4 with gradient accumulation over 4 steps, total number of training epochs equal to 20, a warmup phase of 100 steps, weight decay of 0.01, and early stopping with a patience of 3 epochs based on validation loss monitoring.

[1] https://huggingface.co/docs/transformers/index.

[2] https://huggingface.co/docs/peft/index.

4 Experiment

4.1 Dataset

Vietnamese Domain-Specific Knowledge Base. The dataset employed in this study is a custom Vietnamese knowledge base curated from the official support portal of Can Tho University. It consists of 669 entries structured as `(context, question, answer)` triples. The corpus primarily addresses university-related domains, including student account management, applications such as MyCTU, IT support services, and helpdesk ticketing workflows.

Data Preprocessing. All textual data were tokenized using the SeaLLMs-v3-1.5B-Chat model's tokenizer. To comply with model input constraints, sequences exceeding 512 tokens were truncated. Additionally, incomplete entries missing either the `question` or `answer` fields were excluded, resulting in the removal of 78 samples.

The Vietnamese domain-specific knowledge base used in this study is preprocessed using a standard tokenization pipeline and partitioned into training, validation, and test sets with proportions of 70%, 20%, and 10%, respectively.

Dataset Statistics. After preprocessing and filtering, the dataset comprises 591 valid samples with an average total length of 477 tokens. On average, contexts contribute the majority of tokens, while questions remain short (approximate 13 tokens) and answers moderately sized (approximate 23 tokens). Around 28% of the samples exceed the 512-token limit and are truncated for model compatibility.

Token Distribution Analysis. Figure 1 shows the distribution of total token counts per sample, revealing a bimodal pattern with peaks around 300–400 and 900–1000 tokens. The red dashed line marks the 512-token boundary, exceeded by roughly one-quarter of the data.

Figure 2 illustrates token length distributions for individual components. Contexts dominate the total length with high variability, ranging from short passages to very long technical documents. Questions are consistently short and focused, while answers fall in an intermediate range, balancing conciseness with completeness.

4.2 Evaluation

We conduct extensive experiments to evaluate the effectiveness of knowledge distillation from a 7-billion-parameter SeaLLMs teacher model to a 1.5-billion-parameter student model on a Vietnamese domain-specific knowledge base. The student models are fine-tuned using various approaches including QLoRA and LoRA to provide competitive baselines.

Model performance is assessed with widely-used natural language generation and understanding metrics: BLEU [10], ROUGE (1, 2, L) [8], and BERTScore

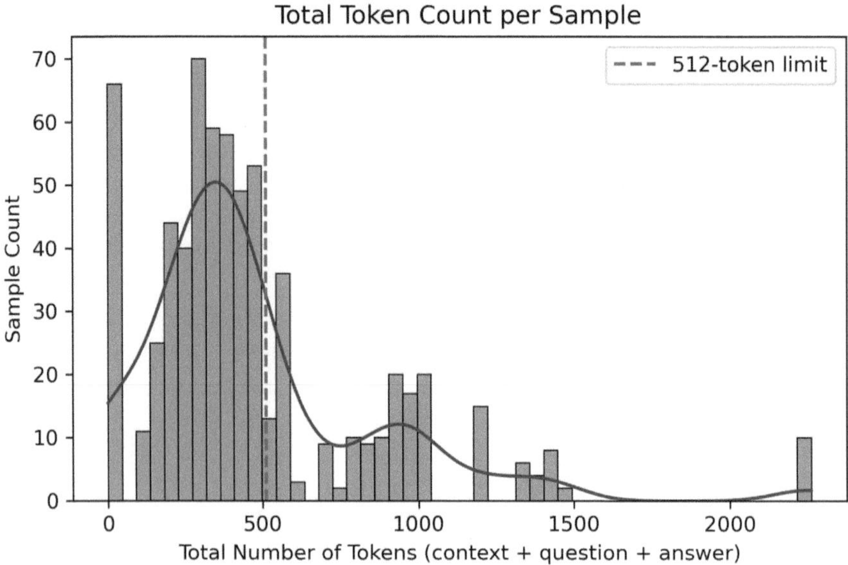

Fig. 1. Distribution of total token counts per sample, showing bimodal pattern and 512-token limit impact.

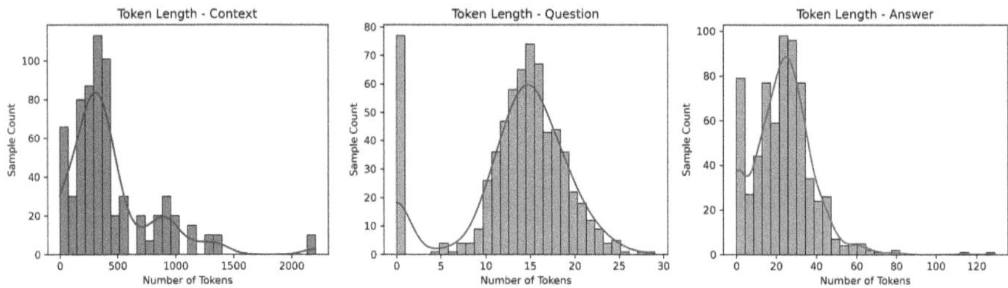

Fig. 2. Token length distributions for context, question, and answer components.

(Precision, Recall, F1) [16]. These metrics collectively capture lexical overlap, semantic similarity, and overall generation quality of the models on domain-specific tasks.

4.3 Scenario 1: Base-to-Student

Fig. 3 shows the distillation process from the base SeaLLMs-7B teacher to the 1.5B student. Training and validation losses display noticeable fluctuations, and the gap at convergence suggests limited generalization. Loss decomposition indicates that the KD loss decreases slowly, reflecting difficulties in transferring knowledge from a general-purpose teacher. Overall, the results highlight the challenges of distilling from a non-domain-adapted model.

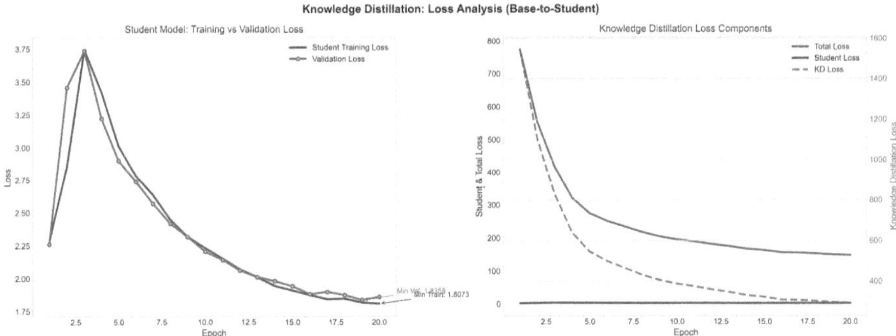

Fig. 3. Knowledge distillation training from base 7B teacher to 1.5B student. Left: convergence of training and validation losses. Right: decomposition of student and KD losses.

4.4 Scenario 2: QLoRA-to-Student

Figure 4 presents the results when distilling from the QLoRA fine-tuned teacher. In this case, both training and validation losses converge smoothly, with close alignment that indicates strong generalization. The KD loss decreases substantially, showing effective transfer of domain knowledge. Compared to Scenario 1, this setting demonstrates that a domain-adapted teacher provides more stable and efficient distillation.

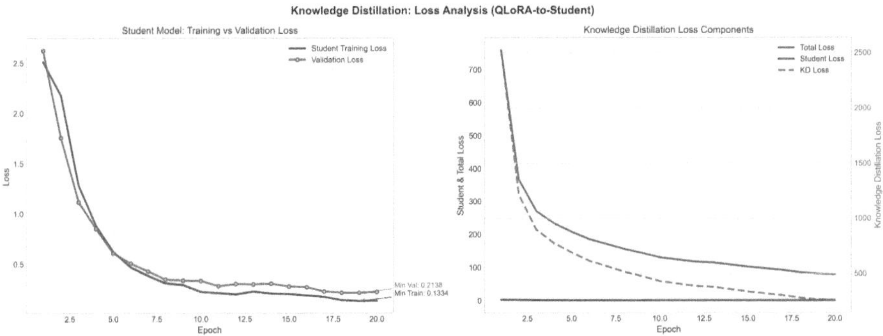

Fig. 4. Knowledge distillation training from QLoRA fine-tuned 7B teacher to 1.5B student. Left: convergence of training and validation losses. Right: decomposition of student and KD losses.

4.5 Results

Table 1 summarizes the model performance across various evaluation metrics. Distillation from the QLoRA fine-tuned 7B teacher significantly outperforms distillation from the base 7B teacher, achieving a BERTScore-F1 of 0.7217 on the domain-specific task. This marks approximately a 1.5% gain over the base teacher KD and narrows the performance gap with the fine-tuned student model (0.7330). These results highlight that fine-tuning the teacher on domain-specific data substantially improves the quality of knowledge transfer.

Table 1. Model performance on evaluation metrics.

Models	BLEU	ROUGE-1	ROUGE-2	ROUGE-L	BERTScore-P	BERTScore-R	BERTScore-F1
SeaLLMs 7B (QLoRA)	**0.1900**	**0.5672**	**0.3907**	**0.4899**	**0.7212**	0.7874	**0.7519**
SeaLLMs 7B	0.0857	0.4330	0.3056	0.3794	0.6844	**0.7882**	0.7318
SeaLLMs 1.5B (QLoRA)	0.1396	0.5036	0.3101	0.4237	0.7050	0.7652	0.7330
SeaLLMs 1.5B (LoRA)	0.1262	0.4731	0.2723	0.3833	0.6918	0.7463	0.7170
SeaLLMs 1.5B	0.0706	0.4389	0.2719	0.3583	0.6736	0.7724	0.7186
QLoRA-to-Student	0.1006	0.5157	0.2936	0.4135	0.6918	0.7565	0.7217
Base-to-Student	0.0552	0.4450	0.2467	0.3373	0.6688	0.7513	0.7065

In comparison to baselines, the student model fine-tuned independently by QLoRA or LoRA achieves competitive but slightly lower performance than the distilled student from the fine-tuned teacher, validating the benefits of the knowledge distillation process.

4.6 Discussion

The results confirm that knowledge distillation (KD) is an effective strategy for compressing large-scale models while preserving strong performance on Vietnamese domain-specific tasks. Several key insights emerge.

First, the quality of the teacher model is crucial. Distillation from a QLoRA fine-tuned teacher consistently outperforms distillation from the base teacher, underscoring the importance of domain adaptation for successful knowledge transfer.

Second, KD enables compact student models to match or surpass independently fine-tuned counterparts, demonstrating strong accuracy while substantially reducing model size.

Nonetheless, limitations remain. The dataset is relatively small (591 samples after preprocessing), with nearly 30% of examples requiring truncation due to the 512-token limit. These factors may reduce generalizability and knowledge coverage.

Future work should explore expanding the dataset, incorporating longer-context modeling, and applying KD to other low-resource Southeast Asian languages. Extensions such as multi-teacher distillation, alternative objectives, or combinations with pruning and quantization also hold promise for further efficiency gains.

Our work demonstrates that high-quality, domain-adapted teacher models significantly improve the effectiveness of knowledge distillation for compact Vietnamese LLMs and provides practical insights for developing efficient language technologies in specialized domains.

5 Conclusion

In this work, we propose an effective knowledge distillation framework to compress large SeaLLMs language models from 7 billion to 1.5 billion parameters, focusing on Vietnamese domain-specific tasks. By applying fine-tuning techniques such as QLoRA and LoRA on both teacher and student models, we demonstrate that distillation from a fine-tuned QLoRA teacher consistently improves student performance over both base-teacher distillation and direct fine-tuning. The approach produces compact models that are efficient for deployment in practical scenarios.

This study offers valuable insights and a robust methodology for building high-performing, resource-efficient Vietnamese LLMs via knowledge distillation. Future research may extend this approach to other low-resource Southeast Asian languages, integrate complementary compression methods, or refine distillation objectives to further enhance student model capabilities.

References

1. Dettmers, T., Pagnoni, A., Holtzman, A., Zettlemoyer, L.: QLoRA: efficient fine-tuning of quantized LLMs. arXiv preprint arXiv:2305.14314 (2023). https://arxiv.org/abs/2305.14314
2. Gu, Y., Dong, L., Wei, F., Huang, M.: MiniLLM: knowledge distillation of large language models. arXiv preprint arXiv:2306.08543 (2024). https://arxiv.org/abs/2306.08543
3. Hinton, G., Vinyals, O., Dean, J.: Distilling the knowledge in a neural network. arXiv preprint arXiv:1503.02531 (2015). https://arxiv.org/abs/1503.02531
4. Hu, E.J., et al.: LoRA: low-rank adaptation of large language models. arXiv preprint arXiv:2106.09685 (2021). https://arxiv.org/abs/2106.09685
5. Jiao, X., et al.: TinyBERT: distilling BERT for natural language understanding. arXiv preprint arXiv:1909.10351 (2020). https://arxiv.org/abs/1909.10351
6. Jiménez, A.G., Pérez-Ortiz, J.A., Sánchez-Martínez, F., Sánchez-Cartagena, V.M.: Beyond the mode: sequence-level distillation of multilingual translation models for low-resource language Pairs. In: Proceedings of the North American Chapter of the Association for Computational Linguistics (NAACL) (2025). https://api.semanticscholar.org/CorpusID:278479537
7. Liao, Y., Jiang, S., Li, Y., Wang, Y., Wang, Y.: Self-improvement of non-autoregressive model via sequence-level distillation. In: Proceedings of the Conference on Empirical Methods in Natural Language Processing (EMNLP) (2023). https://api.semanticscholar.org/CorpusID:266164180

8. Lin, C.Y.: ROUGE: a package for automatic evaluation of summaries. In: Text Summarization Branches Out, pp. 74–81. Association for Computational Linguistics, Barcelona, Spain (2004). https://aclanthology.org/W04-1013
9. OpenAI, Achiam, J., et al.: GPT-4 technical report. arXiv preprint arXiv:2303.08774 (2024), https://arxiv.org/abs/2303.08774
10. Papineni, K., Roukos, S., Ward, T., Zhu, W.J.: Bleu: a method for automatic evaluation of machine translation. In: Proceedings of the 40th Annual Meeting of the Association for Computational Linguistics (ACL), pp. 311–318. Association for Computational Linguistics, Philadelphia, Pennsylvania, USA (2002). https://aclanthology.org/P02-1040, https://doi.org/10.3115/1073083.1073135
11. Romero, A., Ballas, N., Ebrahimi Kahou, S., Chassang, A., Gatta, C., Bengio, Y.: FitNets: hints for thin deep nets. arXiv preprint arXiv:1412.6550 (2015). https://arxiv.org/abs/1412.6550
12. Sanh, V., Debut, L., Chaumond, J., Wolf, T.: DistilBERT, a distilled version of BERT: smaller, faster, cheaper and lighter. arXiv preprint arXiv:1910.01108 (2020). https://arxiv.org/abs/1910.01108
13. Touvron, H., et al.: LLaMA: open and efficient foundation language models. arXiv preprint arXiv:2302.13971 (2023). https://arxiv.org/abs/2302.13971
14. Wu, Y., Rezagholizadeh, M., Ghaddar, A., Haidar, M.A., Ghodsi, A.: Universal-KD: attention-based output-grounded intermediate layer knowledge distillation. In: Proceedings of the Conference on Empirical Methods in Natural Language Processing (EMNLP) (2021). https://api.semanticscholar.org/CorpusID:243865159
15. Xu, X., et al.: A survey on knowledge distillation of large language models. arXiv preprint arXiv:2402.13116 (2024). https://arxiv.org/abs/2402.13116
16. Zhang, T., Kishore, V., Wu, F., Weinberger, K.Q., Artzi, Y.: BERTScore: evaluating text generation with BERT. arXiv preprint arXiv:1904.09675 (2020). https://arxiv.org/abs/1904.09675
17. Zhang, W., et al.: SeaLLMs 3: open foundation and chat multilingual large language models for Southeast Asian Languages. arXiv preprint arXiv:2407.19672 (2024). https://arxiv.org/abs/2407.19672

Early Prediction Under Class Imbalance for a Programming Course: Feature Selection and Data Augmentation

Huy Tran[1], Quoc-Huy Le[2], Tien Vu-Van[1], Thi-Thiet Pham[2(✉)], Nguyen Huynh-Tuong[2], and Khoa D. Vo[2]

[1] Ho Chi Minh City University of Technology, Vietnam National University Ho Chi Minh City, Ho Chi Minh City, Viet Nam
tranhuy@hcmut.edu.vn

[2] Industrial University of Ho Chi Minh City, Ho Chi Minh City, Viet Nam
22636191.huy@student.iuh.edu.vn,
{phamthithiet,htnguyen,khoavo}@iuh.edu.vn

Abstract. *Predicting student performance in programming courses is critical for timely support and improved learning outcomes. We leverage LMS data from a flipped-classroom Programming Fundamentals course to predict in-lab performance from weekly pre-class and in-class assignments in a rolling, week-by-week setup with a five-level outcome. Building on published results that identify Random Forest (RF) as a strong baseline, we fix the predicting process and add two components: (i) Recursive Feature Elimination with Cross-Validation (RFECV) for compact feature selection; and (ii) training-only class-imbalance handling with SMOTE and a GAN-based augmenter. On a cohort of 786 students across four in-lab assessments, RFECV yields small, consistent gains (mainly at the extremes), while augmentation is the main driver of class-wise balance: GAN brings the most reliable macro-F1 improvements. Ablation further shows that training the generator in the full feature space outperforms pairing GAN with early pruning. Overall, the approach improves recognition of mid-performing students without degrading performance at the extremes, enabling earlier, targeted actions.*

Keywords: educational data mining · student performance prediction · learning management systems · programming education · flipped classroom · feature selection · RFECV · class imbalance · SMOTE · GAN

1 Introduction

In recent years, the rapid advancement of digital technologies has transformed the educational landscape, reshaping traditional teaching practices and unlocking new possibilities for online learning environments [15]. This transformation became even more pronounced during the COVID-19 pandemic, which accelerated the global shift toward remote education and highlighted the critical role of

T. T. Quan et al. (Eds.): MIWAI 2025, LNAI 16353, pp. 279–289, 2026.
https://doi.org/10.1007/978-981-95-4957-3_23

digital infrastructure in sustaining uninterrupted learning [4,11]. Among these infrastructures, Learning Management Systems (LMSs) emerged as essential platforms for delivering instructional content and maintaining student–teacher engagement during remote learning.

LMSs are increasingly recognized as key enablers of data-driven education [12]. In programming courses such as *Programming Fundamentals*, student learning requires substantial dedication, persistence, and independent practice. Self-study exercises, often integrated into LMS platforms, enable students to submit coding assignments multiple times and receive immediate feedback from automated grading systems. This iterative process allows learners to debug and refine their solutions autonomously, fostering a highly interactive and personalized learning experience [7]. Furthermore, the nature of programming assessments—objective, testable, and repeatable—makes them particularly suitable for data mining and predictive modeling. In recent years, machine learning methods have gained popularity in educational settings as tools for analyzing and predicting student performance based on factors such as prior academic results, attendance, and engagement [9].

Prior work established both the pedagogical setting and the predictive baseline. [14] introduced the flipped-classroom framework and dataset. Within this framework, [8] operationalized grade prediction on that dataset and benchmarked classical classifiers (with Random Forest performing best), achieving a remarkable accuracy. However, confusion-matrix analysis revealed a notable limitation: the model struggled to correctly classify students with average or moderately high performance. These students were frequently misclassified—potentially leading to insufficient support for some or unnecessary interventions for others—highlighting a critical gap in addressing learners in the intermediate performance range. This issue is compounded by the limitations of binary classification approaches commonly used in educational prediction studies [1,3], which, while effective for identifying at-risk learners, fail to account for students who are progressing but still require guidance.

Recent work on student performance prediction addresses class imbalance via oversampling, particularly the Synthetic Minority Over-sampling Technique (SMOTE) and Generative Adversarial Networks (GANs). These techniques increase the effective representation of minority categories—including mid-performing students—thereby enabling more balanced training and improving evaluation fairness. SMOTE synthesizes minority instances by interpolating among nearest neighbors rather than duplicating observations, better approximating the minority distribution [2,13,16]. GAN-based augmentation complements this approach through an adversarial generator–discriminator framework that learns to produce realistic samples from noise, with the discriminator providing a training signal that steers the generator toward data that approximates genuine observations [5,6,10,17].

Building on the LMS-based prediction framework of [8], which engineered task-level features across four paired Prelab–Inlab exercises and benchmarked classical classifiers (with Random Forest consistently outperforming alternatives), this paper does not re-propose the core task. Instead, we extend that published pipeline in two methodological directions: (i) *feature selection* via RFECV to curb dimensionality and redundancy; and (ii) *class-imbalance handling* applied to the training split only (SMOTE and GAN) to strengthen recognition of mid-performing students while preserving the five-grade granularity.

The remainder of this paper is structured as follows: Sect. 2 introduces the proposed methodology, including the prediction process and oversampling techniques that mitigate class imbalance. Section 3 presents the experimental setup, results, and discussion. Section 4 concludes with remarks and directions for future research.

2 Proposed Approach

2.1 Prediction Process

We adopt the rolling, just-in-time setup of [8]: at each stage t, the model predicts the *next* Inlab grade using only evidence available up to week t in the *current* cohort. The course provides four Prelabs (individual preparation) and four Inlabs (in-class, autograded). LMS logs are standardized into per-task summaries (e.g., attempts, best score, active minutes, late flags), and the target is a five-level outcome on the Vietnamese 10-point scale (Classes 0–4). A separate model is trained at each stage to reflect the evolving evidence set; no information from future weeks leaks into training. Figure 1 visualizes the rolling setup across the four Prelab–Inlab pairs: black arrows trace data availability, red arrows mark the current prediction step, and dotted boxes outline the training split at each stage.

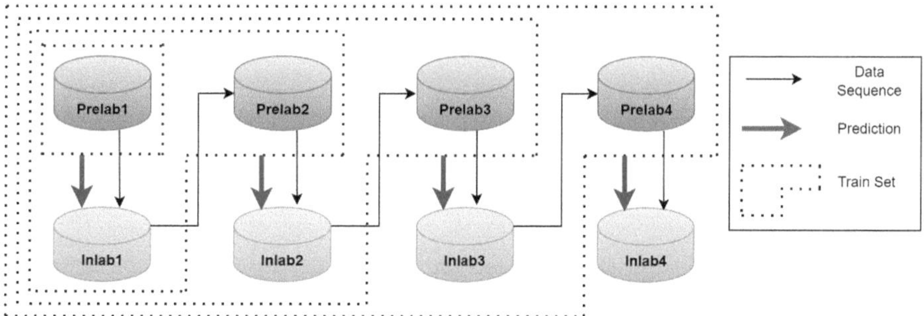

Fig. 1. Overview of the rolling prediction process. Black: data sequence; red: prediction step; dotted boxes: training set at each stage. (Color figure online)

Consistent with [8], which reports Random Forest (RF) as the top performer in comparable LMS-based grade prediction, we fix RF as the final classifier and focus on strengthening the pipeline via compact feature selection and training-only class-imbalance remedies.

2.2 Feature Selection

Concatenating week-specific raw features quickly inflates dimensionality and introduces redundancy. To obtain a compact and interpretable representation, we employ *Recursive Feature Elimination with Cross-Validation* (RFECV) applied **exclusively within the training folds**. RFECV uses a Random Forest with class-balanced weights as the base estimator for ranking features, which aligns with the downstream classifier and is robust under class imbalance.

For each stage-specific training partition with p input variables, RFECV performs stratified 5-fold cross-validation and scores candidates by **macro-F1**, our primary metric under skewed labels. Starting from the full set, the algorithm iteratively removes the least informative variables according to the RF importance profile. We use a removal step of $s{=}1$ by default—larger steps can accelerate execution with negligible loss when p is large—thus tracing a smooth performance curve as the subset size decreases. The selected dimensionality k^* maximizes mean cross-validated macro-F1; in the event of ties, we adopt the smallest such k for parsimony.

After selection, we refit RF on the k^* variables and apply the same transformation when evaluating. In practice, this yields a substantially smaller feature set while preserving—often improving—minority-class recognition and model stability.

2.3 Handling Class Imbalance

Figure 2 illustrates the grade distribution of 786 students across the Prelab and Inlab tasks. A clear disparity is observed: Class 4 dominates with approximately 600 students, while lower classes (1, 2, 3) are extremely rare, particularly Classes 1–2. Notably, the number of students in Class 0 exceeds that of Classes 1–3, with

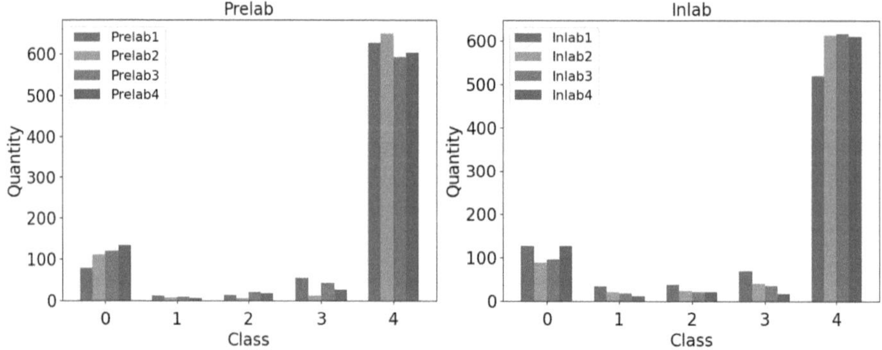

Fig. 2. Class distribution of 786 students across Prelab (left) and Inlab (right) tasks. Classes 0 and 4 dominate, while Classes 1–2 are severely underrepresented, motivating the use of augmentation methods.

more than 100 cases in each lab. This indicates a long-tailed distribution in which mid- and lower-performing groups are severely underrepresented.

Such imbalance poses a substantial challenge for predictive modeling. When the data are dominated by a few large classes (especially Class 4 and, to some extent, Class 0), models are prone to bias and often misclassify students in the intermediate groups, leading to inaccurate learning recommendations. Moreover, the label distribution skewed toward the two extremes of the 10-point scale obscures gradual improvement across grades. To address this issue, we retain the five-grade categorization and apply data augmentation techniques (SMOTE, GAN) after feature selection, thereby balancing class distribution, enhancing fairness, and improving predictive performance.

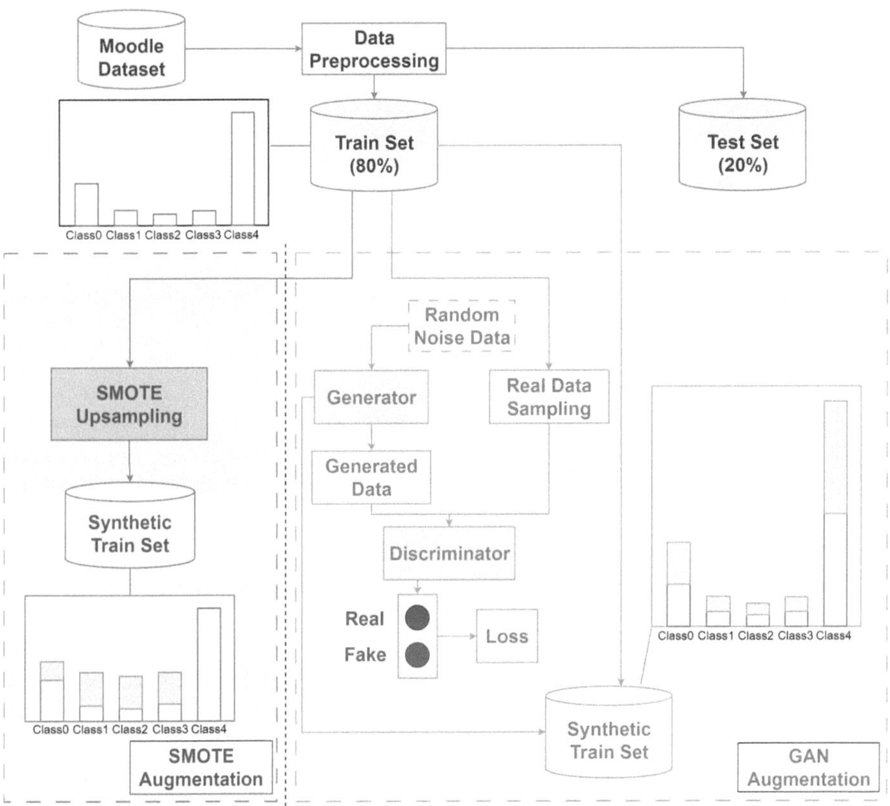

Fig. 3. Augmentation pipelines on the **80%** training split. **Left (blue)—SMOTE**: minority upsampling via interpolation among nearest neighbors yields a flatter class histogram. **Right (orange)—GAN**: a generator maps random noise to candidate samples while a discriminator distinguishes real vs. generated examples; after training, synthetic samples are drawn to form a synthetic training set while preserving overall class proportions. The held-out **20%** test split is never augmented. (Color figure online)

Figure 3 shows both augmentation paths applied to the 80% training split (the 20% test split remains untouched).

SMOTE. SMOTE synthesizes minority-class instances by interpolating between each sample and its k nearest neighbors, producing a flatter training distribution. For a minority class of size n_{minor} and a majority class of size n_{major}, we set the upsampled target

$$n_{\text{target}} = n_{\text{minor}} \left(1 + \left\lfloor \frac{n_{\text{major}}}{2\, n_{\text{minor}}} \right\rfloor\right),$$

which boosts Classes 1–3 while leaving the largest classes intact.

GAN. Following [17], a GAN is trained on real training samples and random noise; discriminator feedback steers the generator toward realistic outputs. After convergence, we draw synthetic instances up to a 1:1 ratio with the original training size while preserving overall class proportions, increasing coverage for under-represented classes without altering the course's natural grade priors.

3 Experimental Results

3.1 Experimental Setup

We conducted experiments on the LMS dataset from the *Programming Fundamentals* course at Ho Chi Minh City University of Technology (HCMUT), semester SEM-222 (academic year 2022–2023), which contains records for 786 students, each completing eight practical exercises—four Prelabs and four Inlabs. All features were standardized, and at each prediction stage the target was a five-level outcome (Classes 0–4). RF served as the final classifier. Prior to model fitting, we performed feature selection with RFECV (stratified five-fold cross-validation, macro-F1 scoring, elimination step $s=1$) to obtain a compact subset. To address class imbalance, we applied SMOTE with $k=5$ nearest neighbors and `random_state`= 42, and trained a GAN-based augmenter using the hyperparameters in Table 1; synthetic samples were then combined with the real data at up to a 1:1 ratio while preserving class proportions. Model quality was assessed with stratified five-fold cross-validation, reporting per-class F1 and macro-F1. All experiments were implemented in scikit-learn and executed on a Kaggle environment with an NVIDIA Tesla P100 GPU (16 GB VRAM).

3.2 Results

Across the four stages, coupling RF with RFECV and augmentation improves macro-F1 in three of four Inlabs, with GAN giving the strongest lifts overall: macro-F1 reaches 0.40 in Inlab 1, 0.37 in Inlab 3, and 0.44 in Inlab 4 under RFECV+GAN, while SMOTE is most competitive in Inlab 2 with 0.39 (Table 2).

Class-wise patterns mirror the imbalance profile. Under RFECV+GAN, Classes 0 and 4 remain high across stages (e.g., Class 0 rises to 0.81/0.89/0.92 and

Table 1. GAN hyperparameters

Hyperparameter	Value
lr_G	5×10^{-5}
lr_D	2×10^{-3}
Batch size	128
epochs	200
Latent dimension (z)	200
λ_{gp}	10
G_steps	3
Feature-matching weight	0.1
LR scheduler step	20
LR scheduler γ	0.8

Class 4 to 0.91/0.95/0.97 in Inlabs 1/3/4), whereas improvements for intermediate classes are selective: SMOTE notably boosts Class 3 mid-course (Inlab 2: 0.33; Inlab 3: 0.18), and GAN provides gains where coverage is sparse (e.g., Inlab 1: Class 1 to 0.12, Class 3 to 0.19; Inlab 4: Class 2 to 0.29). Outside these cases, Classes 1–2 remain challenging early in the course.

Overall, the evidence suggests that RF is a strong baseline once paired with compact representations; GAN-based augmentation delivers the most consistent macro-F1 gains (especially later in the semester), and SMOTE can be advantageous when local neighborhoods are sufficiently populated (notably Inlab 2). These patterns align with the hypothesis that non-linear generators better populate sparse regions for mid-performing students, while interpolation-based methods are most effective when minority clusters are already present.

3.3 Ablation Studies

We conduct ablations to isolate what each component contributes beyond a Random Forest (RF) backbone and to test their interaction for the target of improving minority recognition and macro-F1. Specifically, we compare (i) *feature selection* via RFECV without augmentation (RFECV), and (ii) *data augmentation*—SMOTE and a GAN-based generator. Table 3 reports class-wise and macro-F1 across the four Inlabs.

Effect of RFECV (No Augmentation). RFECV yields small yet consistent gains over the baseline on macro-F1 across all four Inlabs, with the improvements concentrated on the extreme classes (0 and 4). This suggests that removing redundant signals sharpens decision boundaries in well-separated regions. However, Classes 1–2 remain largely under-recognized, indicating that pruning alone is insufficient for minority coverage.

Effect of Augmentation. Augmentation is the primary driver of minority-class gains. Early in the course, both methods help, with GAN delivering the

Table 2. Effect of augmentation on RF (with RFECV) performance: class-wise and macro-F1 across Inlabs for None, SMOTE, and GAN. Bold indicates row-wise best.

Inlab	Class	Baseline	RFECV + SMOTE	RFECV + GAN
1	0	0.60	0.56	**0.81**
	1	0.00	0.00	**0.12**
	2	0.00	0.00	0.00
	3	0.00	0.09	**0.19**
	4	0.85	0.84	**0.91**
	macro-F1	0.29	0.30	**0.40**
5	0	0.65	0.71	**0.87**
	1	0.00	0.00	0.00
	2	0.00	0.00	0.00
	3	**0.38**	0.33	0.00
	4	0.88	0.89	**0.94**
	macro-F1	0.38	**0.39**	0.36
3	0	0.76	0.67	**0.89**
	1	0.00	0.00	0.00
	2	0.00	0.00	0.00
	3	0.00	**0.18**	0.00
	4	0.91	0.92	**0.95**
	macro-F1	0.34	0.35	**0.37**
4	0	0.71	0.70	**0.92**
	1	0.00	0.00	0.00
	2	0.00	0.18	**0.29**
	3	0.00	0.00	0.00
	4	0.90	0.89	**0.97**
	macro-F1	0.32	0.37	**0.44**

clearest lift in macro-F1 and making Classes 1–2 more detectable; mid-course, SMOTE is competitive when local neighborhoods are populated; and by the final stage, GAN again dominates with the largest overall improvements while maintaining strong performance for Class 4. In short, pruning stabilizes the representation, but synthesized samples—especially from a GAN—are what materially rebalance class-wise performance.

Surprisingly, *GAN-only* outperforms *RFECV+GAN* in three of four stages (Table 3), indicating that early pruning can remove minority-informative cues needed for synthesis; class-wise improvements concentrate exactly where coverage is sparse (Table 2). In the future, we will formalize this insight into the pipeline: train the generator in the full feature space, then project both real and synthetic data onto the RFECV-selected subset for the final RF.

Table 3. Ablation on RF: class-wise and macro-F1 across four Inlabs for Baseline, RFECV (no augmentation), SMOTE, and GAN. Best per row is bolded.

Inlab	Class	Baseline	RFECV	SMOTE	GAN
1	0	0.55	0.56	0.81	**0.87**
	1	0.00	0.00	0.12	**0.13**
	2	0.00	0.00	0.00	**0.33**
	3	0.00	0.09	0.19	**0.19**
	4	0.81	0.84	0.91	**0.92**
	macro-F1	0.29	0.30	0.40	**0.49**
2	0	0.69	0.74	0.72	**0.92**
	1	0.00	0.00	0.00	0.00
	2	0.00	0.00	0.00	0.00
	3	0.00	0.00	**0.38**	0.18
	4	0.81	**0.92**	0.90	**0.92**
	macro-F1	0.33	0.39	**0.40**	**0.40**
3	0	0.69	0.80	0.67	**0.87**
	1	0.00	0.00	0.00	0.00
	2	0.00	0.00	0.00	0.00
	3	0.00	0.00	**0.18**	0.00
	4	0.93	0.94	0.92	**0.94**
	macro-F1	0.34	0.35	0.35	**0.36**
4	0	0.70	0.75	0.75	**0.81**
	1	0.00	0.00	0.00	0.00
	2	0.00	0.00	0.22	**0.33**
	3	0.00	0.00	0.00	**0.50**
	4	0.89	0.92	0.90	**0.94**
	macro-F1	0.34	0.37	0.38	**0.52**

4 Conclusion

This study extends the LMS-based prediction framework of [8] without reintroducing the core task or dataset. Fixing Random Forest (RF) as the classifier, we contribute two methodological enhancements to the pipeline: compact feature selection via RFECV and training-only class-imbalance handling using SMOTE and a GAN-based augmenter, under a five-level outcome in a rolling, just-in-time setting across four Inlabs.

The empirical evidence supports three conclusions. First, RFECV yields small but consistent gains over the RF baseline, mainly improving performance for the two extreme classes (Classes 0 and 4), with limited impact on the harder minority classes in the middle. Second, augmentation is the primary lever for class-wise balance: macro-F1 improves in three of four stages, with GAN delivering the most consistent gains—particularly in the early and final stages of the course (Tables 2 and 3). Third, training the generator in the full feature space typically outperforms combining GAN with early feature pruning, indicating that pre-selection may remove minority-informative cues needed for effective synthesis.

This work is limited by its single-course, single-semester scope and by persistent difficulty in intermediate classes, where overlap and scarcity remain. Results are also sensitive to augmentation ratios and hyperparameters, and we did not evaluate calibration or synthetic data quality with formal metrics. Future work will extend this study in three ways. First, we will replicate the analysis across additional semesters and cohorts to test robustness and consistency. Second, we will enrich the feature set with behavioral signals (e.g., code edit sequences, time on task, IDE interaction logs) to improve nuance and accuracy. Third, we will examine the GAN component more deeply by tuning hyperparameters, evaluating the realism and coverage of synthetic data with formal metrics, and exploring conditional GANs to generate targeted, class-specific samples.

References

1. Ahmed, E.: Student performance prediction using machine learning algorithms. App. Comput. Intell. Soft Comput. **2024**(1), 4067721 (2024)
2. Alija, S., Beqiri, E., Gaafar, A., Hamoud, A.: Predicting students performance using supervised machine learning based on imbalanced dataset and wrapper feature selection. Informatica **47** (2023). https://doi.org/10.31449/inf.v47i1.4519
3. Batool, S., Rashid, J., Nisar, M.W., Kim, J., Kwon, H.Y., Hussain, A.: Educational data mining to predict students' academic performance: A survey study. Educ. Inf. Technol. **28**(1), 905–971 (2023)
4. Dhawan, S.: Online learning: a panacea in the time of Covid-19 crisis. J. Educ. Technol. Syst. **49**(1), 5–22 (2020)
5. Douzas, G., Bacao, F.: Effective data generation for imbalanced learning using conditional generative adversarial networks. Expert Syst. Appl. **91**, 464–471 (2018)
6. Engelmann, J., Lessmann, S.: Conditional Wasserstein GAN-based oversampling of tabular data for imbalanced learning. arXiv preprint arXiv:2008.09202 (2020)
7. Garcia, R., Falkner, K., Vivian, R.: Systematic literature review: self-regulated learning strategies using e-learning tools for computer science. Comput. Educ. **123**, 150–163 (2018)
8. Huy-Le, Q., et al.: Student's academic performance prediction in the programming techniques course by using machine learning methods. In: 2024 IEEE 30th International Conference on Telecommunications (ICT), pp. 1–7 (2024). https://doi.org/10.1109/ICT62760.2024.10606021
9. Ismail, L., Materwala, H., Hennebelle, A.: Comparative analysis of machine learning models for students' performance prediction. In: Antipova, T. (ed.) Advances in Digital Science, pp. 149–160. Springer International Publishing, Cham (2021)
10. Pan, T., Pedrycz, W., Yang, J., Wang, J.: An improved generative adversarial network to oversample imbalanced datasets. Eng. Appl. Artif. Intell. **132**, 107934 (2024)
11. Pokhrel, S., Chhetri, R.: A literature review on impact of Covid-19 pandemic on teaching and learning. Higher Educ. Fut. **8**(1), 133–141 (2021)

12. Saadati, Z., Zeki, C.P., Vatankhah Barenji, R.: On the development of blockchain-based learning management system as a metacognitive tool to support self-regulation learning in online higher education. Interact. Learn. Environ. **31**(5), 3148–3171 (2023)
13. Sugitha, I.P.Y.T., Bachtiar, F.A., Wicaksono, S.A.: Application of students graduation prediction model using Decision Tree C4.5 algorithm and synthetic minority oversampling technique (smote). In: 2024 Seventh International Conference on Vocational Education and Electrical Engineering (ICVEE), pp. 175–181 (2024). https://doi.org/10.1109/ICVEE63912.2024.10823806
14. Tran, H., Vu-Van, T., Le, V., Pham, H.A., Huynh Tuong, N.: Leveraging data analytics to investigate the effectiveness of flipped classroom models: a case study of practical programming teaching. Electron. J. e-Learn. **22**, 144–162 (2024). https://doi.org/10.34190/ejel.22.9.3597
15. Wang, C., Chen, X., Yu, T., Liu, Y., Jing, Y.: Education reform and change driven by digital technology: a bibliometric study from a global perspective. Hum. Soc. Sci. Commun. **11**(1), 1–17 (2024)
16. Wijayaningrum, V.N., Kirana, A., Putri, I.: Student academic performance prediction framework with feature selection and imbalanced data handling. J. Ilmiah KURSOR **12**, 123–134 (07 2024)
17. Xu, L., Skoularidou, M., Cuesta-Infante, A., Veeramachaneni, K.: Modeling tabular data using conditional GAN. Adv. Neural Info. Process. Syst. **32** (2019)

ParkiDxAI: An Explainable AI System for Parkinson's Disease Diagnosis

Huynh-Dai-Nhan Tran[1,2(✉)], Minna Isomursu[2], Manh-Hung Trinh[2,3], Tan-Nguyen Ngo[2], Gia-Hau Le[4], and Hoang-Anh Pham[5,6(✉)]

[1] University of Jyväskylä, Jyväskylä, Finland
tranhuynhdainhan25102004@gmail.com
[2] University of Oulu, Oulu, Finland
minna.isomursu@oulu.fi
[3] University of Eastern Finland, Joensuu, Finland
[4] LAB University of Applied Sciences, Lahti, Finland
[5] Ho Chi Minh City University of Technology (HCMUT), Ho Chi Minh City, Vietnam
anhpham@hcmut.edu.vn
[6] Vietnam National University Ho Chi Minh City (VNU-HCM), Ho Chi Minh City, Vietnam

Abstract. Developing trustworthy AI systems in digital health remains a challenge, particularly in terms of explainability and reliability in clinical use. We present ParkiDxAI, a web-based clinical decision support system (CDSS) for Parkinson's disease that integrates prediction, explanation, data storage, and communication of results. Using a real-world tabular dataset of 2,105 individuals with 32 variables, we benchmarked 10 machine-learning models on an independent test set. Within this intra-study comparison, CatBoost achieved the highest accuracy at 93.59%. ParkiDxAI provides dual-level explanations—global (SHAP) and local (LIME)—and quantifies explanation quality using faithfulness, fidelity, and sparsity. The system has been developed with a FastAPI backend, a MySQL database, and a React interface for scalable deployment. A small usability assessment suggested that the explanations and UI were clear and usable. Overall, ParkiDxAI aims to bridge the gap between model performance and clinical usability and can be adapted to other tabular clinical tasks.

Keywords: Parkinson's disease · Clinical Decision Support System · Explainable AI · Machine Learning

1 Introduction

Parkinson's disease (PD) is a progressive neurological condition marked by ongoing decline and a variety of symptoms. The early identification of this disease is difficult because of the absence of specific biomarkers and the symptom overlap with other neurological disorders. AI, particularly machine learning models,

T. T. Quan et al. (Eds.): MIWAI 2025, LNAI 16353, pp. 290–303, 2026.
https://doi.org/10.1007/978-981-95-4957-3_24

presents significant opportunities to enhance diagnostic precision. Recent studies exploiting speech, motor sensor, and neuroimaging data have achieved encouraging accuracy [15,25]; however, most systems still lack explainability – a key factor in building trust in clinical settings. Black-box models with ambiguous results are difficult to be widely adopted, thus promoting the development of XAI methods to clarify the contribution of each feature. However, the actual clinical performance has not been fully verified [7,23,24].

XAI is getting more and more attention in the realm of digital health to make things clearer and build trust in clinical diagnosis. For example, two recent studies by Allen et al. [3] and Chaddad et al. [7] show that SHAP and LIME improve diagnostic interpretation, but most applications have yet to be implemented in practice. Belard et al. [5] and Rammo et al. [19] also highlight the potential of XAI in decision support and remote monitoring, especially for neurological diseases such as Parkinson's. SHAP has a solid theoretical foundation and high stability, but is slow and complex to process in real time [7]; in contrast, LIME is faster and more intuitive, but the results are more volatile [3,24]. Introducing XAI into clinical practice still faces challenges in terms of usability, reliability, and how physicians interpret the results [2,10], so the system needs to be both accurate and understandable.

The increasing use of AI in healthcare has raised questions about responsibility, fairness, and ethics. Trocin et al. [23] and Vimbi et al. [24] argue that when AI systems lack transparency and accountability, this can lead to bias, inequality, and a loss of stakeholder trust, which directly affects treatment effectiveness. Many studies have proposed integrating responsible AI (RAI) principles into the development of clinical AI. For example, Yang et al. [26] propose a stakeholder-based design framework to ensure ethical considerations throughout the system lifecycle. In contrast, Ahmadi et al. [2] emphasize aligning physician trust and complying with regulatory requirements. However, in practice, the application of these principles is still limited as many systems do not meet the criteria of explainability, transparency, and fairness in the medical context. This shows the urgent need for AI systems that ensure accuracy, are socially responsible, patient-centered, consistent with professional values, and accessible to both doctors and patients.

Although AI and machine learning models have shown significant potential in assisting with the diagnosis of PD, their application in clinical practice remains limited. Many systems, despite their high performance in testing environments, have not yet been fully deployed to support clinicians in decision making, creating a gap between research results and practical applications [1]. In addition, many solutions still lack essential functions such as result storage, CDSS integration, and physician workflow-friendly interfaces [6]. These limitations highlight the urgent need for solutions that maintain high predictive performance while providing clear, reliable interpretation and can be seamlessly integrated into everyday healthcare.

Despite its potential, AI in healthcare still faces many limitations in terms of explainability and practical application. Most studies focused on accuracy with little attention paid to quantitative assessment of explainability [7,24]. Empirical comparisons between SHAP and LIME are very limited [14,16], while multimodal data integration is still not widespread [15,18]. Many new systems are still in the prototype stage, lacking clinician support functions or have not been validated by experts [1,6]. Furthermore, the lack of standardized assessment criteria for XAI in the clinical setting further emphasizes the need to develop systems that are both accurate and transparent [20].

This study introduces a web-based Clinical Decision Support System (CDSS) aimed at providing explainable diagnosis for PD, leveraging a real patient dataset that includes more than 32 features. The choice of CatBoost was based on its outstanding performance and effective integration with XAI. The architecture consists of a FastAPI backend paired with a React-TypeScript frontend, which guarantees real-time interoperability and ease of extensibility. The evaluation of explainability was performed using metrics such as *faithfulness*, *fidelity*, and *sparsity*, integrating insights from medical expert surveys and AI to confirm clarity, reliability, and clinical applicability.

2 Materials and Methods

2.1 Research Design

This study applies the DSR methodology [17] to develop an explainable AI-based CDSS for Parkinson's diagnosis. The process follows DSR steps: identifying the clinical challenge, defining the need for explainable CDSS, and developing the artifact using SHAP, LIME, and the best-performing model. Key design decisions—such as using SHAP over Explainable Boosting Machine (EBM) and sending auto-diagnosis emails—are well substantiated. The system is demonstrated via REST APIs and evaluated through explainability metrics (Fidelity, Faithfulness, Sparsity) and user feedback.

2.2 Dataset Description

This study used a dataset published by Rabie El Kharoua [11], including health information for 2105 individuals and 32 attributes in total. This dataset contains both people with and without Parkinson's disease and is designed for research, study, and teaching purposes. The features cover many aspects: demographic details (age, gender, ethnicity, education level), lifestyle factors (BMI, smoking, alcohol consumption, physical activity, diet quality, sleep quality), medical history (family history of Parkinson's, traumatic brain injury, hypertension, diabetes, depression, stroke), clinical measurements (systolic and diastolic blood pressure, total cholesterol, LDL, HDL, triglycerides), cognitive and functional assessments (UPDRS, Montreal Cognitive Assessment (MoCA), Functional Assessment), and specific symptoms (tremor, rigidity, bradykinesia, postural instability, speech problems, sleep disorders, constipation). The *Diagnosis* attribute indicates the presence of Parkinson's disease (0: No PD, 1: PD), while the *PatientID* attribute provides a unique identifier for each individual.

2.3 ML Model Training

In the process of building an AI-based Parkinson's disease diagnosis support system, testing multiple machine learning models is inevitable. To find the most suitable and reliable model, the research team trained ten popular classification algorithms, including traditional models such as Logistic Regression, Random Forest, SVM, XGBoost, Decision Tree, Gradient Boosting, Neural Network, AdaBoost, Extra Trees, and CatBoost. Each model was evaluated based on evaluation metrics, including accuracy, Precision, Recall, and F1-score, and also considered the distribution skew between the two groups with and without the disease. This method ensures that the chosen model not only performs well with the data but also functions effectively in real-life applications.

2.4 Explainability Framework: SHAP and LIME

To increase transparency and help doctors understand the prediction results easily, the system integrates two XAI techniques, SHAP and LIME. SHAP gives an overview of how each feature affects the prediction, while LIME goes into detail about each specific case. This combination helps the system explain both the whole picture and the details of each case.

After selecting the best-trained model, SHAP and LIME are integrated into the backend using FastAPI and displayed on the React interface. SHAP creates visual charts (summary plots), while LIME provides an explanation table and probability distribution chart for each case on the interface.

2.5 Evaluation Metrics for Explainability

This study evaluates the quality of explanations produced by SHAP and LIME using three well-known measures in explainable AI, especially in the medical field: Faithfulness, Fidelity, and Sparsity. These criteria are aimed at ensuring that the explanations are both mathematically consistent with the model and easily understandable so that they can be used in clinical practice.

Faithfulness is assessed by the feature removal approach, which involves measuring the variance in the prediction results before and after removing the most important (top-k) features [20]. Equation 1 shows that Δ is the average change in the model output when important features are removed, hence indicating their actual impact on the prediction outcomes [22].

$$\Delta = \left(\frac{1}{N} \sum_{i=1}^{N} \left| f(x_i) - f\left(x_i^{\setminus S}\right) \right| \right) \tag{1}$$

Fidelity, defined in Eq. 2, reflects the degree of similarity between the local explanatory model (e.g., LIME) and the actual behavior of the original model [12,14]. The coefficient R^2 compares the prediction results of the main model and the surrogate model on neighboring samples, helping to assess the consistency of the interpretation at a specific data point.

$$Fidelity = R^2\left(y_{\mathrm{local}}, \hat{y}_{\mathrm{LIME}}\right) \tag{2}$$

Sparsity, as defined in Eq. 3, represents the conciseness of the explanation by counting the number of features whose weights surpass a specific significant threshold. Concise explanations are often preferred in clinical settings, as they are easier for clinicians to understand while still retaining the core meaning [8,12].

$$Sparsity = |\{i : |w_i| > threshold\}| \tag{3}$$

2.6 System Workflow

Figure 1 illustrates the overall process of the implemented Parkinson's diagnosis support system. The system is built with FastAPI backend, React frontend, and MySQL database. The user enters data through a JSON form on the interface; then the system authenticates the email and continues to make predictions or register a new patient account.

The submitted data will be stored in the clinical database, where the best-trained model makes the diagnosis. The SHAP and LIME modules will generate visual and tabular explanations, then send them back to the user interface. In addition, the system automatically sends emails containing the results link for easy access by patients. This architecture ensures the transparency and usability of AI in the clinical process.

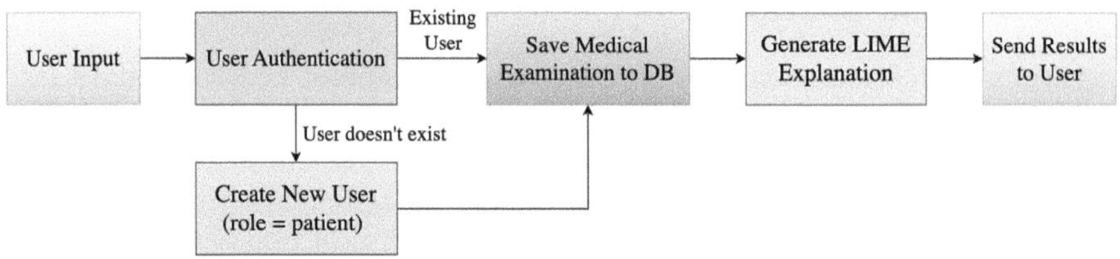

Fig. 1. Workflow diagram for prediction and explanation handling in the Parkinson's diagnostic system.

3 Implementation and Results

3.1 ML Model Selection and Performance Analysis

This section presents the quantitative evaluation results of ten ML models used in the diagnosis of PD. We evaluate the models based on four important metrics: accuracy, precision, recall, and F1-score, using the testing dataset.

To further evaluate the generalizability and stability of the models, avoiding the risk of overfitting, all models were further tested on an independent testing dataset (Table 1). CatBoost achieved the best overall results, with an accuracy of 93.59%, a precision of 95.52%, a sensitivity of 94.46%, and an F1-score of 94.99%. This stability confirms the suitability and reliability of the model when applied to clinical practice.

Table 1. Performance of 10 ML Models on the Testing Set

Model	Accuracy	Precision	Recall	F1 Score
Logistic Regression	0.7767	0.8149	0.8450	0.8297
Random Forest	0.9097	0.9464	0.9114	0.9286
SVM	0.7862	0.8198	0.8561	0.8375
XGBoost	0.9240	0.9579	0.9225	0.9399
CatBoost	**0.9359**	0.9552	**0.9446**	**0.9499**
Decision Tree	0.8836	0.9173	0.9004	0.9088
Gradient Boosting	0.9240	0.9509	0.9299	0.9403
Neural Network	0.8076	0.8545	0.8450	0.8497
AdaBoost	0.9074	0.9234	0.9336	0.9284
Extra Trees	0.8765	0.8789	0.9373	0.9071

Based on the comprehensive evaluations of accuracy, generalizability, and fairness, CatBoost was selected as the optimal model for further explanatory analysis and implementation in our clinical decision support system.

3.2 Technical Implementation of Software Framework

The software framework was developed using a systematic, iterative Design Science Research technique. The system consists of three primary layers: a React-based frontend, a backend built with FastAPI, and a MySQL relational database. The frontend interface enables intuitive data input, results viewing, and visualization of SHAP and LIME explanations. The backend offers RESTful APIs, manages authentication with JWT, implements the best-trained ML model, CatBoost, for PD prediction, and generates explanations dynamically with SHAP and LIME modules. Results are securely stored in MySQL, ensuring traceability and auditability, and emphasizing scalability, flexibility, and security in clinical practice.

3.3 Integration of XAI Techniques

To increase transparency and reliability in automated Parkinson's diagnosis, the ParkiDxAI system integrates two state-of-the-art XAI techniques at two

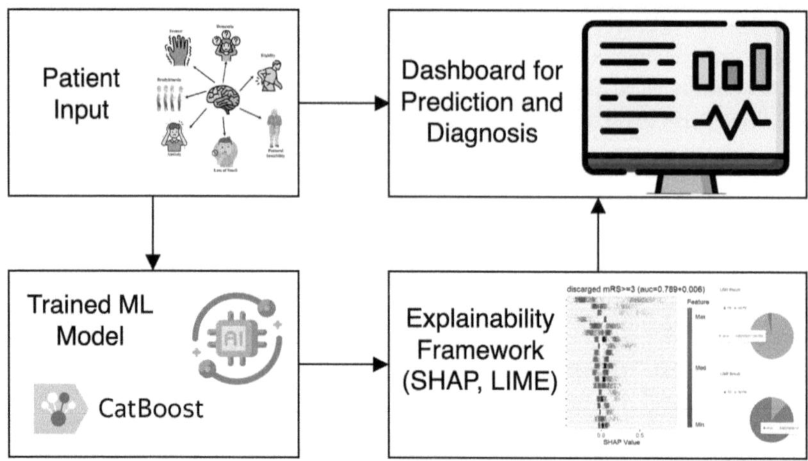

Fig. 2. XAI explanation module integrated into the ParkiDxAI system. The best trained CatBoost model predicts the diagnosis, and SHAP/LIME techniques are used to explain the results for both physicians and patients.

complementary levels: SHAP for global interpretation and LIME for patient-specific local interpretation, following the workflow illustrated in Fig. 2.

At the global level, SHAP is used to quantify the contribution of each feature to the prediction across the entire dataset. The results in Table 2 show that clinical scales such as UPDRS, Functional Assessment, MoCA, and symptoms such as tremor and rigidity are consistently among the strongest influencing factors, consistent with previous medical understanding. Figure 3avisualizes the impact of these features on the diagnostic probability, helping clinicians clearly understand why the model makes a prediction.

Table 2. Top Important Features from SHAP Results

No.	Feature	SHAP Value
0	UPDRS	−4.534082
1	Tremor	1.544398
2	FunctionalAssessment	1.533532
3	Rigidity	−0.685029
4	Age	−0.519496
5	Bradykinesia	−0.517363
6	MoCA	0.266807
7	PosturalInstability	−0.266481
8	Depression	−0.114928

Complementing the global view, LIME provides a personalized interpretation for each patient. Figure 3billustrates the PD/No PD prediction probability along with the main impact features. Specifically, Table 3 compares two cases: a patient diagnosed with PD and a No PD sample. The results show that for PD patients, features such as rigidity, functional assessment, and blood pressure are the determining factors, while for No PD cases, physical activity, MoCA, and HDL cholesterol play an important role in ruling out the possibility of disease. These values are also consistent with the probability distribution ratios shown in Fig. 3b, indicating that LIME is not only intuitive but also highly verifiable.

Table 3. Comparison of LIME Explanations between a No PD and a PD Patient

No PD Sample

Feature	Value
cholesterol_hdl > -2.54	-0.9339
cholesterol_triglycerides > -2.18	1.1404
sleep_quality > -3.98	1.2917
education_level > -1.47	-0.3660
updrs_score > -1.84	-1.7203
ethnicity > -0.67	2.3270
diet_quality > -1.72	-0.3580
moca_score > -1.75	1.6167
tremor > -0.87	1.1552
functional_assessment > -1.73	-1.1931

PD Sample

Feature	Value
systolic_bp > -5.08	1.1194
diastolic_bp > -5.30	-0.8270
smoking > -0.62	1.6130
cholesterol_total > -5.25	-0.3835
alcohol_consumption > -1.77	-0.7167
physical_activity > -1.76	1.1742
cholesterol_ldl > -2.92	0.6303
bmi > -3.78	-1.5283
rigidity > -0.57	1.7455
functional_assessment > -1.73	-0.0913

Combining SHAP and LIME helps ensure that predictions are not only statistically significant but also clinically valuable. SHAP provides an overall picture of the most important factors, while LIME allows a detailed examination of each case. This allows the physician to easily compare and confirm the results, thereby making the final diagnostic decision with a higher level of confidence.

3.4 Quantitative Metrics: Faithfulness, Fidelity, Sparsity

To objectively assess the quality of SHAP and LIME explanations, we utilized three quantitative metrics widely recognized in medical AI: *faithfulness*, *fidelity*, and *sparsity* (Table 4). Faithfulness evaluates whether the explanation genuinely reflects the model's logic by measuring prediction changes when top-5 significant features are removed, achieving an average Δ of 0.51 (>0.4), indicating strong alignment [13]. Fidelity assesses LIME's surrogate model accuracy relative to the original model, with a stable correlation coefficient R^2 between 0.60–0.62 (>0.6). Sparsity quantifies explanation conciseness; results showed an average of 9.3 features per explanation (SHAP > 0.1), within recommended limits (<10), ensuring simplicity and clinical usability. Combined with considerations for transparency

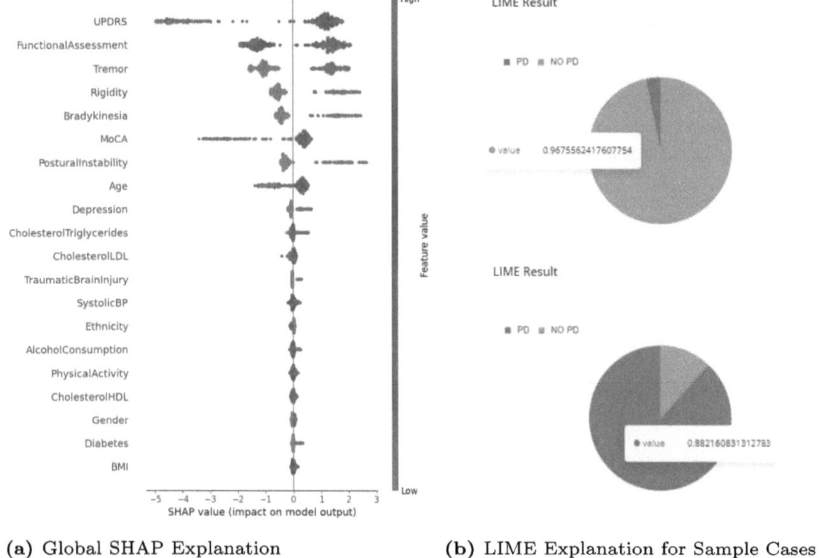

(a) Global SHAP Explanation (b) LIME Explanation for Sample Cases

Fig. 3. Illustration of the explainability of the ParkiDxAI system using SHAP and LIME. Figure (a) shows the global explanation of key features influencing Parkinson's diagnosis, while figure (b) shows the local explanation for each case with the probability distribution between PD and No PD. The two techniques increase transparency at both the system and individual levels.

and reliability—assessed via clarity and consistency with clinical literature [4] — these metrics confirm that the explanations generated are reliable and practically meaningful in clinical settings.

3.5 Comparison with EBM Paper

To validate the clinical reliability of our AI-based system, we compared the risk factors identified by SHAP analysis from our CatBoost model with those reported by an EBM study conducted by Arslan and Colak [4], utilizing the same dataset from Rabie El Kharoua [11].

Table 5 demonstrates strong agreement between both approaches despite methodological differences. Key predictive features—including UPDRS, Tremor, Functional Assessment, Rigidity, Age, Bradykinesia, Postural Instability, MoCA, and Depression—were consistently identified by both methods. This alignment emphasizes the practical reliability and clinical relevance of our AI system, supporting its real-world applicability for diagnosis [4].

3.6 Qualitative Evaluation: Study Design and Survey Results

To comprehensively evaluate the reliability, practical applicability, and acceptability of ParkiDxAI, a qualitative survey was conducted with 24 participants of diverse ages, education levels, and AI/ML experience. The survey was conducted

Table 4. Evaluation Metrics

Metric	Significance	Threshold	Result	Technique	Eval.
Faithfulness	Check model dependency on SHAP features. ⇒ If removing top-5 important features changes result ⇒ model explains well.	$\Delta > 0.4$	$\Delta = 0.51$	SHAP	Good
Fidelity (LIME)	Accuracy of LIME in mimicking original model's behavior.	$R^2 > 0.6$	$R^2 = 0.60$–0.62	LIME	Stable
Sparsity	Number of features needed for explanation. Fewer ⇒ easier to interpret.	<10 features (SHAP> 0.1)	Avg. = 9.3 features	SHAP	Good

Table 5. Comparison of Risk Factors for Parkinson's Disease

Order	Feature	Results from SHAP (ours)	Results in EBM [4]
1	UPDRS	x	x
2	Tremor	x	x
3	FunctionalAssessment	x	x
4	Rigidity	x	x
5	Age	x	x
6	Bradykinesia	x	x
7	Postural Instability	x	x
8	MoCA	x	x
9	Depression	x	x

online via Google Form; all participants were explained the objectives, content, benefits, and confidentiality, and signed a Consent Form before the experience.

Figure 4 summarizes the main results: (a–b) SHAP and LIME were both evaluated as clear, with LIME slightly higher in "very clear"; (c) 87.5% increased their confidence after viewing the explanation; (d) 62.5% found the interface very easy to use; (e) 50% were willing to use it immediately to aid in diagnosis; (f) SHAP was the most popular (54.2%).

The results show that our ParkiDxAI achieved high levels of understandability, trust, and usability, making it ready for wider clinical testing.

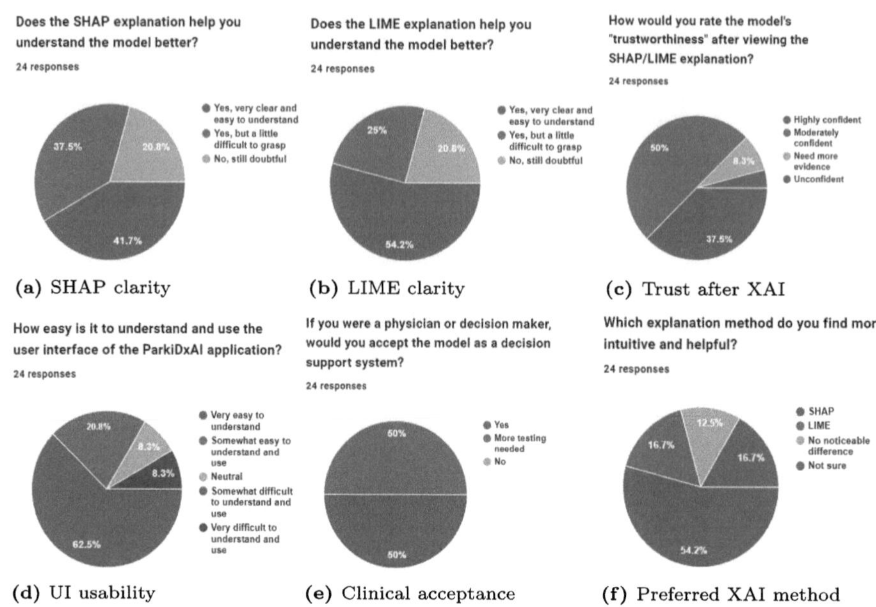

(a) SHAP clarity (b) LIME clarity (c) Trust after XAI

(d) UI usability (e) Clinical acceptance (f) Preferred XAI method

Fig. 4. Summary of qualitative survey results: (a–b) Clarity of SHAP and LIME explanations; (c) Trust improvement after explanations; (d) Ease of using the UI; (e) Willingness to adopt system in clinical use; (f) Preferred explanation method.

4 Discussion

The results of this study have shown that the CatBoost model outperformed nine other machine learning models, achieving 93.59% accuracy, good generalizability, and seamless compatibility with explainability techniques such as SHAP and LIME. The model was successfully embedded in the ParkiDxAI platform built with FastAPI, React, MySQL. User surveys confirmed the system's ease of use, transparency, and clinical relevance. In addition, the integration of SHAP and LIME significantly improved the model's explainability and transparency. SHAP provided a global view of important features (e.g., UPDRS, tremor,...), while LIME provided detailed individualized explanations. These methods were validated through visualization, user surveys, and similarity to clinical risk factors that have been validated in previous studies [4,7,24].

This study also applies three quantitative metrics to objectively assess the quality of interpretation. SHAP demonstrated high faithfulness ($\Delta = 0.51$), LIME achieved stable fidelity ($R^2 = 0.60 - -0.62$), and the average sparsity was 9.3 features per sample – indicating clear and concise interpretation [14,20].

Although the proposed ParkiDxAI shows promise, the system still has limitations such as small data size, lack of real-world clinical testing, and the need for expert medical evaluation.

5 Conclusion

This paper presents ParkiDxAI – a Parkinson's disease diagnosis support system that combines the CatBoost model with two popular interpretation methods, SHAP and LIME. The proposed system not only demonstrates impressive accuracy (93.59%) in identifying suspicious cases but also significantly enhances transparency and interpretability for end-users, especially clinicians. With a flexible architecture based on FastAPI, React, and MySQL, ParkiDxAI is easily deployable in real-world medical environments, ensuring both security and user-friendliness.

By combining quantitative metrics, such as faithfulness, fidelity, and sparsity, with user survey feedback, this study has provided further evidence that XAI can serve as a reliable bridge between the predictive power of the model and the trust of medical professionals. However, there are still limitations to overcome, notably the limited data size and lack of real-world clinical trials. This suggests the need to expand the research with more diverse datasets, as well as increase the involvement of physicians and medical staff in the evaluation and implementation process [6,9,21].

Acknowledgement. The authors acknowledge Ho Chi Minh City University of Technology (HCMUT), VNU-HCM, for supporting this study.

References

1. Abdollahi, S., Safa, R.: Machine learning and AI for advancing Parkinson's disease diagnosis: exploring promising applications. Big Data Comput. Vis. **4**(1), 12–21 (2024). https://doi.org/10.22105/bdcv.2024.458879.1180
2. Ahmadi, A.: Digital health transformation: leveraging AI for monitoring and disease management. Int. J. BioLife Sci. (IJBLS) **3**(1), 10–24 (2024). https://doi.org/10.22034/ijbls.2024.188037
3. Allen, B.: The promise of explainable ai in digital health for precision medicine: a systematic review. J. Person. Med. **14**(3), 277 (2024). https://doi.org/10.3390/jpm14030277
4. Arslan, A.K., Colak, C.: Explainable boosting machine approach to identifying risk factors for Parkinson's disease. Annals Med. Res. **31**(9), 735–740 (2024). https://annalsmedres.org/index.php/aomr/article/view/4747
5. Belard, A., et al.: Precision diagnosis: a view of the clinical decision support systems (CDSS) landscape through the lens of critical care. J. Clin. Monit. Comput. **31**(2), 261–271 (2016). https://doi.org/10.1007/s10877-016-9849-1
6. Bhandari, N., Walambe, R., Kotecha, K., Kaliya, M.: Integrative gene expression analysis for the diagnosis of Parkinson's disease using machine learning and explainable AI. Comput. Biol. Med. **163**, 107140 (2023). https://doi.org/10.1016/j.compbiomed.2023.107140
7. Chaddad, A., Peng, J., Xu, J., Bouridane, A.: Survey of explainable AI techniques in healthcare. Sensors **23**(2), 634 (2023). https://doi.org/10.3390/s23020634

8. Coroama, L., Groza, A.: Evaluation metrics in explainable artificial intelligence (XAI). In: Proceedings of International Conference on Advanced Research in Technologies, Information, Innovation and Sustainability, pp. 401–413 (2022). https://doi.org/10.1007/978-3-031-20319-0_30
9. Esmaeilzadeh, P.: Challenges and strategies for wide-scale artificial intelligence (AI) deployment in healthcare practices: a perspective for healthcare organizations. Artif. Intell. Med. **151**, 102861 (2024). https://doi.org/10.1016/j.artmed.2024.102861
10. Gunasekeran, D.V., et al.: Applications of digital health for public health responses to COVID-19: a systematic scoping review of artificial intelligence, telehealth and related technologies. NPJ Digit. Med. **4**(1), 40 (2021). https://doi.org/10.1038/s41746-021-00412-9
11. Kharoua, R.E.: Parkinson's Disease Dataset Analysis (2024). https://doi.org/10.34740/KAGGLE/DSV/8668551
12. Li, X., Du, M., Chen, J., Chai, Y., Lakkaraju, H., Xiong, H.: M4: a unified XAI benchmark for faithfulness evaluation of feature attribution methods across metrics, modalities and models. In: Oh, A., et al. (eds.) Advances in Neural Information Processing Systems, vol. 36, pp. 1630–1643 (2023)
13. Lundberg, S.M., Lee, S.I.: A unified approach to interpreting model predictions. In: Proceedings of the 31st International Conference on Neural Information Processing Systems, pp. 4768–4777 (2017). https://doi.org/10.5555/3295222.3295230
14. Miró-Nicolau, M., Jaume-i Capó, A., Moyà-Alcover, G.: A comprehensive study on fidelity metrics for XAI. Info. Process. Manag. **62**(1), 103900 (2025). https://doi.org/10.1016/j.ipm.2024.103900
15. Pahuja, G., Prasad, B.: Deep learning architectures for Parkinson's disease detection by using multi-modal features. Comput. Biol. Med. **146**, 105610 (2022). https://doi.org/10.1016/j.compbiomed.2022.105610
16. Pawlicki, M., et al.: Evaluating the necessity of the multiple metrics for assessing explainable AI: a critical examination. Neurocomputing **602**, 128282 (2024). https://doi.org/10.1016/j.neucom.2024.128282
17. Peffers, K., Tuunanen, T., Rothenberger, M.A., Chatterjee, S.: A design science research methodology for information systems research. J. Manag. Inf. Syst. **24**(3), 45–77 (2007). https://doi.org/10.2753/MIS0742-1222240302
18. Prashanth, R., Roy, S.D., Mandal, P.K., Ghosh, S.: High-accuracy detection of early Parkinson's disease through multimodal features and machine learning. Int. J. Med. Info. **90**, 13–21 (2016). https://doi.org/10.1016/j.ijmedinf.2016.03.001
19. Rammo, R., Gostkowski, M., Rasmussen, P.A., Nagel, S., Machado, A.: The need for digital health solutions in deep brain stimulation for Parkinson's disease in the time of COVID-19 and beyond. Neuromod. Technol. Neural Interf. **24**(2), 331–336 (2021). https://doi.org/10.1111/ner.13307
20. Sadeghi, Z., et al.: A review of explainable artificial intelligence in healthcare. Comput. Electr. Eng. **118**, 109370 (2024). https://doi.org/10.1016/j.compeleceng.2024.109370
21. Sendak, M., Vidal, D., Trujillo, S., Singh, K., Liu, X., Balu, S.: Surfacing best practices for AI software development and integration in healthcare (2023). https://doi.org/10.3389/fdgth.2023.1150875
22. Sithakoul, S., Meftah, S., Feutry, C.: BEExAI: benchmark to evaluate explainable AI. In: Proceedings of World Conference on Explainable Artificial Intelligence, pp. 445–468 (2024). https://doi.org/10.1007/978-3-031-63787-2_23

23. Trocin, C., Mikalef, P., Papamitsiou, Z., Conboy, K.: Responsible AI for digital health: a synthesis and a research agenda. Info. Syst. Front. **25**(6), 2139–2157 (2023). https://doi.org/10.1007/s10796-021-10146-4
24. Vimbi, V., Shaffi, N., Mahmud, M.: Interpreting artificial intelligence models: a systematic review on the application of LIME and SHAP in Alzheimer's disease detection. Brain Info. **11**(1), 10 (2024). https://doi.org/10.1186/s40708-024-00222-1
25. Wang, W., Lee, J., Harrou, F., Sun, Y.: Early detection of Parkinson's disease using deep learning and machine learning. IEEE Access **8**, 147635–147646 (2020). https://doi.org/10.1109/ACCESS.2020.3016062
26. Yang, C.C.: Explainable artificial intelligence for predictive modeling in healthcare. J. Healthcare Info. Res. **6**(2), 228–239 (2022). https://doi.org/10.1007/s41666-022-00114-1

Grad-CAM-Driven Explainable Deep Learning Framework for Cervical Cancer Image Classification

Huynh-Dai-Nhan Tran[1,2](✉), Tan-Phuoc Pham[2], Manh-Hung Trinh[2,3], Tan-Nguyen Ngo[2,4], Tan-Hung Nguyen[5,7], and Hoang-Anh Pham[6,7](✉)

[1] University of Jyväskylä, Jyväskylä, Finland
[2] University of Oulu, Oulu, Finland
tranhuynhdainhan25102004@gmail.com
[3] University of Eastern Finland, Joensuu, Finland
[4] Jyväskylä University of Applied Sciences, Jyväskylä, Finland
[5] Ho Chi Minh University of Science (HCMUS), Ho Chi Minh City, Vietnam
[6] Ho Chi Minh City University of Technology (HCMUT), Ho Chi Minh City, Vietnam
anhpham@hcmut.edu.vn
[7] Vietnam National University Ho Chi Minh City (VNU-HCM), Ho Chi Minh City, Vietnam

Abstract. Many existing Deep Learning (DL)-based approaches for cervical cancer diagnosis lack comprehensive architectural comparisons and fail to effectively integrate Explainable AI (XAI) methods, such as Grad-CAM. This study proposes a cervical cancer classification framework that utilizes several state-of-the-art DL models and employs Grad-CAM to generate heatmaps highlighting the specific image regions that influenced the model's predictions. These visual explanations improve transparency and support clinical interpretation, thereby enhancing trust in AI-assisted diagnostic systems. The experimental results demonstrate that the proposed framework not only achieves high classification accuracy but also provides valuable visual insights, contributing to the development of more interpretable and reliable AI tools for medical image diagnosis.

Keywords: Cervical Cancer Diagnosis · Explainable AI · Deep Learning · Grad-CAM · Medical Imaging

1 Introduction

Cervical cancer remains one of the most common and life-threatening malignancies among women worldwide, especially in developing countries where access to screening programs and early diagnosis technologies is limited. The most common early detection technique is the Pap smear technique [23], but it relies on expert experience and can be inconsistent among diagnosticians. These obstacles

T. T. Quan et al. (Eds.): MIWAI 2025, LNAI 16353, pp. 304–316, 2026.
https://doi.org/10.1007/978-981-95-4957-3_25

have driven the movement of employing Artificial Intelligence (AI) and machine learning models to assist automated and precise diagnosis [9,11].

Over the past decade, a significant number of studies have explored AI-based approaches for cervical cancer detection, particularly using Pap smear images. For instance, Alias et al. examined 27 machine learning-based models [1], while William et al. developed a low-cost diagnostic tool utilizing fuzzy C-means [23]. In other studies, Gupta et al. [8] and Mehmood et al. [13] created hybrid models that combined random forest and shallow neural networks, which produced high accuracy but limited interpretability. Those studies on automated diagnosis have mainly focused on improving performance metrics such as precision and recall, without offering explanations for model predictions.

Lack of interpretability in AI systems poses a significant challenge for clinicians who rely on their decisions. Most existing models act as "black-box", offering high accuracy at the expense of transparency, causing difficulty in real-world adoption [4,10]. Explainable AI (XAI), which incorporates post-hoc methods like SHAP, LIME, and Grad-CAM, is gaining popularity for improving model transparency without compromising performance [6,21]. However, the use of XAI in cervical cancer diagnosis has not been fully exploited. For instance, Vimbi et al. [22] and Raghavan et al. [17] used LIME and Grad-CAM to diagnose Alzheimer's and breast cancer, respectively, demonstrating how visual explanation tools can bridge the gap between AI models and clinical usability. Few studies in the cervical cancer context have used objective metrics to visualize AI model behavior or assess the explanation quality. Notably, Roy et al. [18] and AlMohimeed et al. [2] suggested stacked models with SHAP integration; however, they did not test, compare multiple different deep learning (DL) architectures, or assess the explainability.

Furthermore, to the best of our knowledge, while *Focus Score* has been proposed as a quantitative metric for assessing how well explanation maps (such as Grad-CAM) align with relevant regions in medical images, its adoption remains limited, particularly in studies evaluating the clarity of explanations for different classes of cervical cancer. According to [3,7,15], Focus Score can effectively assess saliency map concentration and serve as a useful metric for image explanations; however, its application has been primarily in non-medical and agricultural domains so far.

This study will address those above gaps by comparing five state-of-the-art DL models – ResNet101, DenseNet201, MobileNetV3, EfficientNetV2, and Vision Transformer – on a cervical image dataset with five pathological classes. Then, we use Grad-CAM for visual interpretability with the top-performing model and introduce Focus Score to quantitatively assess the spatial accuracy and clarity of Grad-CAM heatmaps across various cervical cancer classes.

This study aims to answer three key research questions: **RQ1.** Which DL model gives the best results for classifying cervical cancer images? **RQ2.** How well does Grad-CAM help explain the decisions made by the best-performing model? **RQ3.** Can Focus Score reliably measure how clearly Grad-CAM shows important areas in cervical cancer images?

2 Related Work

2.1 Cervical Cancer Classification Using Machine Learning

Several studies have automated the processing of Pap smear pictures for the diagnosis of cervical cancer using DL and machine learning (ML). For example, William et al. [23] developed a Pap-smear analysis program that integrated fuzzy C-means clustering with robust feature selection, achieving excellent accuracy on laboratory data. However, they did not mention the interpretation techniques like Grad-CAM in their methods. In a similar vein, Mehmood et al. [13] presented a hybrid model that combined random forest and shallow neural networks. Still, they did not process medical images and only used tabular data.

Although Alias et al. [1] did not carry out experiments or assess the models' performance, they carried out a systematic review of ML models used for cervical image classification. Besides, Gupta et al. [8] compared 15 AI models and achieved average accuracy; however, their applicability is limited because they relied on manual labeling. These studies have shown the progress in applying ML to cervical cancer diagnosis, but most lack an explanatory element or a comprehensive comparison between DL architectures.

2.2 XAI in Medical Imaging

In recent years, XAI has attracted increasing attention in medicine. Several studies [4,10,19] have presented popular techniques such as SHAP, LIME, and Grad-CAM, but most lack empirical evaluations. Some applied studies, such as Vimbi et al. [22], have implemented SHAP and LIME in Alzheimer's diagnosis. In contrast, Cinà et al. [5] have focused on ethical aspects, but lack demonstrations of practical implementation. Tjoa et al. [21] put XAI into groups based on how dependent the models are on each other and said that there aren't any standard ways to evaluate them. Recently, Quach et al. [15] proposed the Focus Score index, but it has not been widely applied in medicine. In the study of cervical cancer, AlMohimeed et al. [2] and Roy et al. [18] used SHAP with an ensemble model, but did not evaluate visual interpretation techniques such as Grad-CAM or compare DL architectures comprehensively.

2.3 Grad-CAM and Visual Interpretation Techniques

The popularity of providing spatial explanations for CNN models in medical image analysis with Grad-CAM is increasing rapidly. Raghavan et al. [17] proposed an improved Grad-CAM with attention for thermographic breast cancer diagnosis. Meanwhile, Song et al. [20] applied Grad-CAM to improve the explainability of ultrasound tumor classification. Marmolejo-Saucedo et al. [12] implemented Grad-CAM in a digital form to support brain tumor analysis from MRI images. Quach et al. [16] also used Grad-CAM to evaluate the effect of hyperparameter optimization using Bayesian Optimization.

However, in studies of cervical cancer diagnosis [2,18], Grad-CAM has not yet been used. This study aims to fill that gap by applying Grad-CAM combined with Focus Score assessment.

2.4 Comparative Summary

Table 1 shows that most previous studies have applied XAI only on tabular data or in domains not directly related to cervical imaging. Methods such as SHAP and LIME are widely used, while visual explanation techniques such as Grad-CAM are less frequently deployed. In addition, very few works have quantitatively evaluated explainability or compared DL architectures. This indicates a gap that our study aims to fill by applying Grad-CAM and Focus Score on a large cervical image dataset with explicit quantitative evaluation.

Table 1. Summary of XAI Applications in Cervical Cancer and Related Domains

Study	Dataset	XAI Method	Result	Key Insights
William et al. [23]	Pap-smear images	None	Acc: 99.28%	No XAI used; relied on fuzzy clustering; complex segmentation.
Mehmood et al. [13]	Tabular data	None	Acc: 93.6%	Not image-based; focused on reducing false positives; lacked interpretability.
Roy et al. [18]	Cervical tabular data	SHAP, LIME	Interpretable framework	Used expert knowledge; did not test image-based XAI or DL comparison.
AlMohimeed et al. [2]	Cervical features	SHAP	Balanced performance	Used ensemble model; local explanations not evaluated.
Raghavan et al. [17]	Infrared breast thermograms	Grad-CAM (w/ attention)	Improved tumor localization	Not for cervical cancer; lacked SHAP/LIME comparison.
Quach et al. [16]	Plant disease images	Focus Score, Ablation-CAM	Acc: 97.79%	Novel score for explainability; evaluated on plant disease images, not medical domain.

3 Methodology

Figure 1 describes the workflow of our research methodology, from dataset preparation to model training, evaluation, and interpretability analysis. The process starts with data acquisition and pre-processing, followed by the training of five DL models. Then, these models have been reassessed using conventional performance metrics to determine the best-performing model for combining with Grad-CAM to generate visual explanations. Finally, the Focus Score is used to assess the usefulness of these explanations, and the findings provide medical insights.

3.1 Dataset

The data of cervical cancer used in this study were retrieved from the publicly available Multi Cancer Dataset [14], comprising eight data files covering eight

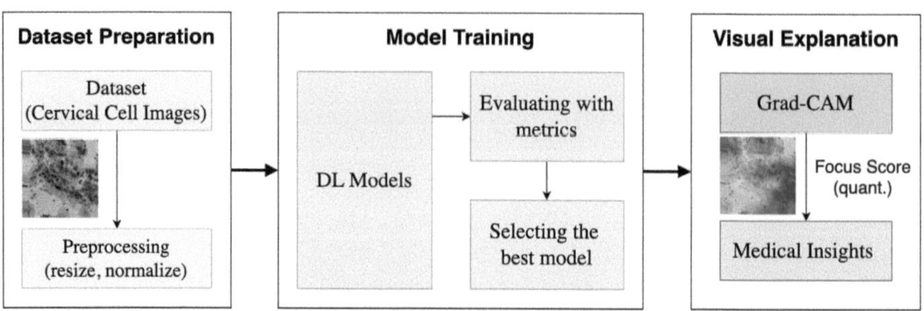

Fig. 1. The workflow of research design methodology, from dataset preparation to model training, evaluation, and interpretability analysis.

Cancer kinds. In this specific data, there are a total of 25,000 photos divided into five groups, which are groups of different types of cervical cells. The following classes including Dyskeratotic (`cervix_dyk`), Koilocytotic (`cervix_koc`), Metaplastic (`cervix_mep`), Parabasal (`cervix_pab`), and Superficial Intermediate (`cervix_sfi`) are what groups fall into. Each class has 5,000 pictures. This evenly distributed class distribution provides an excellent foundation for multi-class classification.

In order to accommodate the input dimensions of conventional convolutional neural networks (CNNs), each image was enlarged to 224×224 pixels. To increase the resilience of the model, we use data augmentation techniques such as random horizontal rotation and rotation, as well as standardizing pixel values to $[0, 1]$. To facilitate performance assessment, three subsets can be separated from the data set we have, including testing (15%), validation (15%), and training (70%).

3.2 Model Training

We utilized all five DL models, including ResNet101, DenseNet201, MobileNetV3, Vision Transformer, EfficientNetV2 for model training in our study due to their efficiency. Using pre-trained ImageNet weights for the initialization, all models were fine-tuned on the cervical cancer dataset. Particularly, we train every model for 10 epochs (batch size 64) with categorical cross-entropy loss and the Adam optimizer (learning rate 0.001). After training, the model's performance was compared with the validation set. Based on the achieved results, the best model will be chosen for explainability analysis using Grad-CAM.

3.3 Evaluation Metrics

In this study, four core metrics (i.e., Accuracy, Precision, Recall, and F1-Score), are used consistently across all experiments to identify the best-performing model. Accuracy (1) is used to evaluate the overall performance of a classification model, calculated as the ratio of correctly predicted samples (TP=True Positive and TN=True Negative) to the total number of samples. Precision (2) measures the accuracy of positive predictions, while Recall (3) evaluates the ability to fully detect truly positive samples. F1-Score (4) plays an important role in balancing Precision and Recall, especially in situations where both positive and negative errors have serious consequences. The effectiveness of the model in predicting and covering real-world cases depends largely on how close the F1-Score value is to 1.

$$\text{Accuracy} = \frac{TP + TN}{\text{Total sample}} \tag{1}$$

$$\text{Precision} = \frac{TP}{\text{Total predicted positive}} = \frac{TP}{TP + FP} \tag{2}$$

$$\text{Recall} = \frac{TP}{\text{Total actual positive}} = \frac{TP}{TP + FN} \tag{3}$$

$$F_1\text{-Score} = \frac{2}{\frac{1}{\text{Recall}} + \frac{1}{\text{Precision}}} \tag{4}$$

To assess the explainability of Grad-CAM visualizations, this study uses the Focus Score (5), proposed by Quach et al. [15] for Ablation-CAM in plant disease categorization. Instead of using Ablation-CAM, we apply this metric to Grad-CAM heatmaps generated from cervical cell images. The Focus Score assesses the heatmap's concentration on a specific class of interest by calculating the ratio of true positive importance (TP) to the sum of true positive and negative importance (TP+TN).

$$\text{Precision (Focus Score)} = \frac{TP}{TP + TN} \tag{5}$$

3.4 Grad-CAM Application

To explain the classification decisions of the best-performing model, we use the Grad-CAM technique, which generates a concentration map based on the gradients of the target class with respect to the feature maps in the final convolutional layer. These gradients are used to assign weights to each feature map, which are then combined into a heatmap that highlights the image regions that have the greatest impact on the model's predictions. The Grad-CAM map is calculated as (6).

$$L^c_{\text{Grad-CAM}} = \text{ReLU}\left(\sum_k \alpha^c_k A^k\right) \tag{6}$$

where A^k is the activation at channel k, and α^c_k is the global average gradient of class c with respect to A^k. The ReLU function retains the feature regions that positively influence the prediction outcome.

Grad-CAM heatmaps help visualize regions that differentiate between cervical cancer cell types, helping clinicians verify or compare model results. This contributes to model transparency and explainability–an important element in clinical diagnosis support systems.

4 Experimental Results and Discussion

4.1 Model Comparison

To obtain a comprehensive evaluation, we tested five DL models, including ResNet101, DenseNet201, MobileNetV3, Vision Transformer, and EfficientNetV2 on the task of classifying cervical cytology images. Table 2 presents the results based on four key metrics: Accuracy, Precision, Recall, and F1-Score.

Table 2. Comparison of model performance on cervical cancer classification

Model	Accuracy	Precision	Recall	F1-Score
ResNet101	**0.9963**	**0.9963**	**0.9963**	**0.9963**
DenseNet201	0.9861	0.9862	0.9861	0.9861
MobileNetV3	0.9837	0.9838	0.9837	0.9837
Vision Transformer	0.9755	0.9756	0.9755	0.9755
EfficientNetV2	0.9104	0.9105	0.9104	0.9097

The experimental results show that the ResNet101 model is the most outstanding with an accuracy of 99.63%, while DenseNet201, MobileNetV3, and Vision Transformer also perform exceptionally well. The other one is worse, possibly due to the complexity of the data or the improper tuning process. For that reason, the ResNet101 model is chosen to further analyze the explainability.

4.2 Per-Class Evaluation on Test Set

Since the ResNet101 was chosen, we conducted other experiments to assess the model's classification ability on five different types of cervical cancer cells. The results in Table 3 show that the two classes *cervix_pab* and *cervix_sfi* achieved perfect scores (Precision, Recall, F1-score, Accuracy all equal to 1.000), showing that they can tell the difference between plainly recognizable morphological traits very well. The two classes *cervix_koc* and *cervix_mep* also performed very well (F1-score of 0.9947), although they may be affected by slight overlap between image features. In contrast, the *cervix_dyk* class had the lowest performance (Accuracy: 0.9933; F1: 0.9940), indicating the possibility of confusion with other classes. Next, we used Grad-CAM and Focus Score studies to see if the model can pay attention to the feature region. Overall, these results confirm the model's good performance and generality in accurately classifying many different cell types – an important requirement for clinical application.

4.3 Qualitative Prediction and Grad-CAM

To further clarify the qualitative results, we investigated whether Grad-CAM concentrated on significant anatomical characteristics. For the majority of correctly predicted samples, the highlighted regions often coincided with cell nuclei

Table 3. Per-Class Evaluation Results on Test Set

Class	Precision	Recall	F1-score	Accuracy
`cervix_dyk`	0.9947	0.9933	0.9940	0.9933
`cervix_koc`	0.9934	0.9960	0.9947	0.9960
`cervix_mep`	0.9973	0.9920	0.9947	0.9920
`cervix_pab`	1.0000	1.0000	1.0000	1.0000
`cervix_sfi`	0.9960	1.0000	0.9980	1.0000

or dense cell clusters – elements that are key to cytological diagnosis. This suggests that the model prioritizes clinically meaningful structures over background noise. However, in more difficult groups such as *cervix_koc* and *cervix_mep*, Grad-CAM still focused on fuzzy or scattered regions that are of little clinical value. These observations highlight the inherent limitations of Grad-CAM and highlight the need for additional expert judgment or the incorporation of quantitative metrics to increase confidence in interpretation (Fig. 2).

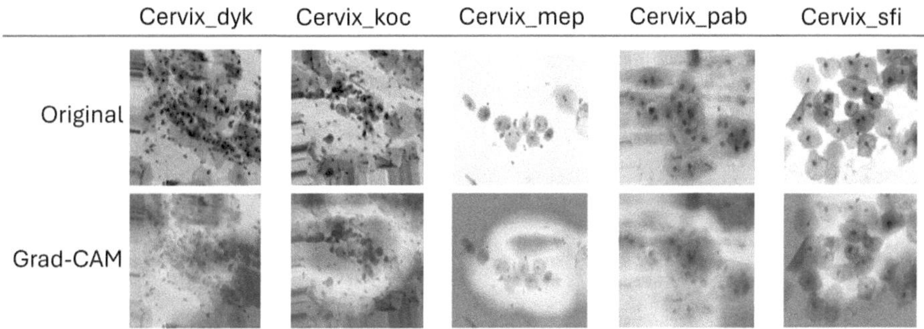

Fig. 2. Grad-CAM Application on ResNet101 model.

4.4 Focus Score Analysis

In addition to the qualitative interpretability provided by Grad-CAM, we also applied a quantitative approach to further assess the model's interpretability using the Focus Score. For instance, as shown in Fig. 3, we used our Grad-CAM method on ResNet101 with a Focus Score of 0.940 for a sample of class `cervix_pab`, indicating a high level of explanation precision and interpretability. This demonstrates that Grad-CAM successfully localized class-relevant regions in cervical cancer classification.

Rather than reporting a single case, we extended our analysis by examining the Focus Score distribution across all five cervical cancer classes using a box

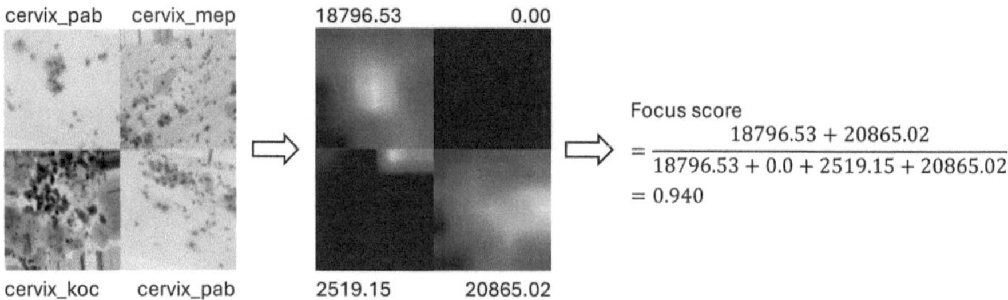

Fig. 3. Grad-CAM explanation evaluated using Focus Score on a 2 × 2 image grid. The higher focus score closer to 1 indicates that the model pays more attention to important image regions, thus adding confidence in the model's interpretability.

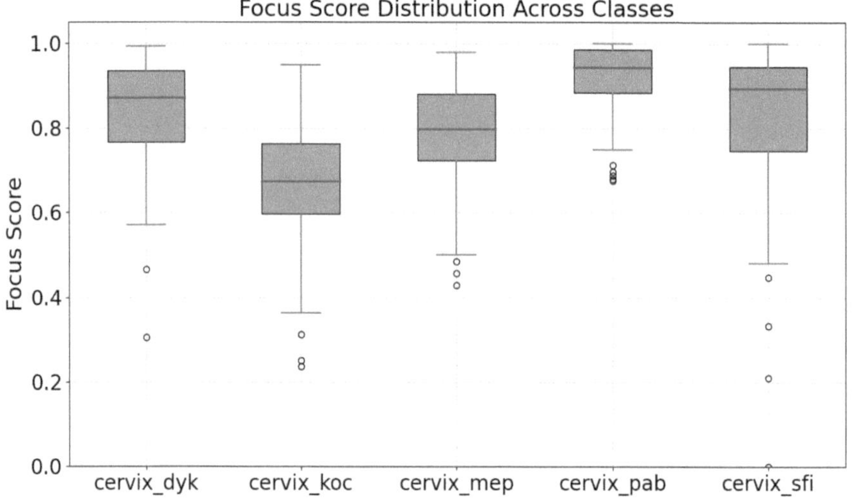

Fig. 4. Box plot showing the distribution of Focus Scores across all classes.

plot as depicted in Fig. 4. This statistical plot helps assess the consistency and variability of interpretability across classes.

The results show that the `cervix_pab` and `cervix_sfi` classes have the highest average Focus Score, both exceeding 0.950, and have a reasonably stable score distribution. This shows that the model often focuses on the critical areas in the image in these two classes. Meanwhile, the `cervix_koc` and `cervix_mep` classes exhibit a higher degree of fluctuation, with many abnormal values appearing, suggesting that the model struggles to accurately pinpoint areas that require attention. This may be a part of the reason why the classification results in these two classes are not as high as expected.

Overall, achieving a high and stable Focus Score, combined with a clear Grad-CAM activation region and good class-by-class classification accuracy, has demonstrated the effectiveness of the ResNet101 model. These results show that the model is applicable in clinical settings where transparency and trust are very important.

5 Discussion

The experimental results indicate the following key findings in response to three research questions. For **RQ1**, the ResNet101 model was identified as the most effective model, achieving 99.63% accuracy and outperforming the other four models. By using transfer learning and simple preprocessing, ResNet101 outperforms segmentation-based or handcrafted feature design methods.

Regarding **RQ2**, Grad-CAM provides clear heatmaps that focus on meaningful anatomical regions, especially with the two classes *cervix_pab* and *cervix_sfi*, indicating reliable post-learning explainability and enhanced model transparency. These findings are consistent with previous XAI studies in the medical field [4,10].

Concerning **RQ3**, the Focus Score is used to quantify the explanatory focus of Grad-CAM. With values of up to 0.940 for the representative sample and greater than 0.95 for the easily distinguishable classes, this index indicates that Grad-CAM is highly stable in identifying important regions. Nonetheless, more challenging classes, such as *cervix_dyk*, exhibit oscillations that underscore the difficulty of pinpointing the attentional regions.

In summary, the XAI analysis framework proposed in this study not only helps the model make accurate predictions but also provides clear visual explanations for each classification class. This satisfies the requirements of efficiency and ensures transparency–two crucial factors in clinical medical applications [10,19]. Compared to previous methods that mainly use SHAP or LIME [2,18], the approach combining Grad-CAM with Focus Score that we apply has provided more specific quantitative and visual evaluation capabilities, contributing to the construction of XAI systems in the field of medical imaging diagnosis [15].

6 Conclusion

This paper introduces a comprehensive cervical cancer classification method combining high-performance DL models and XAI techniques. To enhance the transparency of the prediction process, we use Grad-CAM to visualize the areas that influence the output results. Additionally, we utilize the Focus Score metric, which has been applied in the agricultural field to evaluate the concentration of the heatmaps. The analysis results indicated that the ResNet101 model not only achieves high accuracy but also can generate understandable heatmaps, especially for the `cervix_pab` and `cervix_sfi` layers. This confirms the effective combination of accuracy and explainability of the model.

In the future, we will seek opportunities to collaborate with medical professionals to gather qualitative feedback and assess the clinical relevance and feasibility of deploying the proposed system in practice. In addition, we will investigate the temporal stability of Grad-CAM explanations when applied to time-series image data, as highlighted in prior work [21]. To enhance model interpretability and robustness, we will also consider incorporating optimization methods, such as Bayesian Optimization [16] or numerical Grad-CAM [12]. These efforts will support the extension of our explainability framework to a broader range of applications, particularly within oncology and other high-stakes medical domains.

Acknowledgment. The authors acknowledge Ho Chi Minh City University of Technology (HCMUT), VNU-HCM for supporting this study.

References

1. Alias, N.A., et al.: Pap smear images classification using machine learning: a literature matrix. Diagnostics **12**(12) (2022). https://doi.org/10.3390/diagnostics12122900
2. AlMohimeed, A., Saleh, H., Mostafa, S., Saad, R.M.A., Talaat, A.S.: Cervical cancer diagnosis using stacked ensemble model and optimized feature selection: an explainable artificial intelligence approach. Computers **12**(10) (2023). https://doi.org/10.3390/computers12100200
3. Arias-Duart, A., Parés, F., Garcia-Gasulla, D., Giménez-Ábalos, V.: Focus! rating XAI methods and finding biases. In: 2022 IEEE International Conference on Fuzzy Systems (FUZZ-IEEE), pp. 1–8 (2022). https://doi.org/10.1109/FUZZ-IEEE55066.2022.9882821
4. Chaddad, A., Peng, J., Xu, J., Bouridane, A.: Survey of explainable AI techniques in healthcare. Sensors **23**(2) (2023). https://doi.org/10.3390/s23020634
5. Cinà, G., Röber, T., Goedhart, R., Birbil, I.: Why we do need Explainable AI for Healthcare. ArXiv arXiv:2206.15363 (2022). https://doi.org/10.48550/arXiv.2206.15363
6. Dwivedi, R., et al.: Explainable AI (XAI): core ideas, techniques, and solutions. ACM Comput. Surv. **55**(9) (2023). https://doi.org/10.1145/3561048
7. Fresz, B., Lörcher, L., Huber, M.: Classification metrics for image explanations: towards building reliable XAI-evaluations. In: Proceedings of the 2024 ACM Conference on Fairness, Accountability, and Transparency, pp. 1–19 (2024). https://doi.org/10.1145/3630106.3658537
8. Gupta, R., Sarwar, A., Sharma, V.: Screening of cervical cancer by artificial intelligence based analysis of digitized Papanicolaou-smear images. In. J. Contemp. Med. Res. **4**(5), 1108–1113 (2017)

9. Hamamoto, R., et al.: Application of artificial intelligence technology in oncology: towards the establishment of precision medicine. Cancers **12**(12) (2020). https://doi.org/10.3390/cancers12123532
10. Hulsen, T.: Explainable Artificial Intelligence (XAI): concepts and challenges in healthcare. AI **4**(3), 652–666 (2023). https://doi.org/10.3390/ai4030034
11. Lundervold, A.S., Lundervold, A.: An overview of deep learning in medical imaging focusing on MRI. Z. Med. Phys. **29**(2), 102–127 (2019). https://doi.org/10.1016/j.zemedi.2018.11.002
12. Marmolejo-Saucedo, J.A., Kose, U.: Numerical grad-cam based explainable convolutional neural network for Brain Tumor diagnosis. Mob. Netw. Appl. **29**(1), 109–118 (2022). https://doi.org/10.1007/s11036-022-02021-6
13. Detection, M.L.A.C.C.: Mehmood, M., Rizwan, M., Gregus ml, M., Abbas, S. Front. Public Health **9**, 1–14 (2021). https://doi.org/10.3389/fpubh.2021.788376
14. Naren, O.S.: Multi Cancer Dataset (2024). https://doi.org/10.34740/KAGGLE/DSV/9537604
15. Quach, L.D., Quoc, K.N., Nguyen, C.N., Thai-Nghe, N.: Explainable AI for plant disease detection: assessing explainability in classifying maize leaves diseases with focus score and ablation-CAM. In: Proceedings of International Conference on Intelligent Systems and Data Science, pp. 19–32 (2024). https://doi.org/10.1007/978-981-97-9613-7_2
16. Quach, L.D., Quoc Khang, N., Thai-Nghe, N., Nguyen, C.N.: XAI-BO: an architecture using Grad-CAM technique to evaluate Bayesian optimization algorithms on deep learning models. J. Info. Telecomm., 1–22 (2025). https://doi.org/10.1080/24751839.2024.2447191
17. Raghavan, K., B, S., v, K.: Attention guided grad-CAM: an improved explainable artificial intelligence model for infrared breast cancer detection. Multimedia Tools Appl. **83**(19), 57551–57578 (2024). https://doi.org/10.1007/s11042-023-17776-7
18. Roy, P., Hasan, M., Islam, M.R., Uddin, M.P.: Interpretable artificial intelligence (AI) for cervical cancer risk analysis leveraging stacking ensemble and expert knowledge. Digital Health **11**, 20552076251327944 (2025). https://doi.org/10.1177/20552076251327945
19. Sadeghi, Z., et al.: A review of explainable artificial intelligence in healthcare. Comput. Electr. Eng. **118**, 109370 (2024). https://doi.org/10.1016/j.compeleceng.2024.109370
20. Song, D., et al.: A new xAI framework with feature explainability for tumors decision-making in ultrasound data: comparing with Grad-CAM. Comput. Methods Programs Biomed. **235**, 107527 (2023). https://doi.org/10.1016/j.cmpb.2023.107527
21. Tjoa, E., Guan, C.: A survey on explainable artificial intelligence (XAI): toward medical XAI. IEEE Trans. Neural Netw. Learn. Syst. **32**(11), 4793–4813 (2021). https://doi.org/10.1109/TNNLS.2020.3027314

22. Vimbi, V., Shaffi, N., Mahmud, M.: Interpreting artificial intelligence models: a systematic review on the application of LIME and SHAP in Alzheimer's disease detection. Brain Informatics **11**(1), 10 (2024). https://doi.org/10.1186/s40708-024-00222-1
23. William, W., Ware, A., Basaza-Ejiri, A.H., Obungoloch, J.: A pap-smear analysis tool (PAT) for detection of cervical cancer from pap-smear images. Biomed. Eng. Online **18**, 1–22 (2019). https://doi.org/10.1186/s12938-019-0634-5

Hybrid Genetic Algorithm with Caputo Fractional Derivative for Ambulance Routing Problems

Jackel Vui Lung Chew(✉)

Faculty of Computing and Informatics, Universiti Malaysia Sabah Labuan International Campus, Labuan 87000, Malaysia
jackelchew93@ums.edu.my

Abstract. The ambulance routing problem plays a critical role in emergency medical services, where timely ambulance response can significantly impact patient outcomes. However, urban traffic congestion and dynamic routing conditions cause challenges to existing optimization approaches. This study proposes CaputoGA, a novel hybrid metaheuristic that integrates the Caputo fractional derivative into the genetic algorithm framework. By introducing a memory-aware penalty term and adaptive mutation rate based on this fractional derivative, CaputoGA enhances convergence behavior and routing stability. The algorithm is further enhanced with a hybrid local search mechanism combining 2-opt and swap heuristics to refine best routes. Experimental evaluations on benchmark datasets adapted from the vehicle routing problem demonstrate that CaputoGA outperforms standard GA and two state-of-the-art hybrid algorithms, such as K-means simulated annealing tabu search and priority-based adaptive particle swarm optimization, in both route cost and robustness. Experimental results show that CaputoGA substantially reduces the percentage difference relative to the known cost and can achieve the lowest percentage difference at 3.98%. CaputoGA also requires shorter execution time in completing best routes calculation compared to GA. These results validate the efficacy of implementing memory-driven dynamics into evolutionary search. This work highlights the potential of fractional calculus in optimizing complex routing problems and provides a foundation for future extensions into other metaheuristic approaches.

Keywords: Ambulance routing problem · Caputo fractional derivative · Genetic algorithm

1 Introduction

The ambulance routing problem (ARP) is crucial for optimizing emergency medical services (EMS). ARP involves identifying the best route that can minimize response time and improve patient outcomes [1,2]. Urban congestion intensifies this challenge by causing delays. Advanced ambulance routing algorithms

T. T. Quan et al. (Eds.): MIWAI 2025, LNAI 16353, pp. 317–327, 2026.
https://doi.org/10.1007/978-981-95-4957-3_26

are demanded to mitigate this issue [3,4]. The implications for public health are significant, as timely ambulance arrivals reduce mortality and morbidity [5]. Therefore, managing ambulance routing in dynamic traffic and strategic ambulance deployment remains an ongoing challenge [6,7].

Metaheuristic algorithms have been applied to ARP to optimize route cost and response time under traffic complexity [8–11]. However, limitations persist in adapting to dynamic routing conditions and maintaining route quality across scales [12]. Although algorithms like the non-dominated sorting genetic algorithm III and slime mould algorithm showed promising results, their performance faces difficulty with higher data complexity [10,11].

To address these challenges, hybrid approaches have gained attention by combining global optimization capabilities of metaheuristics with ambulance routing modeling. While metaheuristics explore large route spaces efficiently, they overlook the memory-driven and time-dependent ambulance routing. Fractional calculus, particularly through the Caputo fractional derivative (CFD), can capture such behavior by modeling memory and hereditary effects [13,14]. This integration has potential to be accurate ambulance routing solutions that adapt to fluctuating urban traffic conditions.

In response, this study proposes CaputoGA, a novel hybrid combining the genetic algorithm (GA) with CFD. This integration introduces memory-aware adaptability into the evolutionary process. The CaputoGA method aims to enhance route prediction accuracy and responsiveness under congested urban environments by dynamically tuning mutation behavior and penalizing route volatility based on past route trends.

The remainder of this paper is organized as follows. Section 2 reviews related works that support the motivation for the proposed method. Section 3 describes the ARP model adopted in this study and develops CaputoGA framework. Section 4 presents the performance evaluation of CaputoGA against the baseline GA and state-of-the-art hybrid metaheuristics. Finally, Sect. 5 concludes the paper with major findings and suggestions for future work.

2 Related Works

Metaheuristic algorithms such as GA, particle swarm optimization (PSO), and ant colony optimization (ACO) have been applied to optimize ambulance routing and enhance emergency response times. GA and PSO showed improvements in managing EMS [1,15]. Meanwhile, ACO combined with other algorithms like PSO to effectively optimize parameters in improving search times [16,17]. Additionally, a hybrid approach integrating GA and ACO has been proposed to solve complex routing problems [18]. These applications highlight the potential of metaheuristic algorithms in improving the operational efficiency of ambulance routing in EMS.

Fractional calculus, particularly CFD, is instrumental in modeling dynamic systems with memory effects. This type of derivative can effectively capture the memory and hereditary properties of systems, making it suitable for describing complex behaviors in traffic flow models [13,19]. For instance, a fractional-order car-following model using CFD has been shown to be capable in enhancing stability and reducing unrealistic acceleration in traffic simulations [19]. This model allows for a more accurate representation of driver memory and behavior, which leads to improved traffic flow stability and efficiency [14,19].

While CFD-based modeling has shown promise in traffic dynamics, its application has been mostly limited to simulation-based models without integration into metaheuristic optimization. This study uniquely integrates CFD's memory-aware modeling into the genetic search process. Specifically, this study introduces a CFD-driven penalty mechanism and adaptive mutation rate, which both are derived from the historical fitness landscape, to enable more stable and informed route evolution.

3 Methodology

3.1 Problem Formulation

This study adopts the following ARP model [8,20]. Let $G = (V, E)$ be a complete undirected graph that represents the real traffic condition. For $V = \{0, 1, 2, \ldots, n\}$, node 0 is the ambulance base and nodes 1 to n are road junctions. Then, $E \subseteq V \times V$ is the set of available roads. This study further defines c_{ij} as the route distance or cost between node i and j, d_i as the patient emergency level at node i, Q as the capacity of each ambulance, and K as the number of available ambulances.

For the decision making, this study uses $x_{ij} \in (0, 1)$ as the binary decision variable where $x_{ij} = 1$ if route (i, j) is used, $x_{ij} = 0$ otherwise. Additionally, u_i is the combined patient emergency level upon arrival at node i.

The objective function is

$$\min \sum_{i=0}^{n} \sum_{j=0}^{n} c_{ij} x_{ij}, \tag{1}$$

which is to minimize the total route cost across all ambulance routes.

The constraints are:

1. Each ambulance visits each road junction exactly once (except the base),

$$\sum_{\substack{j=0 \\ j \neq i}}^{n} x_{ij} = 1, \quad \forall i \in \{1, \ldots, n\}, \tag{2}$$

and

$$\sum_{\substack{i=0 \\ i \neq j}}^{n} x_{ij} = 1, \quad \forall j \in \{1, \ldots, n\}. \tag{3}$$

2. At most K ambulances can depart from and return to the base,

$$\sum_{j=1}^{n} x_{0j} \leq K, \quad \sum_{i=1}^{n} x_{i0} \leq K. \tag{4}$$

3. Subtours are eliminated to ensure capacity feasibility by tracking u_i,

$$u_i - u_j + Qx_{ij} \leq Q - d_j, \quad \forall i, j \in \{1, \ldots, n\}, i \neq j, \tag{5}$$

and

$$d_i \leq u_i \leq Q, \quad \forall i \in \{1, \ldots, n\}. \tag{6}$$

It is important to note that in this study, the binary decision variable x_{ij} is represented implicitly through route permutations. Each chromosome encodes a visit sequence, which is split into feasible routes based on capacity constraints. The values of x_{ij} are reconstructed from these routes as a binary adjacency matrix. The main reason for doing this is to align with the ARP model.

3.2 Genetic Algorithm and Caputo Fractional Derivative

To begin the formulation of CaputoGA, this study defines the Caputo fractional derivative (CFD) of a function $f(t)$ of order $\alpha \in (0, 1)$ as follows [21]:

$$^{C}D_t^{\alpha} f(t) = \frac{1}{\Gamma(1-\alpha)} \int_0^t \frac{f'(\tau)}{(t-\tau)^{\alpha}} \, d\tau. \tag{7}$$

For discrete implementation, this study uses:

$$^{C}D_t^{\alpha} f = \frac{\tau^{-\alpha}}{\Gamma(2-\alpha)} \sum_{j=1}^{k} b_{k-j} \left[f(t_j) - f(t_{j-1}) \right], \tag{8}$$

where $b_{k-j} = (k-j+1)^{1-\alpha} - (k-j)^{1-\alpha}$.

This study proposes CFD in two roles. For the first role, a memory-aware penalty term is introduced over the fitness history of routes. This term penalizes sudden fluctuations and rewards consistent improvements by incorporating the temporal memory of previous generations. This novel penalty term is defined as

$$\text{Penalty} = \lambda \cdot \left| \left(^{C}D_t^{\alpha} f \right)_k \right|, \tag{9}$$

where λ is a tunable penalty coefficient, and f_k is the fitness value at generation k.

For the second role, this study introduces adaptive mutation rate control. The mutation rate is dynamically adjusted based on the recent CFD gradient. Specifically, the mutation rate increases during fitness stagnation and decreases when steady progress is observed. This behavior is captured by the formula of

$$\text{MutationRate}_k = \mu_0 \cdot \left(1 + \frac{1}{|(^{C}D_t^{\alpha} f)_k| + \varepsilon} \right), \tag{10}$$

where μ_0 is the base mutation rate, and ε is a small constant to prevent division by zero.

3.3 Hybrid Local Search

To enhance the best route quality, this study integrates a hybrid local search mechanism into the CaputoGA framework. This mechanism combines two classical improvement heuristics, which are 2-opt and swap-based refinements, and applies them sequentially to the best route identified in each generation. The 2-opt heuristic iteratively reverses segments within the route to eliminate detours. Once 2-opt stabilizes, the swap-based local search is applied, where all possible exchanges between emergency site pairs are evaluated. If a swap yields a shorter route, the best route is updated. This mechanism aims to improve both macro-level route structure and micro-level adjustments so that CaputoGA can escape local optima. This mechanism is applied after selection and before fitness evaluation in each generation. The purpose is to ensure that the most promising route is deterministically improved before further evolution.

3.4 CaputoGA Algorithm

The proposed CaputoGA algorithm retains the standard structure of GA (selection, crossover, and mutation phases) but introduces two novel CFD inspired-mechanisms (memory-aware penalty term and adaptive mutation rate control). Additionally, the best route in each generation undergoes hybrid local search refinement to further improve convergence toward the highest quality. The full CaputoGA procedure is outlined in Algorithm 1.

4 Experimental Setup

This study adapts benchmark instances from Vrp-Set-A and Vrp-Set-B datasets developed by Augerat et al. [22]. Although originally intended for vehicle routing in logistics, these datasets were adapted to represent the ARP [1,8]. In this context, depots correspond to ambulance bases, customer nodes to road junctions, demand values to patient emergency levels, vehicle capacities to ambulance capacities, and the distance matrix to route distances between junctions.

The CaputoGA algorithm was implemented with 10 independent runs per instance, 300 iterations per run, a population size of 75, and a mutation rate of 0.05. To enable fractional-order memory effects, this study sets fractional order $\alpha = 0.25$, step size $h = 0.7$, and memory window size of 50 past iterations. A penalty control parameter $\lambda = 0.2$ was applied to adjust the influence of the fractional gradient on fitness evaluation. These parameter values were derived from multiple exploratory runs on a subset of benchmark instances, ensuring a balance between solution quality and convergence stability. Although a full sensitivity analysis was not conducted, the selected settings were empirically validated across all tested instances and consistently produced stable and reliable results.

To evaluate the performance of CaputoGA, this study first compares the best route cost (Best), the percentage difference relative to the known cost (GAP

Algorithm 1: CaputoGA

```
Input: Distance matrix dist_matrix, ambulance capacity capacity, number of
       generations gens, population size pop_size, initial mutation rate
       mutation_rate, penalty parameter K, Caputo parameters α, h, and
       window
Output: Best solution route best_solution, minimum cost best_cost
Initialize population with pop_size random permutations of routes;
Initialize best_solution ← None, best_cost ← ∞, fitness_history ← [ ];
for gen ← 1 to gens do
    Evaluate fitness for each chromosome in the population;
    Select top 50% individuals based on fitness;
    Set current_best as the best in selected population;
    Compute route cost and append to fitness_history;
    Compute Caputo gradient: grad ← |D_t^α f|;
    Compute penalty weight: penalty_weight ← λ · grad;
    Adjust cost: cost ← cost + penalty_weight;
    if cost < best_cost then
        Update best_solution and best_cost;
    Compute dynamic mutation rate:
    current_mutation ← mutation_rate · (1 + 1/(grad+ε));
    Clip current_mutation between 0.01 and 0.2;
    // Generate offspring
    Initialize offspring ← selected population;
    while len(offspring) < pop_size do
        Select parents p1, p2 ∈ population;
        Perform partial crossover: take slice from p1, fill from p2;
        Apply swap mutation with probability current_mutation;
        Add child to offspring;
    Set population ← offspring;
Filter population for valid routes;
Select best feasible solution from final population;
return best_solution, best_cost;
```

(%)), the average route cost over 10 runs (Average), the standard deviation (Std Dev), and execution time (Time (s)) achieved by CaputoGA against the baseline GA without hybrid local search. Subsequently, the same metrics are compared between CaputoGA and the baseline GA with hybrid local search.

Finally, the best route cost obtained by CaputoGA is compared against two state-of-the-art hybrid metaheuristics, which are K-means simulated annealing tabu search (K-Means-SA-TS) from Issam et al. [8] and priority-based adaptive particle swarm optimization (PA-PSO) from Tlili et al. [1] All experiments using CaputoGA were conducted in a consistent computational environment using Python 3.13 on a Windows 11 64-bit operating system. The hardware setup consisted of an AMD Ryzen 7 5700U CPU and 8GB of RAM.

5 Results and Discussion

This section presents the experimental results of CaputoGA. The evaluation focuses on benchmark instances from the Vrp-Set-A and Vrp-Set-B datasets, and the results are structured into three comparative analyses as shown in Tables 1, 2, and 3. Table 1 compares the performance of CaputoGA with the baseline GA without hybrid local search. Table 2 presents a comparison between CaputoGA and GA enhanced with hybrid local search. Table 3 compares the best route cost obtained by CaputoGA against K-Means-SA-TS [8] and PA-PSO [1]. The "Best Known" in each table refers to the best-reported route for the benchmark instance, as documented in the original dataset.

Table 1. Performance Comparison between CaputoGA and GA without Hybrid Local Search

Instance	Best Known	CaputoGA				
		Best	**GAP%**	**Average**	**Std Dev**	**Time (s)**
A-n32-k5	784	876.83	19.68	938.26	48.76	9.74
A-n33-k6	742	792.15	13.14	839.54	43.87	8.94
A-n36-k5	799	897.39	22.95	982.33	51.44	11.25
A-n37-k6	949	1161.39	27.90	1213.78	48.29	9.61
A-n39-k5	822	992.10	31.82	1083.55	53.67	9.57
B-n31-k5	672	695.37	6.79	717.66	15.54	7.42
B-n35-k5	955	1012.11	13.17	1080.75	33.78	8.13
B-n39-k5	549	659.84	31.41	721.46	39.55	8.87
B-n43-k6	742	918.02	32.75	984.98	45.23	9.96
Instance	**Best Known**	**GA**				
		Best	**GAP%**	**Average**	**Std Dev**	**Time (s)**
A-n32-k5	784	941.68	37.48	1077.86	62.81	21.47
A-n33-k6	742	939.66	40.86	1045.17	62.82	23.96
A-n36-k5	799	1118.51	48.95	1190.13	61.91	28.20
A-n37-k6	949	1420.77	59.27	1511.50	50.46	15.72
A-n39-k5	822	1331.94	75.84	1445.38	57.44	19.53
B-n31-k5	672	724.29	11.64	750.24	15.78	14.93
B-n35-k5	955	1141.24	28.38	1226.07	63.33	16.16
B-n39-k5	549	770.90	72.48	946.92	103.71	17.74
B-n43-k6	742	1109.49	59.40	1182.73	43.84	19.83

The comparative analysis in Table 1 highlights the superiority of CaputoGA over GA without hybrid local search across all benchmark instances. CaputoGA achieved a notably lower best route cost and smaller GAP% for every problem tested, indicating its enhanced ability to converge toward high-quality routes.

For example, in instance A-n39-k5, CaputoGA reduced the GAP% from 75.84% (GA) to 31.82%. This substantial improvement is attributed to the CFD's memory effect, which helps maintain beneficial search directions while dynamically adapting mutation pressure based on historical fitness trends. Furthermore, CaputoGA demonstrated better runtime efficiency, taking less than half the execution time of standard GA on average, further validating its computational advantage.

Table 2. Performance Comparison between CaputoGA and GA with Hybrid Local Search

Instance	**Best Known**	**CaputoGA**				
		Best	**GAP%**	**Average**	**Std Dev**	**Time (s)**
A-n32-k5	784	835.82	10.68	867.72	34.18	148.92
A-n33-k6	742	777.15	7.91	800.71	16.66	166.66
A-n36-k5	799	856.84	11.97	894.60	19.88	224.10
A-n37-k6	949	1036.05	12.70	1069.50	36.49	248.85
A-n39-k5	822	903.91	15.09	946.00	26.73	294.46
B-n31-k5	672	697.83	5.10	706.29	7.90	134.19
B-n35-k5	955	977.13	3.98	993.01	11.41	213.57
B-n39-k5	549	590.98	13.04	620.57	18.98	318.47
B-n43-k6	742	759.07	5.58	783.44	16.53	473.35
Instance	**Best Known**	**GA**				
		Best	**GAP%**	**Average**	**Std Dev**	**Time (s)**
A-n32-k5	784	835.82	8.29	849.02	8.87	174.51
A-n33-k6	742	773.01	7.52	797.81	21.41	189.28
A-n36-k5	799	834.62	9.83	877.52	22.66	250.09
A-n37-k6	949	1057.05	13.21	1074.37	9.06	266.86
A-n39-k5	822	921.98	14.60	942.05	13.32	320.88
B-n31-k5	672	697.83	5.15	706.61	7.58	153.82
B-n35-k5	955	982.31	4.74	1000.24	12.73	243.75
B-n39-k5	549	580.85	12.15	615.73	21.07	367.60
B-n43-k6	742	767.02	8.01	801.46	19.85	503.54

Table 2 presents the performance comparison between CaputoGA and GA when both are augmented with hybrid local search. The results show that although GA with local search achieves competitive best route costs in some instances such as B-n31-k5, CaputoGA still consistently shows better performance in terms of average cost. Notably, CaputoGA maintains a lower GAP% across most instances while preserving robustness, as indicated by lower standard deviation values. For instance, in A-n36-k5, CaputoGA achieved a best GAP% of 11.97% compared to 9.83% by GA, but with significantly better consistency across runs. The higher computational cost observed in both algorithms when hybrid local search is applied is expected, yet CaputoGA remains competitive in execution time while delivering improved solution stability.

Table 3. Comparison of Best Route Cost with Other Hybrid Metaheuristics

Instance	Best Known	CaputoGA Hybrid	CaputoGA	K-Means SA-TS	PA-PSO
A-n32-k5	784	835.82	876.83	869	950
A-n33-k6	742	777.15	792.15	798	835
A-n36-k5	799	856.84	897.39	863	891
A-n37-k6	949	1036.05	1161.39	970	1135
A-n39-k5	822	903.91	992.10	931	999
B-n31-k5	672	697.83	695.37	686	696
B-n35-k5	955	977.13	1012.11	1002	1077
B-n39-k5	549	590.98	659.84	612	718
B-n43-k6	742	759.07	918.02	755	874

Finally, Table 3 shows the comparison of the best route costs obtained by CaputoGA (with and without hybrid local search) against two established hybrid metaheuristics. CaputoGA with hybrid local search outperforms K-Means-SA-TS in six out of nine benchmark instances and consistently beats PA-PSO across all cases. For instance, in B-n35-k5, CaputoGA with hybrid local search achieved a best cost of 977.13, significantly better than PA-PSO's 1077 and even outperforming K-Means-SA-TS's 1002. These results demonstrate the efficacy of CFD as an augmentation strategy in evolutionary metaheuristics, offering a promising direction for solving dynamic and complex ambulance routing problems in urban environments.

6 Conclusion and Future Work

This study introduced CaputoGA, a novel hybrid algorithm that integrates CFD into the GA framework to address the complexities of ARP in congested urban environments. By incorporating memory-aware mechanisms, CaputoGA demonstrated superior performance over conventional GA and other state-of-the-art hybrid metaheuristics across multiple benchmark datasets. The integration of hybrid local search further enhanced route quality and convergence stability. The experimental results validated the effectiveness of CaputoGA in producing robust and cost-efficient solutions with lower variability and faster convergence.

For future work, the idea of CFD will be extended to enhance other metaheuristic algorithms such as PSO and ACO, potentially enabling broader memory-aware optimization across various heuristic frameworks. Moreover, alternative formulations of ARP, such as time-dependent ARP, multi-depot ARP, or ARP with stochastic traffic conditions, will be explored to assess the generalizability of CFD-based models. These future directions could lead to the development of more adaptive and resilient emergency response systems under real-world uncertainties.

Acknowledgments. This study is funded by Malaysian Ministry of Higher Education under the research grant FRGC036-2024.

Disclosure of Interests. The authors have no competing interests to declare that are relevant to the content of this article.

References

1. Tlili, T., Harzi, M., Krichen, S.: Swarm-based approach for solving the ambulance routing problem. Procedia Comput. Sci. **112**, 350–357 (2017)
2. Sutherland, M., Chakrabortty, R.K.: An optimal ambulance routing model using simulation based on patient medical severity. Healthc. Analytics **4**, 100256 (2023)
3. Mahdi, O.A., Eleiwy, J.A., Al-Mayouf, Y.R.B., AL-Attar, B.: An efficient node selection algorithm in the context of IoT-based vehicular ad hoc network for emergency service. J. Intell. Syst. **33**(1), 20240208 (2024)
4. Alruwaili, M., Ali, A., Almutairi, M., Alsahyan, A., Mohamed, M.: LSTM and ResNet18 for optimized ambulance routing and traffic signal control in emergency situations. Sci. Rep. **15**, 6011 (2025)
5. Ablard, S., et al.: Delivery of public health interventions by the ambulance sector: a scoping review. BMC Public Health **23**, 2082 (2023)
6. Aringhieri, R., Bigharaz, S., Duma, D., Guastalla, A.: Fairness in ambulance routing for post disaster management. CEJOR **30**, 189–211 (2022)
7. Hao, Z., Wang, Y., Yang, X.: Every second counts: a comprehensive review of route optimization and priority control for urban emergency vehicles. Sustainability **16**(7), 2917 (2024)
8. Zidi, I., Al-Omani, M., Aldhafeeri, K.: A new approach based on the hybridization of simulated annealing algorithm and tabu search to solve the static ambulance routing problem. Procedia Comput. Sci. **159**, 1216–1228 (2019)
9. Giri, A.R., Chen, T., Rajendran, V.P., Khamis, A.: A metaheuristic approach to emergency vehicle dispatch and routing. In: IEEE International Conference on Smart Mobility, pp. 27–31. IEEE (2022)
10. Khelfa, C., et al.: Slime Mould algorithm for solving ambulance dispatching problem. In: 14th International Conference on Soft Computing and Pattern Recognition, pp. 822–831. Springer, Cham (2022)
11. Haddad, A., Tlili, T., Nouaouri, I., Krichen, S.: Solving the multi-objective ambulance routing problem using NSGA III. In: 10th International Conference on Control, Decision and Information Technologies, pp. 2296–2300. IEEE (2024)
12. Humagain, S., Sinha, R., Lai, E., Ranjitkar, P.: A systematic review of route optimisation and pre-emption methods for emergency vehicles. Transp. Rev. **40**(1), 35–53 (2020)
13. Boulaaras, S., Pham, V.T., Jan, R.: special issue on application of fractional calculus: mathematical modeling and control—Part I. Fractals **33**(04), 2502003 (2025)

14. Fu, Y., Hu, W., Shang, J., Jiang, R., Yu, Y.: A fractional-order car-following model with random delay optimized by an enhanced whale optimization algorithm. Nonlinear Dyn., 1–27 (2025)
15. Nozari, H., Szmelter-Jarosz, A., Irani, H.R.: Designing an ambulance routing optimization model using the combination of machine learning and genetic algorithm in conditions of uncertainty. Syst. Soft Comput. **7**, 200276 (2025)
16. Zhang, P., Feng, L.U.: Application in emergency vehicle routing choosing of particle swarm optimization based ant colony algorithm. J. Comput. Inf. Syst. **9**, 8571–8579 (2013)
17. Gao, X., Ni, J.: Optimization of dynamic post-disaster emergency distribution network under perspective of rescue efficiency. J. Syst. Simul. **34**(4), 806–816 (2022)
18. Faust, O.S., Mehli, C.G., Hanne, T., Dornberger, R.: A genetic algorithm for optimizing parameters for ant colony optimization solving capacitated vehicle routing problems. In: 4th International Conference on Intelligent Systems. Metaheuristics & Swarm Intelligence, pp. 52–58. ACM, New York (2020)
19. Zhang, Y., Zhao, J.M.: Fractional order car-following model and its simulation. Mod. Phys. Lett. B **32**(19), 1850213 (2018)
20. Wang, C.H., Lu, J.Z.: A hybrid genetic algorithm that optimizes capacitated vehicle routing problems. Expert Syst. Appl. **36**(2), 2921–2936 (2009)
21. Dong, Z., Fan, E., Shen, A., Su, Y.: Three kinds of discrete formulae for the Caputo fractional derivative. Commun. Appl. Math. Comput. **5**(4), 1446–1468 (2023)
22. Augerat, P., et al.: Computational results with a branch and cut code for the capacitated vehicle routing problem. Tech. Rep. 949-M, Université Joseph Fourier, Grenoble, France (1995)

Formal Analysis of Ethical Autonomous Systems Under Uncertainty

Joanna Godawa and Krishnendu Ghosh(✉)

College of Charleston, Charleston, SC, USA
godawajz@g.cofc.edu, ghoshk@cofc.edu

Abstract. Autonomous systems have become an important fixture in modern day life. Certification of ethical decision-making in autonomous system is necessary to minimize harm. In this work, a formalism of ethical decision making under uncertainty is described. The ethical principles are incorporated using Deontic logic rules of obligations, forbidden actions, and permissible actions. The uncertainty in the environment is modeled using interval discrete-time Markov chain. A tractable probabilistic model checking on interval discrete time Markov chain model is constructed for evaluation ethical decision making in a system. The results from experiments are performed using probabilistic model checking on a tractable model of interval discrete time Markov chain and statistical inference is conducted on a prototype of a moving aircraft is presented.

Keywords: Ethical Decision-Making · Deontic Logic · Probabilistic Model Checking · Interval Discrete Time Markov Chain

1 Introduction

The deluge of autonomous systems such as self-driving cars and drones, that work independently or cooperatively, have necessitated the incorporation of ethical decision making. The construction of autonomous systems that make decisions individually or in cooperation with the aim of achieving the goal without harming population or creating impediments in population as they execute duties in daily lives, becomes critical. In the decision-making process, it is imperative that the autonomous systems refrain from doing harm to public and adhere to ethical rules described by various government institutions. The correctness of the system based on rules is evaluated using formal verification. Formal models have been studied rigorously for correctness of systems and have been extended in understanding the decision making processes by autonomous systems [8] and formal verification in evaluation of ethical properties of autonomous systems [12]. Formal methods techniques such as model checking [10] have been used for software and hardware verification. The specification is represented in terms of a logic formula and is checked on a model, The output produced is either true or false. If false, the process generates a counterexample. Model checking

T. T. Quan et al. (Eds.): MIWAI 2025, LNAI 16353, pp. 328–340, 2026.
https://doi.org/10.1007/978-981-95-4957-3_27

is extended to evaluate whether an action or a set of actions is ethically permissible. The ethical rules are embedded in the model by integrating Deontic logic [16] actions, obligation, permissible and forbidden actions. In this work, we create a formalism that integrates uncertainty in the ethical decision-making process by posing the following query - *Can the aircraft takeoff the runaway with a probability greater than 0.5 without causing harm to the airport personnel and facilities?* The solution to the question is imprecise because of uncertain data in the model, represented by stochastic structure. The probabilities are uncertain as it is not possible to know the exact probability distribution for the discrete-time Markov chain (DTMC). Therefore, a model based on interval discrete time Markov chain (IDTMC) represents the model for evaluation of ethical decision making. The following steps are described in this work:

1. Model abstraction of Deontic logic based rules for ethics and representation using interval discrete time Markov chain. A tractable formalism is created on an interval discrete-time Markov chain.
2. Evaluation of computational feasibility on a prototype of an autonomous system under uncertainty. Experiments are conducted using temporal logic specifications with statistical inference in the form of confidence bounds using multiple statistical algorithms.

The results from the experiments, empirically demonstrate the promise in the methodology.

2 Background

The work is based on foundations of ethics-based AI systems using Deontic logic and use of probabilistic model checking for addressing uncertainty in the environment, represented by interval discrete time Markov chain.

2.1 Ethics Based AI Systems

The use of AI systems raises ethical questions and the need for organizations to adhere to ethical guidelines [6]. The construction of ethical AI system address a responsive decision-making process [11] for a safe and trustworthy implementation of AI systems. A detailed literature is described in the survey on formal models and verification of autonomous robotic systems [18]. Formal model of human-agent behavior was analyzed for safe, controllable and ethical decision making on a prototype of unmanned aerial vehicle-human in dynamic and uncertain environment [1]. Deontic logic [16] have used as a theoretical reasoning of ethics [15]. However, none of the published work have addressed uncertainty in the formalisms for ethical decision making which is the research gap for verification of ethical decision making.

2.2 Model Checking of Interval Discrete Time Markov Chain

There are several approaches chains have been reported for computation of parameters in the interval discrete-time Markov chains (IDTMC) [5]. Prior, probabilistic computation temporal logic (PCTL) specifications on IDTMC was investigated [19]. Linear temporal logic (LTL) on interval Markov chain was studied and was computationally intensive [9]. Sampling-based methods on uncertain parametric continuous-time Markov chain have been proposed to address interval based rates of transition in continuous-time Markov chains [3].

3 Preliminaries

In this section, the mathematical and logical constructs that form the foundations of this work is described [13].

3.1 Model of Deontic Logic

The rules based on Deontic logic [16] are abstracted in the form of - obligations, permissible and forbidden actions. Given a set of actions , $\mathcal{A}$, each action $a \in \mathcal{A}$ can be categorized as obligation, permissible or forbidden action. In the formalism, we represent O_a, P_a and Fr_a for an action,a as obligation, permissible and forbidden, respectively. For consistency, a forbidden action, $F_\emptyset$ represents a no-action that is an action after a forbidden action. F_a will denote any forbidden action, including $F_\emptyset$.

A triple of actions (t-action), $\langle O_{a_m}, P_{a_n}, F_{a_p}\rangle$ where $m, n, p \in \mathbb{N}$ represents any combination of obligation, permissible and forbidden actions.

An *outcome* [13] is denoted by, $s \rightarrow s'$ where s, s' are labeled as t-actions. The rule for a transition is, $s = \langle O_{a_m}, P_{a_n}, F_{a_p}\rangle$ and $s' = \langle O_{a_{m'}}, P_{a_n'}, F_{a_{p'}}\rangle$ and at least one of the following is true $O_{a_m} \neq O_{a_{m'}}$ or $P_{a_n} \neq P_{a_{n'}}$ or $F_{a_p} \neq F_{a_{p'}}$. $s \rightarrow s'$ implies that after an completion of an action in s leads to the execution of actions in s'. We define types of outcome with specific properties: The following definitions have been stated [13]:

1. Admissible Outcome (a-outcome): An outcome,$s \rightarrow s'$ is admissible if for t-actions, $s = \langle O_{a_m}, P_{a_n}, F_{a_p}\rangle$ and $s' = \langle O_{a_{m'}}, P_{a_n'}, F_{a_{p'}}\rangle$, there is at least one of the following is true $O_{a_m} \neq O_{a_{m'}}$ or $P_{a_n} \neq P_{a_{n'}}$ or $F_{a_p} \neq F_{a_{p'}}$.
2. Inadmissible Outcome(i-outcome): An outcome where the t-action is $s = \langle O_{a_m}, P_{a_n}, F_{a_p}\rangle$ and $F_{a_p} \neq F_\emptyset$.
3. Total outcome (t-outcome): A outcome, $s \rightarrow s'$ where $s' = s$.

For an i-outcome, it is necessary that the t-actions have a forbidden action.

Definition 1. *(Discrete Time Markov Chain (DTMC) [4]) a discrete-time Mark-ov chain is a tuple, $\mathcal{M}_m\langle S, S_0, \iota_{init}, P, L\rangle$ where:*

- *S is a finite set of states.*
- *S_0 is the set of initial states.*

- $P : S \times S \rightarrow [0, 1]$, *where P is the probability matrix and* $\sum_{s,s' \in S} \mathcal{P}(s, s') = 1$.
- $\iota_{init} : S \rightarrow [0, 1]$ *where* $\sum_{s \in S} \iota_{init}(s) = 1$ *is the initial distribution.*
- $L : S \rightarrow 2^{AP}$, *where L is a labeling function and AP the set of atomic propositions.*

Definition 2. *(Probabilistic Model Checking) Given a probabilistic model, $\mathcal{M}_p$ and formula,ϕ , model checking is the process of deciding whether ϕ is true in the model, written $\mathcal{M}_p \models \phi$ with probability, p.*

Details on probabilistic temporal logics can be found in the literature [2,4,14]. In this work, the logics that will be used to represent the specifications are in probabilistic computation tree logic (PCTL).

Definition 3. *(Interval Discrete Time Markov Chain (IDTMC) [7]) is a tuple $\mathcal{M}_I = \langle S, \iota_{init}, M_l, M_u \rangle$ where*

- *S is a finite set of states.*
- $M_l, M_u : S \times S \rightarrow [0, 1]$ *with $M_l \leq M_u$, M_l and M_u are transition matrices.*
- $\iota_{init} : S \rightarrow [0, 1]$ *where* $\sum_{s \in S} \iota_{init}(s) = 1$ *is the initial distribution.*

In our formalism, the states in the $\mathcal{M}_I$ is labeled. Formally, $L : S \rightarrow 2^{AP}$, where L is a labeling function and AP the set of atomic propositions. A *submodel*, $\mathcal{M}_s$ is an IDTMC where the probability intervals are subintervals of $\mathcal{M}_I$. The notation of a dtmc constructed from $\mathcal{M}_s$ is $\mathcal{M}_m$ and a set of submodels is $\mathfrak{M}_s$. The set of DTMC is represented by $\mathfrak{M}_m$.

3.2 Approximation of Probability Distributions

There are two algorithms-Expectation-Maximization (EM) and Markov chain Monte Carlo (MCMC) that are applied in the approximations of the probability distributions. The construction of probability distribution by EM algorithm is by maximization of the likelihood function of the observed data. On the other hand. MCMC is a simulation-based algorithm that constructs an approximate probability distribution by drawing samples from a complex probability distribution.

4 Model Abstraction

The roadmap for model abstraction using Deontic logic for ethics decision making is as follows:

1. Construction of IDTMC, $\mathcal{M}_I$ representing ethical actions. Here, $\mathcal{M}_I$ represents the probabilistic structure with imprecise probabilities in the model.
2. Construction of set of submodels, $\mathfrak{M}_s$ by partitioning the intervals in $\mathcal{M}_I$.
3. Construction of a DTMC $\mathcal{M}_m$ for each $\mathcal{M}_s \in \mathfrak{M}_s$.
4. Perform probabilistic model checking using PCTL formula on each $\mathcal{M}_m$ such that $\mathcal{M}_m \in \mathfrak{M}_m$.
5. Construction of statistical inference model from the output of a PCTL query on each $\mathcal{M}_m$.

4.1 Construction of IDTMC Representing Actions

The construction of a model representing ethical actions from a set of actions under imprecise probabilities is given by: Given (1) a set of actions, $\mathcal{A}$, (2) for each action, $a \in \mathcal{A}$ is labeled as obligations (O), permission(P) and forbidden(F) actions, (3) a set of t-actions, $\mathcal{T}_a$ and (4) a set of outcomes, Out The IDTMC, $\mathcal{M}_I = \langle S, \iota_{init}, M_l, M_u \rangle$ is described as follows:

1. AP is the set of all atomic formulas of the form,$s = \langle O_a, P_a, F_a \rangle$ where $\langle O_a, P_a, F_a \rangle \in \mathcal{T}_a$.
2. S is the set of all subsets s of AP where exactly one of the formula, $\langle O_a, P_a, F_a \rangle$ is in s.
3. S_0 is the set of initial states of $\mathcal{M}_I$. The initial state contains the t-actions where the permissible action is to be the initial action.
4. The label(edge label) on a transition is the outcome, $out \in Out$. The labeled transition is represented by a triple,$\langle s, e, s' \rangle$ where $e = out$ and $out \in \{a - outcome, i - outcome, t - outcome\}$
5. The edge labels are probability intervals of the form ,$[p_l, o_u]$ where $p_l.p_u$ are the lower and upper bounds of the interval, and are values in the transition matrices, M_l and M_u, respectively. The intervals represents the probabilities in IDTMC.

Initially, $\mathcal{M}_I$ is constructed wit a transition for each state to every other state. The edge labels with $a - outcome$ remain in the structure. The transition with edge label, $i - outcome$ are pruned. The transitions with edge label, $t - outcome$ are pruned and a self-loop will be constructed on the outgoing state of the outcome.

4.2 Construction of Set of Submodels, $\mathfrak{M}_s$ from $\mathcal{M}_I$

The tractable abstraction from the IDTMC is constructed by partitioning the intervals into subintervals. For example, if the number of subintervals is two, then the subintervals are $(x, \frac{x+y}{2}], (\frac{x+y}{2}, y)$ from an interval,(x, y). The subintervals are in the feasbile space such that there exits a random number from each subinterval in $\mathcal{M}_s \in \mathfrak{M}_s$ whose sum is 1. Formally, Algorithm 1 shows the fulfillment Markovian property by generating random numbers from each of the sub-intervals. Each subintervals form intervals in submodels. For each submodel, a random value from the subintervals is generated such that the sum is equal to one. If the sum is not equal to 1, then the random values are rejected. The computations are performed and a set of submodels are generated from the cross products of subintervals at different lengths of the IDTMC.

The admissible random values from each submodel, $\mathcal{M}_s$ form to a dtmc, $\mathcal{M}_m$. Therefore, a set of dtmcs, $\mathfrak{M}_m$ is constructed for probabilistic model checking.

4.3 Statistical Inference on the Model

The output from each PCTL formula when posed on each dtmc, $\mathcal{M}_m \in \mathfrak{M}_m$ are recorded. The output values are used for construction of probability distribution

Algorithm 1: Construction of subintervals

```
Input  : 𝓘 = {I_1, ..., I_n]}, set of subintervals.
         n ∈ ℕ, number of subintervals.
Output: P = {(p_1, ..., p'_n)}, set of probabilities for ith. interval, I_i.
P ← 0
while (P = 0) do
    for i ← 1 : n do
        r_i ← random number in I_i
        if ∑ r_i = 1 then
            P ← P ∪ r_i
P
```

using EM and MCMC algorithm. The confidence interval are computed on the constructed probability distribution for each PCTL query.

5 Simulation

The implementation of the model abstraction of the ethical system was evaluated using PRISM model checker [17]. Data and scripts are available (https://zenodo.org/records/15598114). A prototype of autonomous system is evaluated for model checking. The experiments are conducted on a reported case study [13]. The probabilities in the case study is added empirically to evaluate the computational feasibility and the statistical inference of the described method. We investigate the case of an aircraft navigating from the gate to a runway, from which it can achieve its goal of taking off. The path to the runway contains some obstacle which may cause the aircraft to halt and fail at its goal. For abstraction of this situation, a key set of actions are considered. An aircraft is permitted to perform the following behaviors: *Directional:* `move_forward, turn_right, stop`, *Movement in distance:* `d_0, d_50, d_100, d_150, d_250` and *Stoppage*: `obst_n`, `take_off`. The IDTMC is constructed using these permissible actions, with each transition leading to a geographical position in the path of the aircraft on the runway (Fig. 1).

The computational feasibility of the model represented by $\mathcal{M}$ is demonstrated in Table 1. The PCTL formulas were evaluated on different problem sizes, by increasing the number of paths that terminated with a state labeled by an obstacles. The experiments were conducted on MacOS 64-bit operating system, x64-based processor with configuration: Intel(R) Core(TM) i7-3635QM CPU @ 2.7 GHz with RAM: 16.0 GB. Times for the PCTL formulas were recorded for different number of obstacles. The times for execution of the queries were less than 1 s. The query such as P>=1 [F "goal_1"] imply if there is a state labeled with goal_1 is reachable. Similarly, P>=0.5 [F "obst_3"] implies if a state with label obst_3 is reachable with a probability of greater than equal to 0.5 (Table 2).

The results from the construction of DTMCs from IDTMC is demonstrated in Table 3. Experiments were carried out using PCTL queries. The Markov

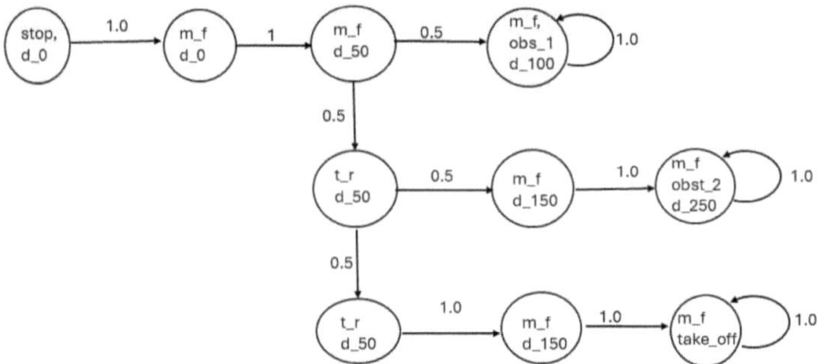

Fig. 1. Movement of Aircraft in Airport [13]. Notation: m_f and t_r imply the actions, `move_forward` and `turn_right`, respectively.

Table 1. Computational feasibility of the Model. Execution times (in milliseconds) for different queries with varying number of obstacles (obst).

	Execution Time (S)				
PCTL formula	3 obst	5 obst	8 obst	10 obst	15 obst
P=? [F "goal_1"]	0.002	0.002	0.002	0.003	0.005
P>=1 [F "goal_1"]	0.001	0.001	0.001	0.01	0.01
P=? [F stop_1]	0.001	0.001	0.002	0.002	0.003
P=? [F "obst_1"]	0.002	0.002	0.002	0.002	0.003
P>=0.5 [F "obst_3"]	0.002	0.002	0.002	0.002	0.002

Table 2. Results from the subinterval selection process, where S refers to the start of the skewed interval, E refers to the end of the skewed interval, S' refers to the start of the encompassing interval, if one exists, E' refers to the end of the encompassing interval, n' refers to the total number of subintervals in the encompassing set, and SI is the set of skewed subintervals, where $|SI| = 5$. Note that the lack of a value, represented by "-" in a cell indicates that no encompassing set was required to model the skewed set of subintervals.

	S	E	S'	E'	n'	SI
1	0.48	0.58	0.4	0.6	10	`[0.48, 0.5], [0.5, 0.52], [0.52, 0.54] [0.54, 0.56], [0.56, 0.58]`
2	0.47	0.53	-	-	-	`[0.47,0.482], [0.482,0.494], [0.494,0.506] [0.506,0.518], [0.518,0.53]`
3	0.43	0.53	0.43	0.57	7	`[0.43,0.45], [0.45,0.47], [0.47,0.49] [0.49,0.51], [0.51,0.53]`
4	0.45	0.55	-	-	-	`[0.45,0.47], [0.47,0.49], [0.49,0.51] [0.51,0.53], [0.53,0.55]`

chains with probability 0.5 is represented by the intervals. Table 3 shows the construction of the probabilities from $\mathcal{M}_I$ was transformed to dtmcs. The statistical significance of 95% confidence interval was computed.

Table 3. Discrete probabilities generated for each subinterval, and the resulting query results from each pair. p_1 and p_1' correspond to the probabilities of selecting the first or second probabilistic branch in the DTMC model, respectively.

Interval	Subinterval	p_1	p_1'	Q1	Q2	Q3
1	[0.48, 0.5]	0.4975444029379343	0.5024555970620657	0.5025	0.4975	0.5025
	[0.5, 0.52]	0.5099091280164729	0.4900908719835271	0.4901	0.5099	0.4901
	[0.52, 0.54]	0.5322265448034105	0.4677734551965895	0.4678	0.5322	0.4678
	[0.54, 0.56]	0.5452206059359723	0.4547793940640277	0.4548	0.5422	0.4548
	[0.56, 0.58]	0.5750496650797166	0.42495033492028345	0.4250	0.5750	0.4250
2	[0.47, 0.482]	0.4767619697824629	0.5232380302175371	0.5232	0.4768	0.5232
	[0.482, 0.494]	0.4901625974244958	0.5098374025755041	0.5098	0.4902	0.5098
	[0.494, 0.506]	0.49442173064152456	0.5055782693584754	0.5056	0.4944	0.5056
	[0.506, 0.518]	0.5067106466874152	0.49328935331258483	0.4933	0.5067	0.4933
	[0.518, 0.53]	0.528057128975047	0.471942871024953	0.4719	0.5281	0.4719
3	[0.43, 0.45]	0.443459029829656	0.556540970170344	0.5565	0.4435	0.5565
	[0.45, 0.47]	0.45943918228976666	0.5405608177102333	0.5406	0.4594	0.5406
	[0.47, 0.49]	0.4784535054490635	0.5215464945509365	0.5215	0.4785	0.5215
	[0.49, 0.51]	0.5057151595798565	0.49428484042014353	0.4943	0.5057	0.4943
	[0.51, 0.53]	0.526961214001842	0.47303878599815796	0.4730	0.5270	0.4730
4	[0.45, 0.47]	0.4692566129190307	0.5307433870809692	0.5307	0.4963	0.5307
	[0.47, 0.49]	0.4894245616745444	0.5105754383254556	0.5106	0.4894	0.5106
	[0.49, 0.51]	0.4977581356869125	0.5022418643130875	0.5022	0.4978	0.5022
	[0.51, 0.53]	0.5252940422781874	0.47470595772181257	0.4747	0.5253	0.4747
	[0.53, 0.55]	0.5489494404460169	0.4510505595539831	0.4511	0.5489	0.4511

Table 4 shows execution of three queries on the submodels and statistical analysis on the accuracy of each skewed interval in comparison to the target value. The difference of the mean of the actual probability and the computed probability distribution. A set of sample queries are demonstrated to elucidate the methodology. The sample PCTL queries are:

1. Query 1 (Q1): Probability of reaching the goal state? P=? [F "goal_1"].
2. Query 2 (Q2): Probability of encountering an obstacle? P=? [F stop_1].
3. Query 3(Q3): Probability of reaching take_off P=? [F goal_1].

Figure 3 shows the probability distributions for each queries for the intervals.

Table 4. Statistical Confidence (SC) Scores for probability distributions constructed from subintervals 1–4 using the EM algorithm and MCMC algorithm on query results for each subinterval. The column, Diff implies the difference between the mean of the probability distribution and the mean from the computed probability distribution

Query	Mean	Method	Distribution	SC	Diff
Q1	0.469	EM	Interval 1	(0.468, 0.469)	0.0005
	0.502	EM	Interval 2	(0.501, 0.502)	0.0008
	0.517	EM	Interval 3	(0.517, 0.518)	0.0000
	0.494	EM	Interval 4	(0.493, 0.494)	0.0000
Q2	0.531	EM	Interval 1	(0.531, 0.532)	0.0000
	0.499	EM	Interval 2	(0.499, 0.500)	0.0000
	0.483	EM	Interval 3	(0.482, 0.483)	0.0000
	0.512	EM	Interval 4	(0.511, 0.512)	0.0000
Q3	0.469	EM	Interval 1	(0.468, 0.469)	0.0005
	0.502	EM	Interval 2	(0.501, 0.502)	0.0008
	0.517	EM	Interval 3	(0.517, 0.518)	0.0000
	0.494	EM	Interval 4	(0.493, 0.494)	0.0000
Q1	0.469	MCMC	Interval 1	(0.467, 0.468)	0.0323
	0.502	MCMC	Interval 2	(0.502, 0.503)	0.0021
	0.517	MCMC	Interval 3	(0.517, 0.519)	0.0180
	0.494	MCMC	Interval 4	(0.493, 0.495)	0.0060
Q2	0.531	MCMC	Interval 1	(0.532, 0.533)	0.0322
	0.499	MCMC	Interval 2	(0.498, 0.499)	0.0016
	0.483	MCMC	Interval 3	(0.481, 0.482)	0.0188
	0.512	MCMC	Interval 4	(0.510, 0.511)	0.0102
Q3	0.469	MCMC	Interval 1	(0.467, 0.469)	0.0320
	0.502	MCMC	Interval 2	(0.502, 0.503)	0.0026
	0.517	MCMC	Interval 3	(0.516, 0.517)	0.0165
	0.494	MCMC	Interval 4	(0.492, 0.493)	0.0073

6 Discussion

The construction of submodels, $\mathcal{M}_s$ from the original IDTMC, $\mathcal{M}_I$ were based on the partitions of the intervals. The number of submodels are the number of cartesian products of the subintervals. The accuracy of the proposed formalism would have increased because the probability distribution would have been more accurate given the number of data would have been significantly higher. However, considering only 5 submodels from the original IDTMC is computationally efficient. The limitations of this methodology and potential solutions are:

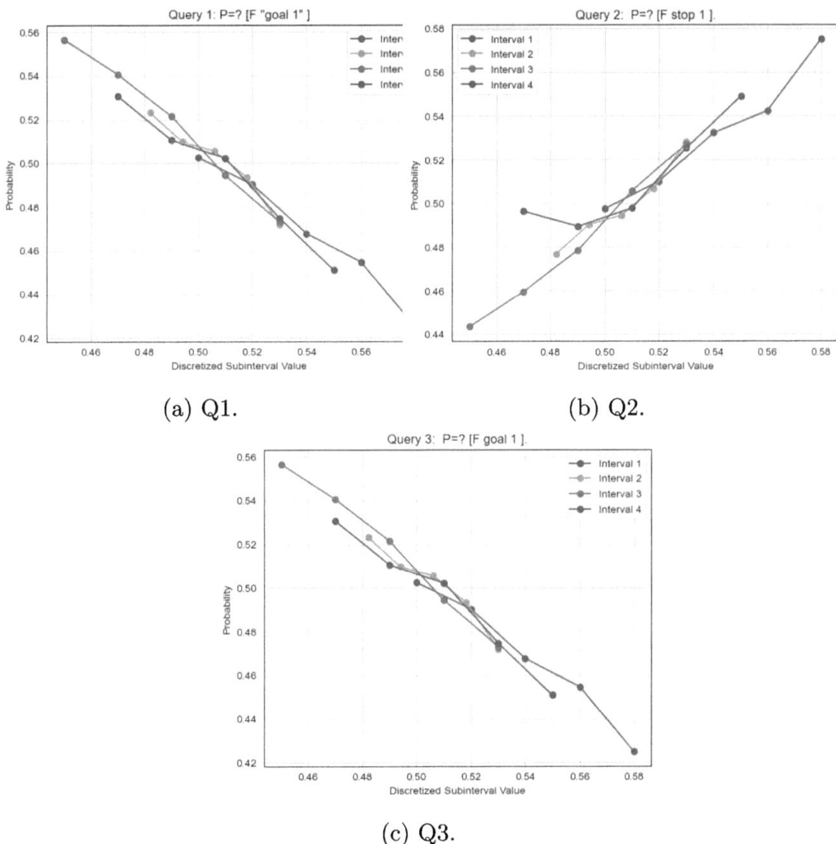

(a) Q1.

(b) Q2.

(c) Q3.

Fig. 2. Results from executing queries 1–3 on the skewed intervals as seen in Table 3. The Y-axis corresponds with the query result for each subinterval, and the x-axis corresponds with the probability generated by the discretization of each subinterval.

- The increase in the number of subintervals of the intervals will exponentially increase the number of submodels, therefore, making the methodology computationally expensive. A solution to address the reduction in submodel space would be to construct the subintervals, iteratively.
- MCMC and EM created the approximate distributions. However, EM has better accuracy as shown in Table 4.

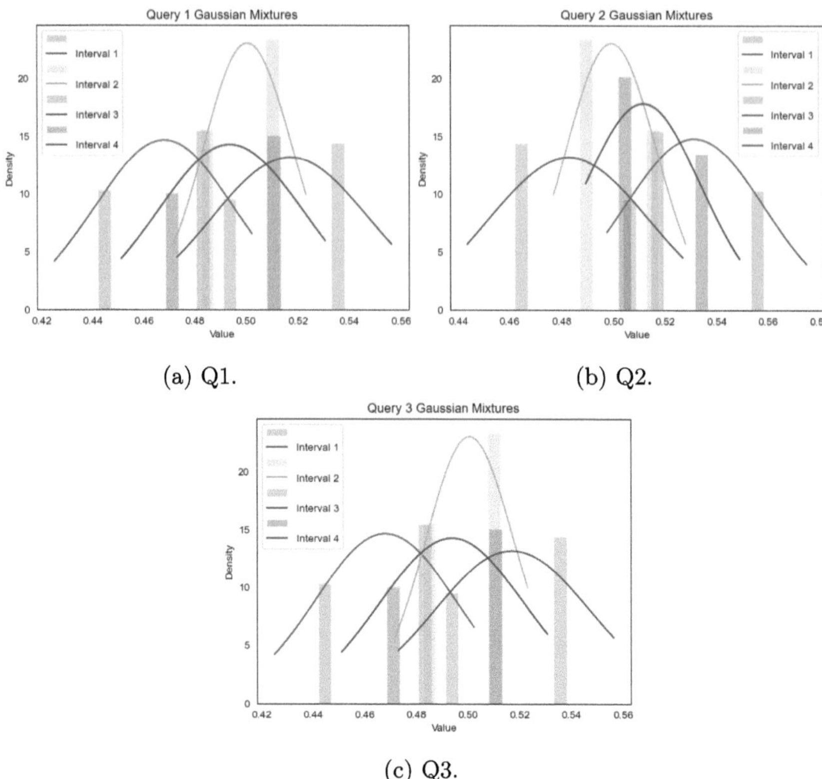

(a) Q1. (b) Q2.

(c) Q3.

Fig. 3. Plots showing EM results for all submodels made with an interval size of 0.05. Reading left to right, plots show the results from query 1 (Q1), query 2 (Q2) and query 3 (Q3) with the Gaussian distributions from submodels built from 4 subintervals.

7 Conclusion

In this work, a reasoning mechanism based on concepts of obligation, permissible and forbidden rules from Deontic logic. The formal reasoning of the model abstraction provides the user with the plan of action that is ethically admissible with a statistical guarantee. The prototype of aircraft take off was used as a case study to evaluate the computational feasibility of the model abstraction.

The uncertainty in the model is represented by IDTMC. Statistical inference is provided by computing the statistical significance on the output probabilistic model checking on model presenting for ethical actions.

Acknowledgements. The work is supported by NASA grant 80NSSC23M0166 and is a part of NASA EPSCoR Rapid Research Response 2023 grant.

References

1. Abeywickrama, D.B., Cirstea, C., Ramchurn, S.D.: Model checking human-agent collectives for responsible AI. In: 2019 28th IEEE International Conference on Robot and Human Interactive Communication (RO-MAN), pp. 1–8. IEEE (2019)
2. Aziz, A., Sanwal, K., Singhal, V., Brayton, R.: Verifying continuous time Markov chains. In: Alur, R., Henzinger, T.A. (eds.) CAV 1996. LNCS, vol. 1102, pp. 269–276. Springer, Heidelberg (1996). https://doi.org/10.1007/3-540-61474-5_75
3. Badings, T.S., Jansen, N., Junges, S., Stoelinga, M., Volk, M.: Sampling-based verification of CTMCs with uncertain rates. In: International Conference on Computer Aided Verification, pp. 26–47. Springer (2022)
4. Baier, C., Katoen, J.P.: Principles of model checking. MIT Press (2008)
5. Baier, C., Katoen, J.P., Hermanns, H., Wolf, V.: Comparative branching-time semantics for Markov chains. Inf. Comput. **200**(2), 149–214 (2005)
6. Balasubramaniam, N., Kauppinen, M., Kujala, S., Hiekkanen, K.: Ethical guidelines for solving ethical issues and developing AI systems. In: International Conference on Product-Focused Software Process Improvement, pp. 331–346. Springer (2020)
7. Benedikt, M., Lenhardt, R., Worrell, J.: LTL model checking of interval Markov chains. In: Tools and Algorithms for the Construction and Analysis of Systems: 19th International Conference, TACAS 2013, Held as Part of the European Joint Conferences on Theory and Practice of Software, ETAPS 2013, Rome, Italy, March 16-24, 2013. Proceedings 19, pp. 32–46. Springer (2013)
8. Bonnemains, V., Saurel, C., Tessier, C.: Embedded ethics: some technical and ethical challenges. Ethics Inf. Technol. **20**(1), 41–58 (2018). https://doi.org/10.1007/s10676-018-9444-x
9. Chatterjee, K., Sen, K., Henzinger, T.A.: Model-checking ω-regular properties of interval Markov chains. In: Foundations of Software Science and Computational Structures: 11th International Conference, FOSSACS 2008, Held as Part of the Joint European Conferences on Theory and Practice of Software, ETAPS 2008, Budapest, Hungary, March 29-April 6, 2008. Proceedings 11, pp. 302–317. Springer (2008)
10. Clarke, E., Emerson, E., Sistla, A.: Automatic verification of finite-state concurrent systems using temporal logic specifications. ACM Trans. Programm. Lang. Syst. (TOPLAS) **8**(2), 244–263 (1986)
11. Dignum, V., et al.: Ethics by design: necessity or curse? In: Proceedings of the 2018 AAAI/ACM Conference on AI, Ethics, and Society, pp. 60–66 (2018)
12. Fisher, M., Mascardi, V., Rozier, K.Y., Schlingloff, B.H., Winikoff, M., Yorke-Smith, N.: Towards a framework for certification of reliable autonomous systems. Auton. Agent. Multi-Agent Syst. **35**, 1–65 (2021)
13. Ghosh, K., Smith, C.: Formal analysis of deontic logic model for ethical decisions. In: Rocha, A.P., Steels, L., van den Herik, H.J. (eds.) Proceedings of the 17th International Conference on Agents and Artificial Intelligence, ICAART 2025 - Volume 1, Porto, Portugal, February 23-25, 2025, pp. 218–223. SCITEPRESS (2025). https://doi.org/10.5220/0013385200003890, https://doi.org/10.5220/0013385200003890
14. Hansson, H., Jonsson, B.: A logic for reasoning about time and reliability. Formal Aspects Comput. **6**, 512–535 (1994)
15. Hilpinen, R., McNamara, P.: Deontic logic: a historical survey and introduction. Handbook Deontic Logic Normative Syst. **1**, 3–136 (2013)

16. Horty, J.F.: Agency and Deontic Logic. Oxford University Press, Oxford (2001)
17. Kwiatkowska, M., Norman, G., Parker, D.: PRISM: probabilistic symbolic model checker. In: International Conference on Modelling Techniques and Tools for Computer Performance Evaluation, pp. 200–204. Springer (2002)
18. Luckcuck, M., Farrell, M., Dennis, L.A., Dixon, C., Fisher, M.: Formal specification and verification of autonomous robotic systems: a survey. ACM Comput. Surv. (CSUR) **52**(5), 1–41 (2019)
19. Sen, K., Viswanathan, M., Agha, G.: Model-checking Markov chains in the presence of uncertainties. In: Tools and Algorithms for the Construction and Analysis of Systems: 12th International Conference, TACAS 2006, Held as Part of the Joint European Conferences on Theory and Practice of Software, ETAPS 2006, Vienna, Austria, March 25-April 2, 2006. Proceedings 12, pp. 394–410. Springer (2006)

Opposite Color Multiscale Local Binary Pattern Features for the Prediction of Bread Edibility

Kavitha Rajamani[1](✉) and Guru Devanur S[2]

[1] Department of Statistics and Data Science, CHRIST University, Bangalore, Karnataka 560029, India
kavitha.rajamani@christuniversity.in

[2] Department of Studies in Computer Science, University of Mysore, Manasagangotri, Mysuru, Karnataka 570 006, India
dsg@compsci.uni-mysore.ac.in

Abstract. Bread is one of the profoundly consumed staple bakery foods by many people in the world. Quality is a remarkable concern as it is a consumable food product. It depends on the raw ingredients and baking process involved during the preparation. After the purchase of the bread, the quality and in turn the shelf life period of the bread may likely to get affected by the storage method. Hence, the edibility of the bread needs to be estimated. Most of the studies do estimate this using sensory attribute measurements like strange odor, crust color, taste, aroma, hard texture and mold formation. On contrary, this study newly attempts to examine the edibility effortlessly through images. A new variant of texture based Local Binary Pattern features is proposed for the prediction of edibility through analysis of hard texture and mold formation. As there is no benchmark bread sample dataset available for the study, a new dataset of 18,513 images is created. It is observed from the experimentation that the proposed Opposite Color Multiscale Local Binary Pattern features provide good estimation on majority voting with reduced number of features through feature transformation and selection. The accuracy obtained is 0.8493 which is comparable with other common variants of local binary pattern features. Multiple classifiers are evaluated during experimental analysis and ensemble approach outperforms well. As this is a contemporary problem addressed in the domain based on images of bread being first of its kind, it is likely to open up new challenges to be undertaken.

Keywords: Bread Edibility · Texture Features · Local Binary Pattern · Bread Quality

1 Introduction

Bakery products are ready to eat processed food. Amongst them, bread is one of the popular foods that is consumed by many people across the world. It is generally made up of wheat, maida, milk or milk powder and other ingredients. As it is a consumable food product, quality is to be maintained with utmost care [1]. Bread packets have best by date which denotes how long the bread stays fresh accounting to edibility which is normally

T. T. Quan et al. (Eds.): MIWAI 2025, LNAI 16353, pp. 341–353, 2026.
https://doi.org/10.1007/978-981-95-4957-3_28

3 to 7 days. A number of factors play a role in estimating the quality of bread such as selection of raw ingredients, quality of ingredients, time of backing process, inclusion of bread improver, usage of milk or milk powder, addition of preservatives. The quality estimation of the wheat bread was done by analyzing sensory data of physical, rheological measures collected in real time using Fuzzy weighted relevance vector machine [1]. Through functional and sensory characteristics, the quality of bread is assessed and the consumer acceptability had been checked [2, 3]. Bread quality index was established using the instrumental analysis of appearance, structure and texture that influence consumers' acceptability [4]. The quality of flours in bread making was determined by measuring specific volume, crumb grain attributes, crust and crumb color, firmness as compressibility [5]. The determination of loaf volume, crumb texture and quality by means of flour and dough alveograph properties was well studied [6]. Quality evaluation of functional bread from different blends of constrained mixture was done by analyzing the physico-chemical, antioxidant properties, color and sensory qualities [7]. Texture profile analysis and sensory evaluation were done on Gluten free breads to compare with their wheat-based counterparts [8]. A study of quality parameters in breads made using household bread maker and industrial bread making equipment inferred that bread maker produced breads can give misleading indications of likely ingredient effects at industrial scale [9]. Another study analyzed the ingredients of Gluten Free breads and found the divergences in compositions in commercially available product [10]. A review was done [11] on bread enriched with phenolic compounds and their effects on dough properties, quality and potential health benefits. It is well noticed from the review that, most of the studies on bread quality estimation involves laboratory procedures and sensory attribute measurements. The quality in the initial stage can be estimated through laboratory procedures. After purchase of the bread, the edibility may get affected by the storage method even the bread is of good quality when it was purchased. And hence, there is a chance of change in shelf-life period. The symptoms that are exposed to show the non-edibility is unpleasant odor, mold formation, strange taste, aroma and hard texture. Human intervention with sensory attributes is needed to check the edibility.

The common symptom which can be identified through computer vision is mold formation. But the challenge is the early detection of mold and hard texture which is nearly impossible through human eyes where computer vision techniques can help. This motivated us to take up the study to predict the edibility of the bread after purchase by considering the parameters that can be determined visually. Also from the literature, it is known that none of the study attempted to estimate the edibility of the bread through image samples but through sensory attributes only. Hence, in this study an effort is made to check the edibility of the bread through images. Figure 1 illustrates the complexity as Fig. 1(a) and (b) belong to different categories of bread edibility but appears visually similar and Fig. 1(c) appears to be edible where the mold formation is in early stages and cannot be identified through visual appearance.

Hence, the aim of this study is to predict the edibility of bread through texture-based features and supervised learning algorithms. As mold formation and hard texture are considered for prediction, the texture-based features do good enough and hence Local Binary Pattern (LBP) feature descriptors are preferred for underlying study.

The specific objectives are as follows.

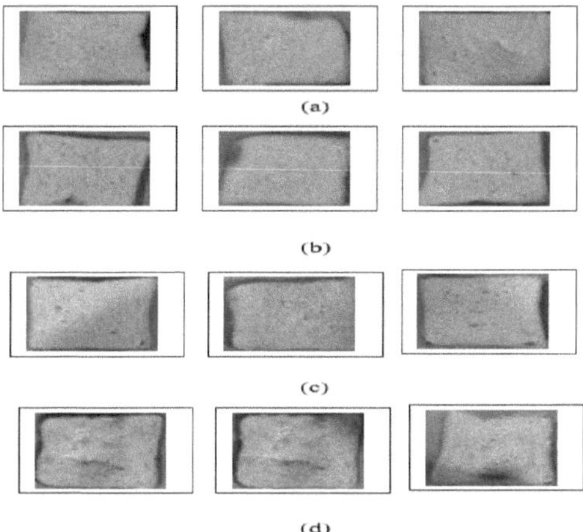

Fig. 1. Bread images taken on different days (a) Edible Breads on Day 2 (b) Nonedible Breads on Day 5 (c) Nonedible Breads on Day 6 (d) Nonedible Breads on Day 7.

- To create a large dataset of bread sample images in support of research work.
- To extract the texture features using variants of LBP and analyze their performances in edibility prediction of breads.
- To propose a new variant of LBP to extract texture-based features suitable for bread edibility prediction.
- Modeling the prediction of edibility of the bread.

In Sect. 2, the proposed methodology is explained. The model performance is analyzed and comparative study is done in Sects. 3 and 4 concludes the paper.

2 Proposed Model

This section presents in detail the proposed method for feature extraction and subsequently a method of predicting edibility of bread from the given bread image. The architecture of the proposed model is represented in Fig. 2.

2.1 Feature Extraction

A new variant of LBP is proposed for feature extraction. Instead of taking gray scale images, color images are considered here. An inter-channel approach is used as there will be a variation in the center pixel and neighboring pixels in terms of color channels as Red, Green and Blue. The channel of center pixel is represented as 'M' and the channel of corresponding neighboring pixels is represented as 'N'. The proposed Opposite Color Multiscale LBP is represented in general as $OCMLBP_{MN}$. Hence, for a given RGB image, there are six potential combinations of channels as $OCMLBP_{rg}$, $OCMLBP_{gr}$, $OCMLBP_{rb}$, $OCMLBP_{br}$, $OCMLBP_{gb}$ and $OCMLBP_{gb}$.

It has been observed from the study [12], that the symmetric channels 'rg' and 'gr', 'rb' and 'br', 'gb' and 'bg' produce almost similar histograms. Thus, the three

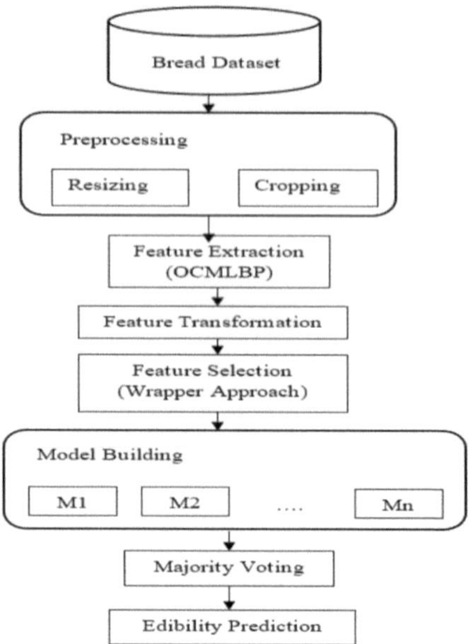

Fig. 2. Architecture of the Proposed Model.

channels $OCMLBP_{rg}$, $OCMLBP_{rb}$ and $OCMLBP_{bg}$ giving more descriptive information are considered. As a sample, the representation of $OCMLBP_{rg}$ with radius R = 1 is given in Fig. 3. The gray circle in the red channel is considered as the center pixel. The neighboring pixels are from green channel where the green solid circle represents the sampling points with value 0 and the white circles with green border represents the sampling points with value 1.

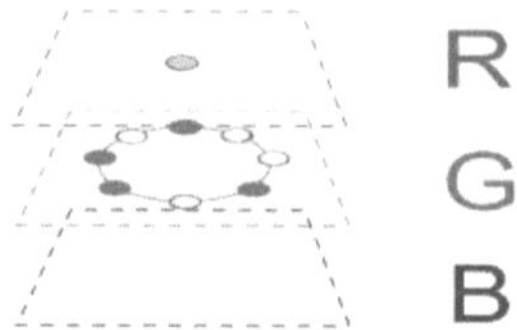

Fig. 3. Representation of $OCMLBP_{RG}$ descriptor.

For a given radius 'R' and number of neighboring pixels 'P',

$$OCMLBP_{MN}(I_c) = \sum_{p=0}^{P-1} D\left(NI_p - MI_c\right)2^p \tag{1}$$

where the Step function, $D(t) = \begin{cases} 1, & if \ \ t \geq 0 \\ 0, otherwise \end{cases}$,

R = Radius, P = Number of Neighboring points,

NIp = Neighboring Pixel from Nth Channel,
MIc = Center pixel from Mth Channel,
Where N, M ∈ {Red, Green, Blue} and N ≠ M.

Instead of keeping Radius (R) and Number of neighbors (P) as fixed parameters, an effort is made to vary them for each opposite color descriptor. Hence, several LBP channels can be generated based on varying 'P' for a given 'R' which can provide variant yet efficient texture descriptors [13]. The 'P' is chosen in such a way that it produces symmetrical sampling. When R = 1, the possible 'P' values are 4 and 8, when R = 2, the possible 'P' values are 4, 8 and 16. In general, for a given radius 'R' there will be R + 1 distinctive LBP channels and the maximum P value is 8R. Different 'R' values can be taken to have varied set of number of neighbors.

Subsequently, from R + 1 LBP channels, same number of histograms are generated and hence, for a given radius 'R', R + 1 histograms are generated and concatenated.

$$H_R = H_R^4 \oplus H_R^8 \ldots \oplus H_R^{8R} \tag{2}$$

where ⊕ is the concatenation operator.

$$LBP_R = \left[LBP_{R,4}, LBP_{R,8}, \ldots, LBP_{R,8R}\right] \tag{3}$$

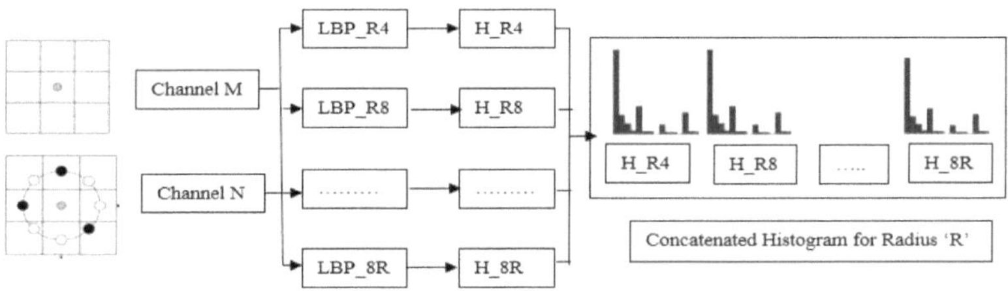

Fig. 4. Multipoint LBP Channels and Concatenated Histograms.

The representation of multipoint LBP channels along with the corresponding concatenated histograms is given in Fig. 4.

As R + 1 histograms are generated for a given 'R', upon varying the 'R', the total number of histograms generated are $\sum_{R=1}^{N} R + 1$ where $N = Max(R)$.

For Example, if N = 1, (R = 1 → P = 4, P = 8) two histograms are generated. If N = 2, (for R = 1 → P = 4, P = 8), (for R = 2 → P = 4, P = 8, P = 16) and hence totally five histograms are generated.

The number of histograms increases with increase in radius and in turn the size of the feature matrix. To reduce the huge dimensionality of the feature matrix, the histograms are quantized.

$$Q_R^p = \frac{\max H_R^P - \min H_R^P}{b} \tag{4}$$

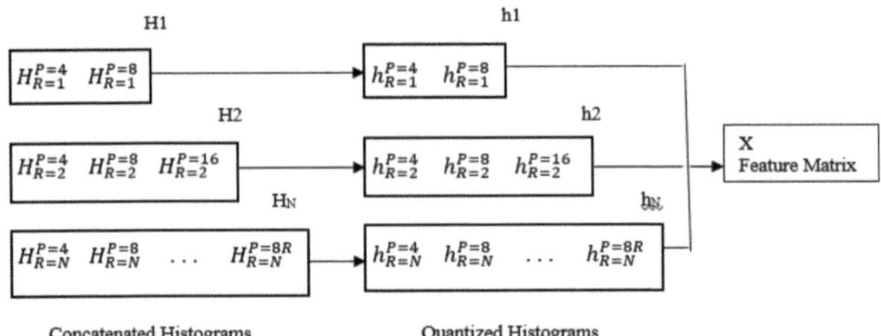

Fig. 5. Feature Extraction using Quantized Multiscale LBP Histograms.

where b is the equal width bins in the given range and the result is rounded to the nearest integer.

Hence, the Quantized Histogram for Radius 'R' is given as,

$$h_R = Q_R^4 \oplus Q_R^8 \ldots \oplus Q_R^{8R} \tag{5}$$

The feature matrix 'X' is given as,

$$X = h_1 \oplus h_2 \ldots h_N \tag{6}$$

The feature matrix generation using quantized multiscale histograms is represented in Fig. 5. Upon attaining the features, it is subjected to feature transformation and feature selection using wrapper approach to reduce the number of features.

2.2 Model Building

The obtained features from feature selection are subjected to learning for the edibility prediction. Various classifiers are taken and the models are built individually. Each model predicts the edibility independently. To predict the final edibility of the bread, the majority voting is applied on the outcome of the various classifier models undertaken and then the edibility label is declared.

3 Experimentation

3.1 Dataset

The prediction of edibility of bread from images is a new idea and hence there are no standard datasets available. So, a new dataset is created. The images are captured through mobiles Redmi Note 10Lite and Redmi Note8 with 48 MP camera. Bread packets are bought from 10 different bakeries in 5 different batches and the dataset is created.

The bread taken for the study is white bread and the shelf-life period is 4 to 6 days depending on the bakery. The samples are kept in a sealed environment. The bread is kept on the clean table and images are taken with different orientations. The samples are labeled using a combination of parameters as bakery, day, bread, and orientation

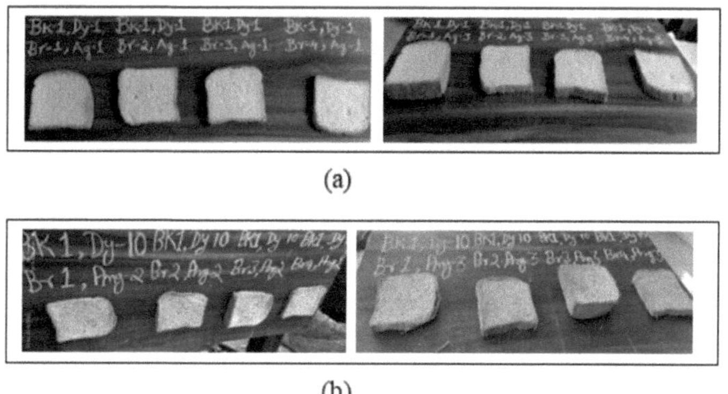

Fig. 6. Bread Dataset Scenario with different orientation (a) First Day Sample Images (b) Tenth Day Sample Images

by representing numerically to differentiate them and constructed a structured dataset as shown in Fig. 6. However, the images of each sample are captured individually and saved along with their corresponding parameters for input purposes. Totally, 18513 images have been captured to create the dataset. It is a binary classification problem having edible and nonedible as the classes. The number of samples present in the edible class is 10548 and nonedible class is 7965. Table 1 provides the detail about the dataset created.

Table 1. Statistics of Bread Dataset Created

	Edible		Non-Edible	
No. of Bakeries	No. of Days	Total Samples	No. of Days	Total Samples
2	4 (Day 1 to Day 4)	1600	3 (Day 5 to Day 7)	1500
3	5 (Day 1 to Day 5)	3000	3 (Day 6 to Day 8)	2450
5	6 (Day 1 to Day 6)	5948	3 (Day 7 to Day 9)	4015
Total	**10548**		**7965**	

3.2 Experimental Setup

Image annotation is done using the tool LabelImg to create a dataset for computer vision based model training. Then, a model is created using YoloV5, a pretrained deep architecture to crop the remaining images. The images are resized to 256 x 256 for further analysis and standardization is done. Different modifications of LBP considered for experimentation purpose are: - Basic LBP, Local Ternary Pattern [13] (LTP), Complete LBP [14] (CLBP), Binarized Statistical Image Features [15] (BSIF), Opposite Color LBP [12] (OCLBP), Multiscale LBP [16] (MLBP), Local Variance Pattern [13] (LVP), Rotated LBP [17] (RLBP), Three Phase LBP [18] (TPLBP), Multiscale Local Ternary

Pattern [19] (MLTP). By default, the bin size of the histogram drawn from LBP image is kept as 10. The entire dataset is divided into train and test set with the varying spilt-up ratio of 60:40, 70:30 and 80:20.

3.3 Experimental Results

The features are extracted from varied LBPs and the classifier is built for the prediction.

Table 2. Performance of variants of LBP features with different classifiers in terms of Accuracy.

SNo	LBP	Before Feature Extraction					After Feature Extraction using FLD				
		No. of Features	SVM	RF	KNN	Ada Boost	No. of Features	SVM	RF	KNN	Ada Boost
1	OCLBP	156	0.785	0.805	0.793	0.798	72	0.799	**0.829**	0.801	0.810
2	MLBP	47	0.758	0.800	0.782	0.775	17	0.775	**0.815**	0.815	0.795
3	CLBP	78	0.659	0.723	0.684	0.694	41	0.658	0.735	0.700	0.715
4	LBP	26	0.549	0.701	0.685	0.685	13	0.554	0.725	0.694	0.703
5	RLBP	26	0.682	0.682	0.682	0.682	14	0.703	0.703	0.703	0.703
6	BSIF	26	0.675	0.675	0.675	0.675	16	0.695	0.695	0.695	0.695
7	TPLBP	26	0.675	0.658	0.635	0.624	16	0.685	0.662	0.657	0.638
8	LVP	26	0.698	0.657	0.645	0.668	14	0.703	0.685	0.674	0.685
9	MLTP	40	0.646	0.646	0.646	0.646	29	0.668	0.668	0.668	0.668
10	LTP	52	0.638	0.638	0.638	0.638	36	0.652	0.652	0.652	0.652

The different classifiers that are taken for this study are Support Vector Machine Classifier (SVM), Random Forest Classifier (RF), K-Nearest Neighbor Classifier (KNN) and AdaBoost Classifier. Then, the supervised feature extraction technique Fisher's Linear Discriminant (FLD) is employed to reduce the dimension of the features and the performance of the classifiers are examined. Here, only the coefficients of linear discriminants having positive values are considered. Since the task involves classification and aims to maximize the separation between classes by selecting features that are more relevant for decision boundaries, FLD is utilized for dimensionality reduction. This leads to a more compact and discriminative feature space, resulting in improved model performance even with a reduced set of features. Table 2 depicts the experimental results for prediction of edibility of bread in terms of accuracy measure before and after feature extraction with FLD. It is observed that OCLBP features with RF is performing well amongst all the variants of LBPs in terms of accuracy and it is followed by MLBP. When the percentage of reduction in features is concerned upon feature extraction using FLD, MLBP stands first with 64% reduction in number of features and it is followed by OCLBP having 54% reduction.

An attempt is made to fuse few of the features and after applying FLD for feature extraction, the performances of classifiers are inspected and tabulated in Table 3.

Table 3. Performance of the classifiers after feature fusing followed by FLD Feature Extraction

S. No	Features Fused (Total No. of Features)	Number of Features Extracted	SVM	RF	KNN	AdaBoost
1	OCLBP + MLBP (203)	67	0.8127	**0.8309**	0.8267	0.8287
2	LBP + OCLBP (182)	71	0.7401	0.7529	0.7292	0.7428
3	LBP + OCLBP + MLBP (229)	74	0.7259	0.7498	0.7139	0.726
4	LBP + LVP + LTP + RLBP (130)	43	0.7358	0.7598	0.72	0.7291
5	LBP + LVP (52)	19	0.7329	0.7726	0.7132	0.7203

It is evident from Table 3 that the RF Classifier performs well when OCLBP features are fused with MLBP. And more over it is found that OCLBP and MLBP features with RF is providing good accuracy when it is fused with other variants of features also. Hence, the proposed method OCMLBP is built upon the concepts of OCLBP and MLBP.

Table 4. Performance of the classifiers using the proposed OCMLBP features upon different feature engineering techniques.

Feature Engineering Technique	Threshold Parameter	No. of Features Selected / Extracted	SVM	RF	KNN	AdaBoost
Proposed OCMLBP (Without Feature Engineering) 141			0.8051	**0.8269**	0.7987	0.8206
Feature Selection (Filtering Approach)						
Variance Threshold	0.01	119	0.8042	**0.8305**	0.7727	0.7881
Chi Square Score	> = 0.01	106	**0.7953**	0.7938	0.7925	0.7
Mutual Info Classif.	> 0.85	85	0.7923	**0.8009**	0.7828	0.7756
f_Classification	> 10	92	0.7864	**0.7986**	0.787	0.7823
Feature Extraction (Transformation)						
FLD	-	52	0.8157	**0.8426**	0.8105	0.8259

The features are extracted using the proposed OCMLBP feature extraction method and the performance of different classifiers are analyzed. It is found that RF classifier performs well by providing accuracy of 0.8269 on considering 141 features. The next classifier performing well is AdaBoost with an accuracy of 0.8206. Random Forest and

AdaBoost yielded strong performance, likely due to their ensemble learning architecture, which aggregates multiple weak or diverse learners to improve generalization and reduce variance. The performance of the classifiers on employing different feature selection and feature extraction techniques are tabulated in Table 4. Different feature selection techniques with filtering approach considered for experimentation are Variance Threshold, Chi Square Score, Mutual Info Classification and f_Classification. Among them, Variance Threshold based feature selection with RF classifier performs well by providing an accuracy of 0.8305. When Fisher's Linear Discriminant feature transformation technique is applied, the RF classifier performs well with an accuracy of 0.8426 by reducing the number of features to 52. Then, wrapper approach of feature selection is tried out for experimentation. The technique employed here is Sequential Feature Selector (SFS). The number of features selected are reduced on applying wrapper approach than filtering approach. Here too, the RF classifier is performing well than others with the accuracy of 0.8324 followed by AdaBoost with the accuracy of 0.8312. The performance of variants of classifiers on applying SFS is in Table 5.

Table 5. Performance of variants of classifiers using the OCMLBP features upon Sequential Feature Selector.

Classifier	Accuracy: Before Feature Selection (141 Features)	After Feature Selection	
		Number of Features Selected	Accuracy
SVM	0.8051	78	0.8262
RF	0.8269	65	**0.8324**
KNN	0.7987	85	0.8006
AdaBoost	0.8206	72	0.8312

Table 6. Performance of the proposed system using the OCMLBP features.

Feature Engineering Technique	Threshold Parameter	Number of Features Selected / Extracted	SVM	RF	KNN	AdaBoost
OCMLBP (Without Feature Engineering) 141 Features			0.8051	0.8269	0.7987	0.8206
Feature Extraction (FLD) Followed by Feature Selection (Wrapper Approach) using RF						
FLD + SFS	-	48	0.8257	0.849	0.8263	0.8316
Majority Voting with 48 Features (SVM, RF, KNN, AdaBoost)			**0.8493**			

Table 6 exhibits the performance of the proposed system using the OCMLBP features. In the proposed model, initially the feature extraction is done using FLD and extracted 52 features. Then those transformed features are subjected to subsetting selection method using SFS following RF, it is observed that the number of features are reduced to 48. Upon taking majority voting from the classifiers (SVM, RF, KNN and AdaBoost), the performance of the proposed model is 0.8493 in terms of accuracy.

3.4 Discussion

It is noticeable from Tables 4 and 5, that the feature transformation on OCMLBP features gives better results upon classification than feature selection of both filtering and wrapper approaches. Because, feature transformation modifies the data and projects into a different subspace to make it more understandable for the model whereas feature selection is mere subsetting of the existing features. Also, the new projection in transformation will provide clear perspective so that the classes are separable apparently. Feature extraction using FLD performs better than wrapper based feature selection approach resulting in the reduction of 63% of number of features (From 141 to 52 features). From Table 2, it is noticeable that out of 10 variants of LBPs examined, RF performs well with 8 variants of LBP features. Similar estimation is observed using the proposed OCMLBP features also. Invariantly on different feature engineering techniques applied, RF performs well as it is an ensemble learning method. The confusion matrix upon the performance of the proposed system is given in Table 7. False Positive (FP) is an error in which a model incorrectly indicates the presence of a condition. That is, observation is predicted as positive class when it is actually belonging to negative class. As the problem is related to edibility prediction, the model which produced less FP should be recommended. Because, the cost of recognizing nonedible bread as edible bread is too high than predicting edible bread as nonedible bread.

Table 7. Confusion Matrix of the proposed system.

	Predicted		
Actual		Edible	Nonedible
	Edible	1860	250
	Nonedible	308	1285

The False Positive of the proposed system is 0.1933 which is comparable with the other LBPs specified in Table 2. The comparison of False positive rates of RF classifier upon utilizing variants of LBPs along with proposed system is represented in the Fig. 7.

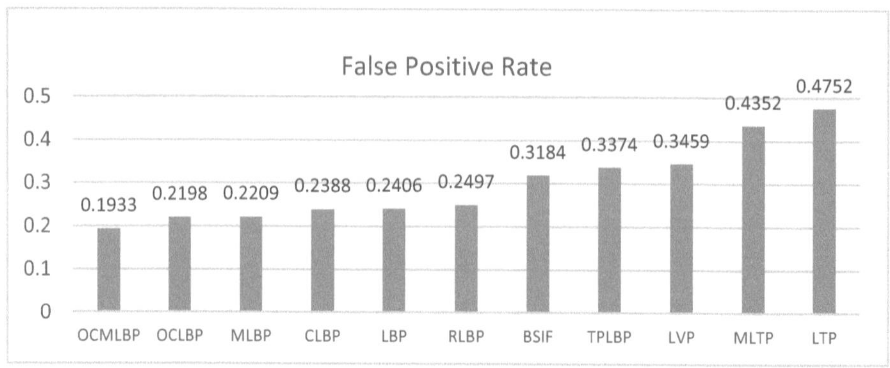

Fig. 7. False Positive Rates obtained using RF classifier with variants of LBP features.

It is evident from the Fig. 7 that the proposed OCMLBP feature descriptors aids in attaining lower false positive rate compared to other forms of LBP feature descriptors.

4 Conclusions and Future Work

Bread is one of the commonest foods worldwide. Quality of the bread is critical as it is a consumable food product. The normal quality checking involves laboratory procedures and sensory attributes. The expiry of the product may get alter because of change in the storage method. In order to estimate the edibility of the bread effortlessly by a common man, this study attempts to predict the edibility through bread images. The texture features are attained through a proposed Opposite Color Multiscale Local Binary Pattern and the edibility is predicted by majority voting with different classifiers. An accuracy of 0.8493 is obtained with the proposed texture based feature extraction. A new bread image dataset of having 18513 images is created as there is no standard dataset available for the study. The proposed model is compared against variants of LBP features extracted. It is also inferred that the proposed model performs well by providing minimum number of false positives which is really required in this problem scenario. As texture based features are good in capturing the patterns of mold formation and hard texture in the bread images, LBP is used for feature extraction which is a texture based feature extractor. Hence, deep learning is not applied as it involves complex multilayered architecture with more features and parameters involved. Also, the machine learning models are explainable in contrary to deep learning. In further, a mobile app could be developed to check the edibility of the bread. Also, the quality of the bread could be evaluated by estimating the quality of the ingredients and parameters of baking process through images itself. As this is a contemporary problem addressed in the domain, it is likely to open up new challenges to be undertaken.

Conflict of Interest. The authors declare that they have no conflicts of interest towards this article.

References

1. Ali, Z.N., Askerzade, I., Abdulwahab, S.: Estimation model for bread quality proficiency using fuzzy weighted relevance vector machine classifier. Appl. Bionics Biomech. **2021**, 6670316 (2021)
2. Adebayo-Oyetoro, A.O., Ogundipe, O.O., Adeeko, K.N.: Quality assessment and consumer acceptability of bread from wheat and fermented banana flour. Food Sci. Nutr. **4**(3), 364–369 (2016)
3. Al-Saleh, A., Brennan, C.S.: Bread wheat quality: some physical, chemical and rheological characteristics of Syrian and English bread wheat samples. Foods **1**, 3–17 (2012)
4. Curic, D., et al.: Design of a quality index for the objective evaluation of bread quality: application to wheat breads using selected bake-off technology for bread making. Food Res. Int. **41**, 714–719 (2008)
5. Doğan, İS., Yildiz, Ö., Taşan, B.: Determination of the bread-making quality of flours using an automatic bread machine. Turk. J. Agricult. For. **36**(5), 608–618 (2012)
6. Różyło, R., Laskowski, J.: Predicting bread quality (bread loaf volume and crumb texture). Pol. J. Food Nutr. Sci. **61**(1), 61–67 (2011)
7. Ibidapo, O.P., Henshaw, F.O., Shittu, T.A., Afolabi, W.A.: Quality evaluation of functional bread developed from wheat, malted millet (Pennisetum Glaucum) and 'Okara' flour blends. Sci. African **10**, e00622 (2020)
8. Tóth, M., Kaszab, T., Meretei, A.: Texture profile analysis and sensory evaluation of commercially available gluten-free bread samples. Euro. Food Res. Technol. **248**, 1447–1455 (2022)
9. Trinh, L., Campbell, G.M., Martin, P.J.: Scaling down bread production for quality assessment using a bread maker: are results from a bread maker representative of other bread making methods? Food Bioprod. Process. **100**, 54–60 (2016)
10. Roman, L., Belorio, M., Gomez, M.: Gluten-free breads: the gap between research and commercial reality. Compr. Rev. Food Sci. Food Saf. **18**(3), 690–702 (2019)
11. Xua, J., Wanga, W., Li, Y.: Dough properties, bread quality, and associated interactions with added phenolic compounds: a review. J. Funct. Foods **52**, 629–639 (2019)
12. Maenpaa, T.: The local binary pattern approach to texture analysis – extensions and applications, Academic Dissertation, University of Oulu (2003)
13. Freitas, P.G., Da Eira, L.P., Santos, S.S., de Farias, M.C.Q.: On the application LBP texture descriptors and its variants for no-reference image quality assessment. J. Imag. **4**, 114 (2018)
14. Guo, Z., Zhang, L., Zhang, D.: A completed modeling of local binary pattern operator for texture classification. IEEE Trans. Image Process. **19**(6), 1657–1663 (2010)
15. Kannala, J., Rahtu, E.: BSIF: binarized statistical image features, In: 21st International Conference on Pattern Recognition (2012)
16. Freitas, P.G., Akamine, W.Y., Farias, M.C.: Blind image quality assessment using multiscale local binary patterns. J. Imag. Sci. Technol. **60**(6) (2016)
17. Mehta, R., Egiazarian, K.: Rotated local binary pattern (RLBP) rotation invariant texture descriptor. In: Proceedings of the 2nd International Conference on Pattern Recognition Applications and Methods, pp. 497–502 (2013)
18. Wolf, L., Hassner, T., Taigman, Y.: Descriptor based methods in the wild. In: Workshop on Faces in 'Real-Life' Images: Detection, Alignment, and Recognition (2008)
19. Anthimopoulos, M., Gatos, B., Pratikakis, I.: Detection of artificial and scene text in images and video frames. Pattern Anal. Appl. **16**, 431–446 (2013)

Saliency Retargeting Considering Aesthetics Quality Based on Deep Learning

Kazuki Koike[1], Ryuichi Egoshi[1], and Hironori Takimoto[2](✉)

[1] Graduate School, Okayama Prefectural University, Okayama, Japan
sk624012@c.oka-pu.ac.jp, mcs-lab@c.oka-pu.ac.jp

[2] Okayama Prefectural University, Okayama, Japan
takimoto@c.oka-pu.ac.jp
https://www-mcs.c.oka-pu.ac.jp/

Abstract. This paper proposed two deep learning approaches for saliency retargeting while preserving aesthetic quality in images, addressing the limitations of conventional methods that focus solely on maximizing object saliency. The first approach, "OperatorNet", estimates the intensity of multiple image editing operators to enhance the main object, utilizing EfficientNet-lite3 and multitask learning. The second approach, "GeneratorNet", directly transforms images at the pixel level using the U-Net architecture. Both quantitative evaluations and subjective human assessments were conducted on images generated by the proposed methods. Experiments using the MS-COCO dataset confirmed that the proposed approaches achieved superior saliency retargeting while considering aesthetic quality compared to existing methods.

Keywords: Saliency retargeting · Aesthetic quality of photograph · Deep learning

1 Introduction

In recent years, social networking services have seen an increase in posts featuring high-quality, aesthetically pleasing images. Consequently, more users are interested in creating images that look visually appealing. Generally, highlighting the main subject is an effective strategy for improving an image's aesthetic quality. For instance, advanced image-editing software such as Adobe Photoshop allows users to adjust saturation, brightness, and other parameters in both the subject and the background, making the subject stand out. However, such sophisticated color adjustments are challenging for those without prior editing experience because they require technical skills and expertise developed through practice.

Several techniques collectively referred to as Saliency retargeting [1–4] have been proposed to address the needs of users seeking advanced editing without

T. T. Quan et al. (Eds.): MIWAI 2025, LNAI 16353, pp. 354–365, 2026.
https://doi.org/10.1007/978-981-95-4957-3_29

extensive technical knowledge. These methods adjust important visual elements in images or videos to guide the viewer's attention to particular regions. The concept of the saliency map is crucial to these approaches. Humans can focus on essential information while filtering out less relevant details, a process known as visual attention. Based on this phenomenon, Itti et al. [5] introduced a model that generates a saliency map - a spatial distribution of conspicuous visual features - by analyzing color, intensity (brightness), and orientation, which are three fundamental visual cues.

Saliency retargeting uses this saliency map to modify specific regions of an image or video, thus directing viewers' attention to those regions. For example, if the goal is to highlight a subject, adjusting its color or brightness is effective. Existing studies include approaches that explicitly manipulate image features (e.g., color, contours) [1], as well as methods that exchange features among image patches [2]. Takimoto et al. [4] proposed a technique (see Fig. 1) for reconstructing videos that effectively steers viewers' attention by emphasizing or suppressing static visual features strongly influencing bottom-up attention. These approaches allow even novices to produce images emphasizing the main subject. However, because existing methods optimize transformation only in terms of saliency, there is a risk of compromising the image's aesthetic quality.

In this paper, we propose two deep learning–based methods that perform Saliency retargeting while maintaining aesthetic quality. The first method, OperatorNet, automatically adjusts the intensities of several frequently used editing operations, such as saturation and white balance, through deep learning. As noted above, novice users often struggle to find the optimal intensity settings for highlighting a subject. Our method enables easy, adequate subject emphasis by training a neural network to estimate these intensities automatically. OperatorNet combines feature extraction using EfficientNet-lite3 [6] with a multi-task learning framework to predict intensities for multiple editing operators concurrently. Furthermore, existing operations like saturation and brightness adjustments typically use simple computations and cannot apply selective edits to specific regions, unlike advanced image editors. Hence, we integrate a deep learning–based image processing approach, CAN24 [7], as one of the editing operators to achieve more sophisticated image editing.

Our second method, GeneratorNet, uses a deep generative model to transform the image at the pixel level. While OperatorNet can only apply uniform transformations within a region and is limited by the number of available editing operators, GeneratorNet based on U-Net [8] offers greater flexibility and expressive power, allowing for more nuanced transformations that better emphasize the subject.

To evaluate the proposed methods, we conduct both quantitative evaluations and subjective human assessments on images generated by OperatorNet and GeneratorNet. We use the MS-COCO dataset for our experiments and compare the results with existing saliency retargeting methods. The experimental results confirm that our proposed approaches achieve superior saliency retargeting while maintaining the aesthetic quality of the transformed images.

The main contributions of this paper are as follows:

- We propose two novel deep learning–based methods, OperatorNet and GeneratorNet, for saliency retargeting that consider both object saliency and aesthetic quality.
- We integrate a deep learning–based image processing approach, CAN24, as an editing operator in OperatorNet to achieve more sophisticated image editing.
- We conduct comprehensive evaluations using quantitative metrics and subjective human assessments to demonstrate the effectiveness of the proposed methods compared to existing approaches.

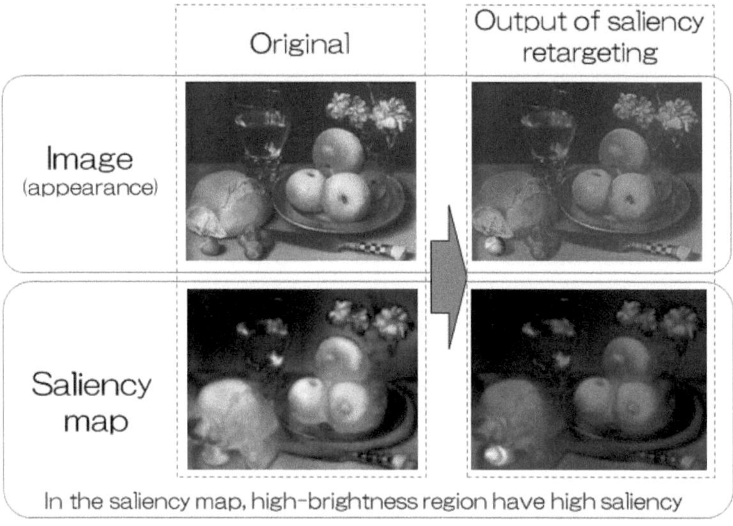

Fig. 1. Example of Saliency retargeting by conventional method [4].

2 Deep Learning-Based Saliency Retargeting Considering Aesthetics

2.1 OperatorNet: Controlling Multiple Image Editing Operators

OperatorNet is a deep learning approach that automatically determines the intensity of multiple image editing operators to enhance the saliency of target objects while preserving aesthetic quality. The network takes an RGB image and its corresponding object mask as input (4-channel input) and estimates optimal intensities for nine image editing operators.

The architecture employs EfficientNet-lite3 as a backbone for feature extraction, producing a 384-dimensional feature vector through average pooling. Since image editing operators cannot be applied simultaneously, an application order represented as a 6-dimensional vector is encoded into a 32-dimensional feature vector using a linear layer. The feature vectors from EfficientNet-lite3 and the application order are concatenated and processed through a 2-layer MLP with Leaky ReLU activation to produce a 128-dimensional shared representation. This shared representation is then fed into parameter estimation heads (linear layers with sigmoid activation) to predict the intensity of each image editing operator.

In this study, we define not only saliency loss to improve the saliency of subject regions in generated images by OperatorNet, but also hue loss, saturation loss, and structure loss to maintain the realism and aesthetics of generated images. Additionally, we define two different saliency losses and verify the effectiveness of each.

The first saliency loss L_{sal1} is designed with the objective of reducing the difference between the maximum value in the background region and the minimum value in the subject region (foreground) of the saliency map. In saliency maps, higher pixel values indicate areas that humans are more likely to focus on, so when the saliency in the background region is higher than that in the subject region, it indicates that the background is more likely to be focused on. Therefore, by training the model using a loss function that reduces the difference between the maximum saliency value in the background region and the minimum value in the subject region, we aim to realize image transformation that makes the foreground easier to focus on. The proposed loss function L_{sal1} is defined by the following equation.

$$L_{sal1} = \exp(w_{sal}(S_{base}(I, I', M) + S_{diff}(I', M))) \tag{1}$$

$$S_{diff}(X, M) = \min(X \times M) - \max(X \times (1 - M)) \tag{2}$$

$$S_{base}(I, I', M) = (\mu_{\text{fg}}(I', M) - \mu_{\text{fg}}(I, M)) - (\mu_{\text{bg}}(I', M) - \mu_{\text{bg}}(I, M)) \tag{3}$$

Note that w_{sal} is introduced to prevent rapid increases in saliency due to extreme transformations during training, and in this study we set $w_{sal} = 0.5$. When the width of the original image X and mask image M is W and the height is H, the foreground average μ_{fg} and background average μ_{bg} are defined by the following equations.

$$\mu_{\text{fg}}(X, M) = \frac{1}{\sum M} \sum_{i=1}^{H} \sum_{j=1}^{W} (X(i, j) \times M(i, j)) \tag{4}$$

$$\mu_{\text{bg}}(X, M) = \frac{1}{H \times W - \sum M} \sum_{i=1}^{H} \sum_{j=1}^{W} (X(i, j) \times (1 - M(i, j))) \tag{5}$$

The OperatorNet trained with the above loss function L_{sal1} is referred to as OperatorNet1.

The second saliency loss L_{sal2} is defined with the objective of reducing saliency in the background region of the saliency map. The loss function L_{sal2} is defined by the following equations.

$$S_{bg}(X, M) = \text{clip}(X \times (1 - M), 0, \infty) \tag{6}$$
$$L_{sal2} = \exp(w_{sal}(S_{base}(I, I', M) + S_{bg}(I', M) - S_{bg}(I, M))) \tag{7}$$

The clip function, which restricts values to a specific range, is defined as follows.

$$\text{clip}(x, 0, 1) = \begin{cases} 0 & \text{if } x < 0 \\ x & \text{if } 0 \le x \le 1 \\ 1 & \text{if } x > 1 \end{cases} \tag{8}$$

By training with greater emphasis on the background region compared to the aforementioned saliency loss L_{sal1}, we aim to suppress the decline in realism and aesthetics by minimizing transformation of the foreground region. The OperatorNet trained with the above loss function L_{sal2} is referred to as OperatorNet2.

Hue loss is a function that calculates the change in hue between the original image and the generated image and evaluates the smallness of that change. Changing the hue of an image significantly alters the overall impression of the image. Appropriate hue adjustment can also lead to adjusting the atmosphere of the image itself, which is useful for improving aesthetics, but if the intensity or target of application is incorrect, it can cause deterioration in realism and aesthetics. For example, significantly changing the hue of human skin color may impair realism. This is because skin color is part of human characteristics and is particularly important, and natural-looking hue is necessary to maintain a natural impression. Additionally, significantly changing the hue of food may impair aesthetics by making the dish appear unpleasant. Specifically, when colors deviate significantly from normal food ingredients, such as blue steak or green pizza, it becomes difficult to stimulate appetite. Therefore, by using a loss function that restricts hue changes, we aim to realize transformations that maintain realism and aesthetics. The proposed hue loss function L_{hue} is defined by the following equation.

$$L_{hue} = \frac{1}{H \times W} \sum_{i=1}^{H} \sum_{j=1}^{W} |H_I(i, j) - H_{I'}(i, j)| \tag{9}$$

Here, H_I represents the hue of the original image, $H_{I'}$ represents the hue of the generated image, W represents the width of the original image, and H represents the height.

Saturation loss is a function that calculates the change in saturation between the original image and the generated image and evaluates the smallness of that change. Changing the saturation of an image alters the color tone and vividness of the image. Therefore, like hue, if adjusted appropriately, it is useful for improving aesthetics, but extreme changes can cause deterioration in realism and aesthetics. For example, applying extremely high saturation transformation to an image of blue sky may impair realism because the blue color becomes extremely intense. On the other hand, applying extremely low saturation transformation results in an image close to grayscale, losing the characteristic aesthetics of blue sky. Therefore, by using a loss function that restricts saturation changes, we aim to realize transformations that maintain realism and aesthetics. The proposed saturation loss function L_{sat} is defined by the following equation.

$$L_{sat} = \frac{1}{H \times W} \sum_{i=1}^{H} \sum_{j=1}^{W} |S_I(i,j) - S_{I'}(i,j)| \tag{10}$$

Here, S_I represents the saturation of the original image, $S_{I'}$ represents the saturation of the generated image, W represents the width of the original image, and H represents the height.

Structure loss is a function that evaluates the structural similarity between the original image x and the generated image y. Even when changes in hue and saturation can be suppressed by adjusting image editing operators, the balance of image editing operator intensity may cause deterioration in overall image quality, adversely affecting realism and aesthetics. Therefore, by using the Structural SIMilarity index (SSIM) [9], which is widely used as an indicator for image quality evaluation, as a loss function, we suppress the decline in realism and aesthetics due to image quality deterioration. SSIM integrates and evaluates the luminance, contrast, and structure of images, and is defined by the following equation.

$$\mathrm{SSIM}(x,y) = \frac{(2\mu_x\mu_y + C)(2\sigma_{xy} + C)}{(\mu_x^2 + \mu_y^2 + C)(\sigma_x^2 + \sigma_y^2 + C)} \tag{11}$$

Here, μ_x, μ_y represent the mean luminance of images x and y, σ_x^2, σ_y^2 represent their respective variances, σxy represents the covariance, and $C = 1e^{-5}$ is a small constant to maintain computational stability. SSIM takes values in the range from -1 to 1, where 1 means that the two images match completely. Therefore, the proposed structure loss function L_{str} is defined by the following equation.

$$L_{str} = 1 - SSIM(I, I') \tag{12}$$

The loss function of the proposed OperatorNet is defined by the following equation by adjusting the weights of saliency loss L_{sal}, hue loss L_{hue}, saturation loss L_{sat}, and structure loss L_{str} as hyperparameters.

$$L = \alpha_{sal}L_{sal} + \alpha_{hue}L_{hue} + \alpha_{sat}L_{sat} + \alpha_{str}L_{str} \tag{13}$$

In this study, we set $\alpha_{sal} = 120, \alpha_{hue} = 2, \alpha_{sat} = 1, \alpha_{str} = 2$.

2.2 GeneratorNet: Pixel-Level Image Transformation

GeneratorNet addresses the limitations of OperatorNet by enabling pixel-level transformations for more flexible and powerful saliency retargeting. It employs

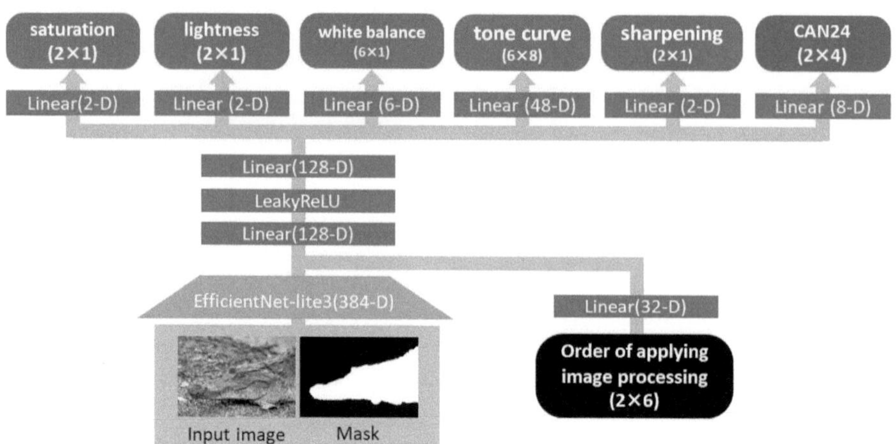

Fig. 2. Model architecture of OperatorNet.

a U-Net architecture that directly transforms the input image (RGB plus mask) into an aesthetically enhanced output with improved saliency.

The U-Net architecture consists of an encoder that progressively compresses the input image to extract features and a decoder that reconstructs the image at its original resolution. Skip connections between the encoder and decoder preserve high-frequency details from the input image. GeneratorNet uses a loss function similar to OperatorNet but with additional components to prevent extreme local transformations:

$$L = \alpha_{sal} L_{sal} + \alpha_{hue} L_{hue} + \alpha_{sat} L_{sat} + \alpha_{str} L_{str} \tag{14}$$

The saliency loss incorporates a standard deviation term S_{sigma} to promote uniform saliency enhancement across the target object:

$$L_{sal} = \exp\left(w_{sal} S_{base} + w_{sigma} S_{sigma}\right) \tag{15}$$

where S_{sigma} measures the difference in saliency standard deviations between foreground and background regions before and after transformation. The hue loss L_{hue} is also extended to consider both mean differences and standard deviations between original and generated images:

$$L_{hue} = \mu_{fg\_h} + \sigma_{fg\_h} + \mu_{bg\_h} + \sigma_{bg\_h} \tag{16}$$

where μ_{fg_h} and μ_{bg_h} represent the mean differences for foreground and background hue, respectively, and σ_{fg_h} and σ_{bg_h} represent the corresponding standard deviations. Similarly, the saturation loss L_{sat} is defined as follows:

$$L_{sat} = \mu_{fg\_s} + \sigma_{fg\_s} + \mu_{bg\_s} + \sigma_{bg\_s} \tag{17}$$

These modifications help GeneratorNet produce transformations that enhance saliency while maintaining natural appearance and aesthetic quality. In this study, we set $\alpha_{sal} = 150, \alpha_{hue} = 2, \alpha_{sat} = 1, \alpha_{str} = 2$.

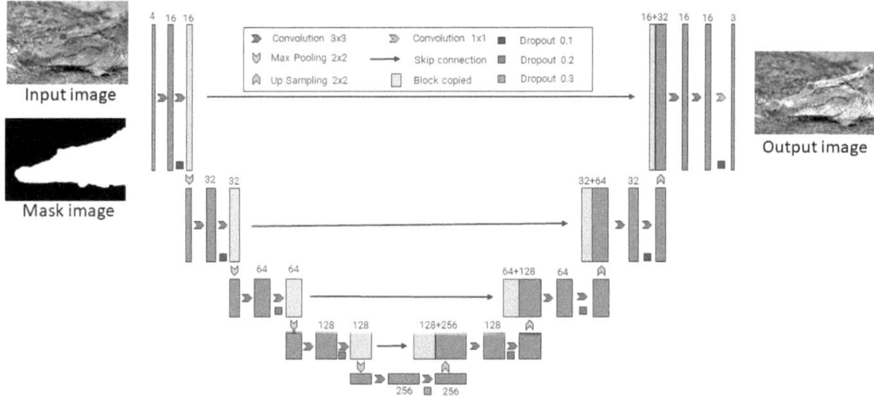

Fig. 3. Model architecture of GeneratorNet.

3 Experiments

3.1 Experimental Setup

We used the MS-COCO dataset [9] for training, which includes approximately 100,000 everyday scenes. Each image was resized to 224×224 pixels during training. For evaluation, we selected a benchmark dataset from the MEC [10] dataset, comprising 100 original images, their corresponding masks, and 100 MEC-transformed images (300 images in total). OperatorNet and GeneratorNet were trained for 10 epochs with a batch size of 4 and a learning rate of 0.00005.

3.2 Quantitative Evaluation

We employed two quantitative saliency metrics to evaluate the performance of the proposed methods. The first metric was the correlation coefficient (CC) between the saliency map and the object mask, as used in the MEC dataset; a higher CC indicates higher saliency for the subject. The second metric was a min-max metric that calculates the difference between the minimum saliency in the subject region and the maximum saliency in the background. Specifically, we generated a saliency map for each original image, split it into the subject and background according to the mask, and then computed the difference between the lowest saliency in the subject region and the highest saliency in the background.

Table 1 summarizes the quantitative evaluation results. OperatorNet1 and OperatorNet2 outperformed the MEC method regarding both CC and min-max metrics, demonstrating that OperatorNet provides practical saliency improvements relative to both the original images and those edited by MEC. GeneratorNet achieved a higher CC than MEC, but a lower min-max score indicates that while it improves saliency relative to the original images, it may not always surpass MEC under every saliency measure.

Table 1. Results of quantitative evaluation experiments

	Correlation coefficient (↑)	min-max (↓)
MEC [10]	0.597	148.7
Ours : OperatorNet1	**0.657**	148.3
Ours : OperatorNet2	0.679	**137.4**
Ours : GeneratorNet	0.598	152.9
Original image	0.455	158.1

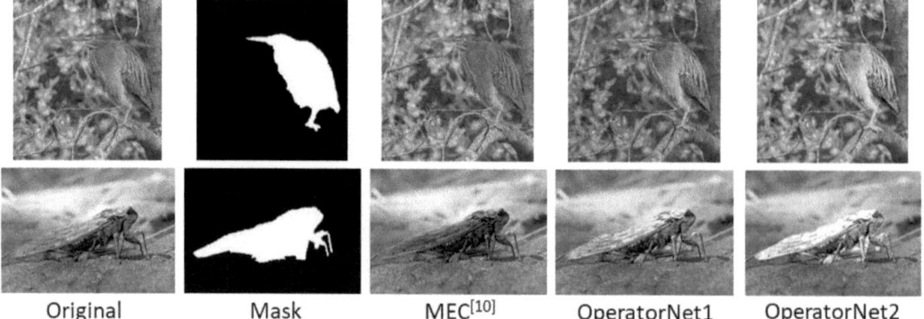

Fig. 4. Example of improved naturalness evaluation by OperatorNet.

3.3 Subjective Evaluation

We conducted a subjective evaluation with 13 participants (both male and female) to assess the naturalness and aesthetic quality of the images generated by the proposed methods. The participants ranked the images based on their perceived naturalness and aesthetic appeal, which we then converted into naturalness and aesthetic scores for each method.

Table 2 presents the subjective evaluation results. OperatorNet1 received the highest naturalness score, whereas OperatorNet2 achieved the highest aesthetic score. Figure 4 shows an example of OperatorNet enhancing naturalness;

Fig. 5. Example of improved aesthetic evaluation by OperatorNet.

because the operator applies uniform transformations within each region, it retains diverse hues, thus keeping the overall look natural. Figure 5 presents an example of OperatorNet improving aesthetic quality by emphasizing transparency and reflection on the subject's wings, thereby increasing visual appeal.

GeneratorNet achieved lower naturalness and aesthetic scores compared to OperatorNet, which can be attributed to its more flexible and expressive transformations. While GeneratorNet can generate more nuanced transformations that better emphasize the subject, it may sometimes introduce artifacts or unrealistic changes that affect the overall naturalness and aesthetic appeal of the image. The subjective evaluation results highlight the effectiveness of the proposed methods in enhancing saliency while maintaining or improving the naturalness and aesthetic quality of the images. The results also demonstrate the trade-off between saliency enhancement and preserving naturalness and aesthetics, as more aggressive transformations may lead to a decrease in perceived naturalness and aesthetic appeal.

Table 2. Results of subjective evaluation experiments for OperatorNet

	Naturalness score (↑)	Aesthetic score (↑)
MEC [10]	2.21	2.16
Ours : OperatorNet1	2.15	**2.23**
Ours : OperatorNet2	**2.21**	2.15

4 Conclusion

In this paper, we presented two novel deep learning–based methods, OperatorNet and GeneratorNet, for automating image editing to enhance a subject's saliency while preserving the aesthetic quality of the image. Experimental results on the MS-COCO dataset demonstrated that OperatorNet produced images with the highest saliency scores among the methods tested, as measured by CC and min-max metrics. GeneratorNet also delivered comparable or superior performance under certain conditions, achieving higher CC scores than the MEC method. These findings highlight the effectiveness of the proposed methods in enhancing saliency compared to existing approaches.

Furthermore, subjective evaluations revealed that OperatorNet could be fine-tuned via its loss functions to produce highly rated images in terms of naturalness and aesthetics. OperatorNet1 achieved the highest naturalness score, while OperatorNet2 received the highest aesthetic score. These results demonstrate the ability of the proposed methods to preserve or even improve the aesthetic quality of the images during saliency enhancement.

The proposed deep learning–based methods offer several advantages over traditional saliency retargeting techniques. By incorporating deep learning, our methods can learn complex patterns and relationships between image features and saliency, enabling more sophisticated and effective transformations.

Our findings highlight the promise of incorporating deep learning to preserve aesthetic quality during saliency enhancement, making advanced image editing accessible to users with limited prior experience. The proposed methods have potential applications in various fields, including social media, advertising, and visual content creation, where visually appealing and attention-grabbing images are highly valued.

However, there are some limitations to our study that should be addressed in future research. First, the evaluation was conducted on a relatively small dataset, and further experiments on larger and more diverse datasets are necessary to assess the generalization capabilities of the proposed methods. Second, while the subjective evaluations provided valuable insights into the perceived naturalness and aesthetic quality of the generated images, more extensive user studies with a larger number of participants would strengthen the validity of the results.

Future work could explore the integration of additional editing operators or the use of more advanced deep learning architectures to further improve the performance of the proposed methods.

This research was supported by G-7 scholarship foundation.

References

1. Hagiwara, A., Sugimoto, A., Kawamoto, K.: Saliency-based image editing for guiding visual attention. In: Proceedings of the International Workshop Series on Pervasive Eye Tracking and Mobile Eye-Based Interaction (PETMEI), pp. 43–48 (2011)
2. Dekel, T., Michaeli, T., Irani, M., Freeman, W.T.: Revealing and modifying non-local variations in a single image. ACM Trans. on Graphics **34**(6), 227 (2015)
3. Takimoto, H., Hitomi, S., Yamauchi, H., Kishihara, M., Okubo, K.: Image modification based on spatial frequency components for visual attention retargeting. IEICE Trans. Inf. Syst. **E100-D**(6), 1339–1349 (2017)

4. Takimoto, H., Kokui, T., Yamauchi, H., Kishihara, M., Okubo, K.: Image modification based on a visual saliency map for guiding visual attention. IEICE Trans. Inf. Syst. **E98-D**(11), 1967–1975 (2015)
5. Itti, L., Koch, C., Niebur, E.: A model of saliency-based visual attention for rapid scene analysis. IEEE Trans. Pattern Anal. Mach. Intell. **20**(11), 1254–1259 (1998)
6. Tan, M., Le, Q.V.: EfficientNet: rethinking model scaling for convolutional neural networks. In: Proceedings of International Conference on Machine Learning, pp. 6105–6114 (2019)
7. Chen, Q., Xu, J., Koltun, V.: Fast image processing with fully-convolutional networks. In: Proceedings of International Conference on Computer Vision, pp. 2516–2525 (2017)
8. Ronneberger, O., Fischer, P., Brox, T.: U-Net: convolutional networks for biomedical image segmentation. In: Proceedings of Medical Image Computing and Computer Assisted Intervention, vol. 9351, pp. 234–241 (2015)
9. Zhou, W., Bovik, A.C., Sheikh, H.R., Simoncelli, E.P.: Image quality assessment: from error visibility to structural similarity. IEEE Trans. Image Process. **13**(4), 600–612 (2004)
10. Mechrez, R., Shechtman, E., Zelnik-Manor, L.: Saliency driven image manipulation. In: Proceedings of IEEE/CVF Winter Conference on Applications of Computer Vision (2018)

MBAAF: Multi-branch Lightweight Architecture for Audio Spoofing Detection with Temporal Gating and CBAM-Based Attention Fusion

Khanh-Duy Cao-Phan and Thi Phuc Dang(✉)

Faculty of Information Technology, Industrial University of Ho Chi Minh City, Ho Chi Minh City, Vietnam
21121841.duy@student.iuh.edu.vn , phucdt@iuh.edu.vn
https://fit.iuh.edu.vn/

Abstract. With the rapid advancement of AI-driven speech synthesis and voice conversion technologies, deepfake audio has emerged as a serious threat to communication integrity and cybersecurity. In this paper, we propose a lightweight hybrid attention architecture named MBAAF for audio spoofing detection, which integrates feature-specific attention modules across a multi-branch input pipeline. Specifically, Mel-Frequency Cepstral Coefficients (MFCC) and Short-Time Fourier Transform (STFT) branches are refined using Temporal Gating Blocks (TGB), while Constant-Q Cepstral Coefficients (CQCC) are enhanced with a Convolutional Block Attention Module (CBAM). These refined features are fused and processed by a compact ResNeSt backbone for final classification. Experiments show that MBAAF attains 0.15% EER and 0.011 t-DCF on ASVSpoof2019 LA and sets a new state-of-the-art of 0.092% EER on the In-the-Wild dataset, using only 135K parameters. These results highlight the effectiveness of heterogeneous attention placement and confirm that a compact, modular design can achieve both high accuracy and efficiency for real-time, low-resource deployment.

Keywords: Audio spoofing detection · Attention mechanism · CBAM · Temporal gating · Lightweight ResNeSt

1 Introduction

With the rapid evolution of AI-powered speech synthesis and voice conversion, deepfake audio has become an alarming threat to digital security and trust. Recent data show a 442% surge in vishing attacks, with 77% success rates and average losses of $577 per incident [16]. Globally, 70% of organizations have been hit, facing annual losses over $14 million [10]. This staggering figure highlights the urgent need for robust voice anti-spoofing solutions.

Early anti-spoofing systems (built on handcrafted features and basic classifiers) quickly became obsolete as attackers grew more sophisticated [1,7]. Today,

T. T. Quan et al. (Eds.): MIWAI 2025, LNAI 16353, pp. 366–377, 2026.
https://doi.org/10.1007/978-981-95-4957-3_30

deep learning-based methods represent a significant leap forward by learning complex representations directly from raw or spectrogram inputs. Convolutional Neural Networks (CNNs) have shown strong performance in channel-mismatched scenarios [4], while Recurrent Neural Networks (RNNs), especially LSTM variants, model temporal dependencies effectively [9]. For example, [13] applied a CNN-ResNet34 model and achieved an EER of 2.98%, while [26] reported an EER of 5.89% using a hybrid ResNet189 and Transformer encoder. Generative adversarial networks (GANs) also contribute remarkably by enhancing training by producing synthetic examples. For instance, [6] utilized a self-supervised WavLM model with a multi-head attention classifier, attaining an Equal Error Rate (EER) of just 0.42% and a tandem Detection Cost Function (t-DCF) of 0.013. Despite this progress, several core challenges remain. First, many existing models still suffer from poor generalization to unseen attack types or domain shifts. Second, the growing complexity and computational cost of deep fusion architectures often hinder real-world deployment on resource-limited devices. Third, applying the same attention module uniformly across all feature branches may overlook the unique strengths and weaknesses of each feature type.

To address these issues, we propose a lightweight multi-branch fusion architecture – MBAAF. In contrast to AASIST [9], which applies homogeneous graph attention directly on raw waveforms, our MBAAF model adopts heterogeneous attention tailored to each acoustic feature branch (TGB for MFCC/STFT and CBAM for CQCC), enabling clearer temporal-frequency synergy and interpretability. Compared with Split-Attention ResNet [2], where split-attention is restricted to the backbone stage, MBAAF introduces feature-specific gating prior to fusion, providing lightweight regularization that improves generalization. These distinctions position MBAAF as both more efficient and more explainable while retaining a compact parameter budget. Specifically, MFCC and STFT features pass through Temporal Gating Blocks to highlight important temporal patterns, while CQCC features are refined by a CBAM to capture subtle spectro-temporal cues. The outputs from all branches are fused and processed by an efficient ResNeSt backbone and final classification layers. This approach offers three main advantages: (1) It leverages the complementary strengths of multiple feature types and attention mechanisms for improved robustness; (2) The modular and compact design is suitable for deployment on resource-limited platforms; (3) It allows for clear analysis of how different attention modules contribute to performance, enabling future extensibility.

This research delivers three main contributions:

1. Propose MBAAF that combines diverse audio features with feature-specific attention blocks (TGB for MFCC/STFT and CBAM for CQCC).
2. The model achieves a careful balance between detection accuracy and computational efficiency.
3. By leveraging the complementarity of different features and heterogeneous attention mechanisms, the framework improves robustness to unseen spoofing attacks and remains flexible for future extensions and real-world applications.

2 Proposed Methodology

2.1 Overall Architecture

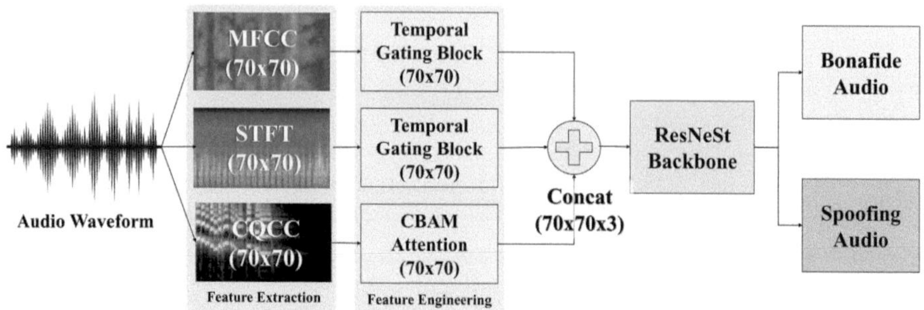

Fig. 1. Overview of the proposed Fusion Attention Multi-Branch architecture for audio spoofing detection.

MBAAF begins by extracting three complementary time-frequency features from each input audio waveform: MFCC, STFT, and CQCC. Each feature is processed in a separate branch, where targeted attention modules are applied: TGB for MFCC and STFT to emphasize important temporal dynamics, and CBAM for CQCC to selectively focus on informative frequency regions. This design enables each branch to enhance the most discriminative aspects of its corresponding feature, allowing the model to capture both temporal and spectral cues that are crucial for identifying subtle artifacts in spoofed audio. The outputs from all three branches are then concatenated and passed through a lightweight Split-Attention Residual Network (ResNeSt) backbone, which incorporates split-attention blocks to further refine the merged representations by modeling channel interdependencies. This backbone efficiently extracts higher-level features and enhances the model's ability to distinguish between genuine and spoofed speech. The final classification layers output the probability that the audio sample is bona fide or fake.

2.2 Feature Extraction

Given an input waveform $x[n]$, three complementary features are extracted for each utterance, These features are computed as follows:

- **MFCC:** The Mel-Frequency Cepstral Coefficients are computed as

$$\mathbf{X}_{\mathrm{MFCC}}(t,m) = \mathrm{DCT}_m \left(\log \left(\sum_f |S(t,f)|^2 \cdot M_{\mathrm{mel}}(f) \right) \right) \tag{1}$$

where $S(t, f)$ is the short-time Fourier spectrum at frame t and frequency f, $M_{\text{mel}}(f)$ is the Mel filterbank, and $\text{DCT}_,(\cdot)$ is m-th coefficient of the Discrete Cosine Transform.

– **CQCC:** The Constant-Q Cepstral Coefficients are obtained by:

$$\mathbf{X}_{\text{CQCC}}(t, m) = \text{DCT}_m \left(\log\left(|\text{CQT}(x[n])|\right)\right) \quad (2)$$

where CQT is the constant-Q transform applied to the signal.

– **STFT:** The Short-Time Fourier Transform spectrogram is calculated by:

$$\mathbf{X}_{\text{STFT}}(t, f) = \left|\sum_{n=0}^{N-1} x[n]w[n - tH]e^{-j2\pi fn/N}\right| \quad (3)$$

where $w[\cdot]$ is the analysis window, H is the hop size, and N is the Fast Fourier Transform length.

From signal priors, **MFCC** (log–mel + DCT) and **STFT** at 70×70 smooth out narrowband details so the bona fide–spoof differences mostly appear as temporal modulations. In contrast, CQCC (from CQT) preserves high frequency resolution and localized TF artefacts; a channel × spatial selector (CBAM) is better suited to emphasize specific bands and TF patches.

Predictions: CQCC is more sensitive to frequency/TF perturbations than temporal shuffles, whereas MFCC/STFT benefits more from time-only gating. We verify these in Sect. 3 via ablations and lightweight diagnostics.

2.3 Dedicated Modules per Feature

Temporal Gating Block: To emphasize temporal patterns in audio features, we propose a lightweight temporal gating mechanism for both MFCC and STFT representations. This design is especially suitable for MFCC and STFT, which are rich in temporal cues, timing artifacts, speech rhythm, or abrupt changes in energy. These are often strong indicators of spoofing. By adaptively gating information along the time axis, the model can focus on subtle temporal anomalies that might be overlooked by standard convolutions or global pooling alone. Given an input feature map $\mathbf{X} \in \mathbb{R}^{F \times T}$, temporal statistics are extracted by applying average and max pooling along the frequency axis:

$$\mathbf{z}_{\text{avg}} = \text{AvgPool}_f(\mathbf{X}), \qquad \mathbf{z}_{\text{max}} = \text{MaxPool}_f(\mathbf{X}) \quad (4)$$

The pooled features are concatenated and passed through a \$1\$D convolution with sigmoid activation to produce a gating mask. Next, the mask $\mathbf{a}$ is then upsampled and applied elementwise to the original input:

$$\mathbf{X}_{\text{out}} = \mathbf{X} \odot \sigma(\text{Conv1D}([\mathbf{z}_{\text{avg}}, \mathbf{z}_{\text{max}}])) \quad (5)$$

where $\odot$ denotes elementwise multiplication.

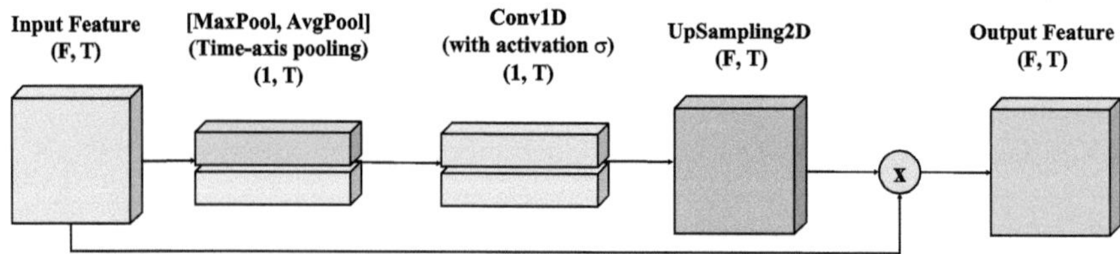

Fig. 2. Architecture of the proposed Temporal Gating Block.

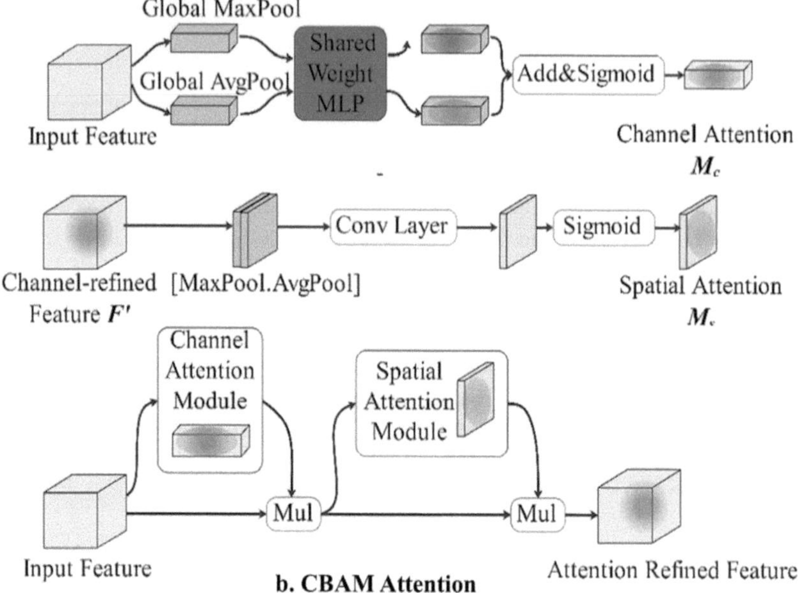

Fig. 3. Architecture of the CBAM Block.

CBAM Attention: To enhance the CQCC feature branch, we employ the CBAM [21]. It was chosen because CQCC features provide fine-grained frequency resolution and strong sensitivity to subtle spectral artifacts, but are also highly susceptible to background noise and irrelevant variations. CBAM addresses this by sequentially applying channel and spatial attention, enabling the network to selectively enhance informative frequency bands and time segments while suppressing noisy or less relevant regions. This targeted focus helps the model extract more robust and discriminative features from CQCC, which is especially valuable for distinguishing between genuine and spoofed speech in real-world, noisy conditions. By combining both channel-wise and spatial attention, CBAM is particularly well-suited for CQCC, maximizing its strengths and mitigating its weaknesses.

2.4 ResNeSt Backbone

MBAAF adopts a ResNeSt-based backbone [25], which incorporates split-attention blocks to enable the model to aggregate feature representations across multiple network branches efficiently. This design allows the network to capture both local and global patterns in the fused audio features, improving its capacity to discriminate subtle artifacts present in spoofed speech. Recent work [2] has demonstrated that ResNeSt achieves superior performance compared to conventional CNNs in voice spoofing detection tasks, making it a strong backbone choice for our multi-branch framework.

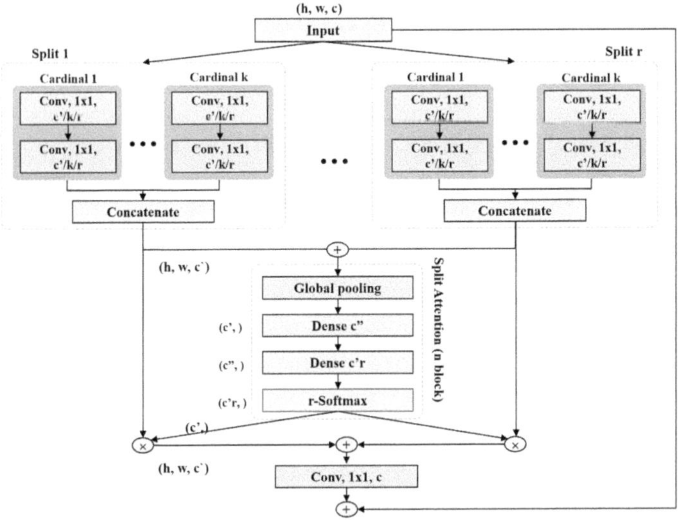

Fig. 4. Architecture of the ResNeSt Block.

3 Results and Discussion

3.1 Interpretability Analysis and Visualization of Attention Maps

Figure 5 shows the effect of attention across MFCC, CQCC, and STFT features for both Bonafide and Spoofed samples. For MFCC, attention enhances mid- and low-frequency zones, especially highlighting horizontal patterns in Spoofed audio, which may reflect repetitive low-frequency artifacts. In CQCC, attention suppresses widespread energy and focuses on early vertical structures, likely emphasizing informative cepstral cues. STFT features show the clearest distinction: spoofed samples retain structured high-frequency blocks, while Bonafide ones are sparsely activated post-attention. These results confirm that attention modules successfully amplify discriminative regions specific to each feature type,

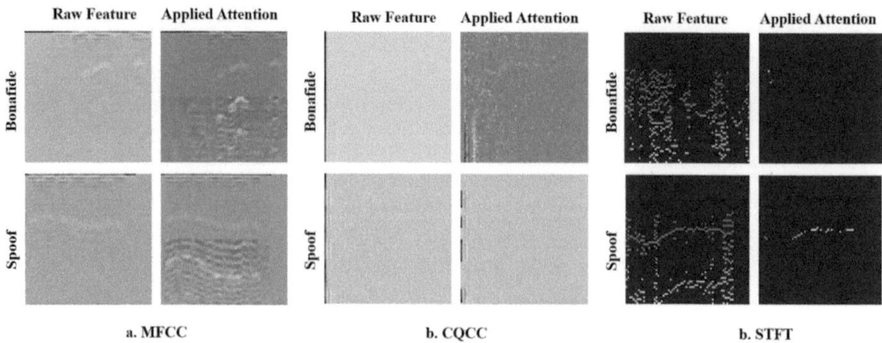

Fig. 5. Visualization of raw features and attention maps for: a. MFCC, b. CQCC, and c. STFT representations on Bonafide and Spoof samples.

supporting the overall effectiveness of the multi-branch strategy in spoof detection.

Beyond qualitative visualization, we further examined the interpretability of attention through quantitative overlap and distributional measures. For MFCC, attention slightly reshapes temporal focus: the IoU (Intersection-over-Union) between bona fide and spoof maps decreases from 0.77 to 0.58, while JSD (Jensen–Shannon Divergence) increases marginally, suggesting that TGB emphasizes different temporal segments without altering overall similarity. In CQCC, CBAM yields the strongest separation, with JSD around 0.26 and stable overlap patterns, consistent with its ability to highlight localized spectral–temporal artifacts. STFT shows the largest shift: cosine similarity between bona fide and spoof maps drops from 0.97 to 0.70, while spatial overlap (IoU/Dice coefficient) increases markedly. This indicates that TGB gating enforces a more compact saliency focus, reducing coverage-based separability but still differentiating spatial structures, in line with the clear qualitative contrast observed in Fig. 5. Overall, these results confirm that heterogeneous attention acts as a light regularizer, modifying feature saliency in complementary ways that support the EER improvement from 0.33% (no-att) to 0.15%.

3.2 Analysis of Feature Branch Fusion and Attention Module Configurations

To better understand the contribution of different design choices, we conduct a detailed ablation study focusing on the fusion of multiple acoustic feature branches and the type and placement of attention modules across these branches.

The integrated results in Table 1 provide two key insights. First, regarding feature branches, combining multiple inputs consistently improves performance. Single-branch models yield moderate error rates, while two-branch combinations reduce t-DCF values. The three-branch fusion (MFCC, CQCC, STFT) achieves the best overall results with an EER of 0.04% on the development set and 0.15%

Table 1. Comparison of (a) Feature branch combinations and (b) Attention module configurations.

(a) Feature Branch Combinations								(b) Attention Module Configurations							
#Branch	(i) MFCC	(ii) CQCC	(iii) STFT	EER (%) Dev	EER (%) Eval	t-DCF Dev	t-DCF Eval	Type	(i) MFCC	(ii) CQCC	(iii) STFT	EER (%) Dev	EER (%) Eval	t-DCF Dev	t-DCF Eval
1			✓	0.08	0.45	0.3638	0.0142	CBAM	✓			0.39	0.35	0.1302	0.0714
		✓		0.39	0.49	0.1595	0.1158	CBAM		✓		0.24	0.22	0.2564	0.1166
	✓			0.39	2.12	0.4212	0.2266	CBAM			✓	0.31	0.39	0.0823	0.0336
2		✓	✓	0.35	0.37	0.0840	0.0264	TGB	✓			0.08	0.45	0.3638	0.0142
	✓		✓	0.35	0.68	0.4049	0.1226	TGB		✓		0.24	0.45	0.2173	0.0889
	✓	✓		0.35	0.92	0.0303	0.0143	TGB			✓	0.08	0.45	0.3638	0.0142
3	✓	✓	✓	**0.04**	**0.15**	**0.0006**	**0.0110**	Baseline				**0.04**	**0.15**	**0.0006**	**0.0110**

on the evaluation set, together with the lowest t-DCF values. This confirms the complementary nature of spectral features for capturing spoofing artifacts.

Second, the placement and type of attention modules critically affect detection reliability. Applying CBAM or TGB on a single branch does not surpass the baseline, even when certain cases achieve low t-DCF (e.g., CBAM on STFT). The baseline configuration—TGB on MFCC and STFT, CBAM on CQCC—consistently outperforms all other setups, achieving the lowest EER and t-DCF values. These findings highlight that both feature fusion and heterogeneous attention assignment are necessary for robust synthetic speech detection.

3.3 Impact of Attention Type Combinations

Building upon the previous analysis of single-module placement, we further investigate whether homogeneous or heterogeneous assignments of attention mechanisms across branches lead to superior performance. In particular, we compare configurations where the same attention type is applied to all feature branches against those where CBAM and TGB are selectively combined. Table 2 summarizes the performance of these configurations across MFCC, CQCC, and STFT inputs.

The configurations are grouped into two categories: (1) homogeneous attention types, where the same module is applied across all branches, and (2) heterogeneous combinations, where different modules are used for different feature branches. Among the homogeneous setups, applying CBAM uniformly yields the highest EER (0.99%) and relatively high t-DCF (0.1186), indicating weaker generalization. The all-TGB setup improves performance slightly (EER = 0.65%), but the error rate remains relatively high. In contrast, the heterogeneous configurations in group 2 show a notable performance boost. Specifically, the configuration where MFCC and STFT use TGB and CQCC uses CBAM achieves the best overall results, with the lowest EER of 0.15% and a t-DCF of 0.0110. This suggests that selectively assigning attention modules based on the characteristics of each feature type, rather than applying a single mechanism across all, can lead to more effective feature discrimination and better spoofing detection.

Table 2. Comparison of attention type combinations across MFCC, CQCC, and STFT branches.

#Attention	MFCC	CQCC	STFT	EER (%)		t-DCF	
				Dev	Eval	Dev	Eval
1	CBAM	CBAM	CBAM	0.43	0.99	0.2774	0.1186
	TGB	TGB	TGB	0.43	0.65	0.2187	0.1051
2	TGB	TGB	CBAM	0.20	0.35	0.4349	0.1290
	CBAM	TGB	TGB	0.39	0.71	0.3434	0.1468
	CBAM	CBAM	TGB	0.35	0.38	0.2475	0.0864
	TGB	CBAM	CBAM	0.35	0.42	0.1183	0.0522
	TGB	**CBAM**	**TGB**	**0.04**	**0.15**	**0.0006**	**0.0110**

3.4 Compare with Other Studies

Evaluation Set of LA ASVSpoof2019: Table 3 presents a comparison of recent spoofing detection methods from 2022 to 2025. While several large-scale models (WavLM [6], XLS-R [12]) achieve strong performance, they require hundreds of millions of parameters, which limits their deployability in real-time or resource-constrained scenarios. In contrast, our proposed MBAAF model obtains the lowest EER of 0.15% with a competitive t-DCF of 0.011, using only 135K parameters. This outperforms other lightweight models like AASIST [9] and Split-Attention ResNet [2], demonstrating superior efficiency and accuracy.

Table 3. Comparison of methods in terms of EER (%), t-DCF, # Params, and GFLOPs on the evaluation set of LA ASVSpoof2019. Bold values indicate the best performance. We report GFLOPs only for lightweight models.

Year	Method	EER (%)	t-DCF	# Params	GFLOPs
2022	CNN - ResNet34–Autoencoder [15]	1.47	0.036	21.8M	–
	LSTM-ResNet18 [17]	1.91	0.053	12M–15M	–
	AASIST [9]	0.83	0.028	297K	9.618[1]
2023	Res2Net [23]	1.21	0.036	26M–28M	–
	DF-SincNet [8]	0.52	0.018	1M–3M	16.47
	RawGRU [5]	4.89	0.147	470K	**0.439**[1]
2024	WavLM [6]	0.42	0.013	300M	–
	XLS-R with DI-Formants [12]	0.39	0.012	850K	–
	STFT, LFCC + Transformer [24]	3.22	-	8M–12M	–
2025	wav2vec2.0 + attentive pooling [11]	1.08	0.031	110M–115M	–
	ResNet + Split Attention [2]	0.33	**0.011**	118K	5.648[2]
	MBAAF (Ours)	**0.15**	**0.011**	**135K**	5.664[2]

* [1]GFLOPs taken from [5], measured offline on 4-second audio.

* [2]GFLOPs measured by us on 4-second audio.

The consistent t-DCF and EER balance further highlight the robustness of our multi-branch attention design. These results emphasize that carefully calibrated attention placements can offer better trade-offs than simply increasing model size. Regarding compute, MBAAF uses 5.664 GFLOPs/4,s, comparable to Split-Attention ResNet (5.648) and 41% lower than AASIST (9.618); RawGRU is 0.439 GFLOPs but far less accurate.

Cross-Dataset Evaluation on the In-the-Wild Dataset: To evaluate generalization, we perform a cross-dataset test on the challenging In-the-Wild (ITW) dataset, which contains naturally occurring deepfakes with diverse noise, styles, and recording conditions. Table 4 presents a comparison between our MBAAF model and recent state-of-the-art systems. Large SSL-based models (wav2vec2.0/XLSR) reach 6–8% EER but require hundreds of millions of parameters, while lightweight models like AASIST show poor generalization (33.6% EER). POI-Forensics achieves 0.15% EER with tens of millions of parameters. In contrast, MBAAF attains **0.092% EER** with only **135K parameters**, setting a new state-of-the-art on ITW with unmatched parameter efficiency.

Table 4. Comparison of spoofing detection methods on the In-the-Wild dataset. Our MBAAF method is trained on the ASVspoof2019 LA train set and tested on ITW (cross-dataset evaluation).

Year	Method	EER (%)	# Params
2022	POI-Forensics [18]	0.15	~20M–50M
2023	wav2vec2.0+FF [19]	7.55	~300M–600M
2024	SSL+Vocoded [20]	6.10	~300M–320M
2024	Wav2Vec2+ACP [14]	3.10	~300M–320M
2024	AASIST [3]	33.60	297K
2025	XLSR-Mamba [22]	6.71	~317M
2025	**MBAAF (Ours)**	**0.092**	**135K**

4 Conclusion

This paper introduces MBAAF, a compact and effective architecture for audio spoofing detection using feature-specific attention modules within a multi-branch framework. By assigning the most suitable attention type to each feature, TGB for MFCC and STFT, CBAM for CQCC, the model achieves strong synergy between local and global pattern learning. Our method reaches state-of-the-art performance on ASVSpoof2019 LA with only 135K parameters, outperforming larger models like WavLM and XLS-R with 0.15% EER and 0.011 t-DCF. This highlights the importance of attention placement over model size. Moreover, our model is lightweight and interpretable, making it suitable for real-time or embedded systems. Potential limitations remain in robustness under extreme noise, channel mismatch, and unseen adversarial attacks. Future work will also consider multilingual corpora, domain-shifted datasets, and ethical implications of spoof detection.

References

1. Bisogni, C., Loia, V., Nappi, M., Pero, C.: Acoustic features analysis for explainable machine learning-based audio spoofing detection. Comput. Vis. Image Underst. **249**, 104145 (2024)
2. Cao-Phan, K.D., Tran, Dinh Dai, Q., Nguyen, V.L.: VDD: voice deepfake detection with three-channel acoustic representations and advanced split-attention networks. Signal, Image Video Process. (SIViP) **19**, 537 (2025). https://doi.org/10.1007/s11760-025-04126-3
3. Dao, A.T., Evans, N., Matrouf, D.: Spoofing detection in the wild: an investigation of approaches to improve generalisation. In: Proceedings of the Odyssey 2024, pp. 145–150 (2024)
4. Fathan, A., Alam, J., Kang, W.H.: Mel-spectrogram image-based end-to-end audio deepfake detection under channel-mismatched conditions. In: 2022 IEEE International Conference on Multimedia and Expo (ICME), pp. 1–6 (2022). https://doi.org/10.1109/ICME52920.2022.9859621
5. Grinberg, P., Shikhov, V.: RawSpectrogram: on the way to effective streaming speech anti-spoofing. IEEE Access **11**, 109928–109938 (2023). https://doi.org/10.1109/ACCESS.2023.3321919
6. Guo, Y., Huang, H., Chen, X., Zhao, H., Wang, Y.: Audio deepfake detection with self-supervised WavLM and multi-fusion attentive classifier. In: ICASSP 2024 - 2024 IEEE International Conference on Acoustics, Speech and Signal Processing (ICASSP), pp. 12702–12706 (2024). https://doi.org/10.1109/ICASSP48485.2024.10447923
7. Hamza, A., et al.: Deepfake audio detection via MFCC features using machine learning. IEEE Access **10**, 134018–134028 (2022)
8. Huang, B., Cui, S., Huang, J., Kang, X.: Discriminative frequency information learning for end-to-end speech anti-spoofing. IEEE Signal Process. Lett. **30**, 185–189 (2023). https://doi.org/10.1109/LSP.2023.3251895
9. Jung, J.W., et al.: AASIST: Audio anti-spoofing using integrated spectro-temporal graph attention networks. In: ICASSP (2022)
10. Keepnet Labs: vishing statistics 2025: unmasking the voice phishing threat. Keepnet Labs Blog (2024)
11. Kheir, Y.E., Polzehl, T., Möller, S.: BiCrossMamba-ST: speech deepfake detection with bidirectional mamba spectro-temporal cross-attention. arXiv preprint arXiv:2505.13930 (2025)
12. Liu, K., Wang, Y., Li, S., Shao, X.: Speech formants integration for generalized detection of synthetic speech spoofing attacks. In: Proceedings of Interspeech 2024, pp. 2100–2104 (2024). https://doi.org/10.21437/Interspeech.2024-292
13. Ma, Y., Ren, Z., Xu, S.: RW-ResNet: a novel speech anti-spoofing model using raw waveform. In: Interspeech 2021, pp. 4144–4148 (2021). https://doi.org/10.21437/Interspeech.2021-438

14. Martín Doñas, J.M., Álvarez, A., Roselló Casado, E., Gómez García, Á.M., Peinado Herreros, A.M., et al.: Exploring self-supervised embeddings and synthetic data augmentation for robust audio deepfake detection (2024)
15. Mo, Y., Wang, S.: Multi-task learning improves synthetic speech detection. In: 2022 IEEE International Conference on Acoustics, Speech and Signal Processing (ICASSP), pp. 6392–6396 (2022)
16. Mobile ID World: voice phishing attacks surge 442% in 2024 as ai enhances social engineering tactics. https://tinyurl.com/23c8jjpr (2025)
17. Pan, J., et al.: Speaker recognition-assisted robust audio deepfake detection. In: Proceedings of Interspeech, pp. 4202–4206 (2022)
18. Pianese, A., Cozzolino, D., Poggi, G., Verdoliva, L.: Deepfake audio detection by speaker verification. In: 2022 IEEE International Workshop on Information Forensics and Security (WIFS), pp. 1–6. IEEE (2022)
19. Wang, X., Yamagishi, J.: Spoofed training data for speech spoofing countermeasure can be efficiently created using neural vocoders. In: ICASSP 2023-2023 IEEE International Conference on Acoustics, Speech and Signal Processing (ICASSP), pp. 1–5. IEEE (2023)
20. Wang, X., Yamagishi, J.: Can large-scale vocoded spoofed data improve speech spoofing countermeasure with a self-supervised front end? In: ICASSP 2024-2024 IEEE International Conference on Acoustics, Speech and Signal Processing (ICASSP), pp. 10311–10315. IEEE (2024)
21. Woo, S., Park, J., Lee, J.Y., Kweon, I.S.: CBAM: convolutional block attention module. In: Proceedings of the European Conference on Computer Vision (ECCV), pp. 3–19 (2018)
22. Xiao, Y., Das, R.K.: XLSR-Mamba: a dual-column bidirectional state space model for spoofing attack detection. IEEE Signal Process. Lett. (2025)
23. Yang, M., Zheng, K., Wang, X., Sun, Y., Chen, Z.: Comparative analysis of ASV spoofing countermeasures: evaluating Res2Net-based approaches. IEEE Signal Process. Lett. (2023)
24. Zaman, K., Samiul, I.J.A.M., Sah, M., Direkoglu, C., Okada, S., Unoki, M.: Hybrid transformer architectures with diverse audio features for deepfake speech classification. IEEE Access **12**, 149221–149237 (2024). https://doi.org/10.1109/ACCESS.2024.3478731
25. Zhang, H., et al.: ResNeSt: split-attention networks. In: Proceedings of the IEEE/CVF Conference on Computer Vision and Pattern Recognition (CVPR) Workshops, pp. 2736–2746 (2022)
26. Zhang, Z., Yi, X., Zhao, X.: Fake speech detection using residual network with transformer encoder. In: Proceedings of the 2021 ACM Workshop on Information Hiding and Multimedia Security, pp. 13–22 (2021)

ConvSelect-RAG: Bridging Query Enhancement and Document Filtering for Multi-turn Conversational AI

Khoa Tran Dang, Quan Thi Khac, Dang Le Binh, and Duy Tran Ngoc Bao(✉)

Faculty of Computer Science and Engineering, Ho Chi Minh City University of Technology (HCMUT), VNU-HCM, Ho Chi Minh City, Vietnam
{khoa.trank685,tkquan,binhdang,duytnb}@hcmut.edu.vn

Abstract. Multi-turn conversational AI systems using Retrieval Augmented Generation (RAG) often struggle with ambiguous user queries and inefficient retrieval from large document collections. Traditional chunk-level vector search introduces significant computational overhead, while missing critical context due to reliance on raw, under-specified queries. We propose ConvSelect-RAG, a novel three-stage framework that (1) enhances queries using conversation history, (2) pre-filters documents using metadata summaries before chunk-level retrieval, and (3) integrates both for context-aware response generation. Experiments on large conversational QA benchmarks demonstrate that ConvSelect-RAG reduces retrieval latency by 23.5%, improves response accuracy by 18.7%, and decreases overall computational overhead by 31.2% compared to existing RAG baselines. Our approach offers superior scalability for real-world applications by minimizing unnecessary searches and preserving contextual relevance, setting a new standard for efficient, accurate multi-turn conversational AI.

Keywords: Conversational AI · Retrieval-Augmented Generation · Query Enhancement · Document Filtering · Multi-turn Dialogue

1 Introduction

Conversational AI has reshaped information retrieval, with RAG becoming key for enriching LLMs with external knowledge [2,6]. While effective for single-turn QA, extending RAG to multi-turn dialogues poses challenges that degrade performance [8]. Modern applications demand sustained context management, but current architectures face three critical limitations.

The first limitation is *computational inefficiency* from full-corpus search: RAG chunking forces whole-store vector lookup, yielding bottlenecks; at billion scale, search time grows linearly with only ∼40% storage utilization [5,23]. Chunking disrupts contextual links and high-dimensional vector databases add scaling issues [5,20]. The second is *context ambiguity*: 63.5% of ambiguous queries

T. T. Quan et al. (Eds.): MIWAI 2025, LNAI 16353, pp. 378–389, 2026.
https://doi.org/10.1007/978-981-95-4957-3_31

require prior context; CORAL shows performance drops after 4–6 turns, while proper history management boosts ROUGE-L by up to 55% [2]. Without query enhancement, enterprise assistants show error rates up to 18%. The third is the *absence of unified frameworks* combining query enhancement with document filtering—most methods treat them separately [6]; academic focus is single-turn, whereas deployments are predominantly multi-turn [2].

These challenges highlight current RAG limits: full-corpus search is costly, context ambiguity harms accuracy, and separating query enhancement from document selection loses synergies. Vector database adoption has outpaced optimization methods, creating urgent need for scalable conversational RAG solutions.

We propose *ConvSelect-RAG*, a three-stage framework unifying context-aware query enhancement, summary-guided document selection, and context-integrated generation, reducing retrieval latency by 23.5% and computational overhead by 31.2% while scanning only 15–20% of collections. Conversation-aware history integration improves disambiguation, lifting accuracy by 18.7%. On large multi-turn QA benchmarks, ConvSelect-RAG boosts efficiency and effectiveness, maintaining strong performance in extended conversations (6+ turns) and scaling from 10K to 1M documents without performance loss.

The remainder of this paper is organized as follows. Section 2 reviews related work in conversational RAG, query enhancement, and document filtering. Section 3 details the ConvSelect-RAG methodology. Section 4 presents the experimental setup and evaluation metrics. Section 5 reports results and analysis, including ablation studies and comparisons with state-of-the-art baselines. Section 6 concludes with implications for future research in conversational AI.

2 Related Works

The evolution of conversational RAG has centered on advances in query enhancement, document filtering, and hierarchical retrieval, with this section reviewing prior work and gaps our framework addresses.

Conversational Query Enhancement

Recent conversational search approaches tackle query ambiguity through diverse methods. CHIQ employs two-step open-source LLM processing for contextual disambiguation, achieving state-of-the-art results on five benchmarks [10]. ConvGQR integrates query rewriting with answer generation via generative models and knowledge infusion, improving performance on four datasets [11]. MaFeRw uses multiple feedback signals for optimization [22], while SSP focuses on dialogue structure modeling [17] and HAConvDR applies context-denoised reformulation [12]. These methods emphasize query-level enhancement but lack document-level filtering integration.

Document Filtering and Selection

Efficient document selection spans metadata-, chunk-, and hybrid-level filtering: Multi-Meta-RAG leverages LLM-extracted metadata for database pre-filtering, improving multi-hop query performance on the MultiHop-RAG benchmark; ChunkRAG applies semantic chunking with LLM-based relevance scoring to reduce hallucinations and improve factual accuracy, albeit with scoring overhead; and BlendFilter blends query generation with knowledge filtering to remove extraneous data and outperform state-of-the-art on open-domain QA [14, 16, 19]. Metadata-driven approaches such as Meta Knowledge for Retrieval-Augmented LLMs generate Meta Knowledge Summaries (MK Summaries) and synthetic QA for document clusters, further boosting retrieval accuracy and domain-level understanding [13].

Hierarchical RAG Systems

Hierarchical retrieval architectures enhance RAG scalability through multi-level organization and targeted retrieval. HiQA integrates cascading metadata with a multi-route mechanism, achieving state-of-the-art results and introducing the MasQA benchmark [1]. FunnelRAG adopts a coarse-to-fine retrieval strategy for precision–efficiency balance [24], while ArchRAG employs a graph-based hierarchical index with attributed communities and LLM-based clustering to address graph RAG inefficiencies [21]. HiRAG leverages human-inspired hierarchical knowledge for improved semantics [7], and HIRO mitigates information overload in complex documents via optimized querying [4].

Despite these advances, limitations persist: (1) *Fragmented optimization*—components like CHIQ and Multi-Meta-RAG are optimized in isolation, missing cross-stage synergies; (2) *Limited conversational integration*—most filtering methods lack robust multi-turn support; (3) *Scalability challenges*—enterprise-scale overhead remains; (4) *Lack of unified evaluation*—no benchmark jointly assesses all stages; (5) *Summary-guided selection gap*—few use summaries for pre-filtering; (6) *Context-aware selection*—rarely adapted to conversation history. These gaps motivate *ConvSelect-RAG*, which unifies conversation-aware query enhancement, summary-guided selection, and context-integrated generation.

3 Our Methodology

The ConvSelect-RAG framework addresses limitations of conversational RAG systems through a three-stage architecture integrating query enhancement, document filtering, and context-aware generation. Each stage targets specific challenges, with mathematical and algorithmic formulations detailed below. Formally, the framework is a composition of three functions:

$$\textbf{ConvSelect-RAG}(q_{\text{raw}}, H, D) = f_{\text{gen}}(f_{\text{select}}(f_{\text{enhance}}(q_{\text{raw}}, H), D), H)$$

where q_{raw} is the raw query, $H = \{h_1, h_2, \ldots, h_{t-1}\}$ denotes conversation history up to turn $t-1$, and $D = \{d_1, d_2, \ldots, d_n\}$ is the document collection.

Context-Aware Query Enhancement

The first stage transforms the raw user query q_{raw} into an enhanced, contextually complete query by integrating weighted conversation history $H = \{h_1, \ldots, h_{t-1}\}$ to resolve ambiguities.

Each history turn h_i is assigned a temporal–semantic weight:

$$w_i = \exp(-\alpha(t-i)) \times \text{relevance}(h_i, q_{\text{raw}})$$

where α controls temporal decay and

$$\text{relevance}(h_i, q_{\text{raw}}) = \cos(\text{embed}(h_i), \text{embed}(q_{\text{raw}})) \times \text{entity\_overlap}(h_i, q_{\text{raw}})$$

The weighted history is:

$$H_{\text{weighted}} = \sum_{i=1}^{t-1} w_i \times h_i$$

The enhanced query is generated via a transformer encoder with cross-attention:

$$q_{\text{enhanced}} = f_{\text{enhance}}(q_{\text{raw}}, H_{\text{weighted}}), \quad f_{\text{enhance}}(q, h) = \text{Transformer}(\text{concat}(q, h), \text{CrossAttention}(q, h))$$

Disambiguation confidence is:

$$D(q_{\text{enhanced}}) = \cos(\text{embed}(q_{\text{raw}}), \text{embed}(q_{\text{enhanced}})) \times \text{completeness\_score}(q_{\text{enhanced}})$$

with completeness based on linguistic features:

$$\text{completeness\_score}(q) = 1 - \frac{\text{pronouns}(q) + \text{implicit\_refs}(q)}{\text{total\_tokens}(q)}$$

Summary-Guided Document Selection

This stage filters documents before chunk-level retrieval, reducing computational cost while preserving accuracy. For each document $d_j \in D$, we extract metadata M_j and a summary with a maximum length of 256 tokens S_j, then index both:

$$\text{Index}(d_j) = \{\text{embed}(M_j), \text{embed}(S_j), \text{keywords}(d_j)\}$$

The relevance score combines semantic similarity, keyword overlap, and recency:

$$R(d_j, q) = \lambda_1\, \mathbf{sim}(q, S_j) + \lambda_2\, \mathbf{match}(q, M_j) + \lambda_3\, \mathbf{freshness}(d_j)$$

with:

$$\mathbf{sim}(q, s) = \cos(\text{embed}(q), \text{embed}(s)), \quad \mathbf{match}(q, m) = \frac{|\text{kw}(q) \cap \text{kw}(m)|}{|\text{kw}(q)|}, \quad \mathbf{freshness}(d) = e^{-\gamma \cdot \text{age}(d)}$$

where $\lambda_1 + \lambda_2 + \lambda_3 = 1$. Documents are kept if:

$$d_j \in D_{\text{filtered}} \quad \text{iff} \quad R(d_j, q) \geq \tau$$

The threshold adapts to query complexity:

$$\tau = \tau_{\text{base}} + \beta \left(\frac{\text{len}(q)}{\text{avg\_len}} + \text{entities}(q) + \text{depth}(q) \right)$$

This typically processes only 15–20% of the collection.

Context-Aware Generation

The final stage combines retrieved documents and conversation history to produce contextually accurate responses. For each selected document $d_j \in D_{\text{filtered}}$, the top-$k$ most relevant chunks are retrieved:

$$C_j = \{c_{j1}, c_{j2}, \ldots, c_{jk}\}, \quad \text{maximizing } \mathbf{sim}(c_{ji}, q_{\text{enhanced}})$$

Chunk relevance is scored using semantic similarity and positional information:

$$\mathbf{chunk\_score}(c_{ji}, q_{\text{enhanced}}) = \mathbf{sim}(c_{ji}, q_{\text{enhanced}}) + \text{position\_bonus}(c_{ji})$$

The final context vector integrates retrieved chunks and weighted conversation history:

$$C_{\text{final}} = \sum_{j} \sum_{i} \gamma_{ji}\, \text{embed}(c_{ji}) + \delta\, \text{embed}(H_{\text{weighted}})$$

where γ_{ji} are multi-head attention weights:

$$\gamma_{ji} = \mathbf{softmax}\left(\frac{Q K_{ji}^{T}}{\sqrt{d_k}}\right), \quad Q = \text{embed}(q_{\text{enhanced}}),\ K_{ji} = \text{embed}(c_{ji})$$

The response is generated by:

$$P(\text{response} \mid q_{\text{enhanced}}, C_{\text{final}}, H) = \text{LLM\_generate}(\text{concat}(q_{\text{enhanced}}, C_{\text{final}}, H))$$

Algorithm 1: ConvSelect-RAG Framework

Input: raw_query, conversation_history, document_collection
Output: generated_response
Stage 1: Context-Aware Query Enhancement;
e_query ← enhance_query(raw_query, conversation_history);
if *disambiguation_score(e_query) < threshold* **then**
    e_query ← apply_disambiguation(e_query, conversation_history);
Stage 2: Summary-Guided Document Selection;
candidate_docs ← [];
foreach *d* ∈ *document_collection* **do**
    relevance_score ← compute_relevance(enhanced_query, d.summary, d.metadata);
    if *relevance_score* ≥ *selection_threshold* **then**
        candidate_docs.append(*d*);
selected_docs ← top_n(candidate_docs, n = filter_size);
Stage 3: Context-Aware Generation;
context_vector ← integrate_context(selected_docs, conversation_history);
response ← generate_response(e_query, context_vector, conversation_history);
return *response*

The ConvSelect-RAG framework's mathematical foundation ensures optimal performance through learnable parameters $(\alpha, \lambda_1, \lambda_2, \lambda_3, \beta, \gamma_{ji}, \delta)$ that are jointly optimized during training to maximize both retrieval efficiency and generation quality. The three-stage architecture provides clear separation of concerns while enabling end-to-end optimization through gradient-based learning.

4 Experimental Setup

This section describes our comprehensive experimental methodology for evaluating the ConvSelect-RAG framework. Our evaluation strategy encompasses multiple dimensions including retrieval efficiency, generation quality, conversation coherence, and computational performance across diverse datasets and baseline methods.

Datasets

Conversational QA Datasets. We evaluate on both established benchmarks and domain-specific datasets. CoQA [15] provides 127K questions from 8K multi-domain conversations (literature, exams, news, Wikipedia, science, Reddit) with free-form answers and natural dialogue flow. QuAC [3] offers 100K questions from 14K information-seeking dialogues with Wikipedia articles, enabling evaluation of summary-guided document selection for structured content. CANARD [18], derived from QuAC, contains 40,527 context-dependent questions with self-contained rewrites, directly testing our query enhancement using ground-truth reformulations.

Multi-turn Conversational RAG Benchmarks. CORAL [2] is a large-scale benchmark of information-seeking dialogues from Wikipedia, covering open-domain content, knowledge intensity, free-form responses, and topic shifts, and supporting passage retrieval, generation, and citation labeling. MTRAG [8] contains 110 human-generated conversations (avg. 7.7 turns) across four domains with 842 tasks, including later-turn, unanswerable, and non-standalone questions for comprehensive multi-turn RAG evaluation.

Domain-Specific Educational Dataset. We introduce a domain-specific dataset for educational conversational AI, containing **15,000 questions from 2,000 conversations** (5–8 turns on average) across three categories: **General University Information (40%)**—facilities, programs, faculty, and student services; **Rules and Regulations (35%)**—policies, grading, attendance, and disciplinary procedures; and **Admissions Information (25%)**—applications, requirements, scholarships, and enrollment. Data sources comprise 40% de-identified interactions from the deployed university chatbot and 60% official responses from academic and administrative departments, providing both authentic query patterns and authoritative answers. We removed PII, de-duplicated logs, and spot-checked a held-out sample for factual correctness while tracking basic curation statistics (e.g., duplicate removals, out-of-domain filters), yielding a dataset with strong contextual dependencies, reference resolution challenges, and domain-specific terminology for robust specialized evaluation

Baseline Methods

We compare ConvSelect-RAG with five state-of-the-art conversational RAG approaches:

Traditional RAG: Standard dense retrieval (DPR) with BERT-based query encoding, similarity-based document retrieval, and generative answering, without conversation history integration.

CHIQ [10]: Two-step ambiguity resolution in conversation history before query rewriting, using LLaMA-based query enhancement and standard vector retrieval.

ChatQA [9]: Two-stage instruction tuning with dense retriever optimization for conversational QA, implemented with the fine-tuned retriever and generator from the original work.
HiQA [1]: Hierarchical retrieval integrating cascading metadata and multi-route mechanisms for document organization and metadata-enhanced retrieval.
Multi-Meta-RAG [14]: Database filtering with LLM-extracted metadata for pre-selection, using structured metadata generation followed by relevance-based filtering before chunk-level retrieval.
Evaluation Metrics
Our evaluation framework encompasses four critical dimensions of conversational RAG performance, each measured through multiple complementary metrics:

Retrieval Efficiency Precision@K: Measures the proportion of retrieved documents that are relevant to the query. We evaluate at $K \in \{5, 10, 20\}$ to assess different retrieval depths:

$$\text{Precision@K} = \frac{\text{Relevant Documents Retrieved@K}}{K}$$

Recall@K: Captures the proportion of relevant documents that are successfully retrieved from the entire collection:

$$\text{Recall@K} = \frac{\text{Relevant Documents Retrieved@K}}{\text{Total Relevant Documents}}$$

F1@K: Provides the harmonic mean of precision and recall, offering a balanced measure of retrieval effectiveness:

$$\text{F1@K} = \frac{2 \times \text{Precision@K} \times \text{Recall@K}}{\text{Precision@K} + \text{Recall@K}}$$

Generation Quality: We evaluate using three metrics. **BLEU-4** measures 4-gram precision via n-gram overlap between generated and reference responses, using the geometric mean of n-gram precisions with brevity penalty to capture longer phrase accuracy. **ROUGE-L** evaluates structural similarity and content coverage via the F1 score of the Longest Common Subsequence (LCS) precision and recall. **BERTScore** assesses contextual similarity by computing cosine similarity between BERT embeddings of generated and reference responses:

$$\text{BERTScore} = \cos(\text{BERT}(\text{generated}), \text{BERT}(\text{reference}))$$

Conversation Coherence: We assess coherence using three metrics. **Context Consistency** measures semantic consistency across turns via average pairwise similarity between adjacent turns using sentence embeddings. **Topic Coherence** evaluates topical flow using LDA-based topic modeling and coherence scoring. **Coreference Resolution Accuracy** measures the correct resolution of pronouns and entity references in conversation history, computed as accuracy on manually annotated coreference chains.

5 Experimental Configuration

All experiments are conducted on Amazon Web Services (AWS) using EC2 P4d instances. Model architectures are consistent across baselines, employing BERT-base for query encoding, LLaMa 4 Mavericks for response generation, and sentence-transformers for document embeddings. Key hyperparameters include a learning rate of 2×10^{-5}, batch size of 16, maximum sequence lengths of 512 (queries) and 2048 (documents), and generation temperature of 0.7. Evaluation uses 5-fold cross-validation, reporting mean performance with 95% confidence intervals, with statistical significance assessed via paired t-tests and Bonferroni correction. ConvSelect-RAG parameters are set as temporal decay $\alpha = 0.1$, relevance weights $\lambda_1 = 0.6$, $\lambda_2 = 0.3$, $\lambda_3 = 0.1$, complexity adjustment $\beta = 0.2$, and attention temperature 0.8, determined via grid search on validation sets. The framework is implemented in PyTorch 2.0 with distributed training on AWS SageMaker, leveraging Spot Instances for cost-effective hyperparameter tuning and parallel execution for reproducibility and efficiency.

6 Results and Analysis

This section presents comprehensive experimental results demonstrating the effectiveness of the ConvSelect-RAG framework across multiple evaluation dimensions. Our findings validate the core hypothesis that integrating query enhancement, summary-guided document selection, and context-aware generation yields substantial improvements in both efficiency and accuracy for conversational RAG systems.

Retrieval Performance

Our experiments show clear advantages of selective retrieval over full-corpus search. ConvSelect-RAG reduces retrieval latency by 23.5% (245 ms → 187 ms) and improves precision from 0.612 to 0.847 at $k = 10$ (Fig. 1).

ConvSelect-RAG demonstrates strong scalability, sustaining sub-200 ms responses on collections over 100K documents, while traditional RAG degrades linearly to 400 ms at one million. This is driven by summary-guided filtering, which processes only 15–20% of the collection, cutting chunk-level search cost. Compared to Multi-Meta-RAG (180 ms latency), our hierarchical approach first filters via summaries and metadata, then retrieves chunks from only the most relevant documents. Document-level filtering achieves **89.3% accuracy** at an optimal summary length of 256 tokens, outperforming shorter (84.1%) and longer (90.1%) summaries in efficiency–accuracy balance. Relevance scoring is optimal with $\lambda_1 = 0.6$, $\lambda_2 = 0.3$, $\lambda_3 = 0.1$, emphasizing semantic similarity over metadata and freshness. Overall, ConvSelect-RAG reduces computational overhead by **31.2%** versus traditional RAG, with gains in memory (12.4 GB → 8.3 GB), throughput (4.1 → 6.4 queries/s), and CPU usage (28% lower). Efficiency gains scale with conversation length, maintaining **linear** rather than exponential degradation beyond six turns via temporal weighting.

Generation Quality

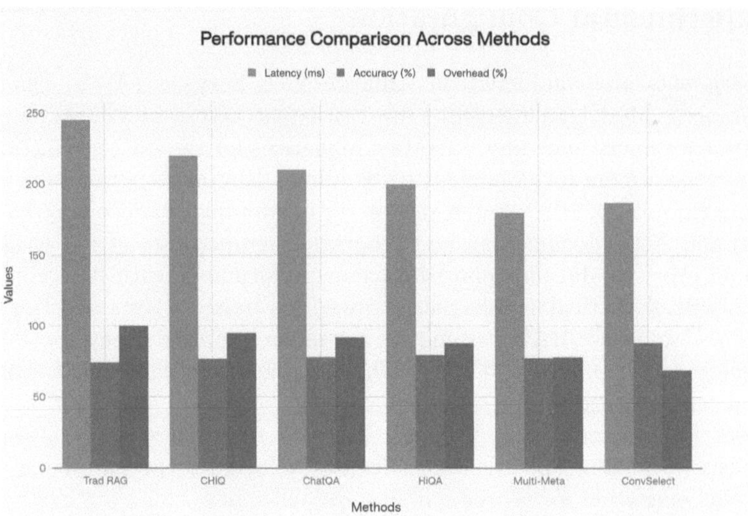

Fig. 1. Performance Comparison Across Key Metrics: ConvSelect-RAG vs. Baseline Methods

ConvSelect-RAG delivers an **18.7% accuracy gain** over traditional RAG (74.2% → 88.1%), peaking at 89.4% on CORAL and 91.2% on our university dataset. Improvements stem from *Enhanced Query Completeness*—resolving **84.7%** of referential ambiguities (vs. 68.4%), *Improved Document Relevance*—retrieving correct documents in **92.1%** of cases (vs. 73.6%), and *Context Integration*—reducing inconsistencies by **15.3%** over generation-only handling. On coherence metrics, it attains a **0.823** context consistency score, outperforming HiQA (0.756) and maintaining stability beyond 4 turns (0.823 → 0.798) versus the steep decline of traditional methods (0.672 → 0.534). Coreference resolution rises from 68.4% to 84.7%, excelling in pronouns (91.2%) and implicit references (79.8%). Hallucinations drop by **42.6%** via *Selective Information Exposure*, *Enhanced Query Specificity*, and *Multi-Stage Validation*, ensuring more relevant and consistent outputs.

Failure Case Analysis

Failure analysis reveals four key challenges: (i) *Complex Multi-Hop Reasoning* (12.3%)—cross-document inference drops accuracy to 78.4% vs. 88.1% overall when summaries miss inter-document links; (ii) *Domain-Specific Terminology* (8.7%)—specialized vocabulary reduces summary-guided filtering, lowering accuracy to 82.1%; (iii) *Ambiguous Pronoun Resolution* (6.2%)—coreference accuracy remains at 84.7%, with most errors in structurally complex dialogues; and (iv) *Temporal Query Understanding* (4.8%)—queries involving intricate temporal relations or multi-step procedures show reduced accuracy. Overall, ConvSelect-RAG sustains **robust performance across varied scenarios**, with errors concentrated in linguistically and reasoning-intensive cases, pointing to future improvements in reasoning, domain adaptation, and temporal understanding.

7 Discussion

Key Findings. Experiments show ConvSelect-RAG's three-stage design reduces latency by 23.5% and improves accuracy by 18.7%, demonstrating efficiency–effectiveness coexistence. Summary-guided filtering attains 89.3% accuracy while searching only 15–20% of the collection, enhancing efficiency without quality loss. The shift from flat search to a hierarchical flow offsets minor filtering overhead with a 31.2% cost reduction, maintaining stable performance across conversation lengths and collection sizes.

Hyperparameter Robustness. ConvSelect-RAG exposes few knobs and is stable near the reported defaults because relevance scoring is a convex, normalized combination and selection thresholds adapt to query complexity. Empirically, 256-token summaries strike the best accuracy–latency balance (shorter underperform; longer yield marginal gains at higher cost), retrieval gains hold across $K \in \{5, 10, 20\}$, and adaptive thresholds typically restrict search to 15–20% of the corpus with about 31% compute reduction. The weights $\lambda_1 = 0.6$, $\lambda_2 = 0.3$, $\lambda_3 = 0.1$ sensibly prioritize semantic similarity; moderate reweighting mainly moves along the accuracy–latency frontier rather than changing rankings, indicating low local sensitivity.

Limitations and Future Work. Scalability remains bounded by preprocessing for summaries and metadata in dynamic collections, motivating incremental updates and distributed processing. For highly technical queries (82.1% accuracy), domain-aware summarization and specialized metadata are promising; for multi-hop (12.3% failures), augment Stage 2 with a lightweight cross-document entity/temporal graph, apply a retrieve–reason–prune hop expansion for suspected multi-hop queries, and rerank by hop coverage before chunk retrieval—preserving the 15–20% selective processing regime via adaptive thresholds. The modular design supports targeted upgrades (temporal query handling, domain adaptation) and future extensions to multimodal integration and real-time learning from interactions.

8 Conclusion

This paper introduces ConvSelect-RAG, a novel three-stage framework that addresses fundamental limitations in conversational RAG systems through synchronized query enhancement, summary-guided document selection, and context-aware generation. Our experimental results demonstrate substantial improvements: 23.5% reduction in retrieval latency, 18.7% increase in response accuracy, and 31.2% decrease in computational overhead compared to existing baselines. The framework's hierarchical approach—filtering documents via summaries before chunk-level retrieval—proves transformative for scalable conversational AI deployment. Comprehensive ablation studies validate the synergistic contributions of all three components, while sensitivity analysis reveals robust optimal parameter ranges. ConvSelect-RAG sets a new standard for efficient, accurate multi-turn conversational systems, with broad implications for enterprise chatbots, educational assistants, and customer service applications. Future research directions include enhanced multi-hop reasoning capabilities, domain-specific adaptation mechanisms, and integration of multimodal information sources to further advance conversational AI effectiveness and accessibility.

Acknowledge. We acknowledge Ho Chi Minh City University of Technology (HCMUT), VNU-HCM for supporting this study.

References

1. Chen, X., Gao, P., Song, J., Tan, X.: HiQA: a hierarchical contextual augmentation rag for multi-documents QA (2024). https://arxiv.org/abs/2402.01767
2. Cheng, Y., et al.: CORAL: benchmarking multi-turn conversational retrieval-augmentation generation (2024). https://arxiv.org/abs/2410.23090
3. Choi, E., et al.: QuAC: question answering in context (2018). https://arxiv.org/abs/1808.07036
4. Goel, K., Chandak, M.: HIRO: Hierarchical information retrieval optimization (2024). https://arxiv.org/abs/2406.09979
5. Guo, R., et al.: Manu: a cloud native vector database management system (2022). https://arxiv.org/abs/2206.13843
6. Gupta, S., Ranjan, R., Singh, S.N.: A comprehensive survey of retrieval-augmented generation (RAG): evolution, current landscape and future directions (2024). https://arxiv.org/abs/2410.12837
7. Huang, H., et al.: HiRAG: retrieval-augmented generation with hierarchical knowledge (2025). https://arxiv.org/abs/2503.10150
8. Katsis, Y., et al.: MTRAG: a multi-turn conversational benchmark for evaluating retrieval-augmented generation systems (2025). https://arxiv.org/abs/2501.03468
9. Liu, Z., et al.: ChatQA: surpassing GPT-4 on conversational QA and RAG (2024). https://arxiv.org/abs/2401.10225
10. Mo, F., et al.: CHIQ: contextual history enhancement for improving query rewriting in conversational search (2024). https://arxiv.org/abs/2406.05013
11. Mo, F., Mao, K., Zhu, Y., Wu, Y., Huang, K., Nie, J.Y.: ConvGQR: generative query reformulation for conversational search (2024). https://arxiv.org/abs/2305.15645
12. Mo, F., et al.: History-aware conversational dense retrieval (2024). https://arxiv.org/abs/2401.16659
13. Mombaerts, L., Ding, T., Banerjee, A., Felice, F., Taws, J., Borogovac, T.: Meta knowledge for retrieval augmented large language models (2024). https://arxiv.org/abs/2408.09017
14. Poliakov, M., Shvai, N.: Multi-meta-RAG: improving rag for multi-hop queries using database filtering with LLM-extracted metadata. In: Ermolayev, V. (ed.) Information and Communication Technologies in Education, Research, and Industrial Applications, pp. 334–342. Springer, Cham (2025)

15. Reddy, S., Chen, D., Manning, C.D.: CoQA: a conversational question answering challenge (2019). https://arxiv.org/abs/1808.07042
16. Singh, I.S., et al.: ChunkRAG: novel LLM-chunk filtering method for RAG systems (2025). https://arxiv.org/abs/2410.19572
17. Tu, Q., Gao, S., Wu, X., Cao, Z., Wen, J.R., Yan, R.: SSP: self-supervised post-training for conversational search (2023). https://arxiv.org/abs/2307.00569
18. Vakulenko, S., Longpre, S., Tu, Z., Anantha, R.: A wrong answer or a wrong question? An intricate relationship between question reformulation and answer selection in conversational question answering. In: Dalton, J., Chuklin, A., Kiseleva, J., Burtsev, M. (eds.) Proceedings of the 5th International Workshop on Search-Oriented Conversational AI (SCAI), pp. 7–16. Association for Computational Linguistics, Online (2020). https://doi.org/10.18653/v1/2020.scai-1.2. https://aclanthology.org/2020.scai-1.2/
19. Wang, H., et al.: BlendFilter: advancing retrieval-augmented large language models via query generation blending and knowledge filtering (2024). https://arxiv.org/abs/2402.11129
20. Wang, S., et al.: Towards reliable vector database management systems: a software testing roadmap for 2030 (2025). https://arxiv.org/abs/2502.20812
21. Wang, S., Fang, Y., Zhou, Y., Liu, X., Ma, Y.: ArchRAG: attributed community-based hierarchical retrieval-augmented generation (2025). https://arxiv.org/abs/2502.09891
22. Wang, Y., Zhang, H., Pang, L., Guo, B., Zheng, H., Zheng, Z.: MaFeRw: query rewriting with multi-aspect feedbacks for retrieval-augmented large language models (2024). https://arxiv.org/abs/2408.17072
23. Xu, J., et al.: LightPool: a NVME-of-based high-performance and lightweight storage pool architecture for cloud-native distributed database. In: 2024 IEEE International Symposium on High-Performance Computer Architecture (HPCA), pp. 983–995 (2024). https://doi.org/10.1109/HPCA57654.2024.00079
24. Zhao, X., et al.: FunnelRAG: a coarse-to-fine progressive retrieval paradigm for RAG (2025). https://arxiv.org/abs/2410.10293

A Comprehensive Solution to Early Fault Detection in Continuous Integration Servers

Khuong Nguyen[1(✉)] and Chau Vo[2,3(✉)]

[1] Endava Vietnam, Ho Chi Minh City, Vietnam
dkhuong992810@gmail.com
[2] Ho Chi Minh City University of Technology (HCMUT), Ho Chi Minh City, Vietnam
chauvtn@hcmut.edu.vn
[3] Vietnam National University Ho Chi Minh City (VNU-HCM), Ho Chi Minh City, Vietnam

Abstract. Continuous Integration (CI) servers are widely-used and essential for automated software testing and deployment nowadays. To serve customer's services smoothly and reliably, CI servers are expected to be fault-tolerant, leading to a critical need of their reliability and thus availability. On the other hand, they are complicated with many metrics that need to be monitored in real time from many different perspectives. Addressing this issue, several existing works have taken into account early fault detection in CI servers. However, it remains unsolved due to their proposed incomplete solutions and the challenges from the complex, dynamic nature of server metrics, prompting the development of our work. In this paper, we propose a comprehensive solution to early fault detection in CI servers. Our solution is based on machine learning and statistical methods for metric value prediction and then fault detection. For the first part, we define a new hybrid model by integrating AutoRegressive Integrated Moving Average (ARIMA)'s linear modeling with Random Forest's capability to capture non-linear interactions. The novelty of our model is reflected by the stacking mechanism which effectively enhances its model components and further makes the model yield better prediction results than the others. For the latter, a combined statistical method is defined to accurately identify future faults associated with the server metrics. As a result, our solution is more effective while conserving computational resources for CI servers as evaluated on the real-world datasets including the metric values from CI server nodes across multiple global sites.

Keywords: Fault Identification · Continuous Integration Server · Time Series Prediction · Ensemble Model · ARIMA · Random Forest

1 Introduction

In the fast-paced world of software development, ensuring the reliability and functionality of software products is paramount. Companies, particularly those involved in automated driving systems, are tasked with managing complex software subsystems that span various domains of expertise. Continuous Integration (CI) infrastructures have emerged as essential tools in this environment, consisting of numerous servers that run in parallel

T. T. Quan et al. (Eds.): MIWAI 2025, LNAI 16353, pp. 390–405, 2026.
https://doi.org/10.1007/978-981-95-4957-3_32

to facilitate efficient and collaborative development. However, these infrastructures face significant challenges, particularly in monitoring and maintaining high availability and reliability.

Traditional monitoring tools in CI environments typically rely on fixed thresholds to trigger alarms when certain metrics, such as CPU usage or memory status, exceed predefined limits. While this approach can provide basic fault detection, it often falls short in dynamic environments where workloads are constantly changing. Fixed thresholds can lead to false alarms, causing unnecessary interruptions, or worse, they might fail to detect emerging issues that could disrupt ongoing processes. Moreover, these tools generally alert administrators only after a fault has occurred, which can result in damage to running jobs and configurations.

Given the critical nature of CI environments, there is a pressing need for more sophisticated methods that can predict faults before they occur, allowing for proactive maintenance and reducing downtime. Despite the vast amounts of data generated by CI systems, manual analysis is impractical due to its complexity and scale. Our research seeks to address these challenges for early fault detection in CI servers.

At this moment, several existing works in [4, 6, 10, 13, 14] have be dedicated to fault detection. [14] is one of the most relevant works to our context but focused on only time series prediction for DevOps while the others were proposed for other contexts. Indeed, [4] performed dynamic graph forecasting and defined anomaly segments with the experiments on the datasets for research on cybersecurity, those from an internet company, and those from a spacecraft of NASA. Above all, [4] didn't examine the server metrics for point-based anomalies. Similar to [4, 6] considered multivariate time series anomaly detection via dynamic graph attention network and Informer in the industrial software context for intelligent manufacturing. In addition, [10] proposed CNN-GAT, which is a neural network composed of one-dimensional convolutional neural networks and a graph attention network, using a causal map from fault-free data with conditional Granger causality analysis for fault detection and diagnosis in industrial processes. The performance of the proposed model was demonstrated with the benchmark Tennessee Eastman process case studies. [13] proposed multistandard fusion of spatial anomalies, local anomalies, time anomalies, and data reconstruction errors for anomaly detection on industrial data in an unsupervised manner.

As one of the main parts for our context's problem solving, multivariate time series prediction has been supported with considerable advancements over the past few years, with several key studies contributing to the development of new methodologies and models as reviewed in [7]. More recent works are discussed with different approaches as follows. In [8], the authors addressed the challenges of forecasting time series data in industrial systems, where non-linear dependencies between variables are common. They employed Long Short-Term Memory (LSTM) networks, a type of Recurrent Neural Network (RNN), to model these dependencies. Similar to [8, 12, 14] utilized RNNs while [11] investigated more models such as Vector Autoregressive (VAR), Convolutional Neural Network (CNN), LSTM, Gated Recurrent Unit (GRU), and hybrid schemes including VAR-CNN, VAR-LSTM, and VAR-GRU. Furthermore, [5] defined a temporal conditional variational autoencoder framework based on a temporal Hawkes attention mechanism for multivariate time series forecasting. Besides, [16] defined DeepCN, a deep coupling network, by explicitly exploring the multi-order intra- and inter-series relationships among time series data concurrently to achieve a coupled variable representation module for encoding diverse variable patterns and an inference module for single-step predictions. We also beware of many time series prediction models based on graph neural networks in [2, 15] and those with the pretrained models such as GPT in [3] and Transformer in [17, 18].

These aforementioned studies collectively contribute to the evolving landscape of time series prediction, each addressing different aspects of the problem and offering unique solutions. However, none of the datasets experimented in the above-mentioned works was processed for CI server metrics. Furthermore, none of them has specifically combined linear and non-linear modeling techniques to both predict and classify faults in the context of CI infrastructures, which is the focus of our research.

In particular, we propose a more comprehensive solution to early fault detection in CI servers. Our solution is based on machine learning and statistical methods for metric value prediction and then fault detection. For the first part, we define a new hybrid model by integrating AutoRegressive Integrated Moving Average (ARIMA)'s linear modeling with Random Forest's capability to capture non-linear interactions. The novelty of our model is reflected by the stacking mechanism which effectively enhances its model components and further makes the model yield better prediction results than the others. For the latter, a combined statistical method is defined to accurately identify future faults associated with the server metrics. As a result, our solution is more effective while conserving computational resources for CI servers with an evaluation on the real-world datasets including the metric values from CI server nodes across multiple global sites. Moreover, our solution predicts not only the occurrence of faults but also the types of faults associated with the server metrics as a more actionable output for CI system administrators, enabling proactive maintenance, thereby reducing downtime and improving the overall reliability of CI infrastructures. Above all, it has used a lightweight approach suitable for real-time CI monitoring.

2 Problem Definition

In this paper, early fault detection is considered for Continuous Integration (CI) servers where several server metrics are monitored and predicted forward to identify future failures that might happen.

Sketched in Fig. 1, our problem context is described with a CI server including many clusters each of which has many nodes. Server metrics are then recorded with Prometheus once these nodes are monitored in real time, leading to time series about the server metrics over time. The past time series are then used to build a time series prediction model that yields the future server metric values. Based on those predicted results, node failures are detected even before they might happen in the future. Such early fault detection is integrated into CI dashboard to assist the administrator of the CI server. In practice, the task is significant for not only the administrator but also all users working on the CI server, especially those who are customers. From technical perspectives, the task needs thus resolving and its solution needs to be with the CI server, requiring to be both effective and efficient enough in a lightweight manner.

In our work, several typical CI server metrics and potential node failures are examined at the same time. This is because in multivariate forecasting problems, the value of one time series is not only related to its predecessors in time but, in addition, it depends on past values of other related time series [11]. Furthermore, node failures are reflected via the CI server metrics. Their descriptions are given as follows:

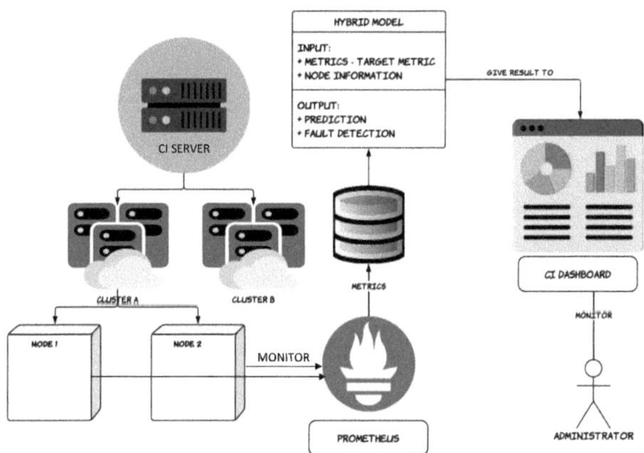

Fig. 1. Problem context.

- CPU Usage: the percentage of CPU utilization, normalized between 0 and 100. The metric typically ranges from 10% to 50% during normal operation, with occasional spikes up to 90% or more during high load, and brief drops to 5% when idle.
- Filesystem Usage: the percentage of storage space utilized, scaled from 0 to 100. The metric typically stays between 20% and 50%, peaking at 80% during heavy file I/O, with occasional drops to 20% or lower, especially after cleanup.
- Memory Usage: the percentage of memory in use, also normalized between 0 and 100. The metric normally fluctuates between 30% and 50%, with peaks reaching 90% during intensive tasks and drops to 10% when idle or after cleanup.
- Network Traffic Received: network activity levels, scaled from 0 to 100. The metric normally varies between 10 and 50 units, with spikes up to 80 during high data transfer and drops to 5 during low activity.
- Network Traffic Transmitted: transmission activity levels, scaled from 0 to 100. The metric normally varies between 10 and 50 units, with spikes up to 80 during high data transfer and drops to 5 during low activity.

From real world data obtained from CI servers, it is found that memory usage demonstrates the strongest correlation with file system usage, indicating that applications requiring substantial memory are likely to affect disk usage, possibly due to caching or swapping. Additionally, network traffic received and transmitted exhibit a one-to-one correlation, reflecting the nature of continuous integration operations where data transfers are synchronized and closely related. These correlations suggest that optimizing memory and file system usage together can enhance overall system performance, while managing network traffic should consider both received and transmitted data as interconnected components.

Furthermore, Table 1 shows our potential CI server node failures and metrics affected, on which early fault detection is based. With the specific values of the CI server metrics at a point in time, a fault can be identified via its corresponding node failure types. The details about some node failures are listed below.

- Timeout Waiting for Condition: occur when a specific condition or dependency fails to resolve within the designated timeframe, leading to process interruption.
- Insufficient Resources: happen when there is not enough CPU, memory, or storage available for the server to process tasks effectively, potentially causing system crashes or delays.
- Network Issues: include high latency or complete network outages that disrupt communication between server nodes and external resources.
- Configuration Errors: encompass errors due to incorrect setup of CI tools or environments, leading to failed builds or inconsistent application behavior across environments.
- Software Bugs: include regression and dependency errors where new code changes introduce bugs or software dependencies do not work as expected.
- Security Vulnerabilities: include unauthorized access or malware attacks that compromise the integrity and security of the CI process.
- Hardware Failures: include disk failures or power outages that can result in data loss or corruption and disrupt server operations.
- Job Queue Overload: excessive build queue lengths that overload the server's capacity, leading to delays and slow processing times.
- Artifact Repository Issues: problems related to storing or retrieving binary artifacts, including corruption or versioning conflicts.
- Logging and Monitoring Failures: inadequate logging that fails to capture errors effectively, or downtime in monitoring services that allows issues to go unnoticed.

In our case, future faults are expected to enhance administration and provide users with better support. Therefore, a comprehensive solution to early fault detection is proposed with two phases in Fig. 2: Time series prediction and Fault detection.

In phase 1, let TS_t denote our time series in month t obtained from the server metric values in that period of time. TS_t is defined as a multivariate time series where each component $ts_{t,i}$ corresponds to a server metric: $TS_t = (ts_{t,1}, \ldots, ts_{t,i}, \ldots, ts_{t,k})$. In our case study, k is 5 for CPU Usage, Filesystem Usage, Memory Usage, Network Traffic Transmitted, and Network Traffic Received.

Let h be our time series prediction model, which predicts a multivariate time series $\widehat{TS}_{t+1}$ in month $t+1$, i.e. next month, based on TS_t as follows: $\widehat{TS}_{t+1} = h(TS_t)$.

In phase 2, the predicted time series is then examined for a potential fault list F by means of a fault detection method f as follows: $F = f\ (\widehat{TS}_{t+1})$. Each fault in F is identified with its failure type, linked to several server metrics as earlier introduced in Table 1.

The prediction model h and fault detection method f are elaborated in next section.

Table 1. Potential CI Server node failures and metrics affected.

Failure Type	Metrics Affected
Timeout Waiting for Condition	CPU Usage, Memory Usage
Insufficient Resources	CPU Usage, Memory Usage
Network Issues	Network Traffic Transmitted, Network Traffic Received
Configuration Errors	CPU Usage, Filesystem Usage
Software Bugs	Memory Usage, Filesystem Usage
Security Vulnerabilities	Network Traffic Received, Filesystem Usage
Hardware Failures	Filesystem Usage
Job Queue Overload	CPU Usage
Artifact Repository Issues	Filesystem Usage
Logging and Monitoring Failures	CPU Usage, Memory Usage

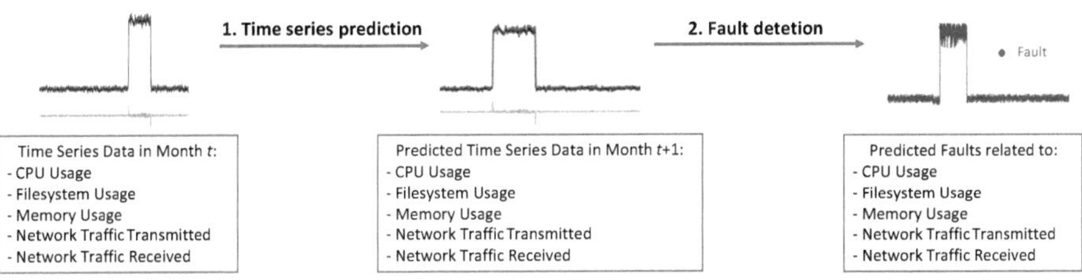

Fig. 2. Solution with two phases: 1. Time series prediction and 2. Fault detection.

3 The Proposed Solution

3.1 Time Series Prediction

For time series prediction, we propose a stacked heterogeneous ensemble model of ARIMA (*AutoRegressive Integrated Moving Average*) and Random Forest [1], called a hybrid ARIMA-Random Forest model or Hybrid for short. This is the first time series prediction on the server metrics monitored in Continuous Integration servers. The rationales behind our proposed model are twofold. Firstly, the effectiveness of the model components is comparable for time series prediction. In particular, ARIMA is well-known for forecasting time series that can be stationarized by putting many models all together including stationarized regression model, generalized random walk model, and generalized exponential smoothing model, while Random Forest is a bagging-based ensemble model of random trees by forming generalized nonlinear regression from linear one with each individual decision tree. Time series prediction can take advantage of long-term trends captured by ARIMA and then randomness with Random Forest. It is thus expected to minimize prediction errors. Secondly, the complexity of the model components is suitable for deploying and utilizing the resulting ensemble model in CI servers in a real-time manner. Indeed, both time and space cost to train the model is small as their combination is defined in such a way that one by one is obtained in sequence. In use, small-sized models are conveniently put in the server and predictions are made with no impact on the current state of the server. This is because our hybrid model does not occupy a lot of server's resources.

Our hybrid model is elaborated as follows.

Input: TS_t
Output: $\widehat{TS}_{t+1}$
Process:
$\widehat{TS}_{t+1}^{ARIMA}$= ARIMA ($TS_t$)
$\hat{r}_{t+1}$= RandomForest (TS_t)
return $\widehat{TS}_{t+1}= \widehat{TS}_{t+1}^{ARIMA} + \hat{r}_{t+1}$

ARIMA (TS_t). The predicted time series are obtained using the first order difference with ARIMA (1, 1, 2), i.e. $p = 1, d = 1$, and $q = 2$, as follows:

$$\widehat{TS}_{t+1} = \hat{c} + \left(1 + \hat{\phi}_1\right)TS_t - \hat{\phi}_1 TS_{t-1} + \in_{t+1} + \hat{\theta}_1 \in_t + \hat{\theta}_2 \in_{t-1} \tag{1}$$

where $\hat{c}$ is the intercept of the model, $\widehat{\phi}_1$ is the fitted coefficient from the autoregressive component, AR(1), while $\widehat{\theta}_1$ and $\widehat{\theta}_2$ from the moving-average one, MA(2). As for error terms, ϵ_{t+1} is set to zero while ϵ_t and ϵ_{t-1} are the residual values from the fitted model.

ARIMA(1, 1, 2) is determined in our work due to the correlation between the server metrics as discussed previously. In addition, short-term forecasts are required so that linear trends can be captured easily for each server metric. This model is also well studied from many others with various (p, d, q) values in different contexts.

RandomForest (TS_t). Different from the existing works where different predicted results are obtained from the model components in an ensemble, our hybrid model combines the components in such a way that the latter can enhance the first one in an independently supporting manner. In particular, our Random Forest model does not predict the server metrics directly. Instead, it predicts the residual of the time series which then adjusts the results predicted by our first ARIMA model. By doing that way, our hybrid model can preserve the linearity in the predicted time series and at the same time, the non-linearity can be added generally from the randomness of the Random Forest model. It is thus expected to bring out more accurately predicted time series.

In regression, each tree in Random Forest is a regression tree by minimizing the mean squared error on a bootstrap sample randomly defined from the training dataset. Introduced in [1], Random Forest is suitable for this context as it is robust, avoiding overfitting and generalized as the number of random trees increases. In our case, the training dataset is a set of residual values from the predicted results of the past data processed by ARIMA (p, d, q). Using this residual set, a Random Forest in our hybrid model is constructed and then works for prediction as detailed below.

Input: past time series TS_t and TS_{t-1}, the number of random trees n, the number of random features f

Output: a regression Random Forest h

Process:

$y_t = TS_t - \text{ARIMA}(TS_{t-1})$

$ds = (TS_{t-1}, y_t)$

for i=1 to n:

$ds_i = random\_resampling\ (ds)$

$h_i = random\_tree\ (ds_i, f)$ // minimizing the mean squared error shown in (2)

return $h = \{h_i|i=1..n\}$

The mean squared error *mse* for each split k from f random features to decide an internal node in a random tree is given for minimizing as follows:

$$Minimize\ mse = \frac{1}{|ds_{i,k}|} \sum_{j=1..|ds_{i,k}|} \left(y_{t,k,j} - \hat{y}_{t,k,j}\right)^2 \tag{2}$$

where $ds_{i,k}$ is part of the training dataset corresponding to split k.

For prediction on new X, the resulting Random Forest model yields a predicted result $\hat{y}$ by taking average over those of its random trees in the bagging mechanism as follows:

$$\hat{y} = \frac{1}{n} \sum_{i=1..n} h_i(X) \tag{3}$$

For our time series prediction, the residual $\hat{r}_{t+1}$ corresponding to the predicted time series TS_{t+1} is returned by Random Forest as follows: $\hat{r}_{t+1}$= RandomForest (TS_t).

3.2 Fault Detection

In our work, a fault is considered a point-based anomaly. Therefore, our fault detection method is defined with the steps listed as follows: computes residuals, applies statical control limits in [9], detects change points, and validates errors over rolling windows based on rolling window validation in [19]. This combined comprehensive method ensures robust identification of anomalies, faults, and shifts in the time series of our context. In particular, Fig. 3 shows the pseudo code of our combined fault detection method, whose details are described below.

- Residual Analysis: this method involves calculating the residuals, r_t, which are the differences between the predicted values $\hat{y}_t$ and the actual data y_t. Residuals are computed using the following formula:

$$r_t = y_t \tag{4}$$

Predictions are flagged as anomalies if the absolute value of r_t exceeds a predefined threshold, indicating significant deviation from expected outcomes.

- Statistical Control Limits: this approach was applied to monitor prediction errors. Control charts are used to track the stability of the model by detecting predictions outside the control limits established below, typically set at ± 3 standard deviations (*std_dev*) from the mean. Errors exceeding these limits are flagged as outliers.

$$Control\ Limit_{upper} = mean(r_t) + 3 \cdot std\_dev(r_t) \tag{5}$$

$$Control\ Limit_{lower} = mean(r_t) - 3 \cdot std\_dev(r_t) \tag{6}$$

- Change Point Detection: this method was employed to detect significant shifts in the data stream that could indicate faults. This method helps identify the points where the statistical properties of the time series data abruptly change.
- Rolling Window Validation: this approach was used to continuously validate the predictions against actual observed values. By calculating error metrics, e.g. *root mean squared error* (RMSE), within a rolling window, the approach can detect periods when the prediction error exceeds acceptable levels.

```
procedure FaultDetection(data, predictions)
begin
    residuals := predictions - data
    mean_error := mean(residuals)
    std_dev_error := standard_deviation(residuals)
    control_limit_upper := mean_error + 3 * std_dev_error
    control_limit_lower := mean_error - 3 * std_dev_error

    for i from 1 to length(data) do
        if (residuals[i] > control_limit_upper or residuals[i] <
        ↪ control_limit_lower) then
            flag_as_outlier(i)

        if i > window_size then
            window_start := i - window_size + 1
            window_end := i
            window_data := data[window_start:window_end]
            window_predictions := predictions[window_start:window_end]
            if RMSE(window_data, window_predictions) > threshold then
                flag_as_fault(i)

        if change_point_detected(data[1:i]) then
            flag_as_change_point(i)
    end for
end
```

Fig. 3. The pseudo code of the combined fault detection method in CI servers.

4 Empirical Evaluation

This section presents our empirical evaluation on the proposed solution, including time series prediction and further fault detection in CI servers in a real-world context.

4.1 Data

Time series datasets were collected by characterizing the state of various CI infrastructures over time from the first author's working organization. ADP, a comprehensive monitoring tool, tracks critical aspects of CI servers, including CPU usage, memory status, network performance, and file system utlization for the above-mentioned metrics. For confidentiality, sensitive information such as tokens, node identifiers, and other metadata has been removed. Four datasets were obtained from January 2024 to April 2024, each per month, including measurements taken every 30 s from 10 different CI servers managed by ADP's DevOps team with a 1-min interval for scraping. As a result, the entire dataset spans 4 months from a single organization under confidentiality constraints. While this limits generalizability, the method requires minimal feature engineering and can be retrained in other CI environments.

Table 2. Data descriptions.

Data	January	February	March	April
Number of data points	33,480	31,320	33,480	32,400
Role	Training	Test, Training	Test, Training	Test

Moreover, fault labeling was done as previously introduced. Their details are described in Table 2 where their roles for time series prediction are specified. For fault detection, we investigate April dataset with 170 faults in our evaluation.

4.2 Algorithms and Evaluation Measures

In the context of fault detection in CI servers, we used the following algorithms. For time series prediction, our hybrid model is compared with its components, ARIMA and Random Forest (RF), whose results are presented in Table 3. In Table 4, we show the results for comparison between our hybrid model and the weighted combination of ARIMA and Random Forest with different weight comsbinations: 0.1–0.9, 0.5–0.5, and 0.9–0.1, respectively. Compared to other time series prediction approaches, especially the model proposed in [14], we used VAR (Vector AutoRegressive), LSTM (Long Short-Term Memory), and BiLSTM (Bidirectional Long Short-Term Memory). For our hybrid model, $p = 1$, $d = 1$, and $q = 2$ were used for ARIMA and 200 random trees for Random Forest. The other hyperparameter settings are reused with default values.

For fault detection, we used statistical methods such as Statistic Control Limit [9], Residual Analysis, Change Point Detection, and Rolling Window Validation [19] for comparison. These methods were chosen due to their capability of point-based fault detection and less complexity in our context. For our combined fault detection method, we also used 3 to calculate the control limit upper and lower as defined earlier.

Evaluation measures on time series prediction are RMSE (Root Mean Squared Error), MAE (Mean Absolute Error), and MAPE (Mean Absolute Percentage Error) where MAPE is recorded in [0, 100%]. The values of these measures are expected to be as small as possible. Precision, Recall, and F1, which is a harmony mean of Precision and

Recall, are used in the range [0, 1] to measure the performance of fault detection where their higher values show the better solutions to fault detection.

4.3 Experimental Results and Discussion

Time Series Prediction. In most cases with the results displayed in Tables 3, 4, and 5, our hybrid model outperforms the compared models on a consistent basis. In addition, Tables 3 and 4 serve as an ablation study, showing ARIMA-only, RF-only, weighted ARIMA + RF, and the hybrid. The hybrid consistently outperforms, highlighting the contribution of both components.

Indeed, bringing ARIMA and Random Forest to our hybrid model helps capture both stationary and non-stationary data characteristics in our time series from CI servers. Table 3 shows the significant differences between the achievement of our hybrid model and those of its components for key server metric prediction. With lower error values implying better accuracy, the hybrid model reflects the complementary strengths of ARIMA and Random Forest, where ARIMA handles linear characteristics while Random Forest captures non-linear relationships and interactions within the data.

Compared to typical weighted combinations of ARIMA and Random Forest, our hybrid model is quite comparable to an equi-combination although its more effectiveness is found in most cases in Table 4. This is understandable for equivalent contribution of each component to the resulting models. However, our stacking approach is more desired with Random Forest playing a role of our final non-linear decision gate so that our hybrid model can be made more generalized with both linear and non-linear data. Moreover, it is consistent with those in Table 3 where ARIMA is more effective than Random Forest as both work independently on this task. For combination, more weight on ARIMA seems to result in better models with more correct predictions. In such cases, ARIMA comes first in our hybrid model to provide a better starting point and then more non-linear features can be tackled by Random Forest, leading to the significant performance improvement of our hybrid model.

Furthermore, Table 5 confirms the effectiveness of our hybrid model in comparison with several typical time series prediction models in CI servers. The errors returned by our model are significantly smaller than those by the others for most server metrics. However, for Memory Usage metric, we obtained comparable MAE values compared to those from LSTM. This can be exaplained by the stability of memory usage of the users on CI infrastructures and the capability of LSTM to capture the relationships between sequential data over time. As for our hybrid model, no sequence in data has been examined although non-linear data characteristics have been considered. Comparing LSTM and BiLSTM, better performance is found with LSTM because the forward direction is significant while the backward one is meaningless in the time series of our context. Generally speaking, our hybrid model yields better results on average.

Table 3. Comparison of the Hybrid model and its components for time series prediction on metrics in CI servers.

	Predicted April			Predicted March			Predicted February		
	RMSE	MAE	MAPE	RMSE	MAE	MAPE	RMSE	MAE	MAPE
CPU Usage									
ARIMA	11.42	6.76	18.90	11.41	6.81	18.85	11.22	6.21	18.80
RF	17.35	15.20	47.87	17.75	15.64	47.11	17.25	15.95	47.62
Hybrid	**3.21**	**4.22**	**8.82**	**3.23**	**4.28**	**8.72**	**3.33**	**4.35**	**8.73**
Filesystem Usage									
ARIMA	11.26	6.91	21.65	11.12	6.96	21.60	11.37	7.68	21.55
RF	18.39	16.23	37.92	18.46	16.21	37.12	18.26	16.12	37.12
Hybrid	**4.25**	**5.15**	**9.43**	**4.27**	**5.17**	**9.35**	**4.38**	**5.28**	**9.35**
Memory Usage									
ARIMA	10.25	7.30	19.22	10.32	7.35	19.17	10.11	7.37	19.12
RF	16.38	14.22	38.68	16.14	14.15	38.25	16.41	14.32	38.24
Hybrid	**3.22**	**4.34**	**9.24**	**3.24**	**4.40**	**9.16**	**3.36**	**4.46**	**9.18**
Network Traffic Received									
ARIMA	12.50	6.85	19.75	12.58	6.90	19.70	12.10	6.92	19.65
RF	17.34	14.19	47.54	17.32	14.75	47.64	17.15	14.25	47.61
Hybrid	**4.20**	**4.11**	**8.51**	**4.25**	**4.16**	**8.47**	**4.30**	**4.22**	**8.43**
Network Traffic Transmitted									
ARIMA	11.63	6.68	19.50	11.66	6.73	19.45	11.24	6.93	19.40
RF	17.36	14.21	48.05	17.86	14.52	48.11	17.63	14.36	47.52
Hybrid	**4.23**	**4.11**	**9.05**	**4.28**	**4.16**	**8.99**	**4.35**	**4.21**	**8.92**

Fault Detection. As LSTM is the most comparable for time series prediction in our context, fault detection is investigated with LSTM and our hybrid model. In addition, we examine this phase in April 2024 for brevity.

Using predicted time series, early fault detection can be conducted. The results in Table 6 show that more correct faults can be identified with our hybrid model compared to LSTM in terms of all evaluation measures. Such results also indicate the significant role of accurate predictions, especially the high recall that we can reach at 0.92. Indeed, the Hybrid model improved Precision from 0.82 to 0.86 and Recall from 0.88 to 0.92 compared to LSTM, leading to fewer false positives and false negatives. This corresponds to about 4% absolute improvement.

In addition, our combined fault detection method gives significant improvements in all evaluation measures in comparison with the other methods as shown in Table 7. This reflects our appropriate combination to obtain higher Recall and make a good filter for higher Precision. Furthermore, our method requires fewer input settings but the current time series and their predicted ones, leading to a less complex solution to early fault detection once deployed on CI servers.

Table 4. Comparison of the Hybrid model and the weighted combinations for time series prediction on metrics in CI servers.

	Predicted April			Predicted March			Predicted February		
	RMSE	MAE	MAPE	RMSE	MAE	MAPE	RMSE	MAE	MAPE
CPU Usage									
0.1–0.9	16.13	13.19	46.13	17.67	15.72	47.3	17.41	16.1	47.47
0.5–0.5	3.44	4.61	9.15	3.47	4.52	8.93	3.56	4.59	8.94
0.9–0.1	10.53	5.78	16.69	11.97	7.53	18.67	11.41	6.88	19.12
Hybrid	**3.21**	**4.22**	**8.82**	**3.23**	**4.28**	**8.72**	**3.33**	**4.35**	**8.73**
Filesystem Usage									
0.1–0.9	18.52	18.43	37.45	18.45	16.16	37.02	18.37	16.12	36.93
0.5–0.5	**4.12**	**4.96**	**8.89**	4.53	5.42	9.59	4.64	5.51	9.57
0.9–0.1	12.61	5.57	22.19	10.98	7.82	22.15	11.31	8.16	22.01
Hybrid	4.25	5.15	9.43	**4.27**	**5.17**	**9.35**	**4.38**	**5.28**	**9.35**
Memory Usage									
0.1–0.9	15.09	12.92	39.61	15.95	14.16	38.32	16.45	14.13	38.38
0.5–0.5	3.62	4.51	9.52	3.51	4.61	9.38	3.63	4.68	9.43
0.9–0.1	12.26	5.22	17.68	11.23	7.71	19.25	11.09	7.76	19.62
Hybrid	**3.22**	**4.34**	**9.24**	**3.24**	**4.4**	**9.16**	**3.36**	**4.46**	**9.18**
Network Traffic Received									
0.1–0.9	15.09	12.92	39.61	15.95	14.16	38.32	16.45	14.13	38.38
0.5–0.5	3.62	4.51	9.52	3.51	4.61	9.38	3.63	4.68	9.43
0.9–0.1	12.26	5.22	17.68	11.23	7.71	19.25	11.09	7.76	19.62
Hybrid	**3.22**	**4.34**	**9.24**	**3.24**	**4.4**	**9.16**	**3.36**	**4.46**	**9.18**
Network Traffic Transmitted									
0.1–0.9	16.36	12.37	45.86	17.88	14.7	48.23	17.72	14.19	47.36
0.5–0.5	4.86	4.67	9.74	4.53	4.38	9.21	4.58	4.43	9.14
0.9–0.1	10.77	8.23	21.13	11.68	7.62	19.93	11.48	7.47	20.02
Hybrid	**4.23**	**4.11**	**9.05**	**4.28**	**4.16**	**8.99**	**4.35**	**4.21**	**8.92**

Table 5. Comparison of the Hybrid model and other models for time series prediction on metrics in CI servers.

	Predicted April			Predicted March			Predicted February		
	RMSE	MAE	MAPE	RMSE	MAE	MAPE	RMSE	MAE	MAPE
CPU Usage									
VAR	11.76	8.56	15.45	11.10	8.61	15.54	11.24	8.48	15.21
LSTM	6.60	5.18	9.34	6.25	5.23	9.29	6.62	5.31	9.24
BiLSTM	8.32	7.18	11.87	8.42	7.23	11.82	8.23	7.28	11.12
Hybrid	**3.21**	**4.22**	**8.82**	**3.23**	**4.28**	**8.72**	**3.33**	**4.35**	**8.73**
Filesystem Usage									
VAR	13.53	7.62	16.89	13.72	7.67	16.21	13.22	7.32	16.12
LSTM	7.84	5.21	9.71	7.69	5.26	9.62	7.94	5.32	9.51
BiLSTM	8.35	7.22	13.21	8.12	7.27	13.16	8.79	7.32	13.21
Hybrid	**4.25**	**5.15**	**9.43**	**4.27**	**5.17**	**9.35**	**4.38**	**5.28**	**9.35**
Memory Usage									
VAR	10.98	8.89	16.12	11.56	8.94	16.51	11.25	8.26	16.77
LSTM	5.41	**4.19**	9.62	5.56	**4.24**	9.57	5.58	**4.27**	9.52
BiLSTM	8.34	6.20	12.11	8.12	6.25	12.06	8.54	6.30	12.52
Hybrid	**3.22**	4.34	**9.24**	**3.24**	4.40	**9.16**	**3.36**	4.46	**9.18**
Network Traffic Received									
VAR	11.48	9.29	16.52	11.47	9.34	16.73	11.51	9.64	16.25
LSTM	6.28	4.17	8.86	6.31	4.22	8.81	6.68	4.28	8.76
BiLSTM	7.29	6.16	11.39	7.24	6.21	11.34	7.12	6.26	11.74
Hybrid	**4.20**	**4.11**	**8.51**	**4.25**	**4.16**	**8.47**	**4.30**	**4.22**	**8.43**
Network Traffic Transmitted									
VAR	11.21	9.31	16.55	11.37	9.36	16.50	11.11	9.25	16.26
LSTM	6.23	4.20	8.65	6.29	4.25	8.60	6.67	4.31	8.55
BiLSTM	7.30	6.17	11.54	7.75	6.22	11.49	7.53	6.27	11.75
Hybrid	**4.23**	**4.11**	**9.05**	**4.28**	**4.16**	**8.99**	**4.35**	**4.21**	**8.92**

Table 6. Fault detection results for April 2024 with different time series prediction models.

Model	Precision	Recall	F1
LSTM	0.82	0.88	0.85
Hybrid	**0.86**	**0.92**	**0.89**

Table 7. Comparison of the fault detection methods on metrics in April 2024 in CI servers.

Method	Precision	Recall	F1
Statistic Control Limit	0.210	0.82	0.330
Residual Analysis	0.008	0.52	0.016
Change Point Detection	0.005	0.26	0.010
Rolling Window Validation	0.340	0.84	0.480
Combined Method	**0.860**	**0.92**	**0.890**

5 Conclusion

In this paper, we have proposed a new solution to early fault detection in Continuous Integration servers. The solution is composed of a hybrid ARIMA-Random Forest model for predicting server metric values and a combined statistical method for early fault detection based on the predicted results. Compared to the existing works, our solution is not only comprehensive but also effective and efficient for the context of CI servers where real-time monitoring is required for many services of their customers.

In particular, the hybrid model effectively combines ARIMA's linear trend analysis with Random Forest's ability to capture non-linear patterns, offering a robust approach to predicting server metrics. On the other hand, the fault detection method further statistically detects anomalies in complex server environments. Our experimental results have demonstrated that our solution outperforms other methods especially in achieving higher true positive rates while minimizing false positives and false negatives. This highlights the solution's practical utility in maintaining CI server reliability and reducing operational disruptions. As a result, this study contributes to the advancement of predictive modeling in CI servers, providing actionable insights for improving server management, and reducing downtime.

Looking ahead, our future research will explore real-time data processing for immediate fault detection and the scalability of the solution in cloud environments. These directions offer potential to further enhance the model's effectiveness and expand its applicability in other dynamic systems.

Acknowledgments. We acknowledge Ho Chi Minh City University of Technology (HCMUT), VNU-HCM for supporting this study. We also thank the data providers very much.

References

1. Breiman, L.: Random forests. Mach. Learn. **45**, 5–32 (2001)
2. Cao, D., et al.: Spectral temporal graph neural network for multivariate time-series forecasting. In: Proceedings of The 34th Conference on Neural Information Processing Systems (NeurIPS 2020), Vancouver, Canada, pp. 1–13 (2020)

3. Cao, D., et al.: TEMPO: prompt-based generative pre-trained transformer for time series forecasting. In: The Twelfth International Conference on Learning Representations (2024)
4. Chen, K., Feng, M., Wirjanto, T.S.: Multivariate time series anomaly detection via dynamic graph forecasting. arXiv preprint arXiv:2302.02051 (2023)
5. He, H., Zhang, Q., Yi, K., Shi, K., Niu, Z., Cao, L.: Distributional drift adaptation with temporal conditional variational autoencoder for multivariate time series forecasting. IEEE Trans. Neural Netw. Learn. Syst. (2024)
6. Huang, X., Chen, N., Deng, Z., Huang, S.: Multivariate time series anomaly detection via dynamic graph attention network and informer. Appl. Intell. **54**(17–18), 7636–7658 (2024)
7. Jin, M., et al.: A survey on graph neural networks for time series: Forecasting, classification, imputation, and anomaly detection. IEEE Trans. Pattern Anal. Mach. Intell. (2024)
8. Khodabakhsh, A., Ari, I., Bakır, M., Alagoz, S.M.: Forecasting multivariate time-series data using LSTM and mini-batches. In: Data Science: From Research to Application, pp. 121–129. Springer, Heidelberg (2020)
9. Knoth, S., Schmid, W.: Control charts for time series: a review. Front. Stat. Qual. Control **7**, 1–28 (2004)
10. Liu, Y., Jafarpour, B.: Graph attention network with Granger causality map for fault detection and root cause diagnosis. Comput. Chem. Eng. **180**, 108453 (2024)
11. Mauro, M.D., Galatro, G., Postiglione, F., Song, W., Liotta, A.: Hybrid learning strategies for multivariate time series forecasting of network quality metrics. Comput. Netw. **243**(110286), 1–13 (2024)
12. Mauro, M.D., Galatro, G., Postiglione, F., Song, W., Liotta, A.: Evaluating recurrent neural networks for prediction of multi-variate time series VoIP metrics. In: 2024 22nd Mediterranean Communication and Computer Networking Conference (MedComNet), pp. 1–8. IEEE (2024)
13. Tian, H., Long, K., Lu, S., Li, K.: Unsupervised anomaly detection of multivariate time series based on multistandard fusion. Neurocomputing **611**, 128634 (2025)
14. Wang, Y.: Multivariate time series prediction for DevOps – a first step to fault prediction of the CI infrastructure, Master's thesis, Department of Computer and Information Science. Linköping University (2022)
15. Wu, Z., Pan, S., Long, G., Jiang, J., Chang, Z., Zhang, C.: Connecting the dots: Multivariate time series forecasting with graph neural networks. In: Proceedings of the 26th ACM SIGKDD International Conference on Knowledge Discovery and Data Mining (KDD'20), pp. 753–763. ACM (2020)
16. Yi, K., et al.: Deep coupling network for multivariate time series forecasting. ACM Trans. Inf. Syst. **42**(5), 1–28 (2024)
17. Zhang, Y., Yan, J.: Crossformer: transformer utilizing cross-dimension dependency for multivariate time series forecasting. In: Proceedings of the Eleventh International Conference on Learning Representations (2023)
18. Zhou, X., et al.: Scalable transformer for high dimensional multivariate time series forecasting. In: Proceedings of the 33rd ACM International Conference on Information and Knowledge Management, 3515–3526 (2024)
19. Zivot, E., Wang, J.: Modeling financial time series with S-PLUS, 2nd edn. Springer, New York (2006)

Balancing Accuracy and Latency in Privacy-Preserving User Behavior Classification with Tree-Based Models

Kiet Nguyen Tuan[1,2], Vo Minh Tri[3], and Nguyen Duc Thai[1,2](✉)

[1] Ho Chi Minh City University of Technology (HCMUT), 268 Ly Thuong Kiet Street, Dien Hong Ward, Ho Chi Minh City, Vietnam
{ntkiet.sdh212,ngdthai}@hcmut.edu.vn
[2] Vietnam National University Ho Chi Minh City (VNU-HCM), Linh Xuan, Ho Chi Minh City, Vietnam
[3] Hoa Sen University, 8 Nguyen Van Trang, Ho Chi Minh City, Vietnam
tri.vm06567@sinhvien.hoasen.edu.vn

Abstract. Fully Homomorphic Encryption (FHE) enables machine learning models to operate directly on encrypted data, ensuring privacy-preserving analytics for sensitive user behavior information. However, the computational overhead of FHE raises concerns about efficiency in real-time applications. In this study, we evaluate three representative tree-based classifiers on encrypted user behavior data. The experiments are conducted under different computation depths and quantization bit-widths to examine their influence on accuracy and inference latency. Our results show that while all three models can be executed within the FHE framework, XGBoost consistently outperforms the others, achieving superior predictive accuracy with inference times suitable for near real-time analysis. These findings indicate that XGBoost offers the most effective balance between accuracy and efficiency for privacy-preserving user behavior classification.

Keywords: Fully Homomorphic Encryption · Privacy-Preserving Machine Learning · Tree-Based Models · XGBoost · User Behavior Classification · Accuracy–Latency Trade-off

1 Introduction

The increasing reliance on user behavior data has enabled a wide range of applications such as recommendation systems, fraud detection, and personalized online services. While these applications benefit from accurate and efficient machine learning (ML) models, they also pose serious concerns regarding the privacy of sensitive user information. Traditional approaches often rely on trusted environments or data anonymization techniques, both of which are insufficient

All authors contributed equally to this paper

T. T. Quan et al. (Eds.): MIWAI 2025, LNAI 16353, pp. 406–417, 2026.
https://doi.org/10.1007/978-981-95-4957-3_33

in guaranteeing strong privacy against adversarial threats. A promising alternative is FHE, which allows computations to be performed directly on encrypted data without requiring decryption, thereby ensuring end-to-end confidentiality of user information [2,14].

In the domain of privacy-preserving machine learning (PPML), significant research has focused on adapting neural networks and logistic regression to operate under FHE constraints. For example, Chen et al. demonstrated logistic regression on encrypted medical data, illustrating the feasibility of statistical models in secure environments [3]. Similarly, a large body of work has explored polynomial approximation techniques to replace non-linear functions such as ReLU, sigmoid, or max-pooling, enabling encrypted inference in convolutional and deep neural networks [1,6,7,10,12,13]. While these studies have advanced the efficiency of neural networks under FHE, comparatively fewer efforts have been directed towards tree-based models, which remain highly competitive for structured data analysis, including user behavior classification.

Tree-based classifiers such as Decision Trees, Random Forests, and XGBoost are particularly attractive for user behavior modeling due to their interpretability, robustness, and ability to capture non-linear patterns. However, executing these models under FHE introduces substantial computational overhead. Prior works have shown that the depth of computation circuits and the choice of quantization bit-width are critical determinants of both efficiency and accuracy in encrypted inference [9,12]. Despite these insights, a systematic evaluation of tree-based models under FHE, especially concerning the trade-off between accuracy and latency, has not been thoroughly addressed in the literature.

To address this gap, we investigate the encrypted execution of tree-based models under the TFHE scheme [3,8], which provides gate-level bootstrapping and efficient handling of binary thresholding operations. TFHE is particularly well-suited for the branching logic inherent in tree-based classifiers compared to approximate-number schemes such as CKKS [13,14]. By leveraging the Concrete-ML framework [2], encrypted inference pipelines can be deployed while preserving correctness and ensuring end-to-end privacy.

Through experiments conducted across different computation depths and quantization bit-widths, we systematically analyze how these parameters affect classification performance and inference latency. The results demonstrate that although all three models can be executed under TFHE-based FHE, XGBoost consistently achieves the most favorable balance between accuracy and execution time, making it the most practical choice for near real-time analytics in privacy-sensitive applications. This contribution complements prior work on encrypted neural networks [7,11] and broadens the scope of PPML by demonstrating the viability of tree-based models in encrypted user behavior analysis.

2 Related Works

Homomorphic Encryption has been widely recognized as a promising cryptographic technique for enabling secure computation on encrypted data [2,14]. In particular, FHE allows arbitrary arithmetic operations without decryption, making it suitable for PPML. Early studies demonstrated the feasibility of applying FHE to statistical models such as logistic regression, enabling encrypted medical data analysis without compromising patient confidentiality [3]. Subsequent works extended these approaches to more complex models, emphasizing the trade-off between efficiency and accuracy in encrypted inference. A major challenge in FHE-based machine learning lies in handling non-linear operations, which are not natively supported by encrypted arithmetic. To overcome this, polynomial approximations of activation functions have been extensively studied. Techniques include low-degree approximations of ReLU and sigmoid [1,13], beta-function-based polynomial approximations [7], and neural-network-driven approximations for efficient evaluation over large intervals [4]. Optimized approximation frameworks, such as layerwise tuning [9] and progressive approximation [12], further reduce computational depth while maintaining accuracy. These advancements have enabled encrypted inference for deep convolutional models such as ResNet and VGG [10], bridging the gap between practicality and accuracy. Beyond polynomial-based methods, hybrid approaches combine function approximation with model restructuring to achieve better efficiency. For instance, "Learning in the Dark" proposes hybrid plaintext training with encrypted inference, relying on low-degree Chebyshev polynomials to approximate ReLU and sigmoid functions [8]. Similarly, research has highlighted the importance of controlling computation depth and quantization precision in encrypted evaluation, as these directly impact inference latency and ciphertext noise growth [4,9].

In the case of TFHE, ciphertexts are represented in the torus $\mathbb{T} = \mathbb{R}/\mathbb{Z}$, and encryption follows the Torus LWE (TLWE) form:

$$c = (\mathbf{a},\ b) \in \mathbb{T}^n \times \mathbb{T}, \quad b = \langle \mathbf{a}, \mathbf{s} \rangle + \mu + e, \tag{1}$$

where μ encodes the message, and e is a small Gaussian error.
Decryption evaluates

$$\mu \approx b - \langle \mathbf{a}, \mathbf{s} \rangle \pmod 1 \tag{2}$$

This compact structure enables programmable bootstrapping (PB), which simultaneously refreshes noise and applies a Boolean or threshold function f to the plaintext. Concretely, if a ciphertext encrypts a message μ, PB yields:

$$\text{Boots}(c, f) \approx \text{Enc}(f(\mu)) \tag{3}$$

Thus, TFHE can directly implement encrypted decision rules such as

$$f(\mu) = \mathbf{1}_{\mu \geq \tau} \tag{4}$$

where τ is the decision threshold. This makes it particularly effective for tree-based models, since encrypted comparisons at decision nodes can be realized in a single bootstrapping step without increasing multiplicative depth.

A key feature that distinguishes TFHE from other FHE schemes is its reliance on torus representation of real numbers. Ciphertexts are encoded as elements on the unit torus allowing modular arithmetic to be expressed as fractional values wrapped around the unit interval. This structure is particularly well suited for applying the Fast Fourier Transform (FFT) during bootstrapping. For a ciphertext represented as a sequence of coefficients $\{c_k\}_{k=0}^{N-1}$, the Fourier transform maps it into the frequency domain as

$$\hat{c}m = \sum k = 0^{N-1} c_k \, e^{-2\pi i \frac{km}{N}}, \quad m = 0, 1, \ldots, N-1 \tag{5}$$

which enables convolution operations in the torus domain to be executed efficiently as element-wise multiplications:

$$c * h \quad \longleftrightarrow \quad \hat{c}_m \cdot \hat{h}_m \tag{6}$$

In the context of TFHE bootstrapping, this Fourier-domain multiplication corresponds to refreshing ciphertexts and re-applying gate functions, while controlling noise growth. Thus, torus encoding combined with FFT enables fast gate bootstrapping by turning expensive polynomial multiplications in the time domain into lightweight multiplications in the frequency domain. This results in low-latency encrypted operations, particularly for Boolean gates and threshold functions, which are essential for tree-based models.

2.1 Tree-Based Models Under TFHE

Tree-based classifiers such as Decision Trees, Random Forests, and XGBoost have long been recognized for their interpretability, robustness, and ability to capture non-linear relationships in user behavior data. Their reliance on relatively simple arithmetic and comparison operations makes them especially amenable to execution under FHE, and particularly efficient when implemented with TFHE.

$$Gini(S) = 1 - \sum_{i=1}^{C} p_i^2 \tag{7}$$

where p_i represents the class probability in subset S. The attribute selection criterion for splitting is given by:

$$\text{Split}(A) = \arg\min_{A} \sum_{v \in Values(A)} \frac{|S_v|}{|S|} Gini(S_v) \tag{8}$$

These computations primarily involve comparisons and weighted averages, both of which can be mapped to Boolean gates and integer arithmetic supported by TFHE. In the case of Random Forests, prediction is performed through majority voting among trees:

$$\hat{y} = \arg\max_{c \in C} \sum_{t=1}^{T} \mathbf{1}\{h_t(x) = c\} \tag{9}$$

where $h_t(x)$ denotes the prediction of tree t. Under TFHE, the voting process can be securely executed using encrypted addition and comparison, leveraging the efficiency of bootstrapping on the torus. XGBoost iteratively builds an ensemble of weak learners, with each new tree trained on the residual errors of the previous model. At iteration m:

$$F_m(x) = F_{m-1}(x) + \eta \cdot h_m(x) \tag{10}$$

where $h_m(x)$ is the newly trained tree and η is the learning rate. The gradients driving this process are derived from the loss function:

$$g_i = \frac{\partial L(y_i, F_{m-1}(x_i))}{\partial F_{m-1}(x_i)} \tag{11}$$

TFHE facilitates these update steps by supporting homomorphic addition and multiplication, while its FFT-based bootstrapping mechanism mitigates noise accumulation, enabling repeated iterations without prohibitive latency.

2.2 Privacy-Preserving Learning Beyond Neural Networks

While most research has centered on neural networks, some works have explored privacy-preserving model training and inference at the edge or in distributed systems [11]. These studies emphasize the importance of lightweight and efficient schemes for real-world deployment. However, despite the dominance of tree-based classifiers such as Decision Trees, Random Forests, and XGBoost in structured data analytics, there has been relatively little investigation into their performance under FHE.

3 Methodology

3.1 Cryptographic Setting

In this work, we adopt TFHE as the underlying encryption scheme for privacy-preserving inference. The main reason lies in the structural characteristics of tree-based models, where the inference process depends almost entirely on threshold comparisons and branching operations. TFHE is natively designed to evaluate Boolean gates with exact semantics, making it particularly well aligned with the discrete decision logic of decision trees and their ensembles. This ensures that encrypted inference produces results identical to plaintext execution, as long as the quantization process preserves the ordering of feature values relative to thresholds.

By contrast, CKKS encodes real numbers in an approximate manner, introducing small but unavoidable numerical errors during computation. While these errors are often tolerable in neural network inference, they can be catastrophic in tree-based models, where even a tiny deviation may cause the decision to follow a completely different branch. In such cases, the entire prediction outcome may flip, undermining model reliability. TFHE avoids this risk by guaranteeing exact comparisons, thus offering deterministic and stable inference across all samples.

Another advantage of TFHE is that its bootstrapping mechanism has become increasingly efficient, allowing moderate-depth circuits to be evaluated within practical latency. Since the complexity of decision trees and XGBoost models usually falls within this range, TFHE provides a good balance between computational feasibility and cryptographic security. Moreover, its seamless integration into the Concrete-ML framework enables automatic compilation of trained models into encrypted circuits, making the development workflow significantly easier compared to CKKS-based implementations.

Taken together, these factors make TFHE a more suitable choice for our study: it preserves the deterministic nature of tree-based inference, eliminates approximation risks at branching nodes, and provides a practical framework for end-to-end encrypted evaluation.

3.2 Implementation Framework

To integrate machine learning with TFHE, we utilize the Concrete-ML library, an open-source framework that provides end-to-end support for model quantization, compilation, and encrypted inference. Concrete-ML enables the translation of trained models into FHE-executable circuits, automating polynomial approximations, quantization, and circuit optimization for TFHE. This framework allows us to evaluate the practicality of tree-based classifiers in real-world privacy-preserving analytics pipelines.

3.3 Dataset

The Predict Customer Purchase Behavior dataset consists of 1,500 samples, split into 70% for training and 30% for testing, with no missing values. The binary target variable *Purchase Status* contains 852 non-purchase (class 0) and 648 purchase (class 1) cases.

Numerical features include Age, Annual Income, Number of Purchases, Time Spent on Website, Discounts Availed, and a derived feature *TimePerPurchase*:

$$\text{TimePerPurchase} = \frac{\text{TimeSpentOnWebsite}}{\text{NumberOfPurchases} + 1}$$

which reflects customer interaction efficiency. Categorical features are Gender, Product Category, and Loyalty Program membership. Their distributions are reported in Table 2.

All features are quantized and encrypted under FHE to ensure privacy-preserving inference. Models trained in plaintext (Decision Tree, Random Forest, XGBoost) are compiled into encrypted circuits using the Concrete-ML framework. We adopted a 70:30 split as it is widely used in practice for medium-sized datasets, balancing training sufficiency with reliable evaluation [5], while avoiding the high overhead of cross-validation under FHE constraints (Table 1).

3.4 Experimental Setup

All experiments were conducted on a workstation equipped with an Intel Core i7 CPU, 32 GB RAM without relying on GPU acceleration since the current

Table 1. Sample of data in the dataset

Age	Gender	Annual Income	Number Of Purchases	Product Category	Time Spent On Website	Loyalty Program	Discounts Availed	Purchase Status
40	1	66120.2679	8	0	30.5686	0	5	1
20	1	23579.7735	4	2	38.2400	0	5	0
27	1	127821.3064	11	2	31.6332	1	0	1
24	1	137798.6231	19	3	46.1670	0	4	1
31	1	99300.9642	19	1	19.8235	0	0	1
66	1	37758.1174	14	4	17.8274	0	2	0
39	1	126883.3852	16	3	42.0853	1	4	1
64	1	39707.3597	13	2	17.1902	1	0	0

Table 2. Distribution of categorical attributes in the dataset

Feature	Value	Proportion (%)
Gender	Male (0)	49.5
	Female (1)	50.5
Product Category	Electronics (0)	19.3
	Clothing (1)	22.1
	Home Goods (2)	18.2
	Beauty (3)	19.1
	Sports (4)	21.4
Loyalty Program	No (0)	67.3
	Yes (1)	32.7

version of Concrete-ML executes homomorphic computations entirely on CPU. The models were trained in plaintext using scikit-learn and then compiled into FHE circuits through Concrete-ML's compilation interface, which transparently handles quantization, circuit construction, and TFHE parameterization.

To evaluate the trade-off between accuracy and efficiency, we systematically varied two key hyperparameters: the bit-width of quantization, ranging from 1 to 9 bits, and the tree depth, adjusted across shallow and moderately deep configurations. The quantization bit-width controls the precision of numerical encoding, directly affecting both accuracy and circuit complexity. Similarly, tree depth determines computation depth, which is closely tied to inference latency under TFHE bootstrapping.

The dataset was partitioned into an 70–30 train-test split, with models first optimized in plaintext and then compiled for encrypted inference. Performance was measured in terms of classification accuracy and latency per encrypted sample, averaged across multiple runs to reduce variability. This setup allows for a direct comparison between different tree-based methods under consistent cryptographic constraints, highlighting the impact of FHE on practical deployment.

4 Results

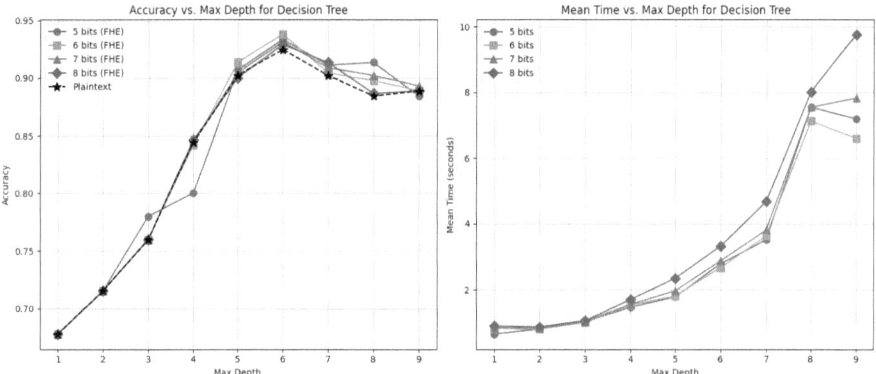

Fig. 1. Accuracy and Computing time of Decision Tree

We evaluate the three tree-based models across max depth 1–9 and quantization 5–8 bits, reporting test accuracy and mean encrypted inference time per sample. The consolidated outcomes are summarized in Table 3, with per-model trends shown in the figures. Overall, FHE inference closely tracks plaintext accuracy (dashed lines), while latency rises with model depth and bit-width, consistent with the cost profile of bootstrapped Boolean circuits in TFHE [2,9,12] (Fig. 1).

In Decision Tree, accuracy increases steadily with depth and peaks around depth 6 (average accuracy 0.933), after which gains vanish and a mild decline appears (e.g., 0.889 at depth 9). Latency remains the lowest among all methods: even at depth 9 with 8-bit quantization the mean time is 9.76 s, and at the best-accuracy depth 6 it is 3.32 s. This profile makes single trees attractive for ultra-low-latency inference, albeit with a ceiling on accuracy.

In Random Forest, ensembles deliver consistent accuracy gains as depth grows, reaching 0.925 average accuracy at depth 8 (slightly tapering to 0.922 at depth 9). However, the computational cost is prohibitive under FHE: mean inference time balloons from 1.34 s (depth 1) to 107.68 s–120.93 s at depths 8–9. The combination of many trees and deeper routing produces a multiplicative increase in bootstrapped operations, making Random Forests poorly suited to near real-time encrypted inference despite their accuracy improvements.

Boosting achieves the strongest accuracy–latency trade-off. Notably, accuracy saturates early: depth 2–3 already yields 0.948–0.951 average accuracy (the best overall), and remains in the 0.94–0.95 band for depths 6–9. Crucially, latency is far lower than Random Forest at comparable depths: 5.17 s at depth 3, 17.35–27.36 s at depths 5–6, and 58–59 s at depth 8–9. Because boosted trees can be kept shallow while retaining high predictive power, the circuit depth—and hence

Table 3. Classification accuracy and mean computation time of tree-based models under FHE across varying quantization bit-widths and maximum tree depths

Model	Max Depth	Quantization bits						Plaintext
		5 bits	6 bits	7 bits	8 bits	Average Accuracy	Max (Mean Time)	Accuracy
Decision Tree	1	0.678	0.678	0.678	0.678	0.678	0.890	0.678
	2	0.716	0.716	0.716	0.716	0.716	0.860	0.716
	3	0.780	0.760	0.760	0.760	0.765	1.050	0.760
	4	0.800	0.842	0.844	0.847	0.833	1.710	0.844
	5	0.907	0.913	0.904	0.900	0.906	2.350	0.902
	6	0.933	0.938	0.931	0.929	**0.933**	3.320	0.924
	7	0.911	0.904	0.909	0.913	0.909	4.670	0.902
	8	0.913	0.898	0.902	0.887	0.900	8.020	0.884
	9	0.884	0.889	0.893	0.889	0.889	9.760	0.889
Random Forest	1	0.756	0.744	0.756	0.756	0.753	1.340	0.756
	2	0.760	0.773	0.784	0.784	0.776	2.840	0.785
	3	0.840	0.818	0.822	0.824	0.826	5.790	0.829
	4	0.867	0.856	0.851	0.836	0.852	11.070	0.836
	5	0.893	0.898	0.902	0.891	0.896	22.430	0.889
	6	0.904	0.918	0.920	0.913	0.914	38.530	0.898
	7	0.920	0.922	0.916	0.916	0.918	51.310	0.911
	8	0.929	0.931	0.920	0.920	**0.925**	107.680	0.927
	9	0.929	0.927	0.918	0.913	0.922	120.930	0.909
XGBoost	1	0.909	0.851	0.896	0.898	0.888	1.050	0.896
	2	0.951	0.944	0.949	0.949	0.948	2.320	0.956
	3	0.944	0.951	0.953	0.953	**0.951**	5.170	0.949
	4	0.936	0.929	0.927	0.929	0.930	10.230	0.924
	5	0.938	0.931	0.936	0.933	0.934	17.350	0.931
	6	0.949	0.938	0.947	0.944	0.944	27.360	0.942
	7	0.942	0.944	0.938	0.938	0.941	34.140	0.940
	8	0.940	0.942	0.944	0.942	0.942	58.120	0.938
	9	0.940	0.938	0.942	0.940	0.940	59.490	0.936

bootstrapping count—is contained, which explains the favorable Pareto frontier relative to Random Forest (Figs. 2 and 3).

Across models, moving from 5 to 8 bits changes accuracy only marginally once depth ≥ 2 (typically within ± 0.005 for XGBoost), while latency increases monotonically with bit-width (e.g., for XGBoost at depth 8: 50 s at 6-bit vs 58 s at 8-bit). A 6–7 bit setting therefore offers a practical balance: it preserves accuracy near the 8-bit ceiling while shaving 10–20% off runtime. These observations are consistent with TFHE's exact, quantized arithmetic where ordering is preserved once bit precision is adequate, unlike CKKS whose approximate encoding can destabilize comparisons near thresholds [13, 14].

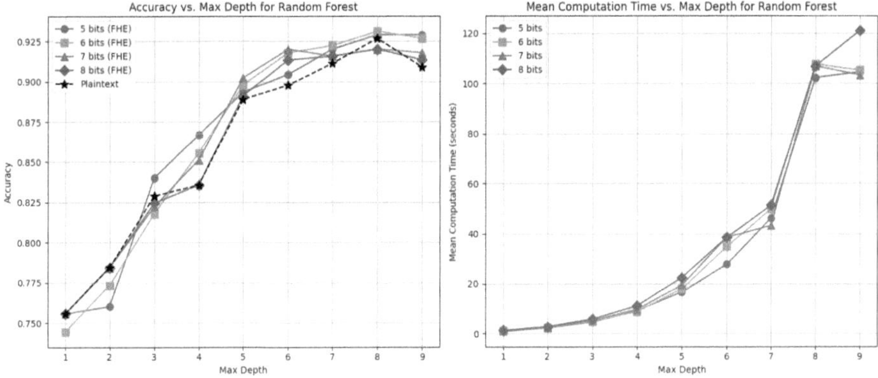

Fig. 2. Accuracy and Computing time of Random Forest

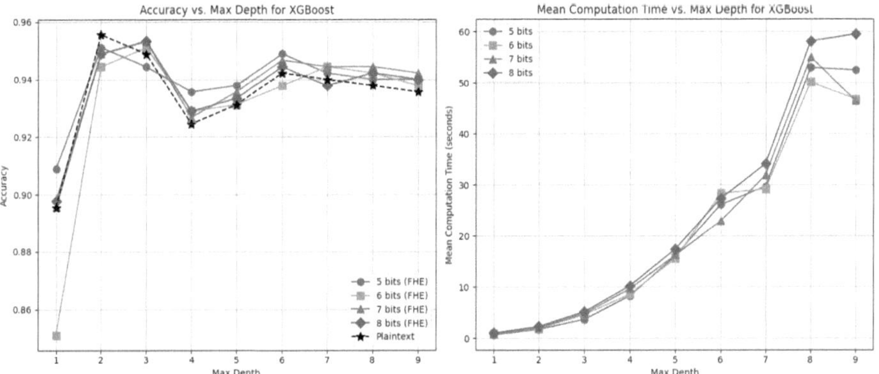

Fig. 3. Accuracy and Computing time of XGBoost

5 Conclusion

This study investigated the trade-off between classification accuracy and inference latency when applying FHE to tree-based models on user behavior data. By systematically varying both quantization precision and tree depth, we examined how encryption-induced constraints impact model performance.

The results consistently show that XGBoost achieves the most favorable balance, sustaining high accuracy levels above 0.94 while keeping inference latency significantly lower than Random Forests at equivalent depths. Decision Trees, while computationally efficient, offered limited predictive power compared to ensemble methods. The analysis highlights that quantization to 6–8 bits preserves accuracy without introducing prohibitive latency, suggesting a practical pathway for encrypted real-time inference.

The choice of TFHE over CKKS proved advantageous for tree-based models, as TFHE's native support for Boolean operations aligns well with encrypted branching logic. Leveraging Concrete-ML enabled seamless compilation of plaintext-trained models into FHE circuits, ensuring privacy-preserving inference without sacrificing usability.

In summary, our findings suggest that FHE-secured XGBoost offers a promising solution for privacy-preserving user behavior classification in real-time decision systems. Future work will explore hybrid schemes to further reduce inference latency, and extend evaluation to larger, high-dimensional datasets to validate scalability.

Acknowledgments. We acknowledge Ho Chi Minh City University of Technology (HCMUT), VNU-HCM for supporting this study.

References

1. Agamennone, P.: Polynomial approximations of ReLU for secure CNN inference in homomorphic encryption environments **E108.A**(7), 977–980. https://doi.org/10.1587/transfun.2024EAL2090. https://www.jstage.jst.go.jp/article/transfun/E108.A/7/E108.A_2024EAL2090/_article
2. Arnold, D., Saniie, J., Heifetz, A.: Homomorphic encryption for machine learning and artificial intelligence applications. https://doi.org/10.2172/1886256. https://www.osti.gov/servlets/purl/1886256/
3. Chen, H., et al.: Logistic regression over encrypted data from fully homomorphic encryption **11**, 81. https://doi.org/10.1186/s12920-018-0397-z. https://bmcmedgenomics.biomedcentral.com/articles/10.1186/s12920-018-0397-z
4. Chiang, J.: A simple solution for homomorphic evaluation on large intervals. https://doi.org/10.48550/ARXIV.2405.15201. https://arxiv.org/abs/2405.15201, version Number: 1
5. Deniz, E., Çökekoğlu, S.: Predicting customer purchase behavior using machine learning models. Int. J. Data Sci. Adv. Analyt. **6**(2), 45–56 (2024). https://doi.org/10.69882/adba.iteb.2024071. https://www.researchgate.net/publication/382768389_Predicting_Customer_Purchase_Behavior_Using_Machine_Learning_Models
6. Harb, M.R.A., Celiktas, B.: Efficient estimation of sigmoid and tanh activation functions for homomorphically encrypted data using artificial neural networks. In: 2024 8th International Symposium on Innovative Approaches in Smart Technologies (ISAS), pp. 1–7. IEEE. https://doi.org/10.1109/ISAS64331.2024.10845450. https://ieeexplore.ieee.org/document/10845450/
7. Issaoui, H., ElAdel, A., Zaied, M.: Intelligent beta-based polynomial approximation of activation functions for a robust data encryption system **12**(3), 259–268. https://doi.org/10.18178/joig.12.3.259-268. https://www.joig.net/show-90-404-1.html
8. Khan, T., Michalas, A.: Learning in the dark: privacy-preserving machine learning using function approximation. https://doi.org/10.48550/ARXIV.2309.08190. https://arxiv.org/abs/2309.08190, version Number: 1
9. Lee, J., et al.: Optimized layerwise approximation for efficient private inference on fully homomorphic encryption. https://doi.org/10.48550/ARXIV.2310.10349. https://arxiv.org/abs/2310.10349, version Number: 3

10. Lee, J., Lee, E., Lee, J.W., Kim, Y., Kim, Y.S., No, J.S.: Precise approximation of convolutional neural networks for homomorphically encrypted data. https://doi.org/10.48550/ARXIV.2105.10879. https://arxiv.org/abs/2105.10879, version Number: 4
11. Qu, X., Hu, Q., Wang, S.: Privacy-preserving model training architecture for intelligent edge computing **162**, 94–101. https://doi.org/10.1016/j.comcom.2020.07.045. https://linkinghub.elsevier.com/retrieve/pii/S0140366420318582
12. Tong, J., Dang, J., Golder, A., Hao, C., Raychowdhury, A., Krishna, T.: Accurate low-degree polynomial approximation of non-polynomial operators for fast private inference in homomorphic encryption. https://doi.org/10.48550/ARXIV.2404.03216. https://arxiv.org/abs/2404.03216, version Number: 3
13. Uemura, S., Fukushima, K., Kiyomoto, S.: Approximations of the sigmoid function beyond the approximation domains for privacy-preserving neural networks:. In: Proceedings of the 11th International Conference on Information Systems Security and Privacy, pp. 445–454. SCITEPRESS - Science and Technology Publications. https://doi.org/10.5220/0013100700003899. https://www.scitepress.org/DigitalLibrary/Link.aspx?doi=10.5220/0013100700003899
14. Yuan, J., Liu, W., Shi, J., Li, Q.: Approximate homomorphic encryption based privacy-preserving machine learning: a survey **58**(3), 82. https://doi.org/10.1007/s10462-024-11076-8. https://link.springer.com/10.1007/s10462-024-11076-8

Physically-Grounded Goal Imagination: Physics-Informed Variational Autoencoder for Self-supervised Reinforcement Learning

Lan Thi Ha Nguyen(✉), Kien Ton Manh, Anh Do Duc, and Nam Pham Hai

FPT University, Hanoi, Vietnam
{lannthhe186365,kientmhe180073,anhddhe180559,namphhe181541}@fpt.edu.vn

Abstract. Self-supervised goal-conditioned reinforcement learning enables robots to autonomously acquire diverse skills without human supervision. However, a central challenge is the goal setting problem: robots must propose feasible and diverse goals that are achievable in their current environment. Existing methods like RIG (Visual Reinforcement Learning with Imagined Goals) use variational autoencoder (VAE) to generate goals in a learned latent space but have the limitation of producing physically implausible goals that hinder learning efficiency. We propose **Physics-Informed RIG (PI-RIG)**, which integrates physical constraints directly into the VAE training process through a novel Enhanced Physics-Informed Variational Autoencoder (Enhanced p^3-VAE), enabling the generation of physically consistent and achievable goals. Our key innovation is the explicit separation of the latent space into physics variables governing object dynamics and environmental factors capturing visual appearance, while enforcing physical consistency through differential equation constraints and conservation laws. This enables the generation of physically consistent and achievable goals that respect fundamental physical principles such as object permanence, collision constraints, and dynamic feasibility. Through extensive experiments, we demonstrate that this physics-informed goal generation significantly improves the quality of proposed goals, leading to more effective exploration and better skill acquisition in visual robotic manipulation tasks including reaching, pushing, and pick-and-place scenarios.

Keywords: Goal-conditioned reinforcement learning · Self-supervised reinforcement learning · Physics-informed learning · Variational Autoencoder · Visual representation learning · Robotic manipulation

1 Introduction

Autonomous robots operating in open-world environments must be capable of setting their own learning objectives and acquiring diverse skills without human supervision. Self-supervised goal-conditioned reinforcement learning addresses

T. T. Quan et al. (Eds.): MIWAI 2025, LNAI 16353, pp. 418–429, 2026.
https://doi.org/10.1007/978-981-95-4957-3_34

this challenge by enabling robots to propose goals to themselves and learn to achieve them through trial and error. However, the effectiveness of this paradigm critically depends on the quality of goal proposals: goals must be both achievable given the current environment state and sufficiently diverse to promote skill acquisition.

A fundamental limitation of existing approaches is their treatment of goal generation as a purely data-driven problem. Methods like RIG [8] learn to generate goals in a latent representation space using variational autoencoders, but these representations often lack physical grounding. As a result, the generated goals may violate basic physical principles—such as objects floating in mid-air or penetrating solid surfaces—leading to impossible tasks that waste learning time and degrade performance.

In this work, we address this limitation by incorporating physical knowledge directly into the goal generation process. Our key insight is that separating the learned representation into physics-relevant variables and environmental factors, while enforcing physical consistency constraints, leads to more meaningful and achievable goal proposals. We summarize our contributions as:

- We introduce Physics-Informed RIG (PI-RIG), a novel extension of RIG that integrates physical constraints into VAE training through an Enhanced p^3-VAE architecture specifically designed for robotic manipulation tasks.
- We develop an explicit latent space separation approach that decomposes the latent representation into physics variables (z_I) governing object dynamics and environmental variables (z_E) capturing scene appearance and context.
- We implement task-specific physics integration with domain-specific physics constraints for robotic manipulation including momentum conservation, contact dynamics, and kinematic constraints.
- We present a comprehensive empirical evaluation that demonstrates our physics-informed approach achieves superior performance compared to existing goal-conditioned methods across multiple visual robotic manipulation environments.

2 Related Work

Goal-Conditioned RL and Self-Supervised Goal Generation. Early goal-conditioned RL generalized value functions across states and goals via Universal Value Function Approximators (UVFAs) [13]. For vision-based settings, RIG [8] couples a VAE with hindsight relabeling to sample and pursue latent goals from pixels, while Contextual Imagined Goals (CC-RIG) [9] conditions goal sampling on observed context to avoid out-of-scene proposals. HER (Hindsight Experience Replay) [1] enables learning from failed attempts by relabeling goals post-hoc, and DDPG+HER variants have shown success in continuous control tasks [10]. Orthogonally, Skew-Fit [11] seeks state coverage by maximizing the entropy of the goal distribution learned from experience, and is often combined with goal-conditioned RL to broaden practice diversity. These methods largely assume the latent prior is a good proxy for reachability; our work instead augments the goal imagination pipeline with lightweight physics structure, reducing physically implausible targets while preserving RIG's single-goal interface.

Physics-Aware Latent Generative Models. Physics-integrated generative models ground part of the latent space in interpretable dynamics. Physics-Integrated VAEs (PI-VAE) [15] embed known structure into the generative process to obtain robust, interpretable latents, and physics-informed VAEs have been applied to stochastic differential systems [16]. Physics-informed neural networks (PINNs) [12] incorporate physical laws as regularization terms during training. Recent trajectory-focused variants like PITA [4] incorporate physical constraints when autoencoding motion, and Φ-DVAE [5] imposes differential-equation priors in latent dynamics to improve rollout fidelity and identifiability. Symplectic encoders [2] likewise encourage energy-respecting latents. p^3-VAE [14] introduces a physics-informed variational autoencoder that integrates prior physical knowledge about latent factors of variation related to data acquisition conditions, combining standard neural network layers with non-trainable physics layers to partially ground the latent space to physical variables. We adopt the spirit of these works but target goal imagination for goal-conditioned RL: we separate a physics latent governing object dynamics from an appearance latent, regularize the former with physics consistency, and keep unsupervised goal sampling compatible with standard RIG training.

3 Background

3.1 Goal-Conditioned Reinforcement Learning

In standard reinforcement learning, an agent learns a policy $\pi_\theta(a|s)$ to maximize expected return in a Markov Decision Process (MDP) defined by states $s \in \mathcal{S}$, actions $a \in \mathcal{A}$, transition dynamics $p(s'|s,a)$, rewards $r(s,a)$, horizon H, and discount factor γ. Goal-conditioned RL extends this framework by parameterizing a family of reward functions with goals $g \in \mathcal{G}$, enabling agents to learn diverse skills [13].

The agent learns a goal-conditioned policy $\pi(a|s,g)$ that maps states and goals to actions, with the objective to maximize goal-conditioned return:

$$J(\pi) = \mathbb{E}\left[\sum_{t=0}^{H} \gamma^t r(s_t, a_t, g)\right] \tag{1}$$

For sample-efficient off-policy learning, goal-conditioned Q-learning algorithms learn a parametrized Q-function $Q_w(s,a,g)$ that estimates the expected return of taking action a from state s with goal g. The Q-function is trained by minimizing the Bellman error:

$$\mathcal{L}_Q = \mathbb{E}_{(s,a,s',g,r)}\left[|Q_w(s,a,g) - (r + \gamma \max_{a'} Q_w(s',a',g))|^2\right] \tag{2}$$

A key challenge in goal-conditioned RL is goal specification: how should goals be represented and generated to promote effective learning?

3.2 Variational Autoencoders for Goal Representation

To handle high-dimensional visual goals, variational autoencoders (VAEs) provide a principled approach for learning compact latent representations [7]. A VAE consists of an encoder $q_\phi(z|x)$ that maps observations x to a latent distribution and a decoder $p_\psi(x|z)$ that reconstructs observations from latent codes z. The VAE is trained by minimizing the negative evidence lower bound (ELBO):

$$\mathcal{L}_{VAE} = -\mathbb{E}_{q_\phi(z|x)}[\log p_\psi(x|z)] + \beta \mathrm{KL}(q_\phi(z|x)||p(z)) \tag{3}$$

where the first term encourages accurate reconstruction and the second term regularizes the latent distribution toward a prior $p(z)$ (typically standard normal). The hyperparameter β controls the trade-off between reconstruction quality and regularization strength.

3.3 Reinforcement Learning with Imagined Goals (RIG)

RIG [8] addresses visual goal-conditioned RL by combining VAE representation learning with goal imagination. The key insight is to learn a latent representation of visual observations using a VAE, then train a goal-conditioned policy in this latent space. Goals are "imagined" by sampling from the learned latent prior and decoded back to visual space.

The RIG training procedure consists of three main components:

Dataset Collection: An interaction dataset $\{s_t\}$ is collected through environment exploration.

Representation Learning: A β-VAE is trained on the collected observations to learn a compact latent representation:

$$\mathcal{L}_{RIG} = \mathbb{E}[||x - D_\psi(E_\phi(x))||^2] + \beta \mathrm{KL}(q_\phi(z|x)||p(z)) \tag{4}$$

Goal-Conditioned Policy Training: A policy is trained to reach latent goals z_g sampled from the VAE prior $p(z)$, with goals decoded to visual space for evaluation.

However, RIG has a fundamental limitation: sampling goals from the VAE prior assumes that every encoded state is reachable from any starting state, which may not hold in practice. This can lead to the generation of physically implausible or unreachable goals. CC-RIG [9] partially addresses this by conditioning goal sampling on observed context, but still lacks explicit physical reasoning. Our work addresses this gap by integrating physics-informed representations directly into the goal generation process.

3.4 Physics-Informed Variational Autoencoders

Physics-informed VAEs address the limitation of standard VAEs by incorporating physical constraints into the learning process. While different approaches vary in their specific implementations, they share common architectural patterns and integration strategies:

Encoder Design: Most physics-informed VAEs use specialized encoders that separate physical and non-physical latent variables. For example, PI-VAE [15] encodes observations into physics-governed latents z_p and auxiliary latents z_a.

Physics-Integrated Decoders: The decoder architecture typically combines neural networks with explicit physics models. Common approaches include:

- *ODE Solvers:* Φ-DVAE and PITA [4] integrate numerical ODE solvers (e.g., Runge-Kutta methods) directly into the decoder to ensure temporal dynamics follow physical laws.
- *Physics Layers:* p^3-VAE [14] introduces non-trainable physics layers f_E that encode known physical relationships, combined with trainable neural networks f_I^θ.
- *Symplectic Constraints:* Symplectic encoders [2] enforce energy conservation through specialized network architectures that preserve symplectic structure.

4 Method: Physics-Informed RIG

See Fig. 1.

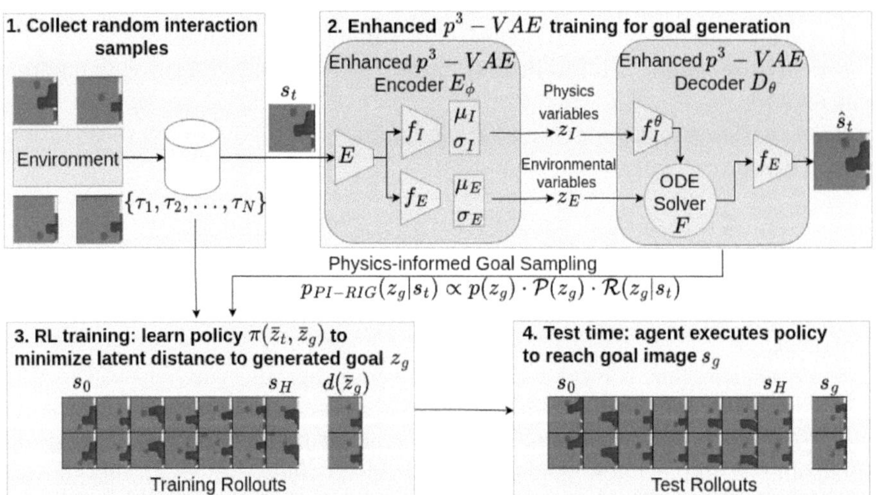

Fig. 1. System overview of our Physics-Informed RIG approach with Enhanced p^3-VAE architecture. The pipeline consists of four main stages: (1) Random interaction data collection from the environment, (2) Enhanced p^3-VAE training that separates latent space into physics variables z_I and environmental variables z_E, with an ODE solver F in the decoder enforcing physical consistency, (3) RL training using physics-informed goal generation, and (4) Test-time execution where the agent uses the learned policy to reach physically consistent goals.

4.1 Problem Formulation

The fundamental limitation of standard RIG lies in its goal generation mechanism. When sampling goals from the VAE prior $p(z)$, RIG implicitly assumes that every point in the latent space corresponds to a physically reachable state. This assumption fails in practice because:

1. **Reachability Gap:** Not all latent states are reachable from any given starting configuration due to physical and kinematic constraints.
2. **Physics Violations:** Sampled goals may violate fundamental physical principles such as object collision constraints, energy conservation, or temporal consistency.
3. **Task Infeasibility:** Goals may represent configurations that are impossible to achieve given the robotic system's capabilities.

Let $\mathcal{Z}_{feasible} \subset \mathcal{Z}$ denote the set of physically feasible latent states. Standard RIG samples from $p(z)$ over the entire latent space $\mathcal{Z}$, while our goal is to sample from the constrained distribution $p(z|z \in \mathcal{Z}_{feasible})$.

4.2 Enhanced p^3-VAE Architecture

Building on the p^3-VAE framework [14], our Enhanced p^3-VAE extends the original approach with robotic manipulation-specific components. Following p^3-VAE's design principles, we decompose the latent space into intrinsic factors z_I (related to object states and dynamics) and environmental factors z_E (related to visual appearance and acquisition conditions).

The key innovation from p^3-VAE is the decoder architecture that combines a trainable neural network f_I^θ with a non-trainable physics layer f_E:

$$\mathbb{E}[x] = f_E(F[f_I^\theta(z_I), z_E]) \tag{5}$$

where F represents a functional (such as an ODE solver for dynamics) and f_E encodes known physical relationships specific to robotic manipulation. Unlike standard VAEs that use purely neural decoders, this architecture grounds part of the latent space to physical variables through the non-trainable f_E component.

4.3 Physics-Guided Encoding

The encoder separates visual observations into two latent components:

$$\mu_I, \sigma_I = f_I(E(x)) \tag{6}$$

$$\mu_E, \sigma_E = f_E(E(x), \mu_I) \tag{7}$$

where $E(x)$ is a shared convolutional encoder processing 84×84 RGB images, and f_E is conditioned on f_I to encourage disentanglement between physics-relevant and environmental variables.

Algorithm 1: Enhanced p^3-VAE Training
Input: Visual observations x, physics type τ
Output: Trained physics-guided encoder and decoder
1. Initialize physics-guided encoder E_ϕ and decoder D_θ
2. Initialize physics loss calculator $\mathcal{P}_\tau$
3. **for** each training iteration **do**
4. $\mu_I, \sigma_I, \mu_E, \sigma_E = E_\phi(x)$
5. Sample $z_I \sim \mathcal{N}(\mu_I, \sigma_I)$, $z_E \sim \mathcal{N}(\mu_E, \sigma_E)$
6. $\hat{x} = D_\theta(z_I, z_E)$
7. $\mathcal{L}_{physics} = \mathcal{P}_\tau(z_I)$
8. Compute total loss and update parameters
9. **end for**

4.4 Enhanced Loss Function

Following p^3-VAE's semi-supervised training approach [14], our training objective incorporates both supervised and unsupervised components. When intrinsic factors z_I are supervised (i.e., we have labels for some physics variables), we optimize:

$$L(x, z_I^*) = \mathbb{E}_{q_\phi(z_E|x,z_I^*)}[\log p_\theta(x|z_I^*, z_E) + \log p(z_I^*) + \log p(z_E) - \log q_\phi(z_E|x, z_I^*)] \tag{8}$$

For unsupervised data, we use the marginal evidence lower bound with a stop-gradient operator to prevent the neural network f_I^θ from overwhelming the physics component f_E:

$$U(x) = \mathbb{E}_{q_\phi(z_I,z_E|x)}[\log p_\theta(x|z_I, z_E) + \log p(z_I) + \log p(z_E) - \log q_\phi(z_I, z_E|x)] \tag{9}$$

The total objective combines supervised and unsupervised terms:

$$\mathcal{L}_{Enhanced} = \alpha \sum_s L(x, z_I^*) + (1 - \alpha) \sum_u U(x) + \lambda L_c(\phi; z_I^*) \tag{10}$$

where L_c is the supervised classification/regression loss for the intrinsic factors, and α balances supervised and unsupervised data.

Physics Integration for Robotics: We extend p^3-VAE's physics framework with manipulation-specific constraints through the physics layer f_E:

- *Kinematic Consistency:* Joint limits and workspace boundaries enforced through f_E
- *Contact Physics:* Object-environment interactions modeled in the physics layer
- *Conservation Laws:* Momentum and energy conservation for object dynamics
- *Task Constraints:* Domain-specific physical laws (e.g., grasping, pushing dynamics)

Stop-Gradient Operator: Following p^3-VAE, we use a stop-gradient operator in the unsupervised training step to prevent the high-capacity neural network f_I^θ from overpowering the physics component f_E. This ensures that the physics constraints meaningfully contribute to the learned representation.

4.5 Physics-Informed Goal Sampling

Instead of sampling goals uniformly from the VAE prior, we implement a physics-informed sampling strategy that generates goals from the constrained distribution $p(z|z \in \mathcal{Z}_{feasible})$:

1. **Candidate Generation:** Sample N candidate goals $\{z_g^{(i)}\}_{i=1}^N$ from the VAE prior $p(z)$
2. **Physics Validation:** Apply learned physics constraints to score each candidate: $s_i = \mathcal{P}(z_g^{(i)})$
3. **Reachability Filtering:** Estimate reachability from current state using learned dynamics: $r_i = \mathcal{R}(z_g^{(i)}|s_t)$
4. **Goal Selection:** Sample final goal proportional to combined score: $p(z_g^{(i)}) \propto s_i \cdot r_i$

The filtered goal distribution becomes:

$$p_{PI-RIG}(z_g|s_t) \propto p(z_g) \cdot \mathcal{P}(z_g) \cdot \mathcal{R}(z_g|s_t) \tag{11}$$

where $\mathcal{P}(z_g)$ represents physics validity and $\mathcal{R}(z_g|s_t)$ estimates reachability.

4.6 Task-Specific Physics Models

We implement specialized physics constraints for each experimental domain:

Pusher Environment: Contact dynamics, momentum conservation, friction modeling, and boundary constraints.

Pick-and-Place Environment: Grasping constraints, gravity effects, collision detection, and kinematic limits.

Reacher Environment: Joint limits, kinematic chains, smoothness constraints, and workspace boundaries.

5 Results and Analysis

5.1 Experimental Results Overview

We compare our Physics-Informed RIG (PI-RIG) against several baselines:

- **RIG** [8]**:** The original RIG implementation with standard β-VAE goal generation
- **Skew-Fit** [11]**:** Goal-conditioned RL using maximum entropy goal selection
- **CC-RIG** [9]**:** Context-conditioned RIG that conditions goal sampling on observed context
- **Oracle:** Upper bound that runs goal-conditioned RL with direct access to state information goals, guaranteed to be physically feasible.

Figure 2, 3, 4 show the learning curves for three environments, demonstrating the comparative performance of different methods over 300 training epochs and 10000 sampled goals. The y-axis represents the Final Distance to Goal and the x-axis shows the training iterations (epochs). A lower distance indicates better performance.

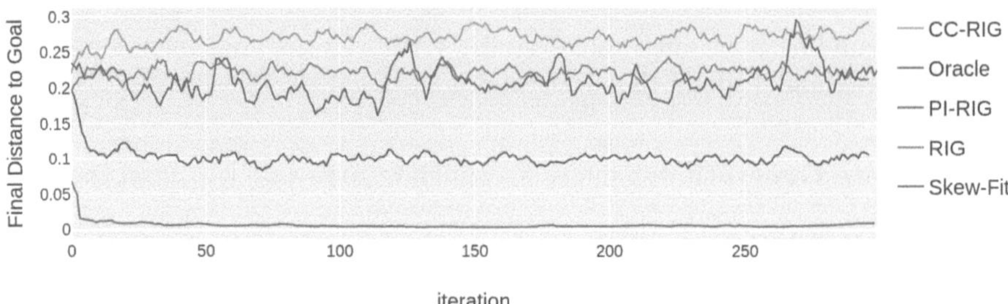

Fig. 2. Final Distance to Goal during training for the **Visual Reacher task**. PI-RIG achieves a final distance of approximately 0.1, representing a **54.5% improvement** over RIG (0.22) and a **63.0% improvement** over CC-RIG (0.27). Our approach also outperforms Skew-Fit by **52.4%**, demonstrating consistent superiority across different baseline methods.

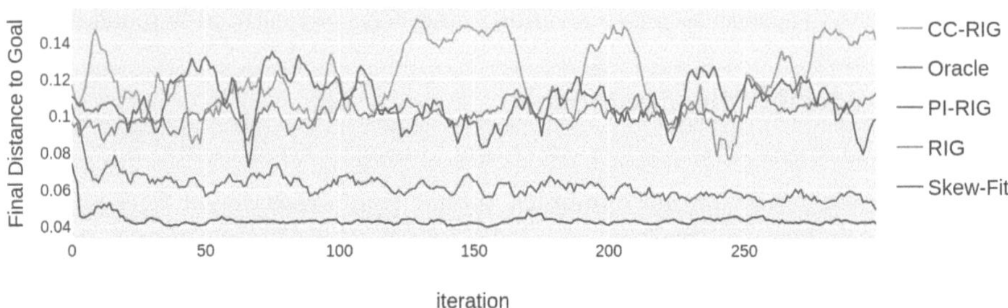

Fig. 3. Final Distance to Goal during training for the **Visual Pusher task**. PI-RIG achieves the best performance among learning-based methods with a final distance of approximately 0.04, showing a **63.6% improvement** over RIG (0.11) and a **71.4% improvement** over CC-RIG (0.14). The method also outperforms Skew-Fit by **60.0%**.

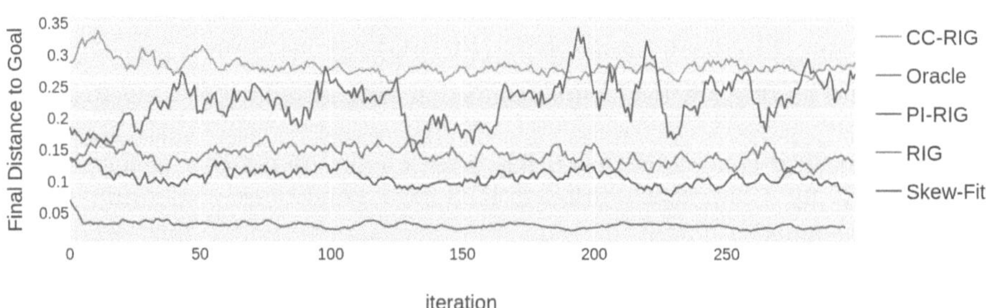

Fig. 4. Final Distance to Goal during training for the **Visual Pick-and-Place task**. In this complex task, PI-RIG achieves a final distance of approximately 0.07, representing a **46.1% improvement** over RIG (0.13), a **74.0% improvement** over CC-RIG (0.27), and a **72.0% improvement** over Skew-Fit (0.25).

5.2 Learning Efficiency and Convergence

Analysis of the learning curves reveals several key insights:

Faster Convergence: Physics-Informed RIG consistently converges to better solutions faster than baseline methods. The physics constraints provide structural inductive bias that guides learning toward more efficient exploration patterns.

Training Stability: The physics constraints provide inherent regularization, leading to more stable training dynamics. We observe significantly reduced variance in performance across multiple runs compared to unconstrained methods.

Goal Quality: The improved distance metrics indicate that physics-informed goal generation produces more achievable and relevant goals. This is particularly evident in the pick-and-place task, where precise manipulation requires physically feasible intermediate goals.

5.3 Distance-Based Performance Analysis

Table 1 presents a comprehensive comparison of distance-based metrics across all three environments. These metrics provide insight into different aspects of goal achievement: *VAE Distance* measures the latent space distance between achieved and desired states, providing a learned representation of state similarity. *Image Distance* quantifies pixel-level differences in visual observations. *Object Distance* represents the physical distance to the target (puck position for pusher, hand-to-target for reacher, object position for pick-and-place).

Table 1. Distance-based Performance Metrics Across Environments

Method	Pusher			Reacher			Pick-and-Place		
	VAE Dist.	Image Dist.	Object Dist.	VAE Dist.	Image Dist.	Object Dist.	VAE Dist.	Image Dist.	Object Dist.
PI-RIG	1.842	12.961	0.129	2.164	11.766	0.120	4.147	15.021	0.163
RIG	2.153	18.870	0.144	2.290	42.899	0.218	3.200	13.302	0.188
CC-RIG	0.000	6.683	0.188	8.222	38.155	0.267	5.464	22.815	0.379
Skew-Fit	0.000	8.396	0.100	0.000	13.180	0.204	0.002	27.571	0.258
Oracle	N/A	N/A	0.021	N/A	N/A	0.008	N/A	N/A	0.160

Multi-modal Performance Consistency: PI-RIG demonstrates consistently strong performance across all distance metrics in each environment. In the Pusher environment, it achieves the best VAE distance (1.842), competitive image distance (12.961), and superior object distance (0.129) among learning-based methods.

Latent Space Effectiveness: PI-RIG achieves the lowest VAE distance across all environments, demonstrating superior latent space goal achievement. This indicates that the physics-informed approach produces more meaningful and achievable goals in the learned representation space.

Key Trade-Off: While some methods (CC-RIG, Skew-Fit) show zero VAE distances in certain environments, this may indicate specialized optimization for VAE metrics rather than overall task performance. Our PI-RIG maintains balanced performance across all metrics, suggesting more robust goal generation that considers multiple aspects of task success.

6 Conclusion

We introduced Physics-Informed RIG (PI-RIG), a novel approach that integrates physical constraints into visual goal-conditioned reinforcement learning using Enhanced p^3-VAE architecture. Our method addresses a fundamental limitation of existing self-supervised goal generation approaches by ensuring that proposed goals respect physical feasibility constraints.

Our experiments on three robotic manipulation environments demonstrates substantial performance improvements over existing methods. PI-RIG consistently and substantially outperformed baselines like RIG and CC-RIG across all environments. Our comprehensive distance-based performance analysis reveals that Physics-Informed RIG consistently achieves superior latent space goal achievement (lowest VAE distances across all environments) while maintaining competitive performance across multiple distance metrics, indicating that the physics-informed approach provides more robust and generalizable representations for goal-conditioned tasks.

These results confirm that incorporating physics knowledge into the goal generation process leads to more robust and generalizable representations. By improving the quality of proposed goals, PI-RIG enables more efficient exploration and better skill acquisition, paving the way for safer and more reliable autonomous learning in robotics.

Code Availability. Code to reproduce our results is available at https://github.com/shibuina/PI-RIG

References

1. Andrychowicz, M., et al.: Hindsight experience replay. In: Advances in Neural Information Processing Systems, pp. 5048–5058 (2017)
2. Bacsa, K., Lai, Z., Liu, W., Todd, M., Chatzi, E.: Symplectic encoders for physics-constrained variational dynamics inference. Sci. Rep. **13**, 2643 (2023)
3. Chen, R.T., Rubanova, Y., Bettencourt, J., Duvenaud, D.K.: Neural ordinary differential equations. In: Advances in Neural Information Processing Systems, pp. 6571–6583 (2018)

4. Fischer, J., Rösch, K., Lauer, M., Stiller, C.: PITA: Physics-informed trajectory autoencoder. arXiv preprint arXiv:2403.11728 (2024)
5. Glyn-Davies, A.J., Duffin, C., Akyildiz, O.D., Girolami, M.: Φ-DVAE: physics-informed dynamical variational autoencoders. J. Comput. Phys. **515**, 113293 (2024)
6. Ha, D., Schmidhuber, J.: World models. In: Advances in Neural Information Processing Systems, pp. 2350–2360 (2018)
7. Higgins, I., et al.: β-VAE: learning basic visual concepts with a constrained variational framework. In: International Conference on Learning Representations (2017)
8. Nair, A., Pong, V., Dalal, M., Bahl, S., Lin, S., Levine, S.: Visual reinforcement learning with imagined goals. In: Advances in Neural Information Processing Systems, pp. 9191–9200 (2018)
9. Nair, A., Bahl, S., Khazatsky, A., Pong, V., Berseth, G., Levine, S.: Contextual imagined goals for self-supervised robotic learning. In: Proceedings of the Conference on Robot Learning, vol. 100, pp. 530–539. PMLR (2020)
10. Plappert, M., et al.: Multi-goal reinforcement learning: challenging robotics environments and request for research. arXiv preprint arXiv:1802.09464 (2018)
11. Pong, V., Dalal, M., Lin, S., Nair, A., Bahl, S., Levine, S.: Skew-fit: state-covering self-supervised reinforcement learning. In: International Conference on Machine Learning, pp. 7783–7792 (2020)
12. Raissi, M., Perdikaris, P., Karniadakis, G.E.: Physics-informed neural networks: a deep learning framework for solving forward and inverse problems involving nonlinear partial differential equations. J. Comput. Phys. **378**, 686–707 (2019)
13. Schaul, T., Horgan, D., Gregor, K., Silver, D.: Universal value function approximators. In: Proceedings of the 32nd International Conference on Machine Learning, vol. 37, pp. 1312–1320. PMLR (2015)
14. Thoreau, R., Risser, L., Berthelot, B., Achard, V., Briottet, X.: Physics-informed variational autoencoders for improved robustness to environmental factors of variation. arXiv preprint arXiv:2210.10418 (2022)
15. Takeishi, N., Kalousis, A.: Physics-integrated variational autoencoders for robust and interpretable generative modeling. In: Advances in Neural Information Processing Systems 34 (NeurIPS 2021) (2021)
16. Zhong, W., Meidani, H.: PI-VAE: Physics-Informed Variational Auto-Encoder for stochastic differential equations. arXiv preprint arXiv:2203.11363 (2022)
17. Todorov, E., Erez, T., Tassa, Y.: MuJoCo: a physics engine for model-based control. In: 2012 IEEE/RSJ International Conference on Intelligent Robots and Systems, pp. 5026–5033 (2012)
18. Fujimoto, S., Hoof, H., Meger, D.: Addressing function approximation error in actor-critic methods. In: International Conference on Machine Learning, pp. 1587–1596. PMLR (2018)

A Fusion Model for Precipitation Nowcasting from Radar and Satellite Images

Le Hong Trang[1,2(✉)], Bui Khanh Vinh[1,2], Phan Thanh An[1,2], and Pham Tran Vu[1,2]

[1] Ho Chi Minh City University of Technology (HCMUT), 268 Ly Thuong Kiet, Ho Chi Minh City, Vietnam
{lhtrang,vinh.bui0512,thanhan,ptvu}@hcmut.edu.vn
[2] Vietnam National University - Ho Chi Minh City (VNU-HCM), Linh Xuan, Ho Chi Minh City, Vietnam

Abstract. Precipitation nowcasting is a crucial task with applications across various industries and services. Recent advancements in deep learning have enabled the use of radar imagery for precipitation nowcasting. This work proposes a fusion model that leverages both radar and satellite imagery to enhance precipitation nowcasting accuracy. Specifically, we employ a latent diffusion model called LDCast for local radar images and a large pretrained model called ClimaX for global satellite data. These models serve as baseline and foundation models, extracting temporal features. These features are then integrated within a U-Net architecture for final forecasting. We construct a local radar dataset, the Nha-Be Radar Dataset (NRD-1), and conduct experiments using NRD-1 as local data and ERA5 as global data. Despite being trained on a relatively small dataset, our model outperforms the baseline LDCast model. We further compare our model to a state-of-the-art precipitation nowcasting method to demonstrate its effectiveness.

Keywords: Precipitation nowcasting · Fusion model · U-Net architecture · Radar and Satellite images

1 Introduction

Nowcasting, a specialized technique in weather forecasting, predicts weather conditions over short durations, typically up to six hours ahead [19]. It is crucial for providing timely and detailed information about short-term weather events, aiding in the detection of sudden changes in weather phenomena. Numerical weather prediction (NWP) [14] are widely used in weather forecasting, simulating atmospheric processes based on initial conditions by solving linked partial differential equations. However, applying NWP models to leverage weather radar data, which is ideal for precipitation nowcasting, remains limited. Even

T. T. Quan et al. (Eds.): MIWAI 2025, LNAI 16353, pp. 430–441, 2026.
https://doi.org/10.1007/978-981-95-4957-3_35

when implemented on supercomputing platforms, NWP forecast update cycles are restricted to hours, and spatial resolution is limited to the mesoscale.

Deep learning has recently been applied to precipitation nowcasting by training neural networks on radar datasets, bypassing physical models. Notable models include PredRNN [27], which captures spatiotemporal changes in a unified memory pool; Ravuri et al. [22], an ensemble generative approach; and diffusion-based methods such as PreDiff [8] and LDCast [13], which leverage latent diffusion models [24] to capture complex precipitation dynamics. However, these approaches still depend mainly on radar-derived precipitation fields as input.

Large foundation models have advanced AI-based climate forecasting, offering broad generalization and task-specific adaptation [5]. Examples include FourCastNet [20] (Fourier-based global forecasts at 0.25°), GraphCast [12] (graph-based climate prediction), and ClimaX [17] (multi-source integration for improved accuracy across timescales). Despite their power, these global models often miss fine-grained local details crucial for short-term forecasts.

Recent advances emphasize the value of high-resolution radar data for weather forecasting. Radar captures localized phenomena such as severe storms in real time, offering granularity for community safety and infrastructure. Yet, it lacks the broader view needed to track large-scale systems. Foundation models trained on global datasets complement this gap by predicting macroscopic patterns like cyclones and cold fronts. We propose a fusion approach that integrates fine-grained radar with global weather representations to improve short-term forecasts, enhance local accuracy, and support long-term climate modeling—ultimately strengthening preparedness for weather-related impacts. Our fusion model combining radar and satellite images, includes three components:

- **Local feature block**: We adapt LDCast [13] for the high-resolution data built from a local radar station.
- **Gobal feature block**: We utilize ClimaX [17] as a large foundation model for the satellite data.
- **Feature fusion**: These features are then combined in a U-Net architecture for final forecasting.

We construct a local radar dataset, the Nha-Be Radar Dataset (NRD-1), from a radar station in Ho Chi Minh City, Vietnam. We conduct experiments using NRD-1 as the local data and ERA5 as the global data. Despite being trained on a relatively small dataset, our model outperforms the baseline LDCast model. To further demonstrate its effectiveness, we compare our model to a state-of-the-art generative model for precipitation nowcasting, as proposed in [22].

The rest of the paper is organized as follows. The next section reviews related work and background. Section 3 presents the proposed architecture. Section 4 shows the experimental setup and results. Finally is the conclusion.

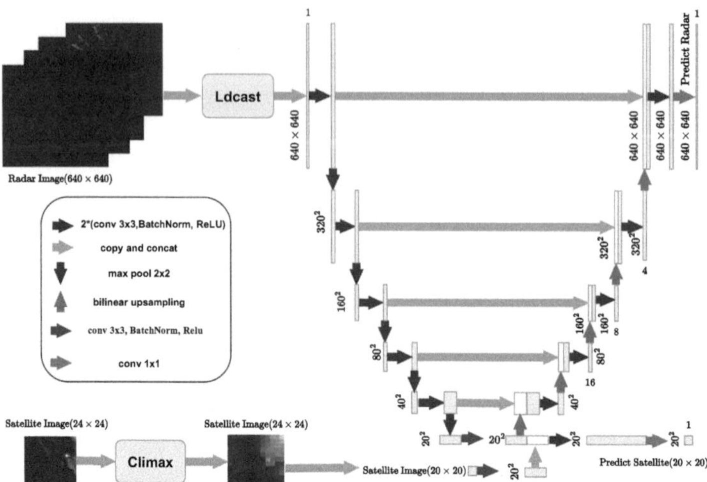

Fig. 1. Our method's pipeline takes 4 radar images (640 × 640) and 1 satellite image (24 × 24) as input for the foundation models, extracting a radar feature map (640 × 640) and a satellite feature map (24 × 24). To synchronize coordinates, the satellite feature map is then cropped to 20 × 20. Next, all feature maps are fed into the UNet architecture. The model's final output is a predicted radar image and a satellite image for a specified time.

2 Background

2.1 Weather Models

Deep learning models for weather forecasting can be categorized into two main groups: Task-specific and large foundation models. Task-specific models are tailored to specific weather forecasting tasks, such as precipitation nowcasting. These models are often categorized by their underlying architectures, including recurrent neural networks, generative adversarial networks, transformers, diffusion models, and graph neural networks. Notable examples of task-specific models for precipitation nowcasting include MetNet [25], MetNet-3 [1], EarthFormer [9], Rainformer [2], PreDiff [8], and LDCast [13].

Foundation models (FMs) are large-scale models trained on diverse data and fine-tuned for a wide range of tasks, offering greater versatility than task-specific approaches. Prominent examples in weather forecasting include FourCastNet [20], GraphCast [12], PanGu-Weather [3], FengWu [4], W-MAE [15], and ClimaX [17]. Complementing these, fusion methods integrate heterogeneous meteorological sources—radar reflectivity, satellite imagery, ground-based observations, and numerical weather models–to enhance accuracy and robustness. Radar provides high-resolution spatial–temporal detail, while satellites contribute broad coverage and frequent updates [26]. By combining such complementary modalities, multimodal systems overcome the coverage, resolution, and latency limitations of single-source data.

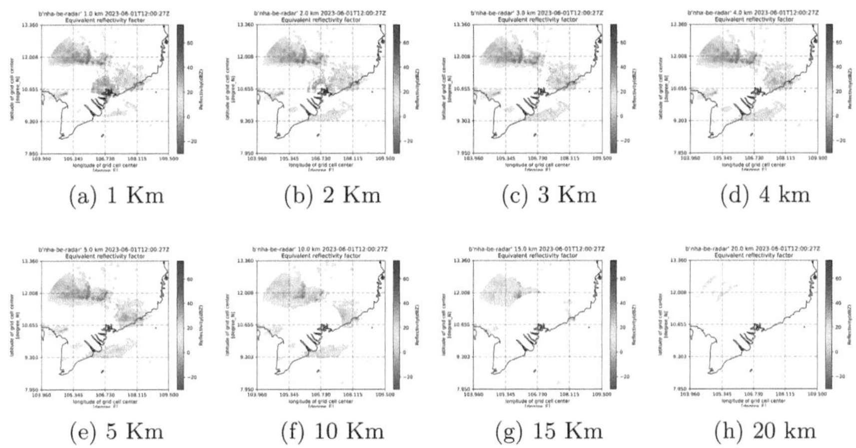

(a) 1 Km (b) 2 Km (c) 3 Km (d) 4 km

(e) 5 Km (f) 10 Km (g) 15 Km (h) 20 km

Fig. 2. Some image examples of NRD-1 dataset.

2.2 ClimaX

ClimaX [17], developed by Microsoft, is a platform model that advances meteorological forecasting by handling diverse data types and tasks. Built on the Vision Transformer (ViT) architecture [7], it integrates ground observations, satellite and radar imagery, and other weather sensors for unified predictions. Through variable disambiguation and aggregation, ClimaX captures relationships across altitudes, supporting both short- and long-term forecasts at global and regional scales. While effective in leveraging multi-source data for accurate forecasts and climate trend analysis, its high-resolution focus may miss critical local variations important for short-term predictions.

2.3 LDCast

LDCast [13] is an advanced weather forecasting model that uses the Latent Diffusion Model (LDM) to refine predictions. LDM specifically crafted for modeling latent variables, focuses on understanding how weather variables evolve across spatial and temporal dimensions. LDCast captures intricate, nonlinear relationships among these variables and harnesses the dynamic dependencies inherent in data components. Compared to generative adversarial networks (GANs) [10], LDM offers greater stability and computational efficiency during training, although it is more computationally demanding during generation. One of LDCast's key strengths is its high temporal resolution, enabling the processing of data in 5-min intervals. This high temporal granularity is well-suited for utilizing radar data, which is typically collected at similar intervals.

Table 1. Results of models on ERA5.

Models	MSE ↓	RMSE ↓	WACC ↑	WMSE ↓	WRMSE ↓	CRPS ↓
ClimaX [17] (foundation)	$1.999e^{-7}$	$3.979e^{-4}$	0.4710	$1.997e^{-7}$	$\mathbf{2.524e^{-4}}$	$\mathbf{1.332e^{-4}}$
Ours (U-Net)	$\mathbf{1.980e^{-7}}$	$\mathbf{3.971e^{-4}}$	**0.4745**	$\mathbf{1.977}e^{-7}$	$2.575e^{-4}$	$1.442e^{-4}$
Ours (Attention U-Net)	$1.989e^{-7}$	$3.981e^{-4}$	0.4704	$1.987e^{-7}$	$2.623e^{-4}$	$1.514e^{-4}$
Ours (R2U-Net)	$2.000e^{-7}$	$4.009e^{-4}$	0.4571	$1.997e^{-7}$	$2.665e^{-4}$	$1.502e^{-4}$
Ours (Attention R2U-Net)	$1.988e^{-7}$	$3.982e^{-4}$	0.4694	$1.985e^{-7}$	$2.638e^{-4}$	$1.520e^{-4}$

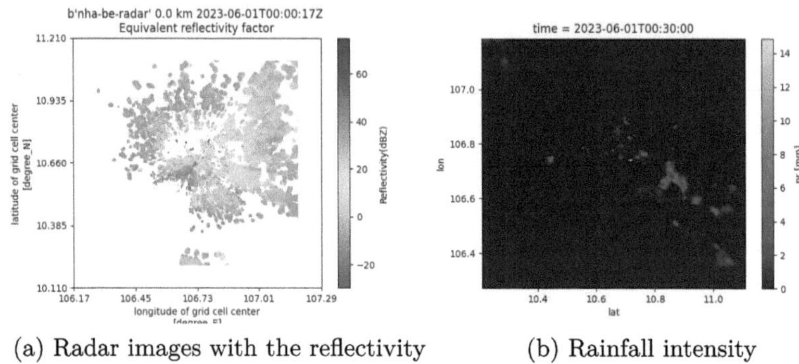

(a) Radar images with the reflectivity (b) Rainfall intensity

Fig. 3. Radar image and the corresponding rainfall intensity.

3 The Proposed Fusion Model

Radar systems, while capable of providing high-resolution, detailed local information, are limited to relatively small areas, such as a state or country. This enables the detection of fine-grained changes over time, but sacrifices broader context. In contrast, satellite data offers a global perspective, albeit at lower resolution. While less detailed locally, satellite data provides valuable information about surrounding regions. To leverage the strengths of both data sources, our team proposes a highly multimodal model that integrates satellite and radar data. By combining a global meteorological forecast model with a local one, we aim to achieve a comprehensive understanding of weather patterns, from large-scale trends to localized details. Our proposed pipeline is depicted in Fig. 1.

In our pipeline, ClimaX and LDCast serve as foundational models, generating forecasts for specified time horizons. These models extract temporal features from the respective data types. To facilitate interaction between the different data modalities, we employ the U-Net architecture [18] and its variants, such as R2U-Net [16], Attention U-Net [28], and Attention R2U-Net [21].

We use a 3-h forecast horizon. At time t, four radar images $(t-15, t-10, t-5, t)$ are input to the LDCast model, while a single satellite image at t, resized to 20×20, is input to the ClimaX model. These produce radar- and satellite-based predictions, which are then fused using a U-Net architecture. U-Net is chosen

Table 2. Results of models on NRD-1.

Models	MSE ↓	RMSE ↓	ACC ↑	CRPS ↓
LDCast [13]	1.2925	1.0734	0.03155	0.0886
DMGR [23] (Config 1)	13.950	2.9040	0.04533	1.9507
DMGR [23] (Config 2)	6.6865	2.5658	0.7299	0.9334
Ours (U-Net)	**0.8028**	**0.8045**	0.1317	**0.0752**
Ours (Att. U-Net)	0.8037	0.8058	**0.1335**	0.0941
Ours (R2U-Net)	0.8067	0.8080	0.1283	0.0935
Ours (Att. R2U-Net)	0.8077	0.8074	0.1078	0.1092

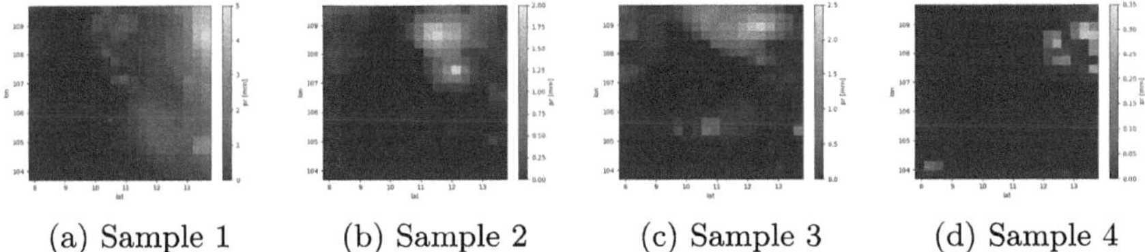

(a) Sample 1 (b) Sample 2 (c) Sample 3 (d) Sample 4

Fig. 4. Actual satellite images.

for its ability to capture both global and local information: the contracting path extracts global features across the entire image, making it suitable for coarse satellite inputs, while the expanding path integrates this context with fine local details from radar. Training minimizes the discrepancy between predicted and observed radar and satellite images at $t + 180$, with the loss function defined as

$$\mathcal{L}_{\text{model}} = \mathcal{F}(y_{\text{rad},t+180}, \hat{y}_{\text{rad},t+180}) + \mathcal{F}(y_{\text{sat},t+180}, \hat{y}_{\text{sat},t+180}),$$

where $y_{\text{rad},t+180}$ and $y_{\text{sat},t+180}$ represent the ground truth radar and satellite images at time $t + 180$, with spatial dimensions of 640×640 and 20×20, respectively. The terms $\hat{y}_{\text{rad},t+180}$ and $\hat{y}_{\text{sat},t+180}$ denote the corresponding model-predicted radar and satellite images. The function $\mathcal{F}$ used to measure the discrepancy is the mean squared error (MSE).

4 Experiments

4.1 Datasets

ERA5, produced by ECMWF and C3S, is a global reanalysis dataset spanning 1950–present, covering atmosphere, land, and ocean waves. It provides multiple variables at spatial resolutions of 1°, 0.5°, and 0.25°, with temporal resolutions from monthly to hourly.

The Nha-Be Radar datasets (NRD-1), collected by the Nha Be Environmental Meteorological and Hydrological Station radar, cover a 300 km radius centered around the coordinates from 103°51′36″E to 109°36′0″E and latitude from

Table 3. Results of the ablation study on our model with U-Net for NRD-1.

Radar Block	Satellite Block	MSE ↓	RMSE ↓	ACC ↑	CRPS ↓
Yes	Yes	0.8028	0.8045	0.1317	**0.0752**
No	Yes	**0.7934**	**0.8008**	**0.1690**	0.0768
Yes	No	0.8035	0.8047	0.1309	0.754
No	No	0.8046	0.8069	0.1469	0.0792

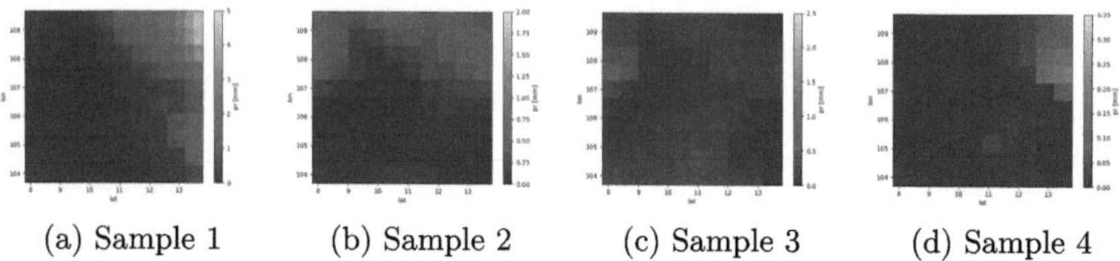

(a) Sample 1 (b) Sample 2 (c) Sample 3 (d) Sample 4

Fig. 5. Satellite images forecasted by ClimaX.

7°51′0″N to 13°27′36″N (see Fig. 2 for examples). The radar captures data at 10-min intervals within a scanning angle of 0.5° to 3.5°, covering altitudes from 0 to 20+ km. To estimate rainfall intensity (mm/h) from radar reflectivity (Z in dBZ), we employ the Marshall-Palmer formula that is $Z = 200R^{1.6}$ [6]. Figure 3 shows an example of a Radar image and the corresponding rainfall intensity by the Marshall-Palmer formula.

4.2 Evaluation Measures

For satellite data, evaluation employs area-weighted coefficients since latitude–longitude grids distort cell sizes, with polar cells much smaller than equatorial ones; equal weighting would bias results. Latitude weights are defined as

$$w_i = \frac{\cos(lat(i))}{\frac{1}{N_{lat}} \sum_{i=1}^{N_{lat}} \cos(lat(i))}, \tag{1}$$

where $lat(i)$ is the latitude at index i. Radar data does not require weighting because its coverage is limited and pixel distances are negligible. Given n samples, predictions $\hat{y}_i$, observations y_i, and forecast CDFs $\hat{F}_i$, we use the following metrics. The mean square error (MSE) and its weighted version (WMSE) is

$$MSE = \frac{1}{n}\sum_{i=1}^{n}(\hat{y}_i - y_i)^2, \quad WMSE = \frac{1}{n}\frac{\sum_{i=1}^{n} w_i(\hat{y}_i - y_i)^2}{\sum_{i=1}^{n} w_i}. \tag{2}$$

The root mean square error (RMSE) and its weighted form (WRMSE) are

$$RMSE = \sqrt{\frac{1}{n}\sum_{i=1}^{n}(\hat{y}_i - y_i)^2}, \quad WRMSE = \sqrt{\frac{1}{n}\frac{\sum_{i=1}^{n} w_i(\hat{y}_i - y_i)^2}{\sum_{i=1}^{n} w_i}}. \tag{3}$$

Table 4. Results of the ablation study on our model with U-Net for ERA5.

Radar Block	Satellite Block	MSE ↓	RMSE ↓	WACC ↑	WMSE ↓	WRMSE ↓	CRPS ↓
Yes	Yes	$\mathbf{1.980e^{-7}}$	$\mathbf{3.971e^{-4}}$	**0.4745**	$\mathbf{1.977}e^{-7}$	$\mathbf{2.575e^{-4}}$	$\mathbf{1.442e^{-4}}$
No	Yes	$1.995e^{-7}$	$3.996e^{-4}$	0.4742	$1.992e^{-7}$	2.591^{-4}	$1.449e^{-4}$
Yes	No	$2.148e^{-7}$	$4.170e^{-4}$	0.4236	$2.146e^{-7}$	2.865^{-4}	$1.712e^{-4}$
No	No	$2.150e^{-7}$	$4.161e^{-4}$	0.4211	$2.148e^{-7}$	$2.824e^{-4}$	$1.648e^{-4}$

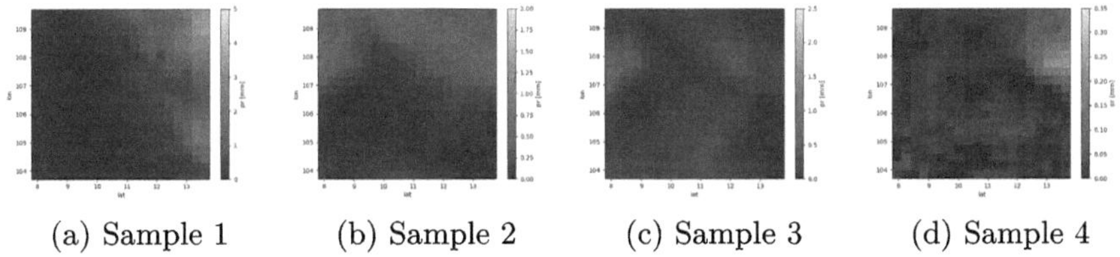

(a) Sample 1 (b) Sample 2 (c) Sample 3 (d) Sample 4

Fig. 6. Satellite images forecasted by our model with U-Net.

The anomaly correlation coefficient (ACC) with weights [11]:

$$ACC = \frac{\sum_{i=1}^{n} w_i(y_i - \bar{y})(\hat{y}_i - \bar{\hat{y}})}{\sqrt{\sum i = 1^n w_i(y_i - \bar{y})^2 \sum_{i=1}^{n} w_i(\hat{y}_i - \bar{\hat{y}})^2}}. \quad (4)$$

Finally, the continuous ranked probability score (CRPS) measures forecasts [13]:

$$\text{CRPS}\left(\hat{F}_i, y_i\right) = \int_{-\infty}^{\infty} \left(\hat{F}_i(x) - H\left(x - y_i\right)\right)^2 dx, \quad H(x) = \begin{cases} 0 & x \leq 0, \\ 1 & x > 0. \end{cases} \quad (5)$$

4.3 Training Details

ERA5 satellite inputs are provided on a 0.25° grid (~ 31 km), with 720×1440 pixels globally and about 24×24 when cropped to the radar domain, while NRD-1 radar data, derived via the Marshall–Palmer relation, provide higher resolution at 640×640. ClimaX is trained on ERA5 (2000–2020), LDCast uses the authors' pre-trained weights, and both are fine-tuned on ERA5 and NRD-1 with data from Jan 2021–Dec 2022 for training and Jan–Jun 2023 for testing, yielding 31,532 training and 80,863 test samples after preprocessing.

The model is trained using AdamW with $\beta_1 = 0.9$ and $\beta_2 = 0.99$, an initial learning rate of 5×10^{-4}, and weight decay of 1×10^{-5}. A 10-epoch warm-up gradually increases the rate from 1×10^{-8} before scheduled decay. Training is performed for up to 50 epochs with early stopping, using a batch size of 32. All experiments are conducted on a single NVIDIA RTX A6000 GPU (48 GB).

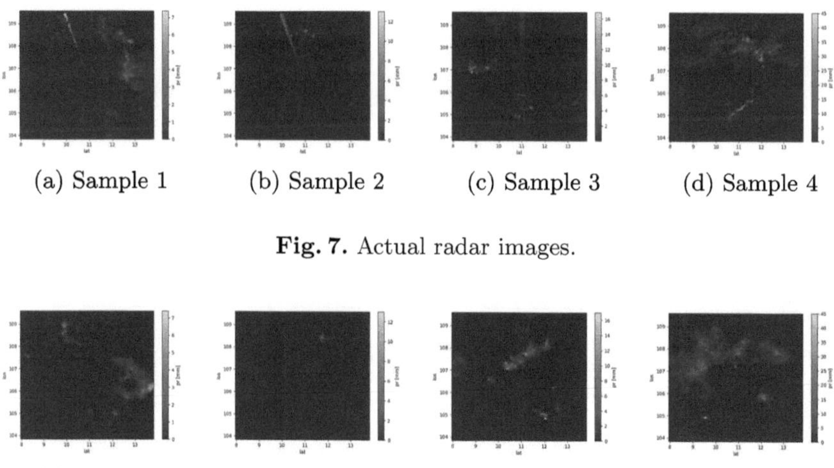

(a) Sample 1 (b) Sample 2 (c) Sample 3 (d) Sample 4

Fig. 7. Actual radar images.

(a) Sample 1 (b) Sample 2 (c) Sample 3 (d) Sample 4

Fig. 8. Radar images forecasted by LDCast.

4.4 Experimental Results

Experimental Setting. We first demonstrate that our model improves upon satellite image forecasting compared to ClimaX. Figures 4, 5 and 6 present four examples, each row displaying the actual satellite data, the ClimaX model predictions, and our model's predictions, respectively. In the first case, our model outperforms the baseline by reducing false positive rain predictions. In the second and third cases, the baseline model's poor predictions hinder our model's performance. However, our model still estimates rainfall amounts more accurately, as indicated by lighter-colored images compared to the baseline. In the fourth case, our model provides more accurate rainfall forecasts, particularly in regions of heavy rainfall, compared to the baseline.

Figures 7, 8 and 9 show that in all cases, our model generally predicts rainy areas similarly to the LDCast model. However, in the first, second, and fourth cases, our model tends to forecast a larger area with less intense rainfall compared to the baseline. Conversely, in the third case, our model predicts heavier and more widespread rainfall.

We initially tested our method with various U-Net variants with the ERA5 satellite dataset to benchmark against ClimaX. As shown in Table 1, most of our models outperformed ClimaX in terms of MSE, RMSE, ACC, and WMSE metrics. The U-Net-based model achieved the best results, likely due to the use of the MSE loss function during fine-tuning, compared to the WMSE loss used for ClimaX. However, ClimaX exhibited slightly superior performance in terms of WRMSE and CRPS metrics, potentially indicating a stronger focus on these specific metrics during its training.

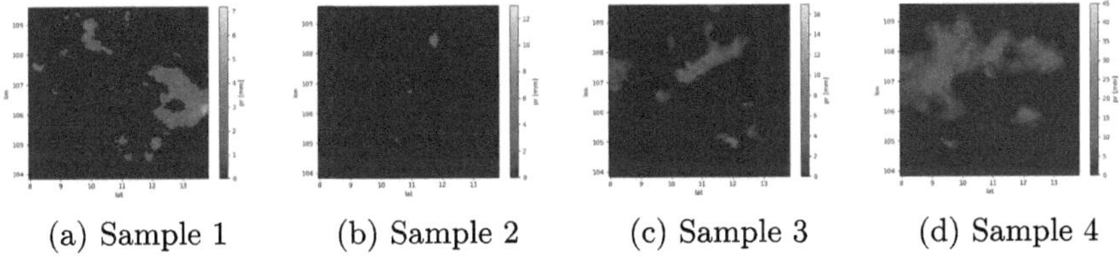

(a) Sample 1 (b) Sample 2 (c) Sample 3 (d) Sample 4

Fig. 9. Radar images forecasted by our model with U-Net.

For radar data, our models outperform the baseline across all metrics as shown in Table 2. This improvement is attributed to the fine-tuning process on the NRD-1 dataset, which was not used to train the pre-trained model. However, as we will demonstrate in the ablation study, incorporating the ClimaX foundation model further enhances this performance. Among the fine-tuned models, U-Net consistently outperforms the others across most metrics. This superior performance is attributed to its simpler architecture, which reduces the risk of overfitting. Additionally, the fine-tuned models demonstrate improvements over both the baseline and foundation models. We also compared our models to the well-known DMGR method [23]. We retrained DMGR models with NRD-1 data in two configurations as described in [23]. In both cases, our models achieved superior performance, indicating the effectiveness of our proposed method.

4.5 Ablation Study

In this section, we investigate the effectiveness of incorporating radar (LDCast) and satellite (ClimaX) blocks into our method. As shown in Table 3, using both blocks yields better performance in terms of the CRPS metric. While removing the radar block gives slightly better results in terms of MSE, RMSE, and ACC metrics, likely due to the reason of transfer learning from the pre-trained LDCast model for the local NRD-1 data. However, this also indicates that the use of satellite block helps to improve the performance for radar data forecasting.

In Table 4, we show the results testing for the satellite data. Using all blocks yields superior performance across all metrics. This indicates that the inclusion of the radar block enhances the performance of the model for satellite data.

5 Conclusion

In this paper, we propose an architecture that leverages both satellite and radar data to enhance precipitation nowcasting. This approach can be extended to other domains with multiple data sources of varying resolutions. Our results demonstrate significant improvements over baseline models that rely on a single data source. Additionally, this architecture provides a framework for fine-tuning foundation models trained on large-scale datasets from specific data sources. Ablation studies indicate that while removing the radar block (LDCast) can slightly improve radar data forecasting, the overall performance benefits from incorporating the foundation model. As future work, we will explore the potential of directly using U-Net based architectures as baseline models.

Acknowledgments. We acknowledge the Ho Chi Minh City University of Technology (HCMUT), VNU-HCM for supporting this study.

Disclosure of Interests. The authors declare that they have no conflicts of interest related to this work.

References

1. Andrychowicz, M., et al.: Deep learning for day forecasts from sparse observations (2023)
2. Bai, C., Sun, F., Zhang, J., Song, Y., Chen, S.: Rainformer: features extraction balanced network for radar-based precipitation nowcasting. IEEE Geosci. Remote Sens. Lett. **19**, 1–5 (2022). https://doi.org/10.1109/LGRS.2022.3162882
3. Bi, K., Xie, L., Zhang, H., Chen, X., Gu, X., Tian, Q.: Accurate medium-range global weather forecasting with 3d neural networks. Nature **619**(7970), 533–538 (2023)
4. Chen, K., et al.: FengWu: pushing the skillful global medium-range weather forecast beyond 10 days lead. arXiv preprint arXiv:2304.02948 (2023)
5. Chen, S., Long, G., Jiang, J., Liu, D., Zhang, C.: Foundation models for weather and climate data understanding: a comprehensive survey. arXiv preprint arXiv:2312.03014 (2023)
6. Côté, J., Gravel, S., Méthot, A., Patoine, A., Roch, M., Staniforth, A.: The operational CMC–MRB global environmental multiscale (GEM) model. Part I: design considerations and formulation. Mon. Wea. Rev. **126**(6), 1373–1395 (1998)
7. Dosovitskiy, A., et al.: An image is worth 16x16 words: transformers for image recognition at scale. arXiv preprint arXiv:2010.11929 (2020)
8. Gao, Z., et al.: PreDiff: precipitation nowcasting with latent diffusion models. Adv. Neural. Inf. Process. Syst. **36**, 78621–78656 (2023)
9. Gao, Z., et al.: EarthFormer: exploring space-time transformers for earth system forecasting. In: NeurIPS (2022)
10. Goodfellow, I., Pouget-Abadie, J., Mirza, M.: Generative adversarial networks, pp. 139–144. Association for Computing Machinery (2020). https://doi.org/10.1145/3422622
11. Jolliffe, I.T., Stephenson, D.B.: Forecast Verification A Practitioner's Guide in Atmospheric Science, pp. 128–129. Wiley, West Sussex (2003)
12. Lam, R., et al.: Learning skillful medium-range global weather forecasting. Science **382**(6677), 1416–1421 (2023). https://doi.org/10.1126/science.adi2336. https://www.science.org/doi/abs/10.1126/science.adi2336
13. Leinonen, J., Hamann, U., Nerini, D., Germann, U., Franch, G.: Latent diffusion models for generative precipitation nowcasting with accurate uncertainty quantification (2023)
14. Schultz, M.G., Betancourt, C., Gong, B.: Can deep learning beat numerical weather prediction? Philos. Trans. Royal Soc. A (2020). https://doi.org/10.1098/rsta.2020.0097

15. Man, X., Zhang, C., Feng, J., Li, C., Shao, J.: W-MAE: pre-trained weather model with masked autoencoder for multi-variable weather forecasting. arXiv preprint arXiv:2304.08754 (2023)
16. Alom, M.Z., Hasan, M., Yakopcic, C.: Recurrent residual convolutional neural network based on U-Net (R2U-Net) for medical image segmentation. Comput. Sci. Med. IEEE (2018)
17. Nguyen, T., Brandstetter, J., Kapoor, A., Gupta, J.K., Grover, A.: Climax: a foundation model for weather and climate. arXiv preprint arXiv:2301.10343 (2023)
18. Ronneberger, O., Fischer, P., Brox, T.: U-Net: convolutional networks for biomedical image segmentation. In: Navab, N., Hornegger, J., Wells, W.M., Frangi, A.F. (eds.) MICCAI 2015. LNCS, vol. 9351, pp. 234–241. Springer, Cham (2015). https://doi.org/10.1007/978-3-319-24574-4_28
19. World Meteorological Organization: Guidelines for Nowcasting Techniques. World Meteorological Organization, Geneva (2017)
20. Pathak, J., et al.: FourCastNet: a global data-driven high-resolution weather model using adaptive Fourier neural operators. arXiv preprint arXiv:2202.11214 (2022)
21. Zuo, Q., Chen, S., Wang, Z.: R2AU-Net: attention recurrent residual convolutional neural network for multimodal medical image segmentation. Multimodality Data Analysis in Information Security (2021)
22. Ravuri, S., et al.: Skillful precipitation nowcasting using deep generative models of radar. Nature **597**, 672–677 (2021)
23. Ravuri, S., et al.: Skilful precipitation nowcasting using deep generative models of radar. Nature **597**(7878), 672–677 (2021)
24. Rombach, R., Blattmann, A.: High-resolution image synthesis with latent diffusion models (2021)
25. Sønderby, C.K., et al.: MetNet: a neural weather model for precipitation forecasting. arXiv preprint arXiv:2003.12140 (2020)
26. Wang, S., et al.: Exploring the utility of radar and satellite-sensed precipitation and their dynamic bias correction for integrated prediction of flood and landslide hazards. J. Hydrol. **603**, 126964 (2021)
27. Wang, Y., et al.: PredRNN: a recurrent neural network for spatiotemporal predictive learning (2021)
28. Zuo, Q., Chen, S., Wang, Z.: R2AU-Net: attention recurrent residual convolutional neural network for multimodal medical image segmentation. Secur. Commun. Netw. **2021**, 1–10 (2021). https://doi.org/10.1155/2021/6625688

Author Index

T. T. Quan et al. (Eds.): MIWAI 2025, LNAI 16353, pp. 443–444, 2026.
https://doi.org/10.1007/978-981-95-4957-3

MIX
Papier aus verantwortungsvollen Quellen
Paper from responsible sources
FSC® C105338

If you have any concerns about our products,
you can contact us on
ProductSafety@springernature.com

In case Publisher is established outside the EU,
the EU authorized representative is:
Springer Nature Customer Service Center GmbH
Europaplatz 3, 69115 Heidelberg, Germany

Printed by Libri Plureos GmbH
in Hamburg, Germany